TEACHER'S EDITION ★ BOOK 2

THE AMERICAN REPUBLIC

★ ★ ★ ★ ★ ★ ★ ★ ★ THIRD EDITION ★ ★ ★ ★ ★ ★ ★ ★ ★

RACHEL C. LARSON, PhD

D1455761

bju press

NOTE: The fact that materials produced by other publishers may be referred to in this volume does not constitute an endorsement of the content or theological position of materials produced by such publishers. Any references and ancillary materials are listed as an aid to the student or the teacher and in an attempt to maintain the accepted academic standards of the publishing industry.

THE AMERICAN REPUBLIC Teacher's Edition
Third Edition

Rachel C. Larson, PhD

Contributing Authors
Carl Abrams, PhD
Dennis Bollinger, PhD
Brian Collins
Lauren Kowalk
Dennis Peterson

Editor
Manda Kalagayan

Bible Integration
Brian Collins
Bryan Smith, PhD

Cover
Drew Fields
Elly Kalagayan
Dave Schuppert

Book Design
Drew Fields

Page Layout
John Cunningham
Melissa Horne
Carol Jenkins
Jennifer Lowry
Ealia Padreganda

Project Managers
Dan Berger
Kevin Neat

Photo Acquisition
Brenda Hansen
Joyce Landis
Holly Nelson

Illustration
Preston Gravely Jr.
Dave Schuppert
Del Thompson

Photograph credits are listed on pages 603–6.

Produced in cooperation with the Bob Jones University Departments of History and Social Studies of the College of Arts and Science, the School of Education, and Bob Jones Academy.

© 2010 BJU Press
Greenville, South Carolina 29614

First Edition © 1988
Second Edition © 2000

ISBN 978-1-59166-706-3

15 14 13 12 11 10 9 8 7 6 5 4 3 2 1

Our Commitment.
Your Confidence.

Creative
Updated look. Colorful, interesting pages.

Credible
Thorough research. Solid content.

Christian
Nothing to conflict with Truth. Everything to support it.

Features of the Book

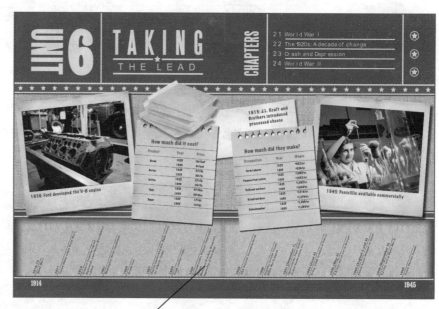

Unit openers offer a glimpse of life during the period covered by the unit, including prices of selected products, wages for selected occupations, and a timeline of major events.

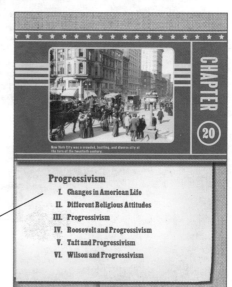

The **chapter outline** lists the major topics that will be covered.

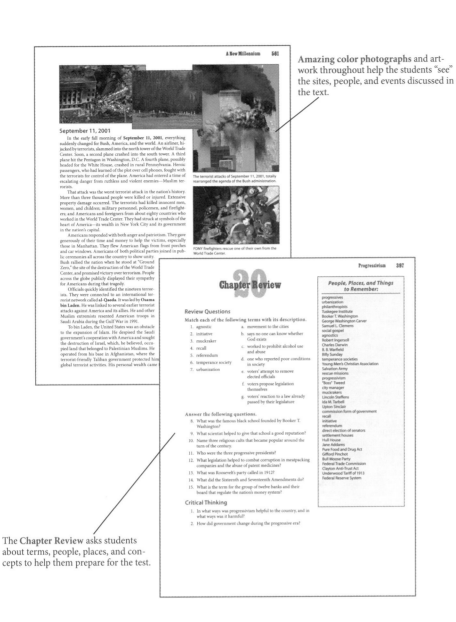

Amazing color photographs and artwork throughout help the students "see" the sites, people, and events discussed in the text.

The **Chapter Review** asks students about terms, people, places, and concepts to help them prepare for the test.

The Teacher's Edition

The teacher's edition of *The American Republic* (third edition) has been designed to help you in your history teaching. Many tools have been provided to allow you to break away from the sometimes stagnant lecture method and give more room for student participation, which is so essential to the junior high student. It is recommended that you begin each lesson with review of past teaching using student feedback to accurately determine whether learning is taking place. The suggested activities are designed as a part of the educational experience and are integral to the text. The materials lists and directions provided should make these suggestions easy to incorporate.

LESSONS AND SCHEDULING

Although some of the third-edition student text will be familiar to those who have used the second edition, we recommend that you read each chapter before beginning lesson plans because some of the chapters have been reorganized, combined, and/or supplemented. Reading each chapter will allow you to note changes and additions to the text as well as any newly available ancillary material. Then you can prepare accordingly.

Each chapter has three to six sections that divide the information into convenient reading assignments. You can combine sections into a single day's lesson or divide them into two or more days, as indicated in the Lesson Plan Chart at the beginning of each chapter.

Your students' ability and interests will determine how you schedule the lessons. The estimated times on the Lesson Plan Chart are only suggestions.

How many chapters should I cover in the first semester?

Most teachers find it convenient to end a semester with a unit break. A natural break occurs after Chapter 16 (Reconstruction), but you will find it difficult to cover all of that material by the end of your first semester. An alternate stopping point is after Chapter 13 (Westward Expansion). This would allow you to begin second semester with Chapter 14 (Storm Clouds over the Nation), which is an appropriate beginning for the second half of the school year.

To the Teacher

The American Republic (3rd ed.) is the eighth book in the Heritage Studies series. It is a survey of United States history, intended to give the junior high student a solid foundation of knowledge about the heritage of this country.

The primary purpose of any Christian course of study is to produce students who are conformed to Christ's image. For the young student who is just discovering his own abilities and responsibilities in life, there might be no more valuable study than the lives of others in the light of Scripture. Throughout the history course are many examples of people who either followed God's standard or failed to do so. From those examples, the student will see the truth of God in action and develop values and principles for living.

General Objectives

The general course objectives can be broken into two categories.

Basic Comprehension Goals

There is basic historical information that all students should understand. By the end of the year, the students should be able to identify the following:

1. God's providence in the seven eras of U.S. history and the outline of major periods within each era.

2. Continuity and change in the six spheres of human activity—politics, economics, religion, society, science, and arts.

3. Continuity and change in foreign relations, including past wars, and the roots of modern foreign policy.

Section quizzes help the students remember what they have learned so far.

Margin info boxes offer intriguing bits of extra information.

Sample page content (inset)

394   Chapter 20

Attempted Assassination of Teddy Roosevelt

On October 14, 1912, John Schrank, who had stalked Roosevelt for thousands of miles, finally got a clear, close-up shot. A stenographer in Roosevelt's entourage deflected the pistol just as Shrank pulled the trigger, probably saving Roosevelt's life. The bullet entered the right side of the candidate's chest but was slowed by a fifty-page speech that was folded double and a steel glasses case. The bullet still lodged three inches inside his chest. Doctors decided against trying to remove it. Roosevelt insisted on delivering his scheduled—but much shortened—speech. He never returned to the campaign trail.

The Election of 1912

Roosevelt had been home less than two months when he hit the campaign trail. He said that he was out to persuade voters to elect progressive Republicans to the House and Senate. But he ended up widening the rift within the Republican Party and building his own support for the 1912 convention. By February 1912, Roosevelt "gave in" to the urging of progressive Republicans and announced, "My hat is in the ring. I will accept the nomination for president if it is tendered to me."

But Taft and his followers had the support of most of the Republican Party leaders. They helped him win the Republican nomination on the first ballot. Roosevelt declared that conservative Taft Republicans had stolen the nomination. So he launched the new Progressive Party. Roosevelt was candidate.

During the campaign, Roosevelt was entering an auditorium in Milwaukee, Wisconsin, to deliver a speech. A gunman came from the crowd and shot him at close range. Against the advice of advisors, Roosevelt went ahead and delivered a brief speech. "It takes more than that to kill a bull moose!" he declared. When Roosevelt announced that he felt "as fit as a bull moose," the Progressive Party was nicknamed the **Bull Moose Party**.

Roosevelt's political ideals were known as "The New Nationalism." If he had won, he would have involved the federal government in still more areas.

The Democrat in the race was New Jersey's progressive governor, Woodrow Wilson. In the campaign he spoke of a "New Freedom." He wanted strict government regulation to restore business competition. Roosevelt and Taft together got more votes than Wilson, but Wilson won because of the split Republican vote. He was the first president to have an earned PhD degree.

Election Results, 1912

Candidate	Party	Popular vote	Electoral vote	Percentage
Woodrow Wilson	Democrat	6,293,152	435	41.8%
Theodore Roosevelt	Progressive	4,119,207	88	27.4%
William H. Taft	Republican	3,486,333	8	23.2%
Eugene V. Debs	Socialist	900,369	0	6%

Section Quiz

1. During his career, Taft headed what other branch of government besides the executive branch?
2. What were the provisions of the Sixteenth and Seventeenth Amendments?
3. The Republican split enabled what Democrat to win the 1912 election?
★ Why was the Bull Moose Party created?

How many days do I spend on a chapter?

Once you have skimmed the teacher's edition and determined your end goal for the semester, look at your school calendar and note how many actual teaching days are available. Most chapters will require five to eight days, which includes a day for review and testing. You can take more or less time per chapter as long as you balance the days to meet your semester goal.

Just a Note

Although this teacher's edition has been designed to assist the instructor in teaching *The American Republic*, it cannot replace teacher preparation. It is a *supplement* of teaching methods, information, and ideas.

Likewise, this manual is not a complete and final authority; it contains only a sample and partial list of suggested sources, methods, background information, and review techniques. It is the teacher's responsibility to select and develop those items that best meet the students' needs.

SIDE MARGIN NOTES

Goals and Objectives

The first information in the side margin of a chapter is a box containing the student goals for the entire chapter. Those general goals are what you want your students to achieve while studying the chapter. Read them carefully to get an overview of the chapter.

Section Objectives

Each section has specific objectives. They are important facts and principles that your students should learn while studying that section. Those objectives are suggestions. You may make changes to the objectives list as necessary to meet the specific needs of your students.

Additional Information

Information provided in the side margins corresponds to information in the nearby text. It is for the teacher's information and can be shared with the students as the teacher deems fit. Such information is designed for enrichment or further expla-

Terms in bold type draw attention to important facts, ideas, people, or definitions.

Maps, charts, and diagrams help the students visualize geographic locations and information.

General feature boxes provide a deeper look at a person, event, or concept mentioned in the text.

4. God's supervision of American church history as God's people have interacted with secular society.

5. The consequences of past decisions, good and bad, that testify that Bible principles are true and that God oversees the course of U.S. history.

6. Major events and dates in each era, including the leading causes and effects of the events.

7. Major individuals of U.S. history, including their roles in the past and lessons for today.

8. Fundamental traits of Americanism—the American dream, limited government, popular culture, the free enterprise economy—and how they have changed over the nation's history.

Basic Skill Goals

In addition to understanding basic historical information, students should develop skills in using information that will help them for the rest of their lives. By the end of the year, they should be able to

1. Define and use basic terms from U.S. history that are essential in understanding and explaining God's providence.

2. Interpret historical maps that are found in atlases of U.S. history.

3. Evaluate historical narratives and original documents for accuracy and historic perspectives.

4. Interpret common tools of historians, such as maps, timelines, graphs, charts, and primary sources.

5. Discern God's providence in any era by showing the impact of physical geography and circumstances on the course of events in U.S. history.

---

nation but is not meant to be included in testing.

BOTTOM MARGIN NOTES

Lesson Plan Chart

As was mentioned, a lesson plan chart is featured at the beginning of every chapter to aid the teacher in scheduling lessons. It is only a *suggested* plan and will vary depending on the teacher's style of teaching, the number of class activities included, and any extracurricular activities that might be included on the school calendar. The chart includes the title of each chapter and section, the main activity in each section, the pages covered by each section, and the suggested

time frame for teaching. The time frame includes a day for review and testing.

Materials List

Also at the beginning of each chapter is a list of materials for the suggested activities in that section. If you do not have access to certain materials, you might choose to skip those activities or design substitute activities.

Teaching Strategies

Suggested teaching strategies are given immediately after the materials list. Many of those activities are labeled with icons to help the teacher identify the type of teaching activity suggested without necessarily reading the entire description. If the activity does

not have an icon, it is most likely a suggested discussion topic. The icons are as follows.

 Art/crafts

 Field trip

 Bible integration

 Web resource

 Additional resources

 Investigation

6. Use the Bible to evaluate social, economic, and political systems or philosophies in any era.

7. Identify the variety of challenges that Christians faced in each era and draw lessons for today.

8. Explain the causes of historic crises, give the Bible's solution, and find parallels to current issues in America.

About National Standards

The seven units in our U.S. history textbook generally follow the ten eras listed in the National Standards for United States History. Our scheme combines (1) the exploration and colonization eras, (2) post-Civil War development of industry and the emergence of "modern" America in the late nineteenth century, and (3) the post-World War II era and the contemporary United States.

Supplementary Materials

Certain materials will help you teach this course. These are noted several times in the teaching ideas of the teacher's text.

Essential Reference Materials
- Wall map of the United States (available from BJU Press)
- Wall map of the world (available from BJU Press)

Additional BJU Press Materials
- *American Republic Student Activities* manual
- Prepared American Republic tests (or Test Builder software)
- *Free Indeed: Heroes of Black Christian History*, highlighting thirteen black leaders in American church history

Contents

★ ★ ★ ★ ★ ★ ★ ★ ★ ★ ★ ★ ★ ★ ★ ★ ★ ★ ★ ★

 Ideas

 CD

 Listening skills

 Special speaker

 Music

 Group activity

 Homeschool activity

 Writing

 Outside reading

 Maps

 Charts and graphs

 Video/DVD

Section Review Answers
At the end of each section are the answers to the review questions and the starred question(s).

Chapter Review Answers
At the end of the chapter are the answers to the chapter review questions.

TEACHING THE AMERICAN REPUBLIC
Your job is to show your students that the subject of history is a living, meaningful, relevant subject in their everyday lives. How do you do that? By making it active. The activities, mental or physical, are attention-getters, interest-sustainers, and long-lasting memory makers that will make Heritage Studies exciting for your students.

Evaluation
Many ways exist for evaluating the students' understanding of the material being taught.

- *Faith of Our Fathers: Scenes from American Church History*, with thirty-two short biographies and essays on key events from American church history
- *American History in Verse*, an inspiring collection of poems that recapture the struggles of our nation's birth and growth (originally published by Houghton Mifflin in 1932)

Additional Reference Materials
- U.S. historical atlas
- World almanac

The Student Text

The student text offers the following features.

Organization

The student text includes twenty-nine chapters divided into seven units. Each chapter has an outlined structure with boldfaced headings. Important terms are also boldfaced.

Unit Divisions

Each of the seven units begins with photos that illustrate important events, pages from a notepad that show how much some everyday items cost and how much selected occupations earned during the time period covered, and a timeline of events covered in the unit.

Feature Boxes

The textbook contains numerous special interest feature boxes that supplement the text. These boxes are designed to spark student interest and to encourage deeper study into particular subjects.

Whatever testing methods you use, be sure to adapt them to the specific needs and abilities of your class and to the material that you have emphasized in your teaching. Do not fall into the habit of giving the same type of questions on all of your tests and quizzes. By varying the type of questions that you use within each test, you will separate students who are having problems understanding a certain type of question from students who are having problems learning the material. Tests should contain enough questions to avoid allowing one section to make or break a student's grade.

Long essay questions are probably not appropriate for this age level, but short (three to five sentences) essays are a good way to help students learn to express their ideas effectively. Take time to explain how to study for and write essay answers before giving the first test. Grade the first essay answers leniently, but gradually increase your expectations on subsequent essay questions. The students' essay-writing ability should improve as they gain experience throughout the year.

Note: Prepared tests are available for *The American Republic* (third edition), or the teacher can make his own tests using Test Builder software available from BJU Press.

Homeschool Ideas

The flexibility inherent in the homeschooling schedule allows parents and students to focus on specific topics of interest to them. As much as possible, allow your child to pursue those interesting topics. Taking field trips to local historical sites, museums, and places of business helps history come alive. (Join other homeschoolers in your area to receive group discounts and guided tours.) Most of the activities generally assumed to be for classroom use can easily be adapted for the smaller setting of the homeschool. Inviting missionaries and older friends or family members into your home to share first-hand experiences from other countries and earlier periods of history or specific events of history adds a personal dimension to otherwise impersonal historical facts. Incorporating other academic disciplines, such as music and literature, broadens the scope

Maps

Numerous maps are included throughout the book, illustrating various periods or helping to explain various events in American history. Refer to these maps often as you teach the material. Many of the maps in the textbook are also found on the CD that accompanies the teacher's edition.

Illustrations

The textbook and the CD that accompanies the teacher's edition contain hundreds of color and black-and-white photographs, drawings, and historic political cartoons. In addition, they include several original illustrations produced by the BJU Press Art Department.

The Constitution

Chapter 7 includes a complete annotated copy of the U.S. Constitution. The student book in no way intends to be a complete text for studying American government, but it provides an introduction and may also stimulate an appreciation for this amazing document.

Section Review Questions

Several questions follow each section. The numbered questions are designed as a reading check of general information from the section. Also included for each section are one or more starred questions that ask the students to go beyond their textbook readings and apply the information they are learning.

Chapter Reviews

Every chapter ends with a fully developed chapter review, including a list of terms. These pages provide students with an opportunity to review factual knowledge covered in the chapter. At the end of the review are Critical Thinking questions that

Pronunciation Guide

★ ★ ★ ★ ★ ★ ★ ★ ★ ★ ★ ★ ★ ★ ★ ★ ★ ★ ★

Vowels

symbol	example	symbol	example
a	cat = KAT	aw	all = AWL
a-e	cape = KAPE	o	potion = PO shun
ay	paint = PAYNT	oa	don't = DOANT
e	jet = JET	o-e	groan = GRONE
eh	spend = SPEHND	oh	own = OHN
ee	fiend = FEEND	u	some = SUM
i	swim = SWIM	uh	abet = uh BET
ih	pity = PIH tee	oo	crew = CROO
eye	icy = EYE see	oo	push = POOSH
i-e	might = MITE	ou	loud = LOUD
ah	cot = KAHT	oy	toil = TOYL
ar	car = KAR		

Consonants

symbol	example	symbol	example
k	cat = KAT	th	thin = THIN
g	get = GET	th	then = THEN
j	gentle = JEN tul	zh	fusion = FYOO zhun

The pronunciation key used in this text is designed to give the reader a self-evident, acceptable pronunciation for a word as he reads it from the page. For more accurate pronunciations, the reader should consult a good dictionary.

Stress: Syllables with primary stress appear in LARGE CAPITAL letters. Syllables with secondary stress and one-syllable words appear in SMALL CAPITAL letters. Unstressed syllables appear in lowercase letters. Where two or more words appear together, hyphens separate the syllables within each word. For example, the pronunciation of Omar Khayyam appears as (OH-mar kie-YAHM).

---

of learning. In pursuing those other interests, however, do not lose sight of the ultimate purpose of the course: to understand the framework of United States history.

Project Ideas

You might want to include extended (long term) student projects in your planning. Such projects give students an opportunity to use the information they are learning throughout the year. It also gives them a chance to demonstrate their creative skills. Ideas include the following:

- Biographical reports, papers, or oral presentations on famous people from the era you are studying. Give the student(s) a check sheet detailing the

requirements of the assignment so that they have every opportunity for success on the project.

- State reports. Each student would research a specific state; write a paper about its geography, resources, and culture; and present an oral report summarizing his or her findings. This is especially helpful if you want to teach your own state's history as you teach U.S. history.

- Art projects. Students would make models of famous structures and prepare a short presentation about their features. For example, they might create maps (flat or 3-D), make early American craft items (samplers, toys, tools, etc.), or make models of wagons, log cabins, or forts.

Why Study American History?

The book you are holding tells the fascinating story of how people from different parts of the world turned a wilderness into the most powerful nation on earth. You may ask, "Why do we have to learn all this stuff about people who lived a long time ago?" That's an important question. This introduction will explain why you should study history from a biblical perspective.

To Teach Us Lessons for Life

As we study the choices of earlier Americans, we learn about the difference between right and wrong, and we see the consequences of both. The main lesson we learn is that humans should trust God and obey Him. Repeatedly, you will discover that those who obey God enjoy His blessing, but those who disobey Him experience His displeasure. In particular, here are some important lessons for life that you will see in this course: (1) hard work and creativity produce wealth, (2) corrupt decisions lead to personal and economic hardship, (3) treating others unfairly weakens society, and (4) those who ignore God are unprepared to face the trials of life. Of course, in a fallen world these lessons are complicated. Sinners sometimes prosper, and good men sometimes suffer. But these lessons still describe in general how God works in human affairs. Learning from these lessons will make you a wiser person.

To Show Us That God Is at Work

The Bible reveals that God made a perfect world without sin and pain. But humans chose to disobey Him, and He has punished us by putting our world under a curse. God, however, has not left us to ourselves. He is working to redeem this world to Himself through His Son and through the people who trust His Son to save them from sin. As we read about the events of history, we must remember that those events are moving this world toward a goal. The Bible teaches that redemption in Jesus Christ is the goal of history. God has planned all that happens in order to establish Christ's kingdom on earth (1 Cor. 15:28; Eph. 1:10–11).

As we study our history, we should ask ourselves how God may be using this nation to carry on His work of redemption. We should not think that Americans are God's specially chosen people, the center of His working in the world. But it is a mistake to assume that God is not using the United States to accomplish His purposes. We should look for the ways in which it seems He has used our nation to spread the gospel and bring His blessings to the rest of the world.

Noticing the ways in which God has used this nation gives us hope for the future. You should also think about how God may use you. You cannot change this fallen, cursed world by yourself. But you can do much good. You can help end abortion, expose corruption, start a church, or raise a godly family. Christians who attempt to do these things are valuable tools in the hands of God.

require students to apply information they have learned in the chapter.

What's the Point?

Ask the students, "What's the point in studying American history? Will it make you more popular? Will it give you a good job?" Guide them to consider the three reasons emphasized in the student text.

Lessons for life—As we study history from a biblical perspective, we learn important lessons for life. Psalm 78 records Israel's history. Its purpose is to encourage the readers to "set their hope in God" (v. 7). Similarly, we teach history because we want the next generation to trust God.

Elaborate on the four specific lessons listed on page xi of the text, noting that each lesson is supported by biblical teaching. Ask the students to comment on each lesson.

God at work in history—Many people do not believe God is at work in our history. To counter this viewpoint, ask the students to consider the following three points: (1) The Bible teaches that God has planned everything to establish Christ's kingdom on earth (1 Cor. 15:28; Eph. 1:10–11); (2) American history is part of everything; therefore (3) God has been using American history to accomplish His plan.

As Christians who love the Lord, we desire to study our past looking for possible explanations of how God has been at work. We cannot determine with certainty what God has been doing. We can, however, offer useful suggestions because we know that God is in control and that His goal is to establish the kingdom of His Son.

To give your students an idea of how these ideas may shape their understanding, engage them in a discussion of events from different periods in American history. With each, (1) describe the event, (2) ask the students what they believe God was doing in this event, and (3) guide them to make connections between what happened and how it may relate to the establishing of Christ's kingdom. Consider using one of the following examples:

- The Mayflower Pilgrims land in Massachusetts instead of Virginia in 1620.

- The American Civil War ends in 1865 with the defeat of the Confederacy.

To Give Us a Sense of Who We Are

A person's memory gives him his sense of identity. A person who does not remember anything about his past does not know who he is—we call this amnesia. But amnesia is not a problem just for individuals. Some societies suffer from this. They know very little about their past—how they became a civilization, what values bind them together, and why some men and women have given their lives to preserve their culture.

Just as a person cannot live normally if he does not know who he is, so a nation cannot function without a clear sense of its past. For a nation to prosper, its citizens must accept the sacrifices that are necessary to hold the nation together. Some of the most notable sacrifices are taxes, laws, and the defense of the nation. These sacrifices can be a burden to those who do not appreciate their country or know what it means to be a citizen.

We have designed this book to be much more than a record of names, wars, and dates. Throughout this course we desire to teach

what it means to be an American. We will present our history as the unfolding of several core values. Americans exist as they do because they tend to value the same ideas. To be a productive, valuable citizen, you must know what these values are. To serve this nation as a Christian, you will need to know how to judge these values with the Word of God in mind.

What Is an American?

The simple answer to this question is someone who lives in America or who is a citizen of the United States. But that answer does not offer much help. It does not tell us what kind of person an American is. To find a more helpful answer, we will need to consider what Americans have tended to love, or—as we will say repeatedly in the following paragraphs—what Americans have tended to *value*.

An American is someone who believes in certain core values. These values forge a common culture and bind a people together. What holds America together is not just a set of laws, a group of police officers, or a government in Washington, D.C. We are held together as a nation mainly by our love for the same ideas. Throughout much of our history, Americans have highly valued the following things.

Freedom

Freedom, also called liberty, is a condition in which a person can make his own choices without fear of harm. Americans value the freedom to worship as they wish, to choose their own jobs, to own whatever property they can afford, and to play a role in their government. When these freedoms are threatened, Americans quickly react.

Is it good to be free? Yes and no. The Bible values liberty (1 Cor. 7:21, 23; Rom. 6:17–22). But it also emphasizes that humans must obey God and His Word. A nation that refuses to submit to God will experience His judgment (Ps. 2:10–12; 9:17). It is good to be free if

---

- New York City and Washington, D.C., are attacked by Islamic terrorists on September 11, 2001.

Cultural identity—Ask the students, "Have you ever read a story in which someone suffered from amnesia?" Allow them to describe the plight of such a person. They may mention that he did not know the people and things he had loved for years, that he was unable to make decisions, and that he could not solve problems.

Ask the students, "What is cultural amnesia?" (*A condition in which people know very little of their culture's past.*) Then ask, "Why is cultural amnesia a bad thing?" (*Cultural amnesia produces the same problems individual amnesia does. The culture does not know*

what it should value, cannot make important decisions, and cannot solve its problems.*)

Ask the students, "How does a person recover from amnesia?" (*His memory must be filled again with content—what has happened to him, what he has done, and what he has loved. But for him to be himself, he must also view this content from his own perspective. If he learns this content from another's perspective, he will not be himself.*)

Conclude this discussion by noting that cultural amnesia is cured in a similar way. If we want to be responsible citizens, we must know our past. But we also need to learn it from a certain perspective. This course will attempt to teach our past with a focus on the core values that have characterized Ameri-

can culture for much of its history. We will also learn to evaluate these values from the teaching of Scripture.

Cultural Glue

Core values are the cultural glue that holds a society together. In order to emphasize this truth with your students, engage them in the following discussion.

Read the following two quotations. Then ask the students what they think they mean.

(1) "The pen is mightier than the sword." (Edward Bulwer-Lytton, playwright)

(2) "What is today a matter of academic speculation begins tomorrow to move armies and pull down empires." (J. Gresham Machen, Bible scholar and preacher)

we choose to please God and help others. It is not good if we use our choices to disobey God and harm others.

Problems arise when people argue that it is more important to be free than to be good. If a nation values freedom over goodness, then freedom is no longer a good core value. This kind of freedom encourages people to do whatever they wish. If people choose to do wrong, they hurt their society. And soon the society questions what is right and values its freedom to do wrong. We see this happen today when people choose to kill unborn children.

For some Americans, freedom has come to mean a freedom from God and religion. We call these people secularists. **Secularism** is the belief that religion has no place in government. They are afraid that if a government is religious, it will be unreasonable. As you read about American history, watch for the slow move away from religion as a central part of society. The America we now live in is far different from the America that once was.

Individualism

Individualism is the belief that a human should think of himself as an individual and not just as a member of a group. An individualist wants to be independent, take care of himself, and take responsibility for his own actions.

God values humans as individuals. He condemns and rewards them individually (Ezek. 18:20; Rom. 2:6–11), and He demands that government do the same (Deut. 24:16). The Bible also teaches that it is the individual's job to use wisdom and hard work to avoid poverty (Prov. 27:23–24; 2 Thess. 3:10). But the Bible also says that it is important to depend on others. Humans must work together—and be generous—if they are to please God. We cannot use individualism as an excuse to act selfishly. Most importantly, humans must depend on God through Jesus Christ for salvation. Those who say they don't need God will find that their own strength, initiative, and wisdom are not enough to carry them through life and beyond.

Lead them to the conclusion that ideas are more powerful than weapons because ideas lead people to invent weapons, form armies, and go to war. Weapons are only tools. Ideas are the driving force that changes the world.

Explain to the students that the most powerful ideas are those that people highly value. New societies form when people who highly value the same ideas join one another in the work of forming a culture. Societies descend into revolution or civil war when the influential citizens cannot agree on what ideas they value.

Conclude by taking a few minutes to demonstrate that the American Revolution and the Civil War were not first and foremost clashes of opposing armies. They were clashes of differing core values. Emphasize with the students that we cannot understand American history unless we understand the core values that have held American civilization together. Then state that in this course, we will study American history as the unfolding of four core values: freedom, individualism, equality, and growth.

Throughout much of our history, Americans have taken pride in their individualism. The story of America is the story of people seeking financial, social, and religious independence. It is the story of explorers, pioneers, inventors, and entrepreneurs.

Equality

Each time we recite the words "One nation under God, indivisible, with liberty and justice for all" in the Pledge of Allegiance, we affirm our pledge to equality. **Equality**, in the sense that we will use the term in this book, is a social condition in which all people are treated in the same way. In America, this means an equal standing before the law, the right of all citizens to vote and own property, and access to education.

The Bible teaches that all people are equally valued because all are made in the image of God (Gen. 1:26–27). Therefore, not even a king may take a person's life or property (2 Sam. 11–12; 1 Kings 21). But the Bible also teaches that a person may lose his right to life, property, or pleasure. If a person disobeys God's moral rules, he deserves punishment. He should not be treated the same as the other citizens. Treating him the same is not justice but injustice.

Americans have always valued equality. The most famous line from the Declaration of Independence affirms equality: "We hold these truths to be self-evident, that all men are created equal." But Americans have often failed to live up to this value. Repeatedly, Americans have not treated minorities—especially Indians and blacks—as fellow image bearers of God. Some of the most difficult struggles of the past two centuries were results of a lack of equality.

Early Americans believed that the best way to preserve equality was to create a republic. A **republic** is a nation ruled by law through representatives chosen by the people. The people choose representatives who work together to craft laws. In America, these laws must agree with the U. S. Constitution. This form of government places limits on those who govern as well as those who are governed. All are under the law. A republic protects the people from a dominating leader. It also prevents small groups from dominating the majority.

Some Americans have come to believe that the republic hinders equality. Increasingly, Americans have tended to favor **democracy**, or rule by majority opinion. Over time, more decisions have been made by the people in general elections. Also, Americans value the majority opinion over the opinion of government officials and even the law.

Democracy has its strengths. But it also has some serious weaknesses. The main weakness is that majority opinion is often wrong. Democracy assumes that the majority opinion is never wrong and that it should always be obeyed. But one of the purposes of government is to restrain evil, even if the evil is the will of the majority of the citizens. As you read this history, carefully trace the movement of this nation from a republic to a democracy.

Growth

Americans love to grow. By *growth* we mean achieving goals—gaining wealth, buying property, changing the environment, and enjoying new experiences.

The desire for growth appears in every period of American history. During the colonial period, Europeans left the security of home in search of new opportunities for wealth, property, and the spread of Christianity. Americans declared their independence from England in order to preserve their liberty and grow according to their own wishes. Soon after, Americans began looking across the continent for more land and the opportunities it provided. In the twentieth century, Americans experienced the growth of their free-market economy, advances in technology, and increased opportunities overseas.

God gives us the desire for growth. In the **Creation Mandate** of Genesis 1:28, He calls us to exercise authority over His earth. But humans are also fallen. So it is easy for this desire for growth to develop into greed and selfishness. While it is good for us to seek growth in many areas, we must be careful not to let growth become an idol. If we replace God with economic, technological, and academic achievement, we will become preoccupied with temporary, material things. The most important achievement for a Christian is growth in Christ as a gift of God's free grace. As you study this history, notice how our desire for growth has helped America—and how it has hurt.

Section Quiz

1. What are three reasons we should study American history?

2. Why are core values important to a civilization?

3. At what point does freedom become a problem?

4. What is individualism?

5. What biblical teaching from Genesis 1 supports the idea of social equality?

6. Why does a desire for growth often develop into greed and selfishness?

★ Explain the difference between a republic and a democracy. What is the main weakness of a democracy?

Section Quiz Answers

1. (1) learning lessons for life, (2) seeing God at work in our world, and (3) gaining a sense of cultural identity

2. They function as the glue that holds a culture together.

3. when people value freedom over goodness

4. the belief that a human should think of himself as an individual and not just as a member of a group

5. the image of God in humans

6. Humans are fallen.

★ A republic is a nation ruled by law through representatives chosen by the people. A democracy is rule by majority opinion. The chief problem with a democracy is that the majority opinion is often wrong.

How much did it cost?

Product	Year	Price
Bacon	1853	11.5¢/lb.
Coffee	1853	13¢/lb.
Peas	1856	71¢/bushel
Salt	1857	4¢/lb.
Springfield musket	1861	$14.93
Bread	1865	4¢/loaf

1859: Edwin Drake drilled the first oil well in Titusville, Pa.

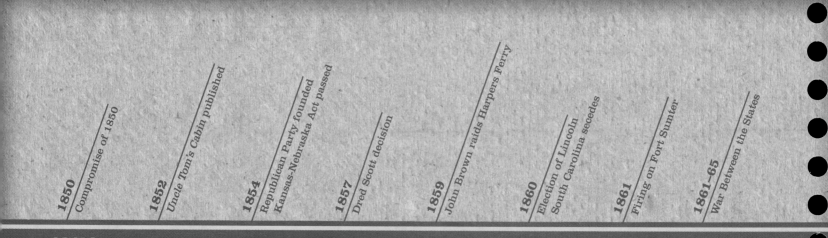

- **1850** Compromise of 1850
- **1852** Uncle Tom's Cabin published
- **1854** Republican Party founded — Kansas-Nebraska Act passed
- **1857** Dred Scott decision
- **1859** John Brown raids Harpers Ferry
- **1860** Election of Lincoln — South Carolina secedes
- **1861** Firing on Fort Sumter
- **1861–65** War Between the States

1858: Hyman Lipman patented a pencil with an eraser on one end.

How much did they make?

Occupation	Year	Wages
Carpenter	1853	$2.00/day
Typesetter	1854	$2.60/day
Brick mason	1855	$2.00/day
Farm laborer	1860	$34.16/month
Blacksmith	1860	$1.62/day
Private in the U.S. Army	1864	$13.00/month

1859: Harriet Wilson became the first African-American woman to publish a novel in the USA.

1863
Battle of Gettysburg
Emancipation Proclamation

1865
Surrender of Lee at Appomattox
Lincoln assassinated
Thirteenth Amendment ratified

1867
Reconstruction Act of 1867

1868
Impeachment of Andrew Johnson
Fourteenth Amendment ratified

1870
Fifteenth Amendment ratified

1876
Disputed presidential election
(Tilden v. Hayes)

1877
Withdrawal of Union troops from
the South

1877

Chapter Goals

Students should be able to

1. Define and use the basic terms of the chapter.

2. Understand how political, economic, and social factors led to sectionalism and the Civil War.

3. Explain the life of slaves in the plantation system, including their reactions to treatment received.

4. Distinguish the different interpretations of the constitutional role of government by the North and the South and explain how they influenced the coming of the Civil War.

5. Explain the significance of the Dred Scott decision, abolitionism, and each party/candidate in the election of 1860 to the sectional controversy.

6. Identify the major leaders of the North and the South during the antebellum years.

7. Explain how the Bible was used to defend and oppose slavery and evaluate the arguments from each side.

Chapter Motivation

A popular topic of discussion is the divisions in America today. These divisions flow from our core values. When the nation's core values diverge, then we have a recipe for civil war. There are issues today where American values are at odds, just as they were then over slavery. What are some examples? *(Answers will vary but could include abortion, legalized gambling, and assisted suicide.)*

The Southern economy was based predominantly on plantation agriculture.

CHAPTER 14

Storm Clouds over the Nation

I. **Differences Between the North and the South**

II. **Slavery in Antebellum America**

III. **The Slavery Issue Intensifies**

IV. **The Election of 1860 and Secession**

V. **Fort Sumter and War**

Chapter 14 Lesson Plan Chart

Section Title	Main Activity	Pages	Days
I. Differences Between the North and the South	Activity 1: Differences Between the North and the South	261–64	½–1 day
II. Slavery in Antebellum America	Activity 3: Frederick Douglass's Escape From Slavery	264–71	1–2 days
III. The Slavery Issue Intensifies	Activity 4: Differing Viewpoints: The Sumner-Brooks Episode	271–74	1–2 days
IV. The Election of 1860 and Secession	Activity 5: Map Work: The Divided Nation	275–77	½–2 days
V. Fort Sumter and War	Activity 6: Account of the Firing on Fort Sumter	277–81	1–2 days
TOTAL SUGGESTED DAYS (INCLUDING 1 DAY FOR REVIEW AND TESTING)			5–10 DAYS

MATERIALS LIST

SECTION I
- CD: Map of Plantation Belt, 1860; Extent of Slavery in the South; Differences Between North and South
- Activity 1 from the *Student Activities* manual

SECTION II
- An anthology of historical documents containing Thomas Dew's argument in favor of slavery
- *Free Indeed: Heroes of Black Christian History* by Mark Sidwell (BJU Press)
- *The Narrative of the Life of Frederick Douglass, an American Slave* by Frederick Douglass

On the surface, the 1850s were a time of unusual growth and prosperity. The population grew rapidly, and food production and manufacturing set records. However, below the surface, differences between the North and South swiftly led to a crisis that threatened the survival of the United States. Previous compromise that had delayed the resolution of these differences would soon prove insufficient to stop the march toward war.

Great problems existed during the **antebellum** (before the war) period. As this period drew to a close, the American nation was coming apart. Americans still held dear the same core values—freedom, equality, individualism, and growth. But they did not agree on how to define these values. Both North and South talked about freedom. The North was concerned that individuals be free from slavery. The South, on the other hand, wanted to keep the states free from federal control. Both sides also talked about equality. The South asserted the equality of the states: the right of each state to make its own decisions in most matters. Northerners, however, thought it was obvious that a culture of slavery could not be a culture of equality. Both North and South valued individualism. Some in the North believed slavery was evil because it kept persons from choosing their own course in life. But Southerners argued that the North was preventing individual whites in the South from living as they had a right to live.

Both North and South valued the growth of their own way of life. The North viewed Southern society as unjust, and the South viewed the North as greedy. Each viewed the other as uncultured. Northerners were afraid that if slavery spread to new states, Southern culture would become dominant. Likewise, Southerners were concerned that by forbidding slavery in the territories, Northern culture would become dominant. Both sides became willing to pay a very high price to expand their own way of life.

I. Differences Between the North and the South

Several issues divided the North and the South. The issues were not new, but some people now saw them as matters of right and wrong. They were not just regional preferences. Continued compromise between the regions seemed impossible.

Economic and Lifestyle Differences

The South was primarily agricultural. It had fewer big towns and villages than the North. It had even fewer cities. Even the largest Southern cities—such as Charleston, Richmond, and Savannah—were relatively small. Those cities had fewer than 40,000 people. Only New Orleans (pop. 150,000) compared to Northern cities in size and diversity. Instead of factories, the South had plantations and farms. They grew cotton, sugar, rice, tobacco, hemp, and other crops. Much Southern business involved agriculture in some way.

In the South the upper class, one percent of the population, was made up of planters owning large plantations and many slaves. This top one percent was the ruling class politically, socially, and economically. Other white farmers owned only a few slaves (generally fewer than ten). A much larger part of the Southern white population, however, owned no slaves at all. (Owners of small farms and other Southerners without slaves made up three-quarters of the white

Slaveholders in the South, 1860

Slaves	Owners	Percentage
1–4	139,718	45.6
5–19	123,085	40.2
20–49	32,882	10.7
50–99	8,170	2.7
100–499	2,251	0.7
500+	14	*

*Less than 1 percent

Section I
Objectives
Students should be able to

1. Describe the differing economies and lifestyles of the North and the South.

2. Explain the differing political views of the North and the South, especially their different interpretations of the roles of the federal and state governments.

• Activity 3 from the *Student Activities* manual

SECTION III
• *American History in Verse* by Burton Stevenson (available from BJU Press)
• Harriet Beecher Stowe's *Uncle Tom's Cabin*
• CD: James Buchanan, 15th President
• Book on John Brown or Bloody Kansas
• Activity 4 from the *Student Activities* manual

SECTION IV
• CD: Party Platform Summaries, 1860; 1860 Political Cartoons; Abraham Lincoln, 16th President; Results of 1860 Presidential Election

• Activity 5 from the *Student Activities* manual

SECTION V
• CD: The Seceding States
• *Scenes from American Church History* (BJU Press)
• Activities 6 and 7 from the *Student Activities* manual

Core Values

The Civil War is a fine example of how American core values can be developed in biblical and unbiblical ways. Christians have the responsibility of evaluating the way these values are understood and lived out. For instance, both North and South valued freedom. Southerners valued the freedom to maintain their own culture and way of life. Some Northerners were concerned that slavery was a blot on a nation that claimed to value freedom. Others were concerned that some Southern efforts to defend slavery encroached on the freedoms of white Northerners (e.g., censoring the mails or the grab for territories). How should a Christian evaluate these conceptions of freedom? A Christian can legitimately value limited government for practical reasons, but a Christian must be opposed to slavery as practiced in the antebellum South for biblical reasons (see side margin pp. 268–69). For instance, a Christian can argue that a limited government with checks and balances is more likely to safeguard against op-

Recurring Issues

The divisive issues that led the country into war in the 1860s were not original to that time period. They had simmered below the surface for many years. One of the best examples of these controversies concerns the social contract. It said that the people of a country voluntarily submit to a ruler for the protection of their natural rights. If he exceeds the appropriate boundaries of his power, however, the people have the right to nullify his laws or even to remove him as the ruler. This issue was raised several times prior to the Civil War, even as far back as the American Revolution, for which the social contract was used as justification. This theory made its way into the Declaration of Independence with the familiar words, "that to secure these rights, governments are instituted among men, deriving their just powers from the consent of the governed; that whenever any form of government becomes destructive of these ends, it is the right of the people to alter or abolish it."

Point out that the slavery issue had not been resolved but merely postponed at the time of the Constitutional Convention. Also lead your students to evaluate the idea of a social contract theory. Note that Romans 13 teaches that all civil power originates with the sovereign God, not with men. Furthermore, God demands that Christians submit as far as they may in obedience to the Lord, even to wicked governments like Nero's. Christians should note that even David, anointed to succeed Saul, did not overthrow Saul's government.

States' Rights

Other instances of appeal to the social contract theory include the Virginia and

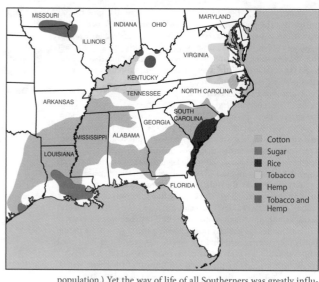

Five generations of slaves on a South Carolina plantation are pictured in this 1862 photograph.

population.) Yet the way of life of all Southerners was greatly influenced by the needs and desires of the slaveholders.

Southerners in general believed that slavery was vital to any stable society. They believed that blacks did not have the intelligence or ability to participate alongside whites in society. Therefore, setting slaves free would result in conditions worse than slavery. The existence of this poor class would lead to crime and class warfare. In time it could also lead to revolution. Southerners also argued that the crime and unrest in Northern cities proved that slavery was good for society.

The North, on the other hand, was heavily industrialized and had mostly free blacks. It had many large cities and towns. Some towns grew so quickly that they struggled to control their growth. New York City's population soared to more than 800,000. Chicago had grown from 4,170 people in 1837 to 112,000 in 1860.

Immigration accounted for much of the North's greater population. More than 2.8 million immigrants had come to America. Seven out of eight of them settled in the North or the West. At first, many of them had to live in filth and misery in the cities. They labored long hours for low wages. The working and living conditions of some Northern workers were so poor that Southerners called them "**wage slaves**." But most immigrants adopted American ways and raised their standard of living.

Immigrants in the North became involved in politics. Some of them held political office. In Boston, New York, and Philadelphia, Irish voters were strong. In St. Louis, Cincinnati, and Milwaukee, Germans were powerful.

The Northern population was mostly merchants, factory workers, and owners of small farms. Four-fifths of the nation's factories were in the North. Although most people were still farmers, mechanized agriculture helped them produce food for nearby towns. Railroads carried food from farms to the cities. They returned with

pression and that such a government will be more conducive to the spread of the gospel. But he cannot argue that a different form of government is sinful. God established Israel first as a confederation of tribes and later as a monarchy. On the other hand, antebellum slavery violated express commands from God.

💻 Teacher Resource: *The Road to Disunion*

An excellent explanation of the events leading up to the outbreak of the Civil War is the two-volume work by William Freehling—*The Road to Disunion: Secessionists at Bay, 1776–1854* and *The Road to Disunion: Secessionists Triumphant, 1854–1861*.

🕸 Prelude to War

Check www.bjupress.com/resources/ for possible links to information on the run-up to the Civil War.

💿 CD: Map of Plantation Belt, 1860

The map on this page of the student text is also available on the CD if you wish to refer to it while teaching this section.

⚖ Debate Ideas

Have your students discuss and/or debate the following topics:

1. States' rights, rather than slavery, was what the Civil War was fought over.

2. The South should have been allowed to secede from the Union.

3. The American Civil War was inevitable.

manufactured goods. Owners of factories, railroads, and other industries became wealthy and influential in Northern society.

Manufacturing by Region, 1860

Region	Businesses	Capital investment ($M)	Workers	Annual value of products ($M)
North	110,843	886	1,147,988	1,655
South	20,631	96	110,721	155

Political Differences

The regions also differed in their political views. Most Northerners followed Hamilton's ideal of a strong federal government. Northerners tended to be more willing to pay higher taxes to provide local and state services. The North also had more wage earners to help pay for such projects.

Most Southerners feared a strong central government. They still believed in Jefferson's ideal that the best government was at the local and state levels. Southerners spent little money on local services. Few of them lived in cities and towns where such services were needed. They did not want to pay taxes for internal improvements that often helped only the North. Southerners also considered education to be a private, parental matter, so the South had few public schools.

The two regions also disagreed sharply about what level of government (federal or state) should have more authority. Most Northerners believed that the Constitution was the nation's highest law under God. The Constitution and federal law overruled any conflicting state and local laws. Northerners based their views on **Article VI** of the Constitution.

Most Southerners disagreed. They argued that the federal government could not overrule the rights of the states. They believed, as Jefferson and Madison had stated in the Virginia and Kentucky Resolutions (see Chapter 8), that government was a contract between a ruling body and the people (the states). They held the Constitution granted only limited powers to the national government. When rulers exceeded the power given to them by the people, the people had the right to nullify those actions or to leave the Union. They could then organize a new government that would respect those limitations and states' rights. Thus, the states' sovereignty (authority) prevailed over national sovereignty. Southerners based their views on the contract theory of government and **Amendment X** of the Constitution.

The South feared losing power in Congress. The North's power increased as its population grew and the population increased westward. Every time a new territory applied for statehood, the South's fears resurfaced. Every new free state admitted to the Union meant more votes against Southern views. If the North gained too large a majority, the South feared the North would restrict the spread of slavery.

The tariff was another issue of disagreement. The tariff was a good revenue source of the U.S. government. The North favored a high tariff, not as a source of revenue but as a means of protecting its industries from foreign imports. The South opposed a high tariff because the South had little industry. Foreign imports and trade

---

Article VI

"This Constitution, and the laws of the United States . . . ; and all treaties made . . . under the authority of the United States, shall be the supreme law of the land; and the judges in every state shall be bound thereby, anything in the constitution or laws of any state to the contrary notwithstanding."

Amendment X

"The powers not delegated to the United States by the Constitution, nor prohibited by it to the states, are reserved to the states respectively, or to the people."

Kentucky Resolutions (Chapter 8), the Hartford Convention at the end of the War of 1812 (margin note in Chapter 9), and South Carolina's Ordinance of Nullification and its accompanying threat of secession (Chapter 11).

Another issue that continually divided North and South was the conflict between industry and agriculture. The conflict was a major factor in differences over the National Bank. It also accounted for the tariff controversy—the desire for a high protective tariff by the North and the strong objection to tariffs by the South. This controversy became heated in 1828 when President John Quincy Adams signed the "tariff of abominations" (Chapter 10). The tariff of 1832, though slightly lower than the 1828 version, was still objectionable enough to provoke the Ordinance of Nullification (Chapter 11).

Article VI

Article VI of the Constitution states that the United States Constitution, together with laws and treaties made under its authority, are the supreme law of the land. Judges throughout the country are to consider the Constitution their final source of authority, even if the laws of the particular states in which they preside are contradictory. Before the war, the Court tended to side with the states. After the war, the Court began to side more often in favor of the national government.

Activity 1: Differences Between the North and the South

Have the students complete this chart as a way of reinforcing the information in this section of the textbook.

CD: Extent of Slavery in the South

Refer to the CD for a map showing degree of slaveholding in the South.

CD: Differences Between North and South

Refer to the CD for a chart showing differences between the North and the South.

Activity 2: Who Has the Greater Authority?

Use this activity to help the students understand the different constitutional emphases of the North and the South.

Section II
Objectives

Students should be able to

1. Explain how slavery in America was different from slavery in other countries.

2. Describe the Middle Passage and life on a Southern plantation, including how slaves were treated.

3. Distinguish between the gang system and the task system.

4. Explain the role of the Bible in the slavery debate.

5. Describe some of the black reactions to slavery, including escape on the Underground Railroad, and their significance to the slavery controversy.

6. Identify key leaders in the abolition movement.

7. Contrast the Northern and the Southern views of slavery.

The Middle Passage

John Newton testified before the British Privy Council in 1788 that it was normal for one-third of the slaves to die on the Middle Passage.

supported its economy; a high tariff hurt trade and made foreign countries less likely to buy the South's crops. Southerners believed that they were, in effect, being forced to pay the tariff to support Northern industry.

Section Quiz

1. What was the main economic focus of the South? the North?

2. What groups of people were most influential in Northern and Southern society?

★ How and why did Northerners and Southerners differ in their philosophy of government? What was the basis of each philosophy?

★ The North and South differed over core values. Which difference was most important? Why?

II. Slavery in Antebellum America

Although slavery is nearly as old as the human race, slavery in antebellum America was different from slavery at other times in history. Hence it was called "the peculiar institution." It differed in the following three ways.

1. It involved only those of African descent.

2. It became a permanent condition for most slaves.

3. It was the result of buying stolen Africans and selling them.

In order to ensure Southern support for the Constitution, the founding fathers had delayed finding a permanent solution to slavery. They counted three-fifths of the total slave population of each state to determine representation. They also guaranteed that Congress would not prohibit the slave trade before 1808.

The demand for cotton in both Europe and the United States encouraged increased Southern production. Slavery also increased. When the government took the first census in 1790, the United States had about 750,000 slaves. By 1860, the cotton boom had pushed the slave population to three and a half million. One of every three Southerners was a slave.

How Slaves Were Acquired

In Chapter 3 you read that most slaves came from the nations on Africa's western coast. Some slaves were captured in raids and sold to traders. Some were prisoners of war captured by warring African tribes, and sold by their enemies into slavery for profit. Slave traders bought African men, women, and children with liquor and various utensils and trinkets.

Perhaps the slave's worst experience was crossing the Atlantic to America. This crossing was called the "**Middle Passage**." (The first passage took the slave to the coast of Africa; the third passage involved the final sale to slave owners in America.) Crowded into shelf-like decks, the Africans were then chained and shackled wrist-to-wrist and ankle-to-ankle. Poorly fed, they usually received gruel and water twice a day. Disease spread quickly because of poor sanitation. Some captives broke down under the stress of the conditions and killed themselves and others. At least one in seven or eight—maybe as many as one in four—died on the voyage.

Growth of Cotton Production, 1792–1860	
Year	Bales produced
1792	4,000
1800	73,222
1820	334,728
1840	1,347,640
1860	3,841,416

Section Quiz Answers

1. agriculture; industry

2. Northern—owners of factories, railroads, and other industries; Southern—owners of large plantations

★ The North generally favored a strong central government. They based their views on Article VI of the Constitution, which states that the Constitution supercedes all state laws. The South believed that the states' rights were more important than national powers based on Amendment X of the Constitution, which stipulates that all powers not delegated to the United States by the Constitution, nor prohibited by it to the states, are reserved to the states respectively, or to the people.

★ Growth of their own way of life; if their own way of life did not grow, the other values would be threatened by the growth of the other side.

Teacher Resources: Plantation Life

Two excellent sources for information about life on a Southern plantation are *Tombee: Portrait of a Cotton Planter* by Theodore Rosengarten and excerpts from Mary Chesnut's *A Diary from Dixie*.

In 1808 the United States became the last major western nation to ban foreign slave trade. (See Article I, Section 9 of the Constitution.) Some slave smuggling did continue, but most new slaves after this time were the children of men and women already living in the United States. Most of the Northern states had abolished slavery by the end of the War for Independence.

Slave Life in the South

The quality of slave life in the South depended on the master, the amount of property he owned, and the kind of system he employed to manage the slaves. Some masters were unquestionably cruel. Others took pride in how well they treated their slaves. But most slaves—even those with kind masters—longed for a different life.

Life on a Southern Plantation

Life on a plantation centered on the master, the overseer, the slaves, and the work. The master instructed the overseer. The **overseer** distributed the work among the slaves and ensured that they did as expected. Sometimes the overseer used verbal or physical threats. Usually he was a hired white man. After it became difficult to find reliable overseers who would work for little pay, some slave owners simply used a trusted slave.

The slaves' work varied with the type of crops grown and the season of the year. Jobs included clearing land, planting seeds, weeding or cultivating, harvesting, cutting wood, and digging ditches. Other jobs included cooking, caring for the master's children, caring

Cotton was packed into bales for shipment to buyers. The cotton plant is in the same family as the hibiscus and okra plants.

Quakers and Slavery

Quakers were opposed to slavery. They refused to use products that were produced by slave labor. However, not all Quakers agreed on the best way to end slavery. Some preferred to watch passively while God worked, but others chose an active role. Some Quakers devised schemes for gradual emancipation. Others aided fugitives traveling the Underground Railroad. Their boldness in that venture is well recorded.

Laura Smith Haviland of Adrian, Michigan, is a good example of a Quaker devoted to the cause of emancipation. She led so many slaves to freedom in Canada that Southern slave owners advertised a reward for her capture. However, Laura eluded restraint, and, together with her family, set up one of the first interracial schools in Michigan.

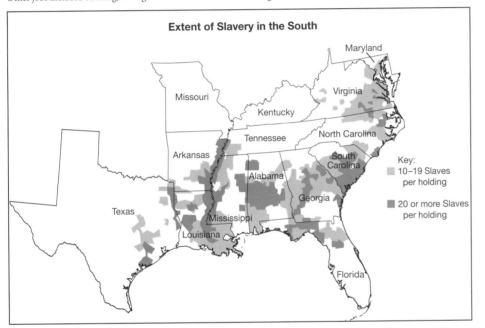

Extent of Slavery in the South

Maryland
Missouri
Virginia
Kentucky
Tennessee
North Carolina
Arkansas
South Carolina
Alabama
Georgia
Texas
Mississippi
Louisiana
Florida

Key:
■ 10–19 Slaves per holding
■ 20 or more Slaves per holding

Thomas R. Dew's "Positive Good" Theory

Have students critique Thomas R. Dew's argument in favor of slavery (or one of John C. Calhoun's speeches on the same topic). These documents are included in many anthologies of U.S. history, and excerpts are available on the Internet. Analyzing these arguments gives the students an opportunity to investigate logical fallacies. Of particular interest are the arguments in behalf of slavery based on the Bible. Evaluate these arguments and demonstrate how they misinterpret Scripture.

Teacher Resource: Slave Religion

An excellent source of information on religion as practiced by the slaves is *Religion in the Old South* by Donald Mathews. Other works include *The Civil War as a Theological Crisis* by Mark A. Noll, and *The Mind of the Master Class: History and Faith in the Southern Slaveholders' Worldview* by Elizabeth Fox-Genovese and Eugene D. Genovese.

Spirituals

Visit www.bjupress.com/resources for a possible link to information about spirituals.

Pastors of Former Slaves

Free Indeed: Heroes of Black Christian History tells the story of Daniel Payne, a black man who was free at birth and became a strong abolitionist and an educator of blacks before, during, and after the Civil War.

"John Jasper" is the story of a slave who was freed at the end of the Civil War and who preached to many.

Traveling to Freedom

Many of the fugitive slaves who traveled the Underground Railroad were men between the ages of sixteen and thirty-five. The Railroad had little organization in the South, so slaves traveling there had to find their own way. A common method of navigation was following the North Star. Another method involved looking for tree moss, which grows only on the north side of trees.

Once they reached the region of Railroad activity, the fugitives could anticipate more assistance. Railroad stations were generally ten or more miles apart. Slaves could identify stations in several different ways. Some indicators were a candle in a window, a lantern in the front yard, a drinking gourd (symbolizing the Big Dipper, which points to the North Star), or a quilt containing the color black hung on a clothesline. Station conductors gave the fugitives food, clothing, and shelter during the day; at night they either told them how to get to the next station or actually took them there.

Average Estimated Cost of a Good Slave, 1798–1859	
Year	Price
1798	$350
1822	$850
1830	$650
1840	$1000
1859	$1300

Slave auctions were big business when cotton was "king."

$100 REWARD!
RANAWAY
From the undersigned, living on Current River, about twelve miles above Doniphan, in Ripley County, Mo., on 3rd of March, 1860, A NEGRO MAN, about 30 years old, weighs about 160 pounds; high forehead, with a scar on it; had on brown pants and coat very much worn, and an old black wool hat; shoes size No. 11.

The above reward will be given to any person who may apprehend this slave against him at the State; and fifty dollars if apprehended in this State outside of Ripley County, or $25 if taken in Ripley county, and this slave returned.
APOS TUCKER.

Owners offered rewards for the return of runaway slaves.

for animals, and repairing tools, fences, dikes, buildings, or other structures.

As mentioned earlier, one factor that affected how slaves were treated was the type of working arrangement used. Some masters used the **gang system**. Their slaves worked in large groups for a set amount of time each day—usually from sunup to sundown or longer—doing whatever the master ordered. Other masters used the **task system**, which most slaves preferred. Under the task system, the overseer gave the slaves specific tasks. Whenever they completed their tasks, they could use the rest of the day to do other things.

Since slaves were the property of the master, they were viewed as an economic investment. In theory, keeping them fit and healthy made good business sense. Their meals, similar to those of poor Southerners, included cornmeal mush or cornbread, fatback (fat from the back of a hog), beans or field peas, and vegetables from the slaves' own gardens. But conditions were not always tolerable. Some masters were inhumane in their treatment of their slaves, and slaves had no legal appeal if they were mistreated. In any case, when all was said and done, they were slaves.

Some slaves, especially those who cared for the master's children, were viewed by their owners as almost members of the family. House slaves (those who worked in the master's house) generally were treated better than field slaves. The smaller the plantation, the closer the slaves and master tended to be. But slaves still had no basic rights other than what their masters granted. Slaves had no standing before the law. Their marriages were not even recognized. Children born to them belonged to the master. Some masters even insisted on naming slave children. What some masters believed to be compassionate care, the slaves viewed as continual interference in their lives.

The typical slave was sold at least once in a lifetime. Some sales were against the master's will, such as when he was forced to sell slaves to pay debts. Many sales meant a heart-wrenching separation from spouses, children, and friends. Slaves especially feared being sold "down the river" to sugar plantations in the lower Mississippi River Valley. Cutting and processing sugar cane was brutal work. Some sugar plantation masters actually worked slaves to death.

Black Responses to Plantation Conditions

Slaves had several ways by which they resisted ill treatment. They would report to the "sick house" whether they were truly ill or not. At other times they might willfully "misunderstand" their master's instructions. They might also work more slowly than they were capable. Or they might purposely break tools so that they could not work while the tools were repaired.

Thousands of slaves ran away. This was a constant problem for many masters. Masters offered large rewards for their slaves' return. The "**Underground Railroad**" offered blacks who could reach the border states a chance of escaping and gaining freedom in the North. This "railroad" was actually a network of people who aided runaway slaves. People called "conductors" hid the slaves by day. At night, they directed them to their next safe location. Conductors at the next "station" did the same thing. In this way, runaway slaves slowly made

Autobiography of a Freed Slave

If you did not have time to read the autobiography of a slave mentioned in Chapter 3, you could do so now. Entitled *The Interesting Narrative of the Life of Olaudah Equiano*, it includes an account of Equiano's "middle passage."

Activity 3: Frederick Douglass's Escape from Slavery

Students are sure to be moved by selections from the poignant autobiography *The Narrative of the Life of Frederick Douglass, an American Slave*, beginning with his lack of knowledge about his age and his separation from his mother in infancy. Activity 3 includes excerpts from this work.

Should Christians Support Civil Disobedience?

The citizens who supported the Underground Railroad practiced civil disobedience. Discuss whether they were right to do so. If slavery took place today, would it be right for a Christian to aid in the Underground Railroad? Some pro-life activists use the same argument to justify breaking the law in order to save the lives of unborn babies. Have your students read the account in Acts 4 where Peter and John respectfully refused to obey the religious/civil authorities. Remind them that the apostles did so with the willingness to suffer the consequences of their decision.

"The Underground Railroad"

their way to freedom. When the Fugitive Slave Act of 1850 required Northern states to return runaways, the Underground Railroad extended its route farther North. Ontario, Canada, became the final destination for many slaves, but some of them actually went south. They developed "maroon" settlements in the swamps of Georgia and northern Florida.

Though slave rebellions seldom occurred, whites still feared them, since by 1860 one-third of the Southern population was enslaved. With this many slaves, a well-organized revolt could become a revolution. Some slaves, such as Nat Turner in Virginia and Denmark Vesey (VEE zee) in South Carolina, led revolts. All such uprisings failed, however. The blacks involved were hanged. The hangings made other slaves less likely to rebel. But the revolts panicked the whites. They slept with guns. They passed even stricter slave codes. Several states even made it illegal to teach slaves to read and write. They feared that ideas of revolt would spread if blacks had those skills.

Several famous black leaders worked against slavery in the troubled years before the war. **Frederick Douglass**, the leading black **abolitionist** (ab uh LISH uh nist; a person who wanted to ban all slavery), escaped from slavery in 1838. He was a talented speaker and lectured against slavery in the North and even in Britain. He used money earned from his lectures to help other escaped slaves. He also wrote an influential autobiography, *The Narrative of the Life of Frederick Douglass*. Douglass risked his freedom because the book told the name of his former master. To escape possible capture, he fled to England. (The British Empire abolished slavery by 1834 due to the untiring influence of abolitionist William Wilberforce.) Sympathizers bought Douglass's freedom. When he returned to the United States, Douglass began publishing an antislavery newspaper, the *North Star*. He also supported women's rights.

After much abuse at the hands of her master, **Harriet Tubman** escaped from slavery in 1849. With the help of Quaker friends, she returned to slave territory nearly twenty times to help other slaves escape. She led about three hundred blacks along the Underground Railroad. She even helped her own parents escape in 1857. A book about her life made her famous as the "Moses" of her people.

Frederick Douglass

Harriet Tubman

Educated Slaves

Explain to your students why the South might have forbidden education to blacks. Remind your students that both Nat Turner and Denmark Vesey (mentioned in both this section and Chapter 12) were intelligent, educated men. Ask your students if such reasons for denying education are justifiable. *(No. Slaveholding was itself sinful. Denying anyone education in order to perpetuate slaveholding was also wrong.)*

The Bible's Role in the Slavery Debate

The issue of the Bible and slavery has remained a key issue for Christians from the early years of the nation through the present. In the nineteenth century, Christians debated whether the Scripture supported slavery or abolition.

At first glance, the Bible seems to support the pro-slavery position. The Pentateuch assumes that Israelites will own slaves (note the fourth commandment), and the New Testament includes instruction to Christian masters and slaves. The suggestion made by some that in Philemon Paul is encouraging Christian masters to free their slaves seems strained.

Many abolitionists, convinced that the Bible condoned slavery, were prepared to discard the Bible because they were sure that slavery was wrong. Others, not ready to abandon the Scripture, unwisely pitted the spirit of the Scripture against its letter. These approaches convinced many Christians of the slaveholding position. If the choice came between anti-slavery and the Bible, they chose the Bible.

Both positions suffered from failing to read the Scripture evidence closely enough. Antebellum slavery was very different from either Jewish or Greco-Roman slavery. For instance, Jewish slaves were freed after six years of service and liberally provided for upon release (cf. Deut 15:12–18). "Slavery" in ancient Israel served in many ways as a social safety-net for the poor and indebted. Greco-Roman slavery was morally a more mixed system, but it too differed greatly from antebellum American slavery. It was not a race-based system of permanent, generational servitude. Slaves could own slaves themselves. They would often work side-by-side with

This sketch was used widely by abolitionists.

William Lloyd Garrison and Horace Greeley were two leading abolitionists.

Blacks in Knoxville, Tennessee

In 1860, nearly half of Knoxville's small population of blacks were free. Of those, 20 percent had skilled jobs. An amazing 28 percent of them owned their own homes. (Robert McKenzie, *Lincolnites and Rebels: A Divided Town in the American Civil War*, p. 35.)

Opposing Views of Slavery

Most Northerners were not abolitionists, and not all those in the South supported slavery. Nevertheless, by the middle of the nineteenth century, clear differences existed between these two sections of the nation on this issue.

Northern Responses to Slavery

Since many Northern states had abolished slavery, most Northerners in the early 1800s were not concerned with slavery. They were more concerned with economic issues. What brought slavery to their attention was its possible spread to new territories and the resulting increase of slave states. Opening western territories to slavery would increase Southern influence in Congress. That would decrease the North's influence.

Northern feelings also changed as abolitionism increased. Abolitionists objected to slavery for moral reasons. They believed slavery violated basic human rights. Abolitionists supported emancipation, paying slave owners whose slaves were freed. This movement was strongest in the New England states.

One vocal abolitionist was **William Lloyd Garrison**. He began a newspaper called the *Liberator*. It advocated an immediate end to slavery without compensation. Garrison also hurt the abolitionist cause by rejecting the Bible because it seemed to condone slavery. Another antislavery journalist was **Horace Greeley**. He published the New York *Tribune*. It opposed slavery and the Fugitive Slave Act. Both men later supported the new Republican Party.

Even though many Northerners opposed slavery, most retained racist attitudes toward blacks. For example, few Northern states allowed free blacks to vote or offered them a public education. Northern states kept blacks from many occupations and public offices. They also assigned them separate areas in churches and other public places. Illinois and Indiana would not even let blacks settle within their borders! Few Northerners desired to go to war to free the slaves.

Southern Responses to Abolitionism

The more the abolitionists opposed slavery, the more Southerners—even those who were not slaveholders—defended it. Some did so to resist the growth of federal power. Others did so because they hoped one day to own slaves. The success of the South seemed to depend on slavery. Many Southern businesses relied on cotton produced by slave labor. Some Southern whites opposed slavery but saw it as a necessary evil. As time went on more Southerners said that slavery was a "positive good." Many believed that their slave society promoted the virtues of honor, courage, duty, and dignity. Some argued that slavery provided educated Southerners the time necessary for spiritual and mental growth. Several also argued that slavery took pagan Africans out of primitive conditions and put them into a Christian setting where they would hear the gospel and perhaps be saved.

Many people in the South supported slavery on constitutional grounds. They believed that, right or wrong, the Constitution recognized slavery. It gave the states, not the national government, primary authority over slavery. To them, the issue was who would regulate slavery—the state governments or the national government.

Other Southerners saw slavery as an issue of economics. The North, they claimed, was trying to end slavery because its businesses, using paid laborers, were unable to compete with the South. If the North could only force the South to use paid labor, too, the North could control the Southern economy. Northern support for a high tariff also hurt the Southern economy and favored Northern industry. Some leaders began to talk of seceding.

Not everyone in the South favored slavery. Small farmers in the Appalachian South opposed slavery because it gave the owners of large plantations greater influence over state governments. Many people from that area later sided with the North on slavery.

Of course, slaves themselves were opposed to the practice of slavery. This is clear because tens of thousands of them attempted to escape. They often revealed how they felt about their condition with songs that came to be known as "**spirituals.**" Songs like "Nobody Knows the Trouble I Seen" and "Sometimes I Feel Like a Motherless Child" expressed the suffering they endured as slaves. Spirituals such as "Steal Away to Jesus" and "Let My People Go" expressed their desire for freedom.

The Bible's Role in the Slavery Debate

Americans during this period were mostly Protestant Christians. This meant that the question of slavery was not merely a political question. It was also a biblical question. The majority of Americans believed that the Bible was God's Word. What it said should have settled the matter. But neither side could agree on what the Bible said.

The slavery issue also split the major religious groups. The Methodists split in early 1844. In the South they formed the Southern Methodist Church. In the same year, the Baptists split over whether slaveholders could be appointed to mission boards or serve as missionaries. The Southern Baptist Convention was formed on May 10, 1845. The Presbyterians split in 1837 and again twenty years later.

Abolitionism and the Bible

The Second Great Awakening sparked many reform movements. Not all Christians were reformers, and not all reformers were Christians. But Christians played a major role in many of the reforms, especially the antislavery movement. Lyman Beecher and Nathaniel Taylor in New England and Charles Finney in New York were among the preachers who sparked the movement. They influenced many future antislavery leaders, including Theodore Weld and Arthur Lewis Tappan.

Most Christians who argued against slavery did not appeal to individual passages of Scripture. They argued from general Bible principles, such as the fact that man was created in the image of God and that Christians were to treat one another as brothers regardless of differences in race or economic condition. As Americans, they believed it should be obvious that the Bible sided with liberty over tyranny.

However, these Christians had difficulty reconciling the general principles of Scripture with specific biblical statements that seemed to condone slavery. Because of this, other abolitionists were willing to reject the Bible altogether.

The Bible and the Defense of Slavery

There were Bible passages that seemed to condone slavery. This led many Christians in the North and South to believe slavery was allowed. The total rejection of the Bible by some abolitionists made these people more suspicious of attempts to justify abolitionism

Spirituals

The following song titles are some of the most famous spirituals:

"'Dis Train"

"Lord, I Want to Be a Christian"

"Do Lord"

"Down By the Riverside"

"Nobody Knows the Trouble I Seen"

"Every Time I Feel the Spirit"

"Go Down Moses"

"In That Great Gettin' Up Mornin'"

"It's Me, O Lord, Standin' in the Need of Prayer"

"Steal Away to Jesus"

"Wayfaring Stranger"

"We Are Climbing Jacob's Ladder"

"We Are Comin', Father Abraham"

"Were You There?"

"Ezekiel Saw the Wheel"

Lyman Beecher preached against slavery in New England.

their masters. Though some were held in deplorable conditions in the mines or galleys, others administered estates and held positions far above poor freedmen. Many of the slaves who served in the cities gained their freedom by their thirties and, because there were no racial differences between slave and free, could move into the broader society. These facts are not intended to minimize the dark sides of Greco-Roman slavery—from the right of the master to kill or torture any slave at will to the degrading practice of referring to slaves of any age as "boy"—but they demonstrate that the New Testament exhortations for Christian masters do not justify antebellum slavery.

Antebellum slavery arose from the slave trade, which fell under the prohibition of Scripture (Ex. 12:16; 1 Tim. 1:10). Southern slavery also contradicted biblical prohibitions against racism (Gen 1:26–27; Mark 12:31; Luke 10:30–37). Furthermore, Southerners could not accurately claim the Bible justified their practice. God commanded his people to free their slaves after six years of service while Southerners held slaves in perpetuity from generation to generation.

The Conflict Among Presbyterians

The most thorough account of the conflict among the Presbyterians was written by Robert Lewis Dabney in *A Defense of Virginia and Through Her of the South*. In it he denounced the slave trade but defended slavery itself. A Northern account of the debate can be found in several articles by B. B. Warfield now printed in *Selected Shorter Writings of Benjamin B. Warfield* in which he argues against the reunion of the northern and southern Presbyterian churches because of the unbiblical Jim Crow laws supported in the South.

John Chavis and Lott Carey

Two other blacks of the early 1800s who had strong Christian testimonies were John Chavis and Lott Carey. Chavis was a free black; he was probably the first black to attend Princeton. He became a teacher and a Presbyterian minister. Carey went to Africa as a missionary after he gained his freedom.

from the Bible. It seemed to these Christians that the abolitionists were trying to avoid the clear teaching of Scripture.

Those who defended slavery used passages such as Leviticus 25:45–46. They concluded from this passage that God permitted slavery. They declared that He also permitted the Israelites to keep foreigners in slavery forever. These defenders of slavery also emphasized that Jesus and the apostles never said anything against slavery. In fact, the apostle Paul told a runaway slave (Philemon) to return to his master. On several occasions New Testament authors tell slaves to obey their masters (Eph. 6:5–8; Col. 3:22–25). Supporters of slavery referred to verses that told slaves to submit to even unjust masters (1 Peter 2:18–25). Masters were told to treat their slaves well (Eph. 6:9; Col. 4:1; 1 Tim. 6:1–2), but masters were never told to release their slaves.

African Americans, the Bible, and Slavery

Religion played a major role in the slave community. Slaves often attended the same churches as their masters. In some churches blacks and whites worshiped together. In other churches the blacks sat in the balcony and whites on the main floor. Some blacks, however, formed their own churches. Some of these churches were independent, but most had white supervisors. Masters feared that the slaves might use their church services to plan revolts. If whites thought that the black churches were a potential threat, they would order them to disband.

John Jasper (1812–1901)

John Jasper spent the first fifty years of his life as a slave, yet he managed to rise to national prominence as a preacher. He was born in Virginia to slaves and worked first on a plantation and then as a factory slave in a tobacco factory. Jasper could only preach with his master's permission, yet he gained a following by preaching at black funerals and twice a month in Petersburg. After gaining his freedom, Jasper started the Sixth Mount Zion Baptist Church and built the congregation to two thousand members. When the church decided to build a suitable structure, Jasper contributed $3,000 of his own money to help pay for the building. He developed a mastery of monologue, and hundreds of people, black and white, came to hear his fascinating preaching. His sermon on Joshua 10 entitled "The Sun Do Move" became the one most requested.

Due to the influence of more than a generation of Bible preaching, African Americans, unlike some white abolitionists, tended to have a very high view of Scripture. But they did not believe the Bible supported American slavery. They argued that the American practice of slavery contradicted the Bible's regulation of the practice. Daniel Coker, a minister, pointed to Genesis 17, which teaches that foreign slaves could become Israelites. Once they were Israelites, he reasoned, they had to be treated like Jews. This meant they would be freed after a few years.

Coker also stated the difference between Israel's slaves and the South's. He noted that the Israelites were not sent by God to distant nations who had no quarrel with them in order to capture them and hold them in bondage forever. Coker pointed to Scripture passages that condemned slavery by means of kidnapping (Exodus 21:16; 1 Tim. 1:10).

Other African Americans noted that, unlike slavery in the Bible, American slavery was racist. The South enslaved only blacks. Many white Southerners justified this condition, asserting that Africans did not have the ability to take part in a white society. However, the Bible clearly condemns racism (Gen. 1:26–27; Mark 12:31; Luke 10:30–37). African Americans pointed out that it also condemns racist slavery.

A Biblical Crisis

Up to this point in American history, most Americans applied the Bible to all areas of society. The debate over slavery brought American culture into a crisis. Americans on both sides of the issue tried to use the Scripture to resolve this problem. But the harder they worked, the more difficult the problem became. They could not agree on what the Bible said. It seemed that the Bible was unable to resolve one of the most important issues in American culture. As a result many educated Americans concluded the Bible was not able to decide issues of national policy. Thus, the Bible would eventually cease to play a leading role in American public life.

Section Quiz

1. What three characteristics distinguished American slavery?
2. Why did thousands of Africans die in the Middle Passage?
3. By 1860, how much of the Southern population was enslaved?
4. Contrast the Northern and Southern viewpoints on slavery.
   ☆ Does the Bible condone slavery as it was practiced in antebellum America?

III. The Slavery Issue Intensifies

The nation had tried to deal with the spread of slavery through compromise. Neither the Missouri Compromise in 1820 nor the Compromise of 1850, however, really solved the problem. All they did was postpone its solution. The slavery issue was like a pot of water with a lid on it sitting on a hot stove. Several incidents brought the issue to a boil.

Uncle Tom's Cabin

One incident was the publication of an innocent-sounding novel— *Uncle Tom's Cabin*, or *Life Among the Lowly*. **Harriet Beecher Stowe**, a Connecticut preacher's daughter, lost a young son to cholera in 1849. She believed that her loss helped her understand how slave mothers felt when their children were sold and taken from them. She vowed to bring the plight of slave families and runaways to public attention.

The Stowes had lived for a while in Cincinnati, Ohio, across the Ohio River from the slave state of Kentucky. She had glimpsed there the plight of fugitive slaves. From that experience, what she read in abolitionist papers, and her imagination, she wrote the novel. It was first published in installments by the *National Era*, an antislavery

UNCLE TOM'S CABIN;
OR,
LIFE AMONG THE LOWLY.
BY
HARRIET BEECHER STOWE.

VOL. I.

ONE HUNDRED AND FIFTH THOUSAND.

BOST
JOHN P. JEWET
CLEVELAN
JEWETT, PROCTOR

Harriet Beecher Stowe was a small, unassuming woman, but her novel produced a great emotional reaction in the North against slavery.

Section III
Objectives
Students should be able to

1. Describe the effect of *Uncle Tom's Cabin* on the nation.
2. Explain the Kansas-Nebraska Act and its effect in Kansas.
3. Name the political party that grew out of antislavery views.
4. Explain the Dred Scott decision and its effect on the nation.
5. Describe John Brown and his activities.

Polarizing Attitudes

Note that each issue discussed in this section had a major role in polarizing attitudes in the United States before the Civil War. Emotions on both sides of the slavery issue were stirred by *Uncle Tom's Cabin*, the Dred Scott case, and John Brown's activity. As more and more anger and hatred were fixed on the South by some in the North, Southern fears and defenses grew accordingly. Likewise, continued reactions and perceived defiance by the South resulted in growing frustration in the North.

Harriet Beecher Stowe

Harriet Beecher Stowe could claim a religious heritage. Her father, brother, and husband were influential religious leaders of the nineteenth century.

Besides her several books, Harriet also wrote a few hymns: "Abide in Me, O Lord," "Still, Still with Thee," "That Mystic Work of Thine," and "When Winds Are Raging." Most of these were published in *Plymouth Collection of Hymns and Tunes*, a book her brother put together.

Section Quiz Answers

1. It was limited to the black race, was a permanent condition for most slaves, and was the result of buying stolen Africans and selling them.
2. For crossing the Atlantic to America, slaves were packed tightly into the lower decks of ships, chained together, and fed sparingly. Poor sanitation led to disease. Many died or took their own lives.
3. one-third
4. Northerners believed slavery to be an injustice and advocated emancipation. Southerners grew increasingly defensive as their way of life came under

attack. They believed slavery to be acceptable, necessary, and perhaps even a "positive good."

☆ No. Antebellum slavery was based on race. The Bible clearly condemns racism (Gen. 1:26–27; Mark 12:31; Luke 10:30–37).

Literature and the Road to War

You will find many poems on the events leading up to and including Fort Sumter in Burton Stevenson's *American History in Verse*.

"The Kansas Emigrants" (John Greenleaf Whittier)

"Brown of Osawatomie" (John Greenleaf Whittier)

"Lincoln, the Man of the People" (Edwin Markham)

"Sumter" (Henry Howard Brownell)

An alternative activity is to have the students read *Uncle Tom's Cabin* and explain why the novel had such a profound impact on the North. At a minimum, consider reading the key scene in Chapter 7 where Eliza carries her child across the Ohio River to safety (after discovering that her child is to be sold). One reason the novel is so powerful is that the slaves are Christians and their masters are unchristian in their treatment of slaves. The patience of Tom, who is trying to

Uncle Tom's Cabin

Considering the circumstances surrounding the publication of *Uncle Tom's Cabin*, its success was phenomenal. The first day it was on the market, it sold three thousand copies. At the end of the first year, it had sold three hundred thousand copies. Eventually, three million copies were in circulation. The book was translated into twenty-two different languages.

Stowe based much of her novel on the life of a slave named Josiah Henson, who wrote an autobiography that detailed his hardships as a slave. Stowe used that information to create Uncle Tom.

Later, during the Civil War, Abraham Lincoln met Stowe and reportedly commented, "So this is the little lady who started this great war."

Kansas and Nebraska Territories

Stephen Douglas was interested in establishing Kansas and Nebraska as territories because of their relationship to a central transcontinental railroad route. Douglas believed that a railroad route through the middle of the country would benefit his state of Illinois, but such a route could not be built until the land through which it would run was organized into territories.

An impediment in the process of organization was the issue of slavery. Douglas proposed popular sovereignty as a compromise. Southerners pointed out that the territory in question fell north of 36° 30', the area designated by the Missouri Compromise as free. They insisted that the Missouri Compromise would have to be declared void if the Kansas-Nebraska Act were to succeed. Douglas finally agreed, which brought strong objections from the Northern states.

paper, from 1850 to 1851. Her story was later released in book form. Within a year, 300,000 copies of the book had sold.

Although *Uncle Tom's Cabin* seems emotional and artificial by today's writing standards, it became one of the most influential novels ever written. The story reached an even wider audience when troupes of actors toured the country performing it. Soon the tragic sufferings of Little Eva, Eliza, and Uncle Tom tugged at the heartstrings of readers and audiences throughout the North and the West. It rallied antislavery opinion. But it angered Southerners because it implied that *all* Southern society was evil. State governments banned the book in the South.

The Kansas-Nebraska Act

When Kansas and Nebraska sought to become states, Congress again faced the slavery issue. Illinois senator **Stephen Douglas** applied the concept of **popular sovereignty** to those territories in 1854. Popular sovereignty was a compromise that would allow the settlers to decide the slavery issue for themselves. Feelings ran so deep, however, that the bill split the political parties.

Douglas's **Kansas-Nebraska Act** passed, but both proslavery and antislavery groups urged their supporters to move west to influence the voting in those states. With proslavery and antislavery groups flooding in, conflict was inevitable. The two sides clashed, especially in Kansas. Kansas suffered such bitter warfare that it got the nickname "Bleeding Kansas." The conflict there was a foretaste of what was to happen nationally.

In May of 1856 events occurred that brought national attention to this territory. On May 21, a group of men attacked Lawrence, Kansas. This town was settled by abolitionists. Since the citizens didn't fight back, the attackers didn't kill them. Instead, the attackers looted and burned the town. Response to this violent attack stiffened resolve and led to further violence.

James Buchanan was elected president in 1856.

The Republican Party

By 1852 the Whigs had split into two factions over slavery: the Cotton Whigs and the Conscience Whigs. After the Kansas-Nebraska Act passed, the Cotton Whigs, the smaller of the factions, joined the Southern Democrats in supporting slavery. The Kansas-Nebraska Act angered Conscience Whigs and Northern Democrats. They joined Free Soilers to oppose the spread of slavery.

In 1854 the antislavery groups formed a new political party: the **Republican Party**. It grew with startling speed. They elected congressmen in their first year. Two years later, they ran their first candidate for president, John C. Fremont. Although Democrat **James Buchanan** defeated Fremont, the Republicans gained national attention and laid the groundwork for the next campaign in 1860.

The Sumner-Brooks Episode

Symbolic of the tensions that were building throughout the country was an incident in Congress in May 1856. Senator **Charles Sumner** of Massachusetts delivered an angry speech about the fighting in Kansas. In the speech he attacked South Carolina senator Andrew Butler. Butler was not present to defend himself.

SOUTHERN CHIVALRY — ARGUMENT versus CLUB'S.

The violence that erupted in the U.S. Senate when Preston Brooks caned Charles Sumner for verbally attacking Brooks's relative Andrew Butler was only a foretaste of future violence.

---

honor Christ in his life, makes the evil lashes of Simon Legree all the more terrible.

 CD: James Buchanan, 15th President

Refer to the CD for information about President James Buchanan.

Newspaper Broadsides

Assign different students to be reporters on events in this chapter. Some students should write for Garrison's abolitionist newspaper *The Liberator*, and others should write for the *Charleston Gazette*, a fiery Southern publication. The articles should be somewhat inflammatory to reflect the divergent views. Topics include Nat Turner's rebellion, the success of *Uncle Tom's Cabin*, passage of the Kansas-Nebraska Act, the founding of the Republican Party, the Dred Scott decision, the deaths of John C. Calhoun and Daniel Webster, and John Brown's raid and hanging. Have the students read their reports aloud. Then have the class discuss the different reporting styles and biases that are evident.

Books on John Brown or Bloody Kansas

Display pictures and read excerpts from a library book on John Brown or Bloody Kansas. To help the students understand the fear and agitation created by his acts of guerrilla warfare, compare those events to modern incidents such as bombings, terrorism, and school shootings in America.

A few days later, South Carolina representative **Preston Brooks**, a relative of Butler's, strode into the Senate chamber. He walked up to Sumner's desk and began to beat him with a cane. Sumner was so badly injured that he did not return to the Senate for more than three years. Some Northerners claimed the episode proved that Southerners were violent brutes. Southerners praised Brooks for defending Southern honor. They sent canes to him to replace the one he broke on Sumner's head.

The Dred Scott Decision

After these events the nation returned to an uneasy calm. But two days after Buchanan took office in 1857, the calmness ended. The Supreme Court heard the case of an elderly black man, **Dred Scott**.

Scott was born into slavery. He was the slave of an army doctor, John Emerson of Missouri. When the army transferred Emerson to military posts in Illinois and Wisconsin, he took Scott with him. Wisconsin was a free state. In 1838 Emerson returned to Missouri, taking Scott with him. When Emerson died, lawyers in Missouri helped Scott sue Emerson's heirs for his freedom. The Missouri Supreme Court had ruled in 1824 that if a slave owner moved to a free state and lived there, his slaves would be free based on the Northwest Ordinance (1787), which banned slavery north and west of the Ohio River. Based on this precedent, Dred Scott's lawyers said that living on free soil had made Scott a free man. Though Scott won in a lower court, he lost the appeals that followed. The case eventually reached the Supreme Court, where **Roger B. Taney,** a Southerner, was the chief justice.

The majority of the justices ruled against Scott. In the ruling Taney wrote that Scott was a slave and not a citizen. Therefore, he did not have the right to sue in the nation's courts. Furthermore, Taney ruled, Scott was not free simply because he had lived in a free state. Taney reasoned that the Fifth Amendment forbade the government from depriving a person of life, liberty, or property without due process of law. He also ruled that the Missouri Compromise had deprived citizens north of 36° 30′ of property, their slaves, and was thus unconstitutional.

The results of the Dred Scott decision were serious. Briefly, the South rejoiced that the Court had upheld slavery and that Congress could not prevent expansion into new territories. Politically, however, the case wrecked any chance of a compromise. The Republicans had suffered a setback, but the antislavery forces would not be silenced. The question of slavery now rested in the hands of voters in new territories. But would each side be willing to abide by their decision?

Compromise became even less likely after Henry Clay, John C. Calhoun, and Daniel Webster died. Those giants of compromise were followed by weak men: Millard Fillmore, Franklin Pierce, Stephen Douglas, and James Buchanan. They lacked the strength, experience, wisdom, and patience to lead the nation in a time of crisis.

John Brown's Attacks on Slavery

John Brown was an abolitionist who went to Kansas to ensure that it did not become a slave territory. When most abolitionists were advocating a peaceful end to slavery, Brown was saying that violence was the only solution. He quoted Hebrews 9:22—"Without shedding of blood is no remission"—to show the price that slaveholders would

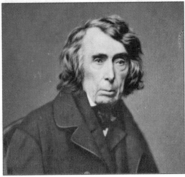

Chief Justice Roger Taney issued the Supreme Court's controversial ruling against Dred Scott.

In introducing the bill, its supporters expected that the more northern of the two territories, Nebraska, would reject slavery while the more southern, Kansas, would accept it, thus maintaining the balance between free states and slave states. Instead, Kansas became the site of a great conflict.

John Brown and Slavery

John Brown was unwavering in his dedication to the cause of abolition and openly advocated unlawful and bloody means to end slavery. Long before the massacres in Kansas and Harpers Ferry, Brown was championing the cause of freedom for the slaves. He actively sought to assist runaways and lived for a time in a community of freed blacks.

Brown settled near Osawatomie, Kansas, in October 1855, during the "Bleeding Kansas" turmoil. Proslavery forces raided Lawrence, a free-soil settlement, in May 1856. Possibly in response to that event, Brown and his sons killed five men at Pottawatomie, a proslavery settlement. After that massacre, Brown led attacks against proslavery armed forces. At one point, he made a raid into Missouri and led out a band of slaves to Canada. All of those activities whetted Brown's appetite to free slaves on a large scale.

The Raid on Harpers Ferry

Brown began his long-anticipated uprising against slavery in October 1859. From his rented farmhouse in Maryland, he and his followers (including thirteen white and five black men) crossed the Potomac River into Virginia. Brown and his men planned to capture and hold Harpers Ferry, including the bridges over the Potomac and Shenandoah rivers that gave access to the town, for two days while scores of slaves left their masters and joined Brown's troops. The swelled ranks would then continue across the countryside, freeing slaves as they went.

Events did not turn out as Brown had hoped. He entered the town on October 16 and seized control of the federal armory. His men cut off access to the town and seized hostages. They set up their headquarters in the fire engine house of the armory complex. Then began Brown's downfall. He was expecting droves of slaves to flock to his side, but they never did. He also underestimated the ability of the Virginians to stop him. Realizing that there was not an immediate response from the local slave population, Brown could have tried to escape. Instead, he insisted on remaining where he was, giving time for local militia to cut off all escape routes. Federal troops were on the scene by the evening of October 17. They stormed the engine house the next morning, killing some of the insurgents and taking the rest into custody. Several men, including Brown, were tried and then executed in Charlestown, Virginia, on December 2.

John Brown took his violence from Kansas to Virginia, hoping to spark a slave rebellion in the South.

U.S. Marines led by Robert E. Lee stormed the engine-house in Harpers Ferry, capturing John Brown.

pay for their support of slavery. His message convinced many people. Frederick Douglass said, "His arguments seemed to convince all; his appeals touched all, and his will impressed all."

Responding to the violence in Lawrence, Kansas, and the attack on Sumner in the Senate, Brown made his first strike against slavery at Pottawatomie (paht uh WAHT uh mee), Kansas, in 1856. He and four of his seven sons murdered five proslavery men there one night. Escaping prosecution for this crime, Brown began to develop a strategy so radical that many abolitionists withdrew their support of him. In the summer of 1859, Brown armed twenty-one men, including four of his sons and two slaves he had freed, and began planning in earnest.

On October 16, 1859, Brown and his little army rode into Harpers Ferry, Virginia (now West Virginia). They took several well-known slaveholders as hostages and seized the federal arsenal (a storage place for weapons). Brown hoped that this action would stir local slaves to rebel and that thousands of other slaves would rally to him as word of his deed spread. No such revolt occurred.

Local militia blocked all of Brown's escape routes. Federal troops led by Colonel **Robert E. Lee** and a young courier named J.E.B. Stuart arrived the next day and demanded that Brown and his men surrender. Brown refused, so the troops stormed the building. Brown was wounded, and two of his sons were killed. Less than two weeks later, Brown was tried. During the trial, he won many admirers, but none of them was on the jury, which convicted him of murder. He was hanged.

Although Brown's attempted revolt failed, his actions had a profound effect on the nation. Southerners feared a slave revolt more than ever. Brown's death made him a martyr for the abolitionist cause. Some Northern soldiers marched off to war singing, "John Brown's body lies a'mouldering in the grave, but his soul goes marching on." Julia Howe used the melody from this song for her hymn, "The Battle Hymn of the Republic."

Section Quiz

1. What famous novel stirred sympathy for the abolitionist cause? Who wrote it?

2. What became the nickname of Kansas as a result of the clash over slavery there?

3. What single issue united the various groups that formed the Republican Party?

4. What were the consequences of Brown's failed raid on Harpers Ferry?

★ What was the significance of the Dred Scott decision?

Section Quiz Answers

1. *Uncle Tom's Cabin*; Harriet Beecher Stowe

2. Bleeding Kansas

3. opposition to slavery or to its spread

4. He was hanged, and abolitionists viewed him as a martyr and intensified their opposition to slavery, while Southerners became more fearful of a slave uprising.

★ It effectively guaranteed slavery in the territories, prohibited citizenship rights to blacks, and voided the Missouri Compromise.

IV. The Election of 1860 and Secession

The tensions that grew during the late 1850s erupted in the election of 1860. The Democratic Party split. New alliances and regional bonds formed. These events influenced the nation for decades.

The Election of 1860

The South was clearly worried about the election of 1860. Southern extremists, called **fire-eaters**, threatened **secession**, to leave the Union, if the Republicans won. The views of the Republicans on almost all issues were in opposition to the interests of the South. Not only views on slavery but also positions on states' rights and the tariff were placing the Republicans at odds with most Southerners.

The Democratic Party was split in the election of 1860, nominating two candidates: Stephen Douglas and John C. Breckinridge.

The Democrats thought that their best chance to capture the White House was to choose a moderate candidate, someone who appealed to both the North and the South. Stephen Douglas seemed to be that candidate. But fire-eaters considered him their enemy and would accept no compromise candidate. The fire-eaters had great influence among Southern Democrats. Rather than unite behind Douglas, they walked out of the convention. Northern Democrats nominated Douglas. Southern Democrats held their own convention. They selected **John C. Breckinridge** of Kentucky. They also adopted a platform (statement of political positions) based on the Dred Scott decision, calling for a federal slave code to protect slavery in all of the territories.

With the Democrats divided, the Republicans had real hopes for victory. In an effort to keep the Union intact, they chose a moderate rather than an abolitionist or a Free Soiler. Their choice was an Illinois lawyer, **Abraham Lincoln**. He had always been a Whig. His hero was Henry Clay. He supported all of Clay's views: a high tariff, a central bank, and government funding of internal improvements. As for slavery, Lincoln had often stated that he did not want to end slavery where it already existed; he just wanted to keep the country united and to prevent the spread of slavery. Lincoln had also debated Douglas during the 1858 senate race in Illinois. Although Douglas won that election, the debates gave Lincoln and his views national exposure.

The Republican Party chose Abraham Lincoln to be its standard bearer.

The rest of the Whigs and a few other voters—most of them in the border states of Delaware, Maryland, Virginia, Tennessee, and Kentucky—were upset with their own parties. They decided to choose **John Bell** of Tennessee as their candidate. He ran under the **Constitutional Union Party**. Bell was for staying in the Union. He thought that slavery could be saved without the states having to secede.

As the election neared, more Southerners began to fear a Republican victory. If that happened, they said, the Southern states should secede and form their own government. They based that view on the concept that the states had voluntarily joined the Union and could, therefore, voluntarily leave it. President Buchanan did nothing to discourage them.

When the votes were tallied, Lincoln had carried the Northern and western states, gaining more popular votes than any other candidate. Douglas was second, followed by Breckinridge and then Bell. Lincoln's victory, however, was far from overwhelming. Douglas and Bell's combined votes were more than Lincoln's. More than

A small number of former Whigs and Southern Unionists chose John Bell to offer the voters a moderate candidate.

Section IV
Objectives

Students should be able to

1. Describe the men involved in the 1860 election and their positions.
2. Identify factors leading to Lincoln's victory in 1860.
3. Describe the formation of the Confederacy.

Southern Democrats

The Southern Democrats called their branch of the party the National Democratic Party.

Seceding States

South Carolina and the other seceding states feared that Lincoln's victory would signal a bolder attack by Northerners on the South and its "domestic concerns." Lincoln had declared that the Union must be preserved and that it could not "endure permanently half slave and half free. . . . It will become all one thing or all the other." The South became concerned that the nation would not become "all slave," and therefore the country would become "all free." Southerners believed that the Declaration of Independence and the Constitution had left them with the option of seceding, and the North would have to prove otherwise by force. After the war Jefferson Davis summarized the South's position by saying, "No alternative remained except to seek the security out of the Union which they had vainly tried to obtain within it. The hope of our people may be stated in a sentence. It was to escape from injury and strife in the Union, to find prosperity and peace out of it." Lincoln and many in the North rejected

 Teacher Resource: Abraham Lincoln

An excellent contemporary perspective on Abraham Lincoln is the biography *Life of Lincoln* by his former law partner, William Herndon.

Newspaper Editorials about Secession

Visit www.bjupress.com/resources for a possible link to contemporary newspaper editorials addressing the question of secession.

"Folly" of Party Splits?

On rare occasions in U.S. history, parties have split and fielded separate presidential candidates. Can the students remember an example of this? (*In 1824 most candidates were elected by state legislatures [Chapter 10]; in 1836 the Whigs selected several candidates and lost to the Democratic-Republicans.*) Students will be seeing other examples of party splits and their consequences.

In each case of a party split, the opposing party has won. So is it worth it for parties to split? The only value of parties is to represent common views, and when people's views diverge too much, then there is no point in their staying in one party. In the end, parties must either appease the diver-

gent view or run the risk of losing power and allowing a third party to take preeminence.

 CD: Party Platform Summaries, 1860

Refer to the CD for summaries of each party's platform during the 1860 election.

 CD: 1860 Political Cartoons

Refer to the CD's political cartoons from the election of 1860 when discussing this part of the chapter.

claims by the South that they had the right to secede. The war would decide the issue.

The Constitution of the Confederacy

When representatives of the seceding states met at Montgomery, Alabama, they immediately wrote a provisional constitution that would set up a temporary government. A smaller committee then met to write a permanent constitution. The constitution, with a few minor adjustments, was passed and adopted by the Montgomery Convention on March 11, 1861. The delegates signed it on March 16, and it then had to be presented to the states for ratification.

The constitution for the Confederacy was very close to the United States Constitution. Most of the differences can be traced to Southerners' dissatisfaction with certain sections of the original document. Many reflect the South's concern for states' rights and slavery. Following are some examples of ways in which the Confederate Constitution was different from the U.S. Constitution.

The president of the Confederacy would serve for six years but be limited to one term. The constitution provided for a national Supreme Court, but one was never established, partially because the Confederate Congress could never agree on whether a Supreme Court should be able to overrule the decisions of state supreme courts.

Four critical provisions protected slavery in the new nation. First, slaveholders had the right to take their slaves unmolested into any other state (see Dred Scott case, where a slave sued for freedom). Second, the fugitive slave provision was made

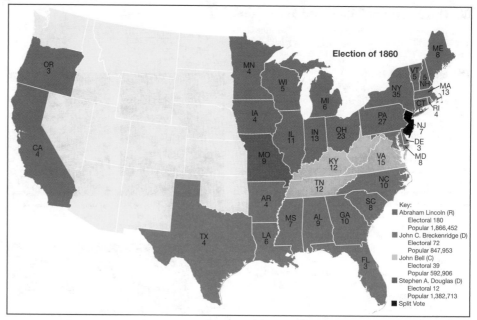

Election of 1860

Key:
- Abraham Lincoln (R)
  Electoral 180
  Popular 1,866,452
- John C. Breckenridge (D)
  Electoral 72
  Popular 847,953
- John Bell (C)
  Electoral 39
  Popular 592,906
- Stephen A. Douglas (D)
  Electoral 12
  Popular 1,382,713
- Split Vote

60 percent of the voters had voted for someone other than Lincoln. Lincoln had failed to carry a single Southern or border state.

The Secession of the Southern States

With Lincoln elected, South Carolina feared that its rights were no longer safe. Hence it voted to secede on December 20. The nation waited for Buchanan's response. Although he believed that secession was illegal, he did not believe in using military force against the seceding states. Instead, he did nothing. He left the problem for Lincoln to solve.

Other Southern states called conventions to consider secession. The states of the deep South—Mississippi, Florida, Alabama, Georgia, Louisiana, and Texas—followed South Carolina's example and voted to secede. South Carolina called a convention of those states in Montgomery, Alabama, on February 1, 1861. There the delegates voted to form the **Confederate States of America**. They wrote their own constitution, using the U.S. Constitution as a pattern. It recognized the "sovereign and independent character" of the states and guaranteed states' rights. It also promised that no law against slavery could ever be passed, allowed cabinet members to take part in legislative debates, and gave the president a single six-year term.

In choosing its leaders, the Confederacy preferred moderates. They hoped to win the support of Southerners who were still unsure about seceding. They elected **Jefferson Davis** of Mississippi—a U.S. senator, hero of the Mexican War, and former secretary of war—as president. They tapped **Alexander Stephens**, a Georgian who had opposed secession, as vice president.

The Confederacy chose Jefferson Davis and Alexander Stephens to be their president and vice president, respectively.

 CD: Results of 1860 Presidential Election

Refer to the CD for a map showing the results of the election of 1860.

 CD: Abraham Lincoln, 16th President

Refer to the CD for information about Abraham Lincoln.

Identify the Border States

The allegiance of the border states was one of the most decisive issues in the course of the Civil War. Refer the students to a map of the period, pointing out the border states. Explain how these states differed from the other states economically and politically. Point out the results of the pivotal 1860 election: Breckinridge won Maryland; Douglas won New Jersey and Missouri; and Bell won Kentucky, Virginia, and Tennessee. (Refer to the map showing the Electoral College results.) Lincoln had to act wisely because volatile public opinion could swing rapidly in the border states that did not vote for him.

Ask the students to identify the geographic importance of each border state if a war

erupted. *(Kentucky provided access to the Ohio River—a crucial trade route; Missouri bordered Illinois and the upper Missouri and Mississippi rivers; and Maryland bordered the federal capital.)* Lincoln helped to ensure Northern victory by successfully maneuvering to keep the border states in the Union.

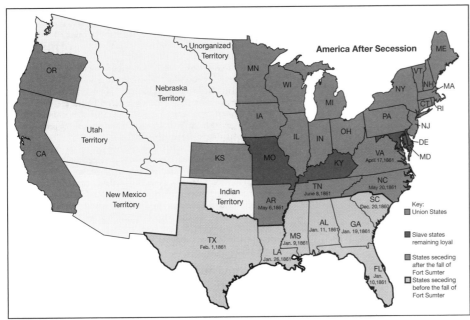

Next, the Confederacy sent commissioners to the Southern states that had not yet seceded. The commissioners hoped to convince them to join the Confederacy. Those states, all Upper South and border states, were taking a "wait-and-see" position on secession. They were not convinced that the election of Lincoln alone was enough to make secession right. The next event in the chain would move them to action.

Section Quiz

1. Who were the four presidential candidates in the 1860 election, and what were their respective political parties?

2. What was Lincoln's public position on slavery?

3. Which state was the first to secede?

4. Who was the president of the Confederacy?

★ What was the political position of the leaders of the Confederacy? Why were such men chosen?

V. Fort Sumter and War

The South's position on secession was that the states had voluntarily joined the Union under the contract theory of government. Each state was a sovereign authority. As long as the national government kept its part of the contract, the states were bound to support it. If the national government failed to keep its part of the contract, however, the states had the right to withdraw from the Union just as they had entered it—as sovereign states.

more extensive. Third, the Confederate government was granted the right to acquire territory, and slavery was automatically protected in any new territory. Fourth, any new states admitted to the Confederacy must be approved by two-thirds of the House of Representatives and the Senate (with the Senate voting by states). The last provision was the compromise that resulted from a heated debate over the admission of new states. Some feared that free states would want to join the Confederacy, and the free state/slave state controversy that disrupted the Union would be renewed. The answer to this dilemma was making a rigorous approval process in Congress a prerequisite for admission into the Confederacy.

Finally, the process for amending the constitution was simpler in the Confederacy. Only three states had to request a change in order for a national convention to be called. (Two-thirds of state legislatures must suggest an amendment in the U.S. Constitution.) And just two-thirds of state legislatures or conventions had to ratify the amendment (as opposed to three-fourths with the U.S. Constitution).

Section V
Objectives

Students should be able to

1. Describe the situation that led to the firing on Fort Sumter.

2. Explain the way the border states were kept in the Union.

3. List the North's advantages as it entered the war.

4. List the South's advantages as it entered the war.

Activity 5: Map Work: The Divided Nation

Have the students complete the map work as a means of reviewing which states seceded and made up the Confederate States of America.

Section Quiz Answers

1. Stephen Douglas—Democratic (Northern), John C. Breckinridge—Democratic (Southern), Abraham Lincoln—Republican, John Bell—Constitutional Union

2. He did not oppose it where it was, but he was against its spread.

3. South Carolina

4. Jefferson Davis

★ Moderates were chosen to lead the Confederacy; moderate leaders tend to draw greater support since they do not hold strongly to controversial opinions. The Confederacy chose moderate leaders to increase its support among Southerners.

Washington Peace Conference

The Washington Peace Conference is not often mentioned, but it does illustrate the truth that not all of the states in the South were initially eager to secede from the Union. While the states of the Deep South were planning a convention to discuss secession in Montgomery, Alabama (see previous section), the Virginia legislature called for a conference in Washington, D.C., to discuss peace. Both groups convened on February 4, 1861. Twenty-one of thirty-four states of the Union attended the Washington Peace Conference. The former president John Tyler chaired the conference, and a series of proposals was drawn up for presentation to Congress. Unfortunately, the secessionists in Montgomery and the Republicans in the United States Congress were so far apart by February 27 (when Congress received the proposals) that the prospects of a peaceful settlement were slim.

Kentucky

Kentucky's decision to remain in the Union was aided by the fact that Lincoln did not send troops into the state until after the Confederacy had violated Kentucky's neutrality by sending in troops first.

Lincoln, however, believed that the Union was permanent and inviolable. Therefore, secession was not possible. No state could pull out once it had joined. Ultimately, the war that came after the South seceded was fought to determine which view would prevail—Lincoln's or the South's.

On March 4, 1861, Lincoln took the oath of office. In his inaugural address, he appealed to the people of the South. "In your hands, my dissatisfied fellow-countrymen, and not in mine, is the momentous issue of civil war." He hoped to reconcile the sections, but he would fight, if necessary, to preserve the Union. He would use the power of government "to hold, occupy, and possess the property and places belonging to the government."

By "property," Lincoln meant the two federal forts in the South where the Stars and Stripes still flew: Fort Pickens at Pensacola, Florida, and **Fort Sumter** in South Carolina's Charleston Harbor. During the last days of Buchanan's presidency, the Confederacy had seized all other federal properties within its borders. Lincoln had been reluctant to suggest the recapture of those seized properties. But the Northern states saw those forts as Lincoln's first test as a president. For Lincoln to control Fort Sumter and Fort Pickens, however, he would have to send supplies to them. How would the South react to that attempt?

Firing on Fort Sumter

Neither Lincoln nor Jefferson Davis sought war. Lincoln hoped the Southern Unionists would bring an end to secession. Davis hoped that Lincoln would see the South was determined to create a new nation and would let them do it. Fort Sumter would test the two sides' willingness to engage in battle.

From South Carolina's view, Fort Sumter was a garrison of foreign soldiers on their territory. To allow the Federal troops to remain provisioned and supplied would be a threat to their independence. From Lincoln's view, withdrawing Federal troops from Federal forts would concede to a rebellion against the United States. Therefore, even though Lincoln's cabinet and General Winfield Scott advised against reprovisioning the fort, he sent a small, unarmed fleet with provisions to Sumter.

Lincoln sent a note to F. W. Pickens, the governor of South Carolina, saying that a supply ship would be arriving at the fort. Pickens relayed the note to Jefferson Davis, and Davis replied that under no circumstances was the fort to be resupplied.

When the Union merchant ship, *The Star of the West*, approached Fort Sumter with supplies, the Confederate cannons around Charleston Harbor fired on it and Fort Sumter. After forty hours of constant bombardment, Major **Robert Anderson**, the Union commander, surrendered the fort.

Neither side wished to be perceived as an aggressor. Even after Sumter both sides resisted issuing declarations of war. Lincoln, however, did issue a call for troops to suppress what he called an "insurrection."

The Call for Troops

Lincoln called for 75,000 volunteer soldiers. The Upper South and border states were forced to decide: would they supply troops to fight their fellow Southerners? Or would they join the Confederacy? First Virginia, then Arkansas and North Carolina, voted to secede

Political Strategy—You Are There

You have an opportunity to test the students' reasoning skills by asking them to rethink the issues that Abraham Lincoln faced during the crisis that precipitated the Civil War. None of his decisions were easy, and solutions were not obvious.

Many American presidents have faced such crises at momentous times in the nation's history (e.g., the Berlin airlift, the Cuban missile crisis, and recent conflicts in Afghanistan and Iraq). Presidents must carefully weigh complex options and their potential consequences. Mistakes can be catastrophic. Good citizens must support their government as they face these crises.

1. After his election and the secession of the seven lower states but before he was sworn into office, what did Lincoln do? (*He said nothing. Some believe he could have voiced his opinion and tried to work closely with Buchanan and Congress, but some of his critics concluded that he did not want to suffer political fallout from any mistakes or catastrophes that might arise.*)

2. After taking office and recognizing Confederate intentions to take Sumter, what did the president do? (*He sent supplies but not troops and wrote the governor; he could have been belligerent and protected the fort with more troops*

and armed ships, but he avoided such provocation.)

3. The states of the upper South did not want to leave the Union even after the firing on Fort Sumter, but the lower states intended to fight to keep out of the Union. What did the president do? (*The president called for troops to put down the rebellion; as a direct result of this momentous decision, political opinion among many in the upper South supported secession.*)

4. The border states still did not want to leave the Union, but they refused to fight against the South. What did the president do? (*The president took each*

The "Stars and Bars," the first official flag of the Confederacy, flew over Fort Sumter after Anderson surrendered it to Southern forces.

and join the Confederacy. Finally, on June 8, the people of Tennessee reluctantly did the same.

Parts of two of the Upper South states opposed secession. Fifty counties of western Virginia resented the tidewater area's greater influence in state politics. Those counties also had the fewest slaves in the state. The people there saw the crisis as their chance to free themselves from tidewater domination. They set up their own state government and applied to Congress for statehood. In 1863 **West Virginia** entered the Union.

Most of the people in the hills and mountains of East Tennessee were Unionists. The slave population was small. East Tennesseans also resented the greater influence of Middle and West Tennessee in state politics.

Lincoln tried to keep other slave states (Kentucky, Missouri, Delaware, and Maryland) from seceding. Like the people of Tennessee, the people of those border states were sharply divided. Delaware was the least likely to secede. But Lincoln feared that the other states might join the Confederacy. He moved quickly to force them to stay in the Union.

Through persuasion and force, Lincoln convinced Kentucky to declare neutrality within the Union. Kentucky was the key to Union access to the Ohio River. In spite of having a pro-Southern governor, Kentuckians were lukewarm to the Confederacy. But neither did they want Northern troops on their soil. They agreed to stay in the Union—but only if Union troops stayed out of Kentucky.

Lincoln sent Union troops into Missouri before the state could vote on secession. Those troops isolated Missourians who favored the South and tried to prevent their fighting against the Union.

Of the four border states, Maryland concerned Lincoln most. If Maryland seceded, the Union capital in Washington, D.C., would be at risk. Lincoln sent Union troops to the state to close bridges to keep out Southern agitators. He declared martial law in the state. That

East Tennessee

The secession vote in Tennessee was complicated and controversial. Voters were asked to vote on two separate issues when they went to the polls: to secede or not to secede and the election of delegates to a secession convention (based on the assumption that secession would be approved). Statewide the vote was against calling a convention by 69,675 to 57,798. The issue of whether to secede was rejected 24,749 for to 91,803 against. But the tide shifted after Lincoln called for troops. Governor Isham Harris defiantly replied that "no gallant son of Tennessee will ever draw his sword" against his fellow Southerners. The legislature voted to call another election to determine if the state would secede, declaring its independence. The statewide vote that time was 104,913 for secession and 47,238 against it. East Tennesseans, however, voted overwhelmingly against secession and even threatened to form their own state, much as West Virginia would do. The governor sent Confederate forces to prevent that from occurring.

state case by case, waiting until the last minute to send troops and letting the South act as the aggressor.)

CD: The Seceding States
Refer to the CD for a map showing the states that seceded in 1860 and those that remained in the Union.

Debate: West Virginia
Moderate a debate among the students over whether the formation of the new state of West Virginia from the original state of Virginia was constitutional. Before beginning the debate, read to the students the following excerpt from Article IV, Section 3.1 of the Constitution: ". . . no new state shall be formed or erected within the jurisdiction of any other state . . . or parts of states, without the consent of the legislatures of the states concerned as well as of the Congress."

Teacher Resources: East Tennesseans and the Civil War
The following books are excellent sources of information on the divided loyalties in East Tennessee before and during the Civil War:
- *Lincolnites and Rebels* and *One South or Many?* by Robert Tracy McKenzie
- *Mountain Rebels: East Tennessee Confederates and the Civil War, 1860–1870* by W. Todd Groce
- *Divided Loyalties* by Digby Gordon Seymour

meant that constitutional rights of citizens were suspended and the military controlled the state. These actions were some of the most controversial of Lincoln's presidency. He justified them because he believed they were necessary to save the Union. The troops held Southern sympathizers against their will. Maryland had little choice but to stay in the Union.

Reasons for Northern Hope

Looking at the resources available to the North and the South, it's obvious that the North had a great advantage. The North had both the means and the manpower to industrialize. This tremendous industrial capacity was the Union's most significant advantage, even more so as the war wore on. The South produced only 10 percent of the nation's manufactured goods and had only 110,000 industrial workers. The North, meanwhile, had 120,000 factories. Consequently, the South had to buy overseas what it could not produce at home. Only at the outset of the war would it have the capital and the freedom to do this. The lack of Southern sea power to maintain its trade routes would soon greatly hinder its war effort. In addition, the North was adding 300,000 immigrants a year to its population, almost as many as the total number of Northern troops killed in the entire war.

Reasons for Southern Hope

If the North had the greatest overall advantage, why did the Confederate leaders think they could succeed as a separate country? The South had at least five reasons for their positive outlook.

1. The South had a simple goal: set up and defend an independent nation. It did not need to conquer the North, capture its capital city, or even defeat Union armies decisively. It only had

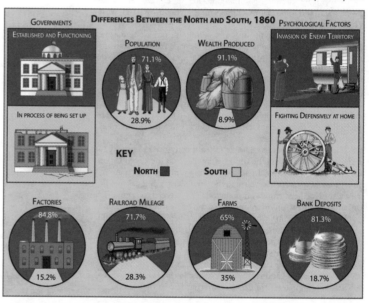

DIFFERENCES BETWEEN THE NORTH AND SOUTH, 1860

GOVERNMENTS — ESTABLISHED AND FUNCTIONING / IN PROCESS OF BEING SET UP

POPULATION — 71.1% / 28.9%

WEALTH PRODUCED — 91.1% / 8.9%

PSYCHOLOGICAL FACTORS — INVASION OF ENEMY TERRITORY / FIGHTING DEFENSIVELY AT HOME

KEY   NORTH ■   SOUTH □

FACTORIES — 84.8% / 15.2%

RAILROAD MILEAGE — 71.7% / 28.3%

FARMS — 65% / 35%

BANK DEPOSITS — 81.3% / 18.7%

Teacher Resource

An excellent account of many of the men who would become leaders on both sides in the Civil War is *The Class of 1846: From West Point to Appomattox* by John Waugh.

Counting the Cost

Every wise nation counts the cost before starting a war (Luke 14:31–32). The text lists five reasons that the South went to war. Can the students think of five reasons that it was wise for the North to go to war? What are five reasons against going to war that each side should have considered?

Divide the students into two groups—North and South—and ask them to look at the maps of the states and evaluate their best strategy for victory. Ask them to condense their ideas into three points. When they are finished, point them to the actual strategies that the two sides adopted (listed on pages 287–88 in Chapter 15).

Lee, the Christian

More information about Lee's Christianity is available in "Robert E. Lee: Christian, Soldier, Gentleman" by Craig Jennings (*Scenes from American Church History*).

Activity 6: Account of the Firing on Fort Sumter

This activity gives a first-hand account of the firing on Fort Sumter and provides a good segue into the next chapter on the War Between the States.

Activity 7: Chapter Review

Use this activity to help the students prepare for the chapter test.

to defend its own territory and outlast the North's will to fight. Also, because the South was so big, the Union armies would have to protect long supply lines to attack and occupy the South.

2. Southerners would be defending their own homes and way of life. Many of the Northerners who were fighting for an abstract concept—"the Union." It would be hard for the Union government to stay on the offensive. The North would have to not only defeat Southern armies decisively but also break the South's will to resist.

3. Confederate leaders thought they would get foreign help. As the source of most of Great Britain's cotton, the South believed that the English would be sympathetic to, if not supportive of, the Southern cause. The South also had more blood connection to Englishmen than did the North, which had more immigrants from non-English-speaking countries.

4. The coastline of the South was long. Although the South had no real navy when the war began, the North would need thousands of ships to block commerce and military supplies from the South.

5. The South believed that its troops were better soldiers. Most of the Confederacy's commanding officers were well trained and battle experienced. Many of them were West Point graduates. In fact, Robert E. Lee, who would become the South's leading general, had been Lincoln's first choice to command the Union armies. Lee, however, turned him down. He was a loyal Virginian and could not bring himself to fight against his state. During the war that would soon break out, the Southern armies produced some of the best generals in American history. Lincoln, on the other hand, went through seven different commanders before he found one who could successfully lead the Union Army.

The South had concluded it could no longer remain in the Union. Throughout the preceding decades, Southerners had watched the Northern way of life gain power and influence. The South had repeatedly looked for ways to check this growth and to ensure the growth of the Southern way of life. In time, however, Southerners faced a troubling choice: live in a nation that did not share their values, or leave the Union and form their own nation. This choice was troubling because both options required great sacrifice. They concluded that the sacrifices of war were more tolerable than having to live in a nation where their values and way of life were threatened.

Section Quiz

1. In what state was Fort Sumter located?

2. What were the four key border states?

3. What was the Union's most significant advantage?

4. List three of the factors that gave the South a fighting chance despite the North's advantages.

★ Why did Lincoln feel that he must hold on to Fort Sumter?

★ Which side began the war, the North or the South?

Section Quiz Answers

1. South Carolina

2. Kentucky, Missouri, Delaware, and Maryland

3. its tremendous industrial capacity

4. (any three) had only to defend itself, deep personal concern, expected foreign help, assumed its long coast would allow the delivery of supplies, good military leadership

★ Holding the fort might help force the South back into the Union. Also it would force the South to make the first aggressive move, thereby preventing the North from looking like the aggressor in the eyes of other nations.

★ From the North's perspective the South began the war by rebelling against federal authority. When the federal government attempted to resupply Fort Sumter, government troops were fired upon. From the South's perspective, the North began the war by insisting on keeping Federal troops within territory that had lawfully left the Union.

CHAPTER REVIEW ANSWERS

Review Questions

1. (a) The North had more industry and factories, the greater population, more large cities, more railroads, more foreign immigration, and it favored free labor and a high tariff; the South had little industry, few railroads, smaller population, few large cities, was heavily dependent on slavery for labor, and favored a low tariff.

(b) The North had a broad interpretation of the Constitution based on Article VI, and favored central (national) sovereignty and much spending on internal improvements; the South had a strict interpretation of the Constitution based on Amendment X, feared a strong central government, favored state and local control of government, and spent little on internal improvements.

People, Places, and Things to Remember:

antebellum
wage slaves
Article VI
Amendment X
Middle Passage
overseer
gang system
task system
Underground Railroad
Frederick Douglass
abolitionist
Harriett Tubman
William Lloyd Garrison
Horace Greeley
"spirituals"
Uncle Tom's Cabin
Harriet Beecher Stowe
Stephen Douglas
popular sovereignty
Kansas-Nebraska Act
Republican Party
James Buchanan
Charles Sumner
Preston Brooks
Dred Scott
Roger B. Taney
John Brown
Robert E. Lee
fire-eaters
secession
John C. Breckinridge
Abraham Lincoln
John Bell
Constitutional Union Party
Confederate States of America
Jefferson Davis
Alexander Stephens
Fort Sumter
Robert Anderson
West Virginia

Review Questions

1. List ways in which the North and the South were different (a) economically and (b) politically.
2. How was American slavery different from any other slave system in the world?
3. Name people in the chapter who played major roles in the abolition movement.
4. What concept did Stephen Douglas introduce as a compromise solution to the slavery controversy in the territories?
5. Which Supreme Court decision was crucial in the slavery controversy?
6. List the candidates in the 1860 presidential election and their respective parties.
7. List the states that seceded and formed the Confederate States of America.
8. Whom did the Confederacy choose to be their president and their vice president?
9. Where were the first shots of the war fired?
10. Which state was added to the Union when it broke away from an existing state?

Critical Thinking

1. Why was slavery a difficult problem for Americans to deal with?
2. How did the slavery question lead to a biblical crisis in American culture?
3. According to the Founding Fathers, did states have the right to secede? Support your answer.

---

2. It involved only the black race, was a permanent condition for most slaves, and was promoted by slave traders seeking profits.

3. William Lloyd Garrison, Horace Greeley, Frederick Douglass, Harriet Beecher Stowe

4. popular sovereignty

5. Dred Scott decision

6. Abraham Lincoln (Republican), Stephen Douglas (Northern Democrat), John C. Breckinridge (Southern Democrat), John Bell (Constitutional Union)

7. South Carolina, Mississippi, Florida, Alabama, Georgia, Louisiana, Texas, Virginia, Arkansas, North Carolina, Tennessee

8. President: Jefferson Davis; Vice President: Alexander Stephens

9. Charleston, S.C., firing on Fort Sumter

10. West Virginia

Critical Thinking

1. Answers will vary but might include such topics as the failure of the Founding Fathers to deal with it early on, the economic impact of abolition on the South, differences of opinion concerning what to do with the freed blacks, the racial attitudes of the North, and the growing conflict between republicanism and the aristocracy.

2. Because people could not agree on what the Bible said, it seemed that the Bible was unable to resolve one of the most important issues in American culture. As a result, many educated Americans began to conclude that the Bible was not able to decide issues of national policy.

3. Answers will vary depending on the students' views of how to harmonize Article VI with Amendment X of the Constitution.

The two-week Battle of Spotsylvania was only one of hundreds of bloody engagements during the war.

The States at War

I. **Gearing Up for War**

II. **Marching into Battle**

III. **Controlling the Waters**

IV. **Continuing the War in the East**

V. **Waging Total War**

VI. **Ending the War**

Chapter Goals

Students should be able to

1. Define and use the basic terms of the chapter.
2. Review the chronology of the events from the Civil War period.
3. Trace the boundaries of the North and the South.
4. Identify major battles and leaders in the war.
5. Analyze the reasons for and effects of the Civil War.
6. Explain the roles played by significant individuals during the Civil War, including Jefferson Davis, Ulysses S. Grant, Robert E. Lee, and Abraham Lincoln.
7. Explain the issues surrounding the firing on Fort Sumter; the battles of Antietam, Gettysburg, and Vicksburg; the Emancipation Proclamation; the assassination of Lincoln; and Lee's surrender at Appomattox.
8. Analyze Lincoln's ideas about liberty, equality, union, and government as contained in his two inaugural addresses and the Gettysburg Address.
9. Explain how the war affected combatants, civilians, and the physical environment.

Chapter Motivation

Ask the students what they know about the Civil War and which side they think was right. Remind them that on both sides were godly people who believed that they had God's blessing in the war. As the students read the chapter, instruct them to look for information that presents viewpoints that differ from their own. It is important to remind your students that the question of who was right is very

Chapter 15 Lesson Plan Chart

Section Title	Main Activity	Pages	Days
I. Gearing Up for War	Activity 1: Comparing Lincoln and Davis	284–88	1–2 days
II. Marching into Battle	Activity 2: Major Battles of the War Between the States	288–91	1–2 days
III. Controlling the Waters	Activity 4: Soldiers' Accounts of the War	291–93	1–2 days
IV. Continuing the War in the East	Activity 5: Lincoln's Gettysburg Address	294–97	1–2 days
V. Waging Total War	Activity 6: Lincoln's Second Inaugural Address	297–301	1–2 days
VI. Ending the War	Activity 8: Chapter Review	301–4	1–2 days
TOTAL SUGGESTED DAYS (INCLUDING 1 DAY FOR REVIEW AND TESTING)			**7–13 DAYS**

MATERIALS LIST

SECTION I
- CD: Selected Bibliography; Timeline of the War; Weapons and Ordnance of the War; The Anaconda Plan; McClellan's Letter to Lincoln
- Activity 1 from Chapter 15 of the *Student Activities* manual

SECTION II
- CD: Battlefield Tragedy, 1862
- Activities 2 and 3 from Chapter 15 of the *Student Activities* manual

SECTION III
- Activity 4 from Chapter 15 of the *Student Activities* manual

complicated. There are some important conclusions we can come to, but to arrive at them, we must study this war carefully from the perspective of a Christian worldview.

Section I
Objectives

Students should be able to

1. Describe the recruitment and activities of soldiers as the war began.
2. Compare the civilian preparations and sacrifices for war in the North with those in the South.
3. List the modern aspects of the Civil War.
4. Describe the main goals involved in the Union and Confederate strategies.

Crittenden's Compromise

John Crittenden attempted to obtain a compromise and avoid the war. His plan involved reinstating the Missouri Compromise boundary for slavery and amending the constitution to guarantee slavery forever where it already existed. Lincoln and the Republicans strongly opposed the amendment.

Difficulties in Raising Armies

Although volunteers rushed to join both armies at the beginning of the war, both sides eventually had to resort to the draft.

In the North, when more soldiers were needed, the national government issued a quota for each state. If the volunteer regiments did not meet the quota, authorities held a draft. They used intense efforts to raise as many volunteer regiments as possible to avoid the unpopular draft. Often cash incentives caused men to join. The

Naming the War

The war between the North and the South has been called by many different names. The two most common names are the Civil War and the War Between the States. Northern sympathizers sometimes called it the War of the Rebellion, the War Against Slavery, the War for Abolition, or the War for the Union. Southern partisans called it the War for Southern Independence, the War of Secession, the War for Southern Rights, the War Against Northern Aggression, and (after the war was over) the Lost Cause. Other names for this war include the following:

- The War for Constitutional Liberty
- The Second American Revolution
- The War for States' Rights
- Mr. Lincoln's War
- The Southern Rebellion
- The War of the Southern Planters
- The Second War for Independence
- The War to Suppress Yankee Arrogance
- The Brothers' War
- The Great Rebellion
- The War for Southern Nationality
- The Yankee Invasion
- The War for Separation
- The Confederate War
- The War of the Southrons
- The War for Southern Freedom
- The War of the North and South
- The Late Unpleasantness

Both sides in the war used advertising, such as this Union recruiting poster, to attract military enlistments.

As war clouds gathered over the nation, Kentucky senator John Crittenden led one last attempt to avoid war and save the Union. Despite his pleas and stirring speeches, Crittenden's compromise plan failed to pass the Senate. The defeat was doubly bitter for Crittenden because his own family was divided over secession. One son, George, became a general in the Confederate army; another son, Thomas, became a general in the Union army.

Throughout the country, families split over the war. Brother fought against brother and father against son in the four years of bloody conflict. Even Lincoln's wife, Mary Todd Lincoln, had relatives who fought for the South.

Devout Christians were on both sides in the war. Each side claimed that God would bless its efforts. But by assuming that God was on their side, many people were fashioning a god as they imagined him. By the end of the war, many in both North and South were confused by the workings of **providence**, God's control over all events. This confusion led to a crisis of faith for some people.

I. Gearing Up for War

After the fall of Fort Sumter, the nation was torn by a bitter four-year war that involved more than seven thousand military actions. About half of them took place in Virginia and Tennessee. But soldiers were not the only people who suffered hardships, death, and destruction. Civilians also suffered.

Turning Men into Soldiers

Stirred by patriotism, thousands of young men joined the armies. In the beginning, both sides relied totally on volunteers. But eventually the flood of volunteers became a trickle. They became so scarce that the armies did not have enough soldiers. Both Lincoln and Davis resorted to drafting men to fill their armies.

Life in the camps was far from exciting. A soldier typically spent 65 percent of his time in camp, 30 percent marching or camping in the open air, and only 5 percent of his time fighting. Some soldiers who were assigned to duty in forts never fired a shot.

Raising Northern Forces

On July 4, 1861, Lincoln called for 500,000 volunteers to enlist for three years. The next year, Congress called "all able-bodied male citizens between the ages of eighteen and forty-five" into state militias. At that time, the states, not the national government, drafted soldiers. Most of the states also paid a large bonus, called a **bounty**, to those who joined.

Because the number of volunteers was insufficient, in March 1863 Congress passed a **conscription** (draft) law to raise a national army. All men between the ages of twenty and forty-five were subject to regular army service. The law exempted certain officeholders and those who were physically or mentally unfit. A draftee could hire a substitute or pay $300 for an exemption. Recent immigrants, who were not subject to the draft, often served as substitutes to earn money. Other immigrants joined to prove their allegiance to their new country.

The system did not work well. At first, more than twice as many men bought substitutes as actually entered the army. Others ran away from service. Furthermore, the draft law caused ill will. Believ-

---

 Civil War Websites

Visit www.bjupress.com/resources for possible links to websites that focus on the Civil War.

 CD: Selected Bibliography

Refer to the CD for a helpful bibliography of resources divided into two categories: books for possible student use and books for teacher use. These resources will be helpful for teaching beyond the textbook and encouraging interested students to study the Civil War further.

CD: Timeline of the War

Refer to the CD for a timeline of major events in the war. Review this with the students periodically to help them grasp a sense of the war's chronology.

ing that the new draft law was unfair, penniless Irish immigrants, already harmed by runaway wartime inflation, rioted for four days in New York City. They vented their anger on local blacks. The mob resented that they were being drafted to free black slaves while the blacks stayed home. Most of the 128 people killed in the riots were blacks.

Raising Southern Forces

Some of West Point's best students joined the Confederate command. They provided able leadership during the war.

Initially the South had no problem getting enough men to fight. In fact, it had more volunteers than could be trained and equipped. Such enthusiasm, however, was short-lived. When the first one-year enlistments were up and no special benefits were offered, the number of recruits declined. In April 1862, the South had to resort to drafting all men aged eighteen to thirty-five. Later, the upper limit was extended to fifty, and men up to sixty-five could be placed in a home guard.

The South's system was not foolproof either. Men had so many ways to get out of service that a War Department clerk joked, "Our Bureau of Conscription ought to be called the Bureau of Exemptions." The most disputed feature of the law was the **Twenty-Negro Law**. It exempted any planter or overseer with more than twenty slaves. Its supporters claimed that those men were needed at home to supervise and control the slaves there. But poor Southerners who were drafted resented that exemption for the rich. It reinforced the idea that it was "a rich man's war but a poor man's fight." Understandably, when the war turned against the South, the South found it even harder to get recruits.

Preparing Civilians for War

The Civil War was a **total war**, one that involved both the military and civilians. Hardly anyone escaped at least some of its effects, and everyone was called upon to sacrifice in some way. In order to fight effectively, both sides needed to mobilize their population. The war especially affected Southerners because most of the fighting occurred on their soil.

In the North

Before the war, the North had begun to widen its industrial base. Women began to enter the work force. Many of the 800,000 immigrants who came to America between 1861 and 1865 worked in Northern factories. When war came, Northern factories produced war materials, including uniforms, blankets, tents, weapons, ammunition, wagons, canned foods, lumber, shovels, steamboats, and surgical instruments.

The war also affected farm production. Although thousands of men left their farms to fight, farm production in the North did not decline. Instead, as the demand for food products increased, farmers began to mechanize even more. This allowed them to produce more food with fewer workers, thus freeing more men to fight. In addition to feeding the Union army, Northern farms began to feed Europeans. For example, 40 percent of England's wheat and flour now came from the North.

The war also strengthened private volunteer groups. Private groups, sometimes called **commissions**, helped to purchase medicines and supply Bibles and other reading material for soldiers.

Southern recruiting posters appealed to patriotism and a desire to protect home and family.

The United States Christian Commission

One of the volunteer groups that sought to provide for soldiers' spiritual and physical needs was the United States Christian Commission (USCC). It was founded in 1861 and served through 1866. The ultimate goal of all its services was to save the souls of Union soldiers.

USCC records show that the Commission had 4,859 "delegates" in its lifetime. During the war, they preached 58,308 sermons and conducted 77,744 prayer meetings. They also wrote 92,321 letters for soldiers—the sick, the wounded, and the illiterate. Because soldiers craved reading material, they gave out large numbers of Bibles, tracts, hymnals, books, magazines, and newspapers. Soldiers had a hard time surviving solely on army rations, so the USCC also prepared a lot of meals.

---

most popular method for wealthier men was to pay a commutation fee or to hire a replacement.

Throughout the war, draft riots broke out in such places as Ohio, Illinois, and Massachusetts. The worst riot, however, occurred in New York City in 1863. During the riots blacks were especially targeted. A mob burned down a black boarding house, a black church, and a black orphanage. Finally, military units fresh from the Battle of Gettysburg arrived and restored order. One hundred or more people were killed in the riots.

Although the South did not experience draft riots as the North did, they still had the problems of inferior soldiers, replacements, and deserters (which dramatically increased near the end of the war). Also, anyone owning 20 or more slaves was exempted from the draft. Just as in the North, some wealthy Confederates hired men to take their place in the draft. However, in 1861, the Confederacy declared conscription into the army for all men between eighteen and thirty-five. Their service would last "for the duration," or until the war was over.

Common Terms of the War

Ensure that your students are familiar with some of the common terms associated with the war, such as the colors blue and gray. Most of the Northern soldiers wore blue uniforms. Many Confederate soldiers wore gray, at least at the beginning of the war, and primarily in the East. Confederate soldiers in the West wore primarily butternut, cloth dyed to a "butternut" brown. By the end of the war, however, many Southern soldiers were wearing whatever clothing they could find because Confederate supplies had been depleted. Northerners were commonly called "Yankees." "Billy

---

The Men Who Led

As was recommended in the previous chapter, an excellent source of information about many of the leading generals on both sides of the war is *The Class of 1846*. Two other good books on the military leaders in the war are *Generals in Blue* and *Generals in Gray* by Ezra Warner.

The "First Modern War"?

The Civil War has been called the "first modern war." Based on their reading, the students should discuss aspects of this war that made it a modern war (e.g., use of railroads for moving troops, telegraph for communication, mines, trenches, wire barricades, rifled guns and cannons, ironclad

ships, balloon observation, photography, and—not mentioned in the text—a submarine). Discuss how each of these advancements changed strategy and tactics.

Religion Among the Soldiers

If you live near Gettysburg, Pennsylvania, you might want to visit the museum of the U.S. Christian Commission there. You might also consider reading Daniel J. Hoisington, ed., *Gettysburg and the Christian Commission* (Roseville: Edinborough Press, 2002).

Yank" became the standard name for any Northern soldier. Southern soldiers were often called "Rebels." "Johnny Reb" was a common name for Confederate soldiers.

Railroads and the War

One technological development that made the Civil War a modern war was the railroad. At the outset of the war, the North had a considerable advantage in both quantity and quality of railroads. Two-thirds of all railroads in America were in the North. An industrial base in the North also allowed it to build new rail lines when necessary. In contrast, no new line was manufactured in the South during the war. When the South needed more tracks, the crews took the materials from less-used sidetracks.

The advantages railroads provided were tremendous. Not only could food and supplies be brought quickly to the front, but whole armies could be moved relatively quickly. Throughout the war, the North was able to shift soldiers from east to west when they were needed. Railroads could also provide the quick communications needed to coordinate attacks. Although the telegraph was already in use, lines could be cut or tapped. On a few occasions, trains were even used to meet direct military objectives. Flat cars with artillery on them bombarded the enemy. Abandoned cars were sent to ram enemy trains or were set on fire and rolled over bridges to burn down the whole structure.

The true value of railroads is shown by their connection to military objectives. In many instances, armies were directed to protect or destroy railroad lines. Colonel John Singleton Mosby of the Confederacy was known for his daring raids behind the Union lines. He left a trail of destroyed rails and trains. Sherman cut into the

Railroads were first used extensively by the military in the Civil War.

Both sides used balloons to observe enemy armies and direct movements on the battlefield.

Many types and sizes of bullets were used in the war.

Commissions sent money home to soldiers' families. They also found food, shelter, and clothing for slaves who had fled from behind Confederate lines.

In the South

The coming of war affected the South in many of the ways it did the North. The South, however, did not have as many factories. Although many of them received government contracts for making weapons, ammunition, and other war materials, they could not produce as much as Northern factories. Neither did the South have a good transportation system for moving those goods from the factories to the war fronts.

Agriculture in the South was severely affected by the war. Large numbers of white farmers and plantation owners entered the army. Later in the war, draft laws required even more of them to enter the army. On many farms, only women were left to oversee farm operations. On plantations, women had to run the plantations and oversee the work of the slaves. This was why the Confederate government passed the Twenty-Negro Law.

In the South, too, volunteer organizations helped soldiers and their families. Churches offered spiritual help. Local women's groups made bandages, socks, and other items. Even after the war, women remained active in caring for wounded veterans and honoring the memory of the fallen Southern soldiers.

Modern Warfare

The Civil War is considered the first modern war. Industry and technology improved weapons, which forced changes in tactics and strategy.

Innovations

For the first time, armies used railroads to move soldiers and equipment quickly. Both armies used cavalry, lightly armed units mounted on horses, extensively. The cavalry served as the eyes and ears of the armies. Cavalry units were scouts, gathering information and tracking the enemy's actions. Another innovation was manned balloons. Balloons could rise high above the surrounding trees or other natural obstructions and allow observers to report on the enemy's movements.

Both governments used the telegraph to communicate with their commanders. For example, almost every evening before he went to bed, Lincoln walked to the War Department to read the dispatches telegraphed from the front lines. That allowed him to stay in close contact with his generals and know what was going on. Because both armies used the telegraph, each was continually trying to destroy the telegraph lines of the other. Both armies also used mines, trench warfare, wire barricades, and other tools against the enemy.

One of the most important innovations was rifling, or making small spiral grooves in the barrels of guns and cannons. Rifling causes the bullet or shell to spin as it leaves the barrel, and that makes it travel in a straighter line, ensuring greater accuracy. Not all guns

CD: Weapons and Ordnance of the War

Refer to the CD for art and photos of many of the common weapons and ordnance used during the war.

or cannons were rifled. Some were smooth-bore weapons. But the greater accuracy of rifled weapons gave armies using them an edge. It also contributed to the higher death rate in this war.

Ironclad warships proved their superiority over wooden vessels. The *Monitor*, a Union iron ship, and the *Merrimac*, an ironclad that the Confederates had renamed the *Virginia*, clashed in the first battle of ironclad naval vessels. The clash ended in a tie, but it marked the beginning of modern naval warfare. The Confederate navy also tried submarines.

Another historic innovation that allows us to see the destruction of the war was photography. Photography had been developed twenty years earlier, but its use was limited. The complicated processes and expense involved prohibited its common use.

By 1861, however, photography was affordable and less complicated. Many soldiers had their pictures taken for loved ones. **Mathew Brady** formed a team of photographers to follow the troops and photograph them. Brady's photographs of corpses on the battlefield shocked Americans. It was the first time that most people had seen war deaths. Brady's photographs continue to give generations of historians revealing archives of the war.

Strategies of War

Determined to keep its independence, the Confederacy was committed to a defensive war. The North, however, would have to take aggressive action in order to prevent the Union from being dissolved. General Winfield Scott developed the **Anaconda Plan** to accomplish this goal and bring the seceded states back into the Union. General Joe Johnston developed the defensive Confederate strategy. The side that accomplished its goals would win the war.

A major innovation of the war was the use of ironclad ships, such as the USS *Monitor*.

The battle between the *Monitor* and the *Merrimac* (*Virginia*) did not have a winner.

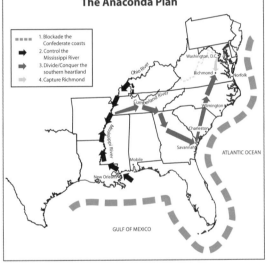

heart of the South by capturing Atlanta, a main railroad hub. In the closing days of the war, the North cut off Richmond by capturing Petersburg, which supplied the city by rail. As the war continued, the South struggled with not only a lack of provisions but also a lack of transportation (rolling stock) to get existing provisions to the troops.

The Face of War

Unlike any previous war, the War Between the States was captured on film for future generations to see. Photography was still in its infancy when the war began. The amount of time for an exposure to be made was at least several seconds, which limited photographers to taking pictures of individuals posing for the camera or on the field after the battle. Any action shots would have blurred badly and been unrecognizable.

CD: The Anaconda Plan and McClellan's Letter to Lincoln

Refer to the CD for a map of the Anaconda Plan and Gen. McClellan's letter to Lincoln about his strategy for conducting the war.

Activity 1: Comparing Lincoln and Davis

Have the students complete this activity as a way of highlighting the similarities and differences between these two leaders. They might have to consult outside resources or later sections of this chapter to complete some of the information.

Section II
Objectives

Students should be able to

1. Describe the activity and results of the First Battle of Bull Run, or Manassas.

2. Explain how McClellan was defeated in the Seven Days' Battle.

3. Describe the activity and results of the Second Battle of Bull Run, or Manassas.

Misconceptions of War

Congressmen, ladies, and other people from Washington expected to be able to picnic and watch the Battle of Bull Run as if it were a sporting event. Southern soldiers expected to whip the Yankees, win the war, and be back home in time for harvest. Northern soldiers had similar expectations, yet the battle actually was only a preview of the horrors of war yet to come, and it set the stage for a long and exhausting struggle.

Battle Names

Several battles of the war are commonly known by two different names. This fact was usually the result of the Northern practice of naming a battle for the nearest feature, such as a creek or a church, and the Southern practice of naming a battle for the nearest town. For example, Bull Run was named by the North for a nearby creek, as was Antietam. The South's names for those two battle sites, however, were Manassas and Sharpsburg. The North named the Battle of Shiloh for a church on the battlefield, whereas the South called it the Battle of Pittsburg Landing.

Union strategy	Confederate strategy
Impose a naval blockade to shut off the South's foreign trade. (International rules of war recognized a blockade as an act of war against another nation.)	Break the Union blockade.
Gain control of the Mississippi River, splitting the Confederacy and cutting off the western states.	Fight a strictly defensive war, making the North the aggressor.
Capture Richmond, the Confederate capital.	Gain diplomatic recognition by Great Britain and France.
Prevent the capture of Washington, D.C.	Restrict shipments of cotton to Britain to help them recognize their dependence on the South.

Section Quiz

1. Why was a draft used by both sides during the war?

2. List some of the names used for the war that occurred between 1861 and 1865.

3. List several innovations introduced during this war. What role did technology play in the war?

★ Compare and contrast the Northern and Southern war strategies.

★ Why did the Civil War cause a crisis of faith for some people?

II. Marching into Battle

After the fall of Fort Sumter, Northerners were eager for something to happen. But the Union army, under seventy-five-year-old General Winfield Scott, was made up of rough, untried recruits. Since many Northerners believed they had a decided edge and could win the war and be home before harvest, the pressure to attack Richmond grew greater. Richmond was only about one hundred miles from Washington, D.C. The press cried, "On to Richmond!" So loud and frequent was the call for action that Congress soon joined the chorus.

The First Battle of Bull Run

Prodded by such pressure, the Union army, led by General **Irvin McDowell**, in July 1861 moved south toward Richmond. The Confederate army, however, was on Bull Run Creek at Manassas Junction, Virginia, about twenty miles south of Washington. McDowell planned to attack it there. Northern journalists, congressmen, and their wives followed McDowell's forces down the Centerville Turnpike. They wanted to admire "the greatest army in the world" and enjoy watching it smash the Rebels while they had picnics.

The Confederates learned of McDowell's advance. Jefferson Davis ordered General **Joseph E. Johnston** to leave the Shenandoah Valley and join Gen. **P. G. T. Beauregard**'s troops at Manassas. On Sunday, July 21, their combined armies clashed with the Federal troops. At first, Union troops fought well. The Confederate army

Gen. Irvin McDowell led Union troops at the first Battle of Bull Run.

Section Quiz Answers

1. because volunteers became too scarce to supply the needed troops

2. Civil War or War Between the States; see the margin box in this section for other possible answers.

3. Answers include rifled weapons, aerial reconnaissance, telegraph, ironclad ships, mines, trench warfare, wire barricades, and photography. It made war more efficient but more deadly.

★ The North wanted to impose a coastal blockade, which the South wanted to break. The North wanted to forcibly cut off all foreign trade to destroy the South's economy; the South wanted to

voluntarily stop cotton shipments to Britain to force recognition. The North planned offensive moves; the South intended simply to defend itself. (Refer to the chart on strategies for other ideas.)

★ People on both sides assumed that God was on their side. When events did not run in their favor, they wondered why God was not fighting for them.

The Chronology of the Civil War

Review the organization of the chapter with your students. Explain that the Civil War is a complex period of history with many battles and events. More books have been

written about this war than any other period of American history, and more are being written every year. Several magazines are also devoted to the ongoing study of the war. (Perhaps obtain and show some of these magazines in class.) Sorting out all of the details requires hours of study, so that is beyond the scope of this course. This chapter, therefore, is just a broad survey of the major events in the war.

A strict chronological study of such a complex period has advantages. But the student also needs to see the flow of events in the three distinct fronts of the war: the war in the East, the war in the West, and the war on the "home front." This chapter combines both approaches in its six sections.

gave ground and seemed to be in disarray. Confederate general Barnard Bee rallied his troops by pointing to General Thomas Jackson nearby. "Look!" Bee shouted to his men. "There's Jackson, standing like a stone wall." Inspired by Jackson's example, the Southerners turned and drove the enemy back. Jackson's brigade had saved the day, and Jackson had earned a nickname: "**Stonewall**" **Jackson**.

The retreat of the Union troops soon turned into a rout when the Northerners panicked. Instead of having supper in Richmond, as they had bragged they would do, the Union soldiers threw down their weapons and equipment and ran for Washington. Dazed spectators joined the stampede. The chaos left Washington unprotected. Some Confederate officers wanted to push on to capture the Union capital. But the Confederate troops were tired and almost as disorganized as their enemies. They could not follow up on their great victory. Besides, Confederate strategy was to fight a purely defensive war. Capturing Washington was not initially an objective.

Generals Joseph Johnston and P. G. T. Beauregard led Confederate armies at Bull Run.

Results of the First Battle of Bull Run

The **Battle of Bull Run** (also called the Battle of Manassas) affected both sides. The North realized that its troops were not yet ready to fight and that the South would not be easily defeated. Lincoln ordered General **George McClellan** to take command of all Union troops protecting Washington and to forge a new army in the East. McClellan soon turned the army into a well-drilled machine. His troops loved him and nicknamed him "Little Napoleon."

The South had won the battle so easily that they became overconfident. They thought that the war soon would be over. They failed to follow up the victory, even after their troops had been refreshed and reorganized.

Hesitation and Loss for the North

The North's goal of taking Richmond proved to be difficult. Lincoln and Congress grew frustrated by McClellan's failure to attack. McClellan claimed that he needed more men and more time. His intelligence service, provided by Allen Pinkerton's Detective Agency, regularly overestimated the strength of the Confederate army. That made McClellan overly cautious. Lincoln finally had had enough of delay. He ordered McClellan to move on Richmond.

McClellan moved his army down the Potomac River and around the Virginia peninsula. They landed between the James and York rivers. Since the Confederates had spent little time fortifying that area, McClellan thought that would be the best place to attack them. The attack caught General Joseph Johnston by surprise. That should have been to McClellan's advantage, but he delayed, believing that he needed more men to win.

But that was only the beginning of McClellan's troubles. Johnston was wounded in an indecisive battle at Fair Oaks. His replacement as commander of the Army of Northern Virginia was General **Robert E. Lee**. Although Lee's troops were outnumbered, he knew his men, his resources, and the area. In a span of seven days, Lee attacked McClellan in six different places and drove the Union army back. McClellan had been nine miles from Richmond on June 25.

Gen. George McClellan was a superb organizer, but he was reluctant to attack.

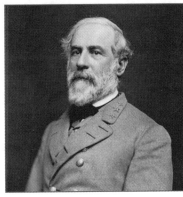

Jefferson Davis found his greatest commander in Gen. Robert E. Lee.

Quaker Guns

The Confederates might not have always had military equipment, but they often made the Union think they did. One reason for McClellan's cautious approach toward Richmond was "Quaker guns." Named for the Quakers' nonviolent beliefs, such "guns" were actually logs painted black or blackened by fire. They were placed on wagon wheels and positioned like cannons. From a distance, the Yankees had trouble telling whether they were real. Finding out could be costly. Occasionally, a real cannon was placed among several Quaker guns. An attacker would have to decide if the one gun firing meant the others were fakes or if it was just measuring distance and gauging range in preparation for a full barrage. Although Quaker guns were used in several places, they brought the biggest embarrassment to McClellan at Centreville.

An eighth-grade study of the Civil War should focus on the difference between the war in the East and the West and on the significance of the most important battles. An understanding of the full chronology and the relationship of events to each other must come with time. The students will cover a more detailed study of the war in eleventh grade U.S. History.

CD: Battlefield Tragedy, 1862
Refer to the CD for a first-hand account of the Battle of Malvern Hill.

The Element of Timing

The Second Battle of Bull Run demonstrated Lee's ability to know when to strike. Dissatisfied with McClellan's lack of progress, Lincoln replaced McClellan with Henry Halleck as general in chief of the Union armies. Halleck decided that the best plan was to pull back McClellan's and Pope's forces and unite them near Washington for a grand assault on the Confederate capital. If McClellan and Pope had united, they certainly would have outnumbered Lee, but Lee had other plans.

When McClellan began to withdraw his forces, he reduced the pressure on Lee to protect Richmond. Thus, the Confederate general had a little time to focus his attack on Pope before the Union armies could unite. In a daring move, Lee divided his force in two. One part, under Stonewall Jackson, moved northwest and attacked Pope's supply base. By the time Pope's forces got there, Jackson was gone. Pope's troops finally caught up with Jackson at the site of the First Battle of Bull Run. Pope attacked Jackson and expected a victory by the next day—but again time was the critical factor.

The other half of Lee's forces, under Major General James Longstreet, showed up on the battlefield the next day. While Pope was busy with Jackson, Longstreet attacked Pope's flank. The result was a major victory for the Confederacy. Once again the Union army retreated from Bull Run toward Washington.

After the Seven Days' Battle, he was back at the tip of the peninsula where he had started the campaign.

Different Names for Battles

Union name	Date(s)	Confederate name
Bull Run	Jul. 21, 1861	Manassas
Wilson's Creek	Aug. 10, 1861	Oak Hills
Pea Ridge	Mar. 7–8, 1862	Elkhorn Tavern
Pittsburg Landing	Apr. 6–7, 1862	Shiloh
Chickahominy	Jun. 27, 1862	Gaines's Mill
Antietam	Sept. 17, 1862	Sharpsburg
Stone's River	Dec. 31, 1862–Jan. 2, 1863	Murfreesboro

The Second Battle of Bull Run

Lincoln ordered McClellan back to Washington and put his army under the command of General **John Pope**, who then launched a new land attack. But Lee decided that the Confederacy could beat Pope before he gained strength.

Lee left half of his army in Richmond. He sent the other half north to keep Pope busy. Meanwhile, **J.E.B. Stuart**, Lee's dashing cavalry commander, raided Pope's headquarters while Pope was

Clara Barton

Clara Barton (1821–1912) is one of the best-known American nurses of all time. Born in Massachusetts, she began her career as a schoolteacher, first in Massachusetts and later in New Jersey. Barton excelled in her job, demanding and receiving wages equal to the male teachers. This was very unusual for the time. After her time as a teacher, she worked at the United States Patent Office in Washington, D.C. Once again, she asked for and received wages at the same level as the men.

With the beginning of the Civil War, Barton volunteered her services for the North. She gained permission to visit the front lines and was aghast at what she found there. She spent the rest of the war doing what she could to help the soldiers. For her work, she earned the title "angel of the battlefield." After the war, President Lincoln asked her to begin a government department to look for missing troops. She also became famous by giving lectures about her experiences.

In 1869, Barton went to Europe. While in Europe, Barton became associated with the International Red Cross, founded in 1864 through the efforts of Jean-Henri Durant. Barton was working with the Red Cross when the Franco-Prussian War broke out in 1870. She helped those in need in that war as well.

Upon her return to America in 1873, she encouraged the United States to agree to the Geneva Convention. The Geneva Convention was a treaty from the International Red Cross protecting the wounded of all sides in a war. Later provisions of the Geneva Convention dealt with civilians, prisoners, and sea warfare. The Senate ratified the Geneva Convention in 1882. This approval also formed the American National Red Cross. Barton was its first president, a post she held for 22 years.

As president, Barton expanded the role of the American Red Cross to aid victims of peacetime emergencies, such as hurricanes, floods, earthquakes, and epidemics. Later, the International Red Cross passed an amendment that made this American endeavor the standard for the whole organization. Barton used her prominent role to support women's suffrage. In 1898, during the Spanish-American War, Barton, then in her seventies, went to Cuba and managed the work there. Barton's leadership style, however, was controlling at times. As a result, other members of the American National Red Cross challenged her leadership around the turn of the twentieth century, and Barton resigned in 1904.

Activity 2: Major Battles

Use this activity at this point to review the battles covered in the narrative so far. You can also use this activity in the remaining two sections of the chapter. The completed activity would also help the students review for the chapter test.

Activity 3: Political Cartoons

Use this activity to help the students understand how newspaper cartoonists of the period viewed events during the war. Relate their shaping of public opinion to the way cartoonists do the same thing today.

gone. Stuart, seeking revenge for losing his favorite hat to Federal troops in a skirmish several days earlier, collected Pope's war chest of $300,000, his dress coat, and the dispatch book that told where Union forces would be going. This gave Lee the advantage he needed.

The Union and Confederate armies met on August 29, 1862, for the second time on the battlefield at Bull Run. Stonewall Jackson's "foot cavalry" (infantry that were so named because they marched so quickly) raced to aid Lee. They covered sixty-two miles in less than forty-eight hours. They jumped into the fight just in time to give the South the victory. The two-day fight, the **Second Battle of Bull Run** (Manassas), again ended with the Union troops fleeing back to Washington. Jackson said that the day had been won "by nothing but the blessing and protection of Providence."

Lee had defeated both the main Union army and the relief army that had come to aid it. He had successfully switched the locale of fighting from Richmond back to Washington. Lincoln sent a disgraced Pope to Minnesota to fight Indians. He put McClellan back in command. McClellan now had a second chance.

Gen. J.E.B. Stuart became Lee's "eyes and ears," twice leading his cavalry around the Union armies and creating panic in Washington, D.C. However, he failed to report to Lee at Gettysburg. This contributed to the crushing defeat of the Confederate forces there.

Section Quiz

1. What key city was the Union army trying to capture?
2. What Confederate commander provided an example of courage that kept Southern troops from retreating at the First Battle of Bull Run?
3. How did each side respond to that Confederate victory?
4. What exceptional Confederate leader overcame McClellan in the Seven Days' Battle?
★ What proved to be a major flaw in McClellan's leadership?

III. Controlling the Waters

The Union's strategy for closing the South's major water transportation links involved two goals. First, they had to blockade the Southern coasts. Second, they had to capture and control the Mississippi River. The North achieved both of these goals quickly. They also found better leadership in the West than had been in charge in the East.

The Union Blockade

On April 19, 1861, only a few days after the fall of Fort Sumter, Lincoln ordered a **naval blockade** of the southern coast from South Carolina to the Mexican border. (The purpose of a blockade is to prevent entry or exit of passengers or commerce.) Later, he extended it northward to the Potomac River. Because of the shortage of ships, however, it was difficult for the Union to maintain a successful blockade. The Secretary of the Navy began a giant ship-buying program and leased or bought just about any vessel big enough to be armed. The North concentrated its blockade on ten major southern ports, each of which had inland connections by rail or river.

The South tried to overcome the blockade with **blockade runners**, ships specially designed to slip through the blockade. They had shallow drafts (little of the ship extended below the water line), so they could dart into shallow inlets to hide. Since the Union ships

Section III
Objectives

Students should be able to

1. Describe the Union blockade and the Confederacy's activity to overcome it.
2. Name the Union general who successfully gained control of the Mississippi River for the North.
3. Identify the last Confederate stronghold on the Mississippi River to fall into Union hands.

The C.S.S. *Alabama*

The most famous of the South's blockade-runners was a British-built ship, the C.S.S. *Alabama*, captained by Raphael Semmes. In 1863, the *Alabama* captured and burned thirty-six Yankee ships. Its raids put fear into Union sailors. After many months at sea, the *Alabama* went to a French port for repairs. While it was there, a Union ship attacked and sank the blockade-runner. In 1871, the United States pressed Britain to accept responsibility for the damage that the *Alabama* and other British-built Confederate raiders had caused during the Civil War. Britain paid the United States $15 million for its failure to exercise "due diligence" over its shipyards.

Section Quiz Answers

1. Richmond
2. Thomas "Stonewall" Jackson
3. The North got a new general and grew more disciplined through increased training. The South became overconfident.
4. Robert E. Lee
★ He was overly cautious and was unwilling to act, wasting opportunities to advance.

Activity 4: Soldiers' Accounts of the War

Have the students read and answer the questions about these two soldiers' accounts of the war to gain a better understanding of the link between the soldiers and the home front during the Civil War.

Blockade runners, such as the *Advance*, were built for speed and near invisibility on the high seas.

needed deeper water to operate, they could not follow them. Blockade runners also had low profiles and usually were painted dull gray, making them blend with the seas and therefore difficult to see. Most of them were steam powered. Some steamers could do eighteen knots (27 mph), enabling them to outrun any Union vessel. Some had powerful engines that burned hard coal, which produced less noticeable smoke.

The best ports for blockade runners had more than one outlet, such as Wilmington, N.C. From such ports the runners, loaded with cotton, usually travelled south to British-held islands. Bermuda and the Bahama Islands were only about three days away. They then transferred the goods to ships that flew the flags of neutral countries. To overcome their ship and manpower shortage, the Confederates hired British ships and young captains from the Royal Navy. The potential wealth to be gained from blockade running made it worth the risks. The Confederates made more than 8,500 successful trips through the blockade. Even in the closing months of the war, some were able to evade the blockade.

In 1861, slipping through the blockade was very easy. Nine of every ten Southern ships got through. But as the months passed, the Union blockade became tougher to get through. As various port cities fell to Union armies, the North had more land bases to make the blockade even more successful. In the spring of 1865, thirty-five fully laden runners carrying $15 million worth of goods sat in Nassau harbor with no ports of call open on the southern coast. Their cargoes would never reach the starving South.

Although the blockade's effectiveness at the war's end was only 50 percent, it hurt the Confederacy greatly. In three years, due to a self-imposed restriction meant to drive up the price of cotton, the South went from exporting ten million bales of cotton a year to shipping only one million bales. However, the Southern strategy to drive up prices and pressure Britain to support the Confederate cause failed. Drained of income, the South had to issue money backed by only faith in its cause. Its credit was weakened, and desperately needed foreign products became nearly unobtainable. Its foreign trade declined by two-thirds. Although the outcome of the war was decided not on the blockade line but on the battlefield, it would have been a far different war if the Union navy had not guarded the coasts of the South.

Taking the Mississippi River

The focus of the North's "War in the West" was controlling the Mississippi River. Controlling it would separate Texas, Arkansas, and Louisiana from the rest of the Confederacy and would also keep the South from using the river. The Union armies could take advantage of the river's transportation opportunities. Union general **William Sherman** called the Mississippi the "spinal column of America."

Gaining the Upper Mississippi

A major factor in the capture of the Mississippi was the leadership of another Union general, **Ulysses S. Grant**. He had retired from

Forts Henry and Donelson

Fort Henry on the Tennessee River and Fort Donelson on the Cumberland River were critical to the defense of the Southern heartland. In fact, Fort Donelson was the main defensive structure separating the Union forces in Kentucky from Nashville.

Grant, who was in command of the Union offensive, thought that his double victory over the two fronts would lead to the collapse of Southern resistance and the ultimate fall of the Confederacy, but he underestimated the determination of Southern forces.

the army earlier but had failed at farming and business. When war broke out, he rejoined the army in Illinois. He believed that the key to success in the West was control of the Tennessee and Cumberland rivers. (These rivers empty into the Ohio River, which in turn flows to the Mississippi.) Leaving Cairo, Illinois, he and his troops moved down to Tennessee and captured Fort Henry on the Tennessee River and Fort Donelson on the Cumberland ten days later. Their fall, followed by the capture of Corinth, Mississippi, and victory in the Battle of Shiloh in April 1862, gave the Union control of the upper Mississippi and access to points south. Grant became a hero. He also gained a nickname: "Unconditional Surrender" Grant.

Gaining the Lower Mississippi

Next, the Union army sought to gain control of the lower Mississippi. That would prevent Confederate use of its Gulf ports. Two Confederate forts, Fort St. Philip and Fort Jackson, on a peninsula below New Orleans guarded the mouth of the river. The Confederacy had also stretched two huge link chains across the Mississippi. They lifted the chains to permit Confederate vessels to pass and then lowered them to snag enemy vessels that might try to get past.

Admiral **David Farragut** of the Union navy devised a plan that, with the aid of a land force led by General Benjamin Butler, captured New Orleans. Farragut bypassed the forts and headed straight for New Orleans. Under cover of darkness, an advance party unhooked the chains. Farragut's gunboats slipped past the forts despite heavy fire from the Confederates. Once past the forts, he scattered and disabled the Confederate fleet. New Orleans fell two days later. Butler's troops remained there to keep it under Union control.

The Union navy moved up the river, capturing first Baton Rouge, Louisiana, and then Natchez, Mississippi. By July 1863, the Union controlled the whole Mississippi River, except for **Vicksburg**, Mississippi.

Vicksburg sat on high bluffs overlooking the river. The Union army attacked the town six times. Each time, Confederate General John Pemberton's Southern troops repelled them, inflicting heavy casualties.

Grant then sought a new strategy. He cut his army loose from its own supply line. He ordered his troops to "carry what rations of hard bread, coffee, and sort we can, and make the country furnish the balance." In a move that surprised Pemberton, Grant moved east to cut Confederate rail access to Vicksburg. Pemberton responded by moving to cut off Grant's supply line, only to find that Grant had none! When Pemberton returned to Vicksburg, he was caught in a trap. Grant could starve Pemberton out by besieging the town.

For six weeks, the Union forces shelled Vicksburg around the clock. Food became so scarce in the town that the people ate mules, rats, and even their family pets. Finally, with no more food and no hope of relief, the Confederate troops surrendered Vicksburg on July 4, 1863. Grant had captured the entire Mississippi in only eighteen months.

Section Quiz

1. Why was it initially difficult for the Union to maintain a successful naval blockade of the South?

Gen. Ulysses S. Grant proved that he could lead armies to victory in the West.

Adm. David Farragut led the Union navy up the Mississippi, helping Grant gain control of Confederate waterways.

Situated on high bluffs over the Mississippi, Vicksburg seemed to be a perfect defensive location.

The Vicksburg Key

Located on the eastern side of the Mississippi, Vicksburg stood as the Confederacy's last major stronghold on the river. If it could be taken, Arkansas, Texas, and Louisiana would be completely cut off from the rest of the Confederacy. Victory would also restore commerce in the river-dependent Ohio and northern Mississippi valleys. The Confederates were also aware of Vicksburg's importance. Eight forts, lines of trenches, and Confederate forces under Major General John C. Pemberton surrounded the city. Swamps to the north of the city made any attack there almost impossible. The best chance for Union victory was to approach the city from the east.

Ulysses S. Grant, the Union general in charge of the Vicksburg campaign, made several attempts to bypass the city.

To get into position to attack from the east, Grant would have to move his men across the Mississippi. Leaving Sherman's force north of Vicksburg, Grant moved most of his forces down the western side of the Mississippi south of the city. A Confederate bombardment prevented him from crossing the river where intended, but he found an unprotected area farther south. The only problem was that Confederate troops in Jackson, Mississippi, might attack Grant's rear, so he moved on them first. Grant swept up toward Jackson, defeating Confederate forces at Fort Gibson and at Raymond. Next he attacked Confederate Joseph E. Johnston's forces at Jackson. Meanwhile, the Confederate forces at Vicksburg left the city to aid Johnston. They were too late. Johnston retreated north before Pemberton could help him.

Section Quiz Answers

1. because of a shortage of ships

Grant turned his forces and headed east toward Vicksburg. At Champion's Hill he defeated Pemberton, who quickly moved the rest of his forces back toward Vicksburg. By the time Grant reached Vicksburg, he was confident that the city would soon be in his hands. However, the Confederates were not ready to surrender. The siege of Vicksburg began on May 19 and lasted almost seven weeks. Pemberton finally surrendered on July 4, 1863. One Confederate chaplain said, "We surrendered to famine, not to them."

Section IV
Objectives
Students should be able to

1. List three reasons Lee moved his forces into Maryland.
2. Describe the circumstances of the Battle of Antietam.
3. Explain the good and bad results of the Battle of Chancellorsville for the South.
4. Describe the circumstances and results of the Battle of Gettysburg.

Antietam
The casualties from this battle made it the single bloodiest day in the history of all America's wars.

2. According to Grant, what was the key to military success west of the Appalachians?
3. What Union naval officer was responsible for breaking through the Confederate chain in the lower Mississippi?
4. What was the last Confederate stronghold on the Mississippi River? On what date did it fall to Union troops?
★ Why did the North want to shut off the South's water links?

The Battle of Antietam was the bloodiest single-day battle of the war. It could have been much worse for the South if McClellan had followed up with another attack.

Gen. Ambrose Burnside suffered a crushing defeat at Fredericksburg.

Losses were heavy on both sides at the Battle of Fredericksburg, but the North lost almost twice as many men as the South.

IV. Continuing the War in the East

In September 1862, Lee took the offensive. He invaded Maryland since many Marylanders were Southern sympathizers. Lee hoped that a Confederate victory there would cause the people to rise up and free it from Union control and free farmers in the grain-rich state to harvest their crops. A victory for the South might also convince Britain to join the Confederate side.

Antietam

Lee divided his army. He sent Jackson up the Shenandoah Valley. He left J.E.B. Stuart's cavalry behind to prevent any pursuit of Lee's army into Maryland.

McClellan had no idea where Lee planned to attack. But two of his soldiers made an amazing discovery. The Union army was crossing an area through which the Confederates had recently marched. A Union corporal and a sergeant saw on the road a bundle of three cigars wrapped in a paper. That paper was a dispatch from Lee that a messenger had lost. It contained orders to Lee's commanders and revealed both Lee's location and the fact that his army was divided. With that information, McClellan hoped to force Lee into a battle before Jackson could return to help Lee.

Less than twenty-four hours later, Lee learned of the lost orders. He was forced to change his plans. He would pull back across the Potomac. But on September 17, 1862, before Lee could escape, McClellan launched a massive attack against Lee near Sharpsburg, along **Antietam** (an TEE tum) Creek. Lee's embattled troops, reinforced by Jackson's foot cavalry, held the line. If McClellan had attacked once more, he might have defeated Lee, but he hesitated. At the end of the day, the Confederates controlled the battlefield. Under cover of darkness, Lee engineered a brilliant retreat and returned to the safety of Northern Virginia. McClellan's failure to pursue Lee's army made this retreat possible.

Since the South did not win an outright victory at Antietam, Britain did not recognize the Confederacy. Since the Union did not lose, Lincoln used the event to issue the Emancipation Proclamation (discussed later). He also replaced McClellan for not following up his attack and winning the battle outright.

Fredericksburg

Ambrose Burnside, McClellan's replacement, had no better success than McClellan. On December 13, 1862, Burnside crossed the Rappahannock River to attack the Confederates entrenched at **Fredericksburg**. Wave after wave of soldiers failed to dislodge the Confederate forces, and the Union army lost twice as many men as the Confederate army.

2. control of the region's waterways: Tennessee, Cumberland, and Mississippi rivers
3. David Farragut
4. Vicksburg; July 4, 1863
★ If the South's water links were closed, then ships could not bring food, weapons, and supplies to Southern troops. The South would also be unable to export cotton and raise money to continue fighting the war.

💿 CD: Battle of Antietam
Refer to the CD for a map detailing the troop movements during the Battle of Antietam.

Union morale dipped to the lowest point of the war. In twenty months, the North had organized a grand army, but no Union general seemed able to win with it. Lincoln tried another general, replacing Burnside with "**Fighting Joe**" **Hooker**.

Chancellorsville

Hooker had 130,000 soldiers to Lee's 60,000. He decided to attack Lee by going west to **Chancellorsville**. The Union forces also had an overwhelming advantage in supplies. An overconfident Hooker boasted, "May God have mercy on General Lee, for I will have none."

Considering that the isolated crossroads was within easy reach of Richmond, Lee took yet another great risk. Once again, he split his army and caught the Federal troops by surprise. The battle, which many historians believe to be Lee's finest, raged for five days. The fifth Union offensive to capture Richmond failed.

Although the South won a major victory at Chancellorsville, it was very costly. During the evening of the first day of battle, Stonewall Jackson was mortally wounded. In the darkness, Confederate soldiers mistook Jackson and his staff, who were out scouting, for enemy cavalry and fired on them. When Lee learned of Jackson's wounds and the amputation of his left arm, he sent word for Jackson to "make haste and get well, and come back to me as soon as he can. He has lost his left arm, but I have lost my right." But Jackson died. Lee and the Confederacy felt the loss keenly. Because of Jackson's skill and unselfish cooperation, he had been worth many regiments to the Confederate cause.

Gettysburg

Lee was buoyed by the victory at Chancellorsville. He decided to make a bold advance into Pennsylvania. Lee believed that if the citizens of the North could feel firsthand the effects of war on their own soil, their support for Lincoln's war would decline. He thought that this strategy would force Lincoln to pull some troops out of the campaign along the Mississippi River and reduce pressure there. Lee also hoped that his famished army could resupply itself as they passed through lush Pennsylvania farmlands. His troops also needed shoes badly. Lee thought, wrongly, that **Gettysburg** had a hidden supply of them.

Lee's Hopeful Advance

In early June, Lee started north, up the Shenandoah Valley. He crossed the Potomac, entered western Maryland, and moved into Pennsylvania. Hooker, even with 90,000 men, did not try to stop Lee. On June 28, in desperation, Lincoln removed Hooker and gave the Army of the Potomac its fifth commander in a year: **George Meade**. Meade was shy and scholarly but well qualified as a general.

On July 1, Lee's advance troops came to the small town of Gettysburg. There they unexpectedly met a Union scouting party. Both armies quickly pulled up along two ridges and prepared to fight. The

Gen. Joseph "Fighting Joe" Hooker bragged about how he would whip the Southern army but later had to eat his words as they soundly defeated him at Chancellorsville.

Although the South won the Battle of Chancellorsville, it cost them one of their greatest generals, "Stonewall" Jackson.

This photo of Gen. Thomas "Stonewall" Jackson was taken less than two weeks before his fatal wounding.

Stonewall Jackson

Thomas "Stonewall" Jackson's name is forever linked to the Southern armies in the East. He was a strict instructor at Virginia Military Institute before the war. He was quite eccentric. For example, he seldom sat down, preferring to read, write, or teach while standing because he thought that sitting compressed the internal organs in an unhealthful way. On the battlefield, he was often seen holding up one hand above his head in the belief that it kept his blood flow balanced.

In spite of his eccentricities, Jackson's courage, fighting ability, and brilliant strategy made him an extremely important leader for the South. Time and again he inspired his infantry regiment to move so swiftly that they surprised the enemy by being where they were least expected. They moved so quickly that they were called "Jackson's foot cavalry." Lee had such confidence in Jackson's ability that he remarked that the South would have won at Gettysburg if Jackson had been there.

Just as important as Jackson's reputation as a soldier, however, was his reputation as a Christian. He was known as a man of faith and prayer. Before the war, he taught a Sunday school class for slaves, in which he taught them to read and love the Bible. In war, he credited the Lord's mercies and his soldiers' bravery for any victories he achieved. His sincere testimony had a profound effect on everyone who knew him. He trained his men to give their best. "Duty is ours; consequences are God's," he often told them. Another of his frequent sayings is "Resolve to perform what you ought; perform without fail what you resolve." (You can find many more quotations in *Stonewall Jackson's Book of Maxims*, edited by James I. Robertson.)

Jackson Biography

Encourage your students to read a biography of Jackson. (One good biography for teacher use, though not on an eighth-grader's level, is James I. Robertson's *Stonewall Jackson*.) A good one for students is *Stonewall Jackson: The Good Soldier* by Allen Tate.

CD: Battle of Gettysburg

Refer to the CD for a series of maps detailing the troop movements on each of the three days during the Battle of Gettysburg.

Which Battle Was the Turning Point of the War?

Ask the students to identify the battle that they think was the turning point of the Civil War and to defend their answers. Which battle turned the tide and made Union victory a near certainty? *(The best choices are the battles of Antietam and Gettysburg, although historians have suggested several other battles as well. A person's answer says much about his understanding of the issues of the war that led to the Union victory.)* Note that Lincoln issued the Emancipation Proclamation after Antietam, ensuring that Britain would stay out of the war.

CD: The Gettysburg Address

Refer to the CD for the complete text of Lincoln's Gettysburg Address.

Activity 5: Lincoln's Gettysburg Address

Use this activity to help the students understand the importance of this short presidential address to both the Civil War era and our own times.

CD: Gettysburg Address Photo

Refer to the CD for a photo of Lincoln's Gettysburg Address.

The Minie Ball

Before the Civil War, soldiers marched into battle in tight formations, firing massed volleys at the enemy and then breaking into bayonet or saber charges. The minie ball made such tactics outdated and suicidal.

The minie ball took advantage of the rifled barrel, which had spiraled grooves that set a bullet spinning, giving it greater distance and precision. The problem was that the bullet had to fit snugly enough in the barrel to make use of the rifling.

Claude-Etienne Minié, a Frenchman, developed a bullet that was cylindrical with a rounded tip. It had grooves on its side to catch those in the rifled barrel. What made the bullet distinctive was its base. Minié left part of the base hollow and inserted a cup-shaped piece of iron here. When the gunpowder behind the bullet exploded, the expanding gasses pushed the cup forward. The cup pushed the sides of the bullet outward so that it would grip the barrel's grooves and start spinning.

On the battlefield, the minie ball changed everything. In the Civil War, 90 percent of battlefield wounds were caused by minie balls. Rifle fire was accurate up to four hundred or five hundred yards. Often men marching toward each other never got close enough for the bayonet charges of old. Artillery units were moved behind the rest of the troops because of the long-distance accuracy of the minie ball. Cavalry units also started to use short-barreled rifles called carbines rather than sabers. After the Civil War, armies began to fight more and more in trenches, which provided cover from accurate weapons of war such as the minie ball.

Gen. George Meade's Union armies clashed with Lee's armies at Gettysburg.

Gen. James Longstreet, Lee's "Warhorse," was in charge of the Confederate right at Gettysburg.

Confederates were on Seminary Ridge; the Union forces stood on Cemetery Ridge about one mile away. At the southern end of Cemetery Ridge were two rocky points called Round Top and Little Round Top. In front of Little Round Top was a field of huge boulders called Devil's Den.

On the first day of the three-day battle, Lee's troops forced the Union lines back but did not break them. The next day, July 2, Lee ordered Gen. **James Longstreet** to attack the Union left on the Round Tops. Longstreet delayed his attack. When he finally pushed his men through a peach orchard, a wheat field, and Devil's Den toward the Round Tops, he was beaten back. Lee planned an assault on the Union center. Several of his officers, including Longstreet, advised that they attack instead on the Union left again. Lee overruled them.

High-Water Mark of the Confederacy

Lee's attack on July 3 began late but with the heaviest bombardment the South had delivered in the war. Then early in the afternoon, 15,000 troops under Gen. **George Pickett** began marching in formation across a mile-wide cornfield toward the Union lines. Protected behind a low stone wall, the Union soldiers fired into the ranks, killing hundreds. The human destruction became especially severe whenever the Confederates slowed their march to cross fences and then re-form. The Union cannons, shooting at point-blank range like giant shotguns, mowed down the Confederate ranks. Still the Confederates came. As they neared a stone wall from behind which the Federal troops were firing, the Southerners turned toward a group of trees in the center of the Union line. They shouted the "Rebel yell" and charged straight into the Union line. They reached the stone wall and fought hand to hand. The slaughter was horrific.

Pickett's men had given their all, but they were unable to break the Union line. They straggled back across the cornfield. "**Pickett's charge**" lasted less than fifty minutes, but the casualties were shocking. The Union lost 2,332 men. The South lost more than 3,000. Pickett lost all fifteen of his regimental commanders, including two brigadier generals and six colonels. When Pickett got back to the

Many historians consider Pickett's charge at Gettysburg to have been the "high-water mark of the Confederacy."
Gettysburg Cyclorama, Courtesy Gettysburg Foundation

Confederate lines, Lee ordered him to regroup his division for the expected Union counterattack. Pickett replied sadly, "General Lee, I have no division."

The counterattack never came. Meade did not know that the Confederates were nearly out of ammunition. The next day, in a downpour, Lee's tattered army withdrew into Virginia. The Confederate army was stretched over seventeen miles but returned without the slightest harassment from the Union army. Meade missed a golden opportunity to deal Lee's army a decisive blow, possibly even taking it out of the war.

Because Meade showed no effort to follow up on his victory at Gettysburg, Lincoln replaced him with a general from the West who had proven that he could fight: Ulysses S. Grant. William T. Sherman was appointed to take Grant's place in the West.

The three-day Battle of Gettysburg (July 1–3, 1863) was the bloodiest battle of the entire war.

Section Quiz

1. What discovery prevented Lee from surprising and defeating the Union army at Antietam?

2. What valuable Confederate leader was mortally wounded during the Battle of Chancellorsville?

3. Who led the famous but futile Confederate charge at Gettysburg?

4. Whom did Lincoln name as the new commander of Union forces in the East following the Battle of Gettysburg?

★ What did Lee think would be the benefit to the South of opening conflict in Northern territory?

V. Waging Total War

By 1863, both sides were growing weary of the war. Despite early Confederate successes at Fort Sumter and Bull Run, conditions in the wartime South quickly deteriorated. The Union blockade resulted in severe shortages. And Confederate money lost its value, resulting in outrageously high prices. By 1864, bacon sold for twenty dollars a pound and flour for one hundred dollars a barrel. The longer the war lasted, the more difficult the situation became.

Many Northerners too were tired of the war and wanted to negotiate peace. But Lincoln wanted to win. He and his advisors believed that freeing the slaves, destroying as much Southern property as possible, and winning the 1864 election might all help to end the war.

The Emancipation Proclamation

Lincoln realized that he needed a new cause to revive support for the war. By adding the goal of freeing the slaves to the goal of preserving the Union, Lincoln hoped to convince the people that this war was worth the blood of thousands of Americans. So in September 1862, after Antietam, he issued the **Emancipation Proclamation**. It would take effect January 1, 1863. Even then, it would free slaves only in Confederate-held areas. The proclamation would not free slaves in the border states or any other areas then under Federal control. Also,

Lincoln got the approval of his cabinet before he issued the Emancipation Proclamation.

Section V

Objectives

Students should be able to

1. Explain the purpose and effects of the Emancipation Proclamation.

2. Define *total war*.

3. Describe the way the North carried on a war of attrition through the activities of Sheridan and Sherman.

4. Identify the candidates in the 1864 presidential election and their respective parties, and explain the results of the election.

Effects of Total War

Because Confederate money had so little value, some people used a barter system, trading goods for food. Then scarce goods disappeared altogether. To fight inflation and provide war materials, the South used taxes in kind, which required the producers to send one-tenth of their products—hogs, corn, or whatever they had—directly to the Confederate government. This further complicated the economic situation.

Substitutions became common. Rye, sweet potatoes, okra seeds, and even peanuts were used to make coffee. As medicines grew scarce, the woods became the South's medicine chest. For example, Southerners could no longer import quinine to treat malaria, so a less effective mixture of red pepper, table salt, and tea took its place.

Since cotton could be neither sold nor eaten, Jefferson Davis tried to get planters and farmers to grow corn. One Georgia newspaper wrote, "Plant corn and be free, or plant cotton and be whipped!" But even if Southern farmers did produce enough food, the South's poor transportation

Section Quiz Answers

1. Two of McClellan's men found lost orders that disclosed Lee's location and the fact that he had divided his army.

2. Stonewall Jackson

3. Gen. George Pickett

4. Gen. Ulysses S. Grant

★ It would give Northern citizens first-hand knowledge of the destructiveness of war and encourage them to decrease their support for the war. It also would allow Lee to resupply his army from the agricultural bounty of the Pennsylvania countryside.

The Emancipation Proclamation

Project the text of the Emancipation Proclamation onto a screen for the class to read. Discuss the provisions of the proclamation and the politics involved. Why would Lincoln free the slaves in unconquered areas of the South and invite them to join the Union military? (An online transcript of the proclamation is available on the National Archives website.)

Biblical Evaluation of Total War

President Lincoln saw the Emancipation Proclamation as a tool enabling him to pursue total war against the South. Total war aims to completely destroy the enemy. One troubling characteristic of total war is the targeting of civilians and their property in order to demoralize the enemy and drive them to unconditional surrender. Sherman's march to the sea and the burning of Atlanta are the two most memorable acts of the total war waged by the Northern army. Engage the students in a discussion of the morality of total war. Is it justifiable? Consider the following:

1. Lincoln felt he had exhausted the limited war option. He believed he could

system often prevented the produce from reaching its destination.

Farmers and planters often struggled more than those in other occupations. The Confederate government took livestock, mules, horses, and carriages as well as tools and buckets for the war effort. Southerners either used what they could make or did without.

Emancipation Proclamation

Note that prior to the Emancipation Proclamation the North was not fighting a war to free the slaves. Some people perceived the war to be against slavery, but the stated purpose was simply to preserve the Union, and that was the reason most of the Northern soldiers gave. Neither did the South declare itself to be fighting to preserve slavery but rather to preserve states' rights and the integrity of their states and the Confederacy.

The Emancipation Proclamation, however, changed the outlook of many people toward the war, encouraging Northerners to fight for the new cause.

Blacks in the Confederate Armies

Blacks served in the Confederate armies only in noncombatant (nonfighting) jobs, such as cooks, wagon drivers, laborers, and personal servants to officers. The Confederate Congress ignored advice from such commanders as Gen. Patrick Cleburne that blacks be used in the Southern armies. By March 1865, however, when the South experienced a severe manpower shortage, the Confederate Congress passed a bill to draft 300,000 blacks. The first two black companies astounded Southern whites with their skill at arms. But no blacks fought for the Confederacy because the war ended before blacks could take the field.

if any Confederate states quit fighting before January 1, they could keep their slaves. Not one state, however, quit.

The proclamation gave the Union a measurable goal. Instead of fighting merely for the Union, Northerners were now waging war "to make men free." The proclamation hurt the South's war efforts because many slaves left their masters. As word spread that slaves who reached Northern lines would be free, thousands of slaves fled from their masters. It also ended all Southern hopes of recognition from Britain, since most of the British opposed slavery. Moreover, the proclamation paved the way for public acceptance of the total end of slavery, which came with the Thirteenth Amendment.

Because they would be fighting to end slavery, blacks were given a real reason for joining the fight. To be captured in a Union uniform would mean almost certain enslavement, but more than 190,000 blacks fought on the Union side.

Blacks faced prejudice wherever they were. Black Union soldiers were not treated the same as white soldiers. Until 1864, black soldiers were paid less and got medical care far below the norm. As a result, the death toll for blacks ran 37 percent higher than that of whites. Blacks also were assigned the most mundane tasks, and no blacks were appointed as officers. Black troops were commanded by white officers.

Sgt. William H. Carney

The 54th Massachusetts was the first all-black regiment in the Union army. Sergeant William Carney, a member of the regiment, received the Congressional Medal of Honor for his actions during the attack on Fort Wagner in Charleston, S.C. He was the first black soldier to receive it. The following is an account of his heroism.

After an exhausting march, and without the troops having had time for food, the bombardment began. The line of battle was formed with the Fifty-fourth Massachusetts assigned to the post of honor and danger, in front of the attacking column.

Suddenly such a terrific fire was opened on the regiment when as-

cending the wall of the fort with full ranks that, using the words of Sergeant Carney, "they melted away almost instantly" before the enemy's fire.

During the attack, Colonel Robert G. Shaw, commanding the brigade, was killed. So disastrous was the fire that the brigade was compelled to retire; but Sergeant Carney, who was with the battalion in the lead of the storming column, and who, with the regimental colors, had pressed forward near the colonel leading the men over the ditch, planted the flag upon the parapet, and, lying down in order to get as much shelter as possible, for half an hour, until the second brigade came up, kept the

colors up all the time. He received a severe wound in the head. When this brigade retired, he, creeping on his knees, having by this time received a wound in the thigh also, followed them, but still held up the flag. Thus he held the flag over the wall of Fort Wagner during the conflict of two brigades, and received two wounds.

When he entered the field hospital where his wounded comrades were, they cheered him and the colors. Nearly exhausted from the loss of blood, he exclaimed, "Boys, the old flag never touched the ground!"[1]

[1] Booker T. Washington, "Heroes in Black Skins," *Century Magazine*, September 1903.

The Destruction of the South

Lincoln found in Grant a general who was willing not only to fight but also to do whatever it took to win. To Grant and Sherman, that meant waging total war, a **war of attrition** to wear down and even to destroy the South completely if necessary.

not win this war unless it became a total war. (From a Christian perspective two questions must be asked. Is the war itself just, and is the way in which the war is being fought just?)

2. God commanded the Israelites to fight a total war against the Canaanites in Deuteronomy 7:1-2. (As the Sovereign over all the earth, God can command His people to fight such a war to punish a people for their sins, but He does not give blanket permission to all nations to exterminate their enemies.)

3. What do Amos 1:3, 6, 9, 11, 13 teach about the way that wars should be fought? (Even though the wars con-

ducted by these nations were probably unjust, God also singles out the way these nations conducted their wars as a reason for their punishment. In other words, God cares about the way that people fight wars.)

Politics and War

Every war that the students study has a political side with a direct bearing on the course of the war. It is impossible to understand modern conflicts without understanding how public opinion affects military decisions. Lincoln had to issue his Emancipation Proclamation after a military victory lest it appear to be the last cry of a defeated country. He also had to choose his wording

to have maximum effect without offending political supporters in the Union's border states.

Another political side to the war was the ever-present concern about "the next election." Generals in both the South and the North did everything they could to affect the outcome of the election—the South wanted the Northerners to be too war-weary to continue, while the North wanted to hand the nation some encouraging victories. Can the students think of any other examples of the impact of public opinion in wars they have already studied or will study? (*During World War II, the Japanese assumed that a few quick victories would make the Americans weary of war and sue for peace before*

The blockade cut off foreign supplies from the Confederacy. Union control of the Mississippi prevented aid from the West. Now Union armies began to invade the very heart of the Confederacy, destroying everything in their path.

Sheridan in the Shenandoah Valley

Lee was aware of Northern war weariness. Hoping to capitalize on it, he sent Jubal Early and his cavalry north. Lee did not expect Early to win any major battles, but he hoped to create anxiety in the North. From their base in the Shenandoah Valley of Virginia, Early's troops raided Maryland farms for supplies and livestock. In July 1864, they rode to the outskirts of Washington, D.C. The threat he posed kept some of Grant's troops near Washington and out of the fight against Lee.

But Early's raid also led Grant to send **Philip Sheridan** into the Shenandoah Valley with his cavalry, a decision that would have a grave effect on the South. "Leave nothing to invite the enemy to return," Grant ordered Sheridan. "Destroy whatever cannot be consumed. Let that valley be left so that crows flying over it will have to carry their own rations."

Sheridan followed his orders with grim efficiency. He not only defeated Early's outnumbered army three times but also destroyed the valley that had fed Lee's army for three years. His men came from nowhere, killing livestock, burning barns and houses and crops, and striking terror throughout the valley. Civilians suffered greatly. Lee's armies had even more trouble finding food.

Rosecrans in Tennessee

Grant was leading Union forces across Tennessee from the Mississippi River to Chattanooga (chat uh NOO guh) in southeastern Tennessee. At the head of Grant's armies was Gen. William Rosecrans, who chased the Confederates under Gen. Braxton Bragg south of Chattanooga to **Chickamauga** (chik uh MAH guh) Creek. (*Chickamauga* is a Cherokee word meaning "river of death.") Bragg requested reinforcements from Lee. Lee sent General Longstreet with 11,000 soldiers. On September 19, 1863, shortly after Longstreet's arrival, the Confederates slammed against the Union line. Longstreet's men broke through and sent the Federal troops scurrying back to Chattanooga in a rout resembling that at the First Battle of Bull Run. Union general **George Thomas**, however, was unaware of what was happening to the rest of the Union army. He held firm against repeated Confederate attacks. His determined stand saved the Union army from disaster and won him a nickname: "the Rock of Chickamauga."

The Battle of Chickamauga was one of the bloodiest battles in the West during the war. The Union lost 1,600, but the South lost 2,300. Their victory had been a costly one.

The Confederates surrounded the Union troops in Chattanooga. They captured the high ground on Lookout Mountain and Missionary Ridge and besieged the city. Bragg learned that Grant and Sherman were approaching Chattanooga from the west. Before they could reinforce Rosecrans, Davis wanted Longstreet to move northeast to Knoxville to free that town, a Confederate stronghold in Unionist East Tennessee, from Union control. Longstreet moved with less than 15,000 troops into unfamiliar territory against a larger army. He chased Ambrose Burnside's army into Fort Sanders in Knoxville and besieged the town.

Gen. William Tecumseh Sherman was a supporter of the idea of total war.

Gen. Philip Sheridan stripped the Shenandoah Valley of anything that could be of use to the Southern armies, causing great suffering for innocent civilians.

After the Battle of Chickamauga, Gen. George Thomas was nicknamed "the Rock of Chickamauga."

---

the United States could put its industrial muscle to work. Also, the Communists in North Vietnam based their strategy on simply wearing down public support for the Vietnam War, and their strategy worked.)

The Unglamorous Side of War

Play the name game. Ask students to name the first five things that pop into their head when they hear the name "Civil War." They may say some of the generals or land battles, but it is very unlikely that they will mention any of the events mentioned in this section.

As the first modern war, the American Civil War was a "total war." Total wars have a decidedly unglamorous side: the need to starve the enemy nation of goods and supplies and

to make civilians suffer in an effort to get them to pressure leaders to end the war.

Scorched-Earth Policy

Ask the students if Sheridan's action reminds them of any other war. Remind them that they learned in World Studies (seventh-grade Heritage Studies) that the Russian people practiced a scorched-earth policy as they retreated before the German people. Compare the effects of Sheridan's and the Russian people's actions. Were they effective against the enemy?

 CD: Medical Care During the War

Refer to the CD for photos of various types of medical equipment used during the Civil War.

CD: Female Spies

Refer to the CD for photos of females who were spies for each of the sides during the war. (You might consider asking for female volunteers to research the lives of these women.)

Gen. William Rosecrans was badly beaten at the Battle of Chickamauga when he moved troops from one place to another in a miscalculation of where the enemy would strike. They struck the place from which he had just moved the troops!

Union forces broke the siege of Chattanooga by smashing Confederate lines on Missionary Ridge (in foreground) and Lookout Mountain (in background).

Burning of Atlanta

Ironically, the burning of Atlanta ultimately led to the rise of the "New South." Atlanta became a modern city.

Copperheads

Throughout the Civil War, Lincoln faced opposition from anti-war Democrats known as Copperheads. Their name came from critics who likened them to copperhead snakes, always ready and willing to strike. Instead of fighting the name, the Copperheads kept it and even wore copper lapel pins showing the head of liberty.

Their opposition to Lincoln came in part as a response to early Union defeats and general war weariness. Some of them thought that victory was unachievable and that peace was a greater goal than

CD: Lookout Mountain and Chattanooga

Refer to the CD for a map detailing troop movements during the battles of Lookout Mountain and Chattanooga.

On November 29, Longstreet, acting on inaccurate information about the fort's defenses, launched a dawn attack. The battle, which lasted only about twenty minutes, was a terrible mistake. The Union troops had cut down all trees around the fort and strung telegraph wire about ankle high between the stumps. The attackers, running in the dark, tripped on the wire. At the base of the fort's walls the Union soldiers had dug a deep, wide ditch. The Confederates tumbled into it. Because the ground was frozen, they could not climb out. For the Union soldiers it was like shooting fish in a barrel. Longstreet called off the attack. Nearly 900 soldiers had been killed, 780 of them Confederates.

Just before Longstreet attacked Fort Sanders, he had heard rumors that Grant and Sherman had arrived in Chattanooga. The rumors proved true. Longstreet had taken so long in Knoxville that he could not return to Chattanooga to help Bragg. On November 23, Grant ordered his troops to break out of Chattanooga. The Union army struck the Confederate right flank on Missionary Ridge and assaulted Lookout Mountain in what became known as the "battle above the clouds." They dislodged the Confederate defenders and sent them retreating into Georgia. Tennessee was thus in Union hands.

Sherman's March to the Sea

When Grant was called to lead the Union armies farther East, he left Sherman in charge of the western command. He ordered him to chase Bragg's army and to "break it up, and to get into the interior of the enemy's country as far as you can, inflicting all the damage you can." Sherman proved to be good at carrying out this order.

Meanwhile, Davis replaced Bragg with Gen. Joseph Johnston. Johnston retreated before Sherman's pressure, hoping to make a stand. But every time Johnston set his forces for a stand, Sherman threatened to flank and surround him, so Johnston retreated again. Davis tired of waiting for Johnston to attack. He replaced him with Gen. John Bell Hood, who promptly lost a costly battle to Sherman in Atlanta. By September 1, Hood realized that he could save his army only by abandoning Atlanta. The loss of Atlanta, a major railroad center, was devastating to the South.

Sherman could not hold Atlanta and protect his long supply line too. He got Grant's permission to burn the city. His army left only ruins when it left Atlanta on November 10, 1864. Sherman divided his army into four columns and sent them by four different roads toward Savannah on the Atlantic coast. His commanders carried maps that carefully marked every village and plantation along the sixty-mile-wide band between Atlanta and Savannah. Sherman's orders were "to forage liberally on the country during the march," keeping a ten-day supply on hand at all times. Everything they did not need, they were to destroy. Sherman wrote to Grant outlining his plan and promising that he would "make Georgia howl."

Sherman's written orders to his commanders said that Union soldiers were not to enter private dwellings or "commit any trespass" unless local bushwhackers molested them. Since the locals almost always did, wholesale destruction resulted. Confederate and Union deserters, called **bummers**, added to the problem, following the army, pillaging and burning whatever the army did not destroy. Sherman made little attempt to stop them. As a result, his **March to the Sea** caused a great deal of bitterness among the people of the South, especially those in Georgia.

By December 10, Sherman's army had reached Savannah. The city fell easily. Sherman telegraphed Lincoln that he was presenting him Savannah as a Christmas gift. He then turned north to march across the Carolinas and join Grant in Virginia. His men devastated that area as well, leaving behind even more bitterness.

The Election of 1864

Northerners were weary of war. They wanted peace. Horace Greeley wrote that nine-tenths of all Americans were "anxious for peace, peace on almost any terms." Radical Republicans believed that Lincoln was too generous with the South. Northern Democrats criticized him at every turn. They considered many of his actions violations of the U.S. Constitution and the separation of powers. Lincoln also faced opposition in his bid for reelection. Former Union general George McClellan was running on a peace ticket. Lincoln told his cabinet that he did not think he would be reelected.

But Lincoln had political skills. He picked Senator **Andrew Johnson**, a Democrat from Tennessee, to be his running mate. He believed that Johnson could help him bring the Southern states back into the Union more easily after the war was over.

The people sensed this fact more than the politicians did. Lincoln also had some men who helped to turn the tide for him: Sherman, Sheridan, and Farragut. Their victories in the fall of 1864 increased Lincoln's popularity and led to his victory over McClellan. Lincoln also moved to ensure that the army in the field could vote absentee, a fact that may have helped immensely.

Section Quiz

1. What was the provision of the Emancipation Proclamation?
2. Why did Lincoln issue the Emancipation Proclamation?
3. In which Tennessee town did the "battle above the clouds" take place?
4. Which Southern city did Sherman present to Lincoln as a Christmas gift?
5. Who ran on a "peace ticket" in the 1864 election?
6. Why did Lincoln choose Democrat Andrew Johnson to be his running mate in 1864?
★ What was the general strategy behind Sheridan's Shenandoah Valley campaign and Sherman's March to the Sea? Was this strategy morally justifiable?

VI. Ending the War

After the South's defeat at Gettysburg, the tide of the war turned in favor of the North. However, the war still threatened to drag on for years.

In his second inaugural address, Lincoln (circled in this photo) sought to reach out to the South and demonstrated humility regarding God's providence in the war.

Excerpt from Lincoln's Second Inaugural Address

"Fondly do we hope, fervently do we pray, that this mighty scourge of war may speedily pass away. Yet, if God wills that it continue until all the wealth piled by the bondsman's two hundred and fifty years of unrequited toil shall be sunk, and until every drop of blood drawn with the lash shall be paid by another drawn with the sword, as was said three thousand years ago, so still it must be said 'the judgments of the Lord are true and righteous altogether.'

"With malice toward none, with charity for all, with firmness in the right as God gives us to see the right, let us strive on to finish the work we are in, to bind up the nation's wounds, to care for him who shall have borne the battle and for his widow and his orphan, to do all which may achieve and cherish a just and lasting peace among ourselves and with all nations."

union among the states. But deeper issues were also at stake. In particular, the Copperheads opposed Lincoln's aggressive use of presidential power. They thought his suspension of habeas corpus was unconstitutional and an abuse of power.

As the 1864 election approached, the Copperheads seemed on the verge of victory. Union armies were making little progress, and more and more soldiers were dying in prison camps. But timely victories by Sherman and Sheridan helped to restore Northern confidence that the war could and would be won. Lincoln also ensured the vote of one of his biggest supporters—the army. Some soldiers were allowed to vote in camp; others were furloughed and returned home to vote. But the Copperheads themselves aided in Lincoln's victory when they chose George B. McClellan, the former leader of the Union army whom Lincoln had dismissed, as their presidential candidate. McClellan had leadership ability and war victories; but he also had views that differed from those of the Copperheads. McClellan was never quite willing to embrace the peace platform. That division weakened the party's chances of winning the election.

Section VI
Objectives

Students should be able to

1. Describe the way Grant finally pressured Lee to surrender.
2. Name the place where Lee surrendered and give the date.
3. Explain why the Civil War was so devastating for the country.
4. Describe the assassination of Lincoln and its consequences.

Activity 6: Lincoln's Second Inaugural Address

Have the students read and study the text of this presidential address to gain a better understanding of how Lincoln proposed to restore the Union following the war.

 CD: Lincoln's Second Inaugural Address

Refer to the CD for the text of Lincoln's second inaugural address. Discuss its contents with the students, focusing especially on his stated intention of dealing kindly with the South after the war in an effort to heal the nation's wounds quickly.

Lincoln, Race, Slavery, and the Constitution

Additional sources of information about Lincoln's real views on slavery and the nature of government and the U.S. Constitution are two issues of *Magazine of History* by the Organization of American Historians. "Lincoln and the Constitution" (January 1, 2007) and "Lincoln, Race, and Slavery" (October 4, 2007).

Section Quiz Answers

1. It declared free the slaves in Confederate-held areas that were still fighting on January 1, 1863.
2. to revive Northern support for the war
3. Chattanooga
4. Savannah, Georgia
5. George McClellan
6. He believed that Johnson, a Southerner, could help bring the South back into the Union more easily.
★ Total war, destroying as much of the countryside as possible so that the South would lose its will to continue fighting; answers will vary.

The Horrors of the Wilderness

The Wilderness Campaign was a series of battles that occurred around Chancellorsville and Spotsylvania, Virginia, between May 5 and May 19 in 1864. The area was well described as a wilderness. The terrain was characterized by thick foliage and periodic swamps. Those geographic features, combined with the thick smoke from thousands of guns firing, made large-unit fighting almost impossible. Authors Hicks and Schultz, in *Battlefields of the Civil War* (p. 183), described the fighting that occurred there: "Flashes of flame, whether single rifles or volleys, might come from anywhere; and to add to the terror, the thickets sometimes ignited. A comparatively mild sprain might be enough to stop a man fleeing; a temporarily incapacitating wound was a death sentence, as men burned alive in the undergrowth. Their screams mingled with the crash of musketry and the yells of the troops; the unmistakable stench of roasting and burning flesh combined with the smell of powder."

Cold Harbor

Grant's attack at Cold Harbor was a big mistake. He lost about twelve thousand men (killed and wounded) in a half-hour battle. Lee lost only about fifteen hundred. One soldier described the battle as "not war but murder." But Grant's army had the reinforcements and supplies to continue the campaign, whereas Lee's did not.

Petersburg

Grant tried to shorten the siege of Petersburg by tunneling under the South's barricades. His men placed four tons of powder at the end of the tunnel and blew a big crater through which they planned to rush Union troops. The Union soldiers tried to

Activity 7: Lee's Farewell to His Troops

Use this activity to help the students gain a better understanding of Lee's affection for his troops and concern for their future well-being and right attitude toward the South's loss.

Grant was called a butcher, even by his own men, following the Battle of the Wilderness.

The Union siege of Petersburg involved a constant bombardment of Confederate lines by huge siege guns such as these.

A Victim of Historic Circumstances?

Wilmer McLean lived on a farm in Manassas and suffered the effects of both battles of Bull Run. Sick and tired of seeing his property destroyed by war, he moved to Appomattox Courthouse—only to have his farm trampled by armies when it was appropriated as the site of Lee's surrender.

The Road to Richmond

By May 1864, Grant was ready to open a new Virginia campaign. His army moved into a heavily wooded area west of Fredericksburg called "**the Wilderness**." There Grant hurled a force of 118,000 men against Lee's scant 60,000. Grant lost about 18,000 men, and Lee lost more than 10,000. Grant's losses were heavier, but he knew that he could more easily replace the men he lost. Lee could not. Northern newspapers and even Union soldiers complained of Grant's callous attitude toward death, calling him "Lincoln's butcher." But Grant believed that if he pressed Lee's army long enough and prevented Lee from maneuvering to fight him, he could wear Lee down and force his surrender. Grant next moved east and then south. Lee marched all night to head him off and caught him at Spotsylvania Courthouse. But Grant moved south again, and Lee had to throw himself and his troops between the Union army and Richmond. Between May 5 and May 12, Grant lost more than 26,000 killed and wounded. At Cold Harbor, Grant committed a costly error by throwing three corps against well-entrenched Confederates. He paid dearly for it. The dead covered five acres. Despite the fact that "Butcher Grant" had lost more than 50,000 men in one month, he continued to press forward. He had no thought of changing his plans. "I intend to fight it out on this line if it takes all summer." Lincoln agreed, telling his cabinet, "I cannot spare this man. He wins."

In June, Grant crossed the James River and moved toward Richmond. To get there, however, he had to take Petersburg. Lee rushed to protect the city, and Grant was able to surround him there and lay siege to the city. Grant was continually being resupplied and reinforced, but Lee's force was getting smaller and weaker every day. The siege would last until April 1865.

Lee realized that he could not hold out much longer. His army had often been hungry during the war, but now it faced starvation. On the night of April 2, 1865, Lee evacuated Petersburg. He hoped to lure Grant into open country and to neutralize Union numbers with superior tactics. But, outnumbered more than two to one, Lee had to fall back.

Surrender at Appomattox

As Lee saw it, his last hope was to link with Johnston's army in upper North Carolina and make one last stand. Perhaps then he could deal Grant a decisive blow. But Sheridan blocked Lee's retreat to the Blue Ridge Mountains. On April 7, Grant approached Lee with an offer to discuss terms of surrender. Both commanders knew that further resistance was hopeless. On April 9, Lee and Grant met in a farmhouse in **Appomattox** (ap uh MAT uks) Courthouse to sign the surrender.

Grant was generous in his treatment of the vanquished army, allowing the officers to keep their side arms and horses. Lee asked that the common cavalrymen and artillerymen—since they had supplied their own horses and would need them to work their farms—be allowed to keep them. Grant agreed. Throughout the surrender process, Grant refused to gloat but rather showed deep respect for the feelings of his former enemies. He did not even ask Lee to surrender his sword, and Lee never offered it. Grant had the Confederate soldiers sign pledges not to take up arms again. Then he issued them provisions enough to get them home.

After Lee's surrender of the South's main army, it was only a matter of time before the other scattered units surrendered. On April 18, Johnston surrendered to Sherman in Durham, N.C. The final army of the Confederacy surrendered in Texas in early May.

The Cost of the War

The Civil War was the most destructive war in American history. Approximately 618,000 soldiers were killed. About one-third of the approximately two million men who served in the war were killed, wounded, or captured. The death rate for Union troops was 23 percent. For Southern troops it was 24 percent. In the South, one-fourth of all manpower of military draft age never returned from the war. (By contrast, in World War II one in sixteen was lost.)

Much personal property had been destroyed, especially in the South. Noncombatants lost homes, farms, and businesses. Roads and farmlands were ruined. Perhaps as important as the human and material loss, however, was the deep bitterness that remained long after the war was over, especially in the South. Distrust and even hatred lingered between the North and the South for decades. The way the North treated the South after the war did little to heal the wounds.

Lee surrendered to Grant in the home of the McLean family in Appomattox.

The Financial and Human Costs		
	Union	Confederacy
Total expenditures	$6,190,000,000	$2,099,808,707
Inflation at worst	$1 gold = $2.59 paper money	$1 gold = $60–70 paper money
Combat deaths	110,100	94,000
Wounded	277,401	194,026
Deaths from disease	224,580	164,000

Lincoln's Assassination

The war would claim one more casualty that affected both sides. On Good Friday, April 14, 1865, President and Mrs. Lincoln went to Ford's Theater in Washington to see a play. **John Wilkes Booth**, an actor and a Confederate sympathizer, slipped into Lincoln's private box and shot the president in the back of the head. Lincoln died the next morning. Booth was later tracked to a barn in Virginia. The barn was burned, and Booth either took his own life or was shot by one of his pursuers.

No one knows what might have happened during the postwar years had Lincoln lived. But Lincoln's second inaugural address had

exit the tunnel, but they piled up in "the Crater," where about four thousand men were killed or captured. The failure of that tactic forced Grant to continue the siege.

Appomattox Courthouse

Appomattox Courthouse was the county seat of Appomattox County, Virginia. Sometimes people refer to the site of surrender as simply "Appomattox."

The McLeans

Wilmer McLean and his family were destined to have a role in the Civil War spotlight even as they sought to escape it. After the first and second battles of Bull Run occurred on their farm in Manassas, they decided to move for their personal safety and the protection of their property. They had hardly gotten used to their new home at Appomattox Courthouse when the armies seemed to follow them. Someone once said that the war began in McLean's backyard and ended in his front parlor. Soldiers carried off practically all of McLean's belongings as souvenirs of the historic surrender site.

Larger Action and Reaction

Lincoln's assassination was actually part of a larger plot to kill several Union government officials, including Vice President Andrew Johnson, Secretary of State William Seward, and General Ulysses S. Grant. John Wilkes Booth settled on his plan after an initial scheme to kidnap the president failed to materialize.

Although Booth was a Southern sympathizer and had helped smuggle medical supplies there, he never fought for the South. That fact bothered him so much that he even referred to himself as a coward. As the war closed, Booth determined to help the South and win personal fame

CD: Comparing Casualty Figures from America's Wars

Refer to the CD for a chart comparing and contrasting the casualties suffered during each of America's wars from the War for Independence through the Iraq War, or "Operation Iraqi Freedom" (current as of 2007).

CD: Reward Poster for Lincoln's Assassins

Refer to the CD for a photo of a reward poster issued for Lincoln's assassins.

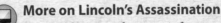

More on Lincoln's Assassination

Two good sources for more information on the plot to assassinate Lincoln and the fate of each of the conspirators are *The Day Lincoln Was Shot* by Jim Bishop and *Manhunt: The 12-Day Chase for Lincoln's Killer* by James L. Swanson.

Bitterness Between Regions After the War

As the students finish studying this chapter, ask them to list some of the decisions and actions that led to so much bitterness for the next century between Southerners and the rest of the nation. Answers might include such points as the South's resentment over (1) the destruction of total war as waged

during Sherman's March to the Sea and Sheridan's raid, (2) the unparalleled loss of life and property, and (3) the devastating economic and social effects of the war on the Southern civilian population. In turn, the North resented (1) the Southerners' decision to secede and (2) the loss of life.

Explain that such momentous sacrifices as those made during the War Between the States do not just suddenly disappear from the nation's memory after a war ends. What keeps those memories alive today? *(national monuments and battlefields; books, magazines, and films on the war and its destruction; historical societies; reenactments; etc.)* Help the students understand how the ramifications of the Civil War lasted for

in one bold stroke. At first, he and his followers, Lewis Powell and George Atzerodt, decided to kidnap Lincoln, take him south, and hold him ransom to win favorable postwar conditions for the South. However, the plot was unsuccessful.

After Lee's surrender at Appomattox, Booth became more desperate. He plotted to kill Lincoln while Atzerodt killed Andrew Johnson and Powell killed William Seward. On April 14, their plot went into action—sort of. Atzerodt got scared and never tried to kill Johnson. Powell was a little more successful. He stabbed and seriously wounded Seward after forcing his way into the sickroom where the secretary of state was recovering from a carriage accident.

But they accomplished their major goal. Booth shot Lincoln and fatally wounded him. In his escape, Booth leaped to the stage and broke his leg. He managed to hobble to his horse and escape. Almost two weeks later, searchers surrounded him in a barn. They set the barn afire and then shot Booth dead as he tried to escape the flames. Powell, Atzerodt, and six other people were charged with conspiracy in the action. All were found guilty by a military court. Four of them were hanged.

Ironically, Booth's actions hurt the South more than they ever helped it. Despite a lack of evidence, some people believed Booth was part of a Confederate conspiracy and called for tougher terms against the South. Other members of the government had been advocating a tough stance toward the South already and found even less opposition with Lincoln out of the way. Booth's bullet ensured that Reconstruction would be harsh for the South.

Booth thought he was doing the South a favor by killing Lincoln, but he probably only increased the South's woes.

States That Felt the War the Most

The following states are ranked in order of the number of military actions that took place within their borders:

Virginia	2,154
Tennessee	1,462
Missouri	1,162
Mississippi	772
Arkansas	771

emphasized "malice toward none." His terms for re-admission of the Southern states to the Union were generous. Andrew Johnson, Lincoln's successor, determined to continue the course set by Lincoln. But the Radical Republicans who won control of both houses of Congress in 1866 were not as kind; they wanted to make the South suffer. They also wanted to ensure that blacks got some rights. In the long run, Booth's action might have done the South more harm than Sherman's army had done.

Lincoln was buried in his hometown of Springfield, Illinois, on May 4, 1865. The country then turned to deal with problems that it had never before faced. Those problems continued to plague the nation for the next hundred years. In some ways, they are still with us today.

The Mysteries of Providence

The Civil War forced people to struggle to understand the mysteries of providence. During the war, Northerners were puzzled at their continued military failures. If their cause was right, why was God not honoring them with victory? After the war Southerners were distraught at their defeat. How could God refuse to answer the prayers of godly men such as Robert E. Lee and Thomas "Stonewall" Jackson? Some on both sides lost faith in God. Others concluded that God did not always give victory to those in the right.

Different from either of these positions was that of Abraham Lincoln. In the middle of the war, He reasoned that God's ways are not always man's ways: "In great contests each party claims to act in accordance with the will of God. Both *may* be, and one *must* be wrong. God can not be *for* and *against* the same thing at the same time. In the present civil war it is quite possible that God's purpose is something different from the purpose of either party."

Section Quiz

1. Why did Grant continue pursuing Lee despite the heavy losses the Union army was suffering?
2. What strategic city did the Union need to take before it could attack Richmond?
3. Where did Lee surrender his army?
4. Who assassinated Lincoln?
★ Why is it difficult to determine whose side God is on during a war?

---

more than a century. (Some of them are still evident even today.) The "Solid South" became a solid voting bloc for Democrats. The Southern states, once the richest in the Union, collapsed economically and did not begin to recover for another half century.

Also, explain that other nations that have endured civil strife, such as those in the Balkans, do not easily forget either. Discuss why many Southerners show more interest in the Civil War than those in other parts of the country. *(Southerners have always honored family and traditions, and it is impossible for them to think of their past without thinking of the Civil War. The war reminds Southerners of both heroism and disappointment.)*

Section Quiz Answers

1. Grant knew that he could replace the men he lost but that Lee could not. Grant also believed that he could wear Lee down and force him to surrender.
2. Petersburg, Va.
3. Appomattox, Va.
4. John Wilkes Booth
★ Because God's purpose in any war could be different than the purpose of any side.

Activity 8: Chapter Review

Use this activity to help the students prepare for the chapter test. You might also consider using the chart in Activity 2 and various maps in the student text and on the CD.

Chapter Review 15

Review Questions

1. The fall of which city in the West gave the Union control of the entire Mississippi River?

2. What name is given to Sherman's devastating trip through the South?

3. What place was the site of two early battles won by the South?

4. Which two ships were the first ironclads to clash in warfare?

5. What document did Lincoln issue in an attempt to make Union soldiers more willing to fight?

6. Which man pioneered the use of photography in an American war?

7. During which battle of the war did a general lead a bloody charge that is considered the "high-water mark" of the Confederacy?

8. Which battle was the bloodiest one-day battle in the war?

Critical Thinking

1. How did the First Battle of Bull Run show that the people misunderstood what the war would be like?

2. Why did the North win the war?

3. How was the Civil War different from other previous wars?

4. How did John Wilkes Booth's assassination of President Lincoln result in tragic unintended consequences for the South?

People, Places, and Things to Remember:

providence
bounty
conscription
Twenty-Negro Law
total war
commissions
Mathew Brady
Anaconda Plan
Irvin McDowell
Joseph E. Johnston
P. G. T. Beauregard
"Stonewall" Jackson
Battle of Bull Run
George McClellan
Robert E. Lee
John Pope
J.E.B. Stuart
Second Battle of Bull Run
naval blockade
blockade runners
William Sherman
Ulysses S. Grant
David Farragut
Vicksburg
Antietam
Ambrose Burnside
Fredericksburg
"Fighting Joe" Hooker
Chancellorsville
Gettysburg
George Meade
James Longstreet
George Pickett
Pickett's charge
Emancipation Proclamation
war of attrition
Philip Sheridan
Chickamauga
George Thomas
bummers
March to the Sea
Andrew Johnson
the Wilderness
Appomattox
John Wilkes Booth

Lincoln's Memo

The following is a private memo penned by Lincoln before his death. It is a model for interpreting the role of providence in history. Lincoln neither denies the role of providence, nor does he draw unwarranted conclusions about what God is providentially doing. This is the complete text, part of which is quoted in the student edition.

"The will of God prevails. In great contests each party claims to act in accordance with the will of God. Both may be, and one must be wrong. God can not be for and against the same thing at the same time. In the present civil war it is quite possible that God's purpose is something different from the purpose of either party—and yet the human instrumentalities, working just as they do, are of the best adaptation to effect this purpose. I am almost ready to say this is probably true—that God wills this contest, and wills that it shall not end yet. By His mere great power on the minds of the now contestants, He could have either saved or destroyed the Union without a human contest. Yet the contest began. And having begun, He could give the final victory to either side any day. Yet the contest proceeds."

CHAPTER REVIEW ANSWERS

Review Questions

1. Vicksburg

2. March to the Sea

3. Bull Run (or Manassas)

4. *Monitor* and *Merrimac* (or *Virginia*)

5. Emancipation Proclamation

6. Mathew Brady

7. Gettysburg

8. Antietam

Critical Thinking

1. Answers might include the following ideas. Spectators went out to watch the battle. Soldiers from both sides thought they would win quickly. Everyone discovered that war is deadly. The conflict would not be decided in one day or one battle.

2. Answers might include the following ideas. The North had more men, more resources, more money, and more industrial capacity. Eventually, all of these factors wore down the South and forced it to surrender.

3. Answers might include new technology, more accurate weaponry, and total war.

4. With the death of President Lincoln, the Radical Republicans determined to punish the South. (More details will emerge in the next chapter.)

Chapter Goals

Students should be able to

1. Analyze the different plans for Reconstruction, their aims, and their effects on political and social life.

2. Evaluate legislative reform programs of the Radical Reconstruction Congress and reconstructed state governments.

3. Identify the purposes of the Freedmen's Bureau and the effects of its actions.

4. Compare and contrast Radical Reconstruction and Bourbon Reconstruction.

5. Describe the economic difficulties faced by the United States during Reconstruction.

6. Explain the social problems facing the South during Reconstruction and evaluate their impact on different groups.

7. Trace the origins and effects of the Ku Klux Klan.

8. Define and use the basic terms of the chapter.

9. List new developments in the South as the region recovered.

10. Examine the plight of blacks after the Civil War and the enduring problems of racial inequality and racism.

Chapter Motivation

Imagine how difficult it would be if your city had a civil war. One part of the city wants everyone to stay together; the other part wants to form a separate city. The part that opposes splitting the city wins the war. It then faces the difficult task of healing the division and getting both sides to work together peacefully for

The major cities of the South lay in ruins following the war.

CHAPTER 16

Reconstruction

I. **Reconstruction and the South**

II. **Presidential Reconstruction**

III. **Radical Reconstruction**

IV. **Bourbon Reconstruction**

V. **Recovery in the South**

Chapter 16 Lesson Plan Chart

Section Title	Main Activity	Pages	Days
I. Reconstruction and the South	Activity 1: Lee and Johnson: Their Post-War Attitudes	307-8	1 day
II. Presidential Reconstruction	Activity 2: Major Events of Reconstruction (time line)	308–11	1–2 days
III. Radical Reconstruction	Activity 4: Interpreting a Reconstruction-Era Political Cartoon	311–17	2–3 days
IV. Bourbon Reconstruction	Discussion of Elections and the Electoral College	317–19	1–2 days
V. Recovery in the South	Activity 8: Chapter Review	319–22	1–2 days
TOTAL SUGGESTED DAYS (INCLUDING 1 DAY FOR REVIEW AND TESTING)			6–10 DAYS

MATERIALS LIST

SECTION I
- Activity 1 from the *Student Activities* manual

SECTION II
- CD: Andrew Johnson, 17th President
- Activity 2 from the *Student Activities* manual

SECTION III
- *Free Indeed: Heroes of Black Christian History* (BJU Press)
- CD: Check Used to Purchase Alaska; Ulysses S. Grant, 18th President
- Activities 3–4 and 6 from the *Student Activities* manual

Just weeks before the end of the weary conflict and his own tragic death, Lincoln had given his second inaugural address, which urged "malice toward none" and "charity for all." But the passage of time brought only more malice and less charity. The wounds of the war were deep, and it would take many years before many would even begin to heal. Some scars would linger for more than a century.

I. Reconstruction and the South

The period from the end of the Civil War to 1877 is called **Reconstruction**. It was a difficult time of reuniting the nation and trying to solve the nation's postwar problems.

The South's Need for Reconstruction

For Northerners, life after the war was not much different from life before the war. The North had lost thousands of men, and it felt that wound deeply, but industry had progressed. Immigration continued to add to the Northern population. Little Northern property had been damaged in the war, so returning soldiers could go back to their farms or jobs with little hindrance.

The situation in the South, however, was totally different. It had lost not only many of its young men but also its slaves. Its labor force, therefore, was entirely disrupted, and there was no wave of immigrants adding to the work force.

The South had suffered severe property damage. Sherman, Sheridan, Grant, and other Union generals left many Southern cities—Atlanta, Columbia, Richmond, and others—in ruins. The South's fields were stripped bare in many areas. Its livestock had been taken or destroyed. Homes, businesses, and railroads were demolished. After the war, little remained with which the South could rebuild. Moreover, its citizens were demoralized and bitter. With the plantations destroyed, many formerly wealthy Southerners found themselves in poverty. "None of us can realize that we are no longer wealthy," one Southern lady said, "yet thanks to the Yankees, the cause of all unhappiness, such is the case."

Not only was the South's plantation system dead, but also the money that remained was worthless. The South had almost no U.S. currency; Confederate paper money was worthless. The South was bankrupt, and its economy was destroyed.

The South also faced the challenge of integrating the freed slaves, or **freedmen**, into their society. More than four million Southern blacks needed jobs, but white Southerners had no money to pay them. Neither were the freedmen particularly eager to return to the same work they had done as slaves. Slaves had been vital to the South's economy before the war, but the freedmen lacked an important role in the postwar South. Yet they were there, and they needed to be given a place in Southern society.

The South also had to reestablish its state governments. The Union victory had removed governments that had been in control during the Confederacy. New governments had to be formed, and they, in turn, would have to deal with the problems and conditions in the South.

All of these problems were major concerns of the federal government. The central question was who—the president, Congress, or the states—would control the methods for solving the problems of Reconstruction.

Reconstruction was originally intended to be a time of picking up and putting together the pieces in the South to restore its economy and society. Instead, it became a time of bitterness during which some Northerners and unscrupulous Southerners took advantage of the condition of the South for their own self-interests.

At the end of the war, Confederate paper money was worthless.

the good of the city. Think how hard this would be. Talk about problems that would occur between the two sections. Relate this to Reconstruction. Ask your students to look for both successes and failures in the management of Reconstruction.

Core Values

Reconstruction revealed tensions in the area of core values. Southern whites who had fought a war to gain independence and freedom were now under military rule. African Americans were legally free, but many were bound in a kind of servitude through sharecropping. The federal government tried to ensure equality and freedom for black citizens, but the value of individualism caused many to resist the expansion of the national government.

Long-Term Consequences

The war had many lasting consequences. Two of the most important were these. First, the national government assumed a much greater role in American life while the individual states became proportionally less important.

Second, the terminology used to refer to the country changed. Before the war, the United States had been referred to in the plural (e.g., "the United States *are* a federal union"). After the war it was referred to in the singular (e.g., "the United States *is* a republic"). This shows the primacy of the national government over the states.

Section I
Objectives

Students should be able to

1. Define *Reconstruction.*
2. List the three phases of Reconstruction.

SECTION IV
- CD: Party Platform Summaries; Electoral College Results of the Election of 1876; Rutherford B. Hayes, 19th President

SECTION V
- CD: Ku Klux Klan
- Activities 5 and 7–8 from the *Student Activities* manual

Debate Idea

Have your students discuss and/or debate the following proposition: Booth made the South's problems worse by assassinating Lincoln.

Activity 1: Lee and Johnson: Their Post-War Attitudes

Use this activity to highlight the attitudes that Robert E. Lee and Andrew Johnson took after the war.

Bitter Feelings

The deep feelings regarding the Civil War did not result solely from the four years of military conflict or the defeat of the Confederacy. Many came from the following years of "political war" that decided how a conquered South and its people should be treated.

An Ongoing Power Struggle

The period of Reconstruction began an ongoing power struggle between Congress and the president. It also led to a struggle between disenfranchised Confederates and the Radical Republican governments established by the Union. Caught in the middle were the freedmen, who generally sided with the Republicans but had to deal with their former masters in gaining jobs.

Section II
Objectives

Students should be able to

1. Describe Lincoln's Ten Percent Plan.
2. Name the bill that Congress tried to pass in reaction to Lincoln's plan.
3. Compare Johnson's plan for Reconstruction with the plans of Lincoln and the Congress.
4. Explain the position of the Radical Republicans.

Ten Percent Plan

When Lincoln announced his Ten Percent Plan, he had swift Reconstruction on his mind. The plan was intended to shorten the war by weakening the South's will to fight. Lincoln's plan made it very easy for the Southern states to rejoin the Union. The plan that would be supported by the

Phases of Reconstruction

The dates of Reconstruction typically cover the twelve years from 1865 to 1877. That was when the federal government directly supervised the rebuilding of the South. In a larger sense, however, Reconstruction continued at least until the turn of the century as Southern state governments continued to deal with the special problems of their region. This larger period divides into three phases:

Phase 1 (1865–67)	Presidential Reconstruction (Lincoln and Johnson)
Phase 2 (1867–76)	Radical (Congressional) Reconstruction
Phase 3 (1877–1900)	Bourbon (Redeemers') Reconstruction

Section Quiz

1. What was the postwar era called?
2. What was the purpose of this era?
3. What were its three phases?
★ How was the postwar economic situation in the South different from what it was in the North?
★ How did the waging of total war increase the difficulty of Reconstruction?

II. Presidential Reconstruction

For a while, Lincoln and Johnson directed the process of Reconstruction. This was the time of **Presidential Reconstruction**. Even before the war ended, Lincoln had developed a plan for bringing the seceded states back into the Union. Lincoln believed that the Southern states, by seceding, had committed an act of rebellion. His duty as commander in chief was to quell their insurrection. Once this was done, he had the power under the Constitution to pardon their wrongdoing. Johnson was going to follow Lincoln's plan.

Lincoln's Plan and Congress's Reactions

In December 1863, Lincoln announced his **Ten Percent Plan**. He would use it to reconstruct the areas of the South that were already under Union control. The plan offered pardons to former Confederates who would swear to support the Constitution and the Union. When ten percent of the total voters who were registered in a state in 1860 had taken the oath, that state could form a new government, write a new state constitution, and be restored to the Union. They could even regain their seats in Congress. By the spring of 1864, three occupied states had met those easy terms. Tennessee, Louisiana, and Arkansas were ready to reenter the Union.

Radical Republicans Object

Lincoln's plan, however, met resistance from a group known as **Radical Republicans**. They believed that the plan treated the South too kindly. Contrary to Lincoln's stated wishes, they wanted the South to be treated as a conquered foreign nation, not as err-

Section Quiz Answers

1. Reconstruction
2. to reunite the nation and to attempt to solve the South's postwar problems
3. Presidential Reconstruction (1865–67), Radical (Congressional) Reconstruction (1867–76), Bourbon (Redeemers') Reconstruction (1877–1900)
★ The Northern economy actually grew after the war. Industry increased, and property loss was small. Returning soldiers could go right back to work, and immigrant laborers helped to replace workers lost in the war. But the Southern economy was devastated. Severe property damage—to farms, industry,

and railroads—kept soldiers from returning immediately to farming and kept industries from resuming operations. Immigrants were not interested in the South, and freed slaves had to find a new place in society and the economy.
★ The level of destruction made Reconstruction an overwhelming and financially draining task. The breadth of destruction embittered Southerners.

Information Online

Check www.bjupress.com/resources/ for possible links to websites related to the Reconstruction era.

ing brethren. They were not ready to forgive the South for the war. Rather, they wanted the South to continue being punished and punished severely. They also believed that if Southerners were let off too easily, they would try to regain the influence in Congress they had possessed before the war.

Radicals won some moderate Republicans to their views. Because these groups did not want to see Confederates back in Congress, they refused to readmit the three states under Lincoln's plan.

The Radicals also reacted to the increase of executive (presidential) powers during the war. During the war, Lincoln had made many decisions without initially asking Congress. It is worth noting that when Congress came into session in 1861, they approved Lincoln's actions and wrote legislation to support some of his policies. However, the Radicals asserted that Lincoln had gone beyond his powers as president. Now they wanted to shift the balance of power back in favor of Congress.

The Wade-Davis Bill

In 1864, Congress developed its own Reconstruction plan: the **Wade-Davis Bill**. By their strict plan, a state could reenter the Union when 50 percent of the voters who had been registered in 1860 had taken the oath of allegiance. People who wanted to vote or hold political office had to swear that they had never supported the Confederacy voluntarily. The states had to abolish slavery. They had to rescind (take back) their acts for secession. And they had to abandon claims that the federal government should repay them for debts incurred during the war.

The Wade-Davis Bill passed both houses. Congress was clearly asserting its intention to be in control of readmitting states and reseating members of the legislative branch. Lincoln, however, disagreed. Rather than sending Congress a formal message listing his objections, Lincoln exercised the pocket veto (see Chapter 7), which effectively killed the Wade-Davis Bill.

The conflict between Congress and Lincoln had not yet been resolved when Lincoln was shot. Andrew Johnson was left to battle with Congress for control of Reconstruction.

Andrew Johnson Takes Over

Vice President Andrew Johnson had been born in poverty in North Carolina. He was apprenticed to a cruel tailor but ran away to Tennessee. There he met and married his wife, who was a teacher. While he worked in his tailor shop in Greeneville, Tennessee, she taught him to read and write. His tailor shop was also a place where local townsmen discussed politics. Johnson became a staunch Democrat and began to climb the political ladder. He was elected first to local offices, then to the U.S. House of Representatives, and eventually to the U.S. Senate.

Johnson opposed Tennessee's vote to secede in 1861. He was the only Southern senator not to resign his Senate seat. When Nashville fell, Lincoln named Johnson military governor of Tennessee. Later, in a shrewd political move, Lincoln chose Johnson to be his running mate. Johnson's public statements won him the support of Radical Republicans. He once said that Jefferson Davis and other leading Confederates should be hanged. He assured people that "treason must be made odious" (arousing intense displeasure). When Johnson became president upon Lincoln's death, Congress assumed he would do their bidding.

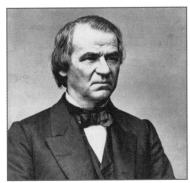

Andrew Johnson became president following Lincoln's assassination and was determined to institute Lincoln's plans for Reconstruction.

Radical Republicans proved to be far more punitive.

Radical Republicans

The Radical Republicans included such Congressional leaders as Benjamin Wade, Charles Sumner, Thaddeus Stephens, Henry Davis, and Benjamin "Beast" Butler. This group was intent on punishing the South. The Radicals had been appalled by the South's attitude toward the dissolution of the Union and its idea that the Constitution granted the right of secession. They so resented the South's having acted on their threat to secede that after the war they were committed to making the South pay dearly for that "transgression."

Wade-Davis Bill

This bill was the brainchild of Benjamin Wade of Ohio and Henry Winter Davis of Maryland. Their bill was, in the words of historians J. G. Randall and David Donald, "a severe measure which made restoration difficult by intrusting the reconstruction of a state not to a minority ready for future loyalty, but to a majority whose Unionism was a matter of past conduct." Note that the bill would have required all Southern voters to swear that they had never supported the Confederacy voluntarily. That requirement would have prevented almost all Southerners from voting, except blacks and people who were loyal to the Union. Therefore, such a restriction would have been especially repugnant to the South and would have caused even greater bitterness.

More on Andrew Johnson

Andrew Johnson was born in North Carolina in 1808 and grew up poor. He was apprenticed to a tailor but ran away. He started his own tailor shop in Greeneville,

Additional Resources: *The Avenger Takes His Place*

An excellent source of information concerning Johnson's succession to the presidency and his conflicts with the Radical Republicans is *The Avenger Takes His Place* by Howard Means. It covers the first forty-five days of Johnson's administration.

CD: Andrew Johnson, 17th President

Refer to the CD for facts on Andrew Johnson.

Tennessee, and married Eliza McCardle, who taught him to read. He enjoyed debating political topics while he worked in the tailor shop. He became a popular stump speaker. His first political office was as a member of the Greeneville council. He went on to serve as a U.S. representative, U.S. senator, and military governor of Tennessee. Lincoln chose him to be his vice presidential running mate in 1864 on the Unionist ticket. Johnson became president following Lincoln's assassination but was never elected president in his own right. After he left the White House, the legislature of Tennessee sent him back to Washington as a U.S. senator.

Democrat or Republican?

Johnson was a Democrat from Tennessee, but he became vice president on a Republican (Unionist) ticket. For this reason he is sometimes listed as a Democrat and sometimes as a Republican. That political situation did not help win Johnson friends among either the Radical Republicans or the Southern Democrats.

Joint Committee on Reconstruction

The three major conclusions of the Joint Committee were as follows:

1. That the States lately in rebellion were, at the close of the war, disorganized communities, without civil government, and without constitutions or other forms, by virtue of which political relations could legally exist between them and the federal government.

2. That Congress cannot be expected to recognize as valid the election of representatives from disorganized communities, which, from the very nature of the case, were unable to

The Lessons of Obstinacy

Johnson's administration is a lesson in the impact of obstinacy. The Bible teaches the value of soft words and the folly of stubbornness. Note the negative impact of Johnson's campaigning during the 1866 elections—his anger helped his enemies. Even if he was right in his views, Johnson's attitude turned the moderates against him and helped the Radicals to pass their program and to impeach him. If possible, make parallels to modern examples of obstinate leaders who end up helping their enemies and hurting themselves.

When Johnson took over the presidency, Congress was out of session. From April to December, he was able to state his ideals and put them into effect without congressional interference. Johnson shared Lincoln's belief that it was impossible for a state to secede. Thus, in his opinion, Confederate states were still in the Union. He believed that individuals had left the Union and that they, not the states, deserved to be punished.

Johnson's Plan

Johnson's plan was first to offer **amnesty** (a group pardon) to Southerners who took an oath of loyalty to the Union. However, he excluded those whose taxable property was more than $20,000. Those people, mostly former larger planters, had to apply to him personally for a pardon. Unpardoned Southerners could not vote, hold office, or reclaim any property seized by the federal government.

Next, the president would appoint provisional (temporary) state governors to hold state conventions. Those bodies would draft new state constitutions that repudiated (rejected, refused to pay) Confederate debts and ratified the **Thirteenth Amendment**, which abolished slavery. When a state had done this and ten percent of its voters had sworn loyalty, Congress would readmit it.

By winter, most of the former Confederate states had met most of Johnson's terms. But South Carolina continued to insist that the federal government honor the debts South Carolina had incurred during the war. Mississippi did not ratify the Thirteenth Amendment. And no Southern state gave voting rights to blacks. So Congress refused to seat Southern representatives. Instead, moderate and Radical Republicans formed their own **Joint Committee on Reconstruction**. They would determine when the Southern states were truly reconstructed.

Republicans' Reaction

Several things in Johnson's plan angered Northern Republicans. First, when Southern states held their elections, most elected former Confederates. Second, many Radicals and others believed that the government should take Southerners' lands and divide them among the newly freed slaves. But Johnson's plan did not include that; nor had Lincoln's.

Third, most of the South's Congressmen were Democrats. Seating the Southern Democrats might put the Republicans in the minority if Northern Democrats sided with the Southerners.

Fourth, some Radicals believed that the war would have been worth the cost only if black Americans got full citizenship rights. "We must see to it," one Radical said, "that the man made free in the Constitution . . . is a free man indeed . . . and that he walks the earth proud and erect in the conscious dignity of a free man." When the Joint Committee held hearings, it found out that the freedmen, instead of being granted more rights, were being denied them through **black codes**.

Black Codes

The black codes established in the postwar South were much like the old slave laws, although they did allow a few new basic rights. Blacks could now sue, be sued, and testify in courts. They were also entitled to legalize their marriages to people of their own race. They could buy, own, and transfer property.

But in trying to control the large population of freed blacks, the codes were very restrictive. They placed blacks in an inferior position to whites, making them, in effect, second-class citizens. The codes were in some ways another kind of slavery.

In some states, for example, blacks could work only as domestic servants or farmers. Some codes forbade blacks to live in towns or cities. The codes seemed to restrict many blacks to the same field work they had done as slaves. Blacks who wanted to practice trades or do anything besides farming had to be apprenticed and often had to get costly licenses. Since few blacks had money, this restriction closed trade doors to them.

Blacks who were not usefully employed could be arrested for vagrancy (wandering around with no job). Blacks who could not pay fines for vagrancy or other crimes could be hired out to anyone who would pay their fines. Some black codes forbade blacks to carry arms, and others told them where they could or could not own property. Southerners argued that the black codes prevented the chaos that could have come from freeing four million slaves at once.

Johnson's Response to the Radicals

Although Andrew Johnson had worked hard to overcome poverty and a lack of formal education, he lacked the tact that the nation needed in leaders at that time. He was firm in his views on Reconstruction. He was determined not to let the Radicals make reunification any harder on the South than it had to be. But when Congress defied his policies, he refused to change. He lashed out at his opponents. His inflexibility often disheartened moderates, driving them into the Radical camp. With most of Congress united against Johnson, the days of Presidential Reconstruction were numbered.

Section Quiz

1. How could Confederate states be restored to the Union under Lincoln's Ten Percent Plan?

2. How did Congress's plan differ from Lincoln's?

3. Who assumed the presidency after Lincoln's assassination?

4. In some ways, the black codes were another form of what former Southern institution? How did they change life for the freedmen?

✶ What were the positive aspects of Johnson's Reconstruction plan? What were the positive aspects of the Radical Republican's plan?

III. Radical Reconstruction

Thaddeus Stevens of Pennsylvania led the Radical Republicans in the House. The Radical leader in the Senate was **Charles Sumner** of Massachusetts. After refusing to seat the Southerners, the Radicals worked to ensure that Congress, not the president, would control Reconstruction. But Johnson vetoed their bills. Johnson's stubbornness drove moderate Republicans to support the Radical Republican agenda. By February 1866, the Radicals had achieved a two-thirds majority in both houses. This allowed them to override Johnson's vetoes.

During Reconstruction, some politicians used posters such as this to play upon the white voters' fear of blacks.

Thaddeus Stevens and Charles Sumner led Radicals in both houses of Congress in pushing for extreme measures to punish the South for the war rather than following Lincoln's more compassionate plan for Reconstruction. Stevens realized that the power of the former slaveholders would not be broken as long as they retained economic power over blacks.

present their claim to representation under those established and recognized rules, the observance of which has been hitherto required.

3. That Congress would not be justified in admitting such communities to a participation in the government of the country without first providing such constitutional or other guarantees as will tend to secure the civil rights of all citizens of the republic; a just equality of representation; protection against claims founded in rebellion and crime; a temporary restoration of the right of suffrage to those who had not actively participated in the efforts to destroy the Union and overthrow the government, and the exclusion from positions of public trust of, at least, a portion of those whose crimes have proved them to be enemies to the Union and unworthy of public confidence.

Section III
Objectives

Students should be able to

1. List and describe the important amendments and legislation passed during Radical Reconstruction.

2. Identify and describe the circumstances of Johnson's impeachment.

3. Name two of Johnson's achievements in foreign affairs.

4. Name the president who followed Andrew Johnson and the problems of that man's administration.

Activity 2: Major Events of Reconstruction

Use this activity to help the students organize the major events of the Reconstruction era chronologically.

Section Quiz Answers

1. by having 10 percent of the registered voters in 1860 take an oath to support the Constitution and the Union

2. Congress wanted 50 percent of voters who had been registered to vote in 1860 to take the oath, new voters to swear that they had not voluntarily supported the Confederacy, the abolition of slavery (ratification of the Thirteenth Amendment), repudiation of Confederate debts, and rejection of the vote to secede.

3. Andrew Johnson

4. slavery; allowed freedmen to sue/be sued, legalized their marriages, and

allowed ownership of property, but always kept them in an inferior position relative to whites

✶ If Johnson had shown some willingness to compromise rather than stubbornly maintaining his positions, he might have improved his relationship with the Radical Republicans or at least kept the moderates on his side. However, that would have come at the expense of the already burdened Southern states.

Balance of Power

Note that when a two-thirds majority of the House and Senate are opposed to a president's views, they have the power to have their way in all legislation (via their power to override vetoes), and the president becomes almost helpless. Of course, the Supreme Court can still declare laws unconstitutional, and therefore it provides a check against too much power.

Freedmen's Bureau

Officially known as the U.S. Bureau of Refugees, Freedmen, and Abandoned Lands, the Freedmen's Bureau faced presidential opposition from the beginning. Johnson claimed that it violated the Constitution. Like Lincoln, Johnson believed that the Confederate states had never really left the Union. Johnson also criticized the Bureau's vague definitions of "civil rights and immunities."

Despite Johnson's opposition, the Freedmen's Bureau went to work and its members labored to help the freedmen establish themselves as productive citizens. Major General Oliver Howard (a Christian) was appointed to be its commissioner. Between 1868 and 1872, the bureau established more than one thousand schools for blacks and spent more than $400,000 for teacher training. Although it had its own courts for cases involving freedmen, those courts were poorly organized and provided little justice. When the bureau was abolished in 1872, its unfinished work was carried on by the Freedmen's branch of the Adjutant General's Office.

Fourteenth Amendment

The Fourteenth Amendment played a key role in the debate over three major legal issues. The first was civil rights. The amendment guaranteed equal protection

Many freedmen attended schools begun by the Freedmen's Bureau.

Radical Republican Legislation

As the Radicals' strength grew, they passed several bills to overcome the black codes and to aid the freedmen in the South. One bill increased the role of the **Freedmen's Bureau**. Another was a constitutional amendment giving blacks full citizenship.

The Freedmen's Bureau

In March 1865, Congress had passed laws to set up a short-term agency called the Freedmen's Bureau to provide aid for refugees. It was the first federal relief agency. It issued rations of surplus army food and clothing to freed slaves and to poverty-stricken whites. The bureau tried to locate jobs for the freedmen and to prevent employers from exploiting them. It also sent agents into the South to establish schools and hospitals for blacks of all ages.

Because Congress assumed that state governments themselves would provide relief services, Congress was to fund the bureau for only one year. But Congress refused to recognize the new state governments, so it voted to keep the bureau going and even to extend its powers. Johnson vetoed two versions of the bill. But the Radicals united to override his second veto. The Freedmen's Bureau continued. Despite the good the bureau was trying to do, both Southerners and some freedmen criticized it. Corruption of bureau officials and slow response to freedmen's needs were common complaints.

The Fourteenth Amendment

Next, Congress voted full citizenship for blacks in the Civil Rights Act of 1866. Because Johnson believed that the Constitution gave the states, not the national government, power over citizenship, he vetoed the act. Congress overrode his veto. But Congress feared that the act would be declared unconstitutional. In June 1866, Congress sought to solve the problem by proposing the Fourteenth Amendment.

The **Fourteenth Amendment** is important for many reasons.

1. It made all persons citizens of both the United States and the state where they resided. It prohibited any state from depriving a person of his life, liberty, or property without due process of law (a proper trial). A state could not deny equal protection of its laws to any person under its jurisdiction.

2. A state's representation in Congress would be based on its whole population. This provision meant that *all* blacks, not just three-fifths, were to be counted to determine the state's representation. States that denied voting rights to blacks would have the number of their representatives in Congress reduced.

3. People who had fought against the United States or held office in the Confederate government were barred from voting or holding office. Congress could pardon them by a two-thirds vote, thus removing those restrictions.

Lessons from the First Federal Relief Agency

The Civil War marked a turning point in the nation's history in more ways than the end of slavery. It ended the nip-and-tuck power struggle between the states and the federal government. Forever after, the federal government reigned supreme, and its size has grown almost unabated ever since. The Reconstruction era is full of warnings about the potential dangers of growing federal power. Ask the students to suggest examples of such warnings.

Among the many modern policies attributed to the war is the first income tax (and the first complaints about unfairness and wrongdoing by tax officers).

Another warning sign was the abuses under the Freedmen's Bureau, a precursor to the New Deal programs under Franklin Roosevelt. While the bureau did a valuable service in helping starving people and protecting freedmen, it had a dark side common to any federal program that spends a lot of money. For one thing, the Radical Republicans used the bureau to "buy votes." Anytime the government hands out benefits, it gets political support from grateful recipients of the aid. (You could also discuss how the Social Security program has been used as a political tool in elections ever since it was started in the 1930s.)

Another dark side of the bureau was graft. With so much money and power, it was impossible to oversee effectively how the money was spent.

"The Veto"

Refer to the CD for a political cartoon about Johnson's veto of the Freedmen's Bureau bill.

4. Congress also refused to assume Confederate debts or accept claims for any costs of freeing the slaves.

When ratified, the amendment would cancel not only black codes in the South but also laws against blacks in some Midwestern states. Johnson urged Southern states to vote against it. He believed that the amendment violated states' rights and was therefore unconstitutional.

Johnson realized that he was powerless as long as the Radicals had a two-thirds majority. So he campaigned against Radical candidates in the 1866 congressional races. He traveled in the North and Midwest, speaking against the Radicals. But his efforts backfired. His audiences heckled him. Instead of ignoring them, Johnson lost his temper and responded harshly. Some people had rejected his Reconstruction plan because they feared it would return former Confederates to power. Now many more became skeptical of his leadership.

When Congress convened in 1867, Reconstruction was even more firmly in Radical hands. **Radical Reconstruction** had begun. By 1868, the Fourteenth Amendment had become law.

Further Radical Reconstruction Rule

Beginning in 1867, the Radical Republicans in Congress, now with an even greater majority, put their program into effect with great speed and little resistance. When the president vetoed their legislation, Congress quickly overrode his vetoes.

Reconstruction Act of 1867

The **Reconstruction Act of 1867** went far beyond the controls that Lincoln and Johnson had wanted. This radical legislation kept the area under martial law. The army was ordered to ensure that the South complied with the congressional mandates. Southerners resented the military occupation.

First, the act divided the South into five military districts, each ruled by a Union general and a provisional governor. Second, it gave blacks the right to vote and hold office. At the same time, the act denied voting rights to those who had served in the Confederacy. Third, Southern states wanting to reenter the Union had to hold open conventions that included both black and white voting delegates. These conventions were to draw up new state constitutions using the guidelines given by Congress. The act also required the states to submit their documents to Congress for approval. Finally, to be readmitted to the Union, states had to ratify the Fourteenth Amendment. When they met those requirements, the troops would be withdrawn.

Scalawags and Carpetbaggers in the South

Few former Southern leaders were eligible to hold public offices because they had served in the Confederacy. Because Congress had opened politics to blacks by its Reconstruction acts, Southern politics experienced great change. New groups took command of the South.

Northerners who came south to help in Radical Reconstruction were called **carpetbaggers**. (The name came from the fact that many of them came south carrying their possessions in small suitcases made of pieces of carpet.) Most carpetbaggers were opportunists who sought financial or political gain. Southerners resented them. A few carpetbaggers, however, were sincere and came because they wanted to help the freedmen change the South. Some of them were former Union soldiers who liked what they had seen of the South and decided to stay.

The carpetbagger came to symbolize Northerners who traveled south to take advantage of the plight of Southerners for their own profit and advancement.

under the law for everyone. That provision was tested in *Plessy v. Ferguson* (1896). Railroads in Louisiana offered blacks and whites "separate but equal" accommodations. A black man challenged the practice in court, but the Supreme Court upheld it. The Court ruled that separating the races did not imply that one was inferior; therefore, both races were receiving the equal protection of the law.

However, in 1954 the Supreme Court changed its mind in *Brown v. Board of Education of Topeka*. In that case, it ruled against segregated schools, declaring that separate institutions were "inherently unequal."

Affirmative action is another civil rights issue for which justification has been sought from the Fourteenth Amendment. In an 1880 case, Justice William Strong affirmed that the Fourteenth Amendment was intended to protect the civil rights of blacks but qualified that the protection was from actions that would harm them. Some people suggest that his opinion supports the idea that separation favorable to blacks, as in preferences assigned as the result of affirmative action, might be acceptable.

A second legal issue was the regulation of business. It grew out of cases involving a meatpacking company that was granted a monopoly by the state of Louisiana. A group of white butchers sued on the grounds that the state was depriving them of property without the due process of law (another clause of the amendment). The Supreme Court decided in the late 1800s that the clause applied only to slaves, but one justice wanted to broaden the definition to include businesses. His view was later adopted, and the amendment was cited as a protection for companies from regulation by states.

Black Christian Leaders

Several black Christian leaders upheld the dignity of their race after the Civil War. One was Matthew Anderson, whose story is told in the article "Matthew Anderson" in *Free Indeed: Heroes of Black Christian History* (BJU Press). The article "Charles Tindley" (also in *Free Indeed*) covers the life of another Christian worker at the beginning of the twentieth century. The article includes four of the popular hymns he wrote. Another account in *Free Indeed* is that of hymn writer Charles Price Jones, who helped found the Holiness movement at the turn of the century.

A third legal issue was the nationalization of the Bill of Rights. As the Constitution was originally written, only the federal government was required to protect the rights listed in the Bill of Rights. In *Adamson v. California* (1947), Justice Hugo Black stated his opinion that the Fourteenth Amendment was intended to apply the Bill of Rights to the states. In other words, the rights that the Constitution required the federal government to protect must also be protected by the states. Black's view was not adopted across the board, but certain key rights were nationalized as he proposed.

Carpetbaggers and Scalawags

Corruption was a major problem in the South during Reconstruction. Although some carpetbaggers and scalawags had a sincere interest in reforming the South, personal interest was often a greater concern. South Carolina's government gives a prime example of this corruption. During Reconstruction more than $200,000 was spent on furniture for the State House. The value of the furniture was no more than $18,000. Bills also approved large sums of money for chairs, mirrors, and food.

Corruption was not limited to the South, however. The state legislatures of Pennsylvania and New York were also filled with corrupt practices. In fact, Northern graft operations were even more organized. Corruption reached its highest levels during the Grant administration.

Tenure of Office Act

The Tenure of Office Act specifically excluded current cabinet members from the applications of that law, but Congress never discussed that fact when they impeached Johnson. That omission clearly demonstrated that their intention was to

Born a slave, Robert Smalls became a steamboat pilot. During the war, he hijacked the boat he was piloting and turned it over to the Union navy. He was elected to Congress during Reconstruction.

Johnson's firing of Secretary of War Edwin Stanton tested the validity of the Tenure of Office Act.

George T. Brown, the Senate Sergeant at Arms, served President Johnson with the summons for his impeachment.

Carpetbaggers took control of Southern politics in some areas for a while. Their most important positive contribution was the capital that they brought with them. Their investments helped bring recovery to the Southern economy.

A white Southerner who supported Radical Reconstruction was called a **scalawag**. Some scalawags had been Unionists during the war. Others endorsed Radical Reconstruction because they believed that it was in the South's best interest. Some of them were prewar Whigs seeking a new party since theirs had collapsed. However, many of them deserved their bad name. Several scalawags saw the postwar situation as a chance for personal gain with the help of Radical Republican support and military protection. Most Southerners looked upon scalawags as traitors.

Although freedmen did not control any state, they did hold offices in every Southern state. They gained the most power in South Carolina. Unfortunately, they had no political experience, so they were sometimes influenced by corrupt white politicians. Radicals often used the black officeholders as puppets. Some whites bribed black officeholders to promote the interests of carpetbaggers and scalawags.

Since Southern whites already resented their former slaves, they were especially critical of black corruption. Most of the blacks who held national political offices—for example, Mississippi senators Hiram H. Revels and Blanche K. Bruce and South Carolina's Robert Smalls—were well-educated men who served with integrity and dignity. But because of the exceptions to that rule, whites tended to look upon all black politicians with suspicion.

Impeachment of Johnson

Although Congress passed its Radical agenda over Johnson's vetoes, he still enforced the laws that were passed. He did so because that was his constitutional duty. As much as Radicals despised Johnson for opposing them, they knew that he was both a loyal Unionist and a consistent defender of the Constitution. Symbolic of that fact were his instructions for his burial. His body was to be wound in the American flag and his head pillowed on a copy of the Constitution.

The Radicals, however, were still unhappy with him. They sought ways to further limit his powers. They feared that Johnson would remove officials who were sympathetic to their views and replace them with his own men. Therefore, they passed the **Tenure of Office Act** in 1867. That act made it illegal to remove any presidential appointee who had been approved by the Senate unless the Senate also approved the dismissal.

Johnson tested the law by firing **Edwin Stanton**, the secretary of war whom Lincoln had appointed. (Stanton had never upheld Johnson's views and now openly sided with the Radicals.) Stanton refused to leave office. He barricaded himself in his office, accepted food through the windows, and cooked for himself. He even slept in his office.

Based on Stanton's firing, Congress believed that it had grounds to **impeach** (bring charges against) Johnson. If he was found guilty of those charges, he could be removed from office. (See Constitution, Art. II, Sect. 4.) In presidential impeachments, the House of Representatives files the charges, the Senate is the trial court, and the chief justice of the Supreme Court presides as the judge. A two-thirds vote is required to remove the president. The only basis for removal is "conviction of treason, bribery, or other high crimes and misdemeanors." A congressional committee did not believe that Johnson was guilty of such crimes, but the Radicals pressed the issue, and the committee referred the accusations to the full House.

On February 24, 1868, the House voted to impeach Johnson. The president's trial began on March 13 and lasted until May 26. Chief Justice Salmon P. Chase presided. Johnson himself never attended the trial. He believed that he had done nothing wrong and that his attendance would only lend credibility to his accusers. Senators sold tickets to the affair, and at times the trial rivaled a theatrical performance.

Senators could not agree. Was the Tenure of Office Act constitutional? Even if it was, did it apply in Stanton's case? Stanton, after all, had been Lincoln's appointee before the Tenure of Office Act was passed. The real issue was that Radicals were trying to get rid of the president because they disagreed with him politically. He had committed no crime, nor had he violated the Constitution. Removing a president for political reasons would set a dangerous precedent. Some senators saw that danger.

Other senators knew that if Johnson were removed, Ben Wade would become president. Wade was the president pro tempore of the Senate and one of the most extreme Radicals. His views on many issues were too shocking for most Americans at that time. (Johnson had no vice president, so, according to the law at the time, the president pro tempore of the Senate was next in line. In 1948, the law was changed to make the Speaker of the House the next in line after the vice president.)

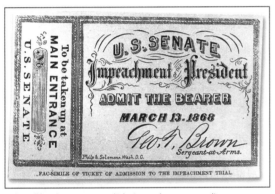

Tickets allowed citizens to watch the impeachment proceedings.

When the final vote was taken, thirty-five senators voted to convict. Nineteen voted to acquit. The Radicals were one vote short of the total needed to remove Johnson. Johnson finished his term. His presidency was preserved, but his reputation was never the same. Years later, the Supreme Court declared the Tenure of Office Act unconstitutional.

The House impeachment managers brought charges against Johnson.

Supreme Court Chief Justice Salmon Chase presided over the impeachment trial in the Senate.

Benjamin Wade actually had a conflict of interest in the impeachment of Johnson because he was in line to become president if Johnson was removed from office.

get rid of a political enemy rather than to seek justice.

Opposition to Impeachment

Of the nineteen senators who voted against conviction, seven were Republicans. Six were against impeachment from the start, but Edmund G. Ross of Kansas was undecided. Knowing that Ross was wavering, supporters of the impeachment threatened him with everything from loss of his seat in the Senate to loss of his life if he did not vote to convict Johnson. Despite the pressure, Ross came to believe that the charges against Johnson were unfounded and voted for acquittal. Johnson remained in the presidency, but neither Ross nor any of the other Republicans who voted against impeachment were ever reelected to the Senate.

New Appointments

Andrew Johnson was eager to remove the radical secretary of war, Edwin Stanton, from his cabinet. Stanton seemed to be working more against Johnson than for him. Johnson first tried to put Ulysses S. Grant into Stanton's position, but the Senate would not approve the appointment. Then Johnson fired Stanton outright and appointed Adjutant General Lorenzo Thomas to fill his post temporarily. Nine of the eleven articles of impeachment from the House were based on Johnson's alleged violation of the Tenure of Office Act.

Grover Cleveland and the Tenure of Office Act

In 1887, President Grover Cleveland declared that only the president had the power to remove his own appointees. The Supreme Court agreed with him and declared the Tenure of Office Act unconstitutional.

CD: Check Used to Purchase Alaska

Refer to the CD for a photo of the check used to purchase Alaska.

Purchase of Alaska

By the mid-nineteenth century, Russia was ready to get rid of its Alaskan territory. Britain and America were starting to push up from the south, and Russia was not eager to defend the territory militarily. Also, Russia was not receiving sufficient profits to justify keeping Alaska. Fur trading, formerly the principal source of revenue from the territory, had declined. Russia had just fought the Crimean War and needed funds, and Alaska seemed to be a worthless drain on the nation's resources.

Secretary of State William Seward was so eager to purchase Alaska that he began negotiations with the Russians even before he received authorization from the president to do so. His preliminary offer to Russia was $5 million, but he found to his surprise that Congress was willing to offer $7 million. Despite the offer and the fact that the treaty passed by a substantial margin, Congress was not excited about the purchase. The treaty was passed in 1867, but an appropriation for the money was not approved until July 1868.

Later generations, however, would praise Seward. He had bought an area that was two times the size of Texas! In that area was a wealth of natural resources that began to be unearthed in 1896 with the Klondike gold strike. (Many of Jack London's stories, including *White Fang* and *The Call of the Wild*, were set in Alaska Territory during the Klondike gold rush.)

Senator Edmund Ross committed political suicide by voting to acquit Johnson, but he followed his conscience and refused to be swayed by partisan pressures.

Secretary of State William Seward's purchase of Alaska from Russia proved to be anything but folly.

Johnson's Achievements in Foreign Affairs

Congress had foiled Johnson's policies at home. But his achievements in foreign affairs were noteworthy. **William Seward**, his secretary of state, ably directed his foreign policy.

In 1864, Napoleon III, the emperor of France, had challenged the Monroe Doctrine by setting up Austrian Archduke Maximilian (MAK suh MIL yun) as the puppet emperor of Mexico. Since the Civil War occupied Lincoln at the time, he could not send troops to evict Maximilian. He could only reprimand the French. In 1866, however, President Johnson moved against the French. He sent fifty thousand veteran troops to the border. The threat of force led to the withdrawal of French troops.

Seward was also an expansionist. He signed a treaty of friendship and commerce with China in 1868. In 1867, he secretly negotiated a treaty with Russia to purchase Alaska for $7 million. When Johnson sought Senate approval of the purchase, the press ridiculed it as "Seward's Folly," "Johnson's Polar Bear Garden," and "Frigidia." But within ten days the treaty went through by a 37–2 vote. In time, the purchase proved to be a great bargain for the United States.

President U. S. Grant

By 1868, Andrew Johnson had lost almost all influence with Republicans. The Republicans chose war hero Ulysses S. Grant to be their presidential candidate. The Democrats were still hampered by both their ties to the old Civil War issues and the Radicals' control of the South. Still, Grant's victory over the Democrats' candidate, New York governor Horatio Seymour, was close. Grant won largely because half a million new black voters voted for him.

The Fifteenth Amendment

Grant rewarded black support by calling for the passage of the **Fifteenth Amendment**. That amendment kept states from denying the vote to any person "on account of race, color, or previous condition of servitude." Passage of the amendment ensured that Republicans stayed in power. It gave them more votes in Northern states that still had antiblack laws. (Although the Radicals had ended Southern

EFFECT OF THE VOTE ON THE ELEVENTH ARTICLE OF IMPEACHMENT.

Cartoonist Thomas Nast showed the contrasting reactions of Johnson (left) and Horace Greeley (right) to Johnson's acquittal.

Do Famous Warriors Make Good Presidents?

Ask the students to name as many presidents as they can who were former generals or other military heroes. *(George Washington, Andrew Jackson, William Henry Harrison, Zachary Taylor, Ulysses S. Grant, Rutherford B. Hayes, Theodore Roosevelt, Dwight D. Eisenhower)* Were any of them good presidents? Why is it often easy for such military leaders to get elected? *(They have name recognition and respect. Note that Colin Powell was a popular choice for president after the U.S. victory in the Gulf War.)* Why is it sometimes hard for good military leaders to be good presidents? *(They are used to giving*

orders, not making compromises and deals to please their supporters.)*

CD: Ulysses S. Grant, 18th President

Refer to the CD for interesting facts about U. S. Grant.

Grant's Legacy

Discuss the ingredients of a man's reputation. Discuss the Bible characters Noah, Saul, David, Solomon, Peter, and Paul. In each case, those men did great wrongs as well as great good. Why do some people keep a good reputation but others do not? What is Grant's reputation? *(He was a good*

general but a terrible president.) Why is he generally well thought of? (He was a humble man; he overcame great obstacles to become commander of all Union armies; and—although the textbook does not mention it—he fought a noble fight against cancer to finish writing his memoirs.)* The lesson for us is that believers *can* overcome the embarrassment of the past. They *can* repent, change their ways, make restitution where applicable, be forgiven, and have a positive influence once again. Yet they always have to live with the consequences of their past wrong deeds throughout their lives.

black codes, they often made little or no effort to end similar laws in the North.) The Southern states still had Republican governments that favored the blacks, so they ratified the Fifteenth Amendment in less than a year. It took effect in 1870, when the last former Confederate states—Georgia, Mississippi, Texas, and Virginia—ratified it and were readmitted to the Union.

The Grant Scandals

Grant served two terms as president. Although a good general might make a popular candidate, he might not be a good president. Grant's terms were marked by political corruption. The corruption, largely the result of greed, was not the president's doing and existed on national, state, and local levels. But when the corruption was uncovered, the president did not punish the guilty. Rather, he allowed them to resign. He believed that prosecution would only further divide the nation. To distract the voters from the scandals, the Republicans called for the people to unite against ex-rebels (whom they tried to get voters to equate with the Democrats). But voters did not want to revive those ill feelings. The Radicals, with their fierce hatred for the South, were losing public support.

Section Quiz

1. What was the first federal relief agency? What groups did it assist?

2. The basic purpose of the Fourteenth Amendment was to provide what for blacks?

3. What type of system did the Reconstruction Act of 1867 establish to enforce Congress's will in the South?

4. Who were the scalawags, the carpetbaggers, and the freedmen?

5. The conflict between Johnson and the Radical Republicans came to a climax when Johnson attempted to remove whom from office? His action was said to be a violation of what law?

6. What significant contributions did Johnson make (or authorize) in foreign affairs?

7. Who won the election of 1868?

✮ What potential danger did Johnson's impeachment trial pose for our system of government?

IV. Bourbon Reconstruction

The people's attitudes toward Reconstruction were changing. Many Northerners had lost interest in the fate of African Americans in the South. They were more concerned with the return to economic prosperity. Others were more interested in the West, its opportunities for expansion, and the Indian wars taking place there. Many people thought that it would be better to abandon blacks and Southerners than to lose the whole country to the turmoil of Radicalism. They believed that peace in the South would be better for business. The country was sick of scandal and controversy. Such attitudes paved the way for **Bourbon Reconstruction**, which was led by conservative Southerners, or "Redeemers."

The Fifteenth Amendment guaranteed the right to vote, and blacks exercised that right under the Radical Republican governments during Reconstruction.

Ulysses S. Grant's administration was tainted by scandals.

Despite the scandals that tainted his administration, Grant did propose major civil service reforms, but many senators did not like them.

Johnson in the Senate

Six years after Johnson left the presidency, he was reelected to the Senate to represent Tennessee. He served only a small amount of his term, however, since he died the same year he took office (1875). As he had requested, his body was wrapped in the U.S. flag and a copy of the Constitution was placed under his head. He is buried in Greeneville, Tennessee.

1868 Election

Grant barely won the election over Democratic candidate Horatio Seymour. Seymour had presided over the Democratic Convention and was not even listed as a candidate until the fifth ballot!

Section IV
Objectives

Students should be able to

1. Identify Bourbon Reconstruction.

2. Describe the circumstances of the disputed election of 1876.

Bourbon Reconstruction

Bourbon was a nickname used to denote a politician who was so conservative that he clung to outmoded ideas. Its primary use was with the Southern Democrats after federal troops were removed from the South in 1877. The Bourbons tried to oust Republicans from governments and return them to control by old-order Democrats. They realized that to do that they had to convince blacks to switch from the Repub-

Activity 3: Saved by One Vote

Use this first-hand account of the vote on President Johnson's impeachment charges to help the students understand how Johnson and his bodyguard reacted to the news.

Activity 4: Interpreting a Reconstruction-Era Political Cartoon

Use this activity to introduce the political cartoons of Thomas Nast and to help the students develop skills in interpreting political cartoons in contemporary context.

Activity 6: Sandhog: Building the Brooklyn Bridge, 1871

Use this activity to give the students an idea of what was involved in building the Brooklyn Bridge during the latter half of the nineteenth century. Help the students to note the working conditions of the period.

Section Quiz Answers

1. the Freedmen's Bureau; freed slaves and poverty-stricken whites

2. citizenship

3. military rule, or martial law

4. scalawags—Southerners who supported Radical Reconstruction; carpetbag-

gers—Northerners who went south to assist in Radical Reconstruction; freedmen—former slaves

5. Secretary of War Edwin Stanton; the Tenure of Office Act

6. He forced the withdrawal of French troops from Mexico, signed a treaty of friendship and commerce with China, and purchased Alaska.

7. Ulysses S. Grant

✮ The charges against Johnson were really political, not criminal. If he had been convicted, the precedent of removing officials for political differences would have been set, upsetting the balance of power between branches.

lican Party to the Democrats, so they tried to court them while giving them as little real power as possible. Blacks continued to be elected to office but in much smaller numbers than during Republican control.

Rutherford B. Hayes

Rutherford B. Hayes was regarded by many as a man of honor and humility. He fought with distinction in the Civil War. He was wounded four times and had a horse shot out from under him four times. When supporters wanted him to run for Congress during the war, he agreed but refused to campaign since he felt that his first duty was to his regiment.

After a term in Congress and three terms as governor of Ohio, Hayes was selected as the Republican candidate for president. Still he did not become puffed up with his success. He did not believe that he would win the election.

Before he took office, Hayes declared that he would seek only one term. He wanted to reform the civil service system, and he knew that he could pursue his agenda more easily if he was not seeking reelection. He chose workers because of their merit. In fact, he angered his own party when he chose a capable ex-Confederate for his cabinet. Congress did not accept the changes in the civil service that Hayes wanted, but he did pave the way for those reforms to be reintroduced and passed in the future.

Technology in the White House

Rutherford Hayes had the opportunity to welcome at least two major inventions to the White House. Thomas Edison brought his phonograph for the president to inspect. And a telephone was installed for the first time in the executive mansion. The problem with having a telephone at

In 1872, **Liberal Republicans** convinced Congress to pardon the rest of the former Confederate leaders. **The General Amnesty Act** pardoned all but a few hundred Confederate leaders. Those who had held federal offices at the time of secession were excluded. This act allowed many former Southern leaders to regain their influence in government.

During this time some blacks, often from the North, participated in Southern politics. Six hundred blacks were state legislators, some served as judges, and others were elected to Congress.

Although the blacks had gained some rights, it was not easy for white Southerners to accept blacks as their legal equals. While blacks and Radicals were able to hang on to offices for a while, they soon found they could not match the organization and experience of Southerners who sought to "redeem the South" from black rule. Southern voters began electing white Democrats to replace blacks and Republicans. Only in areas still occupied by federal troops did Radical Republican governments hold on a bit longer. Grant was growing more reluctant to use troops to quell violence and keep Republicans in power.

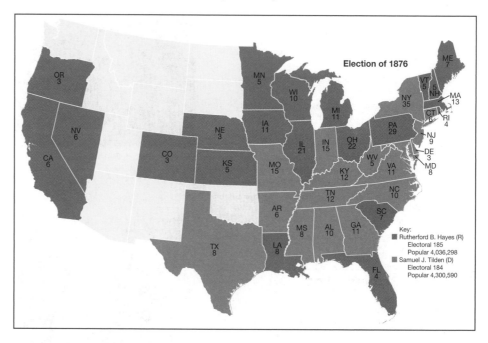

Election of 1876

Key:
Rutherford B. Hayes (R)
  Electoral 185
  Popular 4,036,298
Samuel J. Tilden (D)
  Electoral 184
  Popular 4,300,590

The Disputed Election of 1876

Just as Grant's administration had been marred by scandal, state and local corruption also existed. Both political parties chose reformers as their candidates in the 1876 presidential election. When the votes were counted, Democrat **Samuel J. Tilden** won the popular vote. The Electoral College vote was 184 for Tilden to 165 for his

 CD: Party Platform Summaries
Refer to the CD for summaries of each party's platform during the campaign of 1876.

 CD: Electoral College Results of the Election of 1876
Refer to the CD for a map of the Electoral College Results in the election of 1876.

 Additional Resources: More on the Disputed Election of 1876
A good teacher resource for additional information on the disputed election of 1876 is a book by the late U.S. Supreme Court Chief Justice William Rehnquist: *The Disputed Election of 1876*.

 Rutherford B. Hayes, 19th President
Refer to the CD for interesting facts on Rutherford B. Hayes.

Republican opponent, **Rutherford B. Hayes**. But the results in three Southern states, occupied by federal troops—Florida, Louisiana, and South Carolina—were disputed. Both sides claimed victory in those states, and accusations of election fraud were made. Republicans knew that if Hayes could win the disputed states, he would win the Electoral College by one vote, 185 to 184.

To resolve the dispute, Congress named a special commission of five senators, five representatives, and five Supreme Court justices. Seven commissioners were Republicans, seven were Democrats, and one was an independent. The independent resigned rather than cast the deciding vote. His replacement, a Republican, voted to accept the Republican ballots. Hayes became the president. But before this decision could become final, the Republican-controlled Senate and the Democrat-controlled House of Representatives would need to approve the commission's decision. To accomplish this difficult task, prominent Republicans and Democrats agreed on key compromises. The Republicans would withdraw the last federal troops from the South, and the Democrats would accept the Reconstruction amendments.

The Hayes Presidency

Although the Republicans won the presidency in 1876, the election was the final blow to the harsh Radical Reconstruction. Hayes had sought the support of Southern whites, who favored his economic policies. To gain their support, he embraced policies that they liked. However, Hayes soon found that he had bargained away most of his presidential power. By the time he saw the real picture, it was too late to change his position.

In April 1877, a month after Hayes took office, he withdrew the last troops from the South. With troops no longer supervising elections, the Democrats soon replaced the Republicans in power. With the military gone and white Southern Democrats back in control in the South, Reconstruction effectively ended.

Section Quiz

1. What did the General Amnesty Act do?
2. What action did President Hayes take to please Southerners?
★ What was unusual about the 1876 election? How does it compare with the election of 2000?

V. Recovery in the South

The problems of the South during Reconstruction and efforts to solve them molded Southern life, including the people, economy, and political organization.

Economic Aspects of Reconstruction

Because the war had destroyed the South's plantation system, the freedmen were without jobs. Some of them hoped that the government would seize the old plantations and from those lands give every freed slave "forty acres and a mule." Although some politicians supported such a plan, it was revoked. As a result, many former slaves were not able to support themselves. Farm owners needed laborers to grow crops in the South, but they had no money to pay hired hands.

Tilden and Hayes faced each other in the presidential election of 1876. Hayes won in a tight and disputed race.

Tilden campaign poster

this time, however, was that not many others in Washington had telephones, so there was no one to call.

"Lemonade Lucy"

Hayes's wife, Lucy, set a new standard for modesty and dignity in the White House and Washington, D.C. She was the first First Lady to have a college degree and was considered a "new woman" in that day. Although the Hayeses continued to host receptions and formal balls, these events were more modest and less extravagant than those of previous presidents.

Her new standard was best exemplified in her insistence that no alcoholic beverages be served at the White House. As a result, her critics called her "Lemonade Lucy." She was also popular among the children of Washington politicians and government workers as the hostess of the first White House Easter egg roll.

Section V
Objectives

Students should be able to

1. Describe the sharecropping system that developed in the South.
2. Explain how industry began to grow in the South.
3. Explain why the South became the *Solid South.*
4. Identify the Ku Klux Klan and explain how Congress reacted to it.

Section Quiz Answers

1. pardoned all but a few hundred Confederate leaders
2. He withdrew the last federal troops from South Carolina and Louisiana.
★ There was no clear winner because three states submitted two sets of electoral votes. A special commission had to determine whether the Republican or the Democrat votes would count. In 2000, the U.S. Supreme Court had to determine whether the Florida recount should continue or stop, thereby determining who had won the presidency.

No Heads Rolled!

Perhaps the most amazing fact about the end of the War Between the States is that no heads rolled in its aftermath. In spite of the Radical Republicans' harsh treatment of the South, no leaders of the short-lived Confederacy or its military leaders were hanged for political offenses. The commander of the infamous Andersonville Prison, however, was hanged for murder. Jefferson Davis was imprisoned for a while, but he was eventually released without being charged or put on trial. Contrast this with the typical aftermath of similar events in both the Bible and history, especially European history.

What Next?

The end of this unit is an important place to pause to look both behind and ahead to the remaining eras of U.S. history. Guide the students briefly through the titles of the remaining chapters in the book. Ask the students to summarize the nation's main concerns in the chapters they have covered so far. Now that slavery was dead and the South was no longer the focus of attention, where would the nation direct its energies? Some historians have said that the people needed an enemy to fight, a cause to win. What would become the next great cause, the next great enemy? Note that the industry of the nation, so long distracted by internal division, now exploded with productivity.

Ku Klux Klan

The Ku Klux Klan was founded in 1866. A group of Confederate veterans met at Pulaski, Tennessee, to establish a social fraternity. The name they adopted came from the Greek word *kyklos*, meaning "circle" or "band," and the English word *clan*. Its goal became the defeat of Radical Republicans in the South and the suppression of blacks. The group soon turned to violence to accomplish these goals.

But the Industrial Revolution also introduced new problems, such as an influx of immigrants and demands by organized labor. Now that the nation's borders were complete (except for Hawaii), it also had to decide its role in the changing world, where imperialism was the order of the day. Help the students to understand how those subjects became the natural topics of the next periods of history.

CD: Ku Klux Klan

Refer to the CD for an illustration of Ku Klux Klansmen.

To meet the needs of Southern agriculture, **sharecropping** became common.

Sharecropping

Blacks and poor whites became involved in this new economic system. Sharecroppers farmed small plots owned by planters and paid their annual rent for the use of the land with a part, or share, of the crop they grew. Since sharecroppers had little money, especially at the beginning of the season, they borrowed money for seed and provisions. Often the landlord was their creditor and he also owned the local store. When the harvest came in, the sharecropper "squared up," or settled his account with the creditor. If the sharecropper broke even, he was fortunate. But he often started the next season in debt since interest rates could be as high as 25 percent.

The average sharecropper showed a profit only two years out of twenty-five. As a result, he was locked into a cycle of debt and poverty. He had little chance of breaking out of the cycle. For many freedmen, this seemed to be merely another form of slavery. Under such conditions, the right to vote meant little. Most sharecroppers were more concerned about putting food on their tables.

Industry

Toward the end of Reconstruction, the Industrial Revolution finally reached the South. Southerners had little money for industry, but many Northerners had capital and were eager to make profitable investments. The railroad, steel, and textile industries expanded into the South. Those industries needed laborers. Southerners moved from rural areas to factory towns and cities for those jobs. The South's economy boomed. By 1890, Southerners spoke hopefully of a "**New South**" that would rival the North as an economic force.

One new feature of Southern industry was the **mill town**. Mill towns had some of the same features as plantations. The owner or investors built the workers' housing, usually identical rows of houses near the factory or mill. They often built churches, stores, and doctors' offices in the company towns. They also built company stores, where workers could buy such necessities as food and clothing. Generally, employers in the textile industry hired whole families. For the parents to be hired, they had to agree that their children would also work in the mill. Loom makers lowered the heights of their looms so that children could work them.

Political Trends During Reconstruction

The prosperity of the nation during Reconstruction helped the Republicans retain control of the presidency and usually Congress. Reminding voters of war issues, or "waving the bloody shirt," also helped them stay in power. Republicans were credited with winning the war and freeing the slaves. After the war, Republicans benefited when blacks were allowed to vote and ex-Confederate whites were not. But when the "Redeemers" came to power, the Republican Party declined dramatically in the South.

Because Southerners blamed the war and the hardships of Reconstruction on Republicans, the South sided with the Democrats. For a century, the "Solid South" voted solidly for Democrats.

In 1866, former Confederate soldiers formed a secret organization called the **Ku Klux Klan** (KKK). They were frustrated at having no power; they could not even vote. So the KKK sought ways to oppose Radical Reconstruction. Their goal was to frighten freed-

This cartoon depicts the plight of blacks during Reconstruction.

men and whites sympathetic to the freedmen. The Klan attempted to suppress blacks and prevent them from voting. Their least offensive tactic was to boycott businesses and force them to close.

But the Klan turned to even more threatening means. They rode through black communities at night dressed as white-hooded ghosts. The Klan burned crosses outside the homes of blacks and often beat or killed blacks who opposed them or tried to exercise their civil rights. In 1868, more than 1,300 freedmen were lynched (hung without a legal trial), many of them dragged from their homes at night and lynched in the presence of their families.

Many Northerners and Southern moderates were upset by the Klan's activities. Congress passed two acts—the Force Act in 1870 and the Ku Klux Klan Act in 1871—to deal with Klan abuses. The acts outlawed the use of force to prevent people from voting and gave President Grant the power to place federal troops in polling places to ensure everyone's voting rights. Although the Klan was officially disbanded, in reality it only went underground. It still exists today.

Civil Rights

Congress passed two acts to give blacks citizenship and all of its privileges, or civil rights. The Civil Rights Act of 1866, noted earlier, had granted freedmen the same rights and legal protection as whites, regardless of local laws. A second act, the Civil Rights Act of 1875, guaranteed equal accommodations in public places, such as inns and theaters. It also said that blacks could serve on juries. But the bill did not provide means for enforcing its provisions. The Supreme Court further weakened the legislation in 1883 when it declared that the social provisions of the bill were unconstitutional.

As the years passed, concern for the rights of the blacks declined. The Civil Rights Acts were no longer enforced, although they did serve as precedents for the civil rights acts that were passed in the twentieth century. Meanwhile, blacks found little political equality.

Reforms in the South

Before the war, the South had collected few taxes for public purposes. After the war, both taxes and spending increased. Many people were critical of the high spending of Southern governments. But in many instances the spending seemed to be justified. For the first time, for example, Southern states began providing free public education. They improved prison systems. They developed care for mentally and physically handicapped people and abolished imprisonment for debt.

Reconstruction Evaluated

Reconstruction was not a happy time for anyone. Northerners were not satisfied with its processes or results. Even more Southerners became bitter. The Civil War and Reconstruction changed the South politically, economically, and socially. Not all of the changes came smoothly or tactfully. Although many of the social advances made during Reconstruction were later lost, a foundation for future change had been laid.

Reconstruction was hard on the South. Radicals had treated the South more as a conquered foreign nation than as part of the United States. Even if Congress had followed Lincoln's and Johnson's more compassionate plans, any attempt to rebuild the South would have been difficult, considering how devastated the region was. By harsh

Civil Rights

The Fourteenth and Fifteenth Amendments, along with the Civil Rights Acts of the 1860s and 1870s, may be considered additional attempts to guarantee black Americans their civil rights. These acts and amendments provided a solid framework of laws to protect civil rights, not only for blacks but for all Americans. These acts, however, were overlooked or unheeded for nearly a century. The failure to deal with those issues in the 1800s caused the country to face even greater trials when the abuses were brought to light in the mid-1900s.

Reforms in the South

Most Southerners viewed education, internal improvements, and other such programs listed in this section of the text as the responsibility of families, churches, volunteer societies, private philanthropy, and local governments, not the responsibility of state or national governments.

An Assessment of Reconstruction

The best verdict on Reconstruction was written by Richard Harvey Cain, a black editor in Charleston who also served as a U. S. Representative: "When the smoke and fighting is over, the Negroes have nothing gained, the whites have nothing left, while the jackals have all the booty."

(quoted by Richard M. Weaver, "The South and the American Union" in *The Southern Essays of Richard M. Weaver*)

treatment and corrupt practices the Radicals complicated this already difficult task.

Reconstruction also did not go far enough. Steps were made toward establishing civil rights for blacks. But those rights did not become permanent during Reconstruction. Granting such rights was a major step, but few whites even in the North were willing for blacks to gain significant social and political power. When Southerners regained control of their own governments, many of the civil rights advances were lost.

Reconstruction's chances for success were limited further by great changes that occurred at the same time. America was industrializing, and the industrial age brought its own new problems. In both Reconstruction and the industrial era, people tried to solve those problems in new ways. Sometimes the proposed solutions were merely experiments. When they did not work, they should have been discarded.

The federal government also became a stronger institution after the war and during Reconstruction. Problems that were addressed by churches or voluntary societies in the pre-war years began to be addressed by the federal government. The powers of the centralized government have continued to increase. The Civil War was a turning point for the United States. In government, religion, and society, little was left unaffected by the war.

Section Quiz

1. How did sharecropping get its name?
2. In what kind of community did Southern factory workers sometimes live?
3. What was the purpose of the Ku Klux Klan?
4. Why did civil rights legislation of the late 1800s bring little real change for blacks?
★ What answer could be made to the charge that Reconstruction went either too far or not far enough?
★ Should the government have provided the freedmen with land after the war? Factor Deuteronomy 15:12–14 into your answer.

Additional Resources

An excellent and thorough treatment of the post-war period in the South is *Origins of the New South* by C. Vann Woodward, the "dean" of Southern historians.

Section Quiz Answers

1. Sharecroppers farmed small plots owned by planters and paid rent with a share of their crops.
2. mill towns
3. to frighten blacks and intimidate the freedmen and whites sympathetic to Radical Reconstruction to keep them from voting

4. It provided no measures for enforcement; the Supreme Court declared parts of it unconstitutional; and time eased pressures for reform.
★ Reconstruction was a difficult time, yet no recovery from war would be completely painless. In many instances, the manner in which the Reconstruction measures were taken created problems. On the other side, although racial equality did not become a reality at that time, important legislative steps were taken that set precedents for future action on civil rights.
★ Providing the freedmen with land would have enabled them to become

self-sufficient workers. It could have avoided the quasi-slavery of sharecropping. Though Hebrew slavery was very different from Southern slavery, the Bible does lay down the principle that slaves should not move from slave to free status without the necessary provisions to reestablish themselves in free society.

Activity 5: Writing a Historical Essay

Use this activity to give the students practice in writing a historical essay. You could use it in any section of this chapter where you have time, but the end of this chapter might be a good time.

Chapter Review 16

Review Questions

Match each item with the corresponding man.

1. Ten Percent Plan   A. Ulysses S. Grant
2. impeached president   B. Rutherford B. Hayes
3. secretary of war   C. Andrew Johnson
4. Alaska purchase   D. Abraham Lincoln
5. presidential scandals   E. William Seward
6. withdrew the last federal   F. Edwin Stanton
   troops from the South

Unscramble these letters to find the names of groups involved in Reconstruction.

7. TARGEBACSPREG (Northerners in the South)
8. DEFEMERN (slaves no longer)
9. PRORRASHECEPS (poor farmers)
10. GACLASAWS (despised Southerners)

Match the following legislation and amendments with their effects.

11. Thirteenth Amendment   A. made all persons citizens
12. Fourteenth Amendment   B. used to impeach Johnson
13. Reconstruction Act of 1867   C. abolished slavery
14. Tenure of Office Act   D. gave blacks the vote
15. Fifteenth Amendment   E. put the South under
   military rule

Critical Thinking

1. Why is Reconstruction a good name for the time following the Civil War?
2. How might Reconstruction have been different if Lincoln had lived?

People, Places, and Things to Remember:

Reconstruction
freedmen
Presidential Reconstruction
Ten Percent Plan
Radical Republicans
Wade-Davis Bill
amnesty
Thirteenth Amendment
Joint Committee on Reconstruction
black codes
Thaddeus Stevens
Charles Sumner
Freedmen's Bureau
Fourteenth Amendment
Radical Reconstruction
Reconstruction Act of 1867
carpetbaggers
scalawag
Tenure of Office Act
Edwin Stanton
impeach
William Seward
Fifteenth Amendment
Bourbon Reconstruction
Samuel J. Tilden
Rutherford B. Hayes
sharecropping
New South
mill town
Ku Klux Klan

Activity 7: Eyewitness to KKK Violence, 1868

Use this activity to help the students understand the level of violence experienced by the freedmen during Reconstruction and to give them experience in using eyewitness accounts of historical events.

Activity 8: Chapter Review

Use this activity to help the students prepare for the chapter test.

Chapter Review Answers

Review Questions

1. D
2. C
3. F
4. E
5. A
6. B
7. CARPETBAGGERS
8. FREEDMEN
9. SHARECROPPERS
10 SCALAWAGS
11. C
12. A
13. E
14. B
15. D

Critical Thinking

1. Answers will vary. The South (its homes, businesses, and government) was being rebuilt (reconstructed) after its destruction in the war.

2. Answers will vary. He might have been able to prevent the Radical Republicans from taking control. If the South had accepted his generous proposals, the results might have been less painful and the recovery more complete.

1893: Wrigley's Spearmint and Juicy Fruit chewing gum introduced

WRIGLEY'S SPEARMINT CHEWING GUM

How much did it cost?

Product	Year	Price
Bread	1900	5¢/loaf
	1920	12¢/loaf
Coca-Cola	1900	5¢/bottle
	1920	5¢/bottle
Coffee	1900	13¢/lb.
	1920	50¢/lb.
Eggs	1900	18¢/doz.
	1920	69¢/doz.
Sugar	1900	6¢/lb.
	1920	20¢/lb.

1911: First Indianapolis 500 race held; average speed of winner: 75 mph

1862 Homestead Act passed

1869 Completion of transcontinental railroad

1876 Invention of the telephone
Battle of Little Big Horn ("Custer's Last Stand")

1882 Formation of first trust (John D. Rockefeller)

1887 Interstate Commerce Act passed
Dawes Act passed

1889 Oklahoma Land Rush

1890 Sherman Anti-Trust Act passed

1891 Populist Party formed

1913: Peppermint Life Savers introduced

How much did they make?

Occupation	Year	Wages
Farm Laborer	1900	$247/yr.
	1920	$810/yr.
Manufacturer	1900	34¢/hr.
	1920	88¢/hr.
Health Care Worker	1900	$256/yr.
	1920	$752/yr.
Minister	1900	$731/yr.
	1920	$1,556/yr.
Schoolteacher	1900	$328/yr.
	1920	$970/yr.

WRIGLEY'S **JUICY FRUIT** CHEWING GUM

1897 Alaska Gold Rush

1898 Spanish-American War
Acquisition of Hawaii

1901 Platt Amendment

1903 Panama Canal Treaty signed
Wright brothers' first flight

1911 Triangle Shirtwaist Company fire

1913 Seventeenth Amendment ratified

1914 Opening of Panama Canal

1920 Beginning of Prohibition

1920

Chapter Goals

Students should be able to

1. Define and use the basic terms of the chapter.

2. Understand the impact of immigration on industry and culture in America.

3. Summarize the effect of transportation and technology on industry.

4. Analyze the issues that affect an emerging industrial society.

5. Explain the significance and impact of major entrepreneurs, industrialists, and inventors on American industry.

6. Describe the rise of the labor movement and its major leaders during the age of industrialism.

Chapter Motivation

Unit 5 covers a transitional period in American history. To help the students recognize what the transition was from, ask them to describe the typical American and the typical way of life before the Civil War (covered thoroughly in Chapters 13-14). How is the typical American different today? What major changes had to take place to produce this change? Also list some characteristics of Americans, both good and bad, that have not changed. *(industrious, self-confident, democratic, open to change, idealistic)*

This chapter focuses on the end of an agricultural society and the rise of an industrial society. The next chapter examines the passing of the American frontier and the last icons of the typical "frontier spirit"—miners, homesteaders, cowboys, and Indians. The last two chapters in this unit describe two other major changes in America: its bigger role in world politics

CHAPTER 17

The age of industrialization brought vast changes in transportation, manufacturing, business, and daily life.

Industrialism

  I. **Resources and People**

 II. **Transportation and Technology**

III. **New Ways of Doing Business**

 IV. **Effects of Industrial Expansion**

Chapter 17 Lesson Plan Chart			
Section Title	**Main Activity**	**Pages**	**Days**
I. Resources and People	Activity 1: Emma Lazarus's Most Famous Poem	327–32	1–2 days
II. Transportation and Technology	Activity 2: Eyewitness Tells of "Last Spike" Driving	332–36	1–2 days
III. New Ways of Doing Business	Activity 4: Andrew Carnegie: The Gospel of Wealth	336–38	½–1 days
IV. Effects of Industrial Expansion	Activity 5: Chapter Review	338–43	2–3 days
TOTAL SUGGESTED DAYS (INCLUDING **1** DAY FOR REVIEW AND TESTING)			5½ –9 DAYS

MATERIALS LIST

SECTION I
- *Free Indeed: Heroes of Black Christian History* (BJU Press)
- CD: Workers Loading Logs onto Railcar; James Garfield, 20th President; Chester Arthur, 21st President
- Activity 1 from the *Student Activities* manual

SECTION II
- CD: Directors of the Union Pacific Railroad; Leland Stanford of the Central Pacific Railroad
- A model train
- Special speaker: a model railroading enthusiast

America was a quiet land in the early nineteenth century. It was made up of family farms, small villages, and a few small cities on the Atlantic coast. The middle of the century was consumed with a struggle over how the nation would grow. After the Civil War, the industrial strength of the North set the pattern for the growth to come. By the end of the century, crowded cities, busy factories, and mechanized farms spanned the country.

America's population was swelling. In 1800 it was less than 5.5 million. The 1870 census showed the population to be almost 40 million. By 1910, it reached 92 million. The birthrate was high, but the biggest reason for the growth was immigration. As technology and industry developed, the percentage of Americans living in rural areas declined; the number living in urban areas increased.

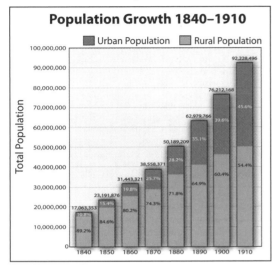

Population Growth 1840–1910

The land area of the United States was also growing. In 1800, only sixteen states were in the Union. By 1900, there were forty-five.

The land and its people were uniquely suited for the large industrial projects. The United States was on its way to becoming the world's greatest industrial power. Its free economy, new industrial techniques, and the ingenuity of its people were turning out a host of products that made life easier.

I. Resources and People

The United States was able to undergo such rapid changes for several reasons. No single factor could have produced such change by itself. Two of the resources that helped the United States produce goods for itself and the world were its raw materials and its labor force.

Natural Resources

God blessed America with abundant natural resources. He gave it fertile soil and almost all the raw materials needed for important

(Chapter 21) and progressive ideas in society and government (Chapter 22).

Section I
Objectives

Students should be able to

1. Describe some of the changes in America during the late nineteenth century.

2. List some of America's natural resources that aided the growth of industries.

3. Describe American immigration during the late nineteenth century.

Frederick Weyerhaeuser: Timber Supplier

Most early settlers could cut enough trees in their immediate area to build their homes. In the late 1800s, however, the demand for timber increased as settlers moved onto the treeless plains and as railroad tracks needed wooden ties.

Frederick Weyerhaeuser (VEYE ur HOU zur) was a young German immigrant working for day wages in a Rock Island, Illinois, sawmill. In 1860, Weyerhaeuser and his brother-in-law, Frederick Denkmann, pooled their earnings, borrowed some money, and bought the sawmill.

Weyerhaeuser expanded the operation northward. Unlike some heads of corporations, Weyerhaeuser was always willing to share the responsibilities with a large circle of capable men. He rarely held more than a 15–20 percent interest in any company, yet his partners took his advice because his past decisions had brought great profits. Weyerhaeuser's most innovative operation was a sales company that served as a nationwide wholesaler,

• Activity 2 from the *Student Activities* manual

SECTION III
• A list of America's wealthiest people from Forbes magazine (can be downloaded from the magazine's website)
• World almanac
• Activities 3 and 4 from the *Student Activities* manual

SECTION IV
• CD: Tenements of New York City
• Newspaper and magazine articles on economic issues
• Activity 5 from Chapter 17 of the *Student Activities* manual

Core Values

The industrial era was an era of growth. The United States had abundant natural resources and a stable government that empowered people to take risks for growing their wealth. They had confidence that government would protect their freedom (it would let them do what they wanted), individualism (it would let them keep their profits), and equality (it would treat them justly before the law). Without this confidence, there is no motive to venture forward and therefore little chance of growth. But with this confidence the American economy boomed.

The economic growth of the country led to growth in immigration. America was already a nation of immigrants. From the beginning, English, Dutch, Germans and others settled the eastern seaboard. But the immigrants in the late nineteenth century brought worries. These people often had different religions (Roman Catholicism and Judaism). Different religions often meant different values, and Americans were concerned about the transformation of their way of life. With the hindsight of history, it is clear that the new immigrants did change the United States. The country moved from being a Protestant nation in the nineteenth century to one that identified itself with Judeo-Christian values in the twentieth century. This diversification of religion in the United States led to religious and cultural pluralism, which in turn has tended to lead to secularism.

handling sawmill products from more than twenty firms. The Weyerhaeuser Sales Company eventually became the world's largest lumber company.

When the forests of the Great Lakes had fallen to ax and saw, Weyerhaeuser sought land elsewhere. James J. Hill, the railroad baron who lived next door to him in St. Paul, Minnesota, sold him nine hundred thousand acres of timberland in the Pacific Northwest for $5.4 million dollars. The value of the land soon quadrupled, and the company moved its headquarters to Tacoma, Washington, where it remains active today.

Weyerhaeuser's giant firms were often criticized because of their methods. His company cut timber, milled it, and then left or sold the scarred land. Vast forests were available at the time, and the company acted in response to public need and to the public policy of that day. Reforestation and conservation have replaced the practice of "cut and run." Innovative uses for wood byproducts also lead to much less waste today.

History of the Immigration and Naturalization Service

As the United States has changed and grown, so have its views on immigrants and its methods of handling them. Immigration first became a federal concern in 1864. Desiring to encourage immigration, Congress created the position of Commissioner of Immigration within the State Department. However, the states still had control over their own immigration affairs, so it was difficult for the commissioner to create one unified national policy. The position went defunct in 1868, but in 1891 the federal government again stepped into the immigration picture by establish-

Deadwood, South Dakota 1876

Logging became a big business in the mountains of the West and Northwest.

industries. A republican form of government, a strong religious and moral basis for decisions and actions, and the free enterprise system proved ideal gifts for the development of those resources. After the purchase of Alaska in 1867, little geographic growth occurred. Hawaii, Puerto Rico, and a few other small areas were added. But available resources grew as new minerals were discovered and regions that were inaccessible before were opened by new means of transportation.

Great **lodes** (a rich deposit or supply) of gold, silver, and copper were found in the Rocky Mountains, the Far West, and Alaska. After the Civil War, thousands of miners and businessmen streamed into the sparsely settled West, hoping to strike it rich. Towns with unusual names like Eureka, Paradise, Coarsegold, Sloughouse, Dinkey Creek, and Whiskeytown flourished briefly near the rich ore veins. When the ore was gone, most miners moved on, leaving behind ghost towns. But some people stayed and found new ways to earn their living.

The rich iron ore deposits of northern Minnesota, the Mesabi (muh SAH bee) and Cuyuna (kuh YOO nuh) ranges, provided raw materials for the growing iron and steel industries. Newly discovered petroleum resources added to America's natural resources. Vast coal deposits provided another important fuel. Water power also proved helpful in producing electricity.

Another important American resource was its timber. Vast forests covering the Northwest and other areas of the country supplied timber for lumber, pulp, and other uses.

Immigration Provides Labor

Developing industries needed workers. Most of the American population was hard at work in the late 1800s, but to expand its industrial production the country needed even more workers. The growing tide of immigrants met that need for laborers.

Immigrants Come to America

Before 1880, most of the immigrants came from northwestern European countries such as Britain, Ireland, Germany, or the Scandinavian countries. Most Europeans crossed the Atlantic by the shortest and cheapest routes. Many traveled first to Liverpool, England, or to Bremen or Hamburg, Germany, where the major steamship companies were located. Steamship companies often used freighters to carry passengers to the United States. They then carried raw materials or manufactured goods back to Europe. The cheapest tickets gave travelers space in steerage, the noisiest, most crowded part of the ship, located under the deck and near the engine and rudder. Passengers brought their food with them in their bundles. Seasickness or disease often made the voyage a miserable experience, and some immigrants lost their lives. People from different walks of life were thrown together under strange conditions. In addition, many came from different countries and spoke different languages.

Some immigrants had been recruited in their homelands by agents of various American companies needing laborers or by the railroads who sought settlers for acres of land grants they wished to

Compare Colonial Settlers and Immigrants

Ask the students whether it is fair to call immigrants "the next generation of settlers." In other words, did the immigrants face the same kinds of challenges as the first Pilgrims and settlers who arrived from England? If so, then it seems reasonable to argue that they have earned an equal place in America by the sweat of their brow. It was not much easier for them to adjust than for the first settlers.

 CD: Workers Loading Logs onto Railcar

Refer to the CD for a photo of trains being used in logging industry.

Welcome to America

Give me your tired, your poor,
Your huddled masses yearning to
*   breathe free,*
The wretched refuse of your teeming
*   shore.*
Send these, the homeless, tempest-
*   tossed, to me,*
I lift my lamp beside the golden door!
(Excerpt from the poem by Emma La-
zarus that is engraved at the base of
the Statue of Liberty)

For Americans, the question
"What is your nationality?" is sometimes hard to answer. Few Americans
can trace their roots to the earliest
inhabitants of this country. Many
Americans have numerous nationali-
ties attached to their family history.

America has experienced several
waves of immigration. The first came
in the early 1700s when German and
Scots-Irish immigrants flooded into
Pennsylvania. The next great immigration occurred during the nineteenth century, when more than
thirty million Europeans flooded into
the United States. At first, the immigrants came from Western Europe.
But by the close of the century, most
of the immigrants came from Eastern
European countries. Many Jews facing persecution in Europe came to
the United Sates in the early 1900s.

The third wave of immigration
began in the 1980s, when Hispanic
and Asian immigrants entered the
nation. Hispanics settled in the
Southwest and Southeast. Refugees
from Haiti and Cuba established
large communities in New York City
and Miami. Southeast Asians settled
primarily on the west coast.

From colonial times to the present, immigration has been a source
of both benefits and problems. Each
group that has become dominant in
a region feels threatened when newcomers enter that area. But newcomers often fill an important place in
society. They bring new skills or are
willing to work at important but low-
paying jobs. By becoming productive
citizens, they encourage growth in
the economy.

Why, then, are people sometimes
so resistant to new immigrants? Three
fears dominate Americans' reactions
to immigration:

1. that the new people will take
    jobs away from American
    citizens
2. that American tax dollars will
    have to pay to take care of un-
    employed foreign-born immi-
    grants, both those who have
    become citizens and illegal
    aliens
3. that immigrants will change
    the nation

---

sell. The companies made contracts with the immigrants, agreeing
to pay their fares if the immigrants would agree to work a specified
length of time for the employer. Many immigrants used most of their
life's savings to come to America. Some immigrants' trans-Atlantic
tickets and even their rail tickets from the port where they landed
were paid for by relatives who had come earlier.

Employers eagerly hired immigrants. Because the
recent immigrants were usually happy just to have
a job, they were generally willing to work for lower
wages than other Americans. They saw their jobs as a
way of getting ahead, which was often impossible in
their home countries. Immigrants who complained
about hours or conditions risked losing their jobs
since there were always newcomers waiting to be
hired. Employers also liked hiring immigrants because most of them worked hard and were reluctant
to join the labor unions.

Ellis Island and Ports of Entry

The largest number of European immigrants
came to America by way of New York harbor at **Ellis
Island**. It served as a temporary stopover for incoming immigrants who used its beautifully designed
great hall, dining room, and hospital. Those who
looked healthy enough to hold a job and who could
prove they had the means to reach distant destinations usually took
the ferry to New Jersey and rode a train inland. Others entered New

The Ellis Island point of entry was one of the first
things immigrants saw as they entered New York
Harbor.

More on Ellis Island

Visit www.bjup.com/resources for
possible links to information about Ellis
Island and the immigrant experience.

The Education of Hyman Kaplan

An interesting and humorous look at the
efforts of early immigrants to become fully
Americanized is the book *The Education of
H*Y*M*A*N K*A*P*L*A*N* by Leo Rosten.
It is a fictional account of one immigrant's
struggles to learn English and assimilate the
ways of his adopted homeland.

Immigration, Good or Bad?

Discuss any modern debates on immigration now raging in state capitals or in
Washington, D.C. The issue has always been
whether to limit the number of immigrants.
Both sides of the debate look to the past to
find support for their positions. Based on
their reading in this chapter, the students
should list the arguments that both sides
might have given during the debate over the
Exclusion Act of 1882 (page 392). Note that
the change in the ethnic background of the
immigrants was one of the major matters
of concern. God told the Hebrews to love
foreigners and treat them well (Exod. 22:21;
Lev. 19:33), and He even expected the hea-

---

ing the Bureau of Immigration under the
Secretary of the Treasury. From this point,
the federal government had the final authority over immigration affairs.

The courts originally handled naturalization, the process of becoming a citizen. It
came under the authority of the executive
branch in 1906. Immigration and naturalization issues were permanently joined
in the Immigration and Naturalization
Service (INS) under the Labor Department
in 1933. The INS reached its final home at
the Justice Department in June of 1940.
Because of the looming threat of war at
that time, the government wanted to have
stronger control over the activities of foreigners entering the country.

Since the Second World War, one major
concern has been preventing illegal immigrant workers from operating in the
country. Another concern is refugees.
Though the United States places a cap on
the number of immigrants it receives each
year, people who are fleeing desperate circumstances are considered to be in a different category. The INS reports that since
1965 the major source of immigration has
shifted from Europe to Latin America and
Asia.

then nation of Moab to accept outcasts from
other nations (Isa. 16:3-4).

The Public Health Service tried to ensure that immigrants did not bring contagious diseases into the United States.

Immigrants generally could bring with them only what they could wear or carry or afford to ship.

York City totally bewildered. Public Health Service doctors assisted the immigrants who were ill. If they could be cured, they were treated and sent on their way as soon as possible.

The immigrant center at Ellis Island operated from 1892 to 1954 and handled the entry of more than seventeen million immigrants. The one-day record for immigrants processed occurred on April 17, 1907, when 11,747 went through the system.

Most immigrants stayed at Ellis Island for an average of only three to five hours. About 20 percent of them encountered problems or questions that required them to stay overnight in dormitory-like facilities until their cases could be resolved. Their accommodations were far better on Ellis Island than they had been on the ship. Often immigrants feared being turned back at Ellis Island, but of the millions who came, the number rejected was less than two percent.

Some immigrants landed in Montreal; others, especially the Irish, entered at Boston. New Orleans was a port of entry for many immigrants who planned to go to the Midwest or the Far West.

Immigrants often settled in neighborhoods of cities where others of their nationality lived. Some of those neighborhoods came to be known by such names as "Chinatown" or "Little Italy." In later years, after immigrants had learned the language and saved enough money, many of them moved to other areas of the city or suburbs and left the inner city to be occupied by newer immigrants.

Immigrants Work to Build America

Immigrants came from many lands, but Ireland provided a large share in the middle to late 1800s. In the 1840s, a potato blight spread across Europe. The plant disease devastated Ireland, where the potato was the major farm crop and food. One-eighth of Ireland's population starved to death or died from diseases caused by malnutrition. Another three-eighths of the people, three million in all, left Ireland. Many of them came to the United States, primarily to Boston and New York City.

The Irish played important roles in the construction of America's transportation systems. An early group of Irish immigrants provided the muscle to build the Erie Canal. Crews of Irishmen were also responsible for laying the track for western railroads. The Irish took these jobs despite a high risk of injury because they saw them as a means to escape their poverty.

Some Irishmen sought altogether different work. Because of previously unstable circumstances, they sought more stable jobs in civic service. Men became policemen or firemen. Irish women became teachers or domestic servants.

Many Chinese also migrated to America. Because American ships traded with China, news of the discovery of gold in California soon reached China. China was overpopulated, and its people faced floods and famines, so many Chinese were attracted to America. Opportunities in the California gold rush brought them in great numbers. As was frequently the case with immigrants, the men came first. Once they had attained their riches, they hoped to return to China and find wives. Instead of mining for gold themselves, many of the Chinese founded businesses such as restaurants and laundries, providing needed services for others. Later, Chinese workers were hired to build western sections of the transcontinental railroad.

Chinese immigrants continued to come, and as long as jobs were available, Americans did not object too much. But when the economic growth slowed, many Americans became hostile. Californians claimed that the Chinese, who were willing to work for lower wages, were getting the jobs that whites deserved. They soon influenced politicians to pass the **Exclusion Act of 1882**, which reduced legal Chinese immigration to a few hundred per year. That act was passed over the veto of President Chester Arthur, who had assumed office after the assassination of James Garfield in 1881.

Northern Europeans also came to America. Political and religious unrest swept the German states during the 1840s. When the revolutions failed in 1848, people left that land. Many of these people had been landowners in Europe, so they had enough money to buy land in the United States when they arrived. They often settled in the farming areas of America's heartland, such as Indiana, Ohio, and Wisconsin. Others found work as lumberjacks in the northern woods, and then they bought farmland soon after.

Scandinavians—Norwegians, Swedes, and Finns—who came to America tended to settle whole towns or counties in Iowa, Minnesota, Wisconsin, and the Dakotas. They had their own newspapers and started their own colleges. Most of them were Lutheran. Some had come to America to protest the policies of their state church back home. Some Swedes, Norwegians, and Finns

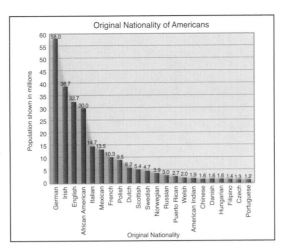

Original Nationality of Americans

Population shown in millions (y-axis)

Original Nationality (x-axis)

Original Nationality	Population (millions)
German	58.0
Irish	38.7
English	32.7
African American	30.0
Italian	14.7
Mexican	13.5
French	10.3
Polish	9.5
Dutch	6.2
Scottish	5.4
Swedish	4.7
Norwegian	3.9
Russian	3.0
Puerto Rican	2.7
Welsh	2.0
American Indian	1.9
Chinese	1.6
Danish	1.6
Hungarian	1.6
Filipino	1.4
Czech	1.3
Portuguese	1.2

The Assassination of President Garfield

President James Garfield had been in office less than four months. The heat in Washington, D.C., was oppressive, and he wanted to get away to the New Jersey seashore for a break. On July 2, 1881, as he walked through the railway station in Washington to catch his train, Charles Guiteau stepped up to him and fired two shots from a revolver before being wrestled to the ground. One bullet grazed the president's arm. The other bullet lodged in his abdomen.

The first doctors to arrive on the scene gave the president brandy and spirits of ammonia (which caused the president to vomit) and probed the entry wound with their fingers and a metal probe. They could not find the bullet but assumed that it was somewhere in his abdomen. The president, who was in great pain, complained of numbness in his legs and feet. The bullet was actually near his spinal column.

Garfield was moved to the White House, and other doctors were consulted. Sixteen different doctors examined him, most of them probing the wound repeatedly with either their fingers or unclean instruments. By the time Garfield finally died (of a heart attack) on September 19, the doctors had turned what initially had been a three-inch-deep wound into a twenty-inch-long, infected gash as they repeatedly searched for the elusive bullet.

Only later did people learn that in a room near where the president had been taken in the railway station after the shooting was a crate. Inside the crate was an experimental instrument that might have saved the president's life: an early version of the X-ray machine.

Guiteau was arrested and tried for assassinating the president. He was disgruntled because he had wanted Garfield to appoint him ambassador to France but had been passed over. In his trial, he claimed that the president's doctors, not he, were responsible for the president's death. His argument, however, carried no weight with the jury. He was found guilty and was hanged on June 30, 1882. Vice President Chester Arthur became president.

"Immigrant" Samuel Morris

Immigrants came from many places and for many reasons. "Samuel Morris" is the story of an African prince who came to study in order to return and teach his native family and tribesmen of Christ. This story can be found in *Free Indeed: Heroes of Black Christian History* (BJU Press).

CD: James Garfield, 20th President; Chester Arthur, 21st President

Refer to the CD for information on presidents James Garfield and Chester Arthur.

Activity 1: Emma Lazarus's Poem

Use this activity to point out the positive aspects of legal immigration for the United States and the valuable contributions immigrants have made to our country's history, economy, and culture.

Section II

Objectives

Students should be able to

1. Explain the need for and the hazard of railroad consolidation.

2. Describe the growth of America's railroad network in the late nineteenth century, including the completion of the transcontinental railroad.

3. Name and describe the significance of key leaders in the early railroad industry.

4. Name two important inventors of the late nineteenth century and explain the significance of their contributions to technology.

Standard Gauge

Early railroad companies often used tracks of a gauge (the distance between the metal rails) that was different from that of other railroads. Whenever trains on a track of one gauge got to the tracks of a railroad that used a different gauge, the cargo on the train had to be unloaded and then placed on a train operating on the different gauge. It made movement of both goods and people a slow, frustrating process.

The Union Pacific Railroad used a gauge of four feet, eight and one-half inches. Gradually, railroads came to accept that measurement as the "standard gauge" for railroads in the later 1800s. (Any rail line that used a gauge less than that was said to operate on "narrow gauge.") Locomotives and rolling stock (rail cars) could move freely from one line to another, making it unnecessary to unload and reload goods and passengers.

worked in logging camps; others worked in the iron mines of northern Minnesota and the copper mines of Michigan.

Immigrants Change American Religion

Protestantism dominated American life before the 1880s. Although immigrants continued to come from the Protestant countries of northern Europe, after 1880 a greater proportion began to arrive from eastern and southern European countries. Other immigrants came from northern Russia and Poland (which was then part of Russia). Only a few immigrants from these countries were Protestant.

By 1920 America was religiously a different country since many immigrants were Catholic, Jewish, or Eastern Orthodox. Many Protestants became concerned about the increased influence of Catholics. Some Catholics, on the other hand, were worried about their children being taught the Protestant religion in public schools. They formed their own parochial (church run) schools. This highlighted the difficulty of including religion in the public life of a nation with multiple religions.

The increasing **religious pluralism** (when a variety of religious beliefs are accepted in a society) played a role in leading the nation further down the road of secularism. If all Americans could not agree on what God had said, they would be discouraged from appealing to His Word to settle disputes about public policy. People still read their Bibles in private, but more and more they felt pressured to ignore the Bible when dealing with matters of public policy.

Section Quiz

1. What was the biggest single reason for the growth of the American population in the nineteenth century?

2. What were two of the factors that helped the industries of the United States to grow?

3. After 1880 many immigrants came from what regions of Europe?

4. Where did many European immigrants go first to be registered?

5. What piece of legislation attempted to limit Chinese immigration?

⭐ Why did established Americans sometimes object to immigrants?

⭐ How did the rise of religious pluralism move the United States down the path of secularism?

II. Transportation and Technology

Two more American resources that helped the land's industries grow were its transportation networks and its technological developments. Promoting the development of these features became an important goal of the country.

Transportation and the Railroads

While steamships were improving transportation for trade with foreign countries, the railroads made it possible for Americans to rapidly travel across the country's immense territory. Railroads also

Immigrants and Religious Pluralism

The student text notes that the immigration of the late 1800s led to religious pluralism and that this pluralism led to the growth of secularism in the twentieth century. Immigration can be a very good thing, but pluralism is a very bad thing. What should Christians do to minimize the growth of pluralism (and secularism) that often results from immigration? (*Christians should labor to evangelize immigrants and immigrant communities in the United States.*)

Section Quiz Answers

1. immigration

2. its supplies of raw materials and its labor force

3. eastern and southern Europe

4. Ellis Island

5. the Exclusion Act of 1882

⭐ Especially during times of financial difficulty, they felt that immigrants took work away from native-born Americans.

⭐ Since Americans could not agree what God said about public policy issues, many began to believe it was best to

exclude the Bible from public policy debates.

Model Trains

Bring a model train to class or ask interested students to help you set up model trains from their homes. If you know someone who is a model railroading hobbyist, ask him or her to speak to the class about the hobby. The person could explain the basis for his or her fascination with trains and share some of the things he has learned.

Another source for a possible speaker is someone from a local hobby shop.

moved America's raw materials to distant factories and distributed the manufactured goods to ready markets.

In 1860 the United States had 30,626 miles of track, but almost all of it was in the East. There were still no railroad bridges across the Hudson, Ohio, or Mississippi rivers. Since a different company built each railroad, each using a different gauge (width) of track, trains could not travel on all tracks. Some railroads used a narrow gauge. Others used a wider gauge. To get goods from one area to another required transferring them from one line to another. Such problems made it difficult to travel by rail or to send freight long distances. Chicago and New York had rails between them, but passengers and cargo had to change cars six times en route. The Civil War revealed the problems and spurred the building of more track and the development of more efficient and economical systems. Perhaps the most significant change was the acceptance of a standard gauge. The accepted width between rails was set at four feet, eight-and-a-half inches, which allowed trains to carry heavier loads and travel at greater speeds.

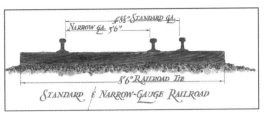
Standardization of track gauge greatly helped the development of railroads in the United States during the last half of the nineteenth century.

Consolidation Helps the Railroads

One means of making railroads more efficient and more economical was **consolidation**, combining small lines. Sometimes this was done through the friendly purchase of one company by another. But more often it was the result of ruthless pressure. Several men sought to gain control of large railroad networks. **Cornelius Vanderbilt**, who already had a steamship line on several of the Great Lakes, dreamed of connecting the Great Lake states to New York City by rail. He forced all of his competitors to sell their railroads to him. He put together a railroad empire.

Other men tried to make fortunes as they built railroad empires. J. Edgar Thompson secretly bought up small lines in Pennsylvania and Ohio. Once he had a base, he cut his rates and drove his rivals out of business. Then he raised his rates. Although small railroads were often hurt by consolidation, the process did help the nation acquire an efficient railroad transportation network.

Government Policy Aids Railroad Building

A second factor leading to the development of a railroad system was government policy. James Gadsden, a South Carolina railroad owner, had become a minister to Mexico under Franklin Pierce. Favoring a southern route from Houston or El Paso to Los Angeles, Congress approved the Gadsden Purchase in 1853. In the 1860s, Lincoln and the Republicans also supported the idea of a transcontinental railroad. But since the South was not in the Union at that time, Congress opted for a central route. They chartered the **Union Pacific** and **Central Pacific** railroads to begin that task in 1864. The Union Pacific laid track westward using Irish workers and war veterans. The Central Pacific laid track eastward using Chinese laborers. Most of the railroad was built after the Civil War.

The Central Pacific faced the trial of crossing the steep Sierra Nevada range. The Union Pacific had its problems, too. Because of a lack of wood on the prairie, most of their ties had to be shipped long distances. A lack of water and the danger of attacks from fierce Plains Indian tribes also hindered their work. The official "wedding

The Union Pacific seemed to have the advantage in the race to complete the transcontinental railroad because they laid track across relatively flat land on the Plains.

Two other important developments for railroads in the same era were sleeping cars and other types of passenger cars developed by George Pullman and the air brake devised by George Westinghouse.

Cornelius Vanderbilt

Cornelius Vanderbilt dropped out of school, borrowed $100 from his mother, bought a boat, and founded his own shipping business, transporting goods from Staten Island to New York City. Thus began his journey to becoming the wealthiest man in America. He paid back his $100 loan in a year—plus $1000. Vanderbilt bought (or built) more boats and gained the nickname "Commodore" when he operated the largest schooner on the Hudson River. He began building steamships. His vessels offered not just transportation but comfort and increasingly luxury. They became known as "floating palaces." By the 1840s, his business had become the largest employer in the United States.

Vanderbilt was nearing 70 when he decided to shift his attentions to building a railroad empire. He began buying small rail lines and combining them: the New York and Harlem Railroad, the Hudson River Railroad, and the Central Railroad. In the first five years, he made $25 million. He lost $1–2 million trying to buy the Erie Railroad but quickly made that up by buying the Lake Shore and Michigan Southern Railroad, the Canadian Southern Railroad, and the Michigan Central Railroad. He had put together the greatest American railroad system and controlled railroading between New York and Chicago.

Biltmore Estate in Asheville, N.C., was built by Vanderbilt's grandson, George.

Additional Resources

Many excellent books are available on the transcontinental railroad and railroading in the United States generally. The following sources would be good starters for giving yourself more information to share with the students when you cover this topic in the chapter:

- John Hoyt Williams, *A Great and Shining Road*
- Stephen Ambrose, *Nothing Like It in the World: The Men Who Built the Transcontinental Railroad, 1863–1869*
- George H. Douglas, *All Aboard! The Railroad in American Life*

- Charleton Ogburn, *Railroads: The Great American Adventure* (published by the National Geographic Society)

Additional Resources

An excellent video on the construction of the transcontinental railroad is the documentary "The Iron Road" from the PBS series *American Experience*. It is narrated by popular best-selling author and historian David McCullough.

Government-Subsidized Railroads

At the time the transcontinental railroad was built, Americans did not universally applaud the idea of a railroad funded by federal loans and lavish grants of public lands. The transcontinental railroad was the first major business endeavor funded by federal subsidies. Today, few people ask, "Was it a wise decision?" but you might consider raising it with your students. In weighing their answer, students should consider the consequences of the deal—the giveaway helped to create a monopoly that would sometimes take advantage of those who needed to use the railroad and would use its wealth to corrupt politicians. Often the original tracks were poorly laid just to get the federal money as quickly as possible. Note also that the rapid expansion heightened tensions with the Indians.

Chinese Laborers

James Strobridge, the man in charge of constructing the Central Pacific Railroad, initially refused to hire Chinese laborers. But white laborers were in short supply, so Strobridge had to accept the laborers who were available and willing to work.

The Chinese soon proved their worth by doing an excellent job of grading railbeds. They became legendary for the speed and quality of their work. Approximately ten thousand Chinese worked on the railroad. More than twelve hundred of them were killed on the job.

James J. Hill's Northern Pacific

Because it was built without any federal land or federal funds, the most unusual railroad of the late 1800s was probably the Great Northern Railroad owned by James J. Hill. He had begun his career as a clerk for a steamboat line. In 1865, he started his own business as a salesman.

Next, Hill bought the almost defunct St. Paul and Pacific Railroad. He envisioned a railroad that stretched from St. Paul, across the Rockies, to the Pacific, and northward into Canada. By January 1879, he had connected St. Paul, Minnesota, to Winnipeg, Canada.

Hill was unlike other railroad magnates in that he built his line in short (200 mile) spans and then stopped to woo farmers and settlers to the end of the line. Once a settlement had developed, he resumed construction on the next span. He also was willing to build "feeder lines" off the main line to service individual mines.

In 1893, his line finally reached the Pacific. When a financial panic in 1893 toppled the Northern Pacific, Hill tried to buy it, too. Instead, it went to J.P. Morgan. Hill

The Union Pacific and the Central Pacific tracks joined at Promontory Point, Utah, on May 10, 1869.

of the rails" took place at Promontory Point near Ogden, Utah, on May 10, 1869.

The railroads received money (in the form of government bonds) for each mile of track laid. They also received land according to the following land grant system. Each railroad got a strip of land four hundred feet wide for the right of way for its tracks. It received in addition two sections of land on alternating sides of the tracks. Each railroad also received 1,280 acres of land for each mile of track it laid. So naturally the railroad companies were highly motivated to lay as much track as possible. The railroads could do whatever they wanted with the land they received. They held onto some lands. More often, however, they sold the lands next to their tracks to eager settlers. The money from the sales helped pay to build the railroad.

The Homestead Act of 1862 also helped railroads. The alternate parcels of land between the sections owned by the railroads belonged to the government. The government sold the land at low prices or made it available for free under the Homestead Act. Thus even more settlers and land speculators came into the region by means of the new railroad lines.

Building Other Lines

Because the men who invested in railroads accumulated enormous wealth, more companies soon sought railroad land grants. In 1864, Congress approved generous land grants to the Northern Pacific Railroad. Finished in 1883, the line joined Duluth, Minnesota, to Portland, Oregon, and Spokane and Tacoma, Washington.

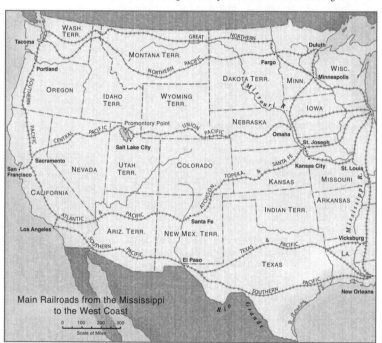

Main Railroads from the Mississippi to the West Coast

A common argument in support of a government-subsidized railroad is that the poor regions of the frontier could not have funded the railroads on their own. But it can be argued that the vast railroad network in the Northeast was not built with federal money. If given time, private enterprise will do a better job, more efficiently and less expensively. Use James J. Hill's Great Northern Railroad mentioned in the text as contemporary evidence that private funds *could* build an efficient railroad system. Have your students apply these lessons to the modern Amtrak system (a government-subsidized passenger rail service).

 CD: Directors of the Union Pacific Railroad

Refer to the CD for a photo of the Directors of the Union Pacific Railroad.

 CD: Leland Stanford of the Central Pacific Railroad

Refer to the CD for a photo of Leland Stanford.

In 1884, a grant to the Atchison, Topeka, and Santa Fe Railroad provided a more southerly route. Another grant allowed the Texas Pacific Railroad to build across Texas, linking to the Southern Pacific at El Paso. When that route was finished, New Orleans was linked by rail with Los Angeles and San Francisco. By 1900, the United States had five transcontinental railroads.

All of those railroads were built primarily with federal grants or subsidies. But **James J. Hill** proved that a large railroad could be built using only private funds. He bought up several railroads and created a line called the **Great Northern Railroad**. In addition to crossing the wheat belt of North Dakota and Montana, his line extended into Canada to help farmers there transport their products to American markets.

Hill not only refused to ask for government funds to build the railroad but also used a radical approach to building and operating it. Rather than climbing over or boring through mountains, his line went around mountains. This allowed him to run longer trains carrying heavier loads. He also kept operating costs low. When many other transcontinental lines went bankrupt in spite of their heavy government subsidies, Hill's Great Northern actually paid its investors a dividend of 5 percent. For his great achievement, Hill is called the "Empire Builder."

James J. Hill proved that a large, effective, and profitable railroad empire could be built without relying on government funds. He built the Great Northern using only private investments.

Technology

Another ingredient critical to the development of American industry was technology—scientific inventions and improved methods of doing things. A strong work ethic and ingenuity resulted in a remarkable ability of Americans to innovate. Americans, often without intending to, fulfilled God's command in Genesis to "subdue" the earth and "have dominion over" it. Many discoveries improved the lives of an increasing number of people. For example, some inventions, such as **Alexander Graham Bell**'s telephone, led to whole new industries and big changes in American life. Other simple inventions, such as rivets for points of stress in Levi Strauss's blue jeans, although minor, are still useful today. The number of patents issued by the U.S. Patent Office shot up, averaging more than 21,000 a year through the 1880s and 1890s.

The increased use of electricity was especially beneficial to the advancement of both industry and technology. **Thomas Edison** promoted the generation of electricity for practical uses. The harnessing of electricity led him to invent many electrical appliances. His incandescent light (light bulb) was among the most important of his 1,093 patented inventions.

Hundreds of other inventors also made important contributions to American industry. The Pullman car made long trips more comfortable with sleeper berths beginning in 1863. However, for the railroad industry, none was more important than **George Westinghouse**'s air brake for trains. That invention in 1869 saved many lives and prevented the loss of thousands of dollars of property.

Thomas Edison patented more than one thousand different inventions.

Edison's light bulb is symbolic of American inventiveness and ingenuity.

Edison Biography

A good source of additional information on the life and work of Thomas Edison is Neil Baldwin's biography *Edison: Inventing the Century.*

later negotiated a merger with Morgan to create the Chicago, Burlington, and Quincy, which ran from St. Louis to Chicago. That meant that Hill's railroads then linked the West Coast with Chicago, St. Louis, Omaha, and Denver. Hill was also involved in creating the Canadian Pacific Railway.

Some people hated Hill, claiming that he had gained his wealth unjustly at the expense of loggers, miners, and farmers. But others praised him as the man who unlocked the wealth of the Great Northwest. He explained his economic views and promoted "scientific agriculture" in a book he wrote titled *Highways of Progress*. When he died, he left an estate worth approximately $63 million.

Bell: Communication Pioneer

Alexander Graham Bell taught teachers of the deaf. As a result of his interest in technical devices to help the deaf, he envisioned the possibility of uniting two hearing aids. From that vision came his invention: the telephone.

Early phone systems were local. In 1892, the Bell Telephone Company formed the first long-distance telephone network, the American Telephone and Telegraph Company (AT&T). AT&T held almost total control of the communications industry until 1985, when the federal government forced it to break up into smaller units.

Edison: Electricity Pioneer

In 1878, Edison began experimenting to find a way to manufacture light bulbs. Edison applied the work ethic to invention, saying, "There is no substitute for hard work. Genius is one percent inspiration, and ninety-nine percent perspiration."

By the time he died in 1931, he owned more than a thousand patents. They included printing telegraph, electric printing machine, stencil pen, brake for electromagnetic motors, addressing machine, method for preserving fruit, vacuum pump, electro-magnetic railway, typewriter, junction box, locomotive for electric railway, process for nickel plating, rotary cement kiln, fluorescent electric lamp, apparatus for grinding coal, and sprocket-chain drive. Most of his inventions were improvements on existing inventions or processes. But a few of them—for example, the alkaline storage battery, the movie projector, and the phonograph—were innovations that led to whole new industries.

Section III
Objectives
Students should be able to

1. Define *capital* (in the economic sense).
2. Name three kinds of business organizations and describe the benefits and limitations of each.
3. Explain the way corporations obtained money to expand industry.
4. Define a trust.
5. Explain the significance of Andrew Carnegie and John D. Rockefeller to the growth of big business.

Andrew Carnegie: Steel

Carnegie's parents were penniless Scottish immigrants. Carnegie himself had spent his childhood as a bobbin winder in a textile factory, earning only twelve and one-half cents a day. In America he got a job as a railroad telegraph boy. Because he

---

Patents
The patent system protected inventions for seventeen years. This helped to encourage innovation.

Andrew Carnegie was a Scottish immigrant who became the world's wealthiest man—and then gave his money away for public causes such as libraries.

From Carnegie's "Gospel of Wealth"
This, then, is . . . the duty of the man of Wealth: First, to set an example of modest, unostentatious living, shunning display or extravagance; to provide moderately for the legitimate wants of those dependent upon him; and after doing so to consider all surplus revenues which come to him simply as trust funds, which he is called upon to administer, and strictly bound as a matter of duty to administer in the manner which, in his judgment, is best calculated to produce the most beneficial result for the community—the man of wealth thus becoming the sole agent and trustee for his poorer brethren, bringing to their service his superior wisdom, experience, and ability to administer—doing for them better than they would or could do for themselves.

Tragically, many Americans came to believe that technology could solve most, if not all, problems. This, along with a growing confidence in science, had a negative spiritual impact on our nation. Men looked to inventors and scientists rather than to God and His Word for answers. When science speculated on matters that disagreed with the Word of God, the Bible was often rejected in favor of scientific theories.

Section Quiz

1. Give three reasons for the difficulty of traveling long distances by rail.
2. What regions of the country did Cornelius Vanderbilt connect with his railroad empire?
3. What did the federal government give railroad companies to aid their building?
4. Name two key inventors of the period and the inventions for which they are best known.
★ What could be the potential danger(s) of railroad empires?

III. New Ways of Doing Business

American industry grew and increased production during the late 1800s. The growth was spurred by competition, new technology, and better management. Companies were constantly looking for ways to improve their production, but improvements often required investment money, or **capital**. Businesses began to find new ways to organize and to obtain capital.

Corporations for Increased Capital

In America's early years, most businesses were either **sole proprietorships** (businesses owned by one person) or **partnerships** (owned by two or more people). Both kinds worked well for small-scale operations.

Proprietorships had the advantages of catering to individual needs. The owner got all the profit, but he also absorbed all the losses and often lacked the funds to expand his business.

Partnerships had the distinct advantage of increasing capital in a business and of sharing the losses of the business. **Andrew Carnegie** built a huge steel empire (selling much of it to the railroads) with the help of multiple partners. They provided him with expertise in areas about which he knew little. He suggested that the epitaph on his tombstone should read: "Here lies a man who was able to surround himself with others far wiser than he."

A big disadvantage of a partnership was that the responsibility for all losses must be shared, even when they resulted from the faults or failures of just one partner. It could lead to the financial ruin of all the partners unless protective measures were taken. Other disadvantages were that all the partners had to participate in the business's legal dealings, and if one partner died or pulled out, the partnership ended.

Another way to organize a business is to incorporate, a method that became very popular in the late 1800s. A **corporation** is formed when a business gains a legal charter and sells stock to many indi-

---

Activity 2: Eyewitness Tells of "Last Spike Driving"

Use this activity to help students understand the events of the ceremonial driving of the "Golden Spike," completing the transcontinental railroad.

Section Quiz Answers

1. Most track was in the East. There were no railroad bridges across the Hudson, Ohio, or Mississippi rivers. And track width (gauge) varied from one set of tracks to another, preventing trains from traveling freely across the land.
2. the Great Lake states and New York City

3. money (government bonds) and land
4. Alexander Graham Bell—the telephone, Thomas Edison—the incandescent light (and other uses for electricity)
★ Large companies, having driven smaller companies out of business and gained a monopoly, raised their rates. This monopoly hurt the consumer as well as the small businessman.

 More on Carnegie
Three potentially useful sources of information on the life and philosophy of Andrew Carnegie are the following books:
- Harold C. Livesay, *Andrew Carnegie and the Rise of Big Business*
- David Nasaw, *Andrew Carnegie*
- Andrew Carnegie and Gordon Hutner, *The Autobiography of Andrew Carnegie and The Gospel of Wealth*

 Question of the Century— What Are the Keys to America's Industrial Success?

Why did the United States become the world's industrial giant? The answer to that

vidual investors. Although the stockholders are essentially the owners, they can lose only the amount they invested in the stock if the corporation fails. If the business makes a profit, the stockholders receive dividends, or payments from that profit.

A corporation is considered a "person" in the eyes of the law, and it can conduct legal dealings without all of its stockholders being present. Also, its existence is not ended by the death of a manager or single stockholder.

Because of such advantages—especially the opportunity to raise large sums of capital quickly—more executives sought to incorporate in the years after the Civil War. Steel, petroleum, and chemical manufacturers are but a few of the many who used the corporate form of business.

Sources of Corporate Money

Company executives realized that they needed large amounts of capital to finance the growth of their ventures. Some people with savings or other wealth became stockholders. The money with which they bought stock provided capital for the corporation. More capital, however, was raised in larger amounts from other sources.

The nation's banking system also helped provide industry with capital. As more Americans entered the work force and the number of businesses grew, the number of bank deposits increased. Banks invested their money in corporations to make more money. They also offered credit to corporations to cover the expansion of industry. Another large-scale source of capital came from life insurance companies that invested the premiums paid by policy holders.

Corporations Find New Ways to Organize

As the corporations grew larger, they needed better internal organization. America's early factories had few executives, usually just managers and bookkeepers. The new large-scale operations, however, required more management, so separate departments to handle each major phase of operations became normal. There were department heads for such responsibilities as purchasing, marketing,

Rockefeller on Money and Moneymaking

John D. Rockefeller became one of the world's richest men through his Standard Oil empire. Some people envied his wealth and tried to make him look bad. Some of them were competitors whom he had driven from business and ruined financially. Journalists called "muckrakers" were especially harsh in their criticism of Rockefeller. One of them asked him how much money would make him happy. He reportedly replied, "Just a little more."

To counter attacks and restore his public image, Rockefeller hired a public relations firm. Part of that campaign involved taking a photograph of him giving a shiny new dime to a little boy on the street. The photo was published in all of William Randolph Hearst's newspapers. The implied message was that Rockefeller was so compassionate that he freely gave money to strangers.

In fairness, some of Rockefeller's competitors had become wealthy when they sold out to him. Many of his managers and executives had also made a great deal of money working for him. Hundreds of workers had jobs in his huge business and were providing for their families. And Rockefeller did give away a lot of his money to the benefit of many people. Those people had a more positive view of Rockefeller. In discussing a biography that he wrote of Rockefeller, historian Ron Chernow concluded that "his good side was every bit as good as his bad side was bad. Seldom has history produced such a contradictory figure."

---

acted quickly to prevent an accident and kept traffic moving in his boss's absence, he was promoted.

Carnegie saved his money and looked for ways to invest it. He believed that steel would be needed to build America. Carnegie got his foot in the door in the steel industry when he invested in the Keystone Bridge Company. Its steel bridges were stronger and easier to construct than wooden bridges and soon replaced them.

Carnegie then started his own steel company, and new uses for the product made his business boom. Structural steel was soon used to build large buildings and even skyscrapers. Barbed wire replaced wooden fences. Wire nails took the place of forged nails. Railroads used steel for rails and railroad cars.

Carnegie was the first captain of industry who viewed productivity and wealth as a means to achieve social goals. He did not believe that his business success resulted just from his ability to beat the competition. He believed that America's industrial supremacy was also the result of the triumph of its form of government over a monarchy.

Carnegie believed that along with wealth came responsibility. He was a wise steward of the wealth he had gained. In his essay "The Gospel of Wealth," Carnegie addressed the duties of the wealthy. Carnegie believed each man had a responsibility to provide for his own family just as the Word of God teaches in 1 Timothy 5:8. Carnegie also believed that the wealthy had a duty to reinvest wealth back into society. "The man who dies . . . rich dies disgraced. Surplus wealth is a sacred trust which its possessor is bound to administer in his lifetime for the good of the community." (However, there is no indication that

---

question is the focus of this section of the chapter. Ask the students to recall the keys to American industrial growth outlined in this chapter—natural resources, immigrant laborers, transportation networks, technological developments, new ways of doing business (corporations), and the competition of capitalism (in the next section). Other nations around the world ask themselves what made American industry so great because they would like to imitate its "keys to success." What do the students consider the most important key to our country's success? (Answers will vary.) Is the United States likely to remain the world's industrial giant, or does another country have the keys necessary to surpass the United States? What aspects of modern American society and

economy might be weaknesses that make it possible for other countries to surpass the United States as the world's greatest industrial power? (Answers will vary.)

The World's Richest People

Forbes magazine publishes an annual list of the world's richest people (also available on its website). Make a photocopy of that list from *Forbes*, or download it from the Internet, and then discuss it in class. Note how the source of great income has changed as the cutting edge of industry has changed. Also raise issues about greed and the ever-present urge to become a millionaire. Proverbs 23:4 warns against setting out to become wealthy (i.e., making achieve-

ment of wealth one's priority), but wealth itself is not evil. Wealth should be seen as a tool to advance the kingdom of Christ (Luke 16:9).

Biggest Businesses Today

Look in a world almanac for the list of the one hundred leading U.S. businesses, along with the fastest-growing businesses (based on revenues). List the top ten or twenty-five businesses and discuss the categories they fall under. Which types of businesses have been around for more than a century? What is the newest type of business?

he ever accepted or promoted the true gospel.)

Carnegie practiced what he preached. He amassed a net worth of approximately $400 million and gave away almost one-third of it ($333 million). He gave the largest amount of it to found libraries. He funded 2,509 libraries in Great Britain, Australia, New Zealand, and the United States. Of those, 1,679 were in the United States and its territories.

John D. Rockefeller: Trust Innovator

During the Civil War, John D. Rockefeller, a bookkeeper in Cleveland, Ohio, was looking for an investment for his savings. Because he believed petroleum would have a role in America's growth, he invested in a refinery with a good profit record. He correctly guessed that the refinery business was the key to success in the oil industry. He also felt that small refineries were cutting profits and that such duplication was wasteful. In 1870, Rockefeller formed the Standard Oil Company by buying the various refineries in his area. He promised the railroads large-scale shipments if they would charge him reduced freight rates. On paper the railroad charged him the public rate, but they gave him a rebate, or "kickback," for each barrel of oil he shipped. Rockefeller's methods, though not illegal at the time, were unfair.

Within two years, Rockefeller had gained control of one-fourth of the refining industry. By 1910, Standard Oil controlled 90 percent of the nation's refineries and 92 percent of the crude oil supply from the Appalachians, the nation's major oil source at the time.

Increased urban population created crowded, unsanitary conditions such as those found in Mullen Alley in New York City.

Large factories produced equipment that allowed the operation of large industries. These workers are making electric railway motors at the Westinghouse Electric and Manufacturing Company.

accounting, financing, and development. Such specialized executives managed businesses more efficiently and made them more profitable.

In 1882, oilman **John D. Rockefeller** and his associates formed Standard Oil, the first **trust**. A trust combined several separate companies into one super-size corporation. The executives of the trust could organize and manage all of the combined companies as they wished. Other industries followed Rockefeller's example and set up trusts of their own in the 1880s.

Section Quiz

1. What is the difference between a proprietorship and a partnership?
2. Who built a huge steel empire by means of a partnership?
3. Name two sources of capital for corporations besides individuals.
4. What is a trust? Who formed the first business trust?
★ What problems of a proprietorship or partnership does a corporation avoid? How?

IV. Effects of Industrial Expansion

The growth of industries brought many changes in how Americans lived. It also changed how the government dealt with industry.

Changing American Life

First, America's trade increased greatly. American foodstuffs and factory products found their way to distant parts of the world. This trade also made many more products available to Americans.

Second, the city population increased greatly. Immigrants swelled the size of cities. As farming became more mechanized, increasing farm production, fewer farm workers were needed. Farmers—or at least several of their children—often moved to towns and cities where other types of jobs were available.

Industrialization magnified urban problems. Air and water pollution, overcrowding, and crime all became more obvious when they were concentrated in one area.

Industrialism also meant that Americans had more leisure time. Some machines freed people from certain types of work. Other machines, labor-saving devices, made work easier. Americans soon found ways to use their extra time. Some played sports. Others watched. New spectator sports like basketball, boxing, and baseball captured the public fancy. Bicycling and tennis also became popular.

Industrialism also affected American family life. Some women had worked outside the home during the Civil War. A few of them continued that work after the war. Others were recruited to work in new or expanding industries. Because inventions made housekeeping easier and less time consuming, some women found time to take other jobs. The number of women in the work force continued to grow in the years that followed, changing the lifestyle of more and more families.

 CD: Tenements of New York City

Refer to the CD for a photo of tenements in New York City.

Activity 3: Ways of Doing Business

Use this activity to help the students distinguish among sole proprietorships, partnerships, corporations, trusts, and holding companies and how they function.

Activity 4: Andrew Carnegie: The Gospel of Wealth, 1889

Use this activity to increase the students' understanding of Carnegie and his philosophy of wealth and philanthropy.

Section Quiz Answers

1. A proprietorship is owned by one person; a partnership is owned by two or more people.
2. Andrew Carnegie
3. banks and life insurance companies
4. a combination of several companies into one super-size corporation; John D. Rockefeller
★ It solves the need for capital by pooling the resources of a group of people. It avoids the potential for losing everything by limiting the amount of a person's loss to the amount of his investment. And it bypasses the legal problems involved in the loss of

a partner by viewing the corporation itself as a person that can continue to live even if stockholders change.

The Role of Economic History

Understanding the development of America's businesses is just as vital to a study of U.S. history as understanding America's exploration and wars. Calvin Coolidge claimed, "The business of America is business." Ask the students to consider the value of understanding the economic history of the United States. For one thing, history provides valuable lessons to young people entering modern businesses. It also gives voting citizens guidance during elections and civic debates.

The Focus on Capitalism

When the United States was founded, it had a capitalist economy. **Capitalism** is an economy in which people are free to invest and make profits on their investments. Businesses are owned by private citizens instead of by the government. Anyone can go into business, competing with others. In competing for personal gain, businesses usually try to sell good products or services so that the business can grow. Poor products or services drive customers away. Competition among businesses in such a capitalistic system helped Americans achieve a high standard of living.

But industrialization revealed some weaknesses in the capitalistic system. Man's evil nature caused some industrialists to run roughshod over their competitors. In some industries, workers labored long hours at dangerous work for low pay while company owners became millionaires. Owners sometimes ignored the biblical rule that "the labourer is worthy of his hire" (Luke 10:7).

During the rapid industrial growth, a philosophy that justified harsh actions became popular. People used Charles Darwin's theory of evolution to defend piling up wealth by any means one wanted. Darwin's theory said that there was a constant struggle in nature. Only the fittest members of the species would survive. Applied socially, this thinking was called **social Darwinism**. Social Darwinists showed little mercy and made no allowance for human weakness. In industry, social Darwinists held that driving weaker competitors out of business was just a part of the struggle for survival. Making a profit, according to their philosophy, might be accomplished by any means possible, even if others were hurt.

Such cruelty makes sense if one believes that humans are simply highly evolved animals. But humans are not animals; they are precious beings made in God's own image (Gen. 1:26-27). Since humans are image bearers of God, it is wrong for humans to be cruel to each other (James 3:9). Humans should instead work hard to make their business endeavors successful, but they should be motivated by a desire to honor God and to help their fellow humans. By freeing humans to make their own choices, a capitalistic system can help a society use labor and investments to serve God and others.

Closely tied to capitalism was the idea of *laissez-faire* economics. Most Americans believed that the best way for a capitalist economy to develop was without any government interference or regulation. Supporters of *laissez-faire* policies argued that government regulation would disturb the fine balance between supply of products and the public's demand for those products. The economy might be ruined. Yet, because individuals and some companies did not love their neighbors by righting wrongs or correcting injustices, people put more and more pressure on the government to do so. Americans grew fearful that large corporations were going to control the nation. They generally preferred that their elected representative in Congress take control instead.

Government Regulation of Business

Americans have long valued equality. The injustices of some business practices during this era challenged the American ideals of equality and justice. Americans turned to the government to regulate these practices. But this solution encroached on the American value of individualism. From this time on there has been a tension in

This 1881 political cartoon depicts monopoly as a snake threatening America's liberty. On the left, John Bull (Great Britain) is telling Uncle Sam (the United States) of the danger and pointing to the snake. On the right in the background, the Capitol is in the grip of the snake's tail.

Modern Economic Issues

Gather articles from newspapers and magazines on the economic issues that are debated today. Compare and contrast these debates with the ones at the end of the nineteenth century. (Note pollution, shortages, and garbage.) Discuss any antitrust suits, such as those against Microsoft (discussed on p. 401) and tobacco companies in the late 1990s.

What labor issues are most often in the news? Have the labor issues changed? Explain why labor unions declined so rapidly during the prosperity of the 1980s and 1990s. New technology allowed more and more Americans to operate their own businesses. Also, labor unions grow when labor-ers are struggling financially, but they shrink when the economy is good.

Debate Ideas

Have your students discuss and/or debate the following:

- Organized labor has increased the dignity of the individual American worker.
- The power to strike is critical to collective bargaining.
- The labor union's accomplishments for the individual worker are overrated.

Report on the Richest People in America

Have students prepare written or oral reports on the richest people in America, either historical people or current people listed in *Forbes* magazine. The main object of the reports is for the students to understand how the people got their wealth, their attitudes about wealth, and how their wealth has affected them.

Microsoft Antitrust Suit

The Sherman Act did not lose its relevance with the passing of the Industrial Age. In fact, the business world continues to feel its effects today. In the 1990s, it was the basis for a lawsuit by the Department of Justice against computer giant Microsoft Corporation.

Microsoft attracted attention by attaching its Internet Explorer web browser to its Windows operating system. The Justice Department said that Microsoft was trying to use an already illegal monopoly in the operating systems market to establish a monopoly in Internet browsers. The idea was that if computer users received a web browser automatically with their operating system, they would not examine other products. That browser could then control a good portion of Internet traffic.

The Justice Department claimed that Microsoft was violating the Sherman Act in two points. First, the company had entered into agreements with computer manufacturers and service providers that required those companies to use Microsoft operating systems exclusively. Second, they had enforced their monopoly through the pressure of their power in the marketplace.

Two other large companies faced antitrust suits in the latter 1900s. AT&T was on trial from 1974 to 1982, at which time it agreed to stop certain activities in exchange for the dropping of all charges. IBM faced thirteen years of litigation, from 1969 to 1982. The case was finally dismissed, but the company did make some concessions that led to a freer computer market.

American political life between individualism and the government's role in ensuring equality and justice in society.

The Interstate Commerce Act of 1887

Ruthless competition among railroads had hurt small shippers and western farmers. So citizens who were dependent on the railroads—such as farmers—demanded government regulation of railroad rates.

Initially, states set up commissions to regulate the rates railroads could charge. Midwestern states such as Illinois and Iowa provided strong enforcement, but other states, such as Massachusetts and Alabama, only gave advisory opinions. Disputes grew as the rulings of some states affected railroad transportation in other states.

When the Supreme Court ruled that states could regulate railroads only within their own state boundaries, not those crossing state lines, Congress felt pressure to act. In 1887, the **Interstate Commerce Act** was passed. This first industry-regulating law was a direct reaction to the unjust practices of the railroads. It directed railroads to set "reasonable and just rates." It also prevented railroads from charging more for short runs that involved little competition than for long runs involving stiff competition.

The **Interstate Commerce Commission** (ICC) was formed to examine complaints and, when necessary, take offenders to court. But when the offenders came to court, the judges usually decided in favor of the railroads. The ICC lost nearly every case filed from 1887 to 1906. Yet the act had an impact since some companies changed their policies to avoid investigations and costly court cases. It set a precedent for the government to organize other independent regulatory agencies. And in later years, as Supreme Court judges changed and more closely reflected public opinion toward business practices, court cases made regulation more effective.

The Sherman Anti-Trust Act of 1890

The public was suspicious of trusts. They felt that their size and power gave them an unfair edge that harmed free enterprise. Large trusts such as Rockefeller's had driven small companies out of business by lowering prices. Once the competition was gone, prices reached new highs. By 1880, both political parties promised to regulate trusts.

In 1890, during Benjamin Harrison's presidency, Congress passed the **Sherman Anti-Trust Act**. The act said, "Every contract, combination in the form of trust or otherwise, or conspiracy . . . in restraint of trade or commerce . . . is declared to be illegal." But since "restraint of trade" was not defined and the courts still favored big business, the act had little effect at first. Its effects were also weakened when trusts devised ways to get around it.

A new form of business consolidation, the **holding company**, was born. The holding company gained control of companies by buying their stock. While member companies kept their names, the holding company made decisions for them in the interest of the entire group, as if it were one giant corporation. The holding companies controlled the businesses as efficiently as the trusts had before them.

Development of Labor Unions

The industrial era also led to the birth of labor unions. Abuses in some factories opened the door to organized protests by the workers.

Many of them began to organize in large groups called **unions** that could stand up to management and demand better wages and working conditions. Although unions showed spurts of growth in this era, it was often uneven. Their advance was hindered by competition for jobs among war veterans and immigrants. Economic depressions occurred in 1873, 1882, and 1893, further limiting union growth.

The Knights of Labor

Uriah P. Stephens began the **Knights of Labor** in 1869. His goal was to form one big union for all workers—skilled and unskilled, men and women. He sought equal pay for men and women, an eight-hour day for workers, safety features, and compensation (payment for loss) for injuries occurring on the job. In 1879, Terence V. Powderly took over the union's leadership. He opposed strikes and believed that the union should not take sides politically. The membership rose from 9,000 in 1879 to 115,000 by 1884. By 1886 the Knights had a membership of 700,000.

But 1886 was a bad year for unions. In Chicago about 80,000 workers, mostly Knights, went on strike for an eight-hour day. The police killed several workers when things got out of hand. Some anarchists (people who oppose government and promote political disorder and confusion) staged a protest rally. The police moved in to break up the meeting. Someone threw a bomb into the crowd, killing a policeman and six spectators. A riot occurred, and eleven more people were killed. The **Haymarket Square Riot**, as it was called, hurt the reputation of the unions because people then linked the union with violence. Membership dropped to just 100,000 in four years.

The American Federation of Labor

A second union, the **American Federation of Labor** (AFL), began in 1881. Its first president was a British-born cigar maker, **Samuel Gompers**. Gompers saw a weakness in the structure of the Knights of Labor and set up his union with different membership requirements. Only skilled workers could join, and dues were high. Women were not allowed to join. Workers joined local craft unions with other people in the same skills. Those local unions then affiliated or associated with state and national groups. Each local union, however, made its own decisions and handled its own funds. The national group provided guidelines.

The AFL also pushed for an eight-hour day and **collective bargaining** (the right of unions to represent workers in negotiations with owners and managers). The AFL did use the threat of strikes. It also used its high membership dues to support the workers when they were on strike and not earning wages. A violent strike over a wage cut at Carnegie Steel's Homestead Plant in 1892 greatly hurt the AFL's attempt to organize in other industries.

Responses to Unions

Employers often opposed unions and their demands. They wanted the right to bargain with workers individually and hated strikes because they hurt production. Courts also opposed unions and often issued **injunctions**, official court orders, to stop strikes, particularly claiming that strikes "restrained trade." The local press also usually sided with employers. Since most of the papers made their money from local advertising, they could ill afford to anger their advertisers. The general public reacted negatively to unions

Samuel Gompers was instrumental in starting the American Federation of Labor.

Views on Labor Unions

The American Federation of Labor and Congress of Industrial Organizations (AFL-CIO) is a voluntary federation of national and international labor unions. It was created in 1955 by a merger of the AFL and the CIO.

The federation is interested in acquiring for its members good wages and benefits and more input from workers in management decisions at work. It supports political activism and community service at home. It also wants to be influential globally in the promotion of its goals (e.g., ending child labor). It wants fairer treatment for all groups, regardless of their race, sex, sexual preference, or any other area of difference.

A voice that speaks against labor unions is the National Right to Work Legal Defense Foundation. That organization works for people who do not want to be forced to join labor unions. It contends that labor unions have undue economic and political influence. Employees should not have to pay dues to support causes they do not agree with or pay fines for acts they committed while being forced into membership. They want to inform employees of legal decisions such as *NLRB v. General Motors Corp.*, which ruled that workers could be forced to pay only "financial core" fees to unions. Those fees support only activities that involve bargaining for workplace issues (wages, benefits, and production decisions); they cannot be used for political or social agendas. (Information on both of these organizations can be found at their websites online.)

because they associated union goals, such as the redistribution of wealth and agitation by lower classes, with socialism. Some people also opposed collective bargaining because it could deprive an individual of his own worth and prevent him or her from making his own choices.

In 1893, a group of employers formed the National Association of Manufacturers to counteract unionism. In 1900, the National Civic Federation was formed. Its leaders, Frank Easley and Marcus Hanna,

Johnstown Flood: The Nightmare of 1889

One of the great disasters in American history occurred in Pennsylvania in 1889. More than two thousand people died in the mining town of Johnstown and in some smaller towns to its north. The killer was a flood resulting from the breaking of an old, neglected earthen dam. To some, however, the killer was actually the negligence of a group of millionaires who owned the dam and refused to make repairs they knew were necessary. These wealthy families were too busy enjoying the lake resort and the hunting and fishing spot created by the formation of Lake Conemaugh (KAHN uh MAW), at the time the largest artificial lake in the world.

The lake was three miles long, one mile wide, and in places one hundred feet deep. It contained twenty million tons of water. The earthen dam, located fourteen miles from Johnstown and at an elevation four hundred feet higher than the town, was thirty-seven years old. It stretched three hundred yards wide and seventy-two feet deep. It was wide enough at the top for a two-lane dirt road. To keep the fish in the lake, the spillways had been closed off. The overflow valves had clogged because of neglect. The few repairs that had been made on the dam had been done by stuffing tree stumps, leaves, and straw into the numerous leaks that had developed since the dam's construction. Several engineers had warned the owners of the dam's deteriorated condition. One company had even offered to pay half the cost

of repairing the structure. Yet nothing had been done.

The people in the towns below had become indifferent as well. They had heard so many times that the dam was breaking that they had lost all concern. No one could convince them that the dam would actually break someday. And even if it did break, they did not believe that the result would be disastrous.

At 3:10 p.m. on May 31, 1889, it happened. After a number of heavy storms, the dam burst. In thirty-five minutes, all twenty million tons of Lake Conemaugh came rushing down the valley in a wave forty feet high and traveling at forty miles an hour. At times it met an obstruction and the water piled higher, once up to ninety feet, and then it burst through again to rush down on the towns below. Along the way it picked up debris that became as deadly as the wall of water itself: twenty-nine locomotives weighing up to eighty tons each, other railroad cars, boiling hot water from the iron works, hundreds of miles of barbed wire from a factory, the bricks and lumber from crushed houses and businesses, along with trees and animals. Because of the debris, the water at the top of the flood wave moved faster than the water at the bottom. Engineers estimated that the crushing force caused by that difference in speeds was as great as the power behind the water flowing over Niagara Falls. Nothing could stand in its way.

Had it not been for the heroic efforts of many of the townspeople, many more lives would have been

lost than actually were. Those who managed to escape the flood stood on the edge and hauled other people out. Some in buildings on the edge of the waters pulled others through windows to the safety of the buildings. Some people even leaped into the rushing waters to make rescues.

Every town along the flood's path was flattened. Finally, the waters were stopped at a bridge in Johnstown, where the debris piled up thirty feet high and covered sixty acres. Behind the debris, Johnstown had become a twenty-foot-deep lake. Then, to make matters worse, the debris caught fire. Some that had escaped drowning but were pinned in the rubble were killed by the fire. Nearly one thousand people were never found.

America and the world came to the aid of the survivors. Clara Barton and her newly formed American Red Cross reacted magnificently to their first major disaster. People from all over the world donated money and food for the needy. The millionaires who owned the lake did little except go into hiding to avoid the press.

In a remarkably short time, Johnstown was rebuilt and again became a thriving iron and steel town. A coroner's investigation held the dam's owners responsible for the flood, but few people sued and no one won a suit against the millionaires. The total damages, staggering in 1889, came to seventeen million dollars. None of the survivors would ever forget the tragic day when neglect and indifference brought a rushing wall of death into unprepared Johnstown, Pennsylvania.

 ### The Beginnings of Modern Marketing

Ask students to volunteer to research and report, either orally or in writing, on the rise of department stores in the late nineteenth and early twentieth centuries. You might assign different students to research Marshall Field, John Wanamaker, R.H. Macy, and J.C. Penney. Discuss with the entire class the differences and similarities between the early versions of those stores and their namesakes today.

The "Golden Rule" Store

J.C. Penney's department store became known as the "Golden Rule" store because he tried to run his stores according to the Golden Rule. Read more about Penney and his business and life philosophy in his autobiography, *Fifty Years with the Golden Rule*.

 ### John Wanamaker, Christian Businessman

John Wanamaker, founder of Wanamaker's department store, was a Christian businessman and Sunday school worker. You can read more about his life and work in *The Business Biography of John Wanamaker: Founder and Builder, America's Merchant*

Pioneer from 1861–1922 by Joseph Herbert Appel.

believed that labor unions were here to stay. The choice then became what kind of union employers would work with. They discouraged anticapitalist, socialist, revolutionary unions. But they encouraged conservative, pro-capitalist unions.

The Dangers of Materialism

Another result of industrialism was an increase in wealth, both nationally and individually. By 1900, the nation had four hundred millionaires. The buying power of the average worker had increased by 50 percent over forty years. People of all classes were living better than they had before. Some people had money to spend on nonessentials.

God's Word does not denounce wealth or money. God promised material blessing to Israel if that nation would keep the covenant He had made with them (Deut. 8:6–10). But in that same passage, God warned the people that their prosperity could cause them to forget Him. The love of money is the source of all kinds of evil (greed and envy, for example; 1 Tim. 6:10). Jesus warned people against making the treasures they collect on earth their god. "Ye cannot serve God and mammon," He said (Matt. 6:24). Instead, wealth is a tool to be used in ways that please God. God's work has first claim on the fruits of one's labor (Prov. 3:9). Scripture also encourages people to work hard so that they can meet their families' needs and also have extra to give to help others (Eph. 4:28). Some of the wealthy became philanthropists (those who give to help those in need). Doubtless, many of them saw philanthropy as a good work that would help them gain merit with God and men. Others had genuinely Christian motives and invested some of their wealth in building churches, contributing to missions, and caring for the sick and needy.

Sadly, in the industrial era, many Americans were not satisfied despite increasing their wealth. They wanted and sought more. Some of the rich competed with one another in showing off their wealth. **Materialism**, putting a higher value on money and possessions than on God and Christlikeness, became a significant American problem. Proverbs 30:8 provides the Christian with the correct attitude toward wealth: "Give me neither poverty nor riches; feed me with food convenient for me."

Section Quiz

1. List five major changes in America that resulted from industrial growth.
2. What is capitalism?
3. How was social Darwinism applied to industry?
4. What industry was regulated by the Interstate Commerce Act of 1887?
5. Why did labor unions emerge? Name two of the earliest ones.
☆ What two core American values were in conflict during this period of U.S. history? What was the cause of this conflict?
☆ How one spends money can reveal one's priorities in life. Give examples of wise and unwise use of money during this period of history.

Department Stores

One development of the nineteenth century that fed Americans' desire for things was the transformation of shopping through the creation of department stores. Department stores offered everything from the practical to the most luxurious of goods, all under one roof. To lure customers inside, stores arranged attractive displays of merchandise in their windows.

Marshall Field of Chicago was one of the giants in the industry. His customers were treated like royalty, regardless—to his credit—of their financial status. Doormen greeted them as they entered the store, and hundreds of workers were available to wait on them and answer their questions. A tearoom offered a nice luncheon for weary shoppers. Company wagons delivered purchases, and unsatisfactory items could be returned. With these enticements, it is no wonder that the consumer was eager to buy.

John Wanamaker opened a store with his name in Philadelphia. Like Field, he introduced many customer-friendly features, including a huge pipe organ on which musicians gave free concerts both during and after regular business hours. Wanamaker was a pioneer in the Sunday school movement in Philadelphia and applied many Christian principles to his business operations.

Another prominent department store pioneer was **J.C. Penney**. He introduced a one-price policy—no haggling or dickering; the customer paid the price marked. He also instituted a liberal return policy if a customer was dissatisfied with the product—no questions asked. He chose to operate his store by the Golden Rule, and

Section Quiz Answers

1. Trade increased; urbanization occurred; urban problems became more noticeable; Americans had more leisure time; and family life changed as many women worked in factories.

2. an economy in which businesses are privately owned, competition is open, and people are free to invest and make profits

3. Profits became most important. Eliminating weaker competitors was just part of the struggle for survival.

4. the railroad industry

5. because of the abuses in some factories (in wages and working conditions); the Knights of Labor and the American Federation of Labor

☆ Equality and individualism; Americans believed that all people should be treated with justice (this is part of equality). When businesses acted unjustly, the government began to regulate businesses. But government regulation encroached on the rights of individuals.

☆ Answers will vary.

Activity 5: Chapter Review

Use this activity to help the students review the chapter in preparation for the test.

Chapter Review Idea

For homework or in class, have the students write ten questions from the text. The questions should include three *who* questions, three *what* questions, two *how* questions, and one *why* question. (You may want them to write the *who* and *what* questions on one piece of paper and the *how* and *why* questions on another piece.) When the students hand in their papers, have them stack the *who* and *what* pages in one pile and the *how* and *why* pages in another.

Divide the class in half by numbering off by twos. Have the "ones" move to one side of the room and the "twos" to the other. Decide which team will answer first. Explain that the *who* and *what* questions will be worth

it quickly became known as the "Golden Rule store."

Christian Principles

During this era it was not uncommon for non-Christians to run their businesses according to Christian principles. This is one of the benefits of a society strongly influenced by Christian ideas. However, one of the dangers of such a society is the possibility of unsaved people thinking they are right with God simply because they live by "Christian principles."

People, Places, and Things to Remember:

lodes
Ellis Island
Exclusion Act of 1882
religious pluralism
consolidation
Cornelius Vanderbilt
Union Pacific
Central Pacific
James J. Hill
Great Northern Railroad
Alexander Graham Bell
Thomas Edison
George Westinghouse
capital
sole proprietorships
partnerships
Andrew Carnegie
corporation
John D. Rockefeller
trust
capitalism
social Darwinism
Interstate Commerce Act
Interstate Commerce Commission
Sherman Anti-Trust Act
holding company
unions
Knights of Labor
Haymarket Square Riot
American Federation of Labor
Samuel Gompers
collective bargaining
injunctions
materialism

Chapter Review 17

Review Questions

Write the word or phrase that best completes each sentence.

1. A business owned by just one person is called a ____.
2. Businesses need large amounts of money or ____ to finance their operations.
3. The Interstate Commerce Act was intended to regulate some of the abuses in the ____ industry.
4. Union members wanted ____ so that the union could negotiate with owners and management.
5. Many of America's turn-of-the-century immigrants landed first at ____.
6. A ____ is an advantageous business organization assembled under a charter by individual stockholders.
7. The theory of ____ was used to support the idea that the biggest and best businesses would survive while others would fall.
8. Uriah P. Stephens first led an early labor union called the ____.
9. The ____ was legislation intended to break up the unfair advantages of trusts.
10. The first transcontinental railroad was completed at ____.

Match these men with their achievements.

11. Alexander Graham Bell
12. Andrew Carnegie
13. Thomas Edison
14. Samuel Gompers
15. John D. Rockefeller
16. Cornelius Vanderbilt

a. invented the incandescent light bulb
b. formed a trust in the oil industry
c. consolidated railroads in the Northeast
d. invented the telephone
e. built a huge steel empire
f. president of the American Federation of Labor

Critical Thinking

1. Should government place controls on industries? Explain your answer.
2. Why is materialism dangerous for those blessed with wealth? How can wealthy people avoid materialism?

---

100 points and the *how* and *why* questions will be worth 200 points. A wrong answer deducts fifty points. When the class period is over, the team with the highest number of points wins.

Chapter Review Answers

Review Questions

1. sole proprietorship
2. capital
3. railroad
4. collective bargaining
5. Ellis Island
6. corporation
7. social Darwinism
8. Knights of Labor
9. Sherman Anti-Trust Act
10. Promontory Point, Utah
11. d
12. e
13. a
14. f
15. b
16. c

Critical Thinking

1. Answers will vary. Because men are sinful, employers will tend to take advantage of their employees, so some regulation is probably necessary. However, the government might abuse its power if given too much authority.

2. Materialism is dangerous for those blessed with wealth because the pleasures gained through the things wealth can provide may crowd out the pleasures gained through close fellowship with God. Wealth also may cause people to think they are self-dependent rather than dependent on God. Wealthy people can avoid materialism by recognizing that wealth is a gift from God and by treating wealth as a tool to be used in service to God and for the benefit of others.

Although the developing West was often wild, settlers enforced law and order to tame it.

CHAPTER 18

The Last Frontier

I. **The Miners**

II. **The Cowboys**

III. **The Homesteaders**

IV. **The Outlaws and the Lawmen**

V. **The Indians**

Chapter Goals

Students should be able to

1. Identify the four main groups that conflicted over land in the West.

2. Define and use the basic terms of the chapter.

3. Compare and contrast the settling of the West with the settling of the original colonies.

4. Trace the patterns of development and settlement of the West for farming, ranching, and mining.

5. Identify profit as the main motive for frontier settlement.

6. Explain the evolution of U.S. Indian policy and the Indian wars and the ongoing problems that those events created.

Chapter Motivation

Ask your students if they think that Americans today would go to an uninhabited planet to homestead if the government were making available free or inexpensive land there. Ask them to explain their answers. In what other countries would people be more likely to take the opportunity to receive free land? *(China, India, and other agrarian and heavily populated societies)* Contrast American society today and American society in the mid-1800s.

Chapter 18 Lesson Plan Chart			
Section Title	**Main Activity**	**Pages**	**Days**
I. The Miners	Activity 1: Mining Methods in the Old West	347–48	1–2 days
II. The Cowboys	Activity 2: A Cowboy in Dodge City, 1882	349–53	2–3 days
III. The Homesteaders	Activity 3: Ranchers and Farmers Collide in Nebraska, 1884	354–58	1–2 days
IV. The Outlaws and the Lawmen	Activity 4: The Death of Billy the Kid, 1881	358–60	1–2 days
V. The Indians	Activity 5: Massacre at Wounded Knee, 1890	360–62	1–2 days
TOTAL SUGGESTED DAYS (INCLUDING 1 DAY FOR REVIEW AND TESTING)			**7–12 DAYS**

MATERIALS LIST

SECTION I

• Copy of Frederick Jackson Turner's essay "The Frontier Thesis"

• Short story by Bret Harte

• Samples of jewelry, gold, silver

• Paper play money

• Activity 1 from the *Student Activities* manual

SECTION II

• Cassette tape or CD of songs of the Old West

• CD: Grover Cleveland, 22nd and 24th President; Benjamin Harrison, 23rd President; Party Platforms, 1884

The term *frontier* refers to the outer fringe of settlement. America's frontier had moved gradually west. First, men moved across the Appalachians. Then they moved on to the Mississippi River. The next frontier, however, was the far West. The discovery of gold and rich lands on the West Coast had lured numbers of settlers west. They had bypassed much of the land from the Mississippi River, across the Great Plains and over the Rocky Mountains, to the Great Basin. These areas remained unsettled until after the Civil War.

Americans now began to migrate West in ever increasing numbers. However, this migration was not to an unoccupied region. The settlers encountered a variety of Indian tribes with a rich diversity of cultures and a total population perhaps exceeding 300,000. In the Southwest, tribes such as the Hopis, Navajos, and Pueblos practiced agriculture. Indian tribes to the North, such as the Chinook and Yurok hunted deer, elk, and moose. The Yakimas and other tribes harvested large quantities of salmon from the rivers. Along the Pacific Coast, the Tlingits hunted and gathered food from the abundant coastal resources. While the removal of these native populations was not inevitable, the Indian way of life would certainly suffer greatly because of the American migration.

The West presented many hindrances to settlement. Western explorers and settlers in wagon trains crossing the plains and deserts believed that the hard soil was not fertile. The climate seemed unsuitable too. The winters were cold, and the summers almost unbearably hot. Even worse, rainfall was scarce. Many areas received less than twenty inches of rain a year. Good water supplies were rarely available to make up for the lack of rainfall. The flow of most of the rivers and the underground water supply rose and fell with the amount of precipitation.

A further hindrance to settlement was the lack of trees on the plains. Not only would it be hard for settlers to get used to the glaring sun, but they could not build the log cabins and wooden houses that had been their homes in the East.

Despite these many discouragements, and an already present Native American population, Americans were committed to settling the West. Going west appealed to people's rugged individualism and desire for growth. In the West a man could determine his own destiny. Free from the constraints of Eastern society, people were able to work hard and enjoy the fruits of their own labor and ingenuity.

Technological advances enabled the move westward. The transcontinental railroad brought change to the Great Plains. With that new form of transportation, people and agricultural products moved easily across the grasslands. As the railroads crisscrossed the prairies, the vast herds of buffalo on which the nomadic Indians depended declined. Railroad crews shot buffalo for meat, both to prevent the buffalo from damaging the track and for the sheer sport.

People of many different nations settled the West. Most of the settlers were whites of European descent. Most notable were the Germans, Irish, and Scandinavians, who settled in remote areas such as the Dakotas. Asians, especially Chinese, came to work on the railroads. More than 200,000 Chinese came between 1876 and 1890. By 1880, as many as 26,000 blacks also had migrated from the South to Kansas. Called "Exodusters," in connection with their Old Testament counterparts, they were fleeing segregation in the South and trying to start life anew in the West. More than half a million blacks lived west of the Mississippi River by that time.

Vast numbers of buffalo herds roamed the Western plains until settlers and city and railroad developers began to threaten their existence.

- Recording of an original radio episode of *The Lone Ranger*
- Books on art of the Old West
- Activity 2 from the *Student Activities* manual

SECTION III
- Materials for making an authentic piece of needlework (cross-stitch, crewel, quilting, etc.) or a completed piece to show in class
- Activity 3 from the *Student Activities* manual

SECTION IV
- Books on outlaws and lawmen of the Old West
- Activity 4 from the *Student Activities* manual

SECTION V
- Eyewitness Book *North American Indians* by David Murdoch
- October 1992 issue of *National Geographic*
- CD: Posters for Buffalo Bill's Wild West Show
- Activities 5 and 6 from the *Student Activities* manual

Core Values
The West epitomizes the core values of individualism, liberty, equality, and growth. The cowboy remains the symbol of the rugged American individual. In American mythology the West is the place where people are free to roam and are free to make a new life for themselves apart from the inequalities of the more structured East. The story of the West is also a story of the growth of the nation. It is the story of the spread of railroads, towns, and families.

Sadly, the desire for growth unrestricted by biblical values can often turn into greed. The West is thus also a story of greed—of men greedy for gold and land. As a result of this greed the American Indians were deprived of their liberty and equality. Time and again, treaties were broken, lands were taken, and the Indians were confined to smaller and smaller reservations.

Americans must continually examine their national values in light of the Word of God.

New inventions and pioneer flexibility also aided the plains settler in his quest to thrive on the prairie. Although earlier writers predicted it would take seventy-five to a hundred years to settle the remaining lands, by 1890 the frontier was closed. The large open spaces of the West became symbolic of American growth and optimism. Tragically, this growth often led to greed. Much of the history of this period is the story of some Americans denying others equality and justice in order to acquire more land or gold. Throughout this story, the native peoples of the West were repeatedly abused.

I. The Miners

The first large incursion of settlers into native populated areas occurred in 1848, when the discovery of gold drew thousands of people to California. When the California gold fields had no more to offer, prospectors turned to other jobs or moved elsewhere to seek their fortunes. Some wandered into the mountain areas of the West that had known few explorers. Many of those people were not disappointed by what they found. For about a generation, the region yielded new riches.

Riches in the West

Several new strikes of gold and silver brought miners to the West. The first big strike occurred in 1859 near Pikes Peak in Colorado, which was then part of the Kansas Territory. Many prospectors raced across the prairie with "Pike's Peak or Bust!" written on their wagons. That strike made few men rich, but it brought attention to the region.

James Finney and Henry Comstock mined gold in northern Nevada, where they struck an even richer vein. At ground level they made $5.00 a day. Two feet down, their take rose to $20.00 a day. At a depth of four feet, they hit heavy blue-black sand. It had gold in it, but the gold did not seem as pure because it was being affected by a blue substance. They did not know what the blue mineral was. Finney and Comstock did not initially realize that they had found the northern end of a rich **lode**, or deposit, of precious metal. They soon learned that the "blue stuff" was nearly pure silver. Over the next thirty years, the **Comstock Lode** yielded more than $400 million worth of precious metals. Fifty-five percent of the wealth was from silver, forty-five percent from gold.

Farther north, the Fraser and Columbia river valleys also yielded rich finds. Strikes in Idaho and Montana along the Bitterroot and Salmon rivers also attracted thousands of miners. Gold was discovered in Helena and Butte, Montana, in 1864. In the 1880s, copper mines were developed in Butte as well. The city is built over a vein that was one mile deep.

In 1876, two soldiers with prospecting experience discovered gold in the Black Hills of South Dakota, an area that belonged to the Sioux Indians. Fortune seekers ignored that fact and soon invaded the area. Although the army had been sent to keep the whites out, it did not. When the government tried to buy back the land from the Sioux—land they had just given them in 1868—two wars with the Sioux followed. Nevertheless, the miners got their claim. The resulting **Homestake Mine** became the world's richest single gold mine.

Miners in the West used various methods to isolate the valuable ores, including the cradle-and-rocker method.

Mining the West

Scale of Miles
0   100   200   300

Columbia R. Ft. Colville
Missouri R.
Walla Walla   Salmon R.   Butte   Helena
Placerville   Bonanza   Deadwood / Black Hills
Silver City   Snake R.
South Pass
Salt Lake City
Virginia City / Comstock Lode   Leadville   Denver
Colorado R.   Pikes Peak
• Santa Fe

◐ Gold
◐ Silver
◐ Gold & Silver

MEXICO

Section I
Objectives

Students should be able to

1. Explain why the Great Plains, Rocky Mountains, and most of the Great Basin were not settled until after the Civil War.
2. Describe the development of mining towns.
3. Describe the various methods used by gold miners during the gold rush days in the West.
4. Explain Westerners' reasons for wanting money backed by silver.

The Log Flume

Strong mine shafts were essential to the safety of a mine. Rotted timbers could easily cause a cave-in, so mine operators had a regular need for new logs to fix potential problems. Sawmills at the top of mountains often provided the logs needed by the mines in the earth below. A quick means of getting those logs from one place to the other was a log flume.

The flume was a chute through which water flowed. The logs were placed in the flume at the top of the mountain, and gravity and the flowing water carried them to the mine below, often at high speeds. It was a generally efficient means of moving the logs to where they were needed.

An 1875 event foreshadowed a future use of the log flume. On a dare, reporter H. J. Ramsdell went with four other men for a wild ride down the flume in an improvised boat. Similar to a log ride in a modern-day amusement park, the flume carried the men down the mountain at breakneck speed. James Flood, one of the riders and part owner of the mine, declared that he

---

The Frontier Thesis

Briefly mention historian Frederick Jackson Turner's "Frontier Thesis" concerning the growth of the American West. If you can obtain a copy of his paper by this title, consider sharing some key excerpts from it with the class.

Bring in Samples of Jewelry

Bring in some samples of gold and silver, and explain why these metals are so valuable (scarcity, beauty, durability).

Share Experiences with Panning

If you or any of the students have experience with panning or mining (e.g., at a tourist attraction), share your experiences in class.

Get-Rich-Quick Schemes

Scheming to get rich quickly, many Americans throw their money into investments that promise fabulous returns. Ask the students whether they know any Bible verses on acquiring quick wealth (e.g., through gambling). (See 1 Timothy 6:6–10.)

Explain to the students that prudent businessmen and bankers usually made more profit from the gold than the miners. Even today, extracting raw materials from the ground is not nearly as profitable as wise investment of money in manufacturing and services. Countries with some of the greatest mineral reserves, such as the Democratic Republic of Congo, are some of the poorest, as different groups war over control of the mineral fields. But the countries that supply the expertise to manufacture goods from the products, such as Japan, are among the wealthiest countries. Abundance of natural resources is clearly not the main reason for America's economic success.

would not make the trip again if he were given the entire mine.

Gold Standard

Describe the gold standard by explaining that every dollar in circulation was either an actual gold piece worth a dollar or other money that was backed by a dollar's worth of gold in the nation's treasury. In other words, the money in circulation was limited to the amount of gold either held by the treasury or circulated in coins. There was a fixed amount of money.

The "silverites" wanted to increase that amount by adding money backed by silver in a similar way to that backed by gold. Because the West had a lot of silver from its mines, such an act would automatically make that region seem "richer." The eventual practical effect, however, was higher prices, which are the natural economic consequence of inflation (an increase in the money supply).

Mining Camps and Boom Towns

Some miners came west alone. But for safety and economy in buying supplies, mining guidebooks suggested four-man companies. Miners gathered in makeshift mining camps, where they lived in tents or hastily constructed brush arbors.

They staked claims quickly. To keep a claim, a miner had to work it one day out of every three. If a miner did not show up after ten days, someone else could take the claim. Of course, the mining claims were not really official because the miners did not own the land. They depended on claim societies that they had organized to protect their interests.

As more people came, businesses came with them. Supply stores and saloons were usually the first such businesses. Soon after, a meeting would be called to plan a town. Streets were drawn out and a town name picked. Lots were drawn for home sites. A church, a school, a miner's union hall, and processing mills for ore soon dotted the town's horizon. Where services were lacking, enterprising people could just about name their own fees. For example, one woman made $18,000 in one year just baking pies for the miners.

A few people made fortunes in mining. Many more made only a living. If the ore ran out or prices dropped, the mines closed down. Often miners, storekeepers, hotel owners, newsmen, and their families left when a mine closed. If everyone left, the empty buildings became weather-beaten over the years and became known as ghost towns. In addition to the mining towns, other ghost towns resulted from abandoned railroad towns, cow towns, lumber towns, and even farm towns across the West.

Silver and the Currency System

The mining of silver and gold aided the growth of the nation's economy. From before the Civil War until 1873, the government had minted both gold and silver coins. Those coins were the nation's money during that time, along with the greenbacks (paper money) printed during the war. When both the greenbacks and the silver coins were phased out, however, the money supply rested on its gold. The country was on the "gold standard."

Naturally, the price of silver plunged sharply once the government quit buying it for coins. Miners were disappointed by this action, and so were many other Westerners. The public began to pressure Congress for legislation that would put into circulation money that was backed by both silver and gold. They wanted more money (which would cause inflation) because they believed it would be easier for them to buy goods and to pay off old debts.

Finally, in 1878, Congress passed the **Bland-Allison Act**. It set the price of silver at a 16:1 ratio (sixteen ounces of silver would equal one ounce of gold) and also required the secretary of the treasury to buy $2 to $4 million a month in silver at the market price. That silver was coined but only into token silver dollars that were still backed by gold in the treasury's vaults. Farmers, silver miners, and mine owners were not satisfied. When six new states that had agricultural and mining interests came into the Union, supporters of the free coinage of silver had more leverage. They were able to force the issue. By 1896, the Democratic Party supported free silver (the use of both gold and silver coinage) in its party platform.

Read a Short Story

Bret Harte is perhaps the best-known author of short stories about the American West. Three frequently reprinted tales are "The Luck of Roaring Camp," "The Outcasts of Poker Flat," and "Tennessee's Partner." If you read one of the stories, be sure to discuss realism. Discuss how literature often handles history and how historical fiction can become part of American history too.

Demonstrate Inflation with Paper Money

Bring in paper money from a board game, along with some dry goods (divided into twenty portions). Put a $1 price tag on each item. Call to your desk "store" three students to represent all of the people in the region. Give them each $5 worth of gold "certificates" (just enough for everyone to buy five items). Now let each of them make a purchase, one at a time. They can spend their money as they wish. Notice that some items sell out while others are left. Ask the students how the shopkeeper would respond to the day's sales. (He would mark up the price of the items that sold quickly, and he would mark down the price of the unpopular items so that he could sell them.)

Now pretend that the government has made silver an acceptable form of money too. Give the three students ten dollars this time—five dollars worth of gold certificates and five dollars worth of silver certificates. Let each

of them come to the store, one at a time, to make purchases. After the first customer leaves, what does the shopkeeper notice? (Half of his goods were sold.) If he sees two more customers approaching his store, what is he likely to do? (Lead the students to understand that a smart shopkeeper will quickly raise his prices on everything that is selling—perhaps more than doubling the prices, depending on how much he sells of an item.)

This situation illustrates why the farmers were demanding silver minting and why the northeastern businessmen wanted only the gold standard. The farmers benefited by having more buying power, though the benefits were only temporary. Today, the gov-

Section Quiz

1. List at least four reasons why people were hesitant to settle the frontier.

2. What system of transportation encouraged the settlement of the frontier?

3. The discovery of what two metals drew thousands into the Great Plains territories?

4. Why did ghost towns emerge?

★ Why did Westerners object to a "gold standard" for the nation's money supply?

★ If you had lived during the days of the gold rush, what role would you have played?

II. The Cowboys

Cattlemen also played an important role in the development of the American West. Acre for acre, they were responsible for taming more of the new frontier than the miners or farmers. And they did so with a relish and a romance that have appealed to people ever since.

The era of the cattle frontier was brief. Although the animals had roamed the Southwest since the Spanish explorers brought the first cattle to the New World, a large scale open range cattle industry did not boom until after the Civil War. The peak of cowboy activity came in the 1880s. By the early 1890s, most of the cowboy legend had passed into history, leaving only the dress and the songs to be copied and idealized by modern Americans. In the twenty-five years that the cattle drives flourished, forty thousand men drove ten million head of cattle over a network of trails. Most of these trails led north from Texas. Seldom mentioned is the fact that almost one-fourth of the cowboys on the cattle drives were African Americans.

The term *cowboy* was a fitting one. Photographs of the era, and there are many, and artwork by such cowboy artists as Charles M. Russell, Frederic Remington, and Olaf Seltzer show faces of young men. Booking and arrest records from cowboy towns show that most were under twenty. Young cowboys spent a few years riding the range or trail and then usually married, settling down as farmers or ranchers.

A Wealth of Cattle

Following the Civil War, Texans realized that the growing herds of longhorn cattle on their lands would bring large prices at market. The Easterners, in ever growing cities, were hungry for beef, and they had the money to buy the cattle. Because no railroads reached to Texas, the only way to get the cattle to market was to walk them to where the railroad lines ended.

The Cattle Trails

Cattle could be sold at a much higher price in the East than in the West. Steers cost $5 when fed on the open range on free public lands. It cost about one cent per mile to drive them north. There they could be sold for between $25 and $50 a head. To take advantage of such profits, cattlemen began to move herds across the Red River in 1866.

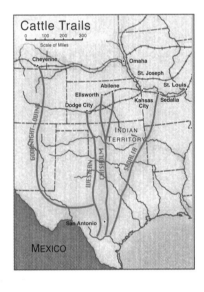

Cattle Trails

ernment controls inflation by controlling how much money it prints. Both sides of the debate continue to use the same old arguments.

Activity 1: Mining Methods in the Old West

Use this activity to help the students understand the various methods used in the West to mine gold and silver.

Section Quiz Answers

1. (any four) infertile soil; severe climate; scarce rainfall; few rivers and an inadequate underground water supply; no trees for lumber and fuel; and hostile Plains Indians

2. transcontinental railroads

3. gold and silver

4. When the ore ran out near a mining town (or the main business died out at other towns), people moved away, leaving the buildings to decay.

★ If all of the nation's money were backed by gold, the federal government would not need to buy silver, and miners would be devastated. Without silver-

backed money, the currency supply would decrease. Westerners thought having more money available would let them buy more and repay debts more quickly.

★ Some may say gold mining, some may mention support industries, and some may think to mention ministerial work. Whatever they say, the question should be an opportunity to teach a lesson in values and economics.

- The West's black powder cartridges produced so much smoke on the first shot that accurate aim thereafter was difficult. (Smokeless powder was not invented until 1895.)
- Cowboys did not carry bullets wrapped around their belts—the bullets would be too heavy, too expensive, and too easily misshapen by lying on them.
- The 1873 Colt Peacemaker, the handgun of choice in the West, was accurate for only fifteen yards.
- Murder was not taken lightly in the real West, even by outlaws. During the entire period, perhaps as few as forty-five murders occurred in the Old West (more murders occur in any one year in Chicago today).
- The fast draw on the street is a myth.
- No one would let the other man "go for his gun first" because reaction time is too slow. Even twenty-five hundredths of a second reaction is too slow to get off a shot against a professional quick-draw artist.
- The eagle feather and warbonnet were Sioux adornments not worn by the Apaches and other fierce Indian tribes.
- Townspeople liked to dress in fancy, well-kept clothes shipped from the East. Even Hickok dressed as an Easterner, not a cowboy, while in Abilene.
- Most people in town were working, not leisurely milling around the streets or in the saloon.
- Most cowboys and gunslingers wore a sort of sombrero, borrowed from the Mexicans, not a Stetson or ten-gallon hat.

Cattlemen quickly learned that longhorn cattle could withstand the dry, hot West, thriving on weeds, cactus, and brush, and going for days without water.

Cattle Brands

With so many cattle grazing freely on the plains and often getting mixed up with the cattle of numerous owners, ranchers had to develop a way to determine which cattle belonged to them. Their solution was branding. They heated a specially designed iron rod to red hot and applied it to the cow's side. The branding iron made a permanent mark on the cow's hide. When the ranchers rounded up the cattle before driving them to market, they separated them according to brands.

Ranchers tried to come up with unique and interesting brand designs that were not easily altered by rustlers, or thieves. Some examples are shown here.

Cattle Brand Designs

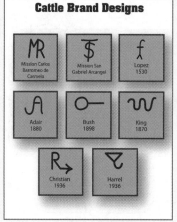

MR — Mission Carlos Barromeo de Carmelo	$ — Mission San Gabriel Arcangel	f — Lopez 1530
A — Adair 1880	O— — Bush 1898	W — King 1870
R→ — Christian 1936	Y — Harrel 1936	

Cattle brands helped owners identify which steers roaming the Western plains belonged to them and foiled would-be cattle rustlers.

The closest railroad at that time reached to Sedalia, Missouri. But cowboys moving north on the Sedalia Trail did not find a warm welcome. First, they had trouble driving the cattle through the forests and brush of eastern Oklahoma and southern Missouri. Second, cattle ticks clung to the Texas longhorns for hundreds of miles. The insects then fell off and attached themselves to stock in Oklahoma and Missouri. Those cattle lacked the immunity of the longhorns. Many animals died from outbreaks of Texas fever. Third, laws were passed to prohibit the passage of Texas herds. Some people also took the law into their own hands. They set up "shotgun quarantines" to keep the longhorns from passing through their lands.

In 1867, Joseph G. McCoy, a shrewd cattle broker from Illinois, built large corrals in Abilene (AB uh leen), Kansas. Using the railroad, which had just reached Abilene, he shipped cattle to the Chicago stockyards. This cut the distance of the long drives and freed the cattlemen from the dangers of armed farmers farther east. It also made the **Chisholm** (CHIZ um) **Trail** the busiest trail north.

The Chisholm Trail took its name from an Indian trader, Jesse Chisholm, who used the 225-mile trail to take supplies to Indian Territory (modern Oklahoma). Although cattle drives became common, they continued to meet difficulties. The trail ran through Indian Territory, and the Chickasaw Indians began levying a grazing tax of up to fifty cents a head on all the cattle driven through. Also, farmers near the trails put up fences to keep the cattle out. This meant less open range and fewer water holes for moving stock. Thus, the cowboys began to swing farther west before heading north. They connected with newly extended railroad lines at Ellsworth and Dodge City, Kansas. The Ellsworth route was a cutoff from the Chisholm Trail. The trail to Dodge City was named the Western Trail.

Two New Mexico ranchers looked for a southeasterly route that would allow them to drive their cattle to the Pecos River and then up the Pecos to the markets in Colorado. Many people thought such a trail was impossible because of one eighty-mile stretch that had no water. But in 1866 Charles Goodnight and Oliver Loving hired eighteen well-armed men, rounded up two thousand head of cattle, and set out for the Pecos. On the first trip they lost nearly four hundred cattle. On their second trip they lost no cattle at all. By 1895, ten thousand head of cattle had taken the **Goodnight-Loving Trail** to western markets. The greatest danger along the route was Comanche Indians, who were on the lookout for free steak on the hoof. In fact, Loving, who had also opened the Shawnee Trail, was killed in an Indian raid on one of his drives.

The Cattle Drive

The heart of the cattle industry and the most important part of a cowboy's job was the trail drive. Getting ready for the drive took careful planning. A rancher or cattle buyer set out to gather a herd in the early spring. The ideal herd size was two thousand head of four-year-olds.

The **trail boss**, who was paid around $125 a month, was in charge of the men, equipment, and animals. His responsibility was to get the herd to market safely. About eight cowboys were hired to work the herd at salaries ranging from $25 to $40 a month. Two were "point" men who rode in the lead. Two "swing" men and two "flank" men rode beside the herd and kept the stock from wandering off. Two "drag" men brought up the rear. Riding in choking dust, they had to keep any weak and tired stragglers moving along. The outfit

---

Songs of the West

Play some songs of the West for your students and discuss the images they reveal. The songs may include "Shenandoah," "Red River Valley," "Home on the Range," "Whoopie-Ti-Yi-Yo," "The Yellow Rose of Texas," and "Cool Water."

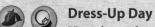

Dress-Up Day

Have the students dress up as characters from the Old West as they study through this chapter. Each should come prepared to share one unusual fact about the person he represents. Stagger the presentations so that the students deliver them on the days when you cover those characters in your class discussion. (You might consider

combining this assignment with the next suggested activity.)

Report on Famous People

Have the students select one person from this unit on whom to do a more in-depth study. They may report on the person either orally or in writing. (You might consider combining this assignment with the previous suggested activity, having the students dress up as their chosen character.)

CD: Grover Cleveland, 22nd and 24th President

Refer to the CD for information on President Grover Cleveland.

CD: Party Platforms, 1884

Use this page to help the students understand the major issues dividing the Republican and Democrat presidential candidates in the election of 1884.

CD: Benjamin Harrison, 23rd President

Refer to the CD for information on President Benjamin Harrison.

The Lone Ranger

Obtain and play a recording of an original radio program of *The Lone Ranger.*

was accompanied by a cook. He hauled the chuck wagon a mile or two ahead of the herd. He stopped and had hot food ready for a tired crew at the end of the day when the herd caught up. The cook's day could start as early as 3:00 a.m. and sometimes lasted until midnight. A **wrangler** was usually the youngest of the hands and was paid the least. He took care of the horses and the riding equipment.

The drive started at daylight and went until dusk—or even later if the trail boss could not find good grass and water. After dinner, a cowboy's work was still not done. They had four two-hour watches at night. Pairs of riders circled the herd, riding in opposite directions, on guard for any signs of trouble. Cowboys hated night riding not only for its loneliness but also because of its dangers. Almost all stampedes, the most frightening and dreaded experience cowboys faced, started at night. The snap of a twig, a strange smell, the flight of a nervous jack rabbit, or a bolt of lightning could set off a stampede. If they could not stop a stampede quickly, the cowboys faced several days of gathering a scattered herd. Even worse, cowboys could be trampled to death by the herd if their horses stumbled and fell in the dust.

The Development of the Meatpacking Industry

The continued success of the open-range cattle industry was assured for a time by the development of a new industry: meatpacking. **Philip Armour** and **Gustavus Swift** led the way in making the meatpacking industry successful. They were willing to try new ideas and ways of doing things.

Philip Armour left his Massachusetts home to build sluices (long boxes for separating ore) for California forty-niners. Later, he went to Milwaukee, Wisconsin, to join his brother selling wholesale grains and provisions. Armour's business boomed when he won a contract to sell barrels of salted meat to the Union armies.

Before and during the war, meat was usually slaughtered locally because the only ways to preserve it for transport were by salting, drying, or pickling. Armour developed meat-packing into a successful large-scale business. After the war, he realized that there would be a large market for meat in eastern cities if he could ship it in large amounts. The trail drives helped supply the cattle he needed, and he used the railroads to ship the meat to the packing plants. Because the cattle were shipped quickly and slaughtered almost immediately, they lost little weight during their journey and yielded large amounts of beef.

In 1875, Armour moved to Chicago and opened a packing plant. Hogs and steers moved down narrow wooden chutes to the slaughterhouse. Inside, they were stunned by a hammer blow on the head. Hung by their hind legs from a moving overhead belt, they moved past men who cut their throats, took out their organs, peeled off their hides and bristles, and cut up the meat.

Armour also saw the possible value of using **by-products**—bones, hide, and other parts of the animal not generally used for meat. Since his company handled many thousands of cattle and hogs a day, it would be better to turn the by-products into something profitable than to discard them. So he hired chemists to find uses for them. They used the fat to make soap; bones to make glue, buttons, and fertilizer; and hides to make shoes and gloves. Someone said that the meatpackers used "every part of a pig but the squeal."

The roundup was the first step in the long cattle drive.

Philip Armour and Gustavus Swift were industrialists who gave the ranchers of the West a financial boost with their meatpacking plants.

- No more than thirty-five thousand cowboys ever hit the cattle trail, and one-third of the cowboys were Mexican or black. Blacks have been excluded from popular accounts and western films, so they are almost ignored in the history of the West.

Roundups

Before they could drive the cattle on the trail, cowboys had to round them up on the range. Before the invention of barbed wire, cows roamed the open range, unrestricted by fences. Calves were born each year, and they had to be added to the herd. The cowboys could tell which cattle belonged to the rancher for whom they were working by his distinctive brand. The big roundup took place in the spring. At that time, new calves were separated from the others and branded.

The roundup could take several weeks. It was a large-scale operation and required careful planning. Hundreds of cowboys participated, all of them overseen by a boss. A cook traveled with the group to feed the men, and wranglers took care of the horses. (Each cowboy had several mounts.)

A typical day involved rising before dawn, eating a quick breakfast of steak and coffee, and heading out on the horses. The cowboys rode out in a circle several miles across. As they worked their way back in, they picked up all the cattle they could find. Some cowboys branched out to search for stragglers while the group continued to move. The circle might contain a thousand cattle by the time the men had returned to their starting point. Then they sorted the calves and branded them. At sundown the men gathered for supper. Shortly after supper, they "hit the sack" in preparation for the work of the next day.

Europeans' Obsession with Things Western

Ask the students why Europeans tend to think of the West when they picture "America." *(primarily because of the portrayals of that region in cowboy movies and TV programs)*

Bring in Collections of Western Art

Bring to class books containing works by Charles M. Russell, Frederick Remington, or Olaf Selter. You or your students might also bring in samples (or pictures) of western décor, which is popular in many areas of the country today.

Myth and Reality

Ask the students to try to summarize the elements in a typical western novel or movie: the strong, silent hero; the Eastern teacher who falls for the hero; the bullying villain; the crime; the chase; the barroom brawl; and the showdown. Discuss some of the common myths described in the margin above and on the next page. Ask the students to identify modern examples of mythmaking by Hollywood.

Public Lands Today

The use of public lands remains a topic of heated debate among individuals, states, and the federal government. Currently, about half of Western land is still owned by the

government, and the Department of the Interior must decide on an equitable way to lease the land for private use by miners, ranchers, and lumber companies. Ask the students to find a recent article on this subject, or bring one in yourself.

Also bring in a map of lands owned by the federal government. Contrary to popular opinion, most of the land is not set aside as parks but is directed by the Bureau of Land Management (BLM).

Life on a Ranch

Most ranches today are relatively small and family operated. Few hire cowboys. Ask a local farmer or rancher (a friend or fellow church member perhaps)

Old Blue

On every cattle drive, one steer usually became the leader of the herd. A good steer who was not edgy or temperamental was a great asset to a trail boss. One of the most famous travelers on the Goodnight-Loving Trail was such a steer named Old Blue. People said that Old Blue knew the trail up to Dodge City better than his owner, Charles Goodnight. For eight years, sometimes twice a year, Old Blue led a herd up the trail to market. Supposedly, he never shied or stampeded. Old Blue was rewarded for his leadership abilities by being spared from the slaughterhouse. He lived to the ripe old age (for a steer) of twenty. Today his horns are on display in a museum in Canyon, Texas.

Refrigerator Cars

George Henry Hammond put ice in a railroad car to send fresh beef to Boston in 1877. But since the meat had lain directly on the ice, it had discolored. Later, someone designed a rail car with bunkers, ice tanks, and heat-proof doors. Then someone designed a refrigerator car that carried ice in V-shaped containers at the ends of the car. The design of the car helped circulate cool air through the ice container and into the boxcar. The ice tanks could be refilled on sidetracks along the route, usually every twenty-four hours. At first the railroads did not want to build refrigerator cars, so Swift and other meatpackers built their own cars. Soon, fruits and vegetables were also being shipped using refrigerator cars.

Tin Cans

Another major revolution in food preservation in America was the tin can. Before the invention of innovations such as refrigeration and canned foods, people had

to discuss ranch life today and some of the changes since the nineteenth century. Perhaps he can also discuss reasons for entering that line of work (especially if it was based on romantic images he got from reading books or watching movies as a child). Another possibility is to have an adult (or student) describe his or her experiences at one of the dude ranches that have become popular vacation spots in America.

Gustavus Swift believed there was a market for more fresh meat. In 1875, he too set up a meatpacking company in Chicago and began shipping fresh meat across the country. The meatpackers knew that chilled meat, whether frozen in winter or chilled on ice in summer, stayed fresh as long as a month. They put beef on ice in a railroad car and shipped it to Boston. But since the meat had lain directly on the ice, it became discolored. Later, specially designed refrigerator cars with separate ice bins came into common use. Their ability to carry fresh meat long distances from the meatpacking plants boosted the industry.

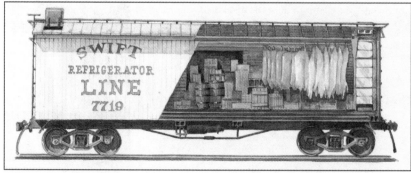

Swift's use of the refrigerator car in the 1870s allowed meat to be transported to Eastern cities and arrive fresh.

The End of the Open Range

By the 1890s, the open-range cattle industry was declining. The last long drive was in 1896. Many factors combined to cause this decline. One problem was a drop in meat prices. With the efficiency of production and the amount of meat produced, meat prices plummeted. It became less profitable to raise livestock.

Overgrazing was also a problem. When more people became involved in the cattle industry, the increased number of cattle grazing made the grasses shorter and scarcer. As the season wore on, the problem became more acute, particularly when there was little rain. In the summer of 1885, especially dry ranges with short grasses left the herds in poor condition. With overgrazing, pure clear springs became stinking mud holes. Harmful weeds replaced lush prairie grasses. Erosion turned cattle trails into ravines.

Even water could prove a danger to the cattle. Sometimes steers broke for water holes or rivers and charged in on top of each other, drowning some of them. Some cattle died while crossing rain-swollen rivers, such as the Colorado, the Brazos, the Red, the Washita (WOSH ih TAW), or the Arkansas. Deadly flash floods were frequent; the sun-baked prairie ground simply could not absorb all of the run-off from sudden thunderstorms.

Droughts and blizzards threatened the cattle as well. When water could not be found, both the cowboys and the cattle suffered terribly. Dehydration made the cattle unmanageable; some even went blind. Winter's cold could freeze the livestock to death if they were stranded in a blizzard without food or shelter.

The summer of 1884 brought severe drought. The winter that followed was the most severe of the century. A raging December blizzard laid a thick coat of ice and sleet over the thin grasses. Cattle drifted south until they reached a 170-mile-long fence that stockmen had built to end earlier feuding with farmers. There thousands of cattle starved or froze to death. More than 10,000 dead cows were found along the fence. More than fifty percent of the stock had died that winter, and the cattle that survived faced another severe drought the following summer.

The cycle of drought and blizzard was repeated again in 1886–87. The weather dealt a blow to the big cattle operations in the West, and they did not quickly recover. President Grover Cleveland, although sympathetic with the troubles of the westerners, replied to requests for government aid by saying, "Federal aid in such cases encourages the expectation of paternal care on the part of the Government and weakens the sturdiness of our national character." This forced American agriculture to face its own problems and adjust to the needs of the market instead of looking to government for immediate help.

Horse thieves and some Indians also plagued the cattle trails. Indians often demanded a toll of beef or horses. If the cowboys refused to pay, the Indians set off stampedes. Horse thieves and cattle rustlers hid along the trail. Stockgrowers' associations tried to rid the plains of such thieves by hanging or shooting them.

Sheep on the Range

One more problem for the cattlemen was sheepherders. The vast vacant grasslands of the plains were as attractive to sheep owners as they were to cattlemen. In 1880, there were about 200,000 sheep in the northern mountain states and territories. By 1890, there were 1.5 million and by 1900, 15 million.

Cattlemen had reached the grasslands first. They were angered as they saw the sheepherders invading the area with their "woolly-backs," as cowboys called sheep. To cowboys on the already overstocked ranges, sheep meant disaster. Cattlemen said that sheep ate grass down to the roots and then trampled what little grass was left behind. They stripped the ground so that no new growth appeared until the next spring's rain. And they fouled water holes, leaving a smell that made cattle refuse to drink.

As grass ran out and tempers grew short, the more numerous cowboys resorted to bullying, intimidating, and even attacking sheepmen and their flocks. Clubbing, shooting, torching, stampeding, and rim-rocking (driving sheep over cliffs) were all effective means of destroying herds. The murder of sheepherders was common too.

Several events eased disputes. The winter of 1886–87 reduced the number of cattle that needed to be grazed. Fencing divided range lands. And some cattlemen found that it was possible for sheep and cattle to share some of the same range lands.

Section Quiz

1. Where did most cattle trails start? How long did the cattle trade flourish?
2. Why did the cattle drivers travel north? List two trails that they used to herd longhorns from the South to the North.

The Candlish Movable Home on the Range

Until the late nineteenth century, sheepherders slept on the ground on blankets. Home on the range was very bumpy and cold. But in 1864, James Candlish, a Wyoming blacksmith, came to the rescue. He took an old wagon and converted it into the first home on wheels, a forerunner of the mobile home. Open in the front, the wagon had a canvas flap to block the wind. In 1892, a hardware company built an improved model that had a stove with an oven, a window, and Dutch doors among its many "conveniences." Soon, most sheepherders, especially on the northern plains, owned their own home on wheels.

Some diehards, of course, thought that the manufacturers were just trying to pull the wool over their eyes. Some sheep ranchers would not even hire herders who used a wagon. One complaint was that the sheepherder who returned to his wagon each night had to herd his sheep back over land already grazed.

But for most of the sheepherders, "home, home, on the range" came with wheels.

The introduction of sheep to the grasslands of the West threatened cattlemen.

---

to eat food almost immediately after it had been picked or slaughtered. This was true of dairy products such as milk, butter, and cheeses, too. The Civil War created an urgent need for ways to store food longer. Soldiers had to be fed. "Necessity is the mother of invention," and the science of canning foods advanced significantly as a result of this need.

Tin cans were a great asset to the cowboy cook on the cattle trail. He was able to fix a greater variety and better quality of food for the hungry cowboys.

Mobile Homes

Americans continued to develop the sheepherders' idea of a home that was mobile. The concept began to be applied to recreation. Some early mobile homes were just cars loaded down with tents and as much camping paraphernalia as they would hold. Others were built specifically for travel, with extra storage shelves or built-in beds. One camper was carved out of a huge log. Another looked like a fancy trolley car and contained fine furnishings.

Although a few mobile homes were very nice, most of them were crudely constructed. Travelers in the late 1920s welcomed Arthur Sherman's two-wheeled, six-by-nine-foot trailer. It contained beds and cooking facilities and could be hitched to a car. One of the best things about the trailer was its price. Since the trailer was mass-produced, it could be sold at a price that the average family could afford.

Although mobile homes lost popularity during the Great Depression (camping out was not as much fun when many people had to "camp out" permanently), they came back into fashion when times got better. Bigger and better vehicles were in demand as Americans continued to earn

---

Activity 2: A Cowboy in Dodge City, 1882

Use this activity to help the students understand what life was like for cowboys, especially when they came to town following the completion of a cattle drive.

Section Quiz Answers

1. Texas; twenty-five years
2. to get to the nearest railhead to ship their cattle east; (any two) Sedalia, Chisholm, Western, Goodnight-Loving

more money and receive more vacation time.

Section III
Objectives
Students should be able to

1. Explain why farmers sometimes fell into conflict with cattlemen.
2. Explain the significance of the Homestead Act.
3. Describe the settlement of Oklahoma.
4. List the problems and hardships faced by prairie farmers.

Pioneer Housing

New homesteaders set up housekeeping in all types of shelters. Besides sod houses, they lived in caves, tents, and canvas homes. There were even cases of families living in the hollowed-out stumps of giant trees.

The day that a family started raising a log cabin was exciting. Construction often became a community activity. Neighboring men worked together cutting logs for the frame. Then they raised the frame into place by attaching ropes to the beams and pulling. Everyone took part in the chinking, filling the cracks between the logs with a material like mud or grass. Neighbors enjoyed food, conversation, and games in addition to their hard work.

Glass Windows

The Homestead Act said that a pioneer family trying to improve on a piece of land must have at least one glass window in their house. Unfortunately for the settlers, it was very difficult to get glass on the frontier. Not everyone could afford such a luxury. To solve their problem, some fami-

3. List four reasons for the decline of the cattle industry.
★ How was the cattle industry benefited by the meatpacking industry?
★ Why does the image of the cowboy remain a symbol of America both at home and abroad?

III. The Homesteaders

Rich lands and the promise of a better lifestyle lured people steadily west. Easterners who had farmed worn-out soil left for the West. They were joined by immigrants, former slaves, and war veterans who were looking for a place to settle down.

Conflict with the Cattlemen

As more farmers went west to stake claims on public lands there, the space left for open-range grazing decreased. Because the homesteaders did not appreciate having their crops overrun by livestock, they put up fences.

For a time, cattlemen fought the homesteaders, cutting the fences and threatening the farmers. There were even some range wars. The cattlemen eventually changed their style. Rather than grazing their cattle on public lands, they took up ranching on their own lands or land that they leased from the government or other owners.

Farmers on the Plains

The **Homestead Act** of 1862 opened western lands for free settlement. Although the 160 acres allowed to a homesteader was hardly enough to sustain a family in those areas, no one seemed to mind. A settler was supposed to build a "12 by 12" house with windows, have a well, improve the land, and live on the homestead for five years. If he met those terms, the land became his. To cheat on the terms, some homesteaders built 12-inch by 12-inch houses or had a house on wheels with a bucket of water on it rolled onto (and off) the land. Some lived on the land only seasonally, which was a legal option.

By making this land available, officials sought to achieve several goals. An increased population would lead to greater stability and eventual statehood. Development of the Plains would also result in expanded economic opportunity. This would lead to additional markets for goods produced in the East.

Settlers could increase their land holdings by purchasing as much as an extra quarter-section (a section was 640 acres) at $1.25 per acre. The smallest amount one could buy was forty acres. That cost $50.00, a large amount in those days. If a pioneer filed a timber claim and planted ten acres in trees, he could add another quarter-section to his holdings. In the first six months after the Homestead Act was passed, settlers gobbled up 224,550 acres of land in Kansas and Nebraska alone.

The railroads sold farmland too, at $2.50 an acre. They sent agents to Europe, spreading news of cheap American lands. The Nebraska and Dakota territorial legislatures also paid immigration bureaus to attract settlers.

The Morrill Land Grant Act of 1862 gave states thirty thousand acres of federal land for every representative and senator they had. The land, or the proceeds from its sale, was to be used to establish

Homesteaders came west seeking a better life and greater opportunities.

3. (any four) a drop in meat prices, overgrazing, drowning in rivers or flash floods, droughts and blizzards, Indians and horse thieves, conflicts with sheepherders
★ By finding new ways of preserving meat and of using cattle to their greatest profitability, meatpackers ensured that cattlemen would be able to sell their livestock.
★ The life of the cowboy symbolizes several core American values: liberty, individualism, and opportunity.

Who Were the Best Settlers?

Ask the students to consider which type of settler was in the best long-term interests of the country: the miner, the rancher, or the farmer. In fact, each of those types of settlers played a valuable part in the settlement of the West. In many ways they needed each other. The "glue" that held the West together was the businessmen in the towns who provided the basic services that everyone needed, but to stay in business the businessmen needed all types of customers. The same is true today. No specific career is "better" for America than any other.

Recruitment Poster

Make a recruitment poster for the railroad lines to encourage Easterners and Europeans to go west.

Samplers and Quilting

Make an authentic sampler or other piece of needlework (cross-stitch, crewel, quilting, etc.). Or perhaps bring in a completed piece to show in class. Historical incidents can also be represented by stitching appliques or by carefully gluing felt shapes onto burlap.

land-grant colleges. Speculators purchased most of the land. They, in turn, sold it to lumber companies, mining companies, and farmers.

The Oklahoma Land Rush

You have read how the government moved the Cherokee and other eastern tribes west in the 1830s. Five tribes from the Southwest, all farming tribes, also were moved to **Indian Territory** (Oklahoma). By the 1880s, most of the desirable farmland in the West had been claimed. Then many of the settlers began to look greedily at the Indian Territory. The railroads, speculators, and land-hungry settlers saw the opportunity to make some money and pressured the federal government to open up Oklahoma to white settlers.

In 1885, the government bought lands in the territory. President Benjamin Harrison announced that some of these lands would be opened to settlers at noon on April 22, 1889. The U.S. Army was on hand to keep the settlers out until the given hour. More than twenty thousand pioneers were poised on the border that day. At the sound of cannons, they raced across the border to claim their land. Those who made their way into the area in that land boom were called "Boomers." (Some had "jumped the gun" illegally and made their claim ahead of time. They were called **Sooners**.) Some 1.9 million acres of land were claimed in a few hours. In 1893, government officials opened for settlement another part of Oklahoma, the Cherokee Strip—where the Indians had just been settled by the same government. Oklahoma gained territorial status in 1890. In 1907, President Theodore Roosevelt welcomed the "Sooner State" into the Union as the forty-sixth state.

Thousands of settlers hoped to claim the best land in Oklahoma and were prepared to find them by train, wagon, or on horseback.

Overcoming the Obstacles to Settlement

As the farmers settled on the plains in the late 1800s, they faced some of the same problems that cowboys and ranchers had faced earlier. But they also faced some new ones. The ways that they overcame those problems demonstrated their perseverance and ingenuity. For Christians, these obstacles provided an opportunity to show the faithfulness of God.

A Lack of Some Resources

Because trees were rare on the plains, wood had to be brought from other places. That made log cabins both expensive and impractical. Some settlers began by living in sod dugouts braced by a few purchased boards. These dreary homes were little more than ditches dug into a hillside and covered with a roof of sod (grass and soil). The **sod house**, however, was a little more pleasant, and it became the classic dwelling on the prairie, especially where there were no hillsides for dug-outs.

A sod house was drier, sturdier, and more comfortable than a dugout. The sod strips used to build it were twelve to eighteen inches wide, three inches deep, and two or three feet long. The sod blocks were staggered like bricks, grass side down, to form the thick walls of the house. Soddies, as such shelters were called, were warm in winter and cool in summer. Usually a lattice of willow branches was woven and covered with clay from a nearby creek bed for the base of

Because trees for lumber were so scarce on the prairie, settlers usually built themselves sod houses.

lies set up a system of sharing. They would pool their resources to buy one glass window and then pass it around. Each family would put up the window long enough for the inspector to check the house, and then they would store the window away to prevent its being broken before other families had the chance to use it. After the inspector left, a durable material would be nailed over the open window frame to protect those inside from the weather.

Caroline Scott Harrison

Caroline Scott Harrison was the first First Lady to adopt a project or cause during her time in the White House. Her project was the renovation of the White House. It had fallen into disrepair and was in serious need of a face-lift.

Caroline wanted to do a complete overhaul, but she could not get the funds that such a project would have required. She was given an allowance for repairs, and she made the most of it. By the time she was finished, the kitchen, flooring, and heating system were all new. Furniture and curtains had been replaced. The president's family had more than one bathroom. And—most exciting of all—the house was lit by electric lights. In the midst of the remodeling, Caroline found many old pieces of presidential china stored away. She brought them out and organized them into the start of the collection that now appears in the White House's China Room.

Well-Drilling Rigs

Steam-powered well-drilling rigs that looked much like oil derricks were available for hire in the later part of the century. Drillers often charged one dollar per foot to drill the wells, however; and because the water table in the Great Plains

  Little House on the Prairie

Share with the students information about Laura Ingalls Wilder and her series of books *Little House on the Prairie*. Perhaps read an excerpt from one of the books. You might also consider showing one or more episodes of the television series based on those books.

Desert Land Act

The Desert Land Act of 1878 offered 640-acre homesteads to farmers who would pledge to irrigate the land. Many of those claims ended up in the hands of stockmen.

Barbed Wire Test

Even after Joseph Glidden had invented a practical version of barbed wire, many ranchers and farmers were not interested in buying it. They simply did not believe that it would work. To try to dispel these doubts, two barbed wire salesmen, John Warne Gates and Pete P. McManus, planned a demonstration of the product in a plaza in San Antonio, Texas.

The men received permission to build a corral using barbed wire. They then arranged for a herd of cattle to be driven into the corral. To the amazement of the skeptical onlookers, the wire held when the cattle charged it. After a couple of encounters, the barbs on the wire convinced the cattle to stay in the corral. Sales of barbed wire shot up.

John Warne Gates later had a role in the establishment of the Texas Company (Texaco) and the American Steel and Wire Company, the first billion-dollar corporation.

Spelling Bees

Being far away from the entertainment of eastern cities, pioneer communities became adept at creating their own amusements. One popular community activity was the school spelling bee.

Noah Webster's "Blue-Back Speller" made the spelling bee possible. First, it estab-

area was often deep, the well-drilling became very expensive for the poor farmer.

the roof. Then sod shingles were laid over it. In heavy rains, however, such roofs leaked water like oversoaked sponges. Debris often fell from the roof, but pioneer wives hung cheesecloth or muslin below the rafters to catch the mud and bugs. Inside walls were whitewashed with a mixture of lime and sand. Tight construction was crucial, not just to keep out the cold but also to deter snakes and field mice. Some sod houses were real works of art. A few, combined with some lumber, were two stories high.

The lack of wood also gave the farmers (called "sodbusters") two other obstacles to overcome. One was scarcity of fuel for fires. Until the railroads brought coal to heat prairie homes, pioneers used corncobs, hay, and even manure ("buffalo chips") as fuel. Another problem was the lack of wood for the split rail fences used back east. Although prairie farmers were generally glad their lands were not rocky, there were no stones to be used for building purposes. There was no practical material for fences until barbed wire was invented.

A sodbuster had to have an adequate water supply. Some settlers set out rain barrels or cisterns to collect rain. Some settled near creeks. Most found water by digging wells, but wells had to be exceptionally deep to reach water in many areas of the dry plains. Even with wells, the farmers could not pump enough water by hand to water their stock and irrigate their crop land. The invention of the **windmill**, however, put the strong breezes of the region to this use. Even wells or rivers were not enough to irrigate many crops. Another means of overcoming the lack of water was raising crops that required less water. Still another solution was using dry-farming techniques, such as the use of mulch to protect what little moisture was in the ground.

Windmill-powered pumps brought scarce water to the surface for use by people and crops in the sometimes-arid West.

Help for the Prairie Farmers

The late 1800s brought many new and helpful developments for western settlers. One was the barbed wire mentioned earlier. Without wood and rocks, fences could not be built. And with cattle grazing contentedly in his corn and wheat, a farmer could not hope to prosper. Plain wire fences were tried, but they failed to hold up when herds pressed on them. Some farmers started thorn hedges, but it often took years for the hedges to become tall enough to do any good. In 1874, an Illinois farmer, **Joseph Glidden**, designed the first practical barbed wire. He used part of a coffee grinder to cut and coil small lengths of wire and then strung the barbs on by hand. Soon a machine was invented to do the work. Within a decade, 120 million pounds of wire were being sold per year.

David Halladay, a Connecticut mechanic, perfected a windmill that helped farmers obtain water. His device pivoted to face the wind and used centrifugal force to adjust the pitch of its wooden vanes. That feature allowed the windmill to withstand the high prairie winds. A crankshaft transferred the mill's rotary motion to force the pump up and down.

Railroads helped ease some of the transportation problems on the vast plains. Many lines built spurs (extensions) to the scattered towns to bring in needed goods and to carry out the farmers' harvests. The lines also made trips to other cities or regions easier.

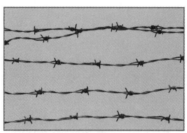

The invention of barbed wire allowed homesteaders and farmers to keep roaming cattle from their property but sometimes led to range wars with the cowboys.

American ingenuity helped the prairie farmer too. Heavier steel plows were designed to cut through the matted sod, and mechanical grain drills planted seeds at the proper depth. Farmers harvested crops using a binder, an improvement on the reaper. After 1850 steam engines provided power for the larger inventions, and threshing crews often traveled through areas with that equipment for harvesting the crops of many farmers. The steam-driven tractor also appeared during the 1890s to aid the farmer.

Hardships of the Prairie Settler

In addition to the lack of some needed resources, homesteaders had to deal with many hazards of prairie life. One such problem arose as more and more western lands were plowed. Especially in dry years, the wind blew tons of exposed topsoil across the dry ground. Keeping a house clean was nearly impossible because the dust settled everywhere. Outside, the dust was blinding. Sadly, the dust was more than an inconvenience. The erosion of precious topsoil left much land infertile. In their eagerness to cultivate more land, settlers created problems of erosion and moisture loss.

Another danger for the sodbuster was prairie fires. What little rain there was came in spring and early summer. As the season wore on, the grasses became dry. The smallest spark from a campfire, chimney, or strike of lightning could turn the prairie into an inferno. Settlers used several methods to put out such fires. Sometimes they used damp clothing and blankets to beat out small fires. At other times farmers used the carcasses of slaughtered livestock, dragging them over the flaming grass. They also lit backfires to slow the progress of the flames. More often, the only thing they could do was go inside the dugouts or soddies and pray. When the flames were fanned by winds, the settler was powerless to stop the spreading fire. The heavy sod of the house and wet sheets over openings might protect people; but it could not keep the crops from going up in smoke.

Hailstorms sometimes did as much damage as fires. They flattened crops, leaving little to be salvaged for harvest. Sometimes the settlers themselves were battered. Another of nature's assaults on the prairie sometimes accompanied rain or hailstorms: tornadoes. These small intense whirlwinds formed by severe thunderstorms destroyed everything in their paths. So many tornadoes occurred on the plains that the region was called "tornado alley." Sodbusters often dug root cellars for protection against such storms. They could also use the cellars for storing food.

Large swarms of locusts and grasshoppers were another scourge. Swarming across the prairies in the 1870s, they devoured everything that grew. "Their fluttering wings," wrote the editor of the *Wichita City Eagle*, "looked like a sweeping snowstorm in the heavens, until their dark bodies covered everything green upon the earth." Other accounts report the locusts covering the ground in a wiggling layer up to six inches deep. They ate crops, grasses, leaves, tree bark, leather boots, harness straps, and even fence posts and door frames. No one knew what caused the swarms to drop from the skies or what caused them to leave, but everyone feared them. Their arrival

One hindrance to settlement in the West was dust storms that destroyed cropland and coated everything in prairie dust.

lished standard spellings of words. Second, it grouped words together according to level of difficulty. This arrangement of progressively harder words was ideal for the organization of spelling bees.

On the frontier, competition between opposing teams was so exciting that the whole community wanted to share in the fun. Anticipation ran high to see whose child would be the local spelling champion.

A Sleighing Song

A favorite winter activity in many places was sleigh riding. Driving up and down the streets of the town with several other sleighs on a frosty winter day was great entertainment.

Sleighs also had potential for danger, however. If something moved into the path of the sleigh, the driver was in trouble because he would be unable to stop quickly. In addition, turning too sharply meant a tumble in the snow for everybody. Also, sleds glided over the snow so quietly that they were in danger of running into each other.

To remedy the potential of collision, sleighs started carrying bells. The bells were typically made of brass or bronze because those metals produced a rich sound. The bells not only increased the safety of the sleighs but also gave sleigh riding the happy sound celebrated in songs such as "Jingle Bells."

Teaching History Through Literature

There are several good historical novels about the hardships of the Old West. *Giants of the Earth* (1927) by O. E. Rölvaag tells the story of an immigrant Norwegian family in South Dakota. The despair in the novel needs to be discussed in class. Other popular novels include *Shane* by Jack Schaefer, *A Lantern in Her Hand* by Bess Streeter Aldrich, and *Prairie Songs* by Pamela Conrad. Share selected excerpts with your class and discuss the experiences of the characters.

Perhaps the most widely known name in Western writing is Zane Grey, who wrote more than 90 books, more than two-thirds of them Westerns.

Why the Farmer's Hardships?

Ask the students to explain why farmers have had such difficulty throughout history—not just U.S. history—in getting fair treatment. The basic reason is that the farming industry is the exact opposite of a monopoly. Farming as a form of competition is called "perfect competition." Ask the students to make a list contrasting a monopoly and a farming business. (There are many farmers; each product is essentially the same no matter who produces it; because there are so many farmers selling their crop, no individual farmer can control the price; and new farmers may enter farming with relative ease.)

The farmer's inability to influence prices became even more pronounced with the advances in transportation and communication. In earlier days, farmers who were experiencing a drought could charge high prices to make up for their diminished crop, but with the advent of railroads, people in a drought-stricken region simply bought food from a different region, leaving local farmers in huge debt. This change raised a new, fundamental question for the American republic: in a free-market, capitalistic country, should the government intervene to help the farmer? The questions raised during the Populist movement are still being asked today.

Section IV

Objectives

Students should be able to

1. Name the most infamous outlaws of the Old West.
2. Name the most famous lawmen of the Old West.
3. Explain why the West gained a reputation as a rough, lawless region.
4. Explain how the reputation of the Old West outlaws and lawmen have shaped foreigners' perception of Americans and the United States.

Dime Novels

Many of the major western legends won their fame or notoriety through the stories told about them in dime novels. Dime novels were serial stories that recorded the adventures—some true and others embellished—of various characters from American history and legend. The books got their name from their initial selling price.

A Life of Violence

For the few outlaws who reformed (such as James Younger), many others died the same way they had lived— violently. Although faced with the opportunity to change, those men persisted in their wicked ways. John Wesley Hardin is one such example.

Hardin was born into the home of a Methodist preacher, and his father hoped that his son would follow him into the ministry. However, young Wesley showed more of an inclination for the pistol than the pulpit. He had a hot temper and was quick to act violently on his impulses. By age twenty-one, he had already committed several murders.

usually meant a two-year crop loss, because the locusts laid eggs that hatched the next year.

Homesteads were often miles from a settlement. Because neighbors were few and the distances between homesteads great, loneliness was a problem. Of course, homesteaders tried to deal with loneliness. For example, pioneers made great efforts to go long distances to churches built in towns.

Mail provided another link to the outside world. After pressure by farmers, the post office began **rural free delivery** (RFD), so that it cost no more to send a letter to a soddie than it did to send one across New York City. Mail-order catalog houses also began. The first, Montgomery Ward and Company, began in Chicago in 1872. Soon afterward, Sears Roebuck and Company started. Those businesses offered settlers a wide array of products that they could order from their catalogs. Most of the products could be delivered to the customer's door. Some were shipped by rail to the nearest town for pickup. Farmers also formed their own social groups. The **Grange**, founded in 1867 by Oliver H. Kelley, began as a social organization. Later, it became a political tool to promote the interests of farmers. The Grange also encouraged the rise of populism, a movement that sought to help farmers solve some of their problems. Eventually this developed into a third-party political movement.

Section Quiz

1. How did the homesteaders react to the cattle drives?
2. What major territory was the last to open to homesteaders?
3. What two important resources did homesteaders often lack?
4. What contributions did Joseph Glidden and David Halladay make to the improvement of prairie farming?
5. List at least five hardships faced by plains settlers.
★ How did the federal government encourage the settlement of the frontier?

IV. The Outlaws and the Lawmen

The settlement of the West occurred faster than government could organize to enforce the law. Without this enforcement, human sinfulness showed itself more frequently. Outlaws manifested the American values of individualism and growth in twisted ways. To control and punish lawbreakers, the government appointed U.S. marshals, federally hired lawmen. Later, towns and communities hired lawmen called sheriffs. Because gunplay was so common, the men hired as lawmen were sometimes gunslingers who were willing to get on the "right side of the law" and use their talent to catch the bad guys. Many of the outlaws and lawmen became legendary.

The Outlaws

Jesse and Frank James

Both of these brothers had been Confederate raiders with a brutal rebel leader named William

Frank James

Jesse James

Activity 3: Ranchers and Farmers Collide in Nebraska, 1884

Use this activity to help the students understand the conflicts that arose between cattlemen and farmers during this period.

Section Quiz Answers

1. They put up fences to keep cattle out of their fields.
2. Indian Territory (Oklahoma)
3. trees and water
4. Glidden—designed the first practical barbed wire, Halladay—perfected a windmill to help get water to the farmers' house and crops
5. (any five) dry and dusty conditions, erosion, fire, hailstorms, tornadoes, locusts and grasshoppers, loneliness
★ by giving away or selling plots of land, some directly to settlers and some to railroads and states

Books on Outlaws and Lawmen

Have the students close their books. Then ask them to name as many famous outlaws and gunslingers from the Old West as they can. Discuss what the students already know about those figures and where they got their information. Display books on the outlaws and lawmen of the West, and allow the students to look up information on those historical figures to distinguish truth from myth.

Quantrill. After the war, they began robbing banks, trains, and stage-coaches in Missouri and other nearby states. Their gang included the four Younger brothers. They claimed that the Northerners had driven them to a life of crime. They gained many sympathizers, who regarded them as modern "Robin Hoods" instead of the thieves that they were. Jesse, whom his friends called Dingus, was shot in the back in 1882 by a "friend" who wanted the reward. Jesse was thirty-four. Frank surrendered five months later, was tried, and was acquitted because of a great deal of political pressure.

Billy the Kid

At the age of seventeen, William Bonney, also known as "Billy the Kid," became involved in the Lincoln County, New Mexico, cattle wars. He fought for an English gentleman, John H. Tunstall, who became a father-figure to the young boy. When a crooked sheriff and his posse murdered Tunstall, Billy swore to get revenge—and he did. By the time he was eighteen, Billy had been charged with twelve murders. Captured by Pat Garrett, a lawman and a former friend of Billy, Billy murdered his two guards and escaped again. In 1881 Garrett tracked him down and killed him. Billy was only twenty-one years old.

Black Bart

Bart was called "the gentleman bandit." Primarily a stagecoach robber, he wore a flour-sack mask with eyeholes, treated everyone with the best of manners, and left a poem at the scene of each of his crimes. Bart was captured in 1883 when a handkerchief he dropped at one job was traced to him. His real name was Charles Bolton. After his release from prison, Bolton disappeared.

The Dalton Gang

Most of the crime spree of the Dalton Gang occurred over an eighteen-month period. All of the gang members were in their twenties. While attempting to rob a bank at Coffeyville, Kansas, in 1892, all except one of them were killed. The survivor, Emmett, had eighteen wounds. After spending fourteen years in prison, he married the girl who had waited for him. They moved to Los Angeles, where Emmett worked as a building contractor, a real estate man, and a movie writer. Outspoken in his condemnation of outlaws, Emmett died in 1937, a respected businessman.

Harry Tracy

Tracy was the subject of one of the greatest manhunts in the nation's history. Pursued throughout the state of Oregon, he could have escaped back to the hideouts in the West, but he seemed to relish the hunt. He stole a boat and sailed around Puget Sound. He then stole a train, had lunch with farmers and their families, joined the posses looking for him, called sheriffs on the telephone to tell them he was in town, and even helped do some of the work on the farms he visited. Eventually cornered by a group of farmers in 1902, Tracy killed himself.

The Lawmen

Tom Smith

Smith served as the sheriff of Abilene, Kansas, before "Wild Bill" Hickock. Smith was actually the man who cleaned up Abilene, and he did it with his fists more than with his guns. The citizens widely

William Bonney, a.k.a. "Billy the Kid"

Pat Garrett

After an encounter that nearly cost him his life, Hardin tried to assume a new identity in Florida, but the law caught up with him three years later. In prison for seventeen years, Hardin eventually settled down to a wise use of his time. He studied theology and became the superintendent of the prison Sunday school. He also studied law and made preparations to take the bar exam. When he was released, he started a legal practice. But he did not sever all of the ties to his former life. He kept company with the wrong crowd and was eventually murdered.

The Lone Ranger

Writers of radio dramas, television shows, and movies about the Old West created many legends. One of those legends, *The Lone Ranger*, aired on radio for the first time in January 1933 and lasted through more than six hundred episodes before ending in 1955. It was so popular that it had spin-off television programs as well.

The narrator's introduction and the accompanying music—the "William Tell Overture"—became fixed in the minds of people all across the country.

Hi-Yo Silver! A fiery horse with the speed of light, a cloud of dust and a hearty Hi-Yo Silver! The Lone Ranger! With his faithful Indian companion, Tonto, the daring and resourceful masked rider of the plains led the fight for law and order in the early West. Return with us now to those thrilling days of yesteryear. The Lone Ranger rides again!

The Lone Ranger's "real" name was John Reid, and he was one of six Texas Rangers who were chasing the dreaded outlaw Butch Cavendish and his gang. The gang laid a deadly ambush for the Rangers, and only Reid, badly wounded, survived. An Indian (Tonto) found him and nursed him back to health. When the Ranger awoke, he asked Tonto what had happened. Tonto explained that all of the other Rangers had been killed. "You only Ranger left. You lone Ranger." At that point, Reid dedicated his life to fighting for justice, and Tonto promised to forever be his faithful companion.

Reid owned a silver mine that provided him with funds and materials for his matched set of silver six-shooters and an endless supply of silver bullets. He named his horse "Silver" and outfitted it with silver shoes.

The Lone Ranger never drank alcohol or smoked, always used correct grammar, and never shot to kill his adversaries. (Remarkably, of the hundreds of foes he faced, he killed only one of them.) He never accepted money from those he helped. He supported himself with the proceeds of his silver mine.

Several people played the Lone Ranger and Tonto characters on the television version, but the most famous duo were Clayton Moore as the Lone Ranger and Jay Silverheels as Tonto. The program premiered on September 15, 1949, and the last episode aired on September 12, 1957.

Section V
Objectives

Students should be able to

1. Name the most famous Indian battle of the late 1800s.
2. Name the most famous Indian chieftains and/or warriors of the period and explain their significance to the events of the period.
3. Explain how the Indians were treated after they surrendered.
4. Describe the U.S. Indian policies used under the Dawes Act.

Wyatt Earp

Bat Masterson

respected him. In 1870 he was killed while trying to arrest a homesteader.

Wyatt Earp
Wherever he was sheriff, Earp was not well liked. He and a brother and some friends killed three cowboys in the famous gunfight at the O.K. Corral in Tombstone, Arizona. The townspeople considered the Earps to be murderers, so Earp and his group left town. Earp died in 1927 at the age of seventy-one.

Bat Masterson
Masterson's first love was gambling. But he also was a rider for the railroads. During his two years as sheriff of Tombstone, Arizona, he did an excellent job of maintaining the peace. Later, he became a sportswriter in New York. In 1905 Teddy Roosevelt made him a deputy U.S. marshal.

The Pinkertons
The Pinkertons established the first "rogues gallery" in 1850 for identifying known outlaws. They also provided intelligence services for the Union during the war. Later, this detective agency hunted down and captured many criminals after the war. The Pinkertons also were used as strikebreakers and union infiltrators.

Bill Tilghman
Like Tom Smith, Bill Tilghman used his guns only when he had to. He was the U.S. marshal in Perry, Oklahoma, for thirty-five years. Tilghman was so well respected by even the outlaws and their gangs that one famous thief refused to let a henchman shoot Tilghman in the back because he was "too good a man." Tilghman was killed in 1924 during the attempted arrest of a drunken man.

Section Quiz

1. Why do you think crime was such a problem in the West?
2. Which Western outlaw was known as the "gentleman bandit" because he was always mannerly and left a poem at the scene of his robberies?
3. Which outlaw was charged with twelve murders by the time he was eighteen?
4. Which of the outlaws discussed in this section committed suicide?
5. What former friend of Billy the Kid ended up killing him?
6. Which lawman had ties to President Theodore Roosevelt?
★ Why would towns hire former criminals to be their sheriffs?
★ How did outlaws distort the American values of individualism and growth?

V. The Indians
When many Americans moved west of the Mississippi River, they did not see themselves as moving into Indian land. Most believed they were settling an American wilderness, a wilderness made American by a series of agreements with France and Spain. However,

---

Activity 4: The Death of Billy the Kid, 1881
Use this activity to give the students additional information about law and order in the West generally and justice as applied to Billy the Kid specifically.

Section Quiz Answers
1. Answers will vary but might include lack of much religious influence and scarcity of law-enforcement officers.
2. Black Bart, or Charles Bolton
3. William Bonney, or Billy the Kid
4. Harry Tracy
5. Pat Garrett
6. Bat Masterson
★ They were quick on the draw and knew how to deal with the bad guys.
★ They pursued their own destiny without regard for lawful society. They sought to increase their own wealth at the expense of others.

Reports on Indian Wars
Have students choose an Indian war to report on. Be sure that at least one student each reports on the battle at Little Bighorn and the massacre at Wounded Knee. *American Heritage* has published a book titled *Indian Wars*, which would be a good source for information.

Nuggets from *National Geographic*
The story of the famous Indian leader Geronimo is told in the October 1992 issue of *National Geographic*. It includes a biographical sketch of the famous warrior and a discussion of popular ideas of that day.

these agreements ignored the needs and desires of thousands of people whose ancestors had lived on these lands for centuries.

Failed Promises and War

When the Indians attempted to defend themselves from American settlement, the U.S. government made new treaties. These treaties promised the Indians peace if they would remain in certain restricted areas of the West. However, illegal prospecting often led to the discovery of gold or silver in these areas. Repeated violations by prospectors and settlers made the treaties worthless. These failed promises led to war.

The Indians became skilled fighters, and the U.S. Army was not used to fighting this kind of unconventional enemy. It responded by waging a total war, destroying Indian villages and sometimes killing women and children. That treatment was similar to what the North had inflicted on the South. Probably the best-known battle of the Indian wars was at Little Big Horn in 1876. Lieutenant Colonel **George Armstrong Custer** misjudged the strength and determination of a group of Sioux warriors. His defeat at Little Big Horn ("Custer's Last Stand") was led by **Crazy Horse** and Gall. **Sitting Bull**, who stayed behind the lines, was the medicine man who inspired the attack.

Sitting Bull of the Sioux; Lt. Col. George A. Custer

Indians Surrender

Indian resistance ended as much from defeat in war as from the destruction of the buffalo herds. The frontiersmen had little sympathy for the Indians. But some Easterners thought that the mistreatment of the Indians was inexcusable. In 1877, President Rutherford B. Hayes admitted in a national address, "Many, if not most, of our Indian Wars have had their origin in broken promises and acts of injustice on our part."

But recognition of the problem did little to change the Indians' plight. The same year that President Hayes made his speech, the peaceful Nez Perce (PURSS) tribe in Idaho, led by **Chief Joseph**, made a desperate attempt to avoid captivity on a reservation by fleeing to Canada. The U.S. Cavalry caught up with the tribe forty miles from the border. They had little choice but to surrender to American troops.

By 1885, all but a few scattered groups of Indians had been forced onto **reservations**, tracts of land set aside for them. One such group was a rebel band of Apache Indians. Their leader, **Geronimo**, who had been captured and then escaped from reservations several times, finally gave up in 1886.

In 1890, as final defeat for the Indians seemed apparent, the Dakota Sioux gathered for a Ghost Dance. The ritual celebrated a time when the Indians envisioned the earth would die and be reborn. The white men would go to another world. The Indians would then get their lands back.

Custer and his Seventh Cavalry are often depicted as victims of Indian brutality, but Custer brought the attack on himself by attacking an Indian village and killing many women and children.

Chief Joseph of the Nez Perce   Geronimo of the Apaches

Custer

Custer is sometimes called a general and sometimes a colonel. This discrepancy results from the fact that he did obtain the rank of brevet general during the Civil War, but after the war he served at the rank of colonel in the cavalry. (A brevet is a temporary promotion in rank without any increase in pay. After a period of time, such as the end of a battle or campaign, the person returns to his original rank.)

A Horse Named Comanche

Each of the men who fought with Custer at the Battle of Little Bighorn was killed. The only survivor of Custer's group was the horse of Captain Keogh, one of Custer's officers. The horse was named Comanche. Although Comanche had seven arrows in his body when found, the horse was nursed back to health at Fort Lincoln in the Dakota Territory. For the service he had rendered, Comanche was given free rein of the fort's grounds and the honor of being saddled for official military occasions (though he was never actually ridden again). After he died, Comanche was preserved and exhibited at the University of Kansas Museum of Natural History in Lawrence, Kansas.

Crazy Horse

For more than fifty years, sculptors in the Black Hills of South Dakota have been working on a monument to honor Sioux chief Crazy Horse. Like nearby Mount Rushmore, the monument is carved out of the stone face of a mountain. Unlike Mount Rushmore, Crazy Horse is intended to be a three-dimensional, full-length statue depicting the Indian chief astride his horse and with an arm outstretched. The completed statue will be 563 feet high and 641 feet long. The head is 87 feet

 Eyewitness Book

The Eyewitness Book *North American Indians*, by David Murdoch, is visually exciting. Show the students some of the old photographs and paintings and see how many of the famous Indian leaders they can name. Try to include some of the Indians they have studied in this chapter.

Mistreatment of Aboriginal Peoples

Since the flowering of the civil rights movement in the 1960s, Americans have become increasingly sensitive to the mistreatment of aboriginal peoples around the world. An aborigine (Latin, "from the beginning") is a member of the earliest known population of a region. As European civilizations conquered the world, they subjugated the aborigines and took their lands. Spanish enslavement of Indians was an especially deplorable example of abuse. Tragically, America's mistreatment of the Indians was similar to the English treatment of aborigines in Australia and the Afrikaners institution of apartheid in South Africa.

The past wrongs against the Indians teach us many lessons. For example, injustice breeds bitterness, has lasting effects, sets a bad example, and becomes a permanent blot on a nation's reputation. The citizens of a great nation must carefully weigh every action their country takes. Also, wrong decisions sometimes create virtually unsolvable problems for the future. The plight of the Indians today has no easy solution. The Indians have already lost their homes and their historic means of livelihood. From the time they were first forced onto reservations, Indians were forced into a state of dependency on government, becoming part of a great welfare program. Liberals, beginning with Franklin Roosevelt, dramatically increased federal aid to the Indians. In the 1980s, conservatives blamed the Indians' problems on their lack of private property and the federal government's socialistic programs. But some conservatives helped to legalize gambling on the reservations as an alternative means of income and thereby created more problems. Joblessness, alcoholism, and drug abuse remain rampant.

tall, and the arm will be nearly as long as a football field. By way of comparison, the four heads on Mount Rushmore are each approximately 60 feet high.

Sculptor Korczak Ziolkowski started the project in the late 1940s and worked on it until his death in 1982. His family kept the work going, and the head was completed in 1998. Private donations and admission fees continue to finance the construction. Crazy Horse was never photographed in his lifetime, so the monument is intended to portray his spirit, not a strict likeness.

Chief Joseph's Surrender Speech

Chief Joseph's words at his surrender on October 15, 1877, are some of the most moving in the history of the U.S. mistreatment of the Indians: "Tell General Howard I know his heart. What he told me before, I have it in my heart. I am tired of fighting. Our Chiefs are killed; Looking Glass is dead, Ta Hool Hool Shute is dead. The old men are all dead. It is the young men who say yes or no. He who led on the young men is dead. It is cold, and we have no blankets; the little children are freezing to death. My people, some of them, have run away to the hills, and have no blankets, no food. No one knows where they are—perhaps freezing to death. I want to have time to look for my children, and see how many of them I can find. Maybe I shall find them among the dead. Hear me, my Chiefs! I am tired; my heart is sick and sad. From where the sun now stands I will fight no more forever."

Treatment of the American Indians

It is easy for us to look at the treatment of the American Indians and recognize the injustice that they faced, just as we look back at the injustice of slavery. Treaties

Burial of Indians killed at Wounded Knee, South Dakota, December 29, 1890.

The Hualapai Indian tribe built the Skywalk over the rim of the Grand Canyon and continues to operate it.

The as-yet unfinished Crazy Horse Memorial in Black Hills, S.D., honors both the warrior Crazy Horse and the Indian peoples who were victims of the white man's westward expansion.

Some of those who participated in the Ghost Dance claimed they received special powers to kill whites, and some claimed the ghost shirts worn at the dance could stop bullets. On December 29, 1890, troops sent to disarm the Indians shot down almost two hundred Sioux at Wounded Knee, South Dakota. That action proved to be the last of many Indian battles. The Indians were conquered.

Indians who had not resisted were made **wards** of the federal government. The government supported them with an annual payment system and placed them under federal protection. Missionaries often offered help for the Indians, meeting their physical needs while also presenting them with the gospel. Tragically, Americans had given the Indians little reason to embrace the white man's God.

The Dawes Act

In 1887, pro-Indian sentiment forced Congress to do something for the Indians. The **Dawes Act** of 1887 assumed that the Indian way of life no longer worked. The government would help Americanize and assimilate (absorb culturally) the Indians into the mainstream of American life. Under the Dawes Act, tribal unions were to be dissolved. Individual Indians were to receive lands and become self-supporting. Each head of a household was assigned 160 acres.

But the reformers, mostly Easterners, did not understand the Indians' needs. First, most western Indians who were given lands had been hunters and traders, not farmers. Second, the lands the Indians had been allotted were very dry. Americans had given them to the Indians because they were undesirable for their own use. Such small plots of arid land could not sustain a family. Third, Indians were not used to the idea of private ownership of land, so the land deeds meant little to them. Also, their basic social units were the tribe and the extended family (several generations of a family, including grandparents, aunts, uncles, and cousins). When these two units were broken down on the reservations, the Indian way of life suffered even more.

All too eager to make money, some greedy whites offered to buy Indian lands. Since Indians now owned the land personally, they had the option to sell it and often did. Not used to a money economy, however, the Indians were easily cheated. When oil was found on Indian lands, speculators bought up even more Indian land.

Section Quiz

1. What kind of warfare did the U.S. Army employ to defeat the Indians?

2. What was probably the most famous Indian battle? Who was defeated during this battle?

3. Name four ways in which the Dawes Act failed to meet the needs of the Indians.

★ Why did Americans believe the West belonged to them? Why did the Indians believe the West was theirs?

For the United States, which claims to be a nation of laws, the plight of the Indians raises many troubling questions. Is the United States obligated to pay reparations for the lands it took from the Indians in violation of its own treaties? If the United States does not honor its treaties, is the law really supreme? Discuss possible answers to these questions with your class.

Activity 5: Massacre at Wounded Knee, 1890

Use this activity to help the students understand the events leading up to and during the atrocity at Wounded Knee.

CD: Posters for Buffalo Bill's Wild West Show

Use these posters to help the students understand how some people, such as "Buffalo Bill" Cody, sought to keep the memory of the Old Wild West alive even as the Indians were being subdued and the West was being tamed.

Dealing with the Indians

Ask for a group of volunteers to research and report to the class on each of the following topics related to the treatment of American Indians throughout American history:

• War and forcible removal

• Segregation on reservations

• Assimilation and Americanization

Section Quiz Answers

1. total war

2. the battle of the Little Bighorn (Custer's Last Stand); George Armstrong Custer

3. Most western Indians had been hunters and traders, not farmers. Lands given to Indians were very dry. Indians had no experience with owning private property. And reservation life destroyed the traditional Indian social units—tribes and extended families.

Chapter Review

Review Questions

Indicate whether each of the following would be most closely associated with the miners, the cattlemen, the homesteaders, or the Indians.

1. windmills
2. Chisholm Trail
3. Comstock Lode
4. wrangler
5. Ghost Dance
6. Dawes Act
7. "Pikes Peak or Bust!"
8. Sooners

Who Am I?

9. I am the colonel killed at the Battle of Little Big Horn.
10. I am the Nez Perce chief who sought refuge in Canada.
11. I am the Sioux medicine man.
12. I am the businessman who sold meat to the Union army.

Which term in each set does not belong with the others?

13. Chisholm, Comstock, Goodnight-Loving
14. ghost town, sod house, windmill
15. by-products, refrigerator car, wrangler

Critical Thinking

1. Why can homesteaders, rather than miners and cowboys, be given more credit for actually settling the frontier?
2. How could the Indians have been treated differently during the settlement of the West?

People, Places, and Things to Remember:

lode
Comstock Lode
Homestake Mine
Bland-Allison Act
Chisholm Trail
Goodnight-Loving Trail
trail boss
wrangler
Philip Armour
Gustavus Swift
by-products
Homestead Act
Indian Territory
Sooners
sod house
windmill
Joseph Glidden
rural free delivery
Grange
George Armstrong Custer
Crazy Horse
Sitting Bull
Chief Joseph
reservations
Geronimo
wards
Dawes Act

were frequently ignored, and the Indians were coerced by various ungodly means to give up land that Americans wanted, whether to extract valuable resources or to provide more land for settlement. Large populations of Indians were decimated by warfare and disease at the hands of many who viewed the Indians as little more than an obstacle to westward expansion. Thankfully, some Christians worked to convert the Indians and help them survive in the changing environment. But many failed to treat the Indians as individuals created in the image of God. In every generation it is a Christian's responsibility to treat others in a way that demonstrates the love of God and to spread the gospel.

Indians Today

There is a special push on the part of many Indian tribes today to preserve the ways of the past. Some still live in their ancestral villages and craft traditional jewelry and ceramics. Others have resurrected tribal languages or ceremonies. Interest in native religion has increased dramatically.

Missionaries endeavor to work among the Indian tribes with mixed results. Generations of alcoholism and government welfare have robbed the once proud Indians of their dignity and have made missionary work among them very difficult. While the labors continue, the work is often slow and the results difficult to measure.

✶ The United States had purchased the land from France or had it ceded to it by treaty with Mexico. The Indians had lived there for centuries.

Activity 6: Chapter Review

Use this activity to help the students prepare for the chapter test.

Chapter Review Answers

Review Questions

1. homesteaders
2. cattlemen
3. miners
4. cattlemen
5. Indians
6. Indians
7. miners
8. homesteaders
9. Gen. George Custer
10. Chief Joseph
11. Sitting Bull
12. Philip Armour
13. Comstock
14. ghost town
15. wrangler

Critical Thinking

1. Answers will vary. They more often settled down to live permanently in an area. The others tended to move around.
2. The federal government could have ensured that every agreement made with the Indians was one that had been agreed to by the Indians (rather than something they were forced to sign). The government could have ensured that every agreement was honored.

Chapter Goals

Students should be able to

1. Define and use the basic terms of the chapter.

2. Review the course of the Spanish-American War.

3. Explain the value of America's acquisitions from the war.

4. Analyze how the decisions of the late 1800s created America's continuing conflict over foreign policy decisions.

Chapter Motivation

Ask your students what prevented America from imperialistic policies prior to this chapter. *(America was still developing and growing as a nation.)* Why do they think America was ready to exert international influence during the late 1800s? *(because it had gained size, its industries were doing well, and it had enjoyed victories over a previously major world power, Spain)* Ask the students to look for the controversies about imperialism in the chapter and to think about why Americans still struggle with the tensions between those who favor isolationism and those who advocate global influence.

Section I

Objectives

Students should be able to

1. Define *isolationism, imperialism,* and *humanitarianism.*

2. Explain the reasons nations were building empires in the late 1800s.

3. Contrast the true gospel with the social gospel.

4. List the early imperial acquisitions of the United States.

CHAPTER 19

President Theodore Roosevelt used U.S. military power as a "big stick" to encourage pro-American governments in Central America and the Caribbean.

America and the World

I. Imperialism in the Late Nineteenth Century

II. The Spanish-American War

III. American Foreign Policy

Chapter 19 Lesson Plan Chart

Section Title	Main Activity	Pages	Days
I. Imperialism in the Late Nineteenth Century	Activity 1: "The White Man's Burden"	365–67	1–2 days
II. The Spanish-American War	Activity 4: The United States Declares War on Spain, 1898	367–72	2–3 days
III. American Foreign Policy	Activity 6: Chapter Review	373–77	1–2 days
TOTAL SUGGESTED DAYS (INCLUDING 1 DAY FOR REVIEW AND TESTING)		5–8 DAYS	

MATERIALS LIST

SECTION I
- CD: Party Platform Summaries, 1892, 1896, 1900
- Biography of D. L. Moody
- *Scenes from American Church History* (BJU Press)
- Historical wall map or atlas
- Activity 1 from the *Student Activities* manual

SECTION II
- CD: William McKinley, 25th President; Cartoon from *Puck*
- *American History in Verse* by Burton Stevenson (available from BJU Press)

Throughout the nineteenth century, America increased its population, built its industries, and expanded its settlement across the continent. As it grew, the nation got stronger and extended its influence. By the turn of the century, the world recognized America as a world power.

I. Imperialism in the Late Nineteenth Century

Definition of Imperialism

During much of the nineteenth century, America focused on itself—solving regional disputes, implementing Reconstruction, settling the frontier, and developing new businesses. The country had little concern for foreign affairs that did not affect it directly. Minding the country's own business and staying out of world politics is known as **isolationism**.

During the late 1800s, however, the United States watched other countries build world empires. Britain, France, Germany, and a few other nations were taking control of foreign lands. Countries that extended their way of life over other peoples, a policy called **imperialism**, could gain greater wealth and power. Would the United States join those imperialist powers by building its own overseas empire?

Reasons for Imperialism

Imperialist countries had several reasons for expanding their control. First, having a large empire gave them *prestige* among the nations. Second, because taking control of foreign lands often required military force, an imperialist power could be proud of its *military strength*. A large and well-trained army was ready to handle the needs of the empire and to defend against enemies. The military also gained important naval bases and army bases around the world in the lands it controlled. Those bases increased the nation's strength as a world power.

Third, imperialism made possible the accumulation of *wealth*. Imperialist countries controlled their colonies' trade and development of natural resources. They sent their own people to oversee the industries of the colonies. They hired natives for low wages and sent the profits to the mother countries, which benefited from mine and plantation production. They also ensured that the colonies bought all of their imports from the mother countries, which held every economic advantage over their colonies. Sometimes the mother countries took advantage of the poverty and ignorance of the native peoples to keep them working for the benefit of the mother countries. Such practices are called **exploitation**.

Fourth, some people in imperialist countries wanted to teach the "uncivilized" peoples of the world how to read and write, especially in European languages. They wanted to share the benefits of Western education, culture, and science so that the colonials would learn to live like Europeans.

Many imperialists also wanted to provide food and health care to the hungry and sick. Such assistance is called **humanitarianism**. Rudyard Kipling thought that this was part of the "white man's burden." This responsibility motivated many Europeans and Americans to take humanitarian aid and Christianity to Asia, Africa, and the

---

The Student Volunteer Movement for Foreign Missions

In 1886, the Student Volunteer Movement for Foreign Missions (SVMFM) began. It was an outgrowth of the Young Men's Christian Association (YMCA). The motto of the SVMFM was "the evangelization of the world in this generation." The SVMFM flourished through the leadership of several college students, especially John Mott and Robert Wilder. Doctrinally, the organization tried to make room for both conservatives and liberals (those who denied clear teachings from the Bible such as the deity of Jesus Christ). That position contributed to its decline after World War I. Until that time, the organization thrived. Other factors contributing to the decline were financial trouble and disagreements among its members. The SVMFM ended in 1966. It had encouraged thousands of college students to preach the gospel throughout the world.

Imperialism Versus Colonialism

The imperialism of the late 1800s can be contrasted with the colonialism of the 1500s to 1700s. That colonialism was usually intended either to establish a colony of people from the mother country in a new land or to collect the gold, spices, or other treasures of the land to bring back to the mother country. The imperialism of the late nineteenth century neither sought new land for the homes of colonists nor intended to strip the land of its treasures. Instead, it subjugated the natives of the land to work for the benefit of the mother country, developed industries and activities that could benefit the mother country, and tried to help the people of the land adjust to the culture and become like the people of the mother country.

British Empire

In the early 1900s the largest empire belonged to Britain. It was said that "the sun never sets on the British Empire" because it ruled countries across the globe—all or part of India, the Malay Peninsula, Canada, Australia, New Zealand, Africa, and the Pacific Islands. France was a strong imperial power as well, with holdings in Africa, Indochina, and the Pacific Islands. Belgium, the Netherlands, Germany, Italy, and Portugal also participated in the imperialist land grab.

New Role for the American Military

Keep in mind during this chapter that with all of America's involvement in the Caribbean and the Pacific in acquiring territories, investing money, building industries, and sending American citizens to oversee its interests, America's military policy changed. Before 1898 America had

---

- February 1998 issue of *National Geographic* magazine
- Facsimile of front page of the *New York Herald* reporting the sinking of the *Maine*
- World map or globe
- Activities 2–4 from the *Student Activities* manual

SECTION III
- CD: Culebra Cut; Map of the Panama Canal; A "Typical" Week for TR
- World map
- Activities 5–6 from the *Student Activities* manual

Core Values

The change in foreign policy from isolationism to imperialism was motivated by the core value of growth. Having spread their culture from the east coast to the west coast, Americans now desired to grow their culture in more distant lands. As they pursued this policy, they were confronted with challenges to their other core values. What if American growth damaged the equality, freedom, and individualism of other peoples? This period should remind believers that Scripture must guide a nation in its view of its core values. Core values are often in conflict. The Word of God, however, can resolve such conflicts.

CD: Party Platform Summaries, 1892, 1896, 1900

This chapter discusses the time period encompassing three presidential elections. The platforms of the major political parties are on the CD. Discuss each of these at some point in the chapter, noting especially any mention of imperialism in the platforms.

a standing army and navy only when they were needed. As a result, the United States was usually unprepared for military action. After the Spanish-American War, however, America's military forces became a permanent fixture. Their new role involved providing protection for land, American citizens, and investments overseas. In time they would become the policemen of the world.

Social Gospel

Impress on your students the fact that providing food, medical aid, and other care for those who are truly in need is a task Christians should perform. However, humanitarian aid is to no avail if people are not reached with the gospel. Those who preach the social gospel say that "Christian" people should help the needy with humanitarian aid, but they overlook the fact that the poor have a greater need that can be met only by salvation through the Lord Jesus Christ. Often the preachers of the social gospel omit this truth because they have not recognized their own sin and need of Christ and because they expect their good works of humanitarianism to satisfy God.

Multiculturalism

During the age of imperialism, western nations tended to believe their cultures were superior to the cultures of the nations they colonized. Today a view called multiculturalism teaches that all cultures are equally good. Multiculturalism recognizes the strengths of other cultures, a point with which Christians could agree. However, the Christian would also assert that all cultures, whether civilized or not, are tainted by sin. Christians must reject the claim that all cultures are equally

D. L. Moody

Pacific. Many of those motivated to provide humanitarian aid were Christian missionaries. Some of these missionaries were simply social reformers. However, there were also many of these missionaries who spread the gospel as they engaged in humanitarian work.

Evangelist **Dwight L. Moody** had a profound influence on both American and British missions through his preaching and recruiting at many universities. In 1886, he invited missions-minded American students to a summer session at his school in Northfield, Massachusetts. In one month, one hundred students pledged themselves to be foreign missionaries. In the next summer session, twenty-one hundred young men and women attended. In 1888, the **Student Volunteer Movement for Foreign Missions** was set up with the goal of "the evangelization of the world in this generation." New advances in transportation and communication made this motto seem possible to achieve. Although it did not reach that lofty goal, its missionaries fanned out across the world. Sadly, within forty years many in that group had strayed from preaching the Bible as God's truth and preached a social gospel instead.

Arguments about American Imperialism

Americans saw the economic benefits and other advantages of empire building. By 1880, they were producing far more food and goods than they could sell at home. They were also looking for new supplies of raw materials. Some people wanted a stronger army and navy. As a result of those issues, Americans began to think about imperialism as an aid to their own country.

But some Americans opposed expansion. The United States was large and lacked few natural resources. It really did not need to acquire many raw materials from lands overseas as other countries did. Moreover, some Americans opposed imperialism, although they may or may not have opposed "Manifest Destiny." Imperialism contradicted their ideals. Americans had fought for their own liberty. Could they now take away the liberty of foreign people? Some people were also concerned because they saw imperialism as a violation of God's Word.

Other Americans supported continued expansion. Some believed that the United States would become a second-rate nation if it did not build an empire. America's raw materials were not unlimited, and new sources of raw materials might be needed. As America produced more manufactured goods, it would need new markets for those products when the market at home became saturated. Naval officials and ship captains thought the nation needed Pacific islands so that American ships traveling west could refuel. Other people believed that the United States needed to extend its military power and position to protect itself from potential enemies.

Acquisitions of American Imperialism

Although the United States did not become imperialistic overnight, it took steps toward imperialism in the last half of the nineteenth century.

Alaska

The United States continued to expand its territory when it purchased Alaska from Russia in 1867. However, unlike all of the land the United States had acquired before that time, Alaska was not connected to the other land areas of the United States. It was a "distant land" bought for America's benefit. Yet, when Alaska was purchased

Teaching History Through Literature

A good biography will give the students a feel for the life and times of D. L. Moody. BJU Press distributes *D. L. Moody* by David Bennett and *D. L. Moody* by Faith Coxe Bailey. Other good biographies of Moody are also available.

Moody, Sankey, and Crosby

You can find more detailed coverage of D. L. Moody and his song leader, Ira Sankey, in and hymn-writer Fanny Crosby in *Scenes from American Church History*.

Journey Back in Time

At times during their study of U.S. history, the students will need an understanding of world conditions to understand events in America. Use a historical wall map or atlas to show the students the world on the eve of World War I.

As the students examine these maps, ask them to compare the world situation at the turn of the nineteenth century with the current world situation. This chapter is an ideal "case study" in which students can test their thinking skills on foreign relations and diplomacy. The students need to understand that foreign affairs are never stable. Friends become enemies, and nations rise and fall. Students will have a better understanding

of their remaining studies of American and world history if you teach them this important lesson now.

Activity 1: "The White Man's Burden"

The British Victorian poet Rudyard Kipling was living in Vermont during the Spanish-American War. He published the poem "The White Man's Burden" in *McClure's Magazine* in February 1899, days before peace was signed with Spain granting the United States control of the Philippines. The pro-imperialist poem has been a source of controversy ever since. Theodore Roosevelt called it "rather bad poetry but good sense from the expansionist point of view." Read and discuss the poem to understand the

in 1867, no one recognized that event as the beginning of American imperialism beyond our natural borders.

As it turned out, Alaska proved to be very beneficial. A gold rush in Alaska in 1897 brought a flood of miners to the area around the Yukon River. It also boosted the economy of the United States. Later, prospectors found silver, copper, and oil in Alaska, thus adding to the nation's resources. Fishing became important to Alaska's economy. Salmon fishing produced far more wealth for the area than gold ever did. Later, Alaska also became important for national defense. In 1959, Alaska became the forty-ninth state.

Midway

Another advance toward America's world empire took place in 1867 when the United States acquired Midway Island. American seamen had discovered Midway Island, northwest of Hawaii, in 1859. It was a far smaller acquisition than Alaska. Midway's strategic importance remained unrealized until it became the focus of a major battle for control of the Pacific Ocean in World War II.

Hawaii

The first *intentionally* imperialistic gain for the United States did not come until early in 1898. In that year Congress annexed the islands of Hawaii. American missionaries and businessmen had gone to the islands in the early 1800s. Businessman Sanford Dole and others built large pineapple and sugarcane plantations and took advantage of the labor of native Hawaiian workers. The Americans also gained influence in the Hawaiian government. In 1893, they forced Hawaii's queen, Liliuokalani (lee LEE oo oh kah LAH nee), from power, declared a republic, and asked the United States to annex them. President Cleveland, however, refused to purchase the islands because the queen had been removed from power illegally. After President McKinley came into office he agreed to the purchase, making Hawaii the next in a series of imperial gains for the nation.

Annexation ceremony in Honolulu, Hawaii, 1898

Section Quiz

1. Define *imperialism*.
2. What were the three major reasons for imperialism?
3. List three reasons for opposition to American expansion in the early 1900s.
4. What 1898 acquisition in the Pacific was America's first intentionally imperialistic gain?
★ What shift in focus was manifested by some missionaries of this period?
★ How did imperialism affect how the native peoples received the gospel?

II. The Spanish-American War

In 1898, America not only added Hawaii to its territories but also entered a war that greatly expanded its overseas empire. Although it was a short and inexpensive war (as wars go), the **Spanish-American War** had huge consequences for American imperialism.

Cuba, less than one hundred miles off the southern coast of Florida, was the cause of a quarrel with Spain. It had been ruled by Spain

good. Scripture provides the Christian historian with the standard by which he is able to evaluate all cultures.

Section II
Objectives

Students should be able to

1. Explain the long-term and immediate causes of the Spanish-American War.
2. Describe the course of the war.
3. List the areas that came under American control as a result of the war.

Sugar and Politics

The profitable sugar cane plantations set up by American businessmen in Hawaii found a strong trading partner in the United States. In fact, Hawaiian exports were allowed into the country duty-free. Problems arose, however, with the passing of the McKinley Tariff of 1890. The tariff eliminated duties on all foreign sugar and, in addition, paid United States farmers two cents for each pound of sugar they produced. Thus, Hawaiian plantation owners lost the advantage they had held over other foreign markets and also faced the competition of cheaper domestic sugar. These owners pushed for Hawaiian annexation with the United States so that their sugar would be considered domestic rather than foreign. Statehood would allow them to compete successfully and turn a profit with their sugar cane.

motives behind imperialism. Which motives, if any, were justified?

Use Activity 1 to help the students understand the responsibilities that imperialism brought to colonial powers. Explain to the students that many people have found this poem to be offensive. Ask them to identify and explain any such passages. Discuss those passages in the context of the Western culture of Kipling's day. Discuss the same passages from the perspective of the nationals whose lands were being occupied. Finally, evaluate these perspectives from a biblical worldview.

Alternative Perspectives

Have your students research the history of Hawaii. Which groups favored annexation then and which opposed it? How did annexation by the U.S. affect Hawaiian culture?

Section Quiz Answers

1. the extension of one's way of life over another people so as to gain wealth and power for the controlling country
2. to build military strength, to gain wealth from raw materials and trade, to help unlearned and poor peoples
3. America did not need the resources; America should not take away the liberty of those lands; America should

not exploit other peoples (contradicted biblical principles).

4. the Hawaiian Islands
★ Rather than preaching salvation through Jesus Christ, they emphasized good works that met physical needs only.
★ Answers will vary.

The Yellow Kid and Yellow Journalism

He started in 1895 as a minor character in the comic strip "Hogan's Alley." But the public liked him. He was named the Yellow Kid after he started appearing in a bright yellow nightshirt. Given his own comic strip shortly thereafter, he communicated with the audience by means of words written on the front of his shirt. New Yorkers were crazy about this youngster from their own streets.

"The Yellow Kid" appeared first as a comic strip in Joseph Pulitzer's *New York World*. Seeing its popularity, William Randolph Hearst hired artist R. F. Outcault to come and draw "The Yellow Kid" for his paper, the *New York Journal*. Not to be outfoxed, Pulitzer hired George B. Luks to continue to draw a Yellow Kid comic strip for the *World*. The intense rivalry that arose between the papers over the character led to the coining of the term "yellow journalism," which referred to any situation in which publishers tried to make their newspapers more exciting in order to compete for subscriptions.

"The Katzenjammer Kids"

"The Katzenjammer Kids" is the oldest comic strip still in syndication. Created in 1897 by Rudolph Dirks, the strip's chief characters, twins Hans and Fritz, continue to operate today with the help of a new artist, Hy Eisman. Sadly, the twins' activities often involve rebellion against authority, either at home or at school.

Comic strips became so popular in twentieth-century America that in 1935 William Randolph Hearst offered his weekend readers a thirty-two-page special comic section.

CD: William McKinley, 25th President

Refer to the CD for information about President William McKinley.

Poetry Corner

You will find the following poems about the Spanish-American War in Burton Stevenson's *American History in Verse*:

- "Cuba Libre" (Joaquin Miller)
- "The Men of the *Maine*" (Clinton Scollard)
- "To Spain—A Last Word" (Edith M. Thomas)
- "Dewey in Manila Bay" (R. V. Risley)
- "The Spirit of the *Maine*" (Tudor Jenks)

for four hundred years but had experienced only about a dozen years of well-run, peaceful, productive existence. Spain had exploited this colony and allowed poor governing by its officials. The United States and other nations tried to help the Cubans and encouraged Spain to improve the situation, but little change occurred.

Causes of the War

Americans watched as the plight and conditions of their Cuban neighbors worsened. They began to think that they must do something to help and viewed the Cubans as oppressed victims.

Cuban Dissatisfaction

The Cubans had long been dissatisfied with conditions in their country. Many of the people suffered from poverty and cruel treatment. In 1895, revolution broke out in Cuba. The revolutionaries had three goals they hoped would lead to eventual independence:

1. to terrorize Cuba
2. to destroy its livelihood (the sugar industry)
3. to draw the United States into the conflict

The revolutionary forces in Cuba also had agents in the United States. They raised money for the revolution. The revolutionaries also fed the American press a steady diet of overblown incidents, all of which they blamed on Spain. They hoped the stories would make Americans angry enough to go to war.

William Randolph Hearst   Joseph Pulitzer

William McKinley

The Yellow Press

The revolutionaries funneled "news" to key newspapers to in order to shape American opinion. Many of those newspapers were themselves locked in fierce competition to sell subscriptions. One way to increase sales was to feed the reading public a steady diet of sensational stories. Reporters twisted news stories, trying to make each one more exciting than the previous. That practice is called **yellow journalism**. Two powerful newspapermen faced off in this struggle: **William Randolph Hearst** (HURST), owner of the *New York Journal*, and **Joseph Pulitzer** (PUL it sur) with the *New York World*. Unfortunately, some of what they reported was either inaccurate or greatly exaggerated. They knew that if they continued to write such stories, they could stir up great interest in a growing conflict. Their news reports stirred the sympathies of readers and made them want to help the Cubans. Many believed that the Cubans were oppressed by Spain. They wanted Cubans to have the freedoms and advantages that Americans enjoyed. Influenced by the press, most Americans favored helping the Cubans rid themselves of Spanish oppression.

American Investment

Another reason for U.S. interest in Cuba was that American businessmen had heavily invested in Cuban sugar plantations and refineries. The investors feared that if the government remained unstable and the terrorist acts continued, they might lose their money. The investors pressured President **William McKinley** to protect their interests.

The Press, Public Opinion, and Comic Strips Too

Joseph Pulitzer, a Hungarian immigrant, had refined his journalistic trade in St. Louis with his powerful paper, the *St. Louis Post-Dispatch*. In 1883 he invaded New York City and bought out the dying *New York World*. Alert reporting, sensational stunts, and vivid pictures helped the *World* make a profit. Pulitzer was a crusader. No matter what the cause, he was able to drum up excitement and inspiration much as a bandmaster does with a band.

Editors across America studied his techniques and imitated them. His most successful imitator, William Randolph Hearst, copied him so well that Hearst soon became Pulitzer's chief competitor. Hearst had been given the *San Francisco Examiner* by his father. When he later inherited his father's millions, he enlarged his base and bought the *New York Journal*. He used some of his fortune to hire writers away from Pulitzer. When news was lacking, Hearst made his own news. He turned reporters into detectives to pursue criminals and made crime columns more exciting. He hired preachers to furnish religious material that would fire editorial controversy.

In 1897, Hearst challenged Pulitzer to a duel for subscribers. The battleground became the events leading to the Spanish-American War. In 1897 artist-reporter Frederic Remington was ready to leave Cuba, believing that there was nothing of importance to report. Pulitzer is said to have cabled him: "Please remain. You furnish the pictures and I'll furnish the war." Hearst entered the journalistic battleground claiming that he was just doing his patriotic duty.

Smaller newspapers copied the style of Hearst and Pulitzer; their pages were filled with the same jingoism (extreme nationalism). Some thoughtful citizens were troubled when they realized that these journalists were not just reporting public opinion, but creating and controlling it. And the issue involved, entry into a war, was deadly serious. This was not the first time the American press had created rather than reflected opinion. But it had never happened before on such a wide scale.

Once this round with Hearst was over, Pulitzer quit the fight and decided to compete on a higher level. He turned his paper into a responsible journal which maintained high standards of journalism. He tried to raise standards for future journalists by endowing a School of Journalism at Columbia University in 1912. Hearst meanwhile created a chain of newspapers and bought magazines. He had political ambitions, but he was widely distrusted, and his ambitions were frustrated.

The Hearst press did leave a lasting legacy to journalism: the funnies, or Sunday comics. Trying to capture working-class families as readers, Hearst's *Sunday Journal* added an eight-page colored Sunday supplement in 1896. Hearst hired the artist who drew Pulitzer's "Yellow Kid" drawings away from him. The *Journal* then published the first real comic strip. Called the "Katzenjammer Kids," it was written by a cartoonist named Rudolph Dirks. Other comics included "Mutt and Jeff" and "Krazy Kat." Editors found that the funnies were the first part of the paper most people read. The funnies became a kind of American folk art expressing what some Americans thought or felt or at least what amused them.

Immediate Causes

As tensions rose over the Cuban situation, two important events spurred the United States into action.

In February 1898, the *New York Journal* published a letter written by **Dupuy de Lôme**, the Spanish minister to the United States. The letter, written to a personal friend of the minister, was never meant for publication. But Cuban rebels stole it and gave it to the Hearst press. The letter described McKinley as "weak and a bidder for the admiration of the crowd, besides being a common politician." At that time, Americans had such high esteem for the presidency that they considered any foreign criticism of the president to be a national insult. The press demanded that Spain be punished. De Lôme resigned, but the furor did not diminish.

The second event occurred less than a week after the de Lôme letter. On February 15, 1898, the **U.S.S. *Maine***, an American warship anchored in Havana, Cuba. The ship was on what the navy called a goodwill mission, and Spain reacted appropriately. However, on February 15 at 9:40 p.m., the *Maine* mysteriously exploded. Two

Hearst's *New York Journal* sought to stir up public support for the war against Spain.

San Simeon

William Randolph Hearst displayed his great wealth and extravagant tastes in his estate at San Simeon, California.

On the estate grounds, he established a private zoo with animals from all over the world, some caged and others roaming freely.

At the top of a large hill, he built La Casa Grande, a magnificent castle in the style of the Spanish Renaissance. He not only created an impressive exterior but also filled the inside of the house with an array of European art treasures, procured through diligent searching by Hearst and his agents and costing millions of dollars. One of the most outstanding rooms is the Refectory, where guests enjoyed the atmosphere of a medieval banquet hall, complete with massive dining table, tapestried walls, and rows of banners.

For family and guest recreation, Hearst built a huge climate-controlled indoor swimming pool as well as an elegant outdoor pool. Part of the architecture surrounding the outdoor pool is the reconstructed facade of an ancient temple.

Though Hearst spent $30 million on the estate, he still had not completed the house to his satisfaction when he died.

The Sinking of the U.S.S. *Maine*

Two other possible explanations for the sinking of the *Maine* are that it was an accident or that it was the work of Cuban terrorists who wanted to create American anger toward Spain. No evidence has been found to prove the cause of the explosion, but some historians believe that the Cubans had the most to gain and are the most likely culprits.

Nuggets from *National Geographic*

The February 1998 issue of *National Geographic* contains the article "Remember the *Maine*?" which gives two possible explanations for the *Maine* explosion and the evidences for each. However, it reaches no conclusive result. Computer simulations show that either explanation is plausible.

Pages from U.S. History

Obtain a facsimile of the front page of the New York *Herald* reporting the sinking of the U.S.S. *Maine*. Share some of the articles with the students, and ask them to identify any indications of biased or sensational reporting.

Bias in the Media

Share recent examples of bias in the media or ask the students to give examples. Also discuss the media's influence on opinion. The media fabricate some "crises" merely by over-reporting an actual incident. (You might obtain examples of such bias by reading former CBS TV reporter Bernard Goldberg's books *Bias: A CBS Insider Exposes How the Media Distort the News* and *Arrogance: Rescuing America From the Media Elite*.)

McKinley's Secret to Political Success

William McKinley won elections to Congress, the governorship of Ohio, and eventually the presidency. He was a highly popular, successful politician. In the presidential election of 1896, he became the first candidate since 1872 to receive a majority of the popular votes. In 1900 he won the largest popular majority that any presidential candidate up to that point had received.

His political success was due in good measure to his personal traits. He was a very courteous man. He was also reasonable. He did not insist blindly on his own way but was willing to look at other sides of an issue. His goal was to bring all sides together. And his skill in compromise was such that he often did just that.

Rough Riders

Lieutenant Colonel Theodore Roosevelt, serving under Colonel Leonard Wood, led a company of soldiers in a successful charge up San Juan Hill in Cuba in 1898. The charge paved the way for an American victory in the Spanish-American War. The men were called the Rough Riders.

Earlier, the term Rough Riders described men who carried messages across the West in the days before the pony express. Buffalo Bill also used the name in his "Wild West Show and Congress of Rough Riders of the World." The Rough Riders who rode in the show were supposedly the top horsemen in the world.

When America declared war on Spain in 1898, the governor of the New Mexico territory offered to send a rifle brigade. His men became the largest contingent of the First United States Volunteer Cavalry. Because many of the cavalrymen had west-

The wreckage of the U.S.S. *Maine* in Havana Harbor

Dewey's naval victory in Manila Bay stirred nationalistic feeling and marked the beginning of U.S. involvement in the Philippines.

Teddy Roosevelt and his "Rough Riders" pose following their victory over the Spanish on San Juan Hill.

officers and 250 enlisted men died in the initial blast. The yellow press concluded that Spain was responsible. Other explanations were possible, but many Americans wanted to blame Spain. They demanded action. The battle cry became, "Remember the *Maine!*"

The president and Congress stalled briefly. Then they issued a resolution that approved the use of force in Cuba to set up a stable government. The resolution included the **Teller amendment**, which said that the United States had no intention of adding Cuba to its empire. They desired only Cuba's independence. That statement gave Americans confidence that further action would only help the Cubans, not further American imperialism.

Some people believe that McKinley yielded to public pressure. McKinley believed that Spain would never grant Cuba independence and that only independence would satisfy the American public. When Congress recognized Cuba's independence (even though Cuba did not yet have its own government), Spain tried to uphold its honor by declaring war on the United States. On April 25, 1898, the United States declared war on Spain.

Most Americans wanted Cubans to have a better life. They honestly thought that the United States could help the Cubans achieve progress. Their interest in Cuba, however, opened the way for expansion of American power and influence and brought the problems of an empire.

The Course of the War

The Spanish-American War was over in one hundred days. The United States was not really ready for a full-scale war, but the Spanish government and army were weak. The United States won every battle fought in this war.

Lack of Military Preparedness

Most of the American soldiers in the war came from the states' volunteers. By late spring, troops had gathered at a military base in Tampa, Florida. Although the war would be fought in a subtropical area, many soldiers had been issued wool uniforms, and some cavalry troops lacked horses. But the invasion force sailed on June 14.

The U.S. army fought bravely. Several regiments, notably the **Rough Riders**, gained special fame. But the navy played the most important role in the war. During the Cleveland presidency, the United States had developed a program to build a fleet of steel ships. Now those ships came in handy. More than anything, the navy's success showed that the United States had arrived as one of the world's great powers.

Battles of the Spanish-American War

Long before war was declared, Assistant Secretary of the Navy **Theodore Roosevelt** sent secret orders to Commodore George Dewey, who was in Hong Kong with the American fleet in the Pacific. Roosevelt told Dewey to prepare for an attack on the Spanish fleet in the Philippines in case war broke out with Spain. The American force arrived in Manila on April 30 and met the Spanish Pacific fleet the next morning. By noon the **Battle of Manila Bay** was over. No Americans died from combat (one engineer died from sunstroke). Spain lost 167 men and much of its Pacific fleet.

The American Caribbean fleet trapped the Spanish Atlantic fleet in the harbor at Santiago, which was then the capital of Cuba. American troops landed near Santiago and stormed into the city.

Activity 2: American Imperialism

Use this activity to help the students understand the scope of American imperialistic activities between 1867 and 1905.

CD: Cartoon from *Puck*

Refer to the CD for a cartoon showing a foreign view of unrest in Cuba.

Activity 3: Sensationalism, Jingoism, and Impartiality

Use this activity to reinforce the existence of media bias and to help the students develop the ability to distinguish between balanced, factual reporting and media bias.

Activity 4: The United States Declares War on Spain, 1898

Use this activity to help the students use a primary source (McKinley's request for a declaration of war).

TR's Rough Riders

A good (though a bit self-promoting) narrative of the involvement of Theodore Roosevelt and his cavalry unit is his book *The Rough Riders.*

They pushed the Spanish back to defenses on **San Juan Hill**. Theodore Roosevelt had resigned his office in the Navy Department to command an all-volunteer cavalry unit called the Rough Riders. He led them in a famous charge up San Juan Hill (ironically, dismounted) and helped defeat the Spanish. The Spanish fleet in the Caribbean lost every one of its ships in a sea battle. On July 17, the Spanish in Santiago officially surrendered. The American army also took Puerto Rico, another Spanish possession, without resistance on July 25.

When the war was officially over in August, fewer than four hundred American soldiers had died in battle or from combat wounds. Disease took a far greater toll—thirteen times as many lives as combat-related causes. More than five thousand soldiers died of typhoid, malaria, yellow fever, or other diseases.

The Treaty of Paris

The Spanish signed a truce on August 12, 1898. Spanish and American diplomats met in Paris on October 1. By December 10, 1898, they had produced a treaty. Spain agreed to give up Cuba and Puerto Rico in the Caribbean and Guam and the Philippines in the Pacific to the United States. The United States gave Spain $20 million.

But a debate erupted in the Senate. Influential anti-imperialists (including Charles Francis Adams, Andrew Carnegie, former presidents Cleveland and Harrison, and authors Mark Twain and William Dean Howells) opposed the treaty. They said the treaty violated the principles of the Monroe Doctrine. Only when William Jennings Bryan supported the treaty and promised Filipino independence did the Senate ratify it. It passed by only two votes.

Consequences of the War

Like it or not, the United States now had an empire—and all of the problems that came with it.

Cuba

The Teller amendment had promised Cuba its independence. But until Cuba was ready for independence, the United States supervised its government. In 1901, Congress passed the **Platt amendment**, strict regulations for Cuba's new government. It kept Cuba from making alliances with countries other than the United States, allowed U.S. oversight of Cuba's financial affairs, and authorized the United States to send forces to Cuba to keep order, if needed. This arrangement was not exactly "independence." It also allowed the United States to establish and keep a navy base in Cuba. The U.S. Navy still uses the base at **Guantanamo Bay** today. (Most recently, "Gitmo," as the Guantanamo Bay base is called, was used to imprison terrorist leaders and enemy combatants captured during the war on terror.)

Despite its reluctance to give up control of Cuba after the war, the United States did much to help the island. Yellow fever was a scourge in the Caribbean. A Cuban doctor, Dr. Carlos Finlay, believed that the disease was carried by mosquitoes. An American army doctor, **Walter Reed**, proved that Finlay was right. Major **William Gorgas** (GOR gus) and a crew of army engineers drained the swamps and low-lying areas and succeeded in getting

> #### Was U.S. Involvement Justified?
>
> It is difficult to make moral judgments in history. Modern people often do not understand the worldview and concerns that motivated people in the previous centuries. Some historians, based on their own modern worldview, have been quick to critique earlier generations. But what makes a current worldview any more valid than an older one? Christian historians have a significant advantage over their secular counterparts. Christians are able to measure all worldviews, both ancient and modern, according to the standard of God's Word. Using biblical principles that deal with honesty and fighting a just war, we can disapprove of the Spanish-American War as an imperialistic action fueled by false news reports and congressional pressure to act.

Walter Reed and William Gorgas's combined efforts led to thousands of lives saved from death by mosquito-borne illnesses.

ern associations, they were called "Rough Riders." Ironically, most of their fighting in Cuba was done on foot since transportation difficulties kept many of their horses in Florida.

After the Rough Riders of San Juan Hill won international fame, Buffalo Bill added a reenactment of their charge to his show. The deceased of the company were given a stone memorial at Arlington National Cemetery in 1908.

Hispanics in Congress

Historian Robert Remini records that "the many territories of the United States sent nonvoting delegates to the House, including the first Hispanic, Joseph Hernandez, a delegate to the 17th Congress, from Florida. He served from September 22, 1822, to March 1823. But the first Hispanic elected to the House proper was Romualdo Pacheco, a Republican from California. He served three terms, starting in 1877. By the mid-1990s, there were seventeen Hispanics in the House—and their number keeps growing" (*The House: The History of the House of Representatives*, p. 265).

William Jennings Bryan

Though William Jennings Bryan never became president, it was certainly not for lack of trying. He ran three times for the presidency (and tried unsuccessfully another time for the Democratic nomination). During one election four different parties supported him as their candidate. However, his message of free silver and other reforms never drew enough voters to enable him to win an election.

Although he did not win the highest office, Bryan did serve two terms in Congress and was appointed secretary of state during Woodrow Wilson's administration.

Locate Acquisitions on a Map

Use a globe or map to locate all of the lands that the United States acquired during and as a result of the Spanish-American War and the era of imperialism.

The Burdens of Victory

Emphasize a primary lesson of this chapter—that foreign wars bring long-lasting commitments and consequences. A country's leaders should weigh the potential long-term costs carefully before going to war. (See Prov. 24:6.) Discuss any recent military actions that have brought long-term obligations (e.g., the invasions of Afghanistan and Iraq and the first Persian Gulf War committed the United States to contribute billions of dollars for rebuilding and defending the freed peoples against the Taliban and terrorists).

Bryan was a powerful orator. In his last years, he spoke and wrote prolifically for the cause of biblical truth, opposing evolution (see discussion of Scopes Trial, Ch. 22) and championing a literal interpretation of the Scriptures.

Yellow Fever

Dr. Carlos Finlay believed that mosquitoes carried yellow fever, while others held that a bacterium caused the disease and that contaminated objects spread it. Dr. Walter Reed led a commission to discover which theory was correct.

A group of soldiers and surgeons volunteered for the experiment. Reed divided the volunteers into two groups. The first group was exposed to the clothes and bedding of yellow-fever victims. The others were either bitten by mosquitoes or exposed somehow to infected blood. All of the men in the second group contracted yellow fever. Reed concluded that a virus caused the disease (this was the first time that a human disease was traced back to a virus) and that mosquitoes of the species *Aedes aegypti* spread it. Identifying the cause of the problem enabled the development of a solution.

McKinley on the U.S. Acquisition of the Philippines

"When next I realized that the Philippines had dropped into our laps[,] I confess I did not know what to do with them. . . . I walked the floor of the White House night after night until midnight; and I am not ashamed to tell you, gentlemen, that I went down on my knees and prayed to Almighty God for light and guidance more than one night. And one night late it came to me . . . (1) That we could not give them back to Spain—that would be cowardly and dishonorable; (2) that we could not turn them over to France or Germany—our commercial rivals in the Orient—that would be bad business and discreditable; (3) that we could not leave them to themselves—they were unfit for self-government—and they would soon have anarchy and misrule over there worse than Spain's was; and (4) that there was nothing left for us to do but to take them all, and to educate the Filipinos, and uplift and civilize and Christianize them, and by God's grace do the very best we could for them, as our fellow-men for whom Christ died."

Emilio Aguinaldo

rid of the water where the mosquitoes bred. The United States also provided food and clothing for the poor and built roads, schools, railroads, and hospitals.

Puerto Rico

The United States gave Puerto Rico aid similar to what had been given to Cuba. Puerto Rico also got special economic considerations such as duty-free trade with the United States. This trade benefited the sugar industry. Puerto Rico was also exempted from paying taxes. By the Jones Act, passed in 1917, Puerto Rico became a territory with a governor appointed by the president and a two-house legislative assembly. In 1952, Puerto Rico asked to become a commonwealth, a freely associated part of the United States. (Some people have pushed for its admission as a state, but most Puerto Ricans have repeatedly voted against that idea.)

The Philippines

Many Americans were unsure about the wisdom of taking the Philippines. It was a land of more than seven thousand Pacific islands. It would be hard for the United States to provide even a basic government to rule such a large area. Since the Filipinos had almost no experience in self-government, the United States would have trouble helping them set up a republican form of government. Opponents also believed that annexation of the Philippines violated the American ideal of liberty. They thought it might even be unconstitutional. Some of them believed that a U.S. presence in the Philippines might lead to a needless war.

But President McKinley believed that if left to itself, the Philippines might fall into anarchy or be taken over by another country. The land would also make a good base for trade with China. In addition, American missionaries could go to help the Filipinos. McKinley's view won, and Congress decided to take over the islands.

Under the leadership of **Emilio Aguinaldo**, the Philippines had long fought against Spanish rule. When the United States won the war, Aguinaldo and his followers expected the United States to grant them independence. The Filipinos were angry when they learned instead that the Americans would simply replace their Spanish rulers. Aguinaldo and his followers decided to fight against the American occupying force. The war lasted for two and one-half years. Suppressing the insurrection cost the United States more time, money, and casualties than had the entire Spanish-American War.

The United States worked to prepare the Philippines for independence by setting up a public school system to teach Filipinos citizenship. They built hospitals, railroads, and power plants. They also greatly improved communication systems. American governors ruled the islands for more than thirty-five years. In 1934, the United States granted the islands commonwealth status. World War II delayed Philippine independence, but they finally got it on July 4, 1946.

Section Quiz

1. What were the two immediate causes of the Spanish-American War?
2. What did the Teller amendment state?
3. How long did the Spanish-American War last?

What If . . .

Ask the students about their knowledge of Cuba, the Philippines, and Puerto Rico from various sources: previous classes, news reports, and missionaries. Fill in holes in their knowledge. Then ask them to consider how different the world would have been if the anti-imperialists had won the debate in Congress or if William Jennings Bryan had come out against acquiring those territories. Note the large part that the Philippines played during World War II and the eventual takeover of Cuba by Communists. Might these countries have taken a radically different course if the United States had not taken responsibility for them?

Section Quiz Answers

1. anger over the de Lôme letter and anger over the sinking of the *Maine*
2. that the United States wanted Cuba to be independent, not part of America's empire
3. one hundred days

4. What were the provisions of the treaty that ended the Spanish-American War?

5. Who was Emilio Aguinaldo? Why did he cause problems for the United States?

★ How did American journalists contribute to the outbreak of the Spanish-American War?

★ How does media influence our perception of the news today? What are some examples of bias in the media?

III. American Foreign Policy

As American interests widened in the late 1800s, U.S. foreign policy changed. The government no longer stayed out of disputes between foreign countries if it was in America's interest to become involved. If American trade and power could be advanced or other countries could be protected from tyranny, the United States got involved. This was especially true in Latin America and eastern Asia. The results of this policy were mixed at best.

In Latin America

Since the proclamation of the Monroe Doctrine, the United States had protected its American neighbors. For example, in 1867, the United States drove French forces out of Mexico. Then, in 1895, the United States mediated a boundary dispute between Venezuela and British Guinea. By 1900, the United States was ready to take its place as leader of the Western Hemisphere.

The Panama Canal

A major goal of the United States in Latin America was to build a canal. American naval officers had been pressing for a canal across Central America. A canal would enable the few ships in the American fleet to defend both the Atlantic and Pacific coasts more easily by moving quickly between the seas. The Spanish-American War helped prove the point. It took two months to sail a warship from Puget Sound in the Northwest to the East Coast by way of Cape Horn (around South America).

The idea of a canal was not new. In 1851, the United States and England had signed a treaty to build a canal that would be open to both nations. The construction of a canal, however, eventually fell to a French company headed by Ferdinand de Lesseps (LES ups), builder of the Suez Canal. The French chose a route across the Isthmus of Panama. But the project took much longer than expected, and many of the workers died of malaria or yellow fever. The French company went bankrupt, and the United States then took over the project.

The United States had thought about building its canal across Nicaragua but decided to build it in Panama. At that time, Panama was part of Colombia, so the United States offered Colombia $10 million for the right to build the canal in Panama and an annual rental fee of $250,000. Colombia refused. It wanted $25 million.

Opposition leaders in Panama wanted independence. America realized that if the Panamanians revolted against Colombia and gained independence, the new Panamanian government would

Dredges work to complete Culebra Cut in what became the Panama Canal.

Section III
Objectives
Students should be able to

1. Explain why the United States wanted the Panama Canal and how it came to build it.

2. Compare Roosevelt's strategy for Latin American foreign policy with that of Taft and Wilson.

3. Describe the foreign activity in China at the turn of the century.

Ferdinand de Lesseps

Ferdinand de Lesseps was both a diplomat and an engineer. As the French consul in Cairo, Egypt, from 1833 to 1838, he became familiar with ideas for a canal that would join the Mediterranean and Red seas. After his retirement from the diplomatic service, he pushed for the organization of the Suez Canal Company and supervised the canal's construction from 1859 to 1869.

After his triumph in Egypt, Lesseps sought a new challenge. In 1881 he formed the Interoceanic Canal Company to build a sea-level canal across the Isthmus of Panama. Engineering difficulties and financial troubles, including charges of mishandling funds, prevented his completion of the project.

---

4. Cuba became independent, and Spain ceded Guam, the Philippines, and Puerto Rico to the United States for $20 million.

5. a leader of Filipino resistance against the Spanish; because he wanted the Philippines to be given independence

★ They wanted to report exciting stories to gain more readers, so they purposely exaggerated events in Cuba to stir up conflict there.

★ News is often portrayed in such a way as to lead the audience to draw false conclusions. Answers to the second question will vary. Try to bring up examples from your local area.

What Makes a Great President?

Ask students what they think makes a great president. Most polls of historians rank Teddy Roosevelt as a "near great" president. (The four presidents generally ranking as "great" are Washington, Jefferson, Lincoln, and Franklin D. Roosevelt—three of whom appear on Mount Rushmore.) Calvin Coolidge, who served during the Roaring Twenties, is usually relegated to the ranks of "below average." Nevertheless, Coolidge was the favorite president of President Reagan (whom many conservatives deeply admire). Why? Reagan considered a great leader to be one who was willing to serve the country's interests by keeping taxes low and government small. Modern historians like to pick

presidents who were strong, assertive, activist presidents. They tend to rank strict constructionist presidents lower. Why? Is an assertive president good for the republic? Is a less activist president necessarily bad? Evaluate Teddy Roosevelt. Was he really great or near great? Or you might want to wait until the next chapter to address this question.

🖥 Detailed History of the Panama Canal

An excellent resource for details of the history of the building of the Panama Canal is David McCullough's book *The Path Between the Seas*.

The Panama Canal

Led by Ferdinand de Lesseps, the mastermind behind the Suez Canal, the French had begun to build a canal across Panama but stopped after near financial ruin and enormous loss of life from diseases. The Americans had also considered such a canal, but they could not decide on the best location for it.

Some people wanted to take over and complete the French project in Panama. Others wanted to cut through Nicaragua to the north. The debate in the Senate hinged on two things. First, Senator Mark Hanna spoke convincingly in favor of Panama, using detailed maps, charts, engineering plans, and endorsements by prominent engineers. Second, during the debates, Mount Pelée in the Caribbean erupted, creating concern about possible volcanic activity in Nicaragua. The Nicaraguans denied that their country had any volcanoes. But then Hanna discovered a Nicaraguan postage stamp that showed an erupting volcano, Momotombo. He bought a bunch of the stamps and mailed one of the stamps to each of the senators shortly before they voted. The tally was 42–34 in favor of the Panama route. Recognizing Hanna's influence over the vote, people began to call it the "Hannama Canal."

Roosevelt's first priority was to solve the problem of disease. He named William Gorgas, a Christian and an authority on tropical diseases, to head the task. Building on the experiments of Walter Reed, another Christian army doctor, Gorgas worked to isolate victims of malaria and yellow fever so that the diseases would not spread, and he also eradicated the two types of mosquitoes that carried the diseases.

James J. Hill, the "Empire Builder" of Great Northern Railroad fame, suggested John Stevens to be chief engineer of the project. Stevens gave Gorgas what he needed to accomplish the health objectives and prepared everything for beginning construction. He tripled the work force, which came from ninety-seven different countries.

Colonel George W. Goethals supervised the actual construction for seven years. The project required sixty-one million pounds of dyna-mite. The most productive month was March 1909, when sixty-eight steam shovels removed more than two million cubic yards. That was ten times the largest amount the French had removed.

To calm public fears about the project, Roosevelt decided to visit Panama himself during the construction. The trip was a public relations coup. He went during November, the peak of the rainy season, so he could see the project under the worst conditions. During his two-week tour, he inspected every conceivable activity. Roosevelt praised the work of the men. According to historian David McCullough, Roosevelt viewed the project "as though it were a mighty battle in which the national honor was at stake" (*The Path Between the Seas*, p. 507). His most famous event was jumping from his train in the rain and climbing aboard a steam shovel. A photographer snapped his picture. The photo appeared in newspapers all across America. Roosevelt died prior to the completion of the canal. The project was completed in 1914 during Woodrow Wilson's presidency.

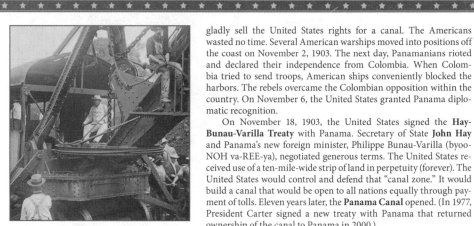

President Theodore Roosevelt visited the Panama Canal during its construction and even posed at the controls of a steam shovel during a rainstorm.

gladly sell the United States rights for a canal. The Americans wasted no time. Several American warships moved into positions off the coast on November 2, 1903. The next day, Panamanians rioted and declared their independence from Colombia. When Colombia tried to send troops, American ships conveniently blocked the harbors. The rebels overcame the Colombian opposition within the country. On November 6, the United States granted Panama diplomatic recognition.

On November 18, 1903, the United States signed the **Hay-Bunau-Varilla Treaty** with Panama. Secretary of State **John Hay** and Panama's new foreign minister, Philippe Bunau-Varilla (byoo-NOH va-REE-ya), negotiated generous terms. The United States received use of a ten-mile-wide strip of land in perpetuity (forever). The United States would control and defend that "canal zone." It would build a canal that would be open to all nations equally through payment of tolls. Eleven years later, the **Panama Canal** opened. (In 1977, President Carter signed a new treaty with Panama that returned ownership of the canal to Panama in 2000.)

CD: Culebra Cut

This photo on the CD shows the beginning of the construction of the Panama Canal in 1904.

CD: Map of the Panama Canal

Refer to the CD for a map of the finished canal.

Activity 5: The Panama Canal

Have the students refer to the feature box on the Panama Canal to answer the questions in this activity.

The Big Stick, Another Perspective

"To Roosevelt" by Ruben Dario, a Nicaraguan poet in the early part of the century, is a representative poem that shows the paradoxical admiration and disdain that Latin Americans held for Roosevelt and his big stick diplomacy.

Progressive Foreign Policies

The foreign policies of the three progressive presidents (Roosevelt, Taft, and Wilson) marked a radical shift from the past (just as progressive social policies—discussed in the next chapter—caused a radical policy shift that is still felt today). How were all three presidents' policies similar? *(They wanted to use the power of the federal government to promote "good" abroad.)* Ironically, the progressives could not agree on the best way to use America's power. Which policy do the students believe would create the most bitterness and long-term harm in America's relations with other countries? *(Answers will vary.)* Foreign policy again became a hot topic after the Cold War ended, as President Clinton shifted back and forth between advancing economic interests and human rights. President George W. Bush became involved in war and nation building at the same time in Afghanistan and Iraq. It is also noteworthy that President Bush was the first president to fund the effort to combat AIDS in Africa.

Theodore Roosevelt and the Big Stick

Theodore Roosevelt, who had become president in 1901, applied his foreign policy in Latin America with the same zest he had showed in his charge up San Juan Hill. He said, "I have always been fond of the West African proverb, 'Speak softly and carry a big stick, and you will go far!'" Roosevelt believed that the United States was the most important nation in the Western Hemisphere. In fact, he believed that the hemisphere was actually an American sphere of influence and that the Caribbean was an American lake. Roosevelt's foreign policy relied on America's military strength to persuade foreign nations to act properly. This philosophy became known as the **"big stick" policy**.

Roosevelt introduced a new diplomatic policy: "Speak softly and carry a big stick."

In 1902, Britain, Germany, and Italy sent warships to blockade Venezuelan ports. They were there to collect unpaid loans. Venezuela asked the United States to intervene. Great Britain asked Roosevelt to mediate. He eagerly obliged, but he saw the incident as a warning that European interests in Latin America were growing. He viewed the European presence as a violation of the Monroe Doctrine. To clear up any misunderstanding, he issued the **Roosevelt Corollary** to the Monroe Doctrine. In that statement, he asserted the U.S. right to be an "international police power" in the Western Hemisphere. When a country was guilty of chronic long-term wrongdoing, the United States reserved the right to intervene and set things right.

Acting on Roosevelt's policy during the next sixty years, the United States sent forces to Cuba, Venezuela, the Dominican Republic, Haiti, Nicaragua, Guatemala, and Mexico. Although the policy protected American interests, many Latin Americans regarded the United States as an unwelcome powerful neighbor, "the colossus of the North."

Dollar Diplomacy and Moral Diplomacy

Other presidents later changed the "big stick" policy. **William Howard Taft** preferred a policy known as **dollar diplomacy**. American money made it possible for Latin American countries to set up industries and helped the people. But if the countries did not follow the wishes of the United States, the money could be withdrawn.

William H. Taft

Woodrow Wilson and Secretary of State William Jennings Bryan turned the policy into **moral diplomacy**. They used negotiation, not threats of force or financial loss, in foreign affairs. They did not want to pressure countries into decisions. They preferred to talk them into following the U.S. example. Wilson believed that "the force of America is the force of moral principle." He tried to promote democratic principles and secure American interests overseas while maintaining peace on all fronts. Wilson's policy, however, was too idealistic. Before he left office, he was forced to send troops into the Dominican Republic, Haiti, and Mexico, and the United States had fought in a world war.

Woodrow Wilson

William J. Bryan

Sagamore Hill

Theodore Roosevelt's home, Sagamore Hill, has twenty-three rooms and is built in the Queen Anne style. His family later gave the estate to the government, and today the National Park Service preserves the homestead as the Sagamore Hill National Historic Site.

The furnishings of the home reflect Roosevelt's interests. His big-game hunting produced several trophies, samples of which are scattered throughout the house. His intellectual interests are apparent as well. His ability to read in three languages would have been put to good use with the approximately six thousand books in the house. Portraits of historical figures demonstrate the importance he placed on the study of history.

While Roosevelt was president, he sometimes used his home for official duties. Before government buildings were air-conditioned, the president, Congress, and the Supreme Court left Washington between April and October. Government business could be transacted from any place, though, with the help of a telephone. Sagamore Hill served quite capably as a summer White House from 1902 to 1908. Most notably, Roosevelt was awarded a Nobel Peace Prize for Russo-Japanese peace negotiations that he conducted in the library at Sagamore Hill.

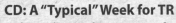

CD: A "Typical" Week for TR

Refer to the CD for a cartoon depiction of a typical week for President Theodore Roosevelt.

American Activity in China

Americans had been somewhat active in China before the Open Door Policy went into effect. In 1844 the Treaty of Wanghai opened five major Chinese ports to American trade. Besides setting low tariffs on American goods, the treaty allowed missionaries to enter China. Over the remaining years of the nineteenth century, missionaries pointed thousands of Chinese to the gospel and started many churches. Because the United States had not been as involved in the exploitation of China as other powers had, U.S. missionaries had much success.

Open Door Policy

Those countries that had fought for spheres of influence in China resisted the Open Door Policy. But Americans believed in the necessity of open, unrestricted commerce. The policy reflected prevailing American sentiment that the United States must promote its principles around the world in order to keep vital trade lines open.

Boxer Rebellion

The Boxer Rebellion actually presented the opportunity for John Hay's Open Door Policy to be put into effect in China. Notice that America's kind treatment of the Chinese after the incident helped create a strong friendship between the two countries.

Christian Principles in Foreign Policy

Both President Wilson and Secretary of State William Jennings Bryan were Presbyterians. They wanted their moral and religious principles to be reflected in the country's policies, both foreign and domestic. You will study more about these two men and how their views influenced their politics in Chapters 20 and 21.

In Asia

In the late 1800s, China was becoming one of the most profitable trading spots in the world. Britain, France, Germany, Russia, and Japan divided China into **spheres of influence**. Each of those countries controlled all of the trading operations within its sphere, or division, of the country. The United States had missed out in that arrangement and was ready to seek some trading opportunities of its own.

China and the Open Door Policy

Some of the foreign powers in China wanted more than control of trade—they wanted land. Japan and some European nations began to seize land and establish colonies. The United States objected to such colonization in China. Americans wanted all of China to be open to everyone.

In 1899, Secretary of State John Hay sent a series of letters to the countries involved in China. His memos formally stated an **Open Door Policy**. No longer would any nation have its own sphere. All of China would be open to all nations equally. No more Chinese land was to be seized. Germany and Japan were not at all eager to follow Hay's policy. But to go against it would risk the wrath of Great Britain and the United States. So Germany and Japan agreed to U.S. demands.

China's regions were not united, and no army existed to protect them. China had no choice but to tolerate the foreign trade invasion. But some Chinese aligned themselves with a secret group called the Society of Righteous and Harmonious Fists that had been formed many years earlier. Foreigners called this group the **Boxers** because one of their rituals was shadowboxing. The Boxers opposed government control of any kind and from any source, whether foreign or domestic. But the empress of China deflected their energies from opposing her government to opposing foreigners.

The Boxers decided to force all foreigners to leave China. The uprising began in rural areas and moved to Peking (now Beijing), the capital of China. The Boxers surrounded the sections of the city where foreigners lived and terrorized the foreigners. They murdered some foreigners. Boxers also attacked and killed many Chinese Christians. The foreigners and Chinese Christians took refuge together and tried to hold out until help could arrive.

The United States acted to protect the lives of its citizens in China. The first relief expedition on June 10, 1900, was forced back. By August, John Hay had put together an international force of twenty thousand men. Those soldiers marched from Tientsin (TIN tsin) to Peking and freed the hostages.

Some of the eleven countries involved thought they should get land. But under the Boxer Protocol, signed on September 7, 1901, none of them did. Ten Chinese officials responsible for the **Boxer Rebellion** were executed. Twenty-five Chinese forts were destroyed. China had to pay damages of $333 million over the next forty years.

The United States put most of its share of the reparations or damage payments into a fund to educate Chinese students in America. Some of the funds were used to build schools and colleges in China. American churches and mission boards also sent personnel and money to China. Because of such efforts, the Chinese were friendlier to the United States than to the other imperialist powers. The United

World Powers Then and Now

The text alludes to all of the major world powers in 1900—Britain, France, Germany, Russia, Japan, China, and the United States. (Britain was more than a world power, however; it can be classified as a superpower.) Perhaps the most objective way to distinguish a world power from a minor power is the amount of money that a country spends on military technology. Based on that criterion, the only superpower today is the United States, and the list of world powers includes the same countries as those in 1900. Note how much the relationship between these world powers has changed. Now China is a Communist country, and Germany is a republic. Locate these countries on a map.

Reports on Relations with China and Japan

Ask the students to bring in an article on current foreign relations with China or Japan. Compare modern issues to the issues in 1900. Note the continuing prominence of trade.

States and China remained friends until the Communists took over that land in 1949.

The United States and Japan

After Commodore Matthew Perry and the U.S. Navy opened Japan to trade with the outside world in 1853, Japan quickly became powerful. In less than forty years, it transformed itself into a modern industrial nation. Japan also gained the technology to become a modern military power.

It is a short step from militarism to imperialism. Japan had demanded a sphere of influence from China. In the Sino-Japanese War (1894–95), Japan easily defeated the Chinese and took the land they wanted. Japan also joined the international force that defeated the Boxers. Then, in 1905, Japan defeated Russia in the Russo-Japanese War.

John Hay and President Roosevelt sought to use American power in Asia to maintain a **balance of power**. Roosevelt could see that Japan might soon be a threat to the rest of the world. He believed that U.S. power could be used to offset Japan's power and that the United States should command the respect of the world. In 1905, he persuaded representatives from Russia and Japan to meet him on a ship anchored off Portsmouth, New Hampshire. There he helped negotiate a treaty that maintained a balance of power in Asia while upholding Chinese independence. For his efforts, he won the Nobel Peace Prize, the first American president to do so.

In 1907, Roosevelt made a dramatic show of American military strength. He sent the entire U.S. battle fleet on a world cruise. Although Congress protested the expense, the Great White Fleet, as the American ships were called (due to their color), sailed. The fleet visited Japanese ports and so impressed the Japanese that their imperialistic designs were curbed for the time being.

Section Quiz

1. Why did American naval officers want the United States to build the Panama Canal?
2. What were the terms of the Hay-Bunau-Varilla Treaty?
3. What famous quotation summarizes Theodore Roosevelt's foreign policy?
4. Who was John Hay? What policy did he propose for relations with China?
5. Who were the "Boxers"?
6. Why did Roosevelt send the U.S. battle fleet on a world cruise?
★ Contrast the diplomatic philosophies of Theodore Roosevelt, William Howard Taft, and Woodrow Wilson.

The Rise of Modern Japan

Emperor Mutsuhito, Japanese ruler from 1867 to 1912, contributed much to the creation of the modern state of Japan. He took the title Meiji, or enlightened rule. His Imperial Charter Oath, issued in April 1868, established the pattern for the Meiji period. According to the oath, the Japanese government would seek to modernize its nation, looking to the West for ideas.

As part of its modernization program, the Meiji government tackled the reform of education, the military, communication and transportation systems, banking, and taxation. The development of industry also received much attention. Industrialists from America and Europe were called in to teach their methods. By the 1920s, zaibatsu (huge family-owned corporations) dominated the business landscape.

The government even reorganized itself. Japan established a constitutional government for the first time in 1889. The emperor became the head of state and supreme commander of the army and navy. He also had the privilege of appointing and overseeing government ministers. But he had to share some of the ruling power with the Diet, a two-house parliament.

A Strong Military—Guarantor of Peace?

Explain to the students the debate over the impact of building a powerful military. Liberals tend to argue that a strong military increases tension and incites a dangerous arms race. Conservatives typically argue that a strong military encourages peace. (Note Reagan's policy of "peace through strength," which is credited with bringing about the downfall of communism and the Soviet Union.) How would the students evaluate the effectiveness of the Great White Fleet?

Section Quiz Answers

1. so they could more easily defend both the Atlantic and Pacific coasts
2. The U.S. would control and fortify a ten-mile-wide strip of land on which a canal would be built. All nations could use the canal by paying a toll.
3. "Speak softly and carry a big stick, and you will go far!"
4. America's secretary of state; the Open Door Policy (All of China would be open to all nations on equal terms.)
5. a secret group of Chinese who were opposed to all foreign activity in China
6. He wanted to make a dramatic show of American military strength to discourage aggressive action.
★ Theodore Roosevelt supported a "big stick" policy. He wanted to force proper behavior through military action. William Howard Taft adopted "dollar diplomacy." His idea was to control other countries through the promise of financial assistance or the threat of its withdrawal. Woodrow Wilson preferred "moral diplomacy," convincing countries to do the right thing through the persuasion of principle.

Around the World with Nellie Bly

Late-nineteenth-century Americans found a heroine in reporter and traveler Nellie Bly. Bly, whose real name was Elizabeth Cochrane, began writing for the *Pittsburgh Dispatch* when she was just a teenager. She changed newspapers more than once during her journalistic career, but the focus of her writing remained the same: exposing corruption. Because of her subject matter, she was not always popular. Twice she was asked to leave a position. But her writing skill always won her another job.

What strongly captured Americans' interest, though, was Bly's trip around the world. Readers were familiar with the fictional travels of Phileas Fogg, a Jules Verne character who went around the world in eighty days. Bly became a real-life Phileas Fogg, but she completed the trip in seventy-two days, six hours, and eleven minutes, traveling on everything from a steamship to a rickshaw. She returned home to great acclaim. Those who would never have the means or inclination to make the trip themselves were able to experience Bly's travels through a commemorative board game.

People, Places, and Things to Remember:

isolationism
imperialism
exploitation
humanitarianism
Dwight L. Moody
Student Volunteer Movement for Foreign Missions
Spanish-American War
yellow journalism
William Randolph Hearst
Joseph Pulitzer
William McKinley
Dupuy de Lôme
U.S.S. *Maine*
Teller amendment
Rough Riders
Theodore Roosevelt
Battle of Manila Bay
San Juan Hill
Platt amendment
Guantanamo Bay
Walter Reed
William Gorgas
Emilio Aguinaldo
Hay-Bunau-Varilla Treaty
John Hay
Panama Canal
"big stick" policy
Roosevelt Corollary
William Howard Taft
dollar diplomacy
Woodrow Wilson
moral diplomacy
spheres of influence
Open Door Policy
Boxers
Boxer Rebellion
balance of power

Chapter Review 19

Review Questions

Match these terms with their descriptions.

1. exploitation
2. humanitarianism
3. imperialism
4. isolationism
5. yellow journalism

a. meeting the physical needs of poor people
b. distorting the news to make it more exciting
c. taking advantage of a people's weakness
d. not getting involved in world affairs
e. taking control of foreign lands

Match each of the items below with the president with whom it is most closely associated.

6. moral diplomacy
7. de Lôme Letter
8. dollar diplomacy
9. "big stick" policy

a. William McKinley
b. Theodore Roosevelt
c. William Howard Taft
d. Woodrow Wilson

Fill in the blanks.

10. The sinking of the _____ helped to trigger the Spanish-American War.
11. The _____ amendment assured Americans that action against Spain was intended to secure Cuban independence and not to build an American empire.
12. _____ was a leader in the Philippines who wanted independence for his land.
13. Secretary of State _____ negotiated a treaty with Panama and helped establish the Open Door Policy with China.
14. Several countries gained trading privileges in areas called _____ in China.
15. The _____ staged a rebellion in China because of their hostility toward foreigners.

Critical Thinking

1. Was humanitarianism a valid objective for American imperialism? Explain your answer.
2. Does the news media still use yellow journalism today? Explain your answer.

Activity 6: Chapter Review

Use this activity to help the students prepare for the chapter test.

Chapter Review Answers

Review Questions

1. c
2. a
3. e
4. d
5. b
6. d
7. a
8. c
9. b
10. U.S.S. *Maine*
11. Teller
12. Emilio Aguinaldo
13. John Hay
14. spheres of influence
15. Boxers

Critical Thinking

1. Answers will vary. It is good to meet people's physical needs, but it is more important to meet their spiritual needs. Humanitarian work should never replace the preaching of the gospel.

2. Answers will vary. Although standards of reporting might be different today, the sensational still draws much attention. (You might mention the slogan "If it bleeds, it leads," which guides much reporting today.)

New York City was a crowded, bustling, and diverse city at the turn of the twentieth century.

Progressivism

I. Changes in American Life

II. Different Religious Attitudes

III. Progressivism

IV. Roosevelt and Progressivism

V. Taft and Progressivism

VI. Wilson and Progressivism

Chapter Goals

Students should be able to

1. Identify changes that occurred in American life at the turn of the century and evaluate their impact on society.

2. Identify the major factors that influenced the change in American attitudes, including challenges to the Christian faith.

3. Identify key social, political, and religious reform movements of the period.

4. Describe the main issues in four presidencies (McKinley, Roosevelt, Taft, and Wilson) discussed in the chapter.

5. Define and use the basic terms of the chapter.

6. Assess how changes in American life and religion paved the way for progressive reforms.

7. Identify progressivism as a new role for government, and explain how it was able to change the thinking of the nation so quickly.

Chapter Motivation

Read Luke 18:23–25 to your class. Ask them why wealth sometimes plays a role in drawing people away from the Lord. *(People tend to trust in their money rather than in the Lord. They feel satisfied and think they have no needs.)*

In this chapter, the students will also see that America's growing secularism drew the nation away from its godly heritage.

Chapter 20 Lesson Plan Chart			
Section Title	**Main Activity**	**Pages**	**Days**
I. Changes in American Life	Activity 2: Booker T. Washington	380–83	2–3 days
II. Increasingly Different Values	Activity 3: Billy Sunday Blasts Liqour	383–87	1–2 days
III. Progressivism	Activity 4: Progressivism	387–91	1–2 days
IV. Roosevelt and Progressivism	Activity 6: The Progressive Presidents	391–92	½–1 day
V. Taft and Progressivism	Activity 5: Roosevelt's Speech Following Assassination Attempt	393–94	½–1 day
VI. Wilson and Progressivism	Activity 7: Find the Message (chapter review)	395–96	½–1 day
TOTAL SUGGESTED DAYS (INCLUDING 2 DAYS FOR REVIEW AND TESTING)			6–11 DAYS

MATERIALS LIST

SECTION I
- Activities 1 and 2 from the *Student Activities* manual

SECTION II
- Copy of "Humanist Manifesto I"
- Special speaker: a rescue mission worker or director
- Biography of Billy Sunday
- Scenes from American Church History (BJU Press)
- Activity 3 from Chapter 20 of the *Student Activities* manual

Section I
Objectives

Students should be able to

1. Describe some general ways in which life was changing at the turn of the century.

2. Name two men involved in black education at Tuskegee Institute and describe their contributions to American society.

Urbanization and the Rest of the Nation

Most of the South, the Great Plains, and the western mountain areas did not participate in extensive urbanization. The South was still 80 percent rural in 1920.

Father of Progressive Education

The rise of modern science and evolution gave a new impetus to secular (nonreligious) education. A new breed of "social scientists" believed that science, not religion, could properly direct mankind's evolution. The leader of so-called progressive education, John Dewey, believed education should teach the child thinking skills to solve life's problems. Dewey was a leader in the philosophical movement known as secular humanism, which denies the existence of God and replaces absolute standards of truth and morality with relative, pragmatic standards based on human experience (i.e., whatever works is right). Humanists affirm the basic goodness and perfectibility of man. In the eyes of humanists, the proper purpose of education is to unleash the good within the student and to free him to a self-realization of his perfection. Obviously, progressive education is directly contrary

The turn of the century was an exciting time for Americans. Those years held good prospects for growth as a world power and as a prosperous nation. Cities and industries were expanding. Technology was making more and more conveniences available to the American people.

Although life in the United States had much to offer, it also held many problems. Greed, dishonesty, immorality, and other sins plagued the nation. Many Americans began trying to right the wrongs and cure the ills. They hoped to "clean up society" and achieve social progress by using government regulatory power. Such people were called **progressives**.

I. Changes in American Life

Life was changing in the United States. New living and working conditions, new opportunities, new possessions, and new attitudes resulted from the changes. They also brought more changes. Some of those changes were pleasant. Others were full of problems.

More People

The U.S. population at the turn of the century was seventy-five million. It was growing by more than a million a year. Most of that growth was absorbed by the cities, and immigration accounted for most of the growth.

By 1900, **urbanization** (UR bun ih ZAY shun; the movement of people to cities) had changed America. Many young people reared in rural areas moved to the cities seeking greater opportunities. Between 1860 and 1910, the percentage of Americans involved in farming decreased from 60 percent to 31 percent. By 1920, more than one-half of Americans lived in cities and towns. Urban areas—especially large cities such as New York, Philadelphia, Boston, and Chicago—became sprawling giants. Inner-city areas were often plagued with crime, poverty, poor sanitation, and crowded tenements (apartments).

Almost all immigrants faced problems adjusting to their new home. In fact, not all first-generation immigrants became "Americanized." But most of their children did. Most of them learned English quickly, but the first few months of their early education were difficult. Few schools of the time offered bilingual education. Many foreign parents actually opposed bilingualism because they wanted their children to become American as quickly as possible. They knew that learning the language was the key to achieving that goal.

The new immigrant groups contributed much to the building of America. They extracted raw materials from the land and became the work force for many of America's diverse new industries. But they brought more than labor. They brought the traditions and customs of their homelands, including their foods, music, and literature. All of these things made America's unique culture more diverse.

More Opportunity

Americans now enjoyed more freedom to improve their lives through education. During much of the 1800s, the only public education available at taxpayer's expense was on the elementary level. In 1860, there were only three hundred high schools in America, and only one-third of them were free to the public. But by 1900, six thou-

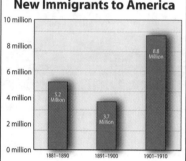

New Immigrants to America

10 million	
8 million	
6 million	
4 million	
2 million	
0 million	

1881–1890: 5.2 Million
1891–1900: 3.7 Million
1901–1910: 8.8 Million

Core Values

After the Civil War, the Bible was no longer seen as an authority for dealing with the problems of society. How then would men and women solve their problems? Increasingly, the answer was science.

This secularism affected the core values of freedom and individualism. During the early twentieth century, some influential Americans argued that people needed to be freed from the bondage of tradition by submitting to science. One key element in this bondage was the Christian religion. Individualism was also a prominent theme. Freed from the biblical teaching that man is a sinner in need of divine grace, man sought to use his own intelligence and knowledge of science to improve his condition.

Continuation of Chapter 12

In many ways, this chapter picks up where Chapter 12 left off, discussing social (as opposed to political) history. A major theme of both chapters is change.

Make a chart comparing modern life to life in 1900. Discuss transportation, commu-

sand tax-supported high schools existed. By 1915, there were twelve thousand.

The same trend was true for higher education. In the middle nineteenth century, upper-class white males were about the only people who attended colleges or universities. But by 1900 more people, including blacks and women, enrolled in college. Those who went to college had more choices of studies. Colleges offered new programs to prepare students for specific professions. Schools in agriculture and the mechanical arts increased, colleges offered more elective courses, and more graduate schools offered advanced training.

Millionaire businessmen helped some of the colleges and universities. They provided endowments (large sums of money) to finance specific programs or salaries. Some even founded schools. Tulane (1834), Cornell (1865), Drew (1866), Vanderbilt (1873), Johns Hopkins (1876), and Stanford (1885) are named for such **philanthropists** (fih LAN thruh pists; wealthy people who donate money to charitable causes). Russell Conwell founded Philadelphia's Temple University (1884) to educate talented young men who wanted to succeed but lacked money. John D. Rockefeller provided funds to found the University of Chicago (1890).

More advanced educational opportunities also opened up for women. It was easier for women to get a college education in the Midwest and the West than elsewhere. They were admitted to most programs and attended classes with men. But in the East women continued to be educated separately in women's colleges. There it was unusual for women to go beyond a basic public education and attend state universities. Those who did had to be strongly motivated to withstand the ridicule of male students.

Blacks could go to college too. But they almost always attended segregated schools founded just for them. The first black university was Ashmun Institute (later renamed Lincoln University in 1866) in Pennsylvania, which opened in 1854. Other African-American colleges included Fisk University in Nashville and Howard University in Washington, D.C., both founded in 1867.

The most famous black school was **Tuskegee** (tus KEE gee) **Institute** in Alabama. It was founded by **Booker T. Washington**, a former slave. The school's philosophy emphasized hard work, self-worth, and self-reliance. Washington hired an Iowa-educated botanist, Dr. **George Washington Carver**, to teach at Tuskegee. Carver, a devout Christian, boosted the school's reputation and finances through not only his teaching but also his scientific experiments. He

Booker T. Washington was dedicated to the education of black Americans and especially emphasized learning a trade.

Tuskegee had a large faculty in 1897.

to Christian education, which attempts to equip redeemed students for living out God's law, especially the Creation Mandate, in whatever vocation God calls them to serve.

Booker T. Washington

When Booker T. Washington was asked to run a school for blacks in Alabama, he was unaware of all the difficulties he would face. However, few men were as well prepared as Washington was for the task. Although born a slave in Virginia in 1856, he went with his parents to West Virginia after emancipation. There he worked in poverty as a coal miner. One day he overheard two men talking about Hampton Institute, a school in Virginia for blacks. He determined to go there to get his education.

He got enough money to get to the school but still had to gain entrance. The head teacher hesitated to admit him as a student because of his poor appearance. As a test, she asked him to sweep out the reception room. Washington swept the room three times and then dusted it four times. Upon examining the room, the head teacher said, "I guess you will do to enter this institution."

To pay his room and board, Washington worked as a janitor for the school. After graduation, he taught at a school in West Virginia, but eventually he returned to Hampton as a staff member. Samuel Armstrong, head of the Hampton Institute, received a letter from men in Alabama asking him to send someone to run a proposed school for blacks in the town of Tuskegee. They assumed he would send a white man, but instead Armstrong sent Washington.

---

nication, agriculture, industry, trade, and religion.

Activity 1: Changing American Life at the Turn of the Century

Use this activity to help the students gain an overview of life and living conditions during the late 1800s and early 1900s.

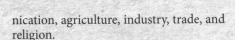 **More on Black Exemplars**

Two Christian exemplars of this period were educator Booker T. Washington and scientist George Washington Carver. Assign the students to read Booker T. Washington's *Up From Slavery*. (An excerpt from the book is part of Activity 2.)

A good biography of George Washington Carver is *God's Ebony Scientist* by Basil Miller. An article-length sketch of Carver's life is "George Washington Carver," *Homeschooling Today* (Nov.–Dec. 2003). A modern double biography of both men is *Unshakable Faith* by John Perry.

Activity 2: Booker T. Washington

Use the excerpts from *Up From Slavery* and Washington's speech to the Cotton States and International Exposition ("Cast Down Your Bucket Where You Are") to help your students understand better Washington's progress from poverty to successfully preparing fellow blacks for productive life and citizenship.

Changing Educational Philosophy in America

As future voters and taxpayers, students need to develop clear convictions about public education. Discuss some of the latest debates about problems in public education—violence, evolutionary teaching, evil teachings about sex, poor scores on national tests, and so on. Also discuss some of the proposed solutions.

Ask the students to imagine the types of arguments Americans (especially Christians) might have used in the late 1800s to attack state-run education. (*The government is not only inefficient but also apt to use its power to promote evil goals. God gave parents, not the government, the responsibility for education.*

When Washington arrived, he found that the only buildings available for the school were an old Methodist church and a nearby shanty. Both were in poor condition, but the school opened with thirty students enrolled. Washington was the only teacher. He recalled "that during the first months of school that I taught in this building, it was in such poor condition that, whenever it rained, one of the older students would very kindly hold an umbrella over me while I heard the recitations of the others."

Eventually, Washington was able to move the entire school to an old plantation. Today Tuskegee University offers forty-nine different degrees in its five colleges: Agricultural, Environmental, and Natural Sciences; Business and Information Science; Engineering, Architecture, and Physical Sciences; Liberal Arts and Education; and Veterinary Medicine, Nursing, and Allied Health. Degrees are awarded at the bachelor's, master's, and doctoral levels. The campus includes about forty-five hundred acres of land and more than one hundred fifty buildings. Enrollment is more than three thousand students, and the school employs about nine hundred people. One of the many famous graduates of Tuskegee is "Chappie" James, the first black four-star general.

Wage Hikes

In 1890, the average work week was 58 hours, and the average hourly wage was 21 cents. In 1910, the work week was 54.6 hours, and the wage was 28 cents. That was a 25 percent increase in total wages over that twenty-year period, with a decrease in working hours as well.

George Washington Carver turned down lucrative offers elsewhere and chose to remain a teacher at Tuskegee, where he exerted a profound influence on many students.

Carver's Humility and Piety

Carver used to enjoy telling how he once asked God to show him the meaning of the universe. God, he said, told him that he wanted to know more than his little mind could grasp. "Ask for something your size." So Carver asked to know what man was made for. "Little one, you are still asking too much. Bring down the extent of your request," God told him. Carver then humbly asked, "God, tell me, then, what the peanut was made for." Then God told him how to take the peanut apart and put it back together again in many helpful products.

(Adapted from *George Washington Carver: God's Ebony Scientist* by Basil Miller, Zondervan, 1943.)

found many uses for the peanut, several uses for clay, and a number of uses for the sweet potato. He also explored ways to use pecans and discovered up to 250 medicinal plants of the South. His work played a role in helping the South become less dependent on cotton. Carver never made a penny from his discoveries, and he did not charge for the advice he gave farmers and housewives.

More Wealth

Education and opportunities to work and advance in business and industry helped many Americans improve their standard of living. Many people who had been penniless immigrants, poor farmers, or poverty-stricken factory workers found a way to improve their situation. Hard work and some business sense could bring financial gain. The fact that a person was born in poverty did not condemn him to stay there. Upward mobility became an attainable goal.

Only a few Americans became millionaires. Some people never escaped poverty. But many Americans joined the ranks of the growing middle class. They had enough money to enjoy a comfortable home, adequate food, and some of the new consumer goods that were being developed. They also had more disposable income. They spent some of it on leisure activities.

More Leisure

In the early 1800s, factories, mines, and other employers often demanded that their laborers work six days a week and for seventy hours or more. Workers began to complain about such long hours. They also complained about poor working conditions and low wages. Their complaints resulted in great changes during the era of progressivism. By 1910, the average workweek had dropped to 54.6 hours. Such a change gave many Americans some leisure time—time they could use to improve or enjoy themselves and their families.

Interest in both spectator and participatory sports mushroomed. Baseball, basketball, and football were all relatively new sports that had developed in the United States. All three were popular, but baseball became the favorite. The first World Series took place in 1903. Baseball greats such as Walter Johnson, Christy Mathewson, "Shoeless" Joe Jackson, and the double-play combination of Joe Tinker, Johnny Evers, and Frank Chance became household names.

In the early 1900s, major league baseball became a popular type of entertainment.

People devalue anything that is free. Government control would spread mediocrity, waste, and radicalism.) Ideas have consequences, and we suffer today from the consequences of progressivism.

Athletes of the Period

Have students volunteer to research and report to the class (either orally or in writing) on some of the leading athletes of this period. Other related topical subjects might include how "Shoeless" Joe Jackson got his nickname, baseball cards of the era, championship teams, and the first World Series.

Is Leisure Time Good?

Discuss the rise of leisure time as a major part of life. The Bible says that we are to work six days, and it generally associates leisure with laziness. But modern conveniences have made it possible for the average citizen to enjoy more leisure time than ever before. Discuss the value of leisure and how God wants us to use our spare time. Have the students look up the following verses and explain how they relate to the subject of leisure and spare time: Mark 6:31; Ps. 90:12; 1 Cor. 7:29–31; Eph. 5:15–16. A recently published work suitable for teachers would be Brian Hand's brief work, *Upright Downtime* (BJU Press).

After baseball, boxing was the most popular sport of the era. Heavyweight fights attracted large crowds. In addition, roller skating and bicycling became new crazes of the day. Many other sports, such as golf and tennis, were also gaining attention.

Concerts, theaters, and amusement parks were other popular forms of entertainment. Interest in opera and classical music surged, especially in areas where European immigrants had settled. Many symphony orchestra members and almost all of the conductors had been born overseas. Immigrants who could afford tickets packed concert halls to hear the music of European composers.

Although reading as a pastime was not new, literature took on new importance in the era. Throughout the 1800s, more people could read and had money for books. Reading became more popular. Americans were especially fond of new American themes and regional settings. The most popular American writer of the day was **Samuel L. Clemens**, whose pen name was Mark Twain. He wrote such famous works as *The Adventures of Tom Sawyer*, *The Adventures of Huckleberry Finn*, and *A Connecticut Yankee in King Arthur's Court*.

Magazines that appealed to literary types were common but expensive (thirty-five cents per issue). Magazines such as *Harper's* and *Atlantic Monthly* never enjoyed wide circulation. But better printing presses and better methods of making paper led to lower prices. Hermann Cyrus Curtis sold *Ladies' Home Journal* for ten cents a copy and *Saturday Evening Post* for only a nickel.

Section Quiz

1. What is urbanization?
2. Who founded Tuskegee Institute, and what is the significance of his work?
3. Who was the famous scientist hired to teach at Tuskegee Institute, and what was his area of expertise?
4. List at least three ways in which American laborers used their newly acquired leisure time.

II. Different Religious Attitudes

America had received a godly heritage from its early Pilgrim and Puritan fathers. Most of the people who came to America after that had a Protestant background. Many of them were not true Christians, but most of them respected the Bible as the Word of God and believed in its moral standards. But immigration during the nineteenth century and the changes in American society greatly altered the nation's religious attitudes.

Challenges to the Faith

Between 1860 and 1910, almost twenty-one million immigrants entered the United States. Some German immigrants were Lutheran. Others were Roman Catholic. Still others were rationalists (those who exalted man's reason above the revelation of God's Word). Most immigrants from Ireland were strong Roman Catholics. The majority of later groups of Scandinavian immigrants were Lutheran. Italian immigrants were usually Roman Catholics. Immigrants from

A Christian Testimony in Baseball

Christy Mathewson pitched for the New York Giants and briefly for the Cincinnati Reds, putting together an impressive record. Using his famous "fade-away" pitch, he won 317 games. He won at least twenty-two games per season for twelve years straight. Four times he won thirty or more games in a single season. His best season was in 1908, when he won thirty-seven games. He compiled a lifetime earned run average of 2.13 and played in the World Series four times (1905, 1911, 1912, 1913). As impressive as his statistics are, he was just as impressive in his Christian testimony. As a devout Christian, he refused to play baseball on Sunday. Because he was such a valuable player, the club owners respected his religious convictions.

Samuel Clemens is better known as Mark Twain.

The First World Series

In October 1903, the Boston Americans (later Red Sox) and the Pittsburgh Pirates played the first World Series.

One interesting point about the series was the size of the ballparks. They were too small for the crowds who wanted to attend the games. Despite the efforts of the police, crowds drifted into the outfield. A few runs were the result of pop fly balls landing in the crowd and allowing for a ground rule of three bases.

Section II
Objectives

Students should be able to

1. Explain how American religion was changing at the turn of the century.
2. Identify various challenges to the Christian faith during the period.
3. Explain the significance of the ministries of B. B. Warfield regarding the confrontation of religious challenges, and Billy Sunday regarding the temperance movement.
4. Identify various reform movements that were influential at the turn of the century.

Immigration

Because immigration changes American culture, Americans have often opposed immigration. People on different sides of the immigration issue have often debated the positive and negative impact of immigration. In most cases the reality is complex; there are both positive and negative results. For instance, in the late nineteenth century many Protestants were concerned about Roman Catholic immigrants transforming American religion and culture. In

---

"Culture Wars" Then and Now

Ask the students to summarize the major subjects of debate in the modern "culture wars." (*education, social welfare, environment, religious freedom, equality, etc.*) How are they similar to the issues being debated during the progressive era? (*Many of them were the same.*) Ask the students to bring in articles on the modern culture wars, or bring in an article yourself. How might those articles have been written in 1910?

Section Quiz Answers

1. the movement of people to cities
2. Booker T. Washington; he emphasized hard work, self-worth, and self-reliance

3. George Washington Carver; uses of the peanut
4. (any three) watching or participating in sports (baseball, basketball, football, golf, boxing); attending concerts, theater performances, amusement parks, and other attractions; reading books and magazines

Enemies of the Gospel

This section reminds students that Christians in America have never been free from attack. It was no easier to be a Christian in past eras than it is today. The purity of the church has always required constant vigilance. Modern Christians have no reason

to grow discouraged by the attacks of the enemy. They must learn to expect such attacks, and they should be encouraged by the example of previous generations.

Ask the students whether they have ever met a member of a cult. Allow volunteers to describe their experiences. Encourage students to recognize that those cults are not really meeting people's needs. The turnover rate in cults such as the Jehovah's Witnesses is drastic. True Christianity offers the only true hope of rest for the human soul.

many ways their worst fears were unrealized. On the other hand, some of those early fears have proven true as the Protestant and Catholic alliance in the culture war has led many Evangelicals to minimize doctrinal differences with Catholics.

Immigration itself is not a positive or a negative thing. Students of history should study immigration in the past for lessons on managing immigration today.

Mary Baker Eddy

The founder of the Christian Science movement was born in Bow, New Hampshire, in 1821. She suffered from several mental and physical illnesses throughout her childhood.

In the 1860s, Eddy became a follower of P. P. Quimby, a doctor of "mental healing." After his death, Eddy claimed much of Quimby's material as her own. Some portions of her book *Science and Health with a Key to the Scriptures* come directly from his writings. After an accident in 1866, she claimed to be healed and to have discovered "Christian Science."

After founding the Church of Christ, Scientist, in 1879, Eddy continued spreading her beliefs through her writings. Those writings were made available in "reading rooms" in many cities. At the age of eighty-eight she founded the *Christian Science Monitor,* a newspaper that still exists today. Despite her death in 1910, the Christian Science movement continued to grow. Today "reading rooms" exist in more than seventy countries.

Charles Taze Russell

In 1852, Charles Taze Russell was born in Pittsburgh. Despite being brought up in the Congregationalist Church, Russell

"Humanist Manifesto I"

"Culture wars" have been fought throughout U.S. history. Modern movements are a natural outgrowth of progressivism and secular humanism. Read portions of the "Humanist Manifesto," published in 1933 and signed by many notables, including John Dewey. Have the students explain how the statements were in keeping with progressive ideas about man's ability to achieve perfection on earth.

Eastern Europe included Mennonites, Russian Orthodox, Catholics, and Jews.

Almost all churches increased their memberships in these years, including the well-known "mainline" denominations such as the Methodists, Presbyterians, and Baptists. When some people began to feel that mainline denominations were too formal and cold or were not meeting their needs, they formed new denominations, such as the Holiness and Pentecostal groups.

During this period several unorthodox groups also emerged. For example, Mary Baker Eddy founded Christian Science, which teaches that "matter and death are mental illusions," as are sin, pain, and disease. Seventh-Day Adventism grew under the leadership of Ellen G. Harmon White. The Watchtower Society (Jehovah's Witnesses) was founded in 1872 by Charles Taze Russell. These groups are all very American. The American value of freedom of religion gave these groups the right to exist, and the American value of individualism made it easier for Americans to turn from traditional, orthodox Christianity to these newer expressions of error.

The Social Gospel

In the late-nineteenth century, a movement called the "social gospel" spread across America. Because the proponents of the social gospel denied doctrines such as the deity of Christ and His sacrificial death on the cross, they were left with only a message of social reform. Consequently, "social gospelers" put their effort into projects such as starting hospitals and rescue missions, gaining equal wages for workers, and helping the poor. These are all good things, but they are not the gospel.

The main proponent of the social gospel was Walter Rauschenbusch (ROU shen boosh) (1861–1918), who wrote *Christianity and the Social Crisis* (1907). Another promoter of the social gospel was Charles M. Sheldon (1857–1946), who wrote *In His Steps* (1896). In this book, Sheldon popularized the question "What would Jesus do?" This question reduced Jesus to little more than a moral example. As a result, those who proclaim a social gospel leave people with no true hope.

The problems that the social reformers sought to correct have only grown in the last century-and-a-half. Many of these problems are complicated by human sinfulness, which the social gospel is powerless to address. Even if humans were able to solve the world's problems, "what shall it profit a man, if he shall gain the whole world, and lose his own soul?" (Mark 8:36).

Liberalism

In the seventeenth and eighteenth centuries, European theologians and philosophers began to emphasize human reason. This led these theologians to judge the Scriptures by what they thought rational. They decided that miracles and other supernatural events were not rational. After all, science had given explanations for many things people had before attributed to the supernatural. Some of them also denied that the Bible had been written by men who were guided by the Holy Spirit as they wrote. Instead they treated the Bible as a purely human book, and they applied the methods used to study the development of folklore to Scripture. This thinking caused them to deny such doctrines as the virgin birth and the deity of Christ. They also denied that God punished Jesus on the cross for people's sins and that He would punish people eternally in hell. These doctrines were deemed unreasonable and unfitting for a loving God. These denials made it unnecessary, in their minds, to preach the gospel of repentance from sin and faith in Christ. Nevertheless, these people still wanted to be considered Christians. Since they had denied the key Christian doctrines, all they had left was a message of Christian ethics—good works. The message of doing good to others without the true gospel of salvation from sin became known as the **social gospel**.

Agnosticism

Some men, called **agnostics**, said that man cannot know if there is a God. The most famous agnostic, **Robert Ingersoll**, traveled the country in the late 1800s giving lectures. People paid to hear him mock true faith. But many people attended his lectures more out of curiosity than agreement.

Darwinism

In 1859, **Charles Darwin** published in England one of the most influential works of the nineteenth century. *Origin of Species* proposed a theory of evolution which argued the variety of species on earth could be explained by the idea of natural selection. His ideas were popularized in the 1870s by the Irish physicist John Tyndall.

Reform and Outreach

Religious liberalism and other common philosophies prompted men to humanitarianism. They also hardened many Americans in their sin. But many Bible-believing teachers, pastors, and evangelists were still preaching salvation through Christ and the authority of the Bible. **B. B. Warfield**, a professor at Princeton Theological Seminary, published many books and pamphlets pointing out the problems with the growing liberalism. He especially opposed the idea that the Bible contains errors. One popular preacher of the day was revivalist **Billy Sunday**, a former professional baseball player whose preaching attacked both liberalism and liquor.

The existence of both liberal religion and true Christianity in American culture led to a mixture of religious goals in the progressive era. Some efforts sincerely sought to reach souls for Christ. Others tried to improve morals or living conditions. Some tried to do both.

Temperance Groups

Abuse of alcohol had become a big problem in many areas of the country. Some immigrant groups were particularly heavy drinkers. Their actions were offensive to many people. Wherever alcoholism occurred, crime, poverty, and abuse of family members increased.

Many religious Americans saw the need to correct the problem. They formed **temperance societies** to fight against the evils of liquor. Most of them were associated with the Women's Christian Temperance Union (1874) or the Anti-Saloon League (1893). The efforts of those societies, combined with the efforts of evangelists who preached against the sin of drunkenness, led to the Prohibition movement.

Interdenominational Organizations

Laymen founded interdenominational organizations that crossed church boundaries. The **Young Men's Christian Association** (YMCA) was formed to provide an entertainment alternative for young people who found themselves in the seducing environment of the big cities. Famed evangelist D. L. Moody was a major force in bringing the YMCA from England to the United States. The "Y," as

Billy Sunday "performed" for his audiences, pacing the platform, leaning over the pulpit, flailing his arms, and even "sliding into base" as a means of getting and keeping their attention.

soon rejected many Bible doctrines, including the reality of hell, the Trinity, the deity of Christ, and Christ's physical resurrection. By 1870, Russell had organized a Bible class that soon named him its "pastor." In 1879, he founded a magazine that eventually became *The Watchtower Announcing Jehovah's Kingdom*. The Jehovah's Witnesses movement is based on Russell's teaching. Today about eighteen million copies of the magazine are distributed worldwide.

As of 2006, the Jehovah's Witnesses claimed 6,613,829 adherents worldwide, 247,631 of whom were baptized. In the United States they claimed 1,035,802 adherents, 28,384 of whom were baptized. They have 12,261 congregations in the United States.

Billy Sunday

Although Billy Sunday grew up as an orphan in Iowa, he became a man twice successful in life—once by the world's standards and then by God's. His amazing running speed led Cap Anson, owner of the Chicago White Stockings, to offer Sunday a tryout. Soon, Sunday was playing baseball for the White Stockings. He helped them win three championships.

But Sunday's baseball career did not last. In 1886, through the ministry of the Pacific Garden Mission, he accepted Christ as his Savior. Eventually, Sunday left baseball to join the ministry full-time. In 1896, he began preaching and holding revival meetings. While he initially spoke in small communities, invitations soon started to come from larger cities. Between 1910 and 1920, Sunday preached in almost every major city in the country.

Sunday's messages focused on Christ and salvation as well as the reality of Satan and

---

Teaching History Through Literature

Several good biographies on the life and times of Billy Sunday are available. They include William T. Ellis's *Billy Sunday* (1959) and Fern Neal Stocker's *Billy Sunday: Baseball Preacher* (1985). BJU Press distributes Betty Steele Everett's *Sawdust Trail Preacher: The Story of Billy Sunday* (1987).

Activity 3: Billy Sunday Blasts Liquor

Use this reading to help the students become acquainted with Sunday's style of preaching.

Defenders of the Faith

For an article about a defender of the faith against liberalism, see "Benjamin Breckinridge Warfield and the Defense of the Scriptures" by Mark Sidwell *in Scenes from American Church History.* That book also includes the stories "Sam Jones, Great Evangelist" by Bob Jones, "A.T. Pierson: Servant of God" by Christa Habegger, and "'Plain Billy Sunday'" by Mark Sidwell. For more extensive information about Warfield, see *B. B. Warfield: Essays on His Life and Thought*, edited by Gary Johnson.

hell. He also attacked the liquor industry, helping to bring about the passage of the Eighteenth Amendment.

Sunday's preaching style was anything but formal. He shouted, stood on chairs, ran across the platform, and even slid on the floor as though stealing a base. Many people were prompted to attend his services for the entertainment they offered, but they got the gospel at the same time.

In 1935, Sunday died of a heart attack. He had preached some three hundred revival campaigns across the United States to about one million people.

B.B. Warfield

Warfield was a Princeton educated theologian who sought to uphold Princeton's demanding scholarship while actively resisting the spread of religious liberalism. He effectively used his pen to defend the authority and accuracy of Scripture against the assaults of various unscriptural schools of thought, including those developed by Friedrich Schleiermacher and Immanuel Kant. Warfield also wrote to refute the growing influence of evolution. His writings helped to lay the foundation for Fundamentalism.

Scofield Bible and Missions

C. T. Scofield (1843-1921), popular Bible conference speaker and advocate of dispensational premillenialism, became affiliated with an independent faith missions board in Latin America. The *Scofield Reference Bible* was created so that missionaries who had little room to carry books in their gear would have access to a variety of useful Bible references in a single source.

Rescue the Perishing

As American cities grew in the 1800s, so did their problems. Sections of large cities such as New York became slums—places where the poor, usually immigrants, lived close together in dirty, noisy tenements. The main forms of "entertainment" in the slums were drinking, gambling, and other vices. These activities drained much of the little money that the people had. Churches tended to move away from the slums and nearer more prosperous and "respectable" people, who could support them.

Some Christians did try to reach the people in the slums. They held services in rented halls, passed out tracts, and tried to witness to the people. One man, Jerry McAuley, wanted to do more. Born in Ireland in 1837, he came to New York City at the age of thirteen. McAuley soon became a thief; at the age of nineteen he was arrested for robbery and sent to prison.

McAuley was converted in prison through the testimony of a former convict. After getting out, McAuley thought that Christians were not doing enough to help the real "down-and-outs"—the drunks, prostitutes, and others who lived in the worst parts of the city. He decided to start a mission, a work located in the slums and designed to rescue people from sin. His Water Street Mission in New York City is usually considered the first rescue mission in the United States.

Probably the most famous rescue mission is the Pacific Garden Mission in Chicago. It was started in 1877 by Colonel George Clark and his wife, Sarah Dunn. D. L. Moody helped to name it. Thousands of people were reached for Christ through the Pacific Garden Mission. In 1886, a half-drunk baseball player named Billy Sunday heard a group of mission workers singing on a street corner. He followed them back to the Garden, where he was converted. Later he became a well-known evangelist.

Other people started rescue missions in other cities. Mel Trotter, for example, began a successful work in Grand Rapids, Michigan, and later helped found missions in other cities. Trotter loved the mission work because he had been saved in a mission. In 1897, he had stumbled into the Pacific Garden Mission. Although it was January, he was barefoot because he had sold his shoes to buy a drink. After he was converted, Trotter dedicated his life to reaching people like himself who had reached the bottom physically, mentally, and spiritually.

Rescue mission work varied in operation from city to city. Usually missions were open day and night to minister to anyone who came in. Services normally consisted of the singing of gospel songs, testimonies of converted sinners from the slums, and simple salvation sermons. The missions also tried to provide hot meals and a place to stay, at least for a night or two. Some more ambitious missions tried to provide work for their people. In those missions the people repaired clothing, made brooms, or did some other kind of work to help pay for their room and board.

Mel Trotter was led to Christ in a rescue mission and went on to minister in a similar mission in Grand Rapids, Michigan.

Archives of the Billy Graham Center, Wheaton, Illinois

it was called, stressed four areas of growth: physical, educational, social, and religious. YMCAs also provided a safe living environment where young Christian men working in big cities could find room and board.

Another group of British origin was the **Salvation Army**. It provided relief for the poor and set up **rescue missions** to convert and rebuild the lives of those people who knew only defeat. Various other groups began rescue missions to work with such people. Probably the most famous rescue mission is Chicago's Pacific Garden Mission, founded in 1877. Other groups set up missions to work with specific immigrant groups.

Foreign Missions and Evangelistic Efforts

Americans were also concerned about sharing the gospel overseas. America sent out more missionary workers than any other country. The religious and cultural impact of Christianity was so great by the end of the nineteenth century that some historians have called it the "Great Century of Christian Missions."

Important throughout the era was the work of evangelists and revival leaders. Camp meetings were held, but tents and brush arbors were abandoned for woodframe tabernacles. Some groups even held

Relate Stories of Local Ministries

Discuss rescue missions and other local ministries that are supported by your church. Students could share their own experiences too. If possible, have a speaker come to share his experiences with those ministries. It would be interesting to find out about the history of the ministry—particularly when it was founded, who founded it, and why.

meetings at modern campgrounds with cabins for the visitors to stay in.

Section Quiz

1. What was one reason for the increased diversity of religious groups from 1860 to 1910?
2. List the three challenges to the faith during this time.
3. What does an agnostic believe?
4. What new book from England most influenced American thinking during this period?
5. What was the purpose of the temperance groups?
6. What type of organization did Christian groups set up to deal with the physical and spiritual needs of those who lived in the slums?
★ How did rationalism lead religion toward the social gospel?

III. Progressivism

Besides its growing spiritual needs, American society was beset with many other problems. Some of the problems were too big for individuals to solve alone. The progressives began to look for help in solving America's problems. More and more they looked to government for the answers. Progressives sought to make life better through reform. Their movement was called **progressivism**. Many Christians supported the progressives and their ideals, especially on moral issues.

Progressive Goals

Progressives sought to end corruption and unfair practices in government, industry, labor, and society. They were able to make permanent changes in the way the cities, the states, and the nation were governed. However, social reforms were much harder to accomplish.

A second goal was to give people more say in governing. Some progressives believed that the evils of government could be cured by making government more democratic. They wanted to give individuals more power over laws and government officials. They also thought that by increasing the number of voters and especially by allowing women to vote they could sweep away government corruption. Some governmental practices that we take for granted today, such as primary elections and voting by secret ballot, were proposed by progressives.

A third goal was to use government to improve the quality of life. Many people thought that government should improve society because government is to be a minister of good (see Rom. 13:4). Fighting crime, prohibiting the making and use of alcoholic beverages, and ending prostitution were among such moral aims. A good example of a progressive is William Jennings Bryan, who was both a Christian and a progressive. Those who embraced the social gospel also looked to government to improve the lives of the poor. However, they followed the logical conclusion of the social gospel that man is basically good and his life can be made better by simply improving his environment. This belief is essentially socialism.

Section III
Objectives

Students should be able to

1. List the aims of the progressives.
2. Describe the social and political corruption that was widespread at the beginning of the Progressive era, including the Tweed ring.
3. Explain the significance of the muckrakers.
4. Describe the major political reforms made during the Progressive era.

Section Quiz Answers

1. immigration of non-Protestant peoples
2. liberalism, agnosticism, Darwinism (or evolution)
3. that we cannot know if there is a God
4. Darwin's *Origin of Species*
5. to fight the evils of liquor (alcoholic drinks)
6. rescue missions
★ Rationalism caused men to question Scripture and to choose the parts they believed were correct and ignore the others. Many rationalists rejected salvation through Christ but believed that doing good was right, so they promoted the social gospel.

Perpetual Discontentment

By 1900, Americans had experienced improvements in living conditions more than in any other period in history. Yet the cry was for "reform." Ask the students to explain what makes people perpetually discontented with their lot in life.

Boss Tweed

Boss Tweed was a leader of the New York City Democratic Party organization called Tammany Hall. Among the many corrupt dealings of Tammany Hall were schemes that charged city and county taxpayers exorbitant amounts of money for city expenses. The excess amounts went into the pockets of Tweed and his friends. One of the biggest schemes involved a new county courthouse that should have cost about $500,000 but ended up with a price tag of more than $8 million. The city's printing bill for two and one half years totaled a staggering $7 million. *Harper's Weekly*, with cartoons by artists such as Thomas Nast, helped bring attention to the corruption. In 1871, Tweed was arrested, tried, and sent to a debtor's prison, where he lived in modest comfort and was even allowed to visit his family when accompanied by his jailer. On one of these visits, Tweed escaped and fled the country. Nearly a year later, he was captured in Spain while working on a Spanish ship. The authorities there had identified him from a famous Nast cartoon. Tweed was returned to prison, where he died two years later.

Triangle Shirtwaist Company Fire

On March 25, 1911, one of New York City's worst disasters occurred. A fire started on the eighth floor of the Triangle Shirtwaist Company. The cause of the fire was never determined, although some people believe that someone carelessly threw a cigarette on the floor. Whatever the cause, the fire spread quickly, fed by the fabric used for shirts.

Although it was Saturday and nearly 5:00 p.m., many women were still working in the building. As news of the fire spread,

Discuss State and Local Reforms

Explain to your students the form of city government in your area and when it was instituted. Also find out whether your state constitution currently allows for recall, initiative, or referendum; find out when these amendments were passed. Also discuss any issues that recently came up for a vote or are coming up soon.

William Marcy "Boss" Tweed

The Tweed Ring dominated New York City politics during the early 1900s.

Fighting Corruption

Corruption was widespread in both government and industry. Progressives fought that corruption through reform.

Government Corruption

Corruption existed at all levels of government. In New York City, William Marcy "Boss" Tweed and his friends defrauded the city of millions of dollars by using city contracts to make large profits. On the state level, officials were bribed to give special favors to certain industries. In Pennsylvania, Standard Oil was accused of doing everything to the state legislature except refining it. On the national level, the Grant administration produced so many scandals that the term *grantism* became a synonym for illegal dealings in public office.

Andrew Jackson had started the spoils system. Presidents who followed him allowed much corruption in the appointment of government employees. That weakness was curbed in the late 1800s by several civil service reforms. They made merit, or ability, not party loyalty, the standard by which jobs were awarded. Yet, even those reforms were not enough to prevent some politicians from doing corrupt things.

Business and Industrial Corruption

Corruption was also rampant in business and industry as was exploitation of natural and human resources. The public, especially Western farmers, felt victimized by the corrupt and unfair practices of the railroads. The railroads had overcharged some customers but offered rebates (money given back) to petroleum shippers. In states where timber was harvested, some lumber companies stripped public lands for their own profit.

Some industrialists were not only dishonest in their business dealings but also unfair and even cruel to their workers. The workers often labored long hours under unsafe conditions, which, in some cases, led to disasters. Perhaps the worst disaster was the Triangle Shirtwaist Company fire in New York City in March 1911. Nearly 150 people, mostly girls and women, died because the doors had been locked to keep the workers on the job until the end of the shift. Another industry with unsafe conditions was the textile industry. Filtering systems in Southern textile mills were rare, so textile workers inhaled cotton lint. Some of them contracted "brown lung" disease and later died from it.

Long hours at low pay were normal. Almost all jobs had the same hours. Employers exchanged lists ("blacklists") of employees who caused trouble or went on strike, so it did little good to try to change jobs. Troublemakers would not be hired. Women and children were also victimized by industry. Early efforts to protect women from some occupations and to forbid children less than fourteen years of age from working failed.

Revealing Social Ills

Living conditions were worst in crowded cities. Rents were high and housing was limited, so the poor huddled together. Small, often one-room, apartments were common for entire families, who sometimes even kept boarders. More than 400,000 residents of New York City lived in windowless tenements. Twenty thousand more lived in damp cellar apartments where their rooms often flooded with water.

Epidemics were common. Diphtheria, smallpox, cholera, typhus, scarlet fever, and tuberculosis took many lives. Even common childhood diseases—measles, mumps, and chicken pox—were dangerous under such conditions. Garbage created a terrible stench and became a breeding ground for germs, rodents, disease, and harmful insects. Even where sanitation departments existed, they could not keep pace with the filth.

Other urban problems included an insufficient clean water supply and a lack of sanitary plumbing. Many tenements did not have running water or indoor bathrooms. People got water from street wells. Because run-off flowed into them, the water was impure. Fire hydrants were opened at certain times for bathing or other uses. Where indoor plumbing did exist, it was usually shared by many people and was undependable.

Housing conditions of the poor were bad, but those of people confined in prisons, mental hospitals, and other institutions were even worse. Filth and cruelty were common.

Filthy, crowded conditions in tenements prompted social reforms among city dwellers.

Instituting Reforms

During this era many city officials had little ability or knowledge for governing. They were also of weak character. To overcome these problems, reformers tried new methods of running city governments. Rather than electing a mayor, some cities hired a trained expert called a **city manager**. His position did not depend on his

---

Muckrakers: Journalists Who Exposed the Worst

If it had not been for muckraking journalists, it is possible that progressivism would have died; certainly it would have been less influential. **Muckrakers**, journalists who exposed society's ills, were given their name by Teddy Roosevelt. But the term was not original with him. It is the name of a character in John Bunyan's *Pilgrim's Progress* who was always looking down and could not look up even when offered a heavenly crown.

Muckraker journalists and authors named specific financiers, industrialists, and congressmen who undermined public interests. Muckraker **Lincoln Steffens** revealed city problems in articles for *McClure's*. Later they were put into a book, *The Shame of the Cities*. Steffens charged Philadelphia politicians with using the votes of "dead dogs, children, and nonexistent persons" to keep themselves in power.

Ida M. Tarbell, a Pennsylvania school teacher turned author, had

Ida M. Tarbell

grown up near Titusville, Pennsylvania, at the height of Standard Oil's attempt to squeeze out its competitors. She later wrote a series of articles on the company's ruthless tactics. In 1903, the articles were printed in a two-volume work, *History of the Standard Oil Company*. Her book led to the court case requiring the company to break apart its holdings.

John Spargo wrote of the ills of child labor and of the poverty that

sent many children to school hungry each day. His work *The Bitter Cry of Children* (1906) aided the passage of child labor laws. Ray Stannard Baker attacked lynching (execution without trial) of blacks in southern states.

Upton Sinclair

Upton Sinclair used his novel *The Jungle* to show that Chicago meatpackers killed diseased cattle and used chemicals and dyes to cover up bad meat. His descriptions were effective enough to spark the final drive for the Pure Food and Drug Act.

---

the women headed toward the fire exits. Several escaped from the eighth and tenth floors. However, the ninth floor became the center of the tragedy. There the exit doors were locked to keep women working until the end of their shift. Nineteen bodies were found next to the locked door.

Other women tried to escape by jumping out the windows. Most died from the fall. Even a safety net brought by firefighters did not help. Too many women jumped at the same time and broke through it. Although two elevators reached the floors on fire, the operators could take only a few women on each trip. In an act of bravery, three men from an adjacent building created a human chain across to a window on the eighth floor. Some women were able to cross on their backs to safety, but the men lost their grip and fell to their deaths.

By the time the fire was put out, 146 people had died. In the aftermath, the New York legislature formed a commission to investigate factory work conditions. Several labor laws resulted.

The Jungle

Although Upton Sinclair's novel *The Jungle* exposed the evils of the meatpacking industry, the author had other reasons for writing. Sinclair meant for his book to focus on the plight of the workers, but people were more concerned about what was going into the meat they ate than about the working conditions of the employees.

Shortly after *The Jungle* was published, the sale of domestic meat dropped by almost half. President Roosevelt sent two agents to see exactly what the health conditions were. Their report was not encouraging. Meat was shoveled off dirty floors and

---

Activity 4: Progressivism

Use this activity to help the students confirm their understanding of the principles of progressivism.

stored in rotting boxcars. Food inspection laws were quickly passed. Sinclair said at the time, "I aimed for the public's heart, and by accident I hit it in the stomach."

Jacob Riis, Muckraker

In 1890, a book titled *How the Other Half Lives* was published. In its pages, author Jacob Riis exposed the condition of inner-city tenements in New York. However, the book's popularity was not so much from its text but from its line drawings, which were based on photographs of the inner city taken by Riis.

Through his photographs, Riis captured scenes of families inside their cramped tenements, homeless children sleeping on the streets, and alleys full of people with laundry hanging from above. Readers were shocked at what they saw. Theodore Roosevelt, then the New York police commissioner, wrote Riis, "I have read your book, and I have come to help." Eventually, public reaction to the book brought about legislation to clean up New York slums.

Hull House

One of the most common misconceptions about Hull House was that the poor lived there. In reality, the residents were wealthy people who wanted to live among the poor and help them improve the neighborhood. Some of the more famous people who stayed at Hull House included Gerard Swope, the future president of General Electric; Charles Beard, historian; and William Lyon MacKenzie King, the future prime minister of Canada.

Jane Addams (center) founded Hull House (below) to help meet the needs of urban women. She also promoted the right of women to vote.

Jane Addams Memorial Collection (JAMC-1921-0049-5597); Photographer: Unknown; Special Collections, University of Illinois at Chicago Library

popularity, so the manager was under less pressure to bow to special interest groups. Other cities tried a **commission form of government**. Voters selected several commissioners, and each was put in charge of a specific area of government. That system made it much easier to detect corruption. Hiring managers and commissioners also allowed for the selection of people with specialized training. The city water or street commissioner, for example, might be a trained civil engineer.

Two states, Oregon and Wisconsin, were leaders in progressive reforms. Oregon reformed so many parts of its government that the package of ideas they tried was called the Oregon System. One new democratic practice was the **recall** of elected officials. If citizens became unhappy with the actions of an elected official, they could get a required number of signatures on a petition and force the official either to resign or to stand for special election, even if his term of office had not yet expired.

Two other government reforms that many states enacted were the initiative and referendum. An **initiative** allowed voters to propose their own legislation. First, a set number of voters' signatures had to be collected on a petition. Next, the proposed law was placed on a ballot and voters accepted or rejected it. A **referendum** (plural, *referenda*), on the other hand, allowed voters to pass judgment on acts already passed by their state legislatures. A similar petition and voting system was used.

One other major government reform was the **direct election of senators**. That reform was enacted in 1913 as the Seventeenth Amendment. It marked a radical departure from the Founders' purposes for our republican form of government. Previously, senators had been elected by state legislatures. The Founders set up the House of Representatives to represent the individual citizens of the various states. The president was to represent the entire union of the states. The Senate was designed to represent the individual state governments. In that way, all levels of government were represented in the national government.

But the progressives wanted to give more power to the voters. They believed that senatorial responsibility belonged to the voters. They also believed that such an approach would put elections out of the reach of corrupt manipulators in state government. But they failed to recognize that senators who were elected directly by the people were more likely to follow the immediate desires of the public rather than stand for what was right for the nation in the long run. As a result, a practical part of America's republican government was lost.

Reformers made many attempts to cure some of the problems of the cities. They responded to the terrible conditions in tenements by founding **settlement houses**. Americans modeled their settlement houses after Toynbee Hall, the first settlement house, which was in the London slum of Whitehall. Besides providing food, clothing, and child care, settlement houses offered recreation and classes to slum area women. America's first settlement house was called Neighborhood Guild. It was founded in 1886 in New York City. Probably the most famous settlement house was Chicago's **Hull House**, which socialist **Jane Addams** founded in 1889. She was assisted by Florence Kelly, who later channeled her energies into law. Her efforts led to the passage of child labor laws in several states.

Other citizens and social groups worked to improve prisons and mental institutions and to aid people in other distressed conditions. Government initially stayed out of most of those social programs, but it began to press for regulation of industries that abused employees and consumers.

Section Quiz

1. List three of the progressives' aims.
2. Who was "Boss" Tweed?
3. List three government reform ideas that gave more control to individual citizens.
4. What was the purpose of Toynbee Hall and Hull House?
★ How did new methods of government help check corruption in cities?
★ Would you have supported the Seventeenth Amendment or opposed it? Why?

IV. Roosevelt and Progressivism

When the issues of corruption, reform, and government regulation and aid were chief concerns, Americans elected three presidents who had progressive goals: Theodore Roosevelt, William Howard Taft, and Woodrow Wilson.

Theodore Roosevelt had been governor of New York when Tom Platt, the Republicans' state political boss, discovered that he could not control him. Platt urged Republicans to nominate Roosevelt for the vice-presidency of the United States in 1900. The vice-presidency was thought to be a political graveyard. Platt hoped that it would keep Roosevelt out of the public eye. But President McKinley was assassinated and Roosevelt became president. Roosevelt was suddenly the constant focus of public attention. He believed that it was "a dreadful thing" to gain the presidency that way. But few people have enjoyed the office as much as Roosevelt did.

Roosevelt had some critics, but he gained a large popular following. He was wealthy and well educated, but his adventures as a cowboy and a soldier allowed him to identify with the people and endeared him to the public. A candy store owner even named a new toy, the Teddy bear, for him.

A graduate of Harvard, Roosevelt spoke several languages and was a prolific writer. He authored more than a dozen books before he became president. By the end of his life, he had written twenty-six books and more than a thousand articles. Roosevelt was also a skilled politician who had many progressive goals. Unlike many Republican leaders of the day, he wanted change and improvement for the nation's government.

The Square Deal

Roosevelt believed that the government should regulate big business and promote competition, better working conditions, and job safety. Roosevelt's views and his efforts to put big business under the government's thumb won him the support of other progressives.

Roosevelt believed that workers should receive just and fair treatment. His labor policy was shown in his handling of the United

Theodore Roosevelt viewed the presidency as his "bully pulpit" to take his reforms to the voting public.

Section IV
Objectives

Students should be able to

1. Describe the rise of Theodore Roosevelt to the presidency.
2. Identify the term that Roosevelt used to describe the goals of his administration.
3. Describe some of the progressive actions of the Roosevelt administration, including the Pure Food and Drug Act and labor relations.

Roosevelt and Big Business

Roosevelt's first blow to big business was aimed at a holding company with a controlling interest in three major railroads. J. P. Morgan, James J. Hill, and Edward H. Harriman had united their genius to run those railroads for high profits. Roosevelt ordered prosecution of the group because they did not serve the "public good." The Supreme Court ruled against the railroads in the Northern Securities Case of 1904. It declared the holding company to be a trust that illegally restrained trade, and it forced the company to subdivide.

Teddy Bears

It is true that the teddy bear gets its name from Theodore Roosevelt, but how it happened is a subject of debate. One of the best-known stories involves a trip the president made to Mississippi in 1902. While he was there settling a border dispute, Roosevelt took some time to go hunting. An advance group of hunters found a bear cub, captured it, and tied it to a tree so that the president could shoot it. When Roosevelt arrived, he refused to

Section Quiz Answers

1. to abolish corruption and unfair practices in government, industry, labor, and society; to give people more say in governing; to use the government to improve the quality of life in America
2. a New York City politician who mishandled city funds and contracts to make money for himself and his friends
3. (any three) recall, initiative, referendum the direct election of senators
4. to provide better living conditions for the poor—food, clothing, child care, recreation, education, housing
★ Because city managers were hired, not elected, they felt less pressure to give in to special interest groups. The commission form of government made it easier to detect corruption because there were several commissioners, each in charge of a specific area of government.
★ Answers will vary.

Teddy Roosevelt's Voice

Visit www.bjupress.com/resources for a possible link to an audio clip of Theodore Roosevelt speaking. Ask the students how they think Roosevelt would fare with that voice in modern politics.

CD: Theodore Roosevelt, 26th President

Refer to the CD that accompanies the TE for information on President Theodore Roosevelt.

Biographies of TR

There are many good biographies that provide additional information about the life and presidency of Theodore Roosevelt. Some of them are listed:

- David McCullough, *Mornings on Horseback* and *The Path Between the Seas* (much information about TR's role in the building of the Panama Canal)
- Edmund Morris, *The Rise of Theodore Roosevelt* and *Theodore Rex*

shoot the captive animal, believing it was unsportsmanlike.

Clifford Barryman, a cartoonist for the Washington Star, heard about the story and used it in one of his cartoons. Soon almost everyone had heard about the bear. A storeowner named Morris Michtom decided to use the story to market a new toy in his Brooklyn store. He and his wife designed and made a toy bear and placed it in the store window with the cartoon and a sign that read "Teddy's Bear."

Roosevelt as Author

Theodore Roosevelt's writing reveals that he had a wide range of interests. Topics on which he wrote ranged from history and politics to biography to outdoor sports. Following is a list of some of his books.

History:
- *The Naval Operations of the War Between Great Britain and the United States—1812–1815*
- *New York City: A History*
- *Winning of the West*
- *The Rough Riders*

Biography:
- *Life of Thomas Hart Benton*
- *Life of Gouverneur Morris*
- *Oliver Cromwell*
- *Theodore Roosevelt: An Autobiography*

Politics:
- *Essays on Practical Politics*

Outdoor Life:
- *Hunting Trips of a Ranchman*
- *American Big-Game Hunting*
- *The Wilderness Hunter*
- *The Strenuous Life*

Gifford Pinchot was a Roosevelt appointee who later stirred controversy under Taft.

Mine Workers' strike in 1902. Workers demanded raises, a shorter workday, and recognition for their union. The strike dragged on for months as management refused to negotiate, and coal shortages caused public discomfort. Instead of siding with the owners and forcing the workers back to the mines, Roosevelt warned that he might use troops to run the coal mines. He also formed a special commission to help settle the dispute. It was the first time that the federal government had worked directly to settle a dispute between labor and management. Roosevelt claimed that he wanted to give both labor and management "a square deal." A compromise reduced the working day for the miners to nine hours and raised pay by ten percent. The question of whether such intervention is a proper use of federal executive powers remains.

Protecting People and Resources

In 1906, Upton Sinclair published the novel *The Jungle*. It exposed corruption in the meatpacking industry. Later the same year, Congress passed the **Pure Food and Drug Act**, which allowed federal inspectors to examine slaughterhouses and meat companies that shipped across state lines. The law also forbade the use of harmful additives.

At that time, patented medicines were widely advertised and available over the counter or by mail. Many of them contained opium derivatives or a high percentage of alcohol. Although those medicines were often useful, they were also addictive. The Pure Food and Drug Act regulated the use of narcotics and required that the contents be listed on product labels. It also made it illegal to make claims about medicines if they could not be verified.

Another issue very dear to Roosevelt's heart was conservation. As an outdoorsman, he readily responded to demands that the government protect lands for future generations to enjoy. America's first national park, Yellowstone, had become federal property in 1872. By 1901, there were three more national parks: Sequoia (sih KWOY uh; 1890), Yosemite (yoh SEM ih tee; 1890), and Mount Rainier (ruh NEER; 1891). When Roosevelt left office in 1909, he had more than doubled the number of national parks.

To protect forests from abuse by loggers, Congress had started a forest reserve system in 1891. Presidents Harrison, Cleveland, and McKinley had all added to the forest acreage, but Roosevelt more than doubled the acreage in reserve. He appointed **Gifford Pinchot** (PIN show), a close friend and a professional forester, chief forester. Pinchot not only helped to preserve America's forest resources but also set up a program to conserve its grasslands.

In 1902, Congress passed the New Lands Act, which permitted the sale of federal lands in arid areas. The money gained through such sales was to pay for irrigation projects to make arid lands more usable.

The End of the Roosevelt Administration

Although Theodore Roosevelt could have run again in 1908, he chose instead to hand-pick the next Republican presidential candidate. That was the first time since Andrew Jackson that a president in power had had enough backing to do so. Roosevelt picked William Howard Taft, who had given him loyal service.

- Theodore Roosevelt, *Theodore Roosevelt, an Autobiography* and *The Man in the Arena: Selected Writings of Theodore Roosevelt*

 Activity 6: The Progressive Presidents

Have the students begin this chart now with Roosevelt and continue as you cover Taft and Wilson in subsequent sections so that they complete the chart by the end of the chapter. At the end of the chapter, this chart will make a good tool in reviewing for the chapter test.

 Labor Relations—An Open Question

The text says of Roosevelt's first-time use of government power to settle a labor dispute: "The question of whether such intervention is a proper use of federal executive powers remains." Look back at the first two paragraphs of this section and have the students debate this question. Is it a proper function of government to intervene in wage disputes between workers and industry? Does it depend on whether an industry is critical to national defense or public safety? Make the question personal. What if a student or his parent had a dispute with his employer? Would he want the federal government to help settle the dispute? Why or why not?

 CD: Theodore Roosevelt Speaking Near Chicago, 1905

Refer to this photo as you discuss TR's succession to the presidency.

Section Quiz

1. How did Roosevelt gain the presidency?

2. What was Theodore Roosevelt's attitude toward big business?

3. What act passed during Roosevelt's administration regulated food and medicine production? What novel prompted Congress to pass this act?

4. What were some of the conservation efforts promoted by Roosevelt?

★ How did the power of the federal government increase during the progressive era? Was the increased power of the federal government good or bad for the country?

V. Taft and Progressivism

William Howard Taft had spent most of his career as a lawyer in the federal court system. Roosevelt had named him civil governor of the Philippines and later secretary of war, but Taft preferred the courts. His lifelong dream was to be chief justice of the Supreme Court. On Roosevelt's advice, he set aside that dream to run for president. (In 1921, nine years after Taft left the presidency, President Harding appointed Taft chief justice.)

Taft was Roosevelt's hand-picked successor, but Roosevelt was soon disappointed in his friend.

Like Roosevelt, Taft believed that government should regulate big business. But when Taft won the 1908 election over Democrat William Jennings Bryan, the course he took as president was somewhat different from Roosevelt's. He followed the advice of Republican leaders more readily, and he did not publicly push progressive reforms. His methods and personality made him seem more casual than Roosevelt. But Taft actually initiated eighty-nine antitrust suits, compared to Roosevelt's forty-three. Taft was not as successful at communicating his successes as Roosevelt had been. People saw only Taft's mistakes. He left office a failure in the eyes of many Americans.

The Taft Administration

Still, Taft could claim many progressive actions. He helped give the Interstate Commerce Commission more control over the railroads. He put telegraph and telephone companies under federal control. He backed reforms in the post office, created the Department of Labor to protect workers, and organized the Children's Bureau to end child labor.

During Taft's term, two progressive amendments were ratified. The Sixteenth Amendment—the income tax—gave government a source of revenue that allowed it to expand its activities greatly. The Seventeenth Amendment required that U.S. senators be elected directly by the people, rather than by the state legislatures.

The Split of the Republican Party

Fighting in the Republican Party threatened Taft's political future. Disputes over the Payne-Aldrich Tariff in 1909 made some Republicans think that Taft had sold out Roosevelt's ideas. A dispute between two of Taft's cabinet members over some western forest lands was the final straw. Taft wanted Gifford Pinchot dismissed from his cabinet. Roosevelt came home from an African safari convinced that Taft had given up his progressive principles.

Section V

Objectives

Students should be able to

1. Describe Taft's activity and success as a progressive president.

2. Explain why the Republican Party split in 1912.

3. Identify Roosevelt's third party and describe the assassination attempt on him during the election campaign.

Sixteenth Amendment

This amendment authorized the federal income tax. For the first time, the federal government could bypass states and their revenue authority and collect revenue directly from workers.

The *Titanic*

During Taft's administration, one of the worst ocean disasters of all time took place. On April 10, 1912, the British luxury liner R.M.S. *Titanic* left Southampton, England, on her maiden voyage. The ship was the largest of its kind, with a length of 882 feet and a displacement of 66,000 tons. The hull was divided into sixteen watertight compartments. People called the ship "unsinkable" because it could remain afloat even with four of those compartments flooded.

The ship headed toward New York City under the command of Captain Edward J. Smith. After forty-three years working on the seas, Smith planned to retire after that voyage. On April 14, around 11:40 p.m., Fred Fleet sighted an iceberg from the crow's nest.

Although the ship turned to avoid a collision, the side of the ship hit the iceberg and ruptured five hull compartments.

Section Quiz Answers

1. He was the vice president when McKinley was assassinated.

2. He thought that government should regulate big business to promote competition and provide better working conditions and job safety for workers.

3. Pure Food and Drug Act; Upton Sinclair's *The Jungle*.

4. the creation of national parks, the expansion of the forest reserve system, and the New Lands Act

★ It was increased through Roosevelt's belief in and use of government regulation. The federal government settled a labor dispute in the coal mining industry, and through the Food and Drug Act, its agents were able to inspect those industries. Answers will vary.

Compare Presidential Successors

Review the list of presidents that students have studied so far (see Appendix, page 588). Which president came from the same party as his predecessor and was the hand-picked successor? *(Martin Van Buren)* What problems did he experience? *(See pages 206-7.)* Now compare his problems to the problems Taft experienced. Note that only strong presidents (Andrew Jackson and Teddy Roosevelt) had enough clout to pick a successful successor. It makes sense that their successors would be "weaker" men and would not satisfy their strong-willed predecessors.

CD: William Howard Taft, 27th President

Refer to the CD for information on President William Howard Taft.

The Sinking of the *Titanic*

A good read and an excellent source of information on the sinking of the R.M.S. *Titanic* is *A Night to Remember* by Walter Lord.

Some researchers believe that only two or three compartments would have flooded if the ship had struck the iceberg head on.

Despite the damage, the ship remained afloat for almost three hours. During that time, distress signals were sent and passengers began to board the lifeboats. Tragically, there was room for only 1,178 of the 2,224 passengers. Some lifeboats entered the water only half full, leaving about 1,500 people to drown or freeze to death in the twenty-eight-degree water.

Four hundred miles from the coast of Newfoundland, the *Titanic* began its last journey—12,500 feet to the ocean floor. It remained unseen by human eyes until 1985, when Robert Ballard's underwater research team discovered the wreckage.

One of the last acts of Congress passed during the Taft administration was a law requiring two radio operators on passenger liners. More people might have been rescued from the *Titanic* had the law been passed sooner. The *Californian* was less than twenty miles from the sinking *Titanic*, but its radio operator was off duty that night and did not receive the distress calls.

Assassination Attempt on Roosevelt

On October 14, 1912, Theodore Roosevelt was in Milwaukee to address a crowd of supporters. As he left his car to enter the auditorium, a man pushed through the crowd and fired a gun at Roosevelt. Roosevelt's stenographer, Albert Martin, rushed to restrain and disarm the gunman.

Meanwhile, Roosevelt fell backward. In a few moments, he got up and told the people not to hurt the gunman, a fanatic named John Crank. Roosevelt had been hit but not fatally. The bullet had gone

Attempted Assassination of Teddy Roosevelt

On October 14, 1912, John Schrank, who had stalked Roosevelt for thousands of miles, finally got a clear, close-up shot. A stenographer in Roosevelt's entourage deflected the pistol just as Shrank pulled the trigger, probably saving Roosevelt's life. The bullet entered the right side of the candidate's chest but was slowed by a fifty-page speech that was folded double and a steel glasses case. The bullet still lodged three inches inside his chest. Doctors decided against trying to remove it. Roosevelt insisted on delivering his scheduled—but much shortened—speech. He never returned to the campaign trail.

The Election of 1912

Roosevelt had been home less than two months when he hit the campaign trail. He said that he was out to persuade voters to elect progressive Republicans to the House and Senate. But he ended up widening the rift within the Republican Party and building his own support for the 1912 convention. By February 1912, Roosevelt "gave in" to the urging of progressive Republicans and announced, "My hat is in the ring. I will accept the nomination for president if it is tendered to me."

But Taft and his followers had the support of most of the Republican Party leaders. They helped him win the Republican nomination on the first ballot. Roosevelt declared that conservative Taft Republicans had stolen the nomination. So he launched the new Progressive Party. Roosevelt was its candidate.

During the campaign, Roosevelt was entering an auditorium in Milwaukee, Wisconsin, to deliver a speech. A gunman came from the crowd and shot him at close range. Against the advice of advisors, Roosevelt went ahead and delivered a brief speech. "It takes more than that to kill a bull moose!" he declared. When Roosevelt announced that he felt "as fit as a bull moose," the Progressive Party was nicknamed the **Bull Moose Party**.

Roosevelt's political ideals were known as "The New Nationalism." If he had won, he would have involved the federal government in still more areas.

The Democrat in the race was New Jersey's progressive governor, Woodrow Wilson. In the campaign he spoke of a "New Freedom." He wanted strict government regulation to restore business competition. Roosevelt and Taft together got more votes than Wilson, but Wilson won because of the split Republican vote. He was the first president to have an earned PhD degree.

Election Results, 1912

Candidate	Party	Popular vote	Electoral vote	Percentage
Woodrow Wilson	Democrat	6,293,152	435	41.8%
Theodore Roosevelt	Progressive	4,119,207	88	27.4%
William H. Taft	Republican	3,486,333	8	23.2%
Eugene V. Debs	Socialist	900,369	0	6%

Section Quiz

1. During his career, Taft headed what other branch of government besides the executive branch?
2. What were the provisions of the Sixteenth and Seventeenth Amendments?
3. The Republican split enabled what Democrat to win the 1912 election?
★ Why was the Bull Moose Party created?

A Mock Interview

Assign groups of students to represent different people from around the country during the 1912 election—Democrats, pro-Taft Republicans, pro-Roosevelt Republicans, and Socialists. Pretend that you are Teddy Roosevelt and that you are going to hold a meeting with "the people." Give the groups a few minutes to prepare questions and to discuss the comments and charges they might make. Then open the floor for questions and comments from the crowd. A citizen must raise his hand and "step up to the podium" to talk to the candidate.

Activity 5: Roosevelt's Speech Following Assassination Attempt

Use this activity to help the students appreciate the pluck of Theodore Roosevelt and his determination to be heard despite being shot. Compare TR's attitude with the humor that Ronald Reagan exhibited when he was shot by John Hinckley.

CD: Electoral College Results, 1912

Refer to the CD for a map showing the results of the Electoral College vote in the 1912 presidential election.

Section Quiz Answers

1. the judicial branch (as chief justice of the Supreme Court)
2. The Sixteenth Amendment created an income tax. The Seventeenth Amendment changed election of U.S. senators from the state legislatures to direct election by the people.
3. Woodrow Wilson
★ because the Republican Party chose Taft again for its candidate, and Theodore Roosevelt and his supporters believed that Taft had betrayed progressive ideals

VI. Wilson and Progressivism

Woodrow Wilson was the son of a Presbyterian pastor. He was born and reared in the South. He believed that there were two sides to every issue, "a right side and a wrong side." He clung stubbornly to principles and refused to compromise. He had confidence in his judgment perhaps because he believed God had led him. He viewed men idealistically. He believed that most people learned from experience and desired to do right. Politically, that view meant that he often underestimated his opposition, whether at home or abroad.

Wilson and Business

At first, Wilson favored less government regulation of business than either Roosevelt or Taft. Rather than try to regulate large trusts, he believed that the government should break them into many smaller companies. He believed that small companies would be less monopolistic and more likely to operate in the public interest.

To deal with big business and get around the courts, which usually decided in favor of big business, Wilson took two steps. First, he set up the **Federal Trade Commission**, a regulatory agency that had power to get data from corporations and to issue orders to stop abuses. Second, Congress passed the **Clayton Anti-Trust Act** of 1914. That act closed some loopholes of the earlier Sherman Anti-Trust Act. It defined the unfair acts for which corporations could be fined or their executives jailed. Both labor unions and farmers' cooperatives were exempt from antitrust laws, so they could lawfully protest unfair practices.

Wilson and Financial Reform

One of Wilson's major accomplishments involved the tariff. The Democrats had gained majorities in both the House and the Senate, so Wilson had support for the reforms he had proposed in his campaign.

Wilson's views on the tariff were consistent with the Democrats' historic position. He believed that a high protective tariff encouraged monopolies and led only to higher prices for consumers. Lowering the tariff would force American businesses to compete with rivals and become more efficient. The **Underwood Tariff of 1913** gave the first major tariff decrease since the Civil War. The tariff rate on imports went down from 40 percent to less than 30 percent.

Congress used the income tax to make up for the loss of tariff revenue. The income tax was a graduated or progressive tax. The more a person earned, the higher the percentage of his income he had to pay. Incomes under $4,000 were not taxed. Annual incomes between $4,000 and $20,000 were taxed at 1 percent. The top bracket was 6 percent on incomes over $500,000. That beginning paved the way for increasingly higher taxes and more government spending.

Another financial reform during the Wilson presidency was the founding of the **Federal Reserve System**. It set up twelve district banks under a national Federal Reserve Board. The Federal Reserve Banks were "bankers' banks." The district reserve banks could increase or decrease the amount of money in circulation. The Board could use its power to control many banking operations throughout the country. Whether intended or not, it allowed one board to manage the nation's economy.

Woodrow Wilson went from college president to governor to president of the United States.

through his overcoat, spectacle case, and folded speech manuscript in his pocket. Although slowed down, the bullet did manage to pierce Roosevelt in the chest. Despite his injury, he insisted on making his speech.

With his vest still stained with blood, Roosevelt had a captive audience for his "brief remarks." Afterward, Roosevelt was rushed to a hospital. But as he had said in his speech, "it takes more than that to kill a bull moose."

Section VI
Objectives
Students should be able to

1. Explain Wilson's dealings with big business.
2. Describe the important changes regarding finances that came during the Wilson administration.
3. Name the two progressive amendments added during the Wilson administration and state their purpose.

Clayton Anti-Trust Act
Among other things, the Clayton Anti-Trust Act made it illegal for firms to charge one price to one customer and a second price to another when that action fostered monopoly. It said buyers did not have to sign contracts stating that they would never deal with the competition. It also made it illegal for the same people to be on the board of directors of several companies involved in the same types of business.

CD: Woodrow Wilson, 28th President
Refer to the CD for information on President Woodrow Wilson.

Why Study Presidents?
Many foreigners wonder why students of U.S. history pay so much attention to individual presidents. Ask students to answer this question. *(Presidential elections bring out the pressing issues that the average citizen cares about, and the presidential candidates aspire to embody or symbolize the aspirations of all people in the nation. Although the power of the president is limited, every president puts his distinct stamp on the course of events in the nation.)* Discuss the current

president. How do his election and administration embody or symbolize the struggles of the average American?

CD: First 1040 Tax Form, 1913
Refer to the CD for a photo of the first 1040 tax form.

CD: Federal Income Tax Rates, 1913–2000
Refer to the CD for a table showing the changes in the income tax rates since that tax became law.

Where Do You Stand?
With the students' help, write on the board all of the accomplishments during Wilson's administration. Then take a vote on each accomplishment to find out how many students would have supported the action and how many would have opposed it. Every student must be ready to defend his vote. Be prepared to give modern examples of similar issues and discuss how conservatives have typically voted.

Federal Reserve System

The Federal Reserve System was the final solution to the problem of keeping and regulating the nation's money. It followed the national bank, pet banks, and independent treasury systems discussed earlier in the book.

Oreo Chocolate Sandwich Cookies

In the same year that Wilson was elected to his first term, the National Biscuit Company introduced what they called a "tea biscuit." Since then, the Oreo cookie has become a popular snack and dessert treat. Its two chocolate wafers are made from Dutch cocoa and embossed with the famous Oreo name. Between the wafers a special icing called "slurry" is added.

Nobody knows for sure where the name for the cookie came from, but it stuck. Today, more than six billion Oreos are produced and consumed each year.

Crossword Puzzles

On December 21, 1913, Arthur Wynne delivered an early Christmas present to the world. The puzzle editor for the *New York World* designed a puzzle of connected blocks in the shape of a diamond. The first crossword puzzle was such a success that the puzzles became a regular feature in the Sunday edition.

As their popularity spread, crossword puzzles began to show up in other newspapers. In 1930, the first *New York Times* crossword puzzle was published. Today, crosswords are found in newspapers around the world, and people still take time out of busy schedules to solve them.

The Nineteenth Amendment

The drive for women's suffrage began before the War Between the States. Throughout the late 1800s, "women suffragettes" campaigned unceasingly for the right to vote. Led by women such as Elizabeth Cady Stanton and Susan B. Anthony, the crusade for women's suffrage was part of an overall campaign for equal rights for women, including control of their own property and custody of children in divorce cases. Anthony's campaign for the vote, however, got the most attention. Although she died fourteen years before it was ratified, the Nineteenth Amendment was often called the "Anthony Amendment" in her honor. Another promoter of women's rights was Jeanette Rankin, who in 1916 was elected to the U.S. Congress as a Republican from Montana, the first female member of Congress. She gained notoriety by voting against U.S. entry into World War I and World War II. She also opposed U.S. participation in the Korean Conflict and in Vietnam.

During Wilson's administration, women received the right to vote.

Federal Individual Income Tax Rates

Year	Bottom bracket		Top bracket	
---	Rate (%)	Taxable income up to	Rate (%)	Taxable income over
1913–15	1	20,000	6	500,000
1919–20	4	4,000	73	1,000,000
1941	10	2,000	81	5,000,000
1944–45	23	2,000	94	200,000
1952–53	22.2	4,000	92	400,000
2000	15	43,850	39.6	288,350

The Election of 1916

As the 1916 election approached, Wilson found himself preoccupied with events in war-torn Europe. His campaign slogan revealed his focus: "He kept us out of war."

When Roosevelt refused to run as a progressive candidate, the Bull Moose Party dissolved. Progressives had to decide whom to follow. Some backed Wilson because of his reforms. Others returned to the Republican fold.

The election of 1916 was very close. Wilson's Republican opponent was former New York governor and Supreme Court justice Charles Evans Hughes. The key state in the election was California. Election returns from that state arrived late, and Hughes went to bed believing that he was the next president. But the next morning, he learned that Wilson had been reelected.

Wilson's Second Term

During his second term, Wilson was forced to focus on foreign affairs and the eventual entry of the United States into World War I. In addition to problems in Europe, Wilson faced problems in Latin America, where he tried to use his moral diplomacy. With all of the focus on foreign affairs, progressive politics fell by the wayside. But two major issues were resolved: Prohibition and women's suffrage. To the delight of prohibitionists, the Eighteenth Amendment, which banned the manufacture and sale of alcoholic beverages, was ratified in 1919. One year later, when the Nineteenth Amendment was ratified, women won the right to vote. But the progressive era in American history was over.

Section Quiz

1. What system set up district banks to manage the nation's economy?
2. What gained most of the national government's attention during Wilson's second term?
3. What two major progressive issues were passed during Wilson's second term?
★ How did the reduction of the tariff make the passage of the Sixteenth Amendment more important?

 CD: Party Platform Summaries, 1916

Refer to the CD for summaries of the parties' platforms for the 1916 presidential campaign.

 CD: Political Cartoons, 1916 Election

Refer to the CD for several cartoons of the 1916 presidential campaign.

The Republican Party Then and Now

Discuss the main tenets of the modern Republican Party (and even read from the party platform written during the last campaign, if you wish to download it from the Internet). Ask the students to make comparisons and contrasts with the party in 1916. Make similar comparisons between the old and new Democratic parties. Note that parties can completely shift sides on such issues as the tariff, control of big business, and welfare.

Section Quiz Answers

1. the Federal Reserve System
2. foreign affairs (Latin American problems and efforts to keep the United States out of World War I)
3. Prohibition and women's suffrage
★ The government needed a new source of income to replace the revenue lost through the tariff reduction. It found that source in the progressive income tax.

Chapter Review

Review Questions

Match each of the following terms with its description.

1. agnostic
2. initiative
3. muckraker
4. recall
5. referendum
6. temperance society
7. urbanization

a. movement to the cities
b. says no one can know whether God exists
c. worked to prohibit alcohol use and abuse
d. one who reported poor conditions in society
e. voters' attempt to remove elected officials
f. voters propose legislation themselves
g. voters' reaction to a law already passed by their legislature

Answer the following questions.

8. What was the famous black school founded by Booker T. Washington?
9. What scientist helped to give that school a good reputation?
10. Name three religious cults that became popular around the turn of the century.
11. Who were the three progressive presidents?
12. What legislation helped to combat corruption in meatpacking companies and the abuse of patent medicines?
13. What was Roosevelt's party called in 1912?
14. What did the Sixteenth and Seventeenth Amendments do?
15. What is the term for the group of twelve banks and their board that regulate the nation's money system?

Critical Thinking

1. In what ways was progressivism helpful to the country, and in what ways was it harmful?
2. How did government change during the progressive era?

People, Places, and Things to Remember:

progressives
urbanization
philanthropists
Tuskegee Institute
Booker T. Washington
George Washington Carver
Samuel L. Clemens
social gospel
agnostics
Robert Ingersoll
Charles Darwin
B. B. Warfield
Billy Sunday
temperance societies
Young Men's Christian Association
Salvation Army
rescue missions
progressivism
"Boss" Tweed
city manager
muckrakers
Lincoln Steffens
Ida M. Tarbell
Upton Sinclair
commission form of government
recall
initiative
referendum
direct election of senators
settlement houses
Hull House
Jane Addams
Pure Food and Drug Act
Gifford Pinchot
Bull Moose Party
Federal Trade Commission
Clayton Anti-Trust Act
Underwood Tariff of 1913
Federal Reserve System

A Close One for Wilson

The 1916 election showed just how important each vote is in an election. If one more person had voted for Charles Evan Hughes in each California district, he would have become the next president of the United States.

Several other elections have been close calls. In the 1884 presidential election, Grover Cleveland defeated James G. Blaine by a majority of 1,047 votes within New York State. John F. Kennedy won the 1960 election by less than 1 percent of the vote in each election district.

In 1988, two Florida congressmen each won their seats by a single absentee vote. A U.S. congressman from Alaska won his seat by eleven absentee votes. With such election results, it is not surprising that politicians spend so much time and effort encouraging people to go to the polls.

Activity 7: Find the Message

Use this activity to help the students prepare for the chapter test.

Chapter Review Answers

Review Questions

1. b
2. f
3. d
4. e
5. g
6. c
7. a
8. Tuskegee Institute
9. George Washington Carver
10. Christian Science, Seventh-day Adventism, Jehovah's Witnesses
11. Theodore Roosevelt, William Howard Taft, Woodrow Wilson
12. Pure Food and Drug Act
13. Bull Moose (or Progressive) Party
14. 16th—allowed a federal income tax; 17th—allowed U.S. senators to be elected directly by the people of the states rather than by state legislatures
15. Federal Reserve System

Critical Thinking

1. Answers will vary. Some abuses were corrected. Some freedom was lost.
2. Answers will vary. Agencies, regulations, and expenses grew.

1936: Ford developed the V-8 engine

How much did it cost?

Product	Year	Price
Bread	1925	10¢/loaf
	1935	6¢/loaf
Butter	1925	57¢/lb.
	1935	38¢/lb.
Coffee	1925	57¢/lb.
	1935	24¢/lb.
Eggs	1925	47¢/doz.
	1935	35¢/doz.
Sugar	1925	17¢/qt.
	1935	14¢/qt.

1914-18 World War I

1917 United States enters World War I

1919 Treaty of Versailles signed
Eighteenth Amendment (Prohibition) ratified

1921 Washington Naval Conference

1925 Scopes trial

1927 Charles Lindbergh's solo flight across the Atlantic Ocean

1929 Stock market crash

1932 Reconstruction Finance Corporation created
Election of Franklin Roosevelt; beginning of New Deal

1915: J.L. Kraft and Brothers introduced processed cheese

How much did they make?

Occupation	Year	Wages
Farm Laborer	1925	$382/yr.
	1935	$324/yr.
Finance/real estate	1925	$1,997/yr.
	1935	$1,632/yr.
Railroad workers	1925	$1,597/yr.
	1935	$1,645/yr.
Retail workers	1925	$1,416/yr.
	1935	$1,279/yr.
Schoolteacher	1925	$1,299/yr.
	1935	$1,293/yr.

1945: Penicillin available commercially

1935 NRA declared unconstitutional

1939 Germany invades Poland; World War II begins

1941 (December 7) Japan attacks Pearl Harbor; United States enters war

1944 (June 6) D-day; Allied invasion of France

1945 (May 8) V-E Day; end of war in Europe

1945 (August 6 and 9) Atomic bombs dropped on Japan

1945 (September 2) V-J Day; end of World War II

1945 United Nations formed

1945

Chapter Goals

Students should be able to

1. Define and use the basic terms of the chapter.

2. Summarize the course of World War I from its beginnings to the Treaty of Versailles.

3. Identify new weaponry used as well as propaganda methods.

4. Identify the major countries and leaders involved in the war, in particular the major American figures.

5. Recognize the failure of imperialist and progressive ideas to solve international problems.

Chapter Motivation

Have the students listen as you read aloud the poem "In Flanders Fields" by Canadian physician John McCrae. (A copy of the poem is available on the Internet or in a public library.) McCrae died of pneumonia while on active duty in France. His poem reminds us of the cost of war and gives a patriotic challenge for people to continue to fight for right. Ask the students to be looking as they study the chapter for ways that the war inspired patriotism.

CHAPTER 21

In 1917, the United States found itself in the thick of Europe's war.

World War I

I. The War as America Watched

II. Effects of the European War on America

III. The United States at War

IV. American Forces "Over There"

V. The End of the War

Chapter 21 Lesson Plan Chart

Section Title	Main Activity	Pages	Days
I. The War as America Watched	Activity 1: Experiences of World War I	401–3	½–1 day
II. Effects of the European War on America	Activity 2: The Sinking of the Lusitania, 1915	403–6	½–1 day
III. The United States at War	Activity 5: U.S. Preparedness: The Run-Up to War	406–8	1–2 days
IV. American Forces "Over There"	Activity 6: The Heroism of Sgt. Alvin C. York	409–11	1–2 days
V. The End of the War	Activity 8: Wilson's Fourteen Points	412–13	½–1 day
TOTAL SUGGESTED DAYS (INCLUDING 1 DAY FOR REVIEW AND TESTING)			4½–8 DAYS

MATERIALS LIST

SECTION I
- Poem "In Flanders Fields" by John McCrae
- Special speaker: a World War I model plane enthusiast
- Models of World War I airplanes
- CD: Airplanes of World War I
- Activity 1 from the *Student Activities* manual

SECTION II
- *American History in Verse* by Burton Stevenson (available from BJU Press)
- April 1994 issue of *National Geographic* magazine

On June 28, 1914, in Sarajevo (SAH rah YEH voh), Bosnia, an assassin shot and killed Archduke Francis Ferdinand, heir to the Austro-Hungarian throne, and the archduke's wife. Most Americans probably asked, "Where is Sarajevo, Bosnia?" Little did they realize how soon Americans' lives would be affected by that event. World War I would soon follow.

The war shocked Americans. For three years—1914 through 1916—the United States watched as "the Great War" ravaged Europe, destroying more property and life than any other war in history to that time. Most Americans believed that the war was Europe's affair. They agreed with President Wilson that Americans should be neutral in word and deed. They hoped that the Atlantic Ocean would shield them from the conflict. Americans had reelected Wilson in 1916 because "he kept us out of war." But on April 6, 1917, hopes for staying at peace were dashed. The United States entered World War I.

I. The War as America Watched

In the beginning, the United States tried to mind its own business and remain aloof from the war. But it could not help seeing the trouble that was brewing in Europe.

Reasons for the War

Europe was in turmoil for several reasons. One reason was *extreme nationalism*. A devotion to and a pride in one's own nation is natural. But some countries had been building a distorted nationalism in their people in the years before the war. Germany, for example, began to believe that it had the right to build and expand no matter what the effect might be on other countries.

Imperialism and *militarism* also contributed to the growing tensions in Europe. Several countries had or wanted large empires. Some of them were willing to go to war to gain control of colonies or nearby territories. Several nations had built large armies to further their imperial goals or protect possessions. Large and powerful military forces threatened weaker neighbors and caused rivals to increase their forces.

Another major reason for the eruption of World War I was the *alliances* of European nations. In an effort to ensure security against aggression, European nations had formed alliances (agreements to support one another militarily). Germany, Austria-Hungary, and Italy, who were united by common imperialistic goals, formed the **Triple Alliance**. Britain, France, and Russia, united by a common fear of Germany, reacted by forming the **Triple Entente** (on TONT; *entente* is French for "agreement"). Those two opposing alliances involved all of the major powers of Europe, so once any of them entered a conflict, all of the others were likely to be drawn in.

The Spark and Spread of the War

The assassination of the Austrian archduke, Francis Ferdinand, ignited the conflict. Russia quickly came to the aid of Serbia, the little Balkan country that Austria-Hungary blamed for the deed. Thus, Russia and Austria-Hungary were soon at war with each other, and the allies of each joined in the conflict.

The assassination of Archduke Francis Ferdinand and his wife sparked World War I.

German soldiers marching to war at the front

The Great War

World War I was called the Great War. It did not become World War I until World War II.

Christmas Truce of 1914

Christmas Day in 1914 was a memorable moment in the war. On that day, opposing soldiers got out of their trenches and met each other on no man's land for a time of joint fellowship. The truce did not last long, but for a brief time the soldiers enjoyed peace.

Shell Shock

War had many ways of wounding or killing soldiers. In addition to physical afflictions, soldiers faced psychological trauma. Many soldiers in World War I suffered from a condition commonly known as shell shock. Having been exposed repeatedly to the noise and horrors of the battlefield, their nervous systems collapsed. With proper rest and treatment, many soldiers could recover from shell shock; however, disturbing memories might return periodically. Other more recent names for shell shock have been battle fatigue or post-traumatic stress disorder.

Slaughter on the Battlefield

The slaughter on World War I battlefields was staggering. On the first day of fighting at the Somme in July 1916, 60,000 British soldiers were killed or wounded. Most of them were lost in the first half-hour of battle. In Belgium in April 1917, the British lost 150,000 soldiers in six days while their front line advanced only a few miles. The dead from the war numbered twice as many as the dead in all the major wars fought from 1790 to 1913.

World War I saw the introduction of many new forms of weaponry, including the tank.

The use of poisonous gases forced the armies to develop counter measures, such as gas masks.

On August 1, Germany declared war on Russia. France joined Russia against Germany and Austria-Hungary two days later. When German armies marched across neutral Belgium to attack France, Britain quickly stepped into the war to help France before the Germans could take the country. Other nations also took sides. Europe quickly found itself involved in a long and bloody war between the **Central Powers**—Germany, Austria-Hungary, Bulgaria, and Turkey—and the **Allied Powers**—Britain, France, Russia, Italy, and later the United States. (Italy switched to the Allied side in 1915.)

The Course of the War

The United States was not involved in the European alliances and rivalries, so it had no reason in the beginning to enter the war. The nation simply watched in horror as soldiers from both sides were slaughtered in the bitter war.

Because Germany led the first major assault of the war, the Allied Powers called the Central Powers the **belligerents**. The two sides soon settled into trenches that stretched from the English Channel to the Rhine River. At the same time, the Russian armies began to attack Germany and Austria-Hungary from the east, but they had little success.

The war dragged on with neither the Central Powers nor the Allies making large gains. Both sides introduced new weapons and equipment that made warfare more efficient and sometimes more brutal.

The British developed the tank, an armored vehicle that could fire shells while moving on caterpillar tracks. It was capable of almost continuous advance over rugged terrain. Soon, the other powers developed their own tanks.

On April 22, 1915, at the Second Battle of Ypres, the Germans unleashed a new deadly weapon: poison gas. Made from chlorine, the gas harmed the nose, throat, and lungs. Poison gases made whole armies temporarily helpless in the face of enemy attacks. Mustard gas, as it was called, soon became the most feared and common gas on the battlefield. About two percent of those who came into contact with it died. As a result, the gas mask was developed and became standard equipment in some war areas.

Fighting also took to the air. For a while, the Germans used zeppelins, large aircraft similar to blimps, to bomb Britain. But zeppelins moved slowly, and airplanes soon replaced them. Airplanes could be used for aerial reconnaissance, bombing, and attacking enemy planes. Aerial battles between planes were called "dogfights." Dogfights were made possible by yet another invention, the machine gun. Machine guns on the planes were synchronized with the airplane's propellers. (Before that development in 1915, pilots could not fire their guns forward without shooting their own propellers.)

Fighter pilots who shot down five or more enemy planes became special heroes called "aces." Manfred von Richthofen, nicknamed "the Red Baron," was Germany's top ace with 80 "kills." Other aces included Great Britain's Mick Mannock (61), Canada's Billy Bishop (72), and France's René Fonck (75). When the United States entered

---

Model Airplanes

World War I is a popular period among model airplane enthusiasts. Ask one or more volunteers to build models of World War I planes (or bring in any models they might have already built) and report what they know about the planes. Another idea is to invite a model plane enthusiast to speak to the class about his or her hobby and to show some World War I–era models.

CD: Airplanes of World War I

Refer to the CD for photos of some of the most frequently used warplanes of World War I.

Display Memorabilia from the War

If the families of any of the students have memorabilia from World War I, such as medals, or uniforms, ask those students to share such items with the class, along with any stories of family members' involvement in World War I.

Activity 1: Experiences of World War I

Have the students begin this activity at this point and continue to fill it out as they study the rest of the chapter. They should complete it by the end of Section V. The completed chart would make a good tool for reviewing for the chapter test.

The Lafayette Escadrille

America's air force had its beginnings in France during World War I. Actually, the first American air squadron was in the French armed forces. The United States did not have an air corps of its own at that time, so many young Americans went to Europe to fly for France. At first, they could join only the French Foreign Legion. French law forbade their enlisting in the regular French forces. The law changed, though, and a group of young and wealthy Americans joined the French Air Corps. (The rich became pilots simply because before the war they were the only ones who had the money to buy planes and learn to fly.)

A group of the American pilots petitioned the French government to form an all-American French squadron. Permission was granted, and in April 1916 the Escadrille Américaine (ES-kuh-DRIL uh-mehr-ih-CAN) was begun. When President Wilson complained that the name violated America's official neutral position, the squadron changed its name to the Lafayette Escadrille. The young men claimed that they were repaying France for the help that the Frenchman Lafayette had given the United States during the War for Independence.

The Lafayette Escadrille began with seven pilots and a lion cub as a mascot. During the war, thirty-eight men served as pilots, and many of them died in their cockpits. When the United States entered World War I, the Lafayette Escadrille became the first American air squadron.

the war, Eddie Rickenbacker became the most famous American ace with 26 kills. (Rickenbacker's total seems small, but one must remember that the other countries' aces were in the war for about three years longer than America's pilots.)

Trucks and automobiles aided the transportation of military goods and personnel. Rifles, cannon, grenades, mines, and other weapons were improved or invented for effective fighting. And for battling on the sea, the Germans perfected the submarine. A German *unterseeboot* (U-boat) could remain unseen while launching a surprise torpedo attack against enemy ships.

Section Quiz

1. What event sparked the start of World War I?
2. List four of the causes of the war's outbreak.
3. What countries composed the Allies? the Central Powers?
4. Which country made the first major assault of the war?
5. What country developed the tank? poison gas?
* Was the use of poison gas an effective form of warfare? Was its use right or wrong?

II. Effects of the European War on America

Although the United States was not participating in the war, it was not totally isolated from the warring nations either. The war affected transportation, trade, and diplomatic relationships with Europe. Americans were concerned with all of those matters.

Eddie Rickenbacker

When Is a War Just?

Just wars have traditionally been defined by the following criteria:

1. Just cause—There must be a moral reason for going to war. Examples include oppression, genocide, and defending oneself from attack or invasion.

2. Comparative justice—Reprisals must not significantly outweigh the original injustice; civilian casualties should be avoided as much as possible.

3. Legitimate authority—Only those who "bear the sword" (Rom 13:4) may wage war or use deadly force (with the exception of self-defense).

4. Right intention—Righting a wrong is a good intention; material prosperity is not.

5. Probability (possibility) of success—There must be hope of winning.

6. Last resort—War should be declared only after diplomacy and other efforts have failed; with the exception of the discovery of an imminent attack (there may not be time for diplomacy and other efforts).

What principles guide action once war has begun?

1. Discrimination—Attack should be directed on the original wrongdoers and those who actively support them, not civilians who bear no responsibility for the original wrongs.

2. Proportionality—Force must be proportional to the original wrong.

3. Minimum Force—Death and destruction should be limited to what is necessary to win the war.

Section Quiz Answers

1. the assassination of Archduke Francis Ferdinand, heir to the Austro-Hungarian throne, and his wife

2. extreme nationalism, imperialism, militarism, and alliances of European nations

3. Allies—Britain, France, Russia, Italy, and the United States; Central Powers—Germany, Austria-Hungary, Bulgaria, and Turkey

4. Germany

5. tank—Britain; poison gas—Germany

* Answers will vary but should include: No, the use of poison gas was not an effective form of warfare. A change of wind direction could send the deadly cloud back onto the army that had dispersed it, or the gas could harm others not involved in the battle. Christians who hold to a Just War Theory would conclude that the use of poison gas violates the principles of proportionality and minimum force.

Would We Be Neutral Today?

Intervention in foreign wars has become so common that Americans think of it as the norm. Help the students see the world as it was at the turn of the nineteenth century and to understand why it seemed so natural for Americans to remain neutral as European countries warred among themselves.

Have the students answer the following questions in two different ways—from a modern perspective and then from the perspective of someone living in 1910. What was the last big war? *(Iraq War; Spanish-American War)* What other big wars have Americans fought in the past fifty years? *(Gulf War, Kosovo intervention, Grenada, Panama, Vietnam; Indian Wars and the Civil War)* What was the last big war on European soil and were Americans involved? *(World War II, yes; the Napoleonic Wars, no)* Who is the greatest world power? *(United States; Great Britain)*

Section II
Objectives

Students should be able to

1. Explain why American interest in the war grew.

2. Describe the British and German policies that violated American neutrality.

3. Describe the two incidents that led to American entry into the war.

Submarines

World War I submarines were vessels of 188 feet or longer, with a crew of twenty-six and the ability to travel underwater on battery and electric power at a speed of eight knots. They carried six torpedoes for military purposes. Today, the submarine is a massive 560 feet long, is powered by nuclear reactors, can travel at twenty-five knots while submerged, and carries ballistic missiles.

Espionage and Sedition Acts

The U.S. government was worried about disloyalty during World War I. Congress passed two acts, one in 1917 and the other in 1918, to prevent un-American activities. The Espionage Act made it illegal to discourage loyalty to the military or to send treasonous mail. The Sedition Act said that Americans could not obstruct the sale of war bonds or make harmful statements about the government, the Constitution, the flag, or the military uniform. Both laws were vaguely worded, leaving them open to interpretation.

Propaganda posters for Germany (top) and Great Britain (bottom) attempted to stir patriotism among the citizens.

Reasons for American Interest

President Wilson had stated that Americans should remain neutral. But maintaining neutrality was difficult for several reasons.

First, American sentiment favored the Allied cause. Although eleven million Americans had some tie to Germany, substantially more had British ties. America's background, its legal system, part of its form of government, and even its language were English. Americans also recalled that another ally, France, had come to America's aid during the War for Independence. Also, Americans had been upset by the German invasion of neutral Belgium.

A second factor was economic. Although American businessmen sold goods and lent money to both the Allied and the Central Powers, more traded with Allied countries, especially Britain. So Americans were more sympathetic to Allied interests just to protect American investments.

Gradually the United States began aiding the Allies. Soon after the outbreak of war, British and French agents placed orders with American firms. They contracted for shipments of grain, cotton, and other supplies. At first, those countries had paid cash for their items and carried them home on their own ships. But when their cash ran low, they asked for and received loans. By early 1917, the United States had loaned Britain more than $1 billion and France over $300 million. The Germans protested that the loans violated neutrality because American-made shells and guns were killing Germans. Wilson, however, chose not to restrict those business deals. He believed that restricting them would help the Central Powers.

Another factor that increased American interest was Allied propaganda. Britain and France controlled the trans-Atlantic cables that brought the news to American newspapers. The Germans had to rely on the still imperfect radio to transmit messages to the United States. The few German messages that did get through did not project a good image to Americans. Because they emphasized hatred and destruction, they aroused more anger than sympathy. The Allies easily won the Americans over just by reprinting German propaganda word for word.

Germany's deeds were also harmful to its relationship with America. When it invaded Belgium, a violation of an earlier treaty, the German government called the treaty "a scrap of paper." The Germans executed about five thousand Belgian civilians who had resisted them. British propagandists were quick to let Americans know about this atrocity and others. They also told about a few that never happened!

Violations of America's Neutrality Rights

The biggest difficulty in maintaining neutrality involved Britain's and Germany's violations of America's neutral rights at sea. Britain was a small island nation, so it was almost totally dependent on overseas trade for raw materials. Over time, Britain had developed the best and largest navy and merchant marine (trading) fleet. The United States had benefited greatly from trade with Britain, and it did not want to lose that trade during the war. The United States wanted to continue trade with Germany, too, but all sea trade with Europe was put in jeopardy by the naval strategies of Britain and Germany.

Early in the war, Britain had laid mines at the entrances to the North Sea to prevent nations from trading with Germany. However,

---

Students should ask themselves why the United States would take sides in foreign wars. Summarize the arguments for U.S. involvement in the most recent war. Were any of those issues at stake before World War I? Should America have remained neutral as long as they did during World War I? Should America stay neutral in most conflicts today?

Poetry Corner

You will find many poems about World War I in Burton Stevenson's *American History in Verse*, including the following:

- "Abraham Lincoln Walks at Night" (Vachel Lindsay)

- "The Road to France" (Daniel Henderson)

- "Armistice Day" (Roselle Mercier Montgomery)

Another poem, which you might consider reading to the class and then discussing, is by Alan Seeger, a Harvard classmate of T.S. Eliot. He died during the war but not before penning a poem of despair—"I Have a Rendezvous with Death." You might also consider reading and discussing Eliot's own poem of despair over World War I—"The Wasteland." A book-length treatment of such despair is *All Quiet on the Western Front* by Erich Remarque. (That book was also made into a film by the same title.)

Mexico and the United States

To see how the Zimmermann telegram looked coded and decoded, visit the website of the National Archives and Records Administration.

instead of trading directly with Germany, some countries, including the United States, sent their goods to the Germans through neutral countries such as the Netherlands, Denmark, or Sweden, who resold them. Such actions angered the British, and they began to stop American shipping bound for neutral nations.

The British were ready to seize anything that could be useful to Germany. American ships were stopped at sea and ordered to British ports for searches. The wasted time pushed up the cost of goods. Sometimes foodstuffs spoiled before they could be delivered. The British claimed this action was necessary because of the danger of attack by German submarines. British firms also made "blacklists" of American firms that they suspected of trading with Germany through neutral nations. Such actions angered Americans because they violated the rights of a neutral country.

But Britain was not the only country to receive America's anger. Realizing that Britain was dependent on foreign trade, too, Germany sought to cut British imports. Rather than using just a blockade, Germany chose to use **unrestricted submarine warfare**. They fired on all ships in a designated war zone around Britain. Attacking neutral ships without giving them a warning and a chance to remove their passengers was a violation of international law. The United States protested Germany's policy as inhumane. Americans also said it violated the concept of freedom of the seas. Germans, however, argued that submarines were at a disadvantage. If they surfaced to give a warning, it was easy for even a merchant ship armed with guns to sink them.

Although the German Embassy put ads in newspapers warning Americans not to travel on British vessels, the warnings were ignored. In May 1915, a German U-boat sank the R.M.S. *Lusitania*, a British liner, without warning off the coast of Ireland. Among the 1,198 who perished were 128 Americans. President Wilson demanded that the Germans apologize and renounce their strategy of unrestricted submarine warfare. He later threatened to withdraw diplomatic recognition if the Germans attacked another passenger ship. Germany cooperated for a while.

Growing American Fears

When the German offensives in France slowed, however, Germany decided that the only way to win the war was to cut Britain's supply lines and force her to surrender. It could accomplish this by using its large fleet of U-boats. The German government announced in February 1917 that it would resume unrestricted submarine warfare. The United States then broke off diplomatic relations with Germany.

The tension caused by submarine warfare was heightened by the discovery of a German plot. Early in March 1917, the German foreign minister, Arthur Zimmermann, sent a telegram to the German minister in Mexico. In it he said that if war broke out between Germany and the United States, Germany would reward Mexico if it entered the war against the Americans. Germany would give Texas, New Mexico, and Arizona back to Mexico.

The Germans accused Britain (perhaps not incorrectly) of shipping war materiel under the U.S. flag to avoid attacks by German submarines.

Unrestricted submarine warfare and the sinking of the *Lusitania* pushed the United States closer to war with Germany.

Jeannette Rankin

Jeannette Rankin was the first woman elected to the U.S. Congress. Elected in 1916 and 1940, she represented her home state of Montana for two terms in the House of Representatives. A determined pacifist, she opposed American participation in both World Wars. She was one of only fifty representatives to vote against the declaration of war against Germany in World War I. After the United States entered the war, however, she supported the sale of Liberty Bonds and voted for the military draft. She was the only member of the House to vote against entry into World War II and the only member of Congress to vote against both wars. She never changed her views on war. She was a founding vice president of the American Civil Liberties Union, a liberal legal organization still going strong today. When Rankin was eighty-seven, she led a march in Washington, D.C., protesting the Vietnam War.

Nuggets from *National Geographic*
For an excellent review of the *Lusitania* findings, see "Riddle of the *Lusitania*" in the April 1994 issue of *National Geographic*. It explains the different theories of why the ship was sunk and how it went down so fast. The article also includes drawings and photographs of the findings.

Activity 2: The Sinking of the *Lusitania*, 1915

Use this first-person account of the sinking of the *Lusitania* to help the students understand the nature of the war through the eyes of one German U-boat captain. Going over the answers to the activity questions can open up opportunities to reinforce the terrible nature of the war.

The President's Difficult Choices

Ask the students to imagine that they are President Wilson or members of his cabinet. List each crisis described in this chapter. Call upon the students to summarize the issues that each crisis raised and the president's alternatives. Wilson vacillated between his role as a potential peacemaker and his need to protect the nation's interests. After each crisis, he could turn his cheek, mediate a peaceful settlement, increase supplies to the opposing side, increase the nation's military preparedness, or declare war. Each alternative had its proponents, and the president faced pressure from all sides. Every president faces crises and difficult decisions. On few occasions do these decisions lead to war (which should be a last resort).

CD: Propaganda Posters of World War I

Refer to the accompanying CD for examples of propaganda posters printed by the different belligerents in World War I.

Activity 3: Objectivity and Propaganda

Use this activity to help the students discern between objective reporting and propaganda.

Section III
Objectives

Students should be able to

1. Explain the way the United States transported supplies to Europe.
2. Describe the way America increased production for the war effort.
3. Explain the way the United States financed the war effort.

Government Agencies and Powers

Note the government agencies and powers that arose in response to the needs of the war. War has often necessitated the temporary expansion of government power. Quite often, however, the powers that the government gained during the crisis do not return to the people once the emergency passes.

American Legion

Established during World War I, the American Legion is the largest veterans' organization in the United States. Twenty officers of the American Expeditionary Force were asked how to improve troop morale. One man suggested a group for veterans, and the result of his suggestion was the American Legion. Today, the group is open to any soldier who served honorably in a major American conflict.

American Junior Red Cross

President Woodrow Wilson announced the creation of the American Junior Red Cross on September 15, 1917. Eleven million young people joined the organization during World War I. They gave money to help children in other countries. They also worked on conservation at home. For

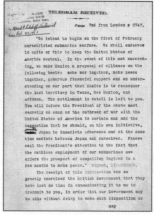

The Zimmermann telegram was the last straw, bringing the United States into the war against Germany.

On April 2, 1917, President Wilson asked Congress to declare war on Germany.

British intelligence intercepted the telegram and notified the United States. The next day, President Wilson asked Congress to arm American merchant ships, and he released the Zimmermann telegram to the public. Americans were outraged. Then German submarines sank three more American merchant ships. The pressure increased even more. Secretary of State William Jennings Bryan pleaded with Wilson, the cabinet, and the American people not to go to war. He wanted to give peace negotiations a chance. When he realized that Wilson was determined to go to war, he resigned in protest.

On April 2, 1917, a solemn President Wilson appeared before both houses of Congress and asked for a declaration of war. Four days later, on April 6, 1917, Congress declared war on Germany. The United States was joining the fight in Europe.

Section Quiz

1. List at least three reasons for the difficulty of American neutrality.
2. How did some American ships attempt to get around Britain's blockade of German ports? What was Britain's response?
3. What German naval policy greatly angered Americans?
★ What was the significance of the Zimmermann telegram?

III. The United States at War

By the time the United States entered the war, the Allies were in a desperate condition. At one time, thanks to the success of Germany's unrestricted submarine warfare, the British people were down to a three-week supply of food.

The United States responded with huge shipments of supplies to Europe. To ensure safe arrival, U.S. ships traveled in groups called *convoys* with destroyer escorts for protection. The destroyers were equipped with antisubmarine weapons, including guns and depth charges. Such protection cut shipping losses. The **convoy system** worked so well that not one of the two million American soldiers bound for Europe was lost at sea. Although American manpower boosted Allied morale, the biggest contribution of the Americans was in providing war materiel. Food, clothing, munitions, ships, and vehicles poured into Europe. The Central Powers were unable to match this production themselves and soon fell behind. But to provide supplies for the Allies, Americans had to gear up for war. The peacetime economy and production needed to be channeled into a great effort for victory.

Lack of Military Preparedness

Americans feared having a strong standing army and had kept the country's military force purposely small. At the beginning of the war, the U.S. military consisted of only 200,000 men. Allied losses in Europe had already exceeded the size of the whole American army. The United States had only four hundred heavy guns and enough ammunition for a nine-hour bombardment. It had no tanks or air force. Suddenly, the United States had to train men, make equipment, and build ships to carry everything to Europe.

Activity 4: America Declares War on Germany, 1917

Use this activity to help the students understand the reasons for declaring war against Germany.

▶ One Voice Against the War

Consider showing the PBS film *Jeannette Rankin: The Woman Who Voted No*, which tells the story of U.S. Representative Jeanette Rankin, the first female member of the U.S. House of Representatives and an ardent pacifist.

Section Quiz Answers

1. (at least three) American sentiment favored the Allied cause; Americans wanted to protect investments with the Allies; Allied propaganda influenced Americans; Britain and Germany violated America's neutral rights.
2. They sent goods to Germany through neutral countries. Britain began stopping and searching American shipping bound for neutral nations.
3. unrestricted submarine warfare
★ Its plot to encourage Mexico to fight against the U.S. in exchange for America's southwestern lands enraged Americans and made them ready to fight Germany.

The Difficulties of Raising an Army

Have the students imagine the problems that the United States faced in gearing up for war. They should list everything that needed to be accomplished and discuss how each of these things could be accomplished.

1. Increase the size of the military from 200,000 to nearly 4,000,000 (use the draft or volunteers)
2. Train the military (open thirty-two camps; keep experienced troops together or use them as trainers)

For the first time since the Civil War, the nation resorted to a draft. Under the Selective Service Act, local draft boards under civilian leadership supplied the men. The system worked well, and there was far less opposition to the draft than there had been during the Civil War. About four million men went into the service. The recruits were trained at thirty-two training camps across the nation.

Production for the War

As America sent its soldiers off to battle, the entire nation had to adjust to the necessities of war. The government had to begin many programs and agencies to coordinate the war effort. Everything the American forces needed had to be obtained or manufactured and transported quickly.

The **War Industries Board** organized industrial production. Factories were transformed to produce the needed war materiel—uniforms, guns, ammunition, vehicles, and medical supplies. The board set criteria to standardize thousands of items and set economic priorities for the nation.

To ensure that the railroads operated efficiently carrying the extra freight and passengers, the United States Railroad Administration took control of all railroads. It organized regional units, set rates and schedules, and set shipping priorities to ensure that weapons, ammunition, and other war materiel reached ports even if nonessential goods had to be held up.

The Fuel Administration had the job of conserving and directing the use of the nation's fuel. It asked civilians to walk more and added "gasless days" to weekly calendars. Auto owners were asked to save gasoline so that trucks could run to carry war goods.

The actions of all of these federal agencies were designed to aid the war effort by coordinating the activities of the nation. The national emergency had reduced the public's resistance to government power and restrictions. With Allied armies facing starvation, increasing America's food production received top priority. Herbert Hoover, who had already gained fame as the organizer of a massive food relief program to Belgium, headed the Food Administration. Rather than force the public to conserve food, the administration set up a voluntary program. Americans were asked to make Mondays wheatless, Tuesdays meatless, and Thursdays porkless. Americans also raised their own vegetables in "Victory Gardens" so that more food would be available for the soldiers. With these efforts huge savings were made. Moreover, the people felt they were a part of the great war effort. Just before the war began, the average annual amount of food shipped to Europe was 7 million tons. By 1919, it had reached 18.6 million tons.

The war also brought changes in the American work force. Four million men were drafted, depleting the normal work force. Because of the urgent need, many women began to work outside the home for the first time. Some gratefully returned home when the war ended, but others continued to work.

Volunteer groups were formed to support the "boys" in France. Memberships in the American Red Cross multiplied as women in local chapters met to roll bandages, knit sweaters or socks, and prepare packages to be sent abroad. Men who could not serve in the military also offered their time to support volunteer efforts.

The labor shortage caused wages to skyrocket, and more jobs were available. Even with high taxes, loan drives, and increased

FEED a FIGHTER
Eat only what you need—
Waste nothing—
That he and his family
may have enough

Although the war was fought in Europe, the citizens of the United States were asked to sacrifice for the war effort.

A Little Bird Named Enza

There was a little bird,

Its name was Enza.

I opened the window,

And in-flu-enza.

In 1918, this was a favorite poem of America's children. But the "little bird named Enza" was no laughing matter. The deadly virus struck many American soldiers either while they were still in training or after they had arrived in Europe. In four months, influenza killed twenty-one million people worldwide, more people than the war killed in four years. At the height of the epidemic, the last week in October 1917, twenty-seven hundred American soldiers died in Europe; twenty-one thousand American citizens died of the flu in the States. But the flu was completely impartial: nearly a quarter of a million Germans died as well.

The flu epidemic left as suddenly and as mysteriously as it had come. By the middle of November 1918, it was over. Ironically, about the same time, so was the war. Some people estimate that more than forty million people died in the four years of World War I, and at least half of those were victims of the "little bird Enza."

---

example, they tended war gardens. Junior Red Crossers continued to serve in World War II.

Dixie Cups

A few years before the war broke out in Europe, an American named Hugh Moore stumbled across an idea for a new kind of cup. He was trying to sell water at a penny a cup. Customers were not especially interested in paying for water, but they did like the paper cups Moore used.

At that time, health issues were receiving much national attention. Previously, the public had shared communal cups or dippers at public drinking places. But when a study revealed the abundance of germs on a public drinking vessel, Americans were shocked. Moore's Health Kups became extremely popular. In 1919, he renamed the product Dixie cups after the Dixie Doll Company near his house. In subsequent years, his invention was used to hold everything from soda to ice cream.

Influenza Epidemic

No one knows for sure where the influenza epidemic started. At the time, most people said it originated in Spain; it was, after all, called Spanish influenza. Many historians today, however, think it began at Fort Riley, Kansas. After a dust storm in March 1917, more than one thousand soldiers became sick with the flu and forty-six of them died. When the regiment was sent to France, the epidemic hit there and spread across the battlefields.

Some units had up to 80 percent casualty rates because of the flu, not the war. Approximately one-third of the American Expeditionary Force died from the disease. On ships bound for Europe, the death rate among troops was 20 percent.

---

3. Supply the military with food, clothes, and weapons (pay private industries or take over industry)

4. Ship the military to Europe (requisition private merchant ships or build more ships)

5. Send the troops into the battle lines (serve as replacements within existing armies or as a separate army)

6. Pay for salaries, equipment, and shipping (raise taxes or acquire loans)

Recruitment Poster

Have the students make World War I recruitment posters using construction

paper, colored pencils or markers, and any other art supplies you have on hand.

Dangers of War

War is often a threat to liberty. The challenges of World War I led to a rapid slide toward socialism in America. In countries where democratic traditions are weak, autocratic governments arise in times of war and often refuse to give up power even after the war is over. America is not immune from this danger as well.

Ask the students to list government actions or policies that led to a loss or limitation of liberties during World War I. *(the draft, standardized products, government determined economic priorities instead of a free*

market, and labor regulations) The student text does not mention other limits created by the Espionage Act, the Trading-with-the-Enemy Act, and the Sedition Act (see side margin note on p. 404). During times of war, uttering, writing, or printing "any disloyal, scurrilous, or abusive language" about the government or armed forces has been viewed as a crime.

Raggedy Ann

Children found new toys to play with in the decade of the Great War. One toy was actually a re-creation of an old favorite, the rag doll. In 1915, cartoonist John Gruelle and his daughter, Marcella, found an old rag doll. They fixed it up and he drew a face on it. What should they name the doll? Gruelle looked up at his shelf of books and saw a collection of poems by James Whitcomb Riley. Among them were "The Raggedy Man" and "Little Orphant Annie." He combined the two names to create Raggedy Ann. Gruelle made up stories about the doll to amuse his daughter and eventually published them as *The Raggedy Ann Stories*. The book and accompanying doll were big hits. Ann got a brother, Andy, in 1920.

Lincoln Logs

War-era children also had the opportunity to build things with their toys. One popular building toy came courtesy of a well-known family in the architectural world. In 1876, Mrs. Anna Wright saw learning toys, including building blocks, used in a demonstration kindergarten. She ordered a set of toys for her son, Frank Lloyd Wright, and he became interested in building. Frank apparently passed on his appreciation for such toys to his son, John Lloyd Wright, also an architect. In 1917, John drew a design for toy-sized logs that kids could use for building. He called them Lincoln Logs.

Patriotic posters such as these sought to get every citizen to do his or her part, including financing the war by buying war bonds.

prices for most goods, Americans were earning more than they ever had. Of course, prices went up for what the government bought too, raising the cost of fighting the war. To keep costs and wages under control, the government created the **War Labor Policies Board** to regulate laborers. Unions were allowed to organize and even showed significant gains in membership during the war years. The board helped settle labor disputes with management. The board also set an eight-hour working day, encouraged fair wages, and set standards for employing women and children.

The shortage of workers and the drop in immigration also provided opportunities for black laborers. More than half a million blacks moved to northern cities during the war. Their migration permanently changed the ethnic makeup of many northern cities. When the war ended, many blacks kept their jobs and remained in the North.

Informing the Public

President Wilson did not want to leave anything to chance. He wanted Americans to know that their cause was just. To unite them behind the war effort, a Committee on Public Information was formed. Headed by journalist George Creel, 150,000 people became involved in a giant propaganda crusade to "advertise America." Talented artists designed war recruitment posters and ads. An army of lecturers appeared at local assemblies and even at silent movies. Called "four-minute men," they gave short talks on any number of patriotic topics and moved crowds to cheers or tears.

Americans' attitude toward the Central Powers or even things distantly related to them became negative. They hated all things German. Although many Germans had been in America for years and had proved their loyalty, some of them were sorely persecuted. Schools stopped teaching German. School orchestras refused to play pieces by German composers such as Bach and Wagner. Sauerkraut was renamed "Liberty Cabbage." Hamburgers were called "Liberty Burgers." And dachshunds were called "Liberty Pups." Mothers whose children caught German measles told the neighbors that they had "patriotic spots" or "patriotic measles."

Paying for the War

The cost of the war was enormous. The United States spent about $24 billion, and the Allies borrowed $8 billion. About one-fourth of the money came from the new income tax and corporate taxes. The rest came from bank loans and loan drives.

Four times during the war the government went to the American people for money, raising more than $18 billion. "Liberty" and "Victory" loan drives were held in every community. Loan chairmen went door to door asking their neighbors to buy bonds. Workers also bought bonds at their places of employment. Buyers received "Liberty Buttons" for their lapels. Goals were set, and great celebrations occurred when the drives went "over the top" (a command given to soldiers when they climbed from the trenches to attack the enemy).

Even children became involved. They sold produce to earn money to finance the war. They bought thrift stamps each week on "stamp day." They could swap a filled thrift card for a $5 savings stamp; they proudly exchanged ten stamps on a card for a $50 bond.

Why Are Loans Necessary?

Governments cannot just "print money" to pay for a war. Traditionally, they have had two options: raise taxes or borrow money. While the U.S. government did raise taxes significantly during World War I, the extra revenue still was not enough to pay for such a large-scale war. To borrow more money, however, the government could not just go to banks. Spare money is scarce in time of war. All Americans, from school children to retirees, had to sacrifice as much as they could. The need for every penny helps to explain the loan drives. The Germans were shocked by how much money America was able to raise and convert into war materiel.

Ask the students why they think the government no longer has loan drives. (*Answers will vary.*) The problem is that modern governments just go into debt and print more money. The result can be inflation, such as the inflation of the 1970s. Even worse is hyperinflation, which occurred in postwar Germany.

Although America got the money it needed through loans, this solution had long-term consequences too. The loans had to be paid back. Once the war was won, people were less willing to sacrifice, and they wanted their money back. The cycle of unpaid debts in the 1920s contributed to the worldwide depression of the 1930s. You can make a personal application, warning students

about the dangers of depending on loans to pay for debt.

 Martial Music

Consider playing for the students some of the musical compositions of George M. Cohan, including "Over There," "I'm a Yankee Doodle Dandy," and "You're a Grand Old Flag." To share with the students the life and other patriotic musical compositions of Cohan, you might consider showing excerpts from the film *Yankee Doodle Dandy*.

Section Quiz

1. What did the Selective Service Act do?
2. What was the purpose of the War Industries Board?
3. Name some of the changes made by the War Labor Policies Board.
4. How did America finance the war?
★ How did the government attempt to unite Americans behind the war?

IV. American Forces "Over There"

The chief role of the navy was to get troops and supplies safely to Europe. Congress had voted for money to enlarge the navy before war broke out. During the war it tried to build or buy more ships to carry men and supplies to the troops fighting in Europe. America's soldiers were needed on the battlefields, particularly those in northern France.

The American Expeditionary Force

The American army in World War I was called the **American Expeditionary Force** (AEF). Although the United States declared war in April 1917, the first American troops, often called **dough-boys**, did not arrive in Europe until the fall of 1917. Most combat troops did not reach Europe until the spring of 1918 because of the period of training and other delays. The minimum training time was three months.

The AEF was commanded by General **John J. Pershing**. Pershing worked under Marshal **Ferdinand Foch** (FOSH), a Frenchman who served as Supreme Allied Commander. The British and French troops were weary and discouraged from three years of war, and the arrival of the "Yanks," as they called the Americans, was a welcome relief.

The Allies wanted to place American doughboys in already existing armies and use them to replace British and French losses, but

John J. Pershing

"No man's land" was the deadly and desolated area between the two armies' trenches.

"Harlem Hellfighters"

Out of the twenty-four million men who registered to serve in the military, about three million were called to serve. Of these, about 350,000 were blacks. During this time military units were segregated by race, and most blacks were relegated to menial tasks. Despite these obstacles, several black soldiers saw combat and some received recognition for their courage under fire. One such group was called the "Harlem Hellfighters." Private Henry Lincoln Johnson, a member of this group, was the first American to be awarded the highly prized *Croix de Guerre* by the French.

Section IV
Objectives

Students should be able to

1. Explain the way the United States financed the war effort.
2. Name the American and the Allied commanders.
3. Trace the American action in World War I.
4. Describe the struggle of Alvin C. York and how he merited the Congressional Medal of Honor.
5. Cite the date of the armistice ending World War I.

George M. Cohan

George M. Cohan wrote one of the most popular patriotic songs of the World War I era—"Over There." Born in 1878, Cohan starred in a vaudeville act with his parents and sister. He later became a composer and lyricist. He found his greatest successes when he focused on patriotic, "flag-waving" themes. Besides "Over There," he also wrote the still-famous songs "I'm a Yankee Doodle Dandy" and "You're a Grand Old Flag." His story is told in the film *Yankee Doodle Dandy*.

The Making of a General

John J. Pershing had a talent for being in the right place at the right time. As a young officer he pushed hard for active service in the field, where opportunities for promotion were great, and he served with distinction in the posts he received. He was awarded a Silver Star for his part in the charge up San Juan Hill in Cuba and was promoted from first lieutenant to captain. After the Spanish-American War, he was assigned to the Philippines.

Activity 5: U.S. Preparedness: The Run-Up to War

Use this activity to help the students understand how the United States prepared for active involvement in World War I.

Section Quiz Answers

1. set up local draft boards under civilian leadership to supply men for military service
2. to organize industrial production for the war effort
3. set an eight-hour workday, encouraged fair wages, and set standards for employing women and children

4. through the income tax and corporate taxes, bank loans, and loan drives
★ It established a Committee on Public Information that promoted the war through printed materials and lectures.

 Video on World War I Battles

Show a video on the U.S. battles of World War I. Such visual reinforcement would help the names of major battles involving the United States—Château-Thierry, Belleau Wood, St. Mihiel, and the Argonne Forest—come alive for the students. Possibilities include the PBS videos *The Great War—1918*, which focuses on American involvement in the war; *Archives of War:*

World War I and the Interwar Years; *The Century*; and *No Man's Land—The Great War*.

More on American Military in World War I

A good grade-level treatment of American military involvement in World War I is Don Lawson's historical summary *The United States in World War I*. Ask a volunteer to read the book and present a report to the class.

There he worked hard to understand and build a rapport with the nationals. He was promoted to brigadier general after a stint as an observer of the Russo-Japanese War, and his leadership in the tracking of Mexican bandit Pancho Villa earned him the rank of major general. Although he never caught the outlaw, he was able to keep the United States out of war with Mexico.

369th U.S. Infantry

Popularly known as the Harlem Hellfighters, members of this New York National Guard regiment served with distinction and overcame racial barriers to play an active and heroic role in several campaigns in 1918, including Champagne–Marne, Meuse–Argonne, Champagne , and Alsace.

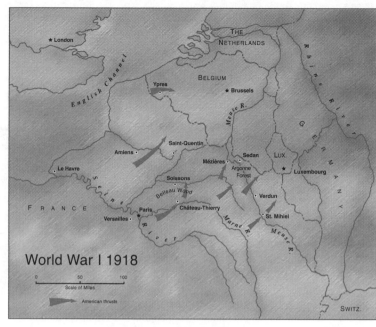

World War I 1918

Pershing refused. Fearing that American morale would suffer, he insisted that the American troops fight as a separate force under the command of American officers. American units were then assigned their own sectors of the front to defend.

Doughboys in Action

By the time the Americans arrived, the Germans had accomplished a major goal—getting Russia out of the fight. The Germans had aided the return of **Vladimir Lenin** to Russia in 1917 after the Russians had already overthrown their czar. Weary of war, the Russians followed Lenin and the Communists in the Russian Revolution. Lenin had promised to the Russians peace and to the Germans Russia's withdrawal from the war. When he gained power, he called Russian troops home and ended support for the Allied cause. Germany then had one less enemy to fight. The German armies that had been fighting the Russians could now be moved to the western front to fight France, Britain, and the United States.

"Uncle Sam's" stern look and pointing finger stirred many Americans to answer the call of the U.S. military, but so did the draft.

The Central Powers launched an all-out offensive on the western front during the spring of 1918. The Germans hoped to reach the English Channel and to take Paris. By June 3, 1918, they had reached the Marne River and were only about fifty miles from the French capital.

The combined American and French forces launched a counteroffensive and pushed the Germans back at a place on the Marne River

CD: American Deaths in World War I and Other Wars

Refer to the CD for a chart showing statistics for the deaths in wars in which the United States has been involved. Compare and contrast the human cost of World War I with the cost in other wars.

called Château-Thierry (shah-TOH tyeh-REE). Next, the Americans moved up to a hunting preserve called Belleau (BEL oh) Wood and stopped the Germans from making a run on Paris from that point. By the beginning of July, Paris was out of danger and the German advance was falling apart. Foch planned and conducted a massive assault at Amiens on August 8. The German general Ludendorff called it "the black day of the German army." Despite heavy German losses, Amiens was not the end of the war.

With more than 250,000 American soldiers arriving monthly, Allied morale climbed. Pershing got permission to apply the separate strength of the U.S. Army as part of the larger counteroffensive. The place was St. Mihiel (SAHN mee-YEL), just south of Verdun. More than half a million doughboys, an air corps of fifteen hundred planes, and thirty-two hundred French and American guns pounded the German army. In forty-eight hours, the battle was over.

Two weeks later, American forces launched an offensive into the Argonne (AHR gon) Forest. Foch had assigned the American troops the worst possible spot. American forces faced a maze of barbed wire, steel, and concrete. The hills and ridges offered almost perfect terrain for a German defensive. Historians have called it "the meat grinder offensive" because of the heavy losses.

By August 8, the British had broken through the German line. Having destroyed German resistance, the Allied troops moved swiftly across France, regaining lost lands for the Allies. The last major American activity took place in late October at Mézières, a link to the main German railway. By the end of September, the German commander, General Paul von Hindenburg, knew that all was lost.

At 11:00 a.m. on November 11, 1918, the slaughter stopped. Germany signed an armistice, or agreement to stop fighting. That date became an American national holiday called **Armistice Day**. (After World War II and the Korean War, the name was changed to Veterans Day, honoring all veterans.)

The war had taken the lives of more than eight million people. Nearly twenty million people had been wounded. The United States had lost 115,000 of its men in its year and a half of activity in the war. More than 200,000 Americans were wounded. Although American casualties were light compared to those of the other major powers, Americans had known the heartache of war. Yet they hoped that this had been the "War to End All Wars" and the "War to Make the World Safe for Democracy." They believed that they had fought for noble goals.

Section Quiz

1. What nickname was given to American troops?
2. Who was commander of the American Expeditionary Force?
3. Who was Marshal Foch?
4. When did the war officially end?
★ Why did the Germans support Vladimir Lenin in his Communist Revolution?

Sgt. York's Medal of Honor Citation

Alvin C. York was a soldier from the hills of north central Tennessee who accepted his being drafted only reluctantly. War violated his conscience. Convinced of its rightness in the case of World War I, he fulfilled his duty to his country, winning the Congressional Medal of Honor in the process. The citation on his medal reads as follows:

"After his platoon had suffered heavy casualties and 3 other noncommissioned officers had become casualties, Cpl. York assumed command. Fearlessly leading 7 men, he charged with great daring a machine gun nest which was pouring deadly and incessant fire upon his platoon. In this heroic feat the machine gun nest was taken, together with 4 officers and 128 men and several guns."

The signatories to the armistice ending World War I pose outside the railcar where they had signed the document.

Sergeant York: Soldier of Christ

You may want to read "Sergeant York: Soldier of Christ" by Mark Sidwell in *Scenes from American Church History*. Another interesting source of information on York is *Sergeant York: An American Hero*. Consider showing the 1941 film *Sergeant York* starring Gary Cooper. Afterward, discuss how York resolved his inner conflict between his conscience and his country's call to duty. Have a volunteer research and discuss York's post-war contributions to his community and state.

Activity 6: The Heroism of Sgt. Alvin C. York

Use this activity to help the students gain an appreciation for the heroism exhibited by York and the honor he received in being awarded the Congressional Medal of Honor. Emphasize the purpose of the award and the rarity of its being awarded. If time permits, refer to other winners of the medal and their deeds that earned that high honor.

Section Quiz Answers

1. doughboys
2. General John J. Pershing
3. a Frenchman who served as Supreme Allied Commander
4. at 11:00 a.m. on November 11, 1918
★ He had promised to pull Russian troops out of the war; Germany could focus on the western front instead of having to divide its forces and fight a two-front war.

Students should be able to

1. Name Wilson's plan for European (and world) peace and the provision he considered the most important.

2. Name the "Big Four" at the peace conference and explain the viewpoint of each.

3. Describe the Treaty of Versailles and America's response to it.

Woodrow Wilson and the Senate

The U.S. Senate disliked the peace plan that Wilson and his allies engineered. A group led by Republican Henry Cabot Lodge especially objected to the provision that the League of Nations would intervene if its members' territory or government was threatened. Senator Lodge had two key objections. First, the United States might not want the League to intervene in some instances. Second, the United States did not want to have an outside organization telling the United States where it had to send troops. Although Wilson listened to a few of the Senate's suggestions, he refused to make significant concessions, thereby ensuring the treaty's defeat.

V. The End of the War

The end of the war brought many questions for the participants. How would Germany and the other defeated countries be treated? Would the victors claim conquered territories and possessions? Could peace be maintained in Europe?

Republican leaders warned that joining the League of Nations would entangle America in Europe's petty conflicts.

Wilson's Fourteen Points

Even before the war ended, Woodrow Wilson had proposed a set of guidelines to help rebuild European peace. His **Fourteen Points** had been announced in January 1918. Most of the points of his program emphasized a just peace and a postwar world in which war would be less likely. The crucial point to Wilson was Point 14, which provided for a **League of Nations**. He idealistically believed that an organization of cooperating nations could talk over problems and settle them peacefully, preventing future wars. Freedom of the seas, a ban against secret agreements, and general disarmament were some of the other key points.

President Wilson spoke of "peace without victory," urging generous terms that would preserve the German nation. He rejected territorial gains for the winners and **reparations**, or payment for damages, by the losers. He said that weak nations should have the right of self-determination—that is, they could choose to be independent.

The Paris Peace Conference

The Allied leaders met at the Palace of Versailles outside Paris on January 18, 1919, to shape the peace. President Wilson represented the United States. He believed that his presence would ensure the victors' acceptance of a just and lasting peace. About two million people welcomed Wilson to Paris, regarding him almost as the savior of Europe. His reception strengthened his resolve to push for a treaty based on his Fourteen Points.

The "Big Four" (left to right): David Lloyd George of Great Britain, Vittorio Orlando of Italy, Georges Clemenceau of France, and Woodrow Wilson of the United States.

But the representatives from the other nations were equally determined. **Georges Clemenceau** (ZHORZH KLEM-un-SOH), the French premier, knew that his country had suffered at German hands in both the Franco-Prussian War and World War I. He wanted to ensure that Germany would never again be strong enough to hurt France. **David Lloyd George** represented Britain. **Vittorio Orlando** represented Italy. Those four men were sometimes called the "Big Four." The defeated nations and Russia were excluded from the peace table, so the treaty has sometimes been called "a victors' peace." Leaving out the losers made them resentful and caused them to reject the treaty's provisions. Germany was forced to sign the **Treaty of Versailles** anyway on June 28, 1919. The other defeated countries signed individual treaties. The 264-page Treaty of Versailles with Germany was very detailed. Against Wilson's wishes, it placed all of the blame for the war on Germany and forced Germany to pay for its actions. Germany had to give up its overseas empire and some of its own land and resources. It had to allow foreign troops to remain on its land. Germany was also forced to pay huge reparations to Britain and France. Although Wilson was disappointed about the details of

---

CD: Map of Europe in 1918

The map of Europe that appears on this page of the student text is also available on the CD.

Activity 7: What God Says About War and Peace

Use this activity to give the students an opportunity to examine their Bibles to see what God has to say about war and peace.

Activity 8: Wilson's Fourteen Points

Use this activity to help the students gain a more complete understanding of Wilson's plan for world peace, the Fourteen Points.

Debate Ideas

Have your students discuss and/or debate one or both of the following propositions:

- A lasting peace after World War I should have been based on Wilson's Fourteen Points.

- The United States should have joined the League of Nations.

Wilson and His Battle for the Treaty

For additional background information about Wilson's frustrating battle with the U.S. Senate over his Fourteen Points and the Treaty of Versailles, see Herbert Hoover's book *The Ordeal of Woodrow Wilson*.

the treaty, he convinced the other leaders to insert a provision for the formation of the League of Nations. Wilson believed that all of the weaknesses of the peace could be worked out through further negotiations in the league.

American Responses

When Wilson returned to the United States, he took the treaty directly to the Senate, whose approval is required for all treaties. Although most Americans probably supported the treaty, many senators were not pleased with it. Wilson had unwisely ignored the Republican leaders in the Senate while he helped formulate the treaty. Now those senators refused to ratify it without some changes. Wilson refused their changes; he wanted all or nothing. The situation became deadlocked. Time passed, and the United States never did ratify the treaty. It simply declared the war to be over. Wilson was further disappointed that the United States did not join the League of Nations.

World leaders met in the Hall of Mirrors at Versailles to sign the formal treaties ending the war.

The Impact of the War

World War I had deep and lasting impacts on the United States. Before the war, Americans generally had been optimistic about the prospects for world peace and the advancement of mankind. Everything had seemed to be getting better and better. But the war had been so horrible that it led to deep pessimism and disillusionment. Progressivism, pacifism, and the hopes of the social gospel now seemed foolish and naïve. Man was getting more brutal and destructive, not better. Many poets, novelists, artists, philosophers, theologians, progressives, and even ordinary Americans became very pessimistic.

World War I also had an important impact on the rise of American Protestant fundamentalism. Conservative preachers and theologians saw the brutality of the German war machine as a direct consequence of the philosophy of Friedrich Nietzsche, the psychology of Sigmund Freud, the economics of Karl Marx, the "science" of Charles Darwin, and German theologians' "higher criticism," which questioned the truth of the Bible. Fundamentalists warned that what had happened in Germany could happen in America. To prevent it, Americans should fight liberalism and modernism in the churches and seminaries. They should fight evolution in the schools.

Section Quiz

1. Who were the "Big Four" at the Paris Peace Conference, and what country did each represent?

2. What treaty stated the conditions for peace with Germany?

3. What key point did Wilson succeed in placing in the treaty?

4. How did the U.S. Senate respond to the treaty?

5. What impact did the war have on American attitudes?

★ What details of the peace process and treaty laid a foundation for German bitterness against the Allies?

Section Quiz Answers

1. Woodrow Wilson—United States, Georges Clemenceau—France, David Lloyd George—Great Britain, Vittorio Orlando—Italy

2. the Treaty of Versailles

3. the formation of a League of Nations (the last of his Fourteen Points)

4. The Senate refused to ratify the treaty without some changes, but Wilson refused to change it.

5. It caused Americans to become pessimistic and led fundamentalists to fight liberalism, modernism, evolution, and secularism in American society.

★ Germany was excluded from the peace discussions. It was forced to accept all of the blame for the war and to pay for its actions by giving up land, accepting occupation by foreign troops, and making large damage payments to Great Britain and France.

People, Places, and Things to Remember:

Triple Alliance
Triple Entente
Central Powers
Allied Powers
belligerents
unrestricted submarine warfare
Lusitania
convoy system
War Industries Board
War Labor Policies Board
American Expeditionary Force
doughboys
John J. Pershing
Ferdinand Foch
Vladimir Lenin
Armistice Day
Fourteen Points
League of Nations
reparations
Georges Clemenceau
David Lloyd George
Vittorio Orlando
Treaty of Versailles

Chapter Review

Review Questions

What significant event happened on each of the following dates?

1. June 28, 1914
2. April 6, 1917
3. November 11, 1918

Who was he?

4. Who was president of the United States during World War I?
5. Who commanded the American Expeditionary Force?
6. Who was commander of all the Allied forces?
7. Who were "the Big Four," and what country did each represent?

Write the appropriate term for each blank below.

When World War I broke out in 1914, Germany, Austria-Hungary, and the nations that sided with them were called the (8) _____, and Britain, France, and the nations that sided with them were called the (9) _____.

Germany's policy of (10) _____ greatly angered Americans. It brought about the sinking of the *Lusitania* and eventually helped to prompt America to enter the war. The American soldiers who arrived in Europe were commonly called (11) _____. They helped the Allies win the war. Fighting stopped on (12) _____ Day.

Allied leaders met at Versailles to draw up a treaty. President Wilson's plan for peace consisted of (13) _____, but most of his plan was rejected, except for the formation of a (14) _____ to help settle international problems. Britain and France especially wanted Germany to pay reparations for the damages caused by the war. The resulting treaty with Germany, called the (15) _____, was never signed by the United States.

Critical Thinking

1. Were the Allied Powers right to blame the entire war on Germany and force it to make huge financial payments to the victors? Why or why not?
2. Should America have joined the League of Nations? Why or why not?

Chapter Review Answers

Review Questions

1. the assassination of Archduke Francis Ferdinand and his wife
2. United States declared war on Germany
3. armistice ended fighting in World War I
4. Woodrow Wilson
5. General John J. Pershing
6. Ferdinand Foch
7. Woodrow Wilson (United States), Georges Clemenceau (France), David Lloyd George (Great Britain), Vittorio Orlando (Italy)

8. Central Powers
9. Allies
10. unrestricted submarine warfare
11. doughboys
12. Armistice
13. Fourteen Points
14. League of Nations
15. Treaty of Versailles

Critical Thinking

1. Answers will vary but might include the following: No, because this laid the foundation for another war (WWII). Others might say that it was right to blame Germany for starting the war, but that Germany should not have been forced to pay such immense amounts to the victors.
2. Answers will vary. It probably would have made little difference since man's organizations can never ensure peace.

CHAPTER 22

The expanding availability of automobiles and the prosperity of the Twenties made America a much more mobile society.

The 1920s: A Decade of Change

I.   The Postwar Environment

II. Prosperity and Materialism

III. The Roaring Twenties

IV. Republican Administrations

Chapter Goals

Students should be able to

1. Define and use the basic terms of the chapter.
2. Identify the three postwar problems discussed in the text.
3. Describe how multiple factors, including economic prosperity, helped bring moral decay.
4. Evaluate the various responses to moral issues in this era including the KKK, those opposed to racism, and Fundamentalism.

Chapter Motivation

With the end of World War I, Americans looked forward to better times. Many expected to get back to a normal life, returning to the ideals and ways of earlier days. Instead, the 1920s became a period of accelerated change, including changes in how Americans worked out their core values. The period was sometimes called the "Roaring Twenties."

During World War I Americans united to wage a war against tyranny. Following the war, many American women sought equality—not just in gaining the right to vote but also in participating in vices once reserved for men, such as smoking, drinking, and swearing. Freedom in the 1920s tragically departed from the traditional American ideal. Rather than seeking freedom for others, many Americans now sought pleasure for themselves. As a result, the 1920s were years when people practiced sin more openly than they had in earlier periods of American history.

Chapter 22 Lesson Plan Chart			
Section Title	**Main Activity**	**Pages**	**Days**
I. The Postwar Environment	Activity 1: The Washington Naval Treaty	416–18	1 day
II. Prosperity and Materialism	Activity 3: The Impact of Technology in the Twenties	419–21	1–2 days
III. The Roaring Twenties	Activity 5: Darrow versus Bryan in the Scopes Trial	422–27	1–2 days
IV. Republican Administrations	Activity 4: Herbert Hoover on the Role of Government	428-29	1 day
TOTAL SUGGESTED DAYS (INCLUDING 1 DAY FOR REVIEW AND TESTING)			5–7 DAYS

MATERIALS LIST

SECTION I
- CD: Warren G. Harding, 29th President; Calvin Coolidge, 30th President; Herbert Hoover, 31st President
- Activities 1 and 2 from the *Student Activities* manual

SECTION II
- CD: The Barnstormers
- Magazines and old books containing pictures or images related to the 1920s
- Special speaker: an antique collector or antique car enthusiast
- Video documentary on Charles Lindbergh
- Activity 3 from the *Student Activities* manual

Section I

Objectives

Students should be able to

1. Describe America's isolationist attitude following World War I.

2. Explain why a short economic depression followed the war.

3. Describe the Red Scare that followed the war.

More on Colonel Edward M. House

Edward M. House, a colonel only by nickname (which he gave to himself), was considered President Wilson's "silent partner" and closest confidant. He was not an official aide or cabinet member, but he perhaps had more influence on Wilson than any other person.

House was a behind-the-scenes operative of the Democrats. Once Wilson was elected and war broke out in Europe, House encouraged "limited preparedness" by the United States. After the war, he was instrumental in drafting Wilson's Fourteen Points and negotiating the Treaty of Versailles. He was more given to compromise, however, than Wilson, who complained that House had "given away everything I had" in the negotiations. Afterward, Wilson rejected House's advice that he try to compromise with the Senate in the debates over ratification of the Treaty of Versailles. House died on March 28, 1938, at the age of 79.

Colonel Edward M. House was called Wilson's "right-hand man."

Warren G. Harding wanted to return the country to normalcy, but his appointees tainted his administration with scandal.

With the end of World War I, most Americans looked forward to better times. Some thought that they could get back to normal life, returning to the ideals and ways of earlier days. Instead, the 1920s became a decade of startling changes, including changes in the way Americans developed their core values. The period was sometimes called the "Roaring Twenties."

In prewar years, progressive Americans had sought to bring about many social changes with the hope of bringing justice and equality to the nation. Then they had allied to wage a war to free the world of tyranny. In the Twenties, many American women sought equality. Beyond just gaining the right to vote, many also embraced masculine vices like smoking, drinking, and swearing. Freedom in the 1920s departed from the traditional American ideal. Instead of seeking to free others from political oppression, many Americans focused on freeing themselves from moral restraints. As a result, the 1920s were years when people practiced sin more openly than they had in earlier periods of American history.

I. The Postwar Environment

America emerged from the war with some attitudes and problems that set the stage for the decade to come. First was a desire to avoid getting involved in foreign conflicts. This brought a return to isolationism. An economic downturn and a growing fear of communism also affected American attitudes.

Isolationism and Peace

President Wilson had diligently sought American approval of the Treaty of Versailles with its League of Nations. Because of his battle with the Senate, he decided to travel across the country and present his views directly to the people. In 1919, during the tour, he had a stroke that left him partially paralyzed and unable to perform his duties for several weeks. His wife and an aide, Colonel Edward House, virtually ran the White House in his stead. No one saw the president, and Mrs. Wilson and Colonel House made most of his decisions for him. He never regained full strength, but he continued to plead for the United States to ratify the treaty and join the League. The Senate and many other Americans, however, feared that membership in the League would draw America into future wars. This fear and a general lack of concern for foreign affairs made most Americans want to isolate themselves from problems outside the United States.

The desire to get back to normal business and to forget about foreign problems produced a strong win for the Republican candidate, **Warren G. Harding**, in the presidential election of 1920. Harding's campaign emphasized a "return to normalcy." He handily defeated James Cox, the Democrat. Ideas of signing the treaty and joining the League were soon forgotten.

Throughout the 1920s, the United States remained true to its isolationist goals in that it stayed out of most foreign affairs. Wishing to cut expenses and to avoid temptation for future war, the government sought a way to trim down its navy. Charles Evans Hughes, Harding's secretary of state, and others believed that one cause of the war had been an arms race. He suggested that the five major powers limit naval shipbuilding. This was done through the **Washington Naval Conference** in 1921–22. Great Britain, Japan,

---

SECTION III
- CD: Results of Enforcing the Volstead Act; The Scopes Trial
- Scenes from American Church History (BJU Press)
- Activities 5–6 from the *Student Activities* manual
- *Scouting* magazine (October 2000)

SECTION IV
- Activities 4, 7, and 8 from the *Student Activities* manual

Lessons in Demobilization

The quick demobilization of the United States after World War I teaches valuable lessons for today. The presidents during that

period, both Democratic and Republican, believed that free enterprise could solve the problems of retooling industries and retraining soldiers. Note that modern presidents proposed expensive federal training programs at the end of the Cold War. But history offers no proof that such efforts help.

How Was Communism a Unique Threat?

This is the first time that the students come face to face with the greatest enemy that the United States ever faced—communism. Ask them to share what they know about communism. Compare and contrast communism with the other threats that the United States has faced. (Note especially the rise of

socialism and violent labor strikes.) Discuss how the attorney general dealt with terrorism then, and discuss measures the United States is taking today against terrorism. In what ways could terrorism undermine a democratic government?

Mrs. Wilson, the First Woman President?

Raise the issue of how Mrs. Wilson and Col. House handled Wilson's incapacity, and discuss how that solution was different from what the Constitution specified. Explain that the 25th Amendment was passed to address such a situation constitutionally. Note that Mrs. Wilson has been called the first woman

France, Italy, and the United States scaled down their navies. For every five British or American ships built, Japan was allowed three, and France and Italy could have one and three-quarters. The treaty, which allowed the United States to cut its budget, delighted Republicans, who were seeking bigger cuts in spending. Japan, however, considered the treaty unfair and later came to resent the United States. In reality, the treaty had little impact because the powers continued to increase their defenses by building smaller ships and submarines that were not limited under the agreement.

Calvin Coolidge became president when Harding died in office. His secretary of state, Frank B. Kellogg, made another attempt to keep America free from the threat of war, optimistically signing the **Kellogg-Briand Peace Pact** with sixty-two other nations in 1928. The countries agreed to outlaw war as a means of settling international disputes. But the treaty was virtually worthless. It had no means of enforcement. It was limited by various nations' self-approved exemptions. Ironically, on the very day that the United States Senate ratified the treaty, it also passed a bill to spend $274 million to build warships. World War II would demonstrate that in a fallen world such approaches to peace are insufficient.

The Red Scare

The rise of communism in Russia at the end of the war was a serious threat to world peace. Although Americans had read of events in Russia leading up to and including the Communist Revolution in 1917, few really were aware of the Communist presence until it involved them directly. Fear of communism began to grow, especially when Americans learned that the Communists intended to spread their rule to other countries. Leaders of the Soviet Union, as the Russian nation had begun calling itself and the surrounding nations it controlled, had organized the **Third International**. That agency for world revolution tried to export communism anywhere by any method. It was already making gains in Germany and Hungary. By 1919, the Communists had two political parties working in America.

One goal of the Communists was to create a struggle between common workers and the property-owning capitalists. Americans began to think of any sign of worker discontent, and strikes in particular, as part of the Communist plot. In April 1919, a wave of anarchist bombings occurred. The post office intercepted letter bombs addressed to thirty-eight prominent businessmen or government officials, including John D. Rockefeller, Justice Oliver Wendell Holmes, and both the postmaster general and the U.S. attorney general. In June, a bomb exploded in front of Attorney General A. Mitchell Palmer's home. In September, an anarchist planted a bomb in front of the New York Stock Exchange. The explosion killed thirty-eight people.

Believing that Communists were involved in the attacks, Attorney General Palmer crusaded for increased government investigation and arrests. Government agents raided the offices of radical organizations and arrested 250 members of the Union of Russian Workers. In December, the Labor Department sent 249 aliens, some of whom were Communists, back to Russia. The arrests and deportations increased until 1920, when Palmer predicted terrorist activity that never occurred. It was now evident that Palmer had overestimated the danger posed by the anarchists. Then, when the Supreme Court

president because she performed the functions of Wilson's office for her husband.

Activity 1: The Washington Naval Treaty

This activity includes excerpts from the Washington Naval Treaty. Use the reading and questions to help the students understand the intentions of the treaty, and then contrast them with what actually happened in subsequent years.

Kellogg-Briand Peace Pact

On August 27, 1928, fifteen key nations renounced war as an instrument of national policy. Forty-eight other nations later joined this pact for peace. Initially, French foreign minister Aristide Briand had proposed a pact between just the United States and France, hoping to enlist America as an ally in the event of another European war. Frank Kellogg knew what Briand was trying to do and instead proposed a treaty for all nations. Briand, of course, supported the popular measure.

Sacco and Vanzetti

Nicola Sacco and Bartolomeo Vanzetti were accused of robbery and murder. They had come to America from Italy in 1908, and neither had become an American citizen at the time of his arrest. In addition, they were radical political anarchists. Their supporters claimed that their ethnic and political backgrounds prevented their receiving a fair trial.

Witnesses for the prosecution identified Sacco as the shooter and Vanzetti as an occupant of the getaway car. In addition, both men were armed at the time of arrest and lied under official questioning. The defense questioned whether prosecution witnesses could accurately identify the criminals after having had only a brief glimpse of them at the scene. Also, Sacco had a reason for carrying a gun, and although the men had lied, they had done so only in response to questions about their radical political activities, which were highly unpopular in America at the time. The defense argued that the robbery was more likely the work of a professional criminal gang, and a convicted bank robber actually confessed to the crime.

Many people were sympathetic to the men at the time of the trial. Opinion today is divided. Tests conducted on Sacco's gun in 1961 suggest that it was the murder weapon. Some have theorized that Sacco was guilty but Vanzetti was innocent. Whatever the truth of the crime, the trial served as a poor example of the American judicial system. The judge denigrated the defendents and seemed to pressure the jury to render a guilty verdict.

Farmers

When farm prices fell after the war, farmers united to seek aid through private

The trial of Sacco (right) and Vanzetti (left) fueled anti-immigrant feelings and fear of anarchy.

ruled that evidence Palmer had collected was gathered illegally, people began to distrust Palmer.

The fear of the Communists increased Americans' resentment of immigrants, many of whom were from southern and eastern Europe, where radical political ideas were spreading. Ill feeling toward both Communists and immigrants combined in a noted court case in 1921. Two Italian anarchists, **Nicola Sacco** and **Bartolomeo Vanzetti**, were arrested and tried for murdering two shoe company employees in a payroll robbery. To this day the facts of the case are disputed, and the trial polarized the nation. The evidence seemed to suggest that at least Sacco was involved in the murder, but the trial was flawed by the biased conduct of the judge. In the end, the defendants were found guilty and were sentenced to death. In 1927 they were executed.

Economic Depression

After the war, the United States experienced a time of economic depression. The high demand for war products had kept industries and farms busy, but when the war was over and demand dropped, business and industry suffered. Because many of the war products were no longer needed, factories had to change over to peacetime industry. That took time and capital. American farms had sent millions of tons of food to Europe during the war, but now Europe could start feeding itself again. American farmers had no market for their great surplus of food.

Unemployment became a problem in the cities. Few jobs were available for soldiers returning home from the war. War industries were closing down. Many Americans believed that blacks and immigrants had taken the jobs that were available. New immigration laws set quotas (fixed numbers) for how many immigrants could enter the United States. Those laws were intended to stop the heavy flow of immigrants, especially those from the Roman Catholic countries of southern and eastern Europe.

American farmers continued to struggle through the 1920s as high production and low prices continued. Representatives of the farming states pressed for government aid and regulation, but Presidents Harding and Coolidge believed that the federal government should not interfere by regulating the farm economy or subsidizing farmers. The Republican strategy of government noninterference proved to be a boon to American companies. Businesses rebounded in the 1920s, setting off a wave of prosperity for the decade.

Section Quiz

1. What did Warren G. Harding stress in his presidential campaign?

2. What did the Washington Naval Conference seek to limit?

3. Why did Americans want to set immigration quotas?

4. What was the Red Scare?

★ How did the 1920s transform the American value of freedom?

Activity 2: The Immigration Act of 1924

Use this activity to help the students grasp the extent of immigration during the 1920s and identify the countries of origin of those immigrants.

Section Quiz Answers

1. a "return to normalcy"

2. naval shipbuilding

3. They were concerned about foreigners taking their jobs.

4. a strong fear of Communist infiltration in America

★ Freedom was transformed from freedom from political oppression to freedom from moral restraint.

Collage

Have your students design and make a collage for this decade. Put photos of historical figures adjacent to symbols or items with which they are associated. Write an explanation of the people and symbols selected, and tell why each is important. Bring in magazines, discarded books, or pictures downloaded from the Internet for students to use, or have them draw their own pictures.

II. Prosperity and Materialism

At the same time the American economy was recovering, technological advances emerged. These new devices were great time-savers. Americans became consumers with more leisure time than ever before.

Technological Advances

Inventions and improvements of industrial products greatly changed the American way of life in the 1920s. The automobile and the application of electricity to household appliances especially revolutionized daily life for many Americans.

The Automobile

The first successful American automobile had been built by Charles and Frank Duryea in 1893. Henry Ford began making cars in 1903. The success of these pioneers prompted other automobile producers to plunge into the business. Although cars had become common before the war, many American families still were without a "horseless carriage." After the war, however, factories geared up to produce cars by the thousands. Families were eager to have their own car, and the prices of all but the luxury models were becoming more affordable. Even if a family did not have enough money to pay for the car in full, they could buy it on the **installment plan** (paying for an item in weekly or monthly payments).

The shift to automobile transportation had many direct effects on Americans. For example, the automobile reduced the isolation of those who lived in rural areas. When town was several hours away by horseback or by horse and wagon, the farmer and his family might venture into town only a few times a year. With a car, however, the whole family could make the same trip in a short time, day or night. Farm families could go to town often to shop or to attend social functions.

The automobile also changed life for many city workers, making it possible for them to live away from the inner-city area where they worked. They could buy a house in the "suburbs" at the edge of the city and commute to and from work by car. With this practice came a by-product of the automobile—traffic jams.

Cars made travel easy for common Americans. As people began to drive everywhere, many other industries arose to meet the needs of the people with cars. Service stations, motels, and drive-in restaurants sprang up along busy highways. Department stores, supermarkets, and other businesses were built where they could be easily reached by car and where they could have large parking lots for their customers.

The Airplane

Although the airplane was not a major form of transportation for most Americans during the 1920s, people admired it for its capabilities. In 1903, Orville and Wilbur Wright had made what

Mass production of the automobile revolutionized American society.

The American public loved heroes such as Charles Lindbergh, who was the first person to fly solo from New York to Paris.

and public channels. The American Farm Bureau Federation began new chapters across the nation. Farm cooperatives were formed to store, market, and ship farm products more efficiently and economically. A "farm bloc" of congressmen from the major agricultural states banded together. They passed two bills to get the government to keep prices above parity (a set level) regardless of the market price. But Coolidge twice vetoed bills for such help. He believed that the government should not be so active in regulating the economy.

Section II
Objectives

Students should be able to

1. Explain the effects of the automobile, the airplane, and electric appliances on life in the 1920s.
2. Describe America's attitude toward business in the 1920s.

Model A

In 1928, Ford began making the Model A, a much-improved car with a four-cylinder engine and a three-speed transmission with reverse. Prices for the Model A ranged from $385 for a coupe to $570 for a top-of-the-line model. And it came in four colors! Designed and priced for the common man, it was built between 1928 and 1931 and became the most common car in America.

Bring in a Collector or Car Restorer

If you know an antique collector or antique car enthusiast, ask him to bring in some items to share with the class. Ask the guest to tell how he got involved in the hobby and some of his activities and unusual experiences.

Advertising over the Years

Study a corporation, perhaps one in your local community or region, that has a history of seventy-five years or more. Design an advertisement for the product at various times (e.g., 1940, 1960, 1980, 2000, and today) to show how it has changed over the years. Interesting products include automobiles, telephones, and radios.

CD: The Barnstormers

Refer to the CD for photos of barnstormers.

The Man Behind Lindbergh's Trans-Atlantic Flight

Tom Rutledge, a 24-year-old engineer with the Wright brothers' airplane engine factory in Paterson, N.J., was assigned to build the engine for Lindbergh's *Spirit of St. Louis*. (At that time, one person built the entire engine, tested it, disassembled it, checked it for wear and other problems, and reassembled it.) Rutledge was disappointed because he wanted to build an engine for a famous person, someone important. At the time, Lindbergh was an unknown. Two other airmen had also applied for the $25,000 prize offered for the first person to fly solo across the Atlantic, one of whom was the famed Admiral Byrd, who had already flown to the North Pole. Yet Rutledge did his job dutifully, faithfully, and conscientiously. And the rest is history!

"Wrong Way" Corrigan

Douglas Corrigan took his first flight in 1925 and became hooked on flying. He took lessons and made his first solo flight in 1926. The next year, Lindbergh made his famous trans-Atlantic flight, and Corrigan was thrilled. In 1935, he applied for permission to make his own trans-Atlantic flight. Officials rejected his application because they did not think his airplane was flight worthy for a trans-Atlantic flight. But they did approve him for a cross-country flight from New York to California.

On July 17, 1935, Corrigan arrived at the New York airport ready to begin his transcontinental flight. The field was shrouded in heavy fog. Airport authorities instructed him to take off in any direction but west because several tall buildings made taking off in that direction dangerous. Corrigan took off eastward, and as his plane

Douglas "Wrong Way" Corrigan was denied permission to fly across the Atlantic but did it anyway, blaming a faulty compass for his "error."

RCA-Westinghouse pioneered production of consumer radio receivers in the early 1920s.

is generally accepted as the first successful machine-powered flight. World War I boosted aviation. Soon the government provided airmail service between major cities. Budding pilots called "barnstormers" put on air circuses at county fairs and took people up for short rides over towns.

The biggest air sensation came in 1927, when a twenty-five-year-old aviator from Little Falls, Minnesota, named **Charles A. Lindbergh** (LIND burg) won a prize for making the first non-stop solo flight across the Atlantic Ocean. He flew his specially designed plane, the *Spirit of St. Louis*, from New York to Paris in thirty-three and one-half hours. When Lindbergh touched down in Paris, he became an instant hero. Called "Lucky Lindy" or "the Lone Eagle," Lindbergh came home to a ticker-tape parade in New York and an invitation to the White House. Wherever he appeared over the next few years, he was mobbed by admiring fans.

Lindbergh's transatlantic flight and the record flights of other pilots did much to encourage air transportation. The first public international passenger carrier was the Pan-American "Clipper." Regularly scheduled commercial flights soon connected all of the major American cities. They also linked America to European and South American capitals.

Electric Wonders

Second only to cars in changing American society was electricity. By 1929, generators were producing more electricity in the United States than in all the other nations of the world combined. Nearly all American cities and towns had electricity by the 1920s. Even a few rural areas had access to it. Americans were ready for not only electric lights but also other electric gadgets.

Inventors added electricity to many existing household appliances such as the ice box, stove, iron, and washing machine. Housewives boasted of having all-electric kitchens, complete with fan, water heater, toaster, coffee percolator, and waffle iron.

Of course, electricity was also applied to industry, where it powered large machines. When applied to the communications network, electricity further improved the quality of American life. The greatest mass communication device of the 1920s was the electric radio.

The basis for the invention of the radio was a sound transmitter invented by an Italian, Guglielmo Marconi (mahr COH nee), in 1895. The "wireless" could transmit messages without using the usual telegraph or telephone wires. Soon inventors began using the wireless to transmit the human voice. The resulting radio provided Americans with hours of news and entertainment. The Westinghouse Company made special home receivers and sold them in quantity during the fall of 1920. Station KDKA in Pittsburgh received its broadcasting license six days before the 1920 presidential elections. The first commercial broadcast—November 2, 1920—announced Harding's election to the presidency.

The radio soon changed the way Americans lived. News, music, entertainment, and advertising reached more than twelve million American homes by 1930. Many Americans listened to comedian

▶ Video Clips of Lindbergh

Make the most of studying Charles Lindbergh as the legend of his day by including portions of a video documentary about his life. Discuss the reasons behind his stardom and the impact of that fame on his life. Many people consider him to be the first superstar of U.S. pop culture.

💻 More on Lindbergh

An excellent source of information on Lindbergh's famous flight is his own autobiography, *The Spirit of St. Louis*. A good general biography is *Lindbergh* by Leonard Mosely.

Tour an Assembly Line

Tour a local assembly line—particularly an assembly line for some of the products mentioned in this chapter.

Activity 3: The Impact of Technology in the Twenties

Use this activity to reinforce the information about technology given in the text.

Jack Benny, singer Rudy Vallee, and comic Will Rogers's home-spun comments and impersonations of Calvin Coolidge. Broadcasts of sports events also gained large popular followings. With Americans from different areas listening to the same programs, some regional differences soon began to fade. The radio drew Americans closer to events and people that affected their lives. They could hear the voice of the president and other leaders, and they could hear broadcasts of events as they happened or shortly after.

Business

Soon after the initial depression that followed the war, America took off on an amazing business boom. Some workers had saved money during the war while wages were high. Others were making money on new businesses. They were all ready to spend it on automobiles, clothes, entertainment, electric appliances, and the other new pleasures of the 1920s. When Americans did not have money, they borrowed it or bought items on credit.

The demand for new industrial goods caused industries to grow. Many manufacturers used the mass production techniques devised by Henry Ford. He placed workers beside a moving conveyer belt, where each performed a certain task or added a certain part to the product. By 1927, the use of the **assembly line** allowed Ford to turn out a new car every twenty-seven seconds. Similar assembly lines turned out refrigerators, phonographs, vacuum cleaners, and countless other consumer goods. Clever advertising campaigns convinced customers that they had to buy more and more of the new products.

Big businesses provided more jobs. Some Americans with money left over after paying routine expenses invested in the stock market. As stockholders were paid larger dividends, more people purchased stocks, even using borrowed money to do so. Other people invested in real estate. Property, especially in Florida, became a tempting deal, as slick promoters portrayed the land as a future resort paradise. Thousands of people speculated on land, buying property and then hoping to resell it for higher prices, although little development took place. Many people went into debt on such get-rich-quick land schemes.

Both public attitudes and government policies favored big business. The general attitude toward big business had been negative from 1880 to 1920, but Americans gained new respect for business and businessmen that bordered on worship. Bruce Barton wrote in *The Man Nobody Knows* that Jesus was the consummate businessman who formed the twelve apostles into a successful business corporation. Calvin Coolidge declared, "The business of America is business." Business and materialism had become the gods of the age. Government rarely interfered with any of the growing business empires of the 1920s. And because the prosperity of business was most important, labor unions gained little when they seemed to be fighting against American business.

Comic Will Rogers was a favorite personality in the early years of radio, quipping about life ("We're all ignorant, just on different subjects.") and poking fun at politicians. ("Be thankful we're not getting all the government we're paying for.")

The application of mass production techniques made consumer products readily available to practically everyone.

climbed, authorities expected him to bank and head west. Instead, he stayed his easterly course and disappeared into the fog. Twenty-eight hours and thirteen minutes later, he landed in Dublin, Ireland, acting surprised when they told him where he was.

Kidnapping of the Lindbergh Baby

It has been called the crime of the century. On March 1, 1932, sometime between 8:00 and 10:00 P.M., twenty-month-old Charles A. Lindbergh Jr. was taken from the second-story nursery of his parents' house near Hopewell, New Jersey. The kidnapper left a ransom note demanding $50,000.

Many people (including Al Capone) offered assistance, but the investigation kept running into dead ends. John F. Condon, a retired educator, volunteered to act as a mediator between the kidnappers and the Lindberghs. He met twice with a man who called himself John, the second time delivering a $50,000 ransom to him. Attempts for recovery ended May 12 when a baby's body was found in a wooded area four miles from the Lindbergh house. Bruno Richard Hauptmann, a German immigrant, was convicted of the crime and executed on April 2, 1936.

Will Rogers

Will Rogers was born November 4, 1879, in Indian Territory (Oklahoma today). He soon became known for his humorous political commentary. He died in a plane crash near Point Barrow, Alaska, in August 1935. Here are some of Rogers's popular sayings:

Debate Idea

Have your students discuss and/or debate the following statement: The business of America has always been business.

- "Broad-minded is just another way of saying a fellow is too lazy to form an opinion."
- "Everybody is ignorant—just on different subjects."
- "The trouble with practical jokes is that they very often get elected."
- "I don't make jokes. I just watch the government and report the facts."

Section III

Objectives

Students should be able to

1. Explain how the 1920s became a time of moral decay.
2. Evaluate some of the responses to the issues of the 1920s.
3. Explain the significance of the Scopes trial.

The Man Nobody Knows

President Coolidge's pointed remark that "the business of America is business" reflected the nation's widespread enthusiasm for business—an enthusiasm that affected even religion.

Bruce Barton, a preacher's son who had become a famous advertising executive, wrote a book, *The Man Nobody Knows*, which portrayed Jesus as a model businessman. Christ, according to Barton, was "the founder of modern business. . . . He picked up twelve men from the bottom ranks of business and forged them into an organization that conquered the world." Christ, Barton said, was a "sociable man" and "the most popular dinner guest in Jerusalem." Barton claimed that Jesus practiced "modern salesmanship," persuading by asking pointed questions, and even advertising by using parables. Barton's favorite quotation from the Bible was Christ's reply to His parents in Luke 2:49: "Wist ye not that I must be about my Father's business?"

The Man Nobody Knows enjoyed great success. In the mid-twenties it was on the bestseller list for two years. Despite its popularity, however, the book revealed the author's lack of knowledge of true Christianity. In a book entitled *The Christ We Know*, conservative Bible teacher A. C. Gaebelein argued that Barton's sketch of Christ struck at the heart of Christianity by denying Christ's incarnation as the Son of God: "Can the conception of Christ as a businessman, as a leader, or advertiser or sociable man, give our conscience rest and bring us nigh unto God? No! Nothing but the blood of Jesus." Furthermore, Barton's book ended with Christ's death, not His resurrection. Clearly *The Man Nobody Knows* misinterpreted Christ's work, but it does show how religion and business were mixed in the 1920s. What Barton wanted to do was bring Christ down to the level of business rather than elevate business to the standards of Christ's teachings.

Pleasure-hungry Americans sought entertainment in the theaters of America during the Twenties.

"Flappers" became symbols of the rebellion of the Twenties.

Section Quiz

1. How did the automobile change life for farmers? for city workers?
2. What American pilot was a hero of the 1920s? What did he accomplish in 1927?
3. What basic mass production technique did Henry Ford introduce?
★ How did the radio help unify American culture? How did electricity change American life and business?

III. The Roaring Twenties

The decade of the Twenties has well earned the label "the Roaring Twenties." These years witnessed a social transformation in the United States. Technological changes led many people to live in cities away from family and friends. This new life weakened social ties and gave people greater leisure time for new entertainments. New ideas about Christianity gained great influence. Much of the literature of this decade contradicted some of the core teachings of the Christian religion. These ideas further transformed American society.

The New Morality

Many Americans revolted against traditional morality during this time. This revolt began among the young people and was most obvious on college campuses. Wild parties, drunkenness, and sexual immorality were not uncommon at many schools. The loose morals of the younger generation are suggested by some of the most popular songs played on the radio: "Hot Lips," "I Need Your Lovin'," and "Burning Kisses."

Section Quiz Answers

1. Farmers were less isolated; they could go to town often to shop or to attend social functions. The car allowed them to be more directly exposed to city lifestyles and habits, including vices. City workers could live away from their inner-city workplaces and drive to work.
2. Charles A. Lindbergh; first to fly nonstop across the Atlantic, from New York to Paris
3. assembly line
★ People from all regions of the country became more alike as they heard the same programs and listened together to the broadcast of national events.

Electricity brought many conveniences to the common person and helped increase speed and efficiency for business.

Parallels to the Modern Church Growth Movement

Discuss the modern church growth movement, which treats the church as a marketing enterprise that should poll the neighborhood and develop programs to satisfy a "target audience." A marketing consultant named George Barna was inspired by the movement to begin surveying religion in America to find out how to reach people with the gospel. He argued that church is a business and that the customers are the "unchurched." His influential books, such as *Marketing the Church: What They Never Taught You About Church Growth* and *User Friendly Churches*, questioned the effectiveness of traditional worship services. He claimed, "If a church studies its market, devises intelligent plans, and implements those plans faithfully, it should see an increase in the number of visitors, new members, and people who accept Christ as their Savior." Since that time, however, even the top leaders of the megachurches are having to admit that numerical growth has not translated into strong Christians (*World* magazine, December 1, 2007).

Discuss the dangers of this movement. What is the scriptural purpose of church services?

Open discussion of sex was encouraged by the popular psychologist **Sigmund Freud**. In his writings Freud emphasized the danger of repressing one's sexual desires and thoughts. Many Americans came to believe that frank talk about sex was necessary for good health and proper behavior.

This same openness was displayed in the major new visual medium of the era—the motion picture. The American film industry exploded in the 1920s. In 1922 about 40 million Americans attended movies. In 1930 the number was 90 million. The romances featured in many of these films glamorized those who crossed traditional boundaries of morality. The American public also seemed to have an insatiable appetite for following the personal lives of the actors and actresses in these films. The immoral lifestyles of these stars became news items followed by many Americans.

Off the screen, many young women adopted the dress and lifestyle of "**flappers**." They delighted in shocking their elders with shorter skirts, slang, new dances, heavy makeup, and drinking or smoking in public. Dancing and jazz were especially popular. The music and dance conveyed the freedom and excitement felt by the youth of the era.

Though the era was roaring along, the literature of the era revealed the despair and disillusionment that lay beneath the surface. T. S. Eliot's *The Waste Land* reflected the hopelessness that followed World War I. Ernest Hemingway wrote stories about people failing to find meaning in life. F. Scott Fitzgerald was himself a symbol of the age. He and his family lived extravagantly, but beneath the glitter lay his alcoholism and his wife's mental illness. Fitzgerald's *The Great Gatsby* told the story of a man corrupted by the new morals of the era.

Greta Garbo (left) and Buster Keaton (right) were two famous stars of silent movies.

Sports

A growing interest in sports was another, less detrimental, result of the growth in leisure time. More people actively participated in athletic events. Still more attended as spectators or listened to them on the radio. Women made names for themselves in sports. In 1926, Gertrude Ederle became the first woman to swim the twenty-two miles across the English Channel. Helen Wills powered her way to glory on the tennis court.

College football drew thousands of fans. Harold "Red" Grange, the "galloping ghost" of the University of Illinois, received the longest ovation in the history of college football when he ran for four touchdowns within twelve minutes. Knute Rockne (ᴺᴼᴼᵀ ᴿᴼᴷ nee), a Norwegian immigrant who became head football coach at Notre Dame, unleashed his players' talents to thrill spectators and radio audiences each Saturday afternoon. His running backs, known as the "Four Horsemen of Notre Dame," dazzled fans and gained fame and glory on the gridiron.

Boxer Jack Dempsey, who was described as having "a neck like a bull, a granite jaw, and fists like iron," drew in the first million-dollar gate (paid attendance) for a sporting event. Horse and auto racing drew crowds. Some people were attracted to such sports, however, not for the excitement, but for a wrong reason—gambling.

The "Four Horsemen" of the Notre Dame football team became legendary.

Despite being knocked down, Gene Tunney was able to get to his feet during a disputed "long count" and defeat boxing legend Jack Dempsey in September 1927.

Gertrude Ederle

When Gertrude Ederle was a young girl, her mother taught her to swim by tying a rope around her and letting her down into the water. Within three days, Gertrude was swimming unassisted. She began swimming competitively while still a girl and had set eighteen world records by the time she was seventeen. She was chosen for the 1924 U.S. Olympic swimming team and went on to win one gold medal and two bronze medals.

Because the water was often choppy and the weather uncertain, the English Channel was a serious challenge for swimmers. Ederle tried to swim the Channel on August 18, 1925, but was disqualified when a fellow swimmer tried to help her, thinking that she was too tired to continue. On August 6, 1926, a rough, stormy day, Ederle successfully swam the Channel in 14 hours and 31 minutes. She was the first woman to swim the Channel and the fastest person to that date. Ederle became deaf later in life but used her talents to teach deaf children to swim. She was inducted into the International Swimming Hall of Fame in 1965.

Bobby Jones

He was not a professional golfer; he was a lawyer. But Bobby Jones was the only golfer ever to win both amateur and open titles in the United States and Britain in the same year—a grand slam. In addition to winning thirteen major championships, Jones is known for founding the Masters tournament.

(See Acts 2:42.) What element of salvation is Barna leaving out? *(Salvation is not a result of good persuasion; it is a result of the Holy Spirit's leading.)*

Activity 6: Sports in the Roaring Twenties

Use this activity to give the students an overview of some of the most prominent sports and sports figures of the Roaring Twenties.

Compare the Roaring Twenties and Today

The number of parallels between the Roaring Twenties and the modern culture wars is surprising. Write down some key facts about this period and ask the students to name some modern parallels. A short sample includes record-setting fads, board games, movies, hairstyles, flappers, sports idols, sensational crimes, speakeasies, bootlegging, gang wars, attacks on Scripture, and the debate over evolution.

St. Valentine's Day Massacre

Al Capone and Bugs Moran were rival gangster leaders in Chicago. In early 1929 Capone associate Jack McGurn told Capone about problems he was having with Moran, and the two planned an assassination. The plan was simple. On February 14, 1929, a bootlegger tricked the Moran gang into meeting him at a garage to buy alcohol at a good price. Capone's hired assassins dressed like police officers and staged a raid on the garage. Moran's gang members lined up against the wall as ordered by the "officers" and were promptly shot. The assassins left the building with some of their own men as "prisoners," climbed into a stolen police car, and drove away, leaving behind six dead and one dying man. Capone and McGurn had impenetrable alibis, and no one was ever charged with the crime. Bugs Moran, the chief target of the assassination, was not in the garage when the massacre occurred.

Capone's Day in Court

Despite Al Capone's well-known criminal activities, the government could not get a conviction on him. Lack of solid evidence, together with intimidation of witnesses and bribery of officials, kept Capone free. With encouragement from President Hoover, however, government officials renewed their efforts to put Capone behind bars. They sought evidence of either income tax evasion or violations of Prohibition. Lawman Eliot Ness and his "Untouchables" pursued the bootlegging portion of Capone's operation.

The government finally moved on Capone in 1931. Not sure how long its case, focusing on the income tax evasion, would hold together, it agreed to allow Capone

New York Yankees slugger Babe Ruth helped make baseball America's game in the 1920s and 1930s.

Another famous name in the sports of the era was a baseball star named George Herman "Babe" Ruth, who played for the New York Yankees and hit more home runs than any other player until Henry (Hank) Aaron in the 1970s. Other famous athletes include Bobby Jones, who won fame as a golfer, and race car driver Barney Oldfield, who not only entered major races but also raced at county fairs. And a horse named Man O'War won twenty of the twenty-one races in which his owners entered him.

Prohibition

Prohibition was also an important issue in the 1920s. Thousands of Americans had rallied to the temperance societies of the 1800s. Many of the progressives of the early 1900s had made Prohibition a major reform issue. By 1915, fifteen states had voted out "demon rum." By 1918, thirty-three states were in the Prohibition column. During the war, when the United States was selling all of its surplus grain to the Allies for food, it was considered unpatriotic to make liquor. The Eighteenth Amendment, which mandated nationwide Prohibition, passed Congress and went to the states for ratification. Its widespread support at the time is evidenced by its quick approval. All the states except Rhode Island and Connecticut ratified it in a little more than a year. In most states, Prohibition won by a large majority. In 1919, the Eighteenth Amendment was ratified. It made illegal the manufacture, sale, transport, import, and export of intoxicating liquors as a beverage.

The **Volstead Act** of 1919 made illegal any beverage with more than 0.5% alcohol content. It also set up a Prohibition Bureau to enforce the law. But it proved difficult to enforce. Although Prohibition was important to American Protestants, including not only evangelicals but also liberal and moderate Christians, it was not popular among many Americans of immigrant ancestry. The Irish, German, and Eastern European immigrants considered alcoholic drinks an essential part of their culture. They resented the outlawing of alcoholic drinks and were unwilling to give them up or help in the enforcement of Prohibition. Also, second- and third-generation immigrants were becoming politically influential. Besides, the Prohibition Bureau had a small budget and only three thousand agents to enforce the law. Soon, other problems also arose.

Whenever authorities found illegal liquor, they arrested the people who possessed it and poured the liquor into the storm sewers.

Illegal taverns called "**speakeasies**" appeared across the nation. The border with Canada, where alcohol was legal, stretched nearly three thousand miles. Officers could not effectively patrol the long border, and liquor flowed across it freely. The Atlantic seaboard also had its share of rum runners. **Bootlegging**, selling illegal liquor, became a big business and made many people rich. Because it was legal to have alcohol for medicinal reasons, some people got it by doctor's prescription. Others made their own home brew in stills or made "bathtub gin."

Violence often accompanied the criminals who organized bootlegging rings. "Scarface" **Al Capone**, leader of a large crime ring in Chicago, and other ruthless criminals organized liquor networks to supply those who wanted liquor and were willing to pay any price for it. With alcohol came other criminal activities, including illegal

CD: Results of Enforcing the Volstead Act

Refer to the CD for charts showing the results of enforcement of the Volstead Act.

Why Was Prohibition a Failure?

Most students will understand from the text that Prohibition was a failure because of lack of government support, but what was the real cause of its failure? (*People need to have their desires changed so they can embrace a biblical worldview on subjects like alcohol consumption.*) What issues does the government have difficulty controlling in the United States today? (*drugs, assisted suicide, abortion*) What should a Christian do about such issues? (*On a personal level, Christians*

ought to evangelize those around them. Cultural change without personal evangelism would be superficial because it only addresses surface problems and would be unloving because it does not meet individuals' greatest need. Christians should also participate in the political process to promote a government that rewards good and punishes bad conduct [Rom. 13:3].) Discuss the Christian's political responsibility and how moral decay affects a nation.

Scenes from American Church History

You might want to read "H. C. Morrison and the Holiness Movement" in *Scenes from American Church History*. Another account

of the religion of that era is "William Jennings Bryan: 'He Kept the Faith.'"

gambling and prostitution. Criminal gangs controlled such activities in certain areas. If a rival gang tried to operate in another gang's territory, a "war" erupted between the gangs. Innocent people were killed, and such crimes shocked the public. Although periodic crackdowns occurred, putting gangsters behind bars was hard. The criminals often refused to testify against each other. They threatened honest citizens who were called as witnesses. They also sometimes bought off corrupt judges and officials.

By the late 1920s, it was apparent that Prohibition was not working. More and more Americans cried out for its repeal. In 1928, the Democrats nominated Al Smith, who called for repeal. Repeal finally came in 1933 under Franklin Roosevelt.

Responses

Many Americans were alarmed by the decline in morals. Some of their responses were negative, such as the revival of the Ku Klux Klan. Other responses were positive, such as a greater emphasis on scriptural truth and doctrinal purity.

The Ku Klux Klan

In the minds of many white Protestants, these moral changes were tied to immigrants, Roman Catholics, and other minorities. Tapping into these fears, a new Ku Klux Klan emerged. Many ordinary, middle class citizens joined the organization with its robes, processionals, and ceremonies. The KKK used high pressure tactics to intimidate politicians and anyone else who differed from the views of the organization. Members began to beat and even murder the Klan's opponents. As the KKK grew more violent, its membership declined.

The KKK was just one example of the racism ingrained in early twentieth century America. For instance, the clubs popular for the jazz performed by African American artists like Louis Armstrong, King Oliver, and Jelly Roll Morton served only whites.

Fighting Racism

Many African Americans moved north, where they found greater employment opportunities. By gathering in northern cities, blacks also gained some political power. Leaders within the black community differed over how to address these remaining challenges of racism. Marcus Garvey, founder of the United Negro Improvement Association (UNIA), argued that whites were incapable of overcoming their racial prejudices. Because of this, Garvey argued that blacks should develop their own cultures entirely separate from those of the whites. Instead of seeking equality in America, he urged emigration to Africa. Garvey's ideas did not take hold in the 1920s, but they are seen as the seeds of the Black Power movement that emerged in the 1960s.

Garvey was opposed by W. E. B. Du Bois, who helped found the National Association for the Advancement of Colored People (NAACP). The NAACP started a journal, *The Crisis*, to educate

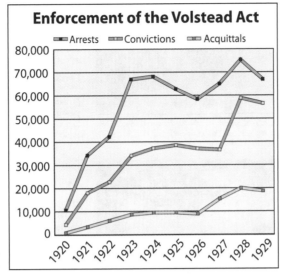

Enforcement of the Volstead Act

■■ Arrests   ■■ Convictions   ■■ Acquittals

(line graph with y-axis values 0, 10,000, 20,000, 30,000, 40,000, 50,000, 60,000, 70,000, 80,000 and x-axis years 1920, 1921, 1922, 1923, 1924, 1925, 1926, 1927, 1928, 1929)

The Ku Klux Klan grew during the 1920s and used deplorable methods to intimidate blacks, Roman Catholics, and immigrants.

to plea bargain for a light sentence. Judge James Wilkerson, however, declared that he was not bound by such a bargain. Capone withdrew his guilty plea and prepared for a trial. Having identified the potential jurors, Capone's men tried to bribe them. In response, Judge Wilkerson switched juries the day the trial started. Capone was sentenced to eleven years in prison. He served eight of those years and then returned to his mansion near Miami, Florida, where he lived until his death in 1947.

Ku Klux Klan

The Ku Klux Klan, founded during Reconstruction but essentially forced out of business, reemerged in 1915. Taking advantage of a wave of patriotism during World War I, Klan organizers supported a native white population and opposed blacks, Catholics, and Jews. The Klan had between four and five million members in the mid-1920s but that number went down quickly afterwards.

Marcus Garvey

Marcus Mosiah Garvey Jr. was, among many things, a publisher, journalist, entrepreneur, black nationalist, and founder of the Universal Negro Improvement Association and African Communities League (UNIA-ACL). He advocated a Pan-African philosophy that sought to have those of African heritage "redeem" Africa from European colonial powers. The concept of African Americans returning to Africa became known as the Colonist Movement. Additional activies included editing the newspaper *The Negro World* and developing the Black Star Line of Delaware. The first ship was named the S.S. *Frederick Douglass*.

W.E.B. du Bois and the NAACP

Du Bois was one of the most influential intellectual leaders and political activists advancing the cause of African Americans in the first half of the twentieth century. In 1910 he became the Publications Director of the NAACP and worked with this organization for twenty-five years. He later left over differences with NAACP leaders Walter White and Roy Wilkins.

The Dyer Anti-Lynching Bill

Leonidas C. Dyer of Missouri initially sponsored this bill opposing lynching ("an extrajudicial punishment carried out by a group of two or more persons") in 1918. The members of the House of Representatives passed this bill in 1922, but southern senators blocked its passage in the Senate. Other legislation to outlaw this evil practice, such as the Costigan-Wagner Bill, has since become law.

American Civil Liberties Union

The American Civil Liberties Union (ACLU) was organized in 1920. Its founders included Clarence Darrow, Felix Frankfurter, Jane Addams, Helen Keller, Norman Thomas, and John Dewey. It was set up as a public interest law firm with the purpose of protecting civil liberties.

Today's ACLU has offices on national, state, and local levels. It pays more than sixty attorneys and, in addition, has available the services of two thousand volunteers. A membership of approximately 275,000 supports the organization.

The ACLU has taken leadership in the defense of such causes as freedom of speech, rights of minorities, abortion and homosexual rights, and separation of church and state (resulting in the removal

Dayton businessmen John Neal (center) and George Rappleyea (right) convinced teacher John Scopes (left) to test the Tennessee anti-evolution law.

William Jennings Bryan (left) and Clarence Darrow (right) during the Scopes trial

The summer heat forced the Scopes trial out of doors, where Clarence Darrow questioned William Jennings Bryan mercilessly in his attempt to discredit the three-time presidential candidate and defender of Christian orthodoxy.

Americans about racial problems. The NAACP also challenged state laws that violated the Fourteenth and Fifteenth Amendments. From 1919 until 1925, the NAACP promoted an anti-lynching bill which would punish law enforcement officers who permitted lynching with five years in prison, a $5,000 fine, or both. Counties that failed to apprehend those who participated in a lynch mob were to be fined $10,000. Those who participated in a lynch mob were to be tried for homicide. The bill never passed due to opposition from many Southern senators, but the publicity surrounding the bill brought public attention to lynching, which helped reduce its frequency.

Fundamentalism

Conservative Christians in the 1920s were concerned about the growth of theological liberalism in the churches. In 1909 concerned pastors and theologians wrote a series of books containing ninety articles defending the inerrancy of Scripture, the deity of Christ, and other fundamental doctrines. A Christian businessman funded the dis-tribution of these books, called *The Fundamentals*, to every Bible teacher, from Sunday school superintendent to seminary professor, in the English-speaking world. These books gave rise to the name **Fundamentalist**.

While firmly supporting historic doctrines of the Christian faith, early Fundamentalists were initially unsure how to handle Darwin's new theory of evolution. Some articles in *The Fundamentals* rejected the theory while others attempted to harmonize some aspects of evolution with Christianity. By the 1920s most Fundamentalists rallied to oppose Darwinism. Fundamentalist opposition to evolution has been symbolized by the Scopes Trial.

Like many other state governments of the time, the Tennessee state legislature had passed a law forbidding high school teachers to teach evolution. Wanting to test such laws, the American Civil Liberties Union said that it would defend any Tennessee teacher who would challenge that law. George Rappleyea approached a number of lawyers and businessmen of Dayton, Tennessee, and convinced them that the publicity of such a trial in Dayton would be good for business in the town. They persuaded a high-school biology teacher, John Scopes, to become the defendant. He taught from a state-approved textbook that included evolution, and authorities arrested him.

In the summer of 1925, the **Scopes trial** turned into the hoped-for gigantic media event. Two hundred reporters converged on the small town of Dayton, and for the first time a trial was covered by radio. One of the prosecutors was William Jennings Bryan, three-time Democratic presidential nominee. Clarence Darrow, a famous trial lawyer and agnostic, defended Scopes. H. L. Mencken (MENG kun), a nationally known reporter who made fun of Christians, called the people of Dayton "gaping primates" and the event in Dayton the "Monkey Trial."

Bryan testified in the trial and was ridiculed by Darrow. While Bryan was a staunch defender of the faith, he did not always handle Darrow's questions well. Bryan was neither a Bible scholar nor a scientist. Darrow managed to confuse him. Darrow's performance seemed to make fundamental Christi-

---

More on the Scopes Trial and the Players in It

A possible source for teacher enrichment on the Scopes trial is *Summer for the Gods* by Edward J. Larson (Basic Books, 1997). Excellent biographies of William Jennings Bryan are *Defender of the Faith: The Last Decade, 1915–1925* by Lawrence Levine (Oxford University Press, 1965) and *A Godly Hero* by Michael Kazin (Knopf, 2006).

CD: The Scopes Trial

Refer to the CD for photos of William Jennings Bryan and Clarence Darrow during the Scopes Trial.

Activity 5: Darrow versus Bryan in the Scopes Trial

This activity describes the confrontation between Clarence Darrow and William Jennings Bryan during the Scopes Trial and includes excerpts from that encounter

anity look foolish. Scopes was convicted of teaching evolution and fined $100, but the trial had made Bible-believing Christians seem ignorant and unscientific.

The Scopes trial allowed intellectuals and the media to announce the apparent demise of Fundamentalism. However, Fundamentalism continued to thrive on the popular level. Though the Fundamentalists were forced to divide from their denominations during the 1920s and 1930s, the separatist groups grew during this period while the mainline denominations declined.

Key to Fundamentalist growth was the network of Fundamentalist schools. Bible institutes like the Bible Institute of Los Angeles (BIOLA), Gordon College of Theology and Missions, and Moody Bible Institute were some of the more influential Bible institutes founded or expanded in the 1920s. These schools provided positive alternatives to liberal denominational schools. Dallas Theological Seminary and Westminster Theological Seminary were both founded in the 1920s to provide advanced doctrinal training for pastors. These seminaries also provided the resources necessary for the battle against theological liberalism. They published popular religious magazines and journals that linked the movement together.

Fundamentalists also became concerned about increased hostility to Christianity in secular colleges and universities. The Bible institutes began to offer a year of preparatory studies in Bible doctrines and Christian living to prepare students for college life. There was still a need, however, for Fundamentalist schools that would provide a full liberal arts education. During his tenure as president (1926–1940), J. Oliver Buswell grew Wheaton College, founded in 1860, into a trusted fundamentalist liberal arts college. Evangelist Bob Jones Sr., while traveling on the preaching circuit, became concerned by accounts of young people from Christian families who lost their faith while in college. He founded Bob Jones College in 1927 as a liberal arts college.

J. Gresham Machen

The Scopes Trial

This famous trial in the 1920s came about through the efforts of the ACLU to challenge laws that forbade the teaching of evolution in schools. Defense attorney Clarence Darrow, an agnostic, skillfully manipulated the proceedings to discredit the biblical account of Creation. Though Scopes was found guilty and received a small fine, many came to believe that the Bible had been discredited and that science provided the answers to questions such as the origin of life. The play, *Inherit the Wind,* later made into a movie, provides a fictional and historically inaccurate account of this trial. For more information, you can visit the Answers in Genesis website and search for information about this trial and the movie *Inherit the Wind*.

(of prayer, Bible reading, and the teaching of Creation from public schools).

J. Gresham Machen

J. Gresham Machen (MAY chun) was Fundamentalism's most respected scholar in the early twentieth century. He studied at some of the best schools in the United States and Europe. Machen was also a professor at Princeton Seminary. He wrote in defense of the virgin birth and the divine origin of Christianity as well as books on God, man, and faith. Machen is best known for his book *Christianity and Liberalism.* In this work, Machen argued that liberalism was not Christianity. Theological liberalism was its own religion.

During the 1920s, he worked hard to prevent the spread of liberalism in the Presbyterian Church (USA). He found his efforts were hindered most by evangelicals. They believed he was harming the unity of the church. This made no sense to Machen, who did not see how forcing non-Christians out of Christian churches and schools harmed Christian unity.

Machen could not stop the Presbyterian Church (USA) from supporting liberal missionaries. As a result, he and some other men started their own independent mission board so believers could give money to Pres-

byterian missions without supporting liberals. In 1929, the Presbyterian Church (USA) reorganized Princeton Seminary to give the liberals greater control. Machen responded by leaving Princeton and helping to found Westminster Theological Seminary in Philadelphia. Because of his stand for the truth, Machen was dismissed from the Presbyterian Church (USA). By 1936 he and other conservatives had formed the Orthodox Presbyterian Church. Machen served as a professor at Westminster and as a leader in the Orthodox Presbyterian Church until his death in 1937.

Section IV

Objectives

Students should be able to

1. Describe the Harding administration.

2. Describe the Coolidge administration and explain why he was a popular president.

3. Name the man who followed Coolidge as president and describe his administration.

Alcohol in the White House

The Eighteenth Amendment prohibited the manufacture, sale, and transportation of alcohol within United States territory. Yet guests at poker parties at the Harding White House were served liquor.

"Silent Cal"

President Calvin Coolidge was famous not so much for what he said as for what he *did not* say. He was called "Silent Cal" for a reason—he did not talk very much. It was not uncommon for him to invite someone to his office and then sit in silence for long stretches of time before dismissing them. Over the fireplace in his home were inscribed the following words:

A wise old owl lived in an oak.

The more he saw the less he spoke.

The less he spoke the more he heard.

Why can't we all be like that wise old bird?

Coolidge's reticence became legendary. At one formal dinner in the White House, a guest sitting beside Coolidge revealed to him that she had bet a friend that she could make the president say more than two words. Coolidge smiled. The woman tried valiantly throughout the evening to make Coolidge say something, but he re-

Section Quiz

1. Why were the 1920s called the "Roaring Twenties"? What does the literature of the era reveal about the satisfaction people gained in such a society?

2. What bill did the NAACP try to have Congress pass?

3. What is "bootlegging"?

4. What famous trial took place as a result of the teaching of evolution? Where did it take place?

★ How did Fundamentalist schools help Fundamentalism grow after the Scopes trial?

IV. Republican Administrations

The presidents of the 1920s reflected the attitudes and goals of their day. They promoted the unhindered growth of business and the general enjoyment of prosperity. The expansion of business and resulting prosperity were indeed enjoyable, but some of the nation's serious problems were brushed aside at the time. Eventually, the fruits of the materialism and selfishness of the era produced a severe crisis for the country.

Warren Harding

Warren G. Harding was a likable, handsome newspaper editor from the small town of Marion, Ohio. He had climbed up the Ohio political ladder, eventually becoming a U.S. senator. The political leaders in the state at that time were called the "Ohio Gang," and Harding did his share of favors for those people to achieve his political success.

Harding had promised to get the country back to normal after the war. That was what the country wanted, so he was easily elected to the presidency.

Once in office, Harding supported most of the popular programs of the day, especially big business. Unfortunately, he appointed many of his political friends to important offices. They were not of the best character, and some of them used the government to promote their own gain. Although Harding may have been honest, his friends tarnished the reputation of his administration. The most prominent criminal was Harding's secretary of the interior, **Albert B. Fall**. Fall persuaded Harding and the secretary of the navy to transfer control of government-owned oil reserves from the Navy Department to the Interior Department. He then leased the reserves at Teapot Dome, Wyoming, and Elk Hills, California, to two oil men, who paid him back with several "loans" totaling $400,000. When Fall's crime was uncovered, he went to prison. He was the first cabinet member in history to be imprisoned for misdeeds in office.

Although Harding was not involved in public scandal for financial gain, he was weak and at fault personally for allowing the law to be disobeyed within the White House. Instead of providing firm direction, Harding allowed national affairs simply to drift along without guidance. By the summer of 1923, however, Harding knew that something was wrong. He told journalist William Allen White, "I have no trouble with my enemies. I can take care of them all right. But my friends, White, they're the ones that keep me walking the floor nights."

Section Quiz Answers

1. Technological advances, automobiles, motion pictures, city life, and moral changes made the decade seem exciting. The literature of the new era reveals the disillusionment and despair beneath the excitement

2. an anti-lynching bill

3. making and selling illegal liquor

4. Scopes trial; Dayton, Tennessee

★ The schools provided training for a new generation. The magazines and journals produced by the schools also linked the movement together.

The Rise of the Republicans

A good source of information about each of the administrations in this section—Harding, Coolidge, and Hoover—is *Republican Ascendancy* by John D. Hicks.

Activity 4: From Progressivism to Normalcy

Use this activity to help the students contrast the progressive presidents of the 1900s and 1910s to the presidents who led the "return to normalcy" during the 1920s. Note that all three progressive presidents—Roosevelt, Taft, and Wilson—are better known than the presidents of the Twenties, primarily because many people, including most historians, tend to rank activist presidents higher

than more passive presidents. Nevertheless, conservative Republicans honor presidents who restrain government power, even if they get no personal glory. Note the popularity of Ronald Reagan, whose administration's foundation was fiscal conservatism and reduction of government bureaucracy and intrusion into private enterprise.

Compare Scandals

Compare the Teapot Dome Scandal with the scandals under Grant and modern examples of scandal (such as Watergate and scandals that plagued Bill Clinton). Can the students find any parallels between the weaknesses of the presidents and the scandals of their respective administrations?

Harding took a vacation to Alaska in 1923. On July 28, on the way back, the president suffered a heart attack. He died on August 2. The **Teapot Dome Scandal** was uncovered only after his death.

Calvin Coolidge

Calvin Coolidge, born in Vermont, had studied law in Massachusetts and entered politics there. He had gained a reputation as a "law and order" man when, as governor of Massachusetts, he took a stand during a Boston police strike in 1919. He declared, "There is no right to strike against the public safety by anybody, anywhere, any time." He forced the police back to work. To a nation that feared disorder and crime, that stand won him admiration.

Succeeding to the presidency on Harding's death, Coolidge was in charge when most of the Harding scandals were revealed. By firmly prosecuting the corrupt officials, Coolidge won enough support to win the presidential election of 1924. Then he continued the basic policies that Harding had supported.

Walter Lippmann, a journalist of the day, said that Coolidge had a "talent for effectively doing nothing" but that "this active inactivity suits the mood" of the country. Coolidge was credited for the prosperity and was enormously popular. He could have won reelection easily, but he did not run. He called a press conference, and reporters gathered eagerly, expecting a major speech from the president. Instead, aides distributed slips of paper that said simply, "I do not choose to run for President in 1928. Calvin Coolidge."

Although business seemed to be successful, ominous conditions were developing. Because of unwise speculation by investors, prices went higher and higher on the stock market. Buying on credit was so popular that millions of Americans were in serious debt. Farmers were still overproducing and receiving low prices for their produce. Those and other features of the American economy would soon lead the nation into calamity. Collectively, unwise individual economic decisions sometimes have far-reaching national consequences.

Herbert Hoover

The nation was still enjoying prosperity when the election of 1928 was held. The Republican candidate, **Herbert Hoover**, was swept into office by a nation satisfied with success. Hoover, a poor, orphaned farm boy, had proved his abilities by becoming a wealthy mining engineer and then devoting his talents to public service. His Democratic opponent, Al Smith, was a Roman Catholic and was against Prohibition. The nation was not yet ready to vote a Catholic into the presidency or to end Prohibition.

Hoover was talented, but he had inherited the seeds of the impending fall from prosperity. The excesses of the Twenties were about to bear the fruit of disaster. Hoover would be saddled with the responsibility for the coming Great Depression.

Coolidge on the Purpose of Taxation

The collection of taxes which are not absolutely required, which do not beyond reasonable doubt contribute to the public welfare, is only a species of legalized larceny. The wise and correct course to follow in taxation is not to destroy those who have already secured success, but to create conditions under which everyone will have a better chance to be successful.

—Calvin Coolidge

President Calvin Coolidge greeting baseball great Walter Johnson

Section Quiz

1. Name the three Republican presidents of the 1920s.
2. What act of corruption is associated with Albert B. Fall?
★ What conditions of the 1920s would help bring the nation's prosperity to an end?

mained tight lipped. At the end of the evening, as the Coolidges were saying goodbye to their guests, the woman shook his hand, and Coolidge spoke his first words to her: "You lose!"

Death in the White House

President Coolidge's two sons were the first Boy Scouts to live in the White House. While playing tennis one day, Calvin Jr. developed a blister on a toe of his right foot. The next day, his entire foot and leg were stiff and painful. He was suffering from a blood infection. Seven different doctors tried to solve the problem, but nothing seemed to work. A few days later, Cal Jr. died.

His parents were devastated. "Silent Cal" became more silent than ever, mourning deeply. "When he went," the president sighed, "the power and glory of the Presidency went with him." The tragic loss undoubtedly influenced Coolidge's decision not to seek reelection.

A Life of Public Service

Before entering the White House, Herbert Hoover had already spent a good part of his life helping others. Traveling around the world as a mining engineer, Hoover was in China during the Boxer Rebellion. While his wife donated her time at hospitals, Hoover directed the building of barricades and at one point risked his life to rescue Chinese children.

At the onset of World War I, Hoover was in London. He helped the American embassy get American tourists home and then, as the result of his good work, received the assignment of feeding occupied Belgium. When America entered the war, he was named the head of the Food Administration, having to balance the food needs of

---

More on the Death of Calvin Coolidge Jr.

For more information on the death of President Coolidge's son, Cal Jr., see the article "The Most Wholesome and Best in the American Boy" in *Scouting* magazine (October 2000).

Activity 7 : Herbert Hoover on the Role of Government

Use this activity to help the students understand Hoover's reasons for acting (or not acting) at the beginning of the Depression and to contrast those views with the diametrically opposite view of an activist government that the New Deal would usher in.

Travel Back in Time

Students perhaps know that in the next two decades the Great Depression and World War II would occur. Ask, "If you could travel back in time, what would you do with the information you know?" Such information could be used for personal financial gain, or it could be used to warn the governments of the world. The challenge would be to make anyone believe you.

Commemorative Stamp

Assign the students to design a stamp that commemorates a historical event or individual in the chapter. They should include a brief explanation why the event or person deserves to be commemorated.

Section Quiz Answers

1. Warren G. Harding, Calvin Coolidge, Herbert Hoover
2. the Teapot Dome Scandal, using government property for his own profit
★ speculation on the stock market, buying on credit, too much farm production for the demands of the market

Activity 8 : Decade of Change

Use this activity as a chapter review to help students prepare for the chapter test.

soldiers at the front with those of civilians back home. After the war, the Allies asked him to organize food shipments for the hungry in Europe.

Star-Spangled Banner

Though written in 1814, "The Star-Spangled Banner" did not become the official anthem of the United States until the twentieth century. In 1916 President Woodrow Wilson ordered that the song be played at all naval and military occasions. And during Hoover's administration (1931), Congress voted to make "The Star-Spangled Banner" the national anthem.

People, Places, and Things to Remember:
Warren G. Harding
Washington Naval Conference
Calvin Coolidge
Kellogg-Briand Peace Pact
Third International
Nicola Sacco
Bartolomeo Vanzetti
installment plan
Charles A. Lindbergh
assembly line
Sigmund Freud
"flappers"
Prohibition
Volstead Act
"speakeasies"
bootlegging
Al Capone
Fundamentalist
Scopes trial
Albert B. Fall
Teapot Dome Scandal
Herbert Hoover

Chapter Review

Review Questions

Match each of these men with the statement or description most closely related to him.

1. Al Capone
2. Calvin Coolidge
3. Albert B. Fall
4. Warren G. Harding
5. Herbert Hoover
6. Charles Lindbergh

  a. America should "return to normalcy"

  b. flew the *Spirit of St. Louis* to Paris

  c. a Chicago gangster

  d. organizer of the Teapot Dome scheme

  e. "the business of America is business"

  f. inherited the fall from prosperity

Answer the following questions about the 1920s.

7. What two international agreements did the United States sign in the 1920s?
8. What was the "Red Scare"?
9. When was the first commercial radio broadcast, and what did it announce?
10. In what ways was racism ingrained in early twentieth century America?
11. What were the shockingly fashionable young women of the 1920s called?
12. When did Prohibition begin, and when did it end?
13. What is bootlegging?
14. In what famous trial was a teacher convicted of teaching evolution but biblical Christianity ridiculed?

Critical Thinking

1. Why is the Roaring Twenties a good name for the 1920s?
2. Why were educational institutions key for the Fundamentalist movement?

Chapter Review Answers

Review Questions

1. c
2. e
3. d
4. a
5. f
6. b
7. Treaty of Washington, Kellogg-Briand Peace Pact
8. a fear of Communist infiltration of America
9. November 2, 1920; Harding's election to the presidency
10. African Americans were barred from various clubs and organizations; groups like the KKK attempted to prevent them from having any political say; they were beaten and even murdered, but Congress could not muster enough votes to pass anti-lynching legislation.
11. flappers
12. 1919; 1933
13. making and selling illegal liquor
14. the Scopes trial

Critical Thinking

1. Answers will vary. The decade was roaring with activity—business, fads, amusements, faster transportation, sensational stories and crimes, etc.
2. Many of the secular schools were using academics to undermine Christianity. Fundamental schools enabled young people to receive an education from a Christian perspective and helped them learn how to counteract the claims of unbelievers.

Unemployed men in bread lines and soup kitchens were a familiar sight during the Great Depression.

CHAPTER

23

The Great Depression

I. The Bubble Bursts

II. FDR and the New Deal

III. The New Deal Faces Opposition

IV. Consequences of the New Deal

Chapter Goals

Students should be able to

1. Explain the difference between Hoover's and Roosevelt's approaches to solving problems of the Great Depression.

2. Define and use the basic terms of the chapter.

3. Summarize the events leading to the Depression.

4. Identify and explain the various New Deal measures and describe their consequences both then and now.

5. Recognize that Americans faced with hard times will choose security over liberty.

Chapter Motivation

Ask the students why they think Americans still remember the Great Depression. Why does it get so much attention? The Great Depression brought the biggest changes—especially in the scope of government— in America since the Civil War. Because no one wants a repeat of that experience, we want to understand its causes. The Great Depression also matters because during those years politicians enacted radical legislation supposedly designed to solve the problems of the Depression, but the repercussions of those actions extended far beyond the economy. Modern Americans need to understand the motives behind such changes and decide whether those changes were positive or negative in the long run.

Chapter 23 Lesson Plan Chart				
Section Title	**Main Activity**	**Pages**	**Days**	
I. The Bubble Bursts	Activity 1: Crash!	432–38	2–3 day	
II. FDR and the New Deal	Activity 2: Roosevelt's First Inaugural Address	438–43	2–3 days	
III. The New Deal Faces Opposition	Activity 5: Huey Long's Plan to "Share the Wealth"	443–46	1–2 days	
IV. Consequences of the New Deal	Activity 8: Chapter Review	446–47	1 day	
TOTAL SUGGESTED DAYS (INCLUDING 1 DAY FOR REVIEW AND TESTING)			7–10 DAYS	

MATERIALS LIST

SECTION I
• Activity 1 from the *Student Activities* manual
• Special speaker (see p. 432)

SECTION II
• CD: Party Platform Summaries, 1932; Electoral College Results, 1932; Franklin D. Roosevelt, 32nd President
• Activities 2–4 from the *Student Activities* manual

SECTION III
• Activities 5–7 from the *Student Activities* manual

Section I

Objectives

Students should be able to

1. List and explain four major causes of the economic crash that marked the beginning of the Great Depression in America.

2. Explain why runs on banks occurred.

3. Describe the conditions that farmers and the unemployed faced.

4. Explain ways that Hoover tried to deal with the Depression and list the results of those measures.

Did the Crash Cause Suicides?

When the stock market crashed in 1929, not only fortunes disappeared but also many Americans' hopes and dreams. Some people feared that they would not be able to support their families. Others dreaded the loss of their lavish lifestyles. Since the crash, stories have abounded of people committing suicide. Did they really?

One sensationalist London newspaper reported that eleven brokers jumped to their deaths from their high-rise offices. According to historian and economist John Kenneth Galbraith, if one believes the London press reports, "speculators were hurling themselves from windows; pedestrians picked their way delicately between the bodies of fallen financiers." He refers to such a report as a "myth" and suggests that humorist Will Rogers might have been responsible for cementing it in the minds of Americans. Rogers used the following quip frequently in his act: "When Wall Street took that tail spin, you had to stand in line to get a window to jump out of."

American businesses seemed to be flourishing as stock prices rose ever higher in 1929. Prices reached a new high in September, but conservative investors were becoming cautious. Stock sellers found fewer buyers. Prices began to slide. By October, brokers' sell orders surpassed their orders to buy. On Thursday, October 24, a record-breaking thirteen million shares changed hands. Prices slid so low that investors lost $9 billion on that "Black Thursday." Many investors, who lost all of their money, could not pay the stock brokers the additional money that they owed. When the investors could not pay, brokers tried desperately to sell the stock, flooding the market still more.

A panic broke out the following Tuesday, October 29, when the stock exchange had orders to sell sixteen million shares. Fortunes made over a period of years vanished in minutes. Some people became so depressed that they took their lives. Prices continued to drop until they finally reached their lowest level on November 13, 1929. The **stock market crash** of 1929 signaled the beginning of the **Great Depression**.

For the next decade, Americans faced a series of problems that reshaped American values and culture. Before the Depression, Americans valued individualism. Part of "the American way" was to value self-reliance. This value resulted in similar ideals of independence, initiative, and responsibility for one's own actions. These beliefs had supported American capitalism, private enterprise, and economic growth. But when the Depression came, many people concluded that self-reliance could not deliver Americans from poverty.

Brokers could keep abreast of moment-by-moment changes in the stock market by reading the ticker-tape machine.

I. The Bubble Bursts

During the 1928 presidential campaign, Herbert Hoover had declared, "We in America today are nearer to the final triumph over poverty than ever before in the history of any land." But millions of Americans were soon unemployed, homeless, and hungry. The Roaring Twenties ended with a national financial collapse that would afflict Americans for more than a decade.

Causes of the Crash

The widespread desire for wealth and pleasure in the 1920s had much to do with the crash that followed, but the financial crisis was caused by a combination of several specific factors.

Economic Slowdown

Despite the air of prosperity in the 1920s, many workers had already begun to face economic woes. Farmers were suffering from low prices before the crash. Textile workers and coal miners were hurt by layoffs as demand for their products declined. Such workers could no longer buy the industrial goods that were filling the market. Many other Americans ran out of credit. As the demand for goods declined, industrial output slowed. Laborers worked fewer hours or were laid off, which reduced incomes and caused hardships. Industries were often interdependent, so when one cut back, others were forced to do the same. Consumer spending had dropped so far that industrial expansion slowed almost to a standstill long before the crash.

Two months after Black Thursday, stockholders had lost $40 billion. Although the market had begun to make some gains by the new

- CD: Electoral College Results, 1936; FDR's Court-Packing Scheme
- Examples of 1930s radio programming

SECTION IV
- CD: Electoral College Results, 1940; Depression and New Deal Statistics
- Activity 8 from the *Student Activities* manual

Core Values:

The Depression challenged the American value of growth. As growth—especially economic growth—seemed to vanish from the United States, other American values began to be reshaped. American individualism, which manifested itself in self-reliance, initiative, and personal responsibility, seemed

inadequate to meet the crisis at hand. Many American leaders concluded they needed to increase the powers of government in order to deliver people from poverty. This led to the surrender of some freedoms. The free market system was not as free as it had been. Now a private business had to compete not only with other businesses but also with the government (an entity with immense financial resources but no obligation to produce a profit). When the government attempted to help an industry, the efficiency of that industry suffered. When the government became involved in American agriculture, farmers were told how much they were allowed to produce, and many became dependent on government subsidies. In order to fund these activities, the government raised

taxes. This gave the government rather than the individual the power to determine how the money would be used.

Activity 1: Crash!

Use this activity, a first-hand account of the 1929 stock market crash, to help the students understand the events of that day and how they influenced the entire U.S. economy for the next decade and longer.

Special Speaker

Invite a person who experienced the Depression to speak to your class, sharing with the students what life was like then.

year, it was not enough to renew confidence, and the country entered a general economic depression.

Overuse of Credit

The use of credit, especially of installment buying, had grown steadily. While credit masked some of the early symptoms of economic illness, its unwise and often unrestrained use made things worse. Before long, people were having to make such high payments on the things they had bought on credit that they could not afford to buy anything new. Auto sales and construction lagged, and workers were laid off. Those people were then unable to meet their payments at all. The merchants who had extended the loans lost money, and their own businesses began to falter.

Speculation

In the late 1920s, newspapers carried accounts of people who had profited from get-rich-quick schemes. Often motivated by greed, those speculators bought real estate or stocks at low prices, hoping to sell them quickly for a much higher price.

Land prices went up in the 1920s, especially in urban areas or near recreational settings as people moved outward to the suburbs. The biggest land boom was in Florida, where the semitropical climate attracted hordes of speculators. Miami alone boasted two thousand real estate offices in 1925. Those who had speculated early and bought good land did make big profits. But others who had bought land on credit eventually found that they could not make their payments. Some people were swindled into buying undesirable land and even swamps. In 1926, hurricanes struck, helping to put an end to the desire to invest in the area. Homes were left vacant, and few sales were made thereafter. Bank failures in Florida climbed when loans were not repaid.

Many Americans who had wisely avoided risky land investments were tempted by stock speculation. Stock prices had risen steadily beginning in 1927. By September 1929, stock prices were 400 percent higher than they had been in 1925. Even people of modest means had an incentive to buy stocks. The ticker-tape machine allowed purchasers to follow price changes almost as they happened.

The number of people "playing the market" grew to about 1.5 million in 1929. But most of them were not buying stocks to collect quarterly dividends. Rather, they wanted to sell stocks for quick profits when the prices rose. Many investors paid scant attention to the earnings of the companies they had invested in, which would have given them an indication of the actual value of the stock. They assumed that stock prices would keep going up no matter what the industries did.

The problem was further complicated because brokers allowed investors to **buy on margin**. The investors or buyers paid only part of the purchase price in cash, usually 10 percent, and borrowed the rest from the broker, using the stock as collateral. The broker borrowed money from banks and corporations to cover loans made to his clients. If the value of the stock went up, there was no problem. The buyer could repay his loan with interest and still gain a profit. But if the stock's value went below the value of the loan, the buyer's margin was "called in." The speculator then had to get more cash or risk losing both the shares and his cash investment. If the buyer could not repay his loan, the broker could take the stock.

An Example of Credit Woes of Consumers and Retail Businesses

G. B. Peterson operated a small country store in rural East Tennessee. He bought goods on credit from a wholesaler in the city of Knoxville. In turn, the farmers of the community bought their supplies from him, many of them making their purchases on credit based on the prospect of future crops. As long as they could raise and sell those crops, they could pay their bills at Peterson's store. When crops failed or prices dropped, however, they could not pay their bills. In turn, Peterson could not pay his wholesale supplier. Eventually, the wholesaler cut off Peterson's credit, forcing Peterson to close the store.

Share Price Growth for Selected Stocks

Company	3/3/28	9/3/29
American Can	77	181⅞
AT&T	179½	304
General Electric	128¾	396¼
Montgomery Ward	137⅞	466½
Union Carbide	145	413⅝

Actually, there is no record of such mass tragedy. About two weeks *before* the crash, the vice president of Earl Radio Corporation did jump from the window of his eleventh-floor hotel room in Manhattan. Later, authorities found a note that he had written that revealed, "Last April, I was worth $100,000. Today, I am $24,000 in the red." Jim Riordan, president of the County Trust Company, shot himself in the head. Rumors spread that he had lost hundreds of thousands of dollars in the crash.

Galbraith wrote, "One can only guess how the suicide myth became established. Like alcoholics and gamblers, broken speculators are supposed to have a propensity for self-destruction. At a time when broken speculators were plentiful, the newspapers and the public may have simply supplied the corollary."

Ticker Tape Machine

The bad news of November 29 was not broken to investors gently. In fact, it rushed toward them, printed on thin sheets of paper from the ticker tape machine.

That little machine was invented in 1867 as a variation of Samuel Morse's telegraph machine. Like the telegraph, it received information by cable, but it also printed the information on strips of paper three-fourths of an inch wide. That feature was valuable for stockbrokers, who needed to stay abreast of stock transactions throughout the day. Little rolls of paper were fed through the machine, which printed the symbol for a stock, the number of shares traded, and the price of each transaction. Each brokerage firm had one of the machines connected to the stock exchange.

Other Causes of the Depression

Explain to your students that determining the causes of events such as the Great Depression is not always as easy as it seems. People behave in predictable ways, so it does not seem fair to blame that entire generation for being greedy, selfish, and shortsighted, although some of the people obviously were. Another explanation for the Depression is the government's radical changes in money policy. Just as the depression of 1837 followed the Specie Circular (see Chapter 11), the Depression of 1929 followed the Federal Reserve's decision to withdraw money from circulation. A free market puts checks and balances on selfish decisions, but government intervention plays havoc with the economy.

Dangers of Credit

Describe life in America before the invention of the credit card. (Credit cards began to become popular in the 1950s and were typically called "charge-a-plates" by the retail stores that issued them.) Before the wide acceptance of credit, people discouraged personal debt, and loans were frowned upon. Most debts were "secured," or backed, by an item of value (collateral) that the borrower would surrender if he or she could not pay the debt. For example, defaulting on a home loan would result in foreclosure, or failure to pay off a car loan meant repossession of the car. Discuss how life has changed since then and the dangers of unsecured loans. Also discuss unwise business practices today. Banks and automobile manufacturers encourage customers to buy on credit. Credit card companies encourage students to apply for cards. Check advance and title loan companies make getting quick loans easy. Solomon warns that "the borrower is servant to the lender" (Prov. 22:7). Discuss ways of avoiding the pitfalls of debt.

Early Depression in Florida

Before 1926, Miami had a booming tourism industry. New housing developments were springing up to accommodate a population that had reached thirty thousand. But that year two hurricanes hit Florida, bringing depression to the region early. Miami was devastated. Whole subdivisions were wiped out. Streets were flooded by six to seven feet of water. More than 243 people died in the two storms.

Ironically, although the hurricanes put South Florida in a depression, they actually helped other areas of the state. In northwest Florida the hurricanes uprooted more than four thousand old power poles. Gulf Power Company was forced to replace the poles, which helped modernize the area.

Rail Hoboes

During the Depression, thousands of people traveled across the United States hidden in or on top of railcars. Most of them were young men, but young women and even whole families used the rails too.

Each hobo had his own reason for riding the rails. The majority of them were out of work and just trying to survive. Some towns were so flooded with homeless people that policemen regularly chased them from the area. They had to move on, and "hopping a train" was an easy way to go. Sometimes families who were unable to support all of their children would send the older ones out on their own. For the children who were turned out, the rails were the best way to travel and search for work. Others simply traveled for the taste of adventure. Now known as "yuppie hoboes," those young people might have even come from wealthy families.

The War Debts Cycle

Illustrate the foreign economic crisis by drawing three arrows that form a circle. The first arrow labeled "German Reparations" points to a second arrow labeled "Allied War Debt," which, in turn, points to "U.S. Loans." The loans to Germany complete the cycle. When the Depression stopped the flow of loans, all the nations in the cycle were hurt.

Share Price Decline for Selected Stocks		
Company	9/3/29	11/13/29
American Can	181⅞	86
AT&T	304	197¼
General Electric	396¼	168⅛
Montgomery Ward	466½	49¼
Union Carbide	413⅝	59

Bank Failures 1929–31

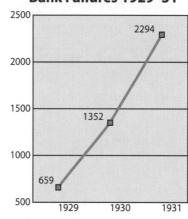

Economic uncertainties prompted thousands of people to withdraw their money from banks, forcing many banks to close their doors.

The system satisfied many people and seemed to stimulate the economy. Stock prices climbed. In March 1928, both the volume and the value of shares traded soared. The boom lasted through the summer of 1929, although economists were baffled because both prices and business profits were falling at the same time.

International Economic Problems

To make matters worse, in 1930 the United States passed the Smoot-Hawley Tariff on foreign goods in order to protect American industries from foreign competition. This was the highest tariff ever passed by the U.S. Congress. Other countries responded by raising their tariffs on American goods. This made it hard for Americans to export.

Without profitable trade, Europe could not repay the more than $11 billion worth of debt owed to the United States. The only source of money for repayment to American creditors was the money they received from German reparations payments. Yet the Germans were too poor to make the large payments demanded by the Treaty of Versailles.

To that complex situation was added the fact that Americans had loaned Germany millions of dollars to rebuild the country. But Germany used the money to make the reparations payments instead. When the crash came, most of the money from those international loans was lost. The end of American credit and prosperity only deepened Europe's already severe depression.

Conditions During the Depression

When the crash came, many Americans lost their confidence in the economy. They saw prosperity disappear. Most of them had little hope that it would return anytime soon. Investments, money, jobs, and homes were no longer safe.

The Run on Banks

People became increasingly afraid that they might lose the money they had deposited in banks. Some people withdrew money from banks to pay their brokers. Others panicked and withdrew all of their money. Banks could not keep pace with the demand. In the last two weeks before Hoover left office, depositors withdrew $1 billion. Banks ran out of cash and were forced to close their doors, some permanently. Others reopened to offer depositors only a percentage of their total deposit.

Banks had unwittingly contributed to the collapse through unwise extension of credit. In September 1927, $1.3 billion was out in loans. By the same month in 1929, the total had risen to $8.5 billion. When many of those loans could not be repaid, the banks ran out of money. By 1931, about five thousand banks had closed their doors. Not all of the failed banks were large, but some were. For example, the failure of the Bank of the United States in New York City affected 400,000 people. During the 1930s, more than 9,000 banks failed. Those that survived were very reluctant to make loans.

Unemployment

Millions of Americans were thrown out of work by the Depression. By 1933, thirteen million Americans—one of every four workers—were unemployed. Some workers kept their jobs but worked only a few days a week or a few hours a day. Others who kept their jobs took wage cuts. Between 1931 and 1933, an average of 100,000 people a week lost their jobs.

People began to buy less because they had less money. As they bought less, inventories of goods increased. Producers had more than they could sell. Prices fell, but no one had money to buy the cheaper goods. The gross national product (GNP; the value of total goods produced in the country) declined. By 1932, the output of the country had fallen to 54 percent of what it had been in 1929. By 1932, steel plants were operating at only 12 percent of capacity.

The loss of a man's job usually meant no steady income for his family. Even so, the family needed food. The mortgage or rent payments had to be made. Any person or business that had given credit was now beating on the door to receive payment. The situation seemed desperate to millions of Americans.

Wives and mothers helped out the best they could. They took in laundry and took cleaning jobs. If families had an empty room or children could double up, they took in renters. They planted gardens and canned vegetables to save on grocery bills. They patched clothing and darned socks. Children wore hand-me-downs. Sometimes unemployed husbands or older sons left home to search for work in other towns.

GNP 1929–32

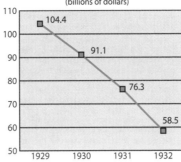

(billions of dollars)

Year	Value
1929	104.4
1930	91.1
1931	76.3
1932	58.5

Depression Unemployment

Year	Labor force	Number of workers unemployed	Unemployed as percentage of labor force
1929	49,440,000	1,550,000	3.14
1930	50,080,000	4,340,000	8.67
1931	50,680,000	8,020,000	15.82
1932	51,250,000	12,060,000	23.53
1933	51,840,000	12,830,000	24.75
1934	52,490,000	11,340,000	21.60
1935	53,140,000	10,610,000	19.97
1936	53,740,000	9,030,000	16.80
1937	54,320,000	7,700,000	14.18
1938	54,950,000	10,390,000	18.91
1939	55,600,000	9,480,000	17.05
1940	56,180,000	8,120,000	14.45

The unemployed with a work ethic, such as this Detroit auto worker, wanted paying jobs, not charity.

Many families could not continue paying the installments on their loans. Because of mortgage foreclosures, some people eventually lost their homes. Some moved to abandoned boxcars or hastily built shacks on the edges of towns. Because they blamed the president and his policies for the country's economic problems, their concentrations of shanties were called "Hoovervilles." (Hoover's name was also attached to other things. A "Hoover flag" was an empty pocket turned inside out, showing that one had no money. A "Hoover blanket" was an opened newspaper that a poor person used for cover as he slept.)

Many people who needed help received aid from those who were better off. Family members helped their relatives. Friends and churches also offered help. People helped each other, trading their skills and materials. Limited help came from local governments. In those days, almost no help came from the federal government.

"Hoovervilles" sprang up in many cities and towns across the nation as the unemployed homeless searched for work.

At the end of the Depression, some hoboes went home; others continued life on the rails. Some went on to be famous. Louis L'Amour (author), H. L. Hunt (oil billionaire), William O. Douglas (Supreme Court justice), and Art Linkletter (television personality) were all hoboes for a time.

Hoovervilles

As the Depression deepened, "Hoovervilles" sprang up across the United States. These poverty dwellings were usually located on the outskirts of major cities, where employment opportunities and services were greater. The homes in the Hoovervilles were built from anything the people could get their hands on. Tents, tar paper, box wood, cardboard, car parts, spare lumber, and scrap metal were all used as building materials.

Hoover-ball

One "Hoover" expression that developed was not related to the Depression. White House physician Admiral Joel T. Boone developed a game called "Hoover-ball" as part of the president's fitness plan. Boone designed the game to be played in a short amount of time to fit the president's schedule and still give a good workout.

The game was played on a court and scored similar to tennis. However, the rules were more similar to those used in volleyball. Teams of 2–4 players used a six-pound medicine ball to score points. A server would throw the ball over the net, and the opponent would have to catch it and throw it back as quickly as possible. Each team would attempt to throw the ball in an area on the court where the opposite team could not catch it.

Today Hoover-ball is still played in certain areas. In Hoover's home state of Iowa, for example, the Hoover-ball National Championship is held at the annual Hooverfest.

Dust Storms

The dust storms that swept through the American plains during the Depression were both natural and man-made disasters. Soil erosion occurs naturally from the winds, but the farmers hastened the process. The wheat they grew replaced the grass of the plains, which had anchored the soil. When droughts came, the soil hardened, crumbled, and blew away in the wind.

The walls of dust created by a dust storm sometimes reached heights of two miles and widths of one hundred miles. Wind carried the dust at speeds of up to fifty miles per hour. When the dust clouds swept over, they blotted out the sun and covered houses and cars. The temperature dropped as much as forty degrees, and the air was thick with static electricity. People got shocked if they touched anything metal.

Some storms carried dust as far as cities on the East Coast. Even ships as far as three hundred miles from the coast sometimes got dusted.

"I Remember the Drought"

The droughts of the 1930s created desperate conditions for farmers. One victim of the droughts recalled his family's situation:

"I know from experience what it means to have no rain. For three years in the thirties we had very, very little rain. There was no pasture for the cows on our dairy farm. My dad chopped down trees so the cows could eat leaves all summer. They would bellow when they heard Dad chopping. We had to make leaf haystacks, which the cows ate in the winter. The grass was so thin Mother used a hand rake and a gunnysack to pick up the hay. The winds blew every day, day after day. The grasshoppers were the only ones who were happy and multiplied easily. They skinned the thistles to live. We poisoned them at every turn. . . . To this day, I still conserve [water] and feel that it's almost a sin to use too much of it because you just don't know when it might be scarce again."

Commodity Prices		
Product	1929	1932
Wheat	$1.05/bu.	39¢/bu.
Corn	81¢/bu.	33¢/bu.
Cotton	17¢/bu.	6¢/lb.
Tobacco	19¢/lb.	10¢/lb.
Total Farm Income	$12 billion	$5 billion

Oklahoma farmers and their families—the "Okies"—left their farms in search of paying work in California, but few places wanted them.

The Depression forced most Americans to lower their living standards. It destroyed the sense of independence and accomplishment of many people. It was difficult for a family's primary breadwinner to be unemployed and unable to support his own family. Some men searched for work in vain and then waited for handouts at soup kitchens or stood in bread lines. Sometimes they gleaned fields, scavenged city dumps, or searched for food in garbage cans. It was not uncommon to see once-prosperous men selling apples on the street corner. A few men tried to escape from their troubles by jumping on freight trains to ride the rails as hobos.

More Farm Problems

Few farmers had been prosperous, even in the booming 1920s. They produced so much grain, livestock, and other farm products that prices had stayed low. Many farmers could not make payments on farmland they had bought or on the cars, equipment, and other items that they had bought on credit. Without higher prices for their products, many of them were in danger of losing their farms.

Conditions for farmers became even worse, especially on the western edge of the Central Plains and on the Great Plains, where dust storms in the "**Dust Bowl**" brought extreme poverty. That area, already semiarid, was first overgrazed by cattle. Then with the increased demand for food during World War I, it had been plowed into farms. Since there had been enough rainfall then, farmers were able to make money.

But droughts came in the 1930s, adding to the farmers' economic woes. First the crops dried up. Next the land turned to dust. Then winds whipped the rich topsoil off the dry, exposed ground. By late fall 1933, "black blizzards" blew from west to east across the country. The clouds of dust darkened skies as far away as Albany, New York. By 1934, the lands from Texas to Canada were ravaged by the dust storms. The soil drifted into banks like snow. Cars had to use their headlights in the daytime. Families put wet towels in window sills and under doors to keep out the choking dust. Livestock died of thirst.

Farmers could not pay taxes or mortgages on their farms. They had to sell them at a loss. Thousands of farm families fled from their homes and moved to areas where farm workers were needed to tend vegetable fields and orchards. California was a popular destination. Many farmers from Oklahoma made the migration in search of jobs, but even California had little work for the "Okies."

Spiritual Questions

During the 1930s, many people wondered if the nation was being judged by God for the 1920s, a decade of unprecedented sinfulness. One businessman wrote in the *New York Times* in 1930, "Business depressions are caused by dissipation, dishonesty, disobedience to God's will—a general collapse of moral character." The connection between the unwise financial choices of the 1920s and the Depression is plain. Less clear is the connection between the Depression and the other sins that characterized the 1920s. Christians recognize, however, that God has control over all things: nations, economies, and even weather. It is His prerogative to judge nations as He pleases.

How Would Your Life Change?

Have the students discuss ways their lives would change if the United States experienced another depression. Discuss ways people could save money and get by during a depression today. Why would many people today be unlikely to tolerate such changes or conditions the way people during the Great Depression did? (*Answers might include lack of personal discipline, lack of willingness to sacrifice, lack of proper education in conservation of resources, and too great a dependence on government.*)

If someone's family already saves money in interesting ways, ask him or her to share examples.

Though one may not be able to prove that the Great Depression was in part God's judgment for sin, the Christian knows that God does judge nations for persisting in sin (cf. Amos 1; Isa. 13–24).

Hoover's Attempt to Solve the Problems

President Herbert Hoover tried to deal with the onset of the Depression by being optimistic. The more people panicked, the more damage was done to the economy, so he tried to encourage Americans to believe that these trials would soon pass and business would boom again. Few people seemed to listen. Stock prices continued to fall as investors tried to sell. Runs on banks continued, and industry remained inactive. Because Hoover was the president, he received most of the blame for what was going wrong.

The Veterans Demand Aid

The veterans of World War I had been promised a life insurance bonus to be paid in 1945. During the Depression, many began to ask the government to pay them part of the face value of their insurance policies at an earlier date. In the spring of 1932, Walter Waters, an unemployed veteran from Oregon, went to Washington, D.C., to pressure Congress to pay the "bonus." Soon men from all parts of the country joined him. About 20,000 veterans became a part of the "Bonus Army." They camped on a muddy, low-lying area near the Potomac River. The men were there most of the summer.

When the Senate defeated the Bonus Bill, many veterans left, but a few thousand stayed. Hoover refused to meet with them, but he did ask Congress to advance them money from their insurance policies so they could get home. Anyone who remained after July 28 was to be evicted. Radicals in the group tried to start a riot. After two policemen were beaten to the ground, two Bonus marchers were killed. Hoover then sent in troops under the command of Douglas MacArthur. The soldiers routed the veterans and set fire to their shacks. Hoover was criticized for treating the veterans harshly.

Hoover's Theory

Hoover believed the best solutions lay in "local responsibility. The best hearts and brains of every community could best serve their neighbors." He believed that creating government agencies to handle the problems would produce more red tape than relief. He thought that federal funds should be used only after all voluntary and local resources were exhausted.

When federal monies were used, Hoover believed that they should be carefully regulated. They should not be given directly to people as a **dole**, or handout. Instead, they should be used for broader projects so that the effects would benefit more people. If cities and states, for example, were given loans to pay for public works projects, they could hire local people who would benefit from the employment.

Hoover did not believe in government regulation of big business. He saw federal control of activities as an invitation to dictatorship, corruption, waste, and inefficiency. He defended personal freedoms against government encroachment. He greatly feared socialism. He also wanted to keep the federal budget balanced, so he was reluctant to spend large amounts of money for aid programs.

Though Hoover emphasized individual responsibility, he also tried to establish programs to help the people. He set up government work projects that employed thousands of men and provided useful

World War I veterans assembled on the Capitol steps demanding their "bonus" early.

Thousands of people lined up outside factories and employment agencies, hoping to be chosen for the few jobs that were available.

Bonus Army

When the "Bonus Army" first arrived in Washington, Police Superintendent Pelham D. Glassford helped provide aid for the more than 20,000 people who demonstrated and allowed some of them to stay in vacant government buildings. However, as the protest wore on, the army got involved. The general directing the operations was Douglas MacArthur, who would later play major roles in World War II and the Korean War. The Bonus Army incident was a dark spot in MacArthur's otherwise outstanding career.

One major question was whether MacArthur disobeyed an order from President Hoover. Hoover sent a message ordering MacArthur to keep his troops from entering the main veteran camp until the women and children had been removed. Did the general even receive the note? His executive assistant, Brigadier General Moseley, claimed that he did, but three other witnesses denied it.

Whatever the case, MacArthur did not apologize for his actions. He believed that what his men did was necessary to prevent a possible overthrow of the government by Communists.

Hoover's Philosophy

President Hoover summarized his philosophy of freedom—and, by extension, of government's role—when he said, "Freedom conceives that the mind and spirit of man can be free only if he is free to pattern his own life, to develop his own talents, free to earn, to spend, to save, to acquire property as the security of his old age and his family." This view is in stark contrast to FDR's desire for government to do all of those things for the individual.

The Challenge of Being a Conservative

Ask the students to answer the question "Why is it easier for progressives/liberals to win the support of voters than it is for conservatives?" Men such as Roosevelt promised to use government money to solve people's problems, but Hoover and other conservatives argued that the job of the American republic is to give individuals the liberty to solve their own problems.

Students need to recognize the tension between security and liberty. Unless leaders govern with God-given wisdom, government tends to provide one or the other but not both. In times of crisis, human nature seeks security at the expense of liberty.

The Founding Fathers placed restraints on human nature's tendency to overreact in a crisis. Students need to be prepared for this danger when new crises arise in the nation.

Discuss how liberal and conservative politicians present their arguments in modern debates. Discuss "crises" that liberals use to appeal for more government programs at the expense of liberty. Why are their arguments so appealing? *(They often cloak their ideas with talk of fairness, equality, safety, and compassion.)* What are some of the most powerful appeals conservatives make? *(liberty, individualism, pride, tradition)*

Demagogues (leaders who appeal to the emotions and prejudices of the people to obtain power) tend to promise and then give

things that, once given, are very hard to take away. For instance, unscrupulous politicians sometimes promise certain benefits that are very expensive (if not unconstitutional) to get a lot of votes. Once those benefits are given, the politician can then appeal to the people in subsequent reelection bids that voting for the opposing candidate might mean losing those benefits. An example of this ploy is the Social Security System, which has become such an ingrained part of American society that even to suggest offering an alternative system is to risk losing votes.

Hoover Dam "High Scalers"

One of the most dangerous jobs in building Hoover Dam was clearing the canyon walls of loose rocks. From ropes secured on top of the canyon, men called high scalers risked their lives to do that job. The men working below could be killed by falling rocks unless the debris was removed. Even pebbles could become deadly when falling from hundreds of feet up.

High scalers had to be agile climbers and unafraid of working at great heights. Many of them were former sailors or circus performers. Because their job was more risky, their pay was 40 percent higher than that of most other workers. High scalers had to maneuver around a network of ropes, air hoses, and electrical lines hanging around them. Often they worked above and below each other, so they had to protect themselves from falling rocks and dropped tools. Those who had hard hats wore them. Others improvised by dipping their soft hats in tar and letting it harden.

Section II
Objectives

Students should be able to

1. Describe the circumstances of FDR's election to the presidency.

2. Explain ways FDR obtained support for his New Deal programs.

3. List the major New Deal programs and their purposes.

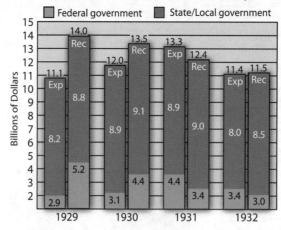

Government Expenditures and Receipts

- ☐ Federal government
- ■ State/Local government

Billions of Dollars

work. Those workers constructed public buildings. In 1931, construction was started on what became Hoover Dam on the Colorado River. The federal government under Hoover also subsidized the building of thousands of miles of roads.

In January 1932, Congress passed Hoover's bill creating the **Reconstruction Finance Corporation**. It loaned up to $2 billion to businesses, industries, and banks for projects to employ more men. That meant that there would be less need for direct relief. Congress also approved the president's request for twelve Federal District Home Loan Banks. Those banks could lend money to loan associations, banks, and insurance companies. In turn, they could aid homeowners who were having trouble making mortgage payments.

Despite his efforts, people continued to criticize Hoover. The steps he took were not dramatic enough to satisfy the many Americans who were still waiting for help. But the measures he took did cost money—money that the government did not have. His efforts to solve the country's woes paved the way for even greater deficit spending.

Section Quiz

1. What were four specific causes of the financial crisis?
2. What does it mean to "buy on margin"?
3. What were "Hoovervilles"?
4. What natural disaster hit farmers on the plains?
5. Why did the "Bonus Army" travel to Washington, D.C.?
☆ How did Herbert Hoover want to handle the nation's financial problems?
☆ What factors indicate that the Great Depression may have been a judgment for sin?

II. FDR and the New Deal

Discontent grew. Hoover began to expand government involvement in the economy in ways that no peacetime president had done before. But Hoover did not seem to be resolving the problem, and the voters were drawn to the optimistic promises of Franklin Delano Roosevelt.

The Election of 1932

The economy was the central issue in the election of 1932, one of the most pivotal campaigns in American history. The Republicans renominated Hoover. The Democrats chose New York governor **Franklin Delano Roosevelt**. Some Americans believed that the regular parties were not solving America's problems and turned to

---

Section Quiz Answers

1. industrial problems, overuse of credit, speculation, and international economic problems

2. to purchase stock by paying part of the price in cash and borrowing the rest from the stock broker, using the stock as collateral

3. areas of shacks that were the dwellings of the poor and homeless (named for Hoover, whom the people blamed for their problems)

4. the "Dust Bowl"

5. to seek early payment of a life insurance bonus that had been promised to veterans of World War I

☆ He preferred that local and volunteer organizations provide relief. Where he did intervene, it was to give money to businesses or state and local governments that could, in turn, create jobs and issue loans to the public.

☆ We know that God sometimes judges nations for their sins. The Great Depression was a national disaster following a decade of openly flaunted wickedness.

 CD: Party Platform Summaries, 1932

Refer to the CD for summaries of the major parties' platforms for the 1932 presidential election.

Activity 2: Hoover versus FDR

Use this activity to help the students understand the differences between the views and policies of Hoover and FDR.

The President's Polio

Stricken with polio in 1921 at the age of thirty-nine, Roosevelt was permanently paralyzed from the hips down. Such personal tragedies tend to make or break a person. Polio helped to make Franklin Delano Roosevelt a historic figure.

For Roosevelt every day was a tremendous struggle. He had to use metal braces just to stand. In order to minimize the effect of his disability on the public, Roosevelt refused to be seen in his wheelchair. He had to be helped to "walk" up to the podium to give his speeches. One time

the podium had not been fastened down, and it and the president went tumbling off the platform into the orchestra pit. Returning to the podium, Roosevelt simply picked up his speech right where he had left off. For traveling, he had a railroad car with a special elevator and a special wheelchair.

Roosevelt's condition also gave him a special burden for the similarly disabled. He was constantly visiting hospitals and working with disabled children or soldiers. He had a car designed with hand controls, and often

he would take a particularly discouraged child for a ride and talk. The child always returned with a positive attitude and a desire to go on. Roosevelt also invested heavily in a treatment center at Warm Springs, Georgia. The springs there had a therapeutic effect on those who used them.

Roosevelt's battle to overcome polio produced in him optimism and a persevering spirit that would enable him to lead the United States through one of its most challenging periods.

even more radical leaders. The Socialist Party nominated Norman Thomas. The Communists ran William Foster.

When the Democrats nominated Roosevelt at their convention, he broke with precedent and addressed the convention directly. In his acceptance speech he offered a "**New Deal**" for the American people without providing any details. Roosevelt promised to cut government spending by 25 percent. He also called on the government to attempt "bold, persistent experimentation." At this point no one knew what these experiments might be—not even Roosevelt himself.

No candidate ran harder than Hoover. He praised "rugged individualism" and encouraged industry and labor to take voluntary action to deal with their problems. But knowing that the people were demanding action, he also pledged more government involvement than ever before. By election day, millions of voters were convinced that Hoover's way had not worked. Roosevelt carried forty-two of the forty-eight states to become the new president. American government would never be the same. Roosevelt's presidency marked a shift from government non-interference and individual responsibility to a government-managed economy and the provision of state welfare.

There are four sources of the New Deal philosophy. One root was *populism*, which promoted farm relief and inflation (the increase in the money supply and an end to the gold standard). In this respect, one can see the influence of William Jennings Bryan.

A second root was *progressivism* as seen in the promotion of government regulation of business. The influence of Theodore Roosevelt and George Norris is seen there.

A third root was the *war mobilization* the country had in World War I. Roosevelt approached the economic crisis of the nation as one would a military foe. Business would be regimented under government control.

Finally, a fourth root was the idea of a *planned economy*. Roosevelt blamed the economic woes on free enterprise and proposed to fight the waste, greed, and inefficiency in that system by government planning.

Assassination Attempt

Shortly before Roosevelt's first inauguration, the president-elect traveled to Miami, Florida. On February 15, Roosevelt was riding through Bay Front Park in a parade. At one point, the car stopped, and Roosevelt sat up on the back seat to give a speech. At that moment, a man in the crowd named Giuseppe Zangara fired five shots from a .32-caliber pistol at Roosevelt. None of the five shots hit FDR because a woman next to Zangara, who was only five feet tall and was standing on a box, pushed him when she realized what he was doing.

The bullets hit four bystanders and the mayor of Chicago, Anton Cermak, who was riding with Roosevelt. Cermak died nearly three weeks later

Zangara was arrested, tried, convicted of murder, and sentenced to death. On March 21, he was executed.

Activity 3: Roosevelt's First Inaugural Address

Have the students read FDR's first inaugural address and answer the questions. Then discuss the speech and their answers to the questions. Emphasize FDR's themes and promises, showing how they were designed to calm the people's fears while foreshadowing the broad expansion of government powers.

The First Modern Politician

Discuss descriptions of President Roosevelt and how he set precedents for a "modern politician" who wins public favor by any means possible. He promised to cut spending while proposing costly programs,

promised vigorous action even when it was unconstitutional, developed a memorable theme—a New Deal, and sought to make the press his ally.

CD: Electoral College Results, 1932

Refer to the CD for a map showing the results of the Electoral College vote for the 1932 presidential election.

CD: Franklin D. Roosevelt, 32nd President

Refer to the CD for more information on Franklin Roosevelt.

Timeline of FDR's Life

Make a vertical timeline of the life of FDR with the dates going up the middle. On one side, place events from the president's personal life. On the other side, place national events that were occurring.

Fireside Chats

Shortly after taking office in March 1933, President Roosevelt addressed the nation in his first radio "fireside chat."

Roosevelt was adept at making his speeches seem very candid and spontaneous. He believed that if he was going to be reaching people in their living rooms, he should speak to them as a neighbor. He chose simple words and phrases, and he made sure that the talks were not too long.

Each fireside chat was carefully crafted. Roosevelt met with a team of professional speechwriters and dictated a rough draft of what he wanted. Then the team would set to work, refining the speech and returning it to the president. Some chats went through as many as twelve revisions before the president gave them. Even then, Roosevelt rarely read them word for word. He ad libbed phrases that came to him as he delivered the chats.

The term *fireside chat* was coined by CBS reporter Hally Butcher just before Roosevelt's second radio address. Other reporters soon began to use the term, and eventually so did Roosevelt.

By the time of his last address on January 6, 1945, Americans were familiar with the sound of Roosevelt's voice and his opening words: "My friends."

The WPA

Historian Clarence Carson wrote that the primary purpose of the Works Progress Administration was "to put people to work and provide them with incomes. The quality of the work, the skill of the workers, or the character of the project was secondary" (*The Welfare State: 1929–1985*, p. 73). This fact became evident to most people,

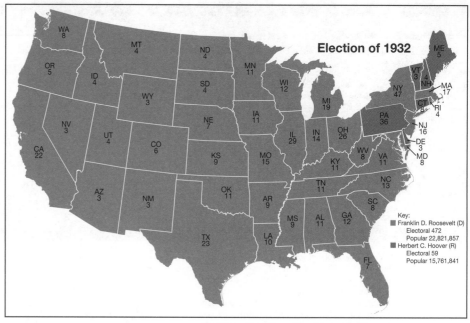

Election of 1932

Key:
- Franklin D. Roosevelt (D)
  Electoral 472
  Popular 22,821,857
- Herbert C. Hoover (R)
  Electoral 59
  Popular 15,761,841

Roosevelt's confidence was contagious, giving Americans hope in the midst of the Depression.

Putting the New Deal into Action

Franklin D. Roosevelt brought optimism to a depressed nation when he took office on March 4, 1933. With confidence he asserted, "This great nation will endure as it has endured, will revive and will prosper. . . . The only thing we have to fear is fear itself. . . . We do not distrust the future of essential democracy. The people of the United States have not failed. In their need they have registered a mandate that they want direct, vigorous action."

Roosevelt and his advisors, a **"brain trust"** of college professors (most from Columbia University), were ready to take that "vigorous action." The president began by proclaiming a **bank holiday**, closing banks temporarily to stabilize banking. Next he called Congress into special session to put his policies into effect. Then he went on the radio for the first of his many **"fireside chats"** to the nation. A good public speaker with an understanding of people, Roosevelt radiated warmth, even on the radio. He got the press on his side by calling numerous press conferences. As his allies, the media could sway public opinion to rally behind his ideas. Soon a long line of legislation set up programs that became FDR's New Deal.

Early New Deal Legislation

Congress, realizing that the American people wanted the action that Roosevelt promised, became his "rubber stamp." It approved almost anything the president proposed. In the first one hundred days, legislation for New Deal programs moved quickly through the Democratic-controlled Congress.

As soon as Congress met after Roosevelt's inauguration, it passed the Emergency Banking Act, which closed all banks temporarily. It

---

Dangers of National Debt

Discuss the Founding Fathers' differing opinions concerning the national debt (see Chapter 8). Focus on the opposition to carrying a national debt. Discuss whether it is ever fair for one generation to borrow from the next generation for its own benefit. (This, of course, would exclude the debt incurred from defensive wars.) In other words, is it right that teenagers today should have to pay interest on debts that previous generations accumulated in the spending spree from the 1960s through the 1990s?

Rule by the Wise Few

Ask the students to discuss how some of the Founding Fathers might have responded to Roosevelt's administration if they had been alive at the time. Note Jefferson's charges against George III and ask whether the same charges could have been made against Roosevelt: "He has erected a multitude of new offices, and sent hither swarms of officers to harass our people and eat out their substance." How might Roosevelt and his "Brain Trust" have defended themselves? *(Times have changed; the emergency calls for emergency measures.)* Note that this attitude is consistent with progressivism's acceptance of the "evolution" of society and government. Ask the students whether the Ameri-

can people of today would accept rule by a "Brain Trust" that proposed dozens of new laws to regulate life in America. *(The answer is surely no, and students need to recognize how shocking Roosevelt's power was.)*

Activity 4: FDR's Fireside Chat, March 12, 1933

Use this activity to help the students gain a greater appreciation for how FDR used his fireside chats to calm the people's fears, communicate his message of big government, and spur support for his New Deal measures.

gave the Treasury Department power to decide which banks were sound enough to reopen. Half of the banks, holding 90 percent of all banking resources, were back in operation by March 15. Only about one bank in twenty remained closed when the banks reopened three weeks later. Confidence returned, and people redeposited more than $1 billion.

In May 1933, Congress approved creation of the Federal Emergency Relief Administration (FERA). That temporary agency (later replaced by the Works Progress Administration, or WPA) had $500 million in federal money to disburse. The agency provided funds for the states to use for relief needs. The money was to be channeled into work relief so that the recipients would work for their pay. However, because the immediate need seemed so great, more of it went out as direct relief than as work relief.

Congress founded the Home Owners' Loan Corporation in June of 1933. That agency bought mortgages from holders and rewrote them on easier payment schedules. By 1936, one-fifth of all mortgaged nonfarm homes had mortgages under that agency. It was one of the most popular New Deal relief acts.

While the general public got relief through FERA and the Home Owners' Loan Corporation, special efforts were made to help farmers. The Farm Credit Administration (FCA) refinanced mortgages for farmers who would have lost their lands. The government also hoped to restore the farmers' purchasing power through the **Agriculture Adjustment Act** (AAA). To raise farm prices, farmers were asked to cut production. Rather than sell their products at a loss, the farmers were told to destroy crops. In 1933, they were asked to plow under between one-quarter and one-half of their crops. Milk was poured into ditches; grain was burned; cattle, sheep, and hogs were killed. Cotton and wool were stored in warehouses and held off the market until greater need would raise the prices.

Many farmers favored the act because they would be paid to co-operate with the plan. The act allowed the government to pay farmers for reducing production. The government also bought surplus crops that it planned to store and sell when prices were higher. Farm income did go up about 50 percent over the next two years.

Despite the AAA's immediate benefits for the farmers, it was soon attacked. When the policies forced farm prices up, consumers had to pay more for their goods. Many of these consumers were already hungry and in need of food. Destroying crops made little sense to hungry people. Moreover, the subsidies for not producing were given to landowners. But where sharecropping was used, the landowners were not the ones who actually farmed the land. The sharecropper who had labored on the land did not receive any benefits. In fact, he often lost money because he had to cut his production. Meanwhile, the landlord received all of the monetary gain.

In 1936, the Supreme Court declared the AAA unconstitutional. Nevertheless, a precedent had already been set. Many farmers became dependent on government subsidies. Farmers would soon regain those subsidies and agricultural regulation, and they would protect them. Conservatives have criticized such policies since they require tremendous taxpayer expense and artificially control the industry.

The **National Recovery Administration** (NRA) was designed to help businesses recover from the effects of the Depression. The goal was to eliminate "wasteful competition" among firms. Codes were

He Refused to Pour Out His Milk

G. B. Peterson not only operated a country store but also ran a dairy farm in Tennessee. When New Deal agriculture agents told local dairy farmers to pour out their milk rather than sell it at a loss, Peterson refused. He knew families in the community, many former customers at his store, who could not afford to feed their families. He took his surplus milk to them and gave it away. As a Christian, he believed it was better stewardship to give away his milk than to pour it in the ditch, which would benefit no one.

The Blue Eagle of the NRA was a short-lived symbol of Roosevelt's attempt at government interference in business competition.

and they came up with several meanings for "WPA," including "We Play Around," indicating a waste of time and resources.

The Blue Eagle

Part of Roosevelt's plan to "sell" the NRA to the American people was its easily recognizable symbol—the Blue Eagle. The presence of the NRA Blue Eagle in a shop window represented that business's compliance with NRA regulations. It was also stamped on items produced by NRA members.

But not everyone was convinced that the NRA was a good idea. Many people saw it as a way for businessmen to set artificial prices. Some people called the Blue Eagle a fascist symbol. Others called it the "Soviet duck."

The NRA finally died in 1935, when the Supreme Court ruled in the Schecter Poultry Corporation case (popularly known as the "sick chicken case") that the NRA was unconstitutional.

TVA's Test-Demonstration Farm Program

FDR wanted to use TVA to attack two problems in the South: soil erosion and poverty. His strategy was to encourage Southern farmers to use fertilizers, diversify their crops, and use new farming techniques (e.g., cover crops and crop rotation). To wage his war, he instructed TVA to introduce the test-demonstration farm program.

TVA worked with county extension agents of the region's land grant colleges to select local farmers who were willing to volunteer for the program. TVA produced experimental fertilizers (three times more concentrated than those commercially

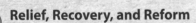

Relief, Recovery, and Reform

Explain the three phases of Roosevelt's program: relief, recovery, and reform. Draw a chart and ask the students to categorize each New Deal program under the appropriate heading. Note that the programs often had overlapping purposes. Discuss which programs met their immediate objectives (√), which were declared unconstitutional (X), and which still exist (*). Mark each with the appropriate symbol on the chart.

The names of all of the programs are not as important as the precedents they set. Students should be able to use these old programs as illustrations when they face debates

about modern-day programs such as Head Start, Social Security, and AmeriCorps.

available) at the World War I-era phosphate plant at Muscle Shoals, Alabama, and provided them to participating farmers at no charge. (Farmers paid only freight and handling charges.) In turn, the farmers agreed to run their farms by a plan developed by the county agent and approved by TVA. The farmers kept detailed records of crops planted, fertilizers used, and the results of each experiment. Then they allowed their farms to be "the schoolrooms of the Valley" as neighboring farmers watched and (hopefully) learned to use the new materials and techniques.

In the next fifteen years, fertilizer use in the Valley grew three times faster than anywhere else in the country. Soil erosion was reduced and soil was more fertile; more acreage was in production; and the soil yielded a greater variety, quantity, and quality of crops. Beef and dairy farming were introduced, and forest management and conservation had improved. TVA farms became places "to visit, to study, to emulate." Even many foreign heads of state visited the farms to learn how they could use the techniques in their own countries.

TVA's Immediate Impact

In the beginning, TVA probably had more of a negative than a positive impact on the people it was supposed to be helping. For example, 15,654 people were forced from their farms and lands when TVA built dams and flooded the valleys behind them. About 2,500 bodies were exhumed and reburied to make way for Norris Lake alone. As for electricity production, the first six dams built were relatively small (ranging from 100 MW to 356 MW generating capacity) compared with those in other non-TVA areas (e.g., Bonneville Dam in Oregon had a generating capacity of

The Cees Get Passing Grades

They planted over 2 billion trees and spent 6.5 million man-hours fighting forest fires. They built over 420,000 dams, fixed up old parks and built new ones, and built or improved miles of trails and access roads. They made thirty dollars a week, twenty-five of which was sent home to help support their families. "They" were the Cees, the young men who worked for the Civilian Conservation Corps.

More than 2.5 million jobless youths were hired by the Civilian Conservation Corps. The CCC was the most popular New Deal program; even the Republicans praised it. It was the first relief agency to go into action. Some have called the Cees "The Tree Army" or "The Soil Soldiers." The program lasted from 1933 until World War II, when most of the young men were called into the armed forces.

The camps for the Cees were directed by army officers. Extracurricular activities were usually oriented toward sports, particularly boxing. Rising time was 5:45 a.m., and taps was at 10:00 p.m. The food had the flavor of army meals, with lots of potatoes and bologna. For most of the men, the time spent in the Cees was rewarding, and for some it was character building. Hard outdoor work kept them busy. The conservation emphasis gave meaning to their efforts. The money sent home to help their families gave them a purpose. It is easy to see why the Civilian Conservation Corps received the most praise of any of Roosevelt's programs.

The CCC workers planted trees, fought fires, worked to prevent erosion, and performed other tasks to help conserve the country's natural resources.

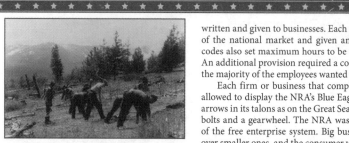

Norris Dam was the first dam completed in the TVA system.

written and given to businesses. Each company was assigned a share of the national market and given annual production quotas. The codes also set maximum hours to be worked and minimum wages. An additional provision required a company to recognize a union if the majority of the employees wanted to form one.

Each firm or business that complied with the NRA codes was allowed to display the NRA's Blue Eagle seal. Rather than clutching arrows in its talons as on the Great Seal, this eagle clutched lightning bolts and a gearwheel. The NRA was soon criticized as a violation of the free enterprise system. Big businesses seemed to be favored over smaller ones, and the consumer was caught in the middle when prices went up. The Supreme Court declared the NRA unconstitutional in 1935.

Another law established the **Civilian Conservation Corps**, which gave jobs to unemployed young men. At the same time, it conserved natural resources. In the seven years of its existence, the CCC employed 2.5 million young men.

In May 1933, Congress also established a permanent New Deal agency with long-range goals. The **Tennessee Valley Authority** (TVA) involved seven southeastern states. It was to provide public power projects on the Tennessee River. It built thirty multipurpose dams to produce and sell electricity, control flooding and erosion, and provide navigable waterways. It also manufactured fertilizer and created recreation areas. Because it involved the federal government in areas where it had never been involved before and put the government in direct competition with private companies, TVA was controversial.

Further Action

Americans were generally pleased that the new president was taking firm action to deal with the Depression. If one measure

Red Flag: TVA

Ask the students why TVA was considered controversial. *(The TVA was a socialistic program. It displaced people and flooded their homes and farms. The TVA put government in the position of competing unfairly with private utilities.)* Discuss the alternatives to government-run utilities. Note that several conservatives in the past called for the privatization of TVA.

🖥 More on TVA

For additional information on the story of the Tennessee Valley Authority, you might want to examine the following resources:

Gordon R. Clapp, *The TVA: An Approach to the Development of a Region.*

Marguerite Owen, *The Tennessee Valley Authority*

David Lilienthal, *TVA: Democracy on the March*

Edwin Hargrove and Paul Conkin, eds. *TVA: Fifty Years of Grass-Roots Bureaucracy*

did not work, Roosevelt quickly tried another one. The actions, however, were not bringing a real economic recovery to the nation, and millions of people were still in need. Roosevelt continued to experiment with new programs that he hoped would solve some of the problems. In 1935, he launched the Works Progress Administration (WPA). That agency put more people to work on construction projects. WPA workers built hospitals, schools, parks, playgrounds, and airports.

Eventually, FDR extended the WPA into other areas, including the arts. Actors, actresses, and directors were employed to put on programs. Authors were hired under the Federal Writers' Project to write historical and geographical guides for the forty-eight states. Artists were hired under a Federal Art Project. They painted murals in public buildings such as post offices. The National Youth Administration (NYA) helped young people. High-school and college students were hired for part-time jobs that enabled them to stay in school. Together, the WPA and NYA provided jobs for almost five million Americans. The WPA was not without its critics, who claimed it was a needless make-work program for loafers.

Up to this point, FDR and his advisors thought the economic problem was overproduction. This meant the attempts to combat the Depression were focused on regulations designed to limit production and the formation of government agencies to create jobs. However, the direction of the New Deal would change in 1935.

Section Quiz

1. Who were the presidential candidates in 1932?
2. What New Deal provisions were made for the nation's farmers?
3. How did the Works Progress Administration and the National Youth Administration provide relief for Americans?
☆ During this crisis Americans moved away from individualism to a welfare state. Was this a good thing? Why or why not?

III. The New Deal Faces Opposition

Although Roosevelt won the presidency with a large popular vote, many people opposed him. Conservatives opposed FDR's programs. Under Roosevelt's New Deal, the government exercised control in areas once reserved for private interests. Conservatives distrusted such governmental control and feared government intrusion into other areas. Under the New Deal, federal officials assumed wide powers over industry and commerce. These were areas that conservatives believed were outside of government's rightful sphere. Roosevelt's agencies were replacing the free enterprise of capitalism with the government regulations associated with socialism. In fact, the federal powers instated during the crisis of the Depression would not be reduced in the decades to come.

Liberals and leftists also opposed FDR because they did not think that his New Deal policies went far enough. They believed that the New Deal needed to be more socialistic, with the government owning certain industries or providing people with an income. Some critics suggested radical plans to redistribute wealth and won many supporters. One such critic was Dr. **Elmer Townsend**, a retired

WPA workers constructed many facilities for city governments, airports, hospitals, roads, and other public areas.

New Deal "Alphabet Agencies"

AAA	Agriculture Adjustment Act
CCC	Civilian Conservation Corps
CWA	Civil Works Administration
FCA	Farm Credit Administration
FERA	Federal Emergency Relief Administration
FHA	Federal Housing Administration
FSA	Farm Security Administration
HOLC	Home Owners' Loan Corporation
NRA	National Recovery Administration
NYA	National Youth Administration
PWA	Public Works Administration
REA	Rural Electrification Administration
SSA	Social Security Administration
TVA	Tennessee Valley Authority
WPA	Works Progress Administration

5,295 MW). The numerous construction projects did provide employment for several thousand people; otherwise, TVA had little immediate positive impact. Historian Jim Powell concluded, "To the degree the TVA had any impact at all, it appeared to be negative. . . . [I]n the half century after the TVA was launched, *economic growth in bordering states, where people didn't get their electricity from the TVA, equaled or surpassed growth within the Tennessee Valley*" (emphasis in original, *FDR's Folly*, pp. 148–49).

Section III
Objectives

Students should be able to

1. Explain why the New Deal met opposition and the major sources of such opposition.
2. Describe the conditions of the election of 1936.
3. Explain FDR's court-packing plan and its significance.

Eleanor Roosevelt

Only two Roosevelts have held the office of president, but a third one also played an important role in the public arena. Eleanor Roosevelt, FDR's wife, made a major contribution to her husband's longevity in the White House. She traveled across the United States promoting the New Deal. In 1933 alone she covered forty thousand miles touting her husband's programs.

Section Quiz Answers

1. Herbert Hoover (Republican), Franklin Delano Roosevelt (Democrat), Norman Thomas (Socialist), and William Foster (Communist)
2. The Farm Credit Administration refinanced farmers' mortgages to help them keep their farms, and the Agriculture Adjustment Act tried to control farm production to raise prices.
3. by providing them with jobs
☆ In favor of government welfare: The government is the one organization that has the ability to produce a lot of aid quickly. During this time it seemed that other organizations that had pre-

viously provided aid were not able to meet the demands of this depression. In favor of individualism: Government programs are often inefficient. Government economic planners are often unable to predict or control the economy. Government involvement crowds out business solutions that might be more effective. Government involvement is difficult to contain once it has begun.

🖥 Voices of Dissent

An excellent coverage of the major opponents of FDR's New Deal, with special emphasis on the fringe movements as opposed to the traditional Republican opposi-

tion, is Brinkley's book *Voices of Dissent*. He devotes much attention to Huey Long, Charles Coughlin, and Elmer Townsend.

Activity 5: Huey Long's Plan to "Share the Wealth"

Use this activity to help the students better understand some of the opposition to FDR's New Deal.

Huey Long

Historian Amity Shlaes referred to Louisana's senator and former governor Huey Long as "perhaps the greatest single political threat to Roosevelt's political coalition" (*The Forgotten Man*, p. 256).

Jesse Owens: 1936 Olympics

In May 1931, the International Olympic Committee awarded the right to host the 1936 summer Olympics to Germany. The United States and several other nations considered boycotting the games because of Nazi Germany's racial practices and belief in the superiority of the Aryan race. German citizens who were Jewish or members of other minorities were unable to participate in the games. In the years leading up to the games, the German sports program focused on demonstrating the superiority of the Aryan race.

While several American Jews did boycott the games, the United States sent an official team. Among the members was a black athlete named Jesse Owens. Owens and several other athletes excelled, delivering a strong blow to the Nazi beliefs. Owens captured four gold medals, a feat that would not be matched until 1984 by Carl Lewis. Besides winning the 100-meter, 200-meter, and 4x100 relay, Owens set an Olympic record in his long jump victory.

A story has persisted that Hitler refused to congratulate Owens on his victories and instead left the stadium. However, some historians have concluded that the insult was probably unintentional.

The *Hindenburg*

With a length of 803.8 feet and a diameter of 135.1 feet, the *Hindenburg* was one of the largest aircraft ever built. Inside her

One of FDR's most formidable opponents was Huey Long, a populist who ran the government of Louisiana as if it were his own kingdom.

Father Charles Coughlin blended his Catholic religious views with his liberal social and political views in his radio sermons.

SOCIAL SECURITY

000 - 00 - 0000

THIS NUMBER HAS BEEN ESTABLISHED FOR

JOHN DOE

Perhaps the most famous legacy of Roosevelt's New Deal was the Social Security system, the expenses of which represent 26 percent of the U.S. federal budget. More money is spent on Social Security today than on national defense.

California medical doctor who designed a plan to help the elderly. His plan required the government to pay each person over sixty years old a $200-a-month pension. The money for the pensions would come from a national sales tax. To receive pensions, retirees had to agree to spend every cent each month. He thought such spending would pump up the economy.

Another opponent was **Huey Long**, a masterful politician (some people said he was a virtual dictator) from Louisiana. He called himself the "Kingfish." He was easily recognized by his white suits, pastel shirts, flamboyant ties, and popular oratory.

As governor of Louisiana, Long built thousands of miles of paved roads. He also provided textbooks for children and pumped life into "his" school, Louisiana State University. Long wanted to confiscate wealth and tax large incomes heavily. He intended to use this money to provide a minimum income of $2,500 for every American. Long promised to make "every man a king" with his "Share the Wealth" plan and exercised total control over the political machine in Louisiana.

Originally a supporter of FDR, Long became an outspoken critic after being elected to the U.S. Senate. He was eager to be president and had written a book titled *My First Days in the White House*. He was assassinated before he got the chance to run.

Another FDR critic with a plan was popular speaker Father **Charles Coughlin** (COG lin). A Detroit priest, he had a nationwide radio broadcast. He suggested inflation, government takeover of certain industries, and a guaranteed living wage for laborers. He also wanted to overhaul the currency system and abolish the Federal Reserve System for regulating the nation's banks.

None of FDR's New Deal programs were as radical as those proposed by Townsend, Long, and Coughlin. The rise of these critics pushed Roosevelt further to the left as he tried to counter his critics' plans. One of Roosevelt's proposals was a government-sponsored insurance plan. Old-age insurance, today called **Social Security**, was only a part of the program. It offered smaller monthly pensions by giving federal aid to the states for the elderly as well as funds for unemployment insurance, aid to dependent children, and public health programs. (Today, the Social Security plan includes Medicare and Medicaid.) It was all to be financed by a federal tax on wages. The employer paid half and the employee paid half.

Roosevelt pushed through Congress the National Labor Relations Act of 1935 (also called the **Wagner Act**). It saved some of the benefits given to labor in the unconstitutional NRA. The NLRA encouraged the growth of labor unions. The largest labor union, the American Federation of Labor (AFL), faced competition from the Congress of Industrial Organizations (CIO). Formed in 1935, the CIO boasted a membership of 3.7 million within two years.

Other regulations intended to help workers came with the Fair Labor Standards Act in 1938. This act established the nation's first legal minimum wage and maximum hours for workers producing goods that crossed state lines. The wage was twenty-five cents per hour, and the workweek was to be forty-four hours. The act also prohibited children under sixteen from working in most industries.

Unions and Freedom of Assembly

The Constitution guarantees freedom of assembly to groups such as labor unions. So why was the National Recovery Administration (NRA) declared unconstitutional, and why did conservatives oppose the Wagner (Labor Relations) Act? The Constitution allows people to join organizations, but it does not allow the federal government to grant special privileges to select organizations. Such favoritism limits the freedom of individuals and the freedom of opposing organizations. If a businessman or laborer dislikes a labor union, he should be free to speak out against it and to cut off all relations with it. Roosevelt's labor laws violated the freedom of businessmen to run their businesses as

they chose. Many conservatives have argued that labor unions should be free to form, but they must earn political clout by attracting voluntary supporters.

Viewpoints on the New Deal

Divide the class into groups representing various perspectives on the New Deal—poor farmers, poor labor, middle class workers, and business owners. Choose one student to represent each of the main nominees for president in 1936. Have each candidate come up with a theme for his campaign and list three main reasons he should be elected (or his opponent rejected). If the candidates

are wise, they will seek reasons that appeal to a majority of voters. Then read each reason and have the different groups vote on whether they would support it. Students should see the difficulty that the Republican nominee faced.

Checks and Balances at Work

Ask the students to explain how the Founding Fathers' system of checks and balances worked during the economic crisis of the 1930s. While the nations in Europe were wracked by political turmoil and rising fascism, Roosevelt was unable to assume dictatorial powers. Congress, although controlled by FDR's own party, refused to go along with his court-packing plan. The courts limited

The Election of 1936

Roosevelt faced considerable opposition in 1936. A group called the American Liberty League sought to block the president's renomination. The Democrats, however, chose Roosevelt on the first ballot. The party platform praised the New Deal and promised additional similar reforms.

Roosevelt's first term transformed the Democratic Party. Many of Roosevelt's policies brought new groups of voters to the Democrats. Until 1935, he had urged businesses, farmers, bankers, and workers to settle conflicts among themselves. After that point Roosevelt endorsed the creation of the National Labor Relations Board. This provided government support for unions to bargain, strike, and boycott in order to gain concessions from employers. Roosevelt's endorsement of these measures resulted in union member support for the Democratic Party.

The Depression hit the poor especially hard. Many poor people were very grateful for the New Deal's financial relief and believed that Roosevelt's programs had saved them from starvation. These people tended to vote Democratic from then on.

Roosevelt's presidency also marked the movement of African Americans from the party of Lincoln to the Democrats. The New Deal was of special importance to blacks. The public works projects offered blacks jobs at the same wages as whites. Though they were not allowed to work with whites and though Roosevelt refused to support civil rights legislation, African Americans believed he was moving things in the right direction for them. Furthermore, Eleanor Roosevelt was an outspoken defender of black rights. In the election of 1936, 75 percent of African Americans voted for Roosevelt. This same percentage had voted for Hoover in the previous election.

The Republicans had lost heavily in the congressional elections in both 1932 and 1934. They lacked a leader and a program to attract voters, so a 1936 win was also unlikely. They ran Alfred M. Landon, who had been a progressive governor in Kansas. Using the phrase "America Is in Peril," the Republicans criticized the New Deal for its overthrow of traditional ways and for betraying its promises to the people.

Although Landon campaigned hard, he carried only two states, Maine and Vermont. Roosevelt beat him by more than eleven million votes. The Congress elected in 1936 was also heavily Democratic.

Alfred M. Landon
KansasMemory.org, Kansas State Historical Society

History of Federal Minimum Wage

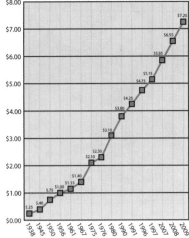

DON'T CRUSH THEM!

Conservative voices of protest against FDR's measures were all but drowned out by the New Deal's popular appeal.

---

metal frame were sixteen gas cells able to hold more than seven million cubic feet of hydrogen. At a top speed of eighty-four miles per hour, the *Hindenburg* could make the trip from Friedrichshafen, Germany, to Lakehurst, N.J., in just a few days.

Passengers aboard the airship traveled in relative comfort. Although the cabins were small and spartan, the passengers spent most of their time in the ship's other rooms. For example, the ship had a fifty-person dining room, a reading-and-writing room, a smoking room, a lounge with a baby grand piano, and a promenade from which passengers could view the earth below.

The *Hindenburg* made ten trips to Lakehurst in 1936. However, during its flight on May 6, 1937, something went terribly wrong. The ship was two hundred feet from the ground and beginning its final descent when flames appeared near the tail. Within seconds, the flames spread over the whole ship, and the *Hindenburg* crashed tail first to the ground. Of the ninety-seven people aboard, thirteen passengers and twenty-two crewmen died. One ground crew member was also killed.

"War of the Worlds"

On October 30, 1938, the Columbia Broadcasting System (CBS) succeeded beyond their wildest expectations in getting listeners' attention. That Sunday evening, the station broadcasted a radio drama titled "War of the Worlds" based on a science fiction novel by H. G. Wells. Orson Welles (no relation to the author) and his team of actors performed a dramatization of an alien invasion of earth. The program began as a fictional musical variety show. It was interrupted at intervals by fictional newscasts with breaking news of the

---

the worst programs of the New Deal. But in response to Roosevelt's threat, the Supreme Court softened its conservatism. (Also, soon after FDR unveiled his court-packing plan, several justices retired, which allowed Roosevelt to replace them with progressive judges and gain a progressive majority on the bench.)

Activity 6: Graphing Negative Numbers

Use this activity to expose students to line and bar graphs with negative numbers and to help the students visualize FDR's deficit spending and the recession of 1937.

Activity 7: Interpreting Political Cartoons of the New Deal Era

Use this activity to help students understand the use of political cartoons to express disagreement with and opposition to FDR's New Deal measures, especially his "court-packing" scheme.

 CD: Electoral College Results, 1936

Refer to the CD for a map showing the results of the Electoral College vote for the 1936 presidential election.

 CD: FDR's Court-Packing Scheme

Refer to the CD for a political cartoon drawn during the New Deal opposing FDR's court-packing scheme.

aliens' landing around New Jersey and attacking people.

At the beginning and throughout the show, the announcer issued notices to clarify that the show was merely a radio drama. However, many people believed the "news" rather than the disclaimers—and panicked.

The incident showed the power of the media to convince people.

Section IV

Objectives

Students should be able to

1. List and explain the major consequences of the New Deal.

2. Explain how the consequences of the New Deal are still evident in American government and society today.

New Deal in Context

If one judges the New Deal in its contemporary context—i.e., in contrast to the dictatorships in Europe at the time: fascist Italy, Nazi Germany, and communist Soviet Union—the New Deal socialism seems rather mild. In light of the dire situation in the United States—25 percent unemployment and the collapse of the banking system—for the government to do nothing was probably not wise. In fact, FDR warned that America might succumb to European-style extremists if Congress did not enact his measures. Even Hoover, a staunch capitalist, had initiated some government efforts to solve the problems. In contrast to previous U.S. history and a strict interpretation of the Constitution, such actions were radical, though not as radical as the actions of European countries. Americans can be thankful that a

FDR's court-packing proposal was sparked by his fear that the Supreme Court was becoming a threat to his New Deal.

Conservatives claimed that the New Deal was not solving the economic problems but merely prolonging them, and the economic slump in the late 1930s seemed to prove their point.

Declining Popularity of the New Deal

Roosevelt's strong win and congressional support encouraged him to challenge the makeup of the Supreme Court. Because it had struck down several New Deal measures, FDR became more critical of the court's conservative nature.

In February 1937, he presented a plan to "pack" the Supreme Court with new justices. He hoped that adding to the number of justices would protect his New Deal measures. Roosevelt requested that the number of justices be increased from nine to as many as fifteen. Each time a justice reached seventy and did not retire, FDR wanted to appoint a new justice. This court-packing plan would have allowed him to add justices who would support his programs.

For the first time, Congress defeated a Roosevelt request. They saw his action as a serious threat to the balance of power among the branches of government. Increasing the court's size in this way would have limited the independence of the judicial branch by giving the president more power to control it.

The New Deal had reached high tide in 1936. In 1937, it ebbed. A **recession** (a slump in business that is considered less serious than a full depression) hit. The decline between September 1937 and June 1938 was one of the worst in American economic history. The stock market dipped and industrial production declined. In early 1937, federal spending had dropped off. That spending reduction cut both personal incomes and the purchasing power that had been artificially sustaining industry's production.

In the second phase of the New Deal, Roosevelt used government spending to get the economy started up, even though it meant going into debt. When the government reduced its spending after four years, the pumped-up economy could not stand on its own. It was becoming evident that the New Deal measures had only covered the problems; they had not brought the United States recovery.

Section Quiz

1. What did old-age insurance come to be called?

2. What groups of voters did the Democratic Party begin to attract in 1935?

3. What Republican candidate ran against Franklin Roosevelt in the 1936 election?

4. Why did Roosevelt want to increase the number of Supreme Court justices?

★ Why could Roosevelt's opponents say that his program for Social Security was a matter of "buying" votes?

IV. Consequences of the New Deal

In 1939, after six years of Roosevelt programs, the United States had not really recovered from the Depression. Prices for farm products were still low. Overall manufacturing production and corporate profits lagged far behind 1929 levels. The stock market had still not reached pre-Depression levels. And nine million Americans were still unemployed.

Because of its high spending, the New Deal had left the country with a record debt. The national debt in 1933 was $2.6 billion. In

---

🎙 Old Time Radio

Obtain one or more recordings of original broadcasts of radio programming during the 1930s. You could include examples from various genres (humor, melodrama, Western, etc.) and even advertisements. Of special interest would be Orson Welles's "War of the Worlds," which you might play (or at least excerpts) to demonstrate the power of radio during that time period.

Section Quiz Answers

1. Social Security

2. the poor, underprivileged, blacks, urban immigrants, workers, and reforming liberals

3. Alf Landon

4. so that he could add justices who would vote to uphold his programs

★ Once the government began such a program, the beneficiaries of the program would view its benefits as a right (entitlement). Thereafter, it would be almost impossible for any candidate who even hinted at reducing or eliminating those benefits to get elected. Any candidate who defended the program would be guaranteed the votes of the beneficiaries or future beneficiaries.

🖥 Teacher Resources

A good source for exposing the problems of FDR's New Deal is Jim Powell's *FDR's Folly: How Roosevelt and his New Deal Prolonged the Great Depression.* Another good source is *The Forgotten Man: A New History of the Great Depression* by Amity Shlaes.

Precedents of the New Deal

Ask the students to list all of the precedents of the 1930s (during both Hoover's and FDR's administrations). Answers will include the expansion of government power over national currency, the end of the gold standard, growth of federal spending, deficit spending and the resulting record debt, increased executive power, increased size

1939, it was $6.5 billion. Excessive spending and unbalanced budgets continued.

The New Deal also brought long-term changes. The government, especially the executive branch, had greatly increased its power. Under Roosevelt, both the size and the scale of the federal government had been greatly increased. The country shifted from an emphasis on individual responsibility and local initiative to meet challenges to an emphasis on government involvement and aid. This shift in emphasis moved the nation away from the volunteerism that characterized the nineteenth century to the welfare state that characterizes the nation today.

Private businesses remained the mainstay of economic activity. However, government had now assumed a major role in providing for individual and national economic welfare. Government had provided special help to farmers and industrial workers. Others would now appeal to the government for aid when future crises occurred.

Positively, the New Deal did improve conditions. Business profits and farm prices were up; unemployment was down from its 1933 high of 24 percent. Annual per capita income had gone up from $678 in 1933 to $925 in 1939. Electricity had been extended to many rural areas, and other public works had improved buildings and parks and encouraged conservation. These benefits, however, had come at an immense price—the growth of federal power and spending.

Roosevelt's money policies had a great effect in the following years. He had taken the United States off the gold standard in 1933. Paper money and coins were no longer convertible into gold coins. This did little to aid the economy at the time. However, it gave the government more power to control the amount of money in the economy and to attempt to minimize future economic downturns.

Perhaps the key positive thing that the New Deal had achieved was the restoration of people's faith and confidence in America. Roosevelt, despite the failures of many of his programs, had offered hope for people who were in a panic. People trusted him to do something about their problems.

Though conservatives have bemoaned the changes brought about during Roosevelt's presidency, Americans continued to enjoy a free nation run by elected officials. In many countries the Depression led to the replacement of democratic governments by dictators. In Europe, the rise of these dictators led to World War II.

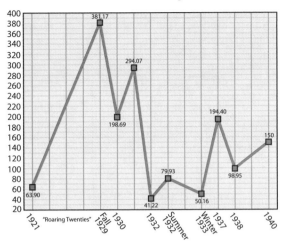

Dow Jones Industrial Average (1920–1940)

The DJIA index shows that the stock market did not reach pre-Depression levels under the New Deal.

Section Quiz

1. What positive things did the New Deal accomplish?
2. What evidence existed that the New Deal had not solved the nation's problems even in 1939?
★ Why did people want to trust the government for assistance?

demagogue like Hitler or Mussolini did not rise to power during the Depression.

Short-Term Consequences

The following actions by the New Deal had short-term consequences on the United States:

1. Broke up the strongest banks and centralized the monetary policy in the Federal Reserve System.
2. Outlawed private ownership of gold.
3. Tripled taxes; people had less money to spend.
4. Spent tax money on relief and public works programs that did not benefit the poorest people.
5. Passed securities laws that did not help investors do better.
6. Increased the cost of practically everything.
7. Destroyed food when people were going hungry.
8. Contributed to higher unemployment.
9. Disrupted large businesses that could have hired thousands.
10. Subverted individual liberties.

Long-Term Consequences

Long-term consequences of the New Deal include the following.

1. *Leftist economic policies*—FDR initiated liberal economic policies that subsequent presidents have continued to use to varying degrees to redistribute personal income.
2. *Federally insured banking*—Federally insured bank deposits tend to give a false sense of security and to reduce any incentive to keep a close eye on

and scope of the federal government, help to farmers and industrial workers, and belief that the public is entitled to government aid during a crisis. Students should see that these precedents continue to affect us today.

 New Deal Consequences
Visit www.bjupress.com/resources for possible links to articles evaluating various aspects of the New Deal.

CD: Electoral Results, 1940
Refer to the CD for a map showing the results of the 1940 presidential election.

CD: Depression and New Deal Statistics
Refer to the CD for several interesting charts and graphs showing Depression and New Deal Statistics.

Activity 8: Chapter Review
Use this activity to help the students prepare for the chapter test.

Section Quiz Answers

1. restored people's faith and confidence in America and its economy; provided jobs for many unemployed people
2. Prices for farm products were still low. Manufacturing production and corporate profits lagged far behind 1929 levels. The stock market had not reached pre-Depression levels. And nine million Americans were still unemployed.
★ The American public got used to having the things the government was giving them and came to expect them as their right. In times of crisis in the future, Americans expected the government to take care of them; they had lost their sense of individual responsibility.

what bankers are doing with one's money.

3. *Knee-jerk reactions to periodic inflation and unemployment*—Rather than allowing the normal business cycle to resolve overexpansion naturally, the government has persisted in interfering, thereby making the problems even greater.

4. *Blindness to problems inherent in the Social Security System*—The earliest beneficiaries got a windfall. The reverse has become increasingly true over the years. The system will soon be bankrupt, but politicians continue to ignore the problem.

5. *Farm subsidies and restrictions*—Such programs still operate today. Average payments to farmers exceed $46,000.

6. *Continued problems for the Tennessee Valley Authority*—These problems include debt, no payment of taxes, exemption from some federal laws, and lack of compensation.

Concluding Thoughts about the Great Depression

Historian Jim Powell wrote, "The Great Depression was a government failure, brought on principally by Federal Reserve policies that abruptly cut the money supply; unit banking laws that made thousands of banks more vulnerable to failure; Hoover's tariffs, which throttled trade; Hoover's taxes, which took unprecedented amounts of money out of people's pockets at the worst possible time; and Hoover's other policies, which made it more difficult for the economy to recover" (FDR's Folly, p. 267). The New Deal merely prolonged and deepened the Depression.

People, Places, and Things to Remember:

stock market crash
Great Depression
buy on margin
"Dust Bowl"
dole
Reconstruction Finance Corporation
Franklin Delano Roosevelt
"New Deal"
"brain trust"
bank holiday
"fireside chats"
Agriculture Adjustment Act
National Recovery Administration
Civilian Conservation Corps
Tennessee Valley Authority
Elmer Townsend
Huey Long
Charles Coughlin
Social Security
Wagner Act
recession

Chapter Review

Review Questions

Define each of the following terms.

1. "Dust Bowl"
2. buying stock on margin
3. dole
4. bank holiday
5. recession

Match each of the following terms with its description.

6. Great Depression
7. Social Security
8. New Deal
9. brain trust
10. Reconstruction Finance Corporation

a. Roosevelt's group of advisors
b. Hoover's aid program
c. "old-age insurance"
d. the 1930s
e. Roosevelt's attempt to bring the nation relief and recovery

What were the full names of the New Deal programs listed below, and what did each one do?

11. AAA
12. NRA
13. CCC
14. TVA

Critical Thinking

1. Is the Social Security program, established during the New Deal, a benefit to the nation? Explain your answer.
2. How did the Depression change Americans?

Chapter Review Answers

Review Questions

1. drought-stricken area of the Plains during the Depression
2. paying part of the price with cash and borrowing the rest using the stock as collateral
3. a handout
4. closing banks temporarily to stabilize the banking system
5. a slump in national business activity; less severe than a full depression
6. d
7. c

8. e
9. a
10. b
11. Agriculture Adjustment Act—asked farmers to cut production to raise prices
12. National Recovery Administration—tried to eliminate "wasteful competition" by regulating businesses
13. Civilian Conservation Corps—hired young men for public works projects such as fighting forest fires, planting trees, and preserving natural habitats
14. Tennessee Valley Authority—power production, flood control, and main-taining navigable waterways in the Tennessee Valley

Critical Thinking

1. Answers will vary. Some students might tout the care of senior citizens and dependents. Others might point out the loss of individual responsibility to save for personal needs, uncontrolled growth of benefits, and the increase in those receiving benefits while the number of tax-paying workers declines.

2. Answers will vary but might include the facts that it destroyed optimism and confidence in the American economy and made them more dependent on government.

Joe Rosenthal's photo of five Marines and a Navy corpsman raising the American flag on Iwo Jima became one of the most recognizable photos of World War II.

CHAPTER 24

World War II

I. **Storm Clouds Gather**

II. **War Erupts**

III. **America Enters the War and Turns the Tide**

IV. **America Wins in the Pacific**

Chapter Goals

Students should be able to

1. Identify the causes and events that led to the outbreak of World War II.

2. Identify major battles and officers in World War II and cite the significance of each.

3. Summarize the course of the war.

4. Define and use the basic terms of the chapter.

Chapter Motivation

At the beginning of class, ask the students how World War II was different from all other wars that they have studied in this course. Challenge the students to look for information and viewpoints in the chapter that they have never known before.

Popularity of World War II Studies

More books have been written about this period of American history than perhaps any other period, except the War Between the States. Numerous magazines and journals are also devoted to its coverage.

Chapter 24 Lesson Plan Chart			
Section Title	**Main Activity**	**Pages**	**Days**
I. Storm Clouds Gather	Activity 1: Prelude to World War II	450–52	1 day
II. War Erupts	Activity 2: The War Begins: Chronological Order	452–56	2 days
III. America Enters the War and Turns the Tide	Activity 4: Life for a Japanese-American Internee	456–62	2–3 days
IV. America Wins in the Pacific	Activity 8: A Marine's Journal from Guadalcanal	463–68	2–3 days
TOTAL SUGGESTED DAYS (INCLUDING 1 DAY FOR REVIEW AND TESTING)			8–10 DAYS

MATERIALS LIST

SECTION I
- Episodes from the *Why We Fight* or *Victory at Sea* video series
- Activity 1 from the *Student Activities* manual

SECTION II
- CD: The Warplanes (specifically the German planes)
- Activity 2 from the *Student Activities* manual

SECTION III
- December 1991 issue of *National Geographic*

Section I
Objectives

Students should be able to

1. Describe the rise of dangerous leaders and parties in Germany, Italy, and Japan.
2. Name the Latin American foreign policy of the United States in the 1930s.

Fascism

Hitler and Mussolini introduced fascist governments to their countries. However, fascism was not new. Earlier societies and philosophers had promoted the state over the individual. In ancient Sparta, men were taken at an early age and placed in military training schools. Individuals had greater loyalty to the city-state than to their families. In the nineteenth century, the German philosopher Hegel argued that a person was important only as part of the state, not as an individual. Another nineteenth-century philosopher, Nietzsche, promoted fascism through his belief that man could become perfect by forcibly exerting his will.

Facism succeeded in Germany and Italy for a number of reasons. In both countries, charismatic leaders inspired the people and used propaganda to promote fascism. The depressed economic conditions in both countries made the people more willing to accept change. And in the case of Germany, the harsh conditions set by the Treaty of Versailles after World War I caused people to blame others for their problems.

Essentially, fascism exerted strong central control over all economic activity of the country. The government did not actually own businesses or industries—private ownership continued—but it told owners

Benito Mussolini forced fascism on the people of Italy and tried to revive the glory of the country by establishing an empire.

Japan invaded Manchuria in 1931 and then the main part of China in 1937.

As Americans struggled to overcome the problems of the Great Depression, they also watched some troubling events overseas. Many Europeans, suffering from the Depression and great political turmoil, were dissatisfied with economic conditions. They seemed willing to surrender freedoms to dictators who promised to solve the problems. Japan and the United States disagreed increasingly over trade issues. The role of China in their trade was an especially thorny topic. Events in both Europe and Asia soon reached the boiling point. Once again, the world faced war.

I. Storm Clouds Gather

Although Americans fighting in World War I had believed that they were fighting a "war to end all wars," in less than twenty-five years Americans were back on the battlefields of not only Europe but also Asia. Many conditions led to the conflict. The troubles had begun almost before the guns of World War I had cooled.

Not everyone was pleased with the outcome of World War I. The peace settlements had satisfied only a few of the participants. Most countries did not get all they wanted from victory or lost too much in defeat. Some of this dissatisfaction led to the rise of three strong imperialist countries in the 1930s—Italy, Japan, and Germany.

Italian Fascism

Italy was disappointed after World War I. It had switched to the Allied side during the war but did not get the lands it expected. In addition, postwar Italy had many economic and political problems. In 1922, **Benito Mussolini** seized power. His followers called him *Il Duce* (DOO chay; "the leader"). His party opposed communism and promoted extreme nationalism and totalitarian rule by a fascist state. Italian **fascism** (FASH ihz ihm) was an economic and political system in which the totalitarian government allowed private ownership of property but heavily regulated all economic activity. All activities had to support and further the goals of the state.

Mussolini started military groups across Italy. Most notable were his "Black Shirts," thugs who ensured that his wishes were carried out. The school system was dedicated to teaching young people their duty to the state. Mussolini maintained popular support by building efficient railroads and major highways, providing houses and lands for sixty thousand peasants, and making other improvements. Although he denied freedom to the people, he promised to give Italy back the pride of a bygone era by establishing a "Second Roman Empire." Such promises initially caused his followers to rank him with Julius Caesar. Italians admitted he took many of their freedoms, but they also noted he made the trains run on time!

Mussolini began building his foreign empire in 1935. Italian soldiers crossed the Mediterranean and attacked the African land of Ethiopia. Tribesmen with spears and rifles faced Italy's modern war machine. The world watched in horror, but no one helped Ethiopia. The League of Nations failed to punish Italy beyond imposing weak economic sanctions. That made Mussolini bolder. On April 7, 1939, his forces invaded Albania. Again, the world did nothing.

Japanese Militarism

Japan's industrial and military power had been growing since the turn of the century. Military leaders steadily gained control of

---

- CD: The Warplanes (Japanese and American planes); The Attack on Pearl Harbor; U.S. Propaganda Posters; U.S. Leaders; Women in the War; Japanese Relocation and Internment; European Theater, 1943–44; The Battle of the Bulge
- Activities 3–6 from the *Student Activities* manual
- Materials for making a recruitment poster
- February 2008 issue of *American History* magazine
- Recordings of World War II songs
- A recording of "God Bless America"
- Special Speaker: World War II veteran

SECTION IV
- Activities 7–9 from the *Student Activities* manual
- CD: World War II in the Pacific; The Doolittle Raid; Pacific Carriers; Amphibious Assaults; Japanese Carrier *Yamato*; The End Approaches; Harry Truman, 33rd President; The Cost of America's Wars

Why Study This War?
Explain the value of understanding the causes of World War II. As with all wars, we study the causes so that we can avoid another war like it. Ask the students whether a new world war would be likely today. If not, why not? If so, where might it be fought, and who would fight on each side? Help them to

contrast the conventional warfare of World War II and unconventional warfare, such as guerrilla warfare and the global war against terrorism.

Discuss Rogue Nations
Under their fascist leaders, Germany, Italy, and Japan became "rogue nations." A rogue nation ignores fundamental principles of international relations. They willingly use any means necessary to increase their power. The two most common types of rogue nations are Communist countries, such as North Korea, and radical Muslim nations, such as Iran. Ask the students to consider U.S. relations with the fascists during the

the government. They wanted to increase Japanese power in China and other areas of East Asia and the Pacific. The military leaders believed that Japan deserved greater recognition as a world power. They convinced the Japanese people that the United States threatened Japan's growth and that Japan should gain control of the trade and resources of East Asia.

After World War I, the League of Nations assigned Japan to govern some of Germany's Pacific islands. In 1931, Japan fortified the islands, invaded China, and took over the northern region called Manchuria. The United States opposed Japan's conquest of Manchuria and asked the League to act against Japan. But the League's action proved to be ineffective. Japan stayed in Manchuria and renamed the region Manchukuo. But no American possessions in the Pacific were yet threatened, so the United States only strengthened slightly their defenses in the Philippines.

But some American fighter pilots decided to help the Chinese repel the Japanese invaders. Under the leadership of General Claire Lee Chennault, they formed a force called the American Volunteer Group. They were better known as the "Flying Tigers." They were also celebrated for their airplanes—P-40s with their noses painted to resemble a shark's mouth.

German Nazism

Germany was the country that was most upset by the Treaty of Versailles. That settlement had placed on Germany all of the blame for the war and had stripped the country of its strong army, its self-respect, some of its land, and its colonial possessions. The treaty had also forced Germany to make large payments to the Allies as reparations. Humiliated by those terms, Germany struggled through the 1920s. From the midst of the downcast German people, however, arose a man who gave Germany a false hope for future greatness.

Adolf Hitler preached against the injustice of the Treaty of Versailles, blamed the Jews for Germany's problems, and declared the superiority of the German race. Hitler also organized the National Socialist German Workers Party, or **Nazi Party**, which he led. He denounced communism (which Germans greatly feared at that time) and proposed a strong, organized Germany that would become a powerful leader in the world. Although his book, *Mein Kampf* ("My Struggle"), clearly revealed his views and intentions, few who read this book took it seriously.

Although at first many Germans did not accept Hitler, he became increasingly popular. Calling Hitler the *Führer* (FYOOR uhr; "leader"), his supporters believed Hitler's claim that he was building a Third Reich (empire) that would last for a thousand years. They believed that Hitler would restore Germany to its rightful place in the world. The German people enthusiastically accepted the promises Hitler made in his speeches. In addition to these hopes of restored German greatness, Nazi rallies generated great excitement through music, speeches, and elaborate pageantry. Some people continued to mistrust Hitler, but their influence was not strong enough to reverse his power.

As the economic depression deepened, German despair grew in the early 1930s. Riding the wave of dissatisfaction, Hitler and the Nazis swept into power. He became the German chancellor in 1933 and was given the powers of a dictator. Hitler soon violated the Treaty of Versailles by sending troops into the Rhineland near

The Flying Tigers

The Flying Tigers of the American Volunteer Group in their P-40 fighter planes patrolled the skies over China and Burma to hinder the Japanese advances there. Always outnumbered and short on parts, the Tigers' tactics were deadly. For every P-40 shot down, the Flying Tigers shot down fifteen Japanese planes.

Adolf Hitler used national socialism (Nazism) to restore Germany's power and take over much of Europe.

how to run their operations for the greater public good and taxed them heavily to achieve the government's goals. The government also maintained strict control of the educational system and process.

Japan's Leadership

Although Emperor Hirohito was the supreme leader of Japan, military warlords held practical control over all national policy, foreign and domestic. General Hideki Tojo was the leading Japanese military officer active in Japan's expansion of power.

Hitler's Ruse

Hitler cleverly avoided the restrictions of the Treaty of Versailles as he trained Germans for eventual service in his armies. He organized youth groups and sports groups with the underlying purpose of military training. The Hitler Jugend (Hitler Youth) gave young men from age fourteen to eighteen the opportunity to go on military excursions with real army units. Younger boys eagerly wore the uniforms of the Jungvolk (Young Folk). "Hiking clubs" became popular and taught the Young Folk to march in formation and obey orders like military men. The 1936 Olympic games were held in Munich, and they gave the Germans the opportunity to train for pistol and rifle teams. The League of Air Sports trained pilots and supervised glider clubs under the leadership of Hermann Göring, the eventual head of the Luftwaffe (German Air Force).

1930s. Are modern rogue nations or their leaders any less dangerous?

🖥️ 📹 World War II Background

Several excellent World War II video documentaries give general background and summary material about the war. You might consider showing excerpts from some of the following videos (or those listed elsewhere in this chapter of the TE):

• *Why We Fight* (several different episodes that explain how the war came about; originally shown to U.S. servicemen; directed by Frank Capra, who is famous for the movie *It's A Wonderful Life*; includes much original film footage)

• *Victory at Sea* (twenty-six episodes that cover the progress of every aspect of the war; contains original action footage)

Use the videos over several days, showing pertinent excerpts each day as you progress through the chapter. This will help make the war more real to your students.

For a good general print resource for personal memories of the war on both the battlefront and the home front, see *"We Pulled Together . . . and Won!"* by Reminisce Books.

🖥️ General Surveys of World War II

Some excellent sources of information about World War II are *Reader's Digest Illustrated Story of World War II*, *The United States in World War II* by Don Lawson, and

The Story of the Second World War by Katharine Savage.

🎨 🎩 Model Show and Tell

Consider the following two chapter projects.

1. Ask volunteers to build models of World War II-era equipment and present them to the class with explanations of their capabilities and use. Examples might include warplanes, tanks, ships, and submarines.

2. Ask volunteers to research and report (either orally or in writing) on one of the following American leaders in World War II: Eisenhower, Patton,

Hitler and the Jews

Hitler and his Nazi henchmen preached the false doctrine of Aryan supremacy. They acted on that belief by persecuting the Jews. First, they made life difficult for the Jews, hoping they would leave Germany voluntarily. Next, they forced them to live in inhuman conditions in ghettos. Then, they began expelling them. Finally, Hitler instituted the "final solution"—he imprisoned the Jews in concentration camps where they were treated as slave laborers. As Allied armies got ever closer to the prison camps and it became obvious that Hitler would lose the war, he ordered mass exterminations in gas chambers.

Shoah

Many Jews avoid using the term *Holocaust* and prefer the Hebrew word *Shoah* (catastrophe) instead. *Holocaust* was a Greek term that originally meant "burnt offering." Many Jewish people find it offensive because it might imply that the Jews died as a burnt offering to God.

Section II
Objectives

Students should be able to

1. Describe German expansion and the policy of appeasement.
2. Trace Hitler's successful advances in Europe as the war began.
3. Describe the Battle of Britain.
4. Explain the failure of Hitler's invasion of the Soviet Union.
5. Describe American opinions and policies as the United States watched the war unfold.

Clark, Bradley, MacArthur, Stilwell, or Nimitz.

 God Is My Co-Pilot

The students might enjoy reading *God Is My Co-Pilot* by Robert Scott, one of the original Flying Tigers of the American Volunteer Group. Scott was also instrumental in founding and operating the Museum of Aviation in Warner Robins, Georgia. If your school is located in that area, you might consider a field trip there. The museum has a wide range of vintage and modern aircraft on display, as well as an excellent section on World War II pilots.

France. Hitler also organized German men and boys into groups for military training. In addition, he ordered German scientists to develop new weapons and war materials. Hitler's power and ambition soon threatened world peace.

Mussolini, Hitler, and the Japanese warlords became allies in 1940. Both Mussolini and Hitler had formed fascist governments, strong dictatorships that stressed nationalism, power, and expansion. They formed an alliance. Later, when Japan joined them, their pact became known as the Rome-Berlin-Tokyo Axis, or the **Axis powers**.

Roosevelt's Foreign Policy

The United States knew about the growing powers of Hitler, Mussolini, and the Japanese military leaders and recognized them as threats to the delicate balance of world peace. But the isolationism of the 1920s still prevailed in the 1930s. Most Americans were more concerned about domestic problems than foreign affairs. They hoped that the limits established by naval treaties and peace pacts signed by major nations in the 1920s would discourage war. Americans wanted the League of Nations to act against the threats to peace. But the League proved to be weak and unable to restrain villainous nations effectively.

President Roosevelt wanted the United States to take a major role in foreign affairs. But without popular support, he could do little about the trouble brewing overseas. He made progress, however, in U.S. relationships with the countries of Latin America. President Hoover had initiated a "**Good Neighbor Policy**" in dealings with those lands, and Roosevelt continued that policy. Instead of marching into Latin American countries with a big stick when troubles arose, as Theodore Roosevelt had done, the United States let these countries handle their own affairs. Those countries had grown tired and suspicious of U.S. intervention, so the Good Neighbor Policy did much to improve relations with them.

Section Quiz

1. What two European leaders built strong military dictatorships after World War I?
2. What part of China did Japan conquer?
3. What was the general attitude of Americans toward foreign affairs in the 1930s?
4. What new policy was the United States following in its dealings with Latin America?
★ How did the end of World War I prepare Germany for the start of World War II?

II. War Erupts

In the late 1930s, the world watched as Hitler began his conquest of European territory. His actions soon made France and Britain realize that they had to do something.

Activity 1: Prelude to World War II

Use this activity to help the students understand how the actions of Italy, Germany, and Japan led to war.

Section Quiz Answers

1. Adolf Hitler and Benito Mussolini
2. Manchuria
3. isolationism—they were more worried about problems at home than abroad
4. "Good Neighbor" policy
★ Feeling that everything had been taken away from them and staggering under the weight of a huge debt, Germans were ready for a leader like Hitler who expressed their grievances and seemed to offer the return of self-respect.

Germany Expands

Other nations had not protested Hitler's disregard of the Treaty of Versailles, so Hitler violated it again. In 1938, he proposed uniting Austria (a German-speaking land) with Germany. The Treaty of Versailles forbade *Anschluss*, the uniting of Germany and Austria. But in four weeks Austria came under Hitler's control. Foreign powers still did nothing. He next demanded the Sudetenland, an area along the border of Czechoslovakia. He claimed that the 3.5 million Germans who lived there "deserved to be a part of the Fatherland." But he had secretly ordered his military to invade Czechoslovakia if he did not gain it peacefully by October 1, 1938. Hitler promised that this demand would be "the last territorial claim I have to make in Europe."

Hitler, Neville Chamberlain (the British prime minister), and other European leaders met in conference in Munich, Germany. Chamberlain thought that if Europe appeased Hitler (gave in to his demand) they would avoid conflict and preserve peace. When Chamberlain returned to Britain and announced that they had achieved "peace for our time," many Europeans agreed. However, **Winston Churchill**, who would soon replace Chamberlain as prime minister, disagreed. He warned, "You chose dishonor, and you will have war!"

Hitler took the Sudetenland peacefully, but **appeasement** did not work. About six months later, Hitler took all of Czechoslovakia by force. Europe realized that Hitler intended to keep increasing his power and his empire. No European nation was safe.

Next, Hitler wanted Poland. Both Britain and France warned him that his demand would lead to war. Hitler ignored them. "Our enemies are little worms," he said. "I saw them at Munich." But Hitler worried that the Soviet Union would also protest his actions. Fighting too much of Europe at once would be folly. So in August he signed a nonaggression pact with **Joseph Stalin**, the dictator of the Soviet Union. The two leaders agreed not to attack each other as they both expanded their territory. The stage was set for the beginning of World War II.

Chamberlain sought to appease Hitler at the Munich Conference.

War Envelops Europe

On September 1, 1939, after weeks of posturing and provocation, Hitler unleashed his war machine on Poland. Hundreds of bombers soared over Poland. Divisions of armored vehicles, called *panzers*, and thousands of soldiers moved in to take control. The Soviet Union also attacked Poland from the east. Within hours, Poland had lost almost all hope for avoiding defeat. A few Poles continued to resist for several weeks, but the fall of Poland was complete before the month ended. The world had seen a new type of warfare—**blitzkrieg** ("lightning war").

Britain and France, the **Allies**, knowing that Hitler had to be stopped, declared war on Germany on September 3, 1939. They rushed to prepare their armies, but little fighting took place for eight months. Then on April 9, Hitler's forces invaded Denmark and Norway. On May 10, 1940, Hitler staged another blitzkrieg, sending his forces into Belgium, the Netherlands, and Luxembourg. The Belgians and the Dutch, unable to stand against Hitler's strong armies, soon collapsed.

German panzer units roared across the Polish border on September 1, 1939.

Churchill on Appeasement

Winston Churchill criticized British Prime Minister Neville Chamberlain for his attempts to appease Hitler. He defined an appeaser as someone who feeds a voracious crocodile, hoping it will eat him last.

Blitzkrieg

The military philosophy of blitzkrieg ("lightning war") was based on lessons learned from World War I and the Spanish Civil War (1936–39). It was a coordinated attack using combined air, land, and sea forces. Its key characteristics were speed, mobility, flexibility, and the exploitation of circumstances and conditions.

The blitzkrieg was dependent on total air superiority, which was achieved by heavy coordinated attacks on all enemy air bases as the first stage of the attack. Simultaneously, paratroopers were dropped behind enemy lines to cut lines of communication, create confusion, and prevent enemy retreat. Forces would feign attacks in several areas at once, thereby distracting the enemy from the area where the focused attack would fall. These were followed by penetrating thrusts by multiple overwhelming mechanized divisions supported closely by bombers and fighter planes. Those coordinated assaults would then use pincer movements to surround and seal off enemy strongholds, thereby preventing those troops from escaping or reinforcing troops elsewhere.

Poland, 1939

Hitler's "lightning war" was first demonstrated in Poland on September 1, 1939. Fifty years earlier, the blitzkrieg would not have been possible. The development of the internal combustion engine changed everything. No longer did troop movement depend on how fast men could

---

Discuss Appeasement

The main lesson of this section is the danger of appeasement. It is clearly wrong for a nation or an individual to back down on its obligations, no matter what the threat. The Allies were bound by the Versailles treaty to respect the boundaries of Czechoslovakia.

Students should also consider the flip side of appeasement. When should the United States ignore evildoers in the world? Supporters of U.S. intervention around the world constantly raise the specter of "appeasement" as an argument against isolationism. But students need to understand that it is often difficult to know when it is appropriate to commit military forces and when other options should be considered.

The Uncertainties of War

Emphasize to the students that although some people tried to warn about the rise of Hitler's military machine, no one foresaw the full possibilities of a blitzkrieg. The Allies' lack of preparedness led to the collapse of Poland, the Low Countries, and France and the near annihilation of the British army.

Ask the students to discuss the surprising course that other wars have taken in U.S. history. In particular, recall that in the Civil War the North thought that they could beat the South in a matter of weeks. Students need to look for other examples of unwise optimism as they read about later wars, such as Korea, Vietnam, and the Persian Gulf.

CD: The Warplanes

Refer to the CD for photos of some of the major German warplanes used in the blitzkrieg. (This source also provides photos of American and Japanese warplanes and you should refer to them when they are mentioned later in the chapter.)

march or ride horses or where rail lines ran. Trucks could move men and artillery across almost any kind of terrain. Planes could drop paratroopers behind enemy lines. Tanks offered protection, mobility, and firepower as German troops swept over enemy territory.

Today, it is hard for us to imagine armies without mechanized forces, but at that time tanks, trucks, and airplanes were new in the war arena. Hitler used those elements to the fullest to take over large portions of Europe with relative speed.

Dunkirk

The evacuation of the Allied troops from Dunkirk was made possible by the bad weather. That protection of the Allied troops from almost certain annihilation is often cited as an instance of providential control over history.

The Influence of Winston Churchill

Sir Winston Churchill became the man of the hour during Great Britain's greatest trial. His oratory did much to inspire the British people.

"I have nothing to offer but blood, toil, tears and sweat," he declared. "We have before us an ordeal of the most grievous kind. We have before us many long months of toil and struggle.

"You ask what is our policy. I will say, it is to wage war with all our might, with all the strength that God can give us, to wage war against a monstrous tyranny never surpassed in the dark, lamentable catalogue of human crime."

"We shall not flag or fail. We shall go on to the end. We shall fight in France, we shall fight on the seas and oceans, we shall fight with growing confidence and growing strength in the air. We shall defend our

The British refused to be broken by the onslaught of Nazi bombers during the Battle of Britain.

RAF pilots in their Spitfires (shown here) and Hurricanes thwarted *Luftwaffe* plans to break the spirit of the British.

Next, the Germans bypassed France's heavily fortified Maginot Line and moved into France through the Ardennes Forest. Britain rushed soldiers and equipment to help France, but the Allied army of 338,000 men was forced to retreat to northern France. They were trapped near the port of Dunkirk. The Germans sought to cut off any escape across the English Channel. Having trapped the Allies, the German army halted. The German air force, the *Luftwaffe*, would finish them off.

But bad weather kept German planes from bombing the trapped armies. The British rushed every available boat to Dunkirk. They used fishing boats, steamers, yachts, and even lifeboats to evacuate the Allied army. Fishermen, dockworkers, merchants, and farmers all helped ferry the army across the Channel to safety. They had to leave almost all of the armies' weapons, vehicles, and equipment behind. On June 14, 1940, German troops entered Paris. France surrendered. The Nazis allowed a degree of self-government in the south in Vichy and the French colonies in North Africa—as long as the French puppets did what the Nazis wanted.

Meanwhile, Mussolini announced that Italy was joining Germany in the fight against the Allies. He intended to gain more land from an Axis conquest of Europe.

Britain Stands Alone

After France fell, Britain stood alone against the fascists. Most people expected the Germans to invade and conquer the British Isles. In fact, Hitler had a plan to do just that. Operation Sea Lion called first for the *Luftwaffe* to gain control of the skies by wiping out the British Royal Air Force (RAF). Next, the *Luftwaffe* would bomb port cities and beaches in preparation for the final phase—the amphibious landing of troops.

But the *Luftwaffe* experienced stiffer opposition than expected from British fighter planes. The RAF shot down many German planes. Hitler ordered devastating bombing raids on English cities, including the capital, London. Many of those bombing attacks targeted civilians and were designed to break the British will to resist. The attacks began in July 1940 and lasted for one year. This deadly period became known as the Battle of Britain.

The RAF fought courageously to protect Britain from the bombings. Because of a shortage of pilots, RAF pilots made as many as five sorties (flights) a day to defend their homeland. Their efforts prevented the fall of Britain. The new prime minister, Winston Churchill, said of the RAF, "Never in the field of human conflict was so much owed by so many to so few." Had the attacks continued, the outcome might have been different. But Hitler grew impatient, and the British determination persuaded him to seek another approach to victory.

Hitler Turns Against the Soviet Union

Hitler was mired in a stalemate in Great Britain, but he was winning elsewhere. German armies controlled Hungary and Rumania by the spring of 1941. Turkey signed a treaty of neutrality. In early summer, Hitler swept into southeastern Europe. Bulgaria, Yugoslavia, and Greece soon joined the list of Axis victims.

Hitler then made a decision that would have tremendous consequences. He ordered his armies to attack the Soviet Union. Hitler took this major step because he believed the Soviets would change sides and come to Britain's aid. Hitler wanted to crush the Soviet Union before it could turn on him. He also needed Soviet resources. Hitler ignored warnings by his generals that opening another front, or battleground, in the East was unwise. Expanding the war into the Soviet Union late in the summer could be dangerous. On June 22, 1941, Operation Barbarosa, the blitzkrieg against the Soviet Union, began. Hitler thought he could defeat the Soviets in just eight weeks.

At first, the Russian people accepted Hitler's armies as a relief from the terrors of Stalin's Communist rule. But they soon learned that the Nazis were not friendly. Germans ravaged Soviet towns and tortured Russian civilians. The Russians began to practice a "scorched earth" policy. Instead of leaving crops and livestock that Hitler could use to feed his men, the retreating Russians burned their crops and killed their animals. The supplies the German army had hoped to capture were gone. The farther the Germans advanced, the longer their supply lines stretched.

By mid-October German troops were only forty miles from Moscow. They had killed more than two million Russians. The autumn days grew shorter and temperatures grew colder, but Hitler refused to stop his offensive and wait until spring for further action. He did not want to give Stalin more time to strengthen his defenses. The Germans marched on with only their summer uniforms and lightweight oil for their vehicles. Ironically, a century before, Napoleon had been in the same situation and found that the Russian winter was far more dangerous than Russian troops. On December 6, as the freezing Soviet winter closed in, Soviet troops attacked Hitler's cold and weary forces and broke through the German lines. The Germans were forced to retreat. The Russian military and the Russian winter had kept Hitler from defeating the Soviet Union.

American Sympathies and Fears Grow

Americans watched events in Europe with increasing alarm. The European dictators had made clear that they were opposed to any form of republican government. Some Americans feared that if Britain fell, Germany might try to wage war on the United States. Americans generally opposed Hitler and wanted the Allies to win. However, most Americans wanted to avoid direct participation in the war. Reflecting American sentiment, Congress had passed a series of neutrality acts in the 1930s. Therefore, American options to help the Allies were limited.

In 1939, Congress had allowed the Allied powers to buy war materials from American companies if the Allies paid cash and carried the supplies on their own ships. Congress also passed a Selective Service Act (military draft) in 1940. Young men aged twenty-one to thirty-five were required to register for possible military service. Some 375,000 men were drafted and started training to be ready for a possible attack. But since the armistice in 1918, America had not been concerned with building a strong armed force. So the new soldiers had to train with old or substitute equipment until new pieces were available.

Many Americans still feared war and wanted to avoid it at all costs. The America First Committee, with such prominent members as Charles Lindbergh, and other organizations pleaded for American neutrality. Roosevelt ran for a third term as president in 1940. Because of the fear of war, he had to promise to keep American boys

Europe, 1941

island, whatever the cost may be. We shall fight on the beaches, we shall fight on the landing-grounds, we shall fight in the fields and in the streets, we shall fight in the hills. We shall never surrender!"

Other Heroes

Although the pilots of the RAF are given the most credit for winning the Battle of Britain, many other people helped. Radar operators kept track of incoming German planes and quickly alerted the RAF. That information was vital considering how few British pilots were available. It also kept the pilots in the right place at the right time.

All along the coast, a series of long-range radar towers created an invisible net. Once a radar operator detected an aircraft, he or she relayed the information to Fighter Command Headquarters. Trained civilians also kept track of the plane visually, using binoculars and height-measuring equipment. At Fighter Command, personnel plotted the information on a huge map of the coast. All around the map, workers used long sticks to move markers representing planes and flight groups. A balcony above the map allowed the higher-ranking British officers to see exactly what was happening across the coast and to make decisions based on the situation.

Where? How Far?

In anticipation of a German invasion, the British government ordered the removal of signs which indicated the direction of and distance to towns and cities. That tactic was intended to confuse the Germans if they ever invaded.

America First

The existence of the America First Committee, led by such prominent men as Charles Lindbergh, is surprising to modern Americans. The group seems to have been shortsighted and profascist. But in reality, many of their leaders were attempting to continue America's tradition of isolationism. Divide the class and have them argue the two sides of the debate that raged in 1940. Lindbergh was willing for Britain to fall to the Nazis. Why? (*It was widely believed that Soviet Communism was at least as dangerous as Nazism, and isolationists hoped the two evil systems would destroy each other.*)

Liberty Ships

When Great Britain needed help getting food, equipment, and war supplies from America, the United States did not have enough ships to carry it all. A British engineer gave the Americans his design for a large, quickly built ship that became known as the Liberty ship. By the end of the war, American shipyards were turning out a Liberty ship every forty days or less.

Read more about the building of Liberty ships in *Military History* (Jan.–Feb. 2008). Or visit www.bjupress.com/resources/ for a possible link to a couple of interesting websites devoted to preserving the story of the Liberty ship.

Section III
Objectives

Students should be able to

1. Name the event that brought the United States into the war.
2. Describe ways in which Americans went to work for the war effort.
3. Describe ways in which Americans produced or conserved materials for the war effort.
4. Explain the "Hitler first" policy.
5. Trace the Allied operations in North Africa, Italy, and France.
6. Explain the significance of the Normandy invasion.
7. Describe the defeat of Germany.

America Goes to War

For months before the Pearl Harbor attack, President Roosevelt had actually been hoping for an event that would bring the United States into the war. The American public, however, was reluctant to enter the war without some kind of clear attack on the United States itself. Roosevelt had even sent American naval patrols nearer and nearer to Europe, hoping to provoke a German attack, but Hitler had been careful not to give the United States an excuse to enter the war while he was busy with other enemies. After Pearl Harbor, however, Hitler had no choice but to fight the Americans too.

Following the attack on Pearl Harbor, the U.S. government was reluctant to release detailed statistics or photographs of the damage inflicted for fear that it would embolden the Japanese. Newspapers cooperated by not publishing such photos.

Liberty Ships such as this were included in the Lend-Lease agreement between the United States and Great Britain.

Hideki Tojo not only was the head of Japan's military but also became its prime minister.

The American flag flew defiantly as the U.S.S. *Arizona* burned from the fatal strike by Japanese bombers.

out of a foreign war, a war that did not directly involve the United States. He won the election.

As the Battle of Britain threatened to crush the Allies in the summer of 1941, Roosevelt decided that Britain desperately needed more help. He sought a way for the Allies to obtain vital war equipment from the United States more easily. Congress complied by approving the **Lend-Lease Act**. That act allowed the president to send equipment to any nation in which such equipment might support American defense. Rather than paying for the equipment with money, the countries could pay with property, services, or equipment for American use. This way, the United States received land for seven air bases throughout the British Empire in exchange for war supplies sent to Britain.

Americans also began to realize that Germany and Italy might not be their only enemies. Japan had joined the Axis powers and was pursuing an empire in Asia. Japanese forces had already entered Southeast Asia. Their next target might be Australia, New Zealand, or the Philippines. Japan and the United States were also disagreeing more frequently over economic and trade issues.

Roosevelt decided to retaliate. He froze all Axis assets in the United States. Then he forbade almost all trade with Japan. The strain between the two nations increased as Japan continued to expand its power in defiance of American interests. If Japan could not trade with America for the resources it needed, it would take them from its Pacific neighbors. On October 17, General Hideki Tojo became prime minister of Japan. In late November 1941, Japanese diplomats arrived in Washington for talks. At the same time, Japanese aircraft carriers were sailing northwestward across the Pacific.

Section Quiz

1. With what major power did Hitler make a nonaggression treaty that he later broke?
2. Hitler's invasion of what country actually triggered World War II?
3. Which countries did Hitler capture between September of 1939 and June of 1940?
4. What was the German strategy in the Battle of Britain?
5. How did the RAF defend Britain?
6. What was the Lend-Lease Act? How did it attempt to preserve American neutrality in the war?
✯ Why was Hitler's decision to invade the Soviet Union unwise? Why did he do it anyway?

III. America Enters the War and Turns the Tide

On Sunday morning, December 7, 1941, planes from the Japanese carriers in the Pacific bombed the U.S. naval and air bases at **Pearl Harbor** in Hawaii. Nineteen American ships were sunk or dis-

Activity 2: The War Begins: Chronological Order

Use this activity to help the students develop a chronological understanding of the events of the war. Refer to this chart throughout the chapter as you study each event, and have the students complete it as they go.

Section Quiz Answers

1. the Soviet Union
2. Poland
3. Denmark, Norway, Belgium, the Netherlands, and Luxembourg

4. to drive Britain's Royal Air Force from the skies and to force a surrender by inflicting heavy damage on civilians
5. by making as many as five flights a day to repel the Luftwaffe
6. An agreement that the United States would provide needed supplies for the Allies in return for property, services, equipment, or other items useful to the United States; it attempted to preserve neutrality by assisting the Allies without officially siding with them or being directly involved in the war.
✯ In opening another front, the Germans had to divide their forces; it is always more difficult to make progress with

a divided focus. In addition, the timing of the attack put Germany in the middle of the Soviet Union as the dangerous Russian winter closed in. Hitler hoped to capture valuable resources and to end British hopes that the Soviets would come to their aid.

 Nuggets from National Geographic

"Pearl Harbor: A Return to the Day of Infamy" in the December 1991 issue of *National Geographic* covers the story of the immediate cause of America's entrance into World War II. The article is accompanied by good pictures and memoirs.

FDR's Declaration of War Request

Yesterday, December 7, 1941—a date which will live in infamy—the United States of America was suddenly and deliberately attacked by naval and air forces of the Empire of Japan. . . .

❀❀❀

Yesterday the Japanese Government also launched an attack against Malaya. Last night Japanese forces attacked Hong Kong. Last night Japanese forces attacked Guam. Last night Japanese forces attacked the Philippine Islands. Last night the Japanese attacked Wake Island. And this morning the Japanese attacked Midway Island.

❀❀❀

Hostilities exist. There is no blinking at the fact that our people, our territory, and our interests are in grave danger.

With confidence in our armed forces—with the unbounding determination of our people—we will gain the inevitable triumph—so help us God.

I ask that the Congress declare that since the unprovoked and dastardly attack by Japan on Sunday, December 7, 1941, a state of war has existed between the United States and the Japanese Empire.

—President Franklin D. Roosevelt
December 8, 1941

---

abled. Nearly two hundred planes were destroyed. More than two thousand men were killed, and more than one thousand more were wounded. The treacherous surprise attack prompted Roosevelt to address Congress the next day, requesting a declaration of war. He called December 7, 1941, "a date which will live in infamy."

The second wave of the Japanese assault on Pearl Harbor met a wall of anti-aircraft fire.

Congress declared war. (The Senate vote was 82–0 and the House vote was 388–1, with Jeanette Rankin casting the only nay vote.) These events thrust America into a worldwide conflict that became known as World War II. Germany and Italy, who with Japan made up the Rome-Berlin-Tokyo Axis, also declared war on the United States. No longer neutral, America became directly involved in a fight against all of the Axis powers.

Equipping America to Fight

The damage inflicted by the Japanese was severe. The silver lining in the dark cloud of the attack was that the American carrier fleet was at sea that morning and escaped the attack. Those carriers and their warplanes would haunt Japan in the coming days. Still,

Dorie Miller, Hero at Pearl Harbor

Doris "Dorie" Miller was an African American mess attendant aboard the U.S.S. *West Virginia* at the time of the attack on Pearl Harbor. He was awarded the Navy Cross medal for his courageous actions on that fateful day. The citation says in part, "While at the side of his Captain on the bridge, Miller, despite enemy strafing and bombing and in the face of a serious fire, assisted in moving his Captain, who had been mortally wounded, to a place of greater safety, and later manned a machine gun directed at enemy Japanese attacking aircraft until ordered to leave the bridge."

Internees Finally Recognized

When orders came for the internment of all Japanese-Americans, 440 Japanese-Americans were students at the University of Washington. Forced to withdraw, these students lost the chance to finish their studies and earn their degrees. Finally, in February 2008, the university officially recognized the wrong done to those students in forcing their withdrawal and agreed to award them honorary baccalaureate degrees.

Rosie the Riveter

World War II brought about an important societal change as women took over many of the jobs formerly filled by men when the men joined the military. Women worked not only in clerical or medical positions but also in industrial work. The symbol of the huge female work force became known as "Rosie the Riveter." For example, the aircraft industry hired about half a million female workers to build fighter planes, bombers, and cargo planes. Female pilots were also used to ferry new planes to air bases around the country.

Tin Cans in the North Atlantic

Liberty ships that crossed the North Atlantic with food and war materiel—first for the Allies and later for U.S. forces—were extremely vulnerable to attack by Nazi U-boats, which roamed the sea in "wolf packs." To offer some protection, the Liberty ships sailed in formation in convoys, and U.S. destroyers (sometimes called "tin cans" by the men who served aboard them) surrounded the Liberty ships and searched for the enemy subs. Duty aboard such warships was cold and dangerous but critical to the war effort.

CD: The Warplanes
Refer to the CD for photos of some of the major Japanese warplanes.

CD: The Attack on Pearl Harbor
Refer to the CD for photos of Pearl Harbor during and after the Japanese attack.

More on Pearl Harbor
Two excellent detailed accounts of the Japanese attack on Pearl Harbor are *Day of Infamy* by Walter Lord and *At Dawn We Slept* by Gordon Prange.

An accurate dramatic presentation of the attack is the film *Tora! Tora! Tora!* (Note: this film has Japanese subtitles and is very long, so you might want to play only excerpts that deal with the actual attack.)

Activity 3: FDR's Request for a Declaration of War Against Japan
Use this reading activity to help the students appreciate the scope of the Japanese attack on the United States and understand the determination that FDR and Congress exhibited in declaring war on Japan.

CD: U.S. Propaganda Posters
Refer to the CD for examples of U.S. propaganda posters, including recruitment posters. Have the students construct their own recruitment posters for World War II.

CD: U.S. Leaders
Refer to the CD for photos of some of the major leaders of the U.S. military during World War II.

CD: Women in the War
Refer to the CD for photos of WACs in various war-related jobs.

"Miracle Meat"

With millions of soldiers in the field during World War II, the U.S. military needed a food that was easily transported and did not need refrigeration. To supply that need, it turned to a product that Hormel Foods had developed in 1937. The product was called SPAM, short for "spiced ham." It was made of pork shoulder (which was not selling well at the time and was going to waste), ham, salt, water, sugar, and sodium nitrite. It was packaged in 12-oz. tin cans and could be fried, broiled, or eaten cold right from the can because it was precooked. It provided much-needed calories and supplied almost one-quarter of the recommended daily allowance of fat.

SPAM was shipped to Europe via Lend-Lease to help alleviate the food shortage. By 1940, 70 percent of all Americans had tried it. When the United States entered the war, soldiers carried it with them. The GIs called it "miracle meat," "mystery meat," or "ham that failed the physical." But when they were hungry on the battlefield, it tasted pretty good. American, British, and Russian troops consumed more than 100 million pounds of SPAM during the war.

GIs had only one flavor of SPAM, but today it comes in several different flavors, including Classic, Lite, Less Sodium, Hickory Smoke Flavored, Oven Roasted Turkey, Hot & Spicy, Spread SPAM with Cheese, SPAM with Bacon, and SPAM with Honey. Nearly seven billion cans have been sold in forty-one countries. More than 122 million cans are sold every year, more than 100 million of them in the United States. The largest U.S. consumers of SPAM are Hawaiians, who eat an average of twelve cans per person per year.

Are you a girl with a Star-Spangled heart?

JOIN THE WAC NOW!

THOUSANDS OF ARMY JOBS NEED FILLING!   Women's Army Corps United States Army

Women became an important part of the American war effort.

Japanese American Heroes

After Pearl Harbor, many people questioned the loyalty of Japanese Americans. The government discharged the approximately 5,000 who were in the military at the time. Some of them petitioned the government, however, saying that they wanted to do their part to defend America. General George Marshall agreed and approved the formation of two Japanese American units. The 100th Infantry Battalion made its motto "Remember Pearl Harbor." The 442nd Infantry Regimental Combat Team had the motto "Go for Broke." By the end of the war, 33,000 Nisei were in uniform. They served with distinction in Italy and France and were among the most decorated units in the war. The Nisei soldiers were awarded 22 Medals of Honor, 53 Distinguished Service Crosses, 1 Distinguished Service Medal, 588 Silver Stars, 5,200 Bronze Stars, 22 Legions of Merit, 12 Croix de Guerre, 9,486 Purple Hearts, and 7 Presidential Unit Citations.

the United States had much to do to prepare itself for the long fight ahead.

Manpower to Wage the War

Anger and patriotism swept the nation. Volunteers swarmed army and navy recruiting stations. In all, about sixteen million Americans—one in eleven—joined the military. Americans who sincerely believed that war was wrong registered as **conscientious objectors** and served in the medical corps or in other noncombatant roles.

Women also became involved in the war effort in military or civilian jobs. Some served in the Women's Army Corps (WACS). Others joined the Women's Naval Reserve or the Women Accepted for Voluntary Emergency Service (WAVES). The Women Air Force Service Pilots (WASP) helped to fly aircraft from the factories to the air bases where they were needed. Women were not assigned to combat roles, but they did serve overseas, especially in tasks that freed men to fight.

More women also joined the work force, taking the places of men who were drafted. Posters featuring "Rosie the Riveter" were used to recruit women to join work forces everywhere. Some women joined the Red Cross. Others worked with the USO (United Service Organizations), entertaining troops and providing other services.

Black Americans joined the work force in larger numbers than ever before. Jobs that were closed to them suddenly opened. Blacks also enlisted in all-black units in the armed forces.

While African Americans were provided with some increased opportunities during World War II, Americans of Japanese ancestry—even those born in the United States—were rounded up and moved to internment camps. That forced relocation proved to be an over-reaction prompted by fear and suspicion. However, this fear was not based on any facts. The government had no indication that Americans of Japanese descent were going to be disloyal. Yet as a result of this policy, most Japanese Americans lost their jobs. Japanese farmers lost their produce, and Japanese merchants were forced to sell their stores at low prices. All were stripped of their rights as American citizens.

Japanese Americans were transported inland to internment camps.

 ### "Rosie the Riveter"

For more information on women who served in war production industries, the symbol of which became "Rosie the Riveter," see the February 2008 issue of *American History* magazine.

Songs of the War

Play World War II-era songs to the class. Obtain examples of songs by the Andrews Sisters, who also appeared in several films made during the war, including *Private Buckaroo*, which includes the song "Three Little Sisters" (or "Tell It to the Marines"). Other war songs include "Goodbye Momma, I'm Off to Yokohama" and "To Be Specific, It's Our Pacific."

National Hymn: "God Bless America"

Play a recording of the song "God Bless America" by Kate Smith (if possible). (Although "God Bless America" was not composed during the Thirties, that is when it became famous. Irving Berlin wrote the song in 1918 and laid it aside. But in 1938, as war in Europe approached, Berlin decided to write a song of peace. He pulled out "God Bless America," improved it, and then gave Kate Smith exclusive rights to sing it.) Afterward, discuss the lyrics and why some people believe that this song, rather than "The Star-Spangled Banner," should be the national anthem of the United States. Also

discuss how it regained popularity after the terrorist attacks on September 11, 2001.

 ### CD: Japanese Relocation and Internment

Refer to the CD for photos related to the relocation and internment of Japanese-Americans after the attack on Pearl Harbor.

More on Japanese Internment

Visit www.bjupress.com/resources/ for possible links to more detailed information about the relocation and internment of Japanese-Americans.

Beginning on February 1, 1943, Japanese Americans could enlist for military service too. They trained as an all-Nisei (American-born Japanese) force. Yet, because of their Japanese ancestry and lingering doubts about their loyalties, most Nisei fought in Europe. A few Japanese Americans did intelligence work in the Pacific. They helped crack the secret Japanese telegraph codes.

Materiel to Fight the War

The United States entered the war without enough materials or preparation. But Americans rose to meet the challenge. They soon retooled factories to produce war goods. For example, auto plants converted to producing jeeps and tanks. People worked as teams and sacrificed for the war effort. They doubled production in less than four years. By 1945, American industry had produced more than 300,000 planes. It had built 100,000 tanks and self-propelled guns and 2.5 million military trucks. American industry cranked out 1.1 million rifles and carbines, 400,000 artillery weapons, and 50 billion rounds of ammunition.

Shipbuilders set to work to increase the United States' naval and merchant marine fleets. They built ships dubbed "Liberty Ships" at the rate of one every three and a half working days. Those ships carried war materiel to the far-flung fronts. Aircraft carriers, destroyers, submarines, and other vessels also were built with amazing speed.

To meet the ever-increasing need for war materiel, Americans at home had to sacrifice during the war. After 1942, automobiles were no longer made for private sale. Gasoline, oil, meat, butter, sugar, coffee, shoes, and most canned or frozen goods were **rationed** (restricted in use) because of shortages. Americans received books of ration stamps. They could buy a rationed item only if they had an unused stamp for it. When scarce products were available in stores, there were often long lines to buy them. Little was thrown away. Drives to collect tin cans, waste paper, aluminum, and scrap iron to aid the war effort became common.

Many Americans added to their food supply by planting "Victory Gardens" in backyards, along edges of parking lots, in zoos and parks, and in window boxes. By 1943, these gardens supplied Americans with a third of all their vegetables. Those efforts ensured that more food was available for the men fighting in the war. Americans also bought war bonds to help pay for the war effort.

The supply lines used to carry goods to the armed forces stretched around the globe. In addition to supplying its own forces, the United States supplied much of the Allied forces. President Roosevelt called the United States "the arsenal of democracy."

Mapping the Strategy of the War

As commander-in-chief of all American armed forces, the president mapped the country's overall war strategy. He sought help from leading military officers and advisors. Roosevelt also met with Churchill. They held their first meeting secretly aboard an American destroyer off the coast of Newfoundland in August 1941, before the United States had joined in the war. Later talks near Washington, D.C., made public the Allied leaders' "Hitler-first" policy. That made the Allies' first priority the defeat of Nazi Germany. The United States agreed that the Germans were the biggest threat to the Allies. Once Hitler was defeated, they would focus on defeating Japan.

In other meetings, Allied leaders discussed their military strategy and how to deal with the problems they would face after the war.

American naval yards built warships at a record pace.

American industry began turning out warplanes at an amazing rate.

Americans' purchases of many goods were limited by the requirement that they use ration stamps for each purchase.

Activity 4: Life for a Japanese-American Internee

Use this activity to increase the students' appreciation for the hardships endured by innocent Japanese-Americans who were relocated to internment camps during World War II.

CD: The Warplanes

Refer to the CD for photos of some of the major American warplanes used in World War II.

World War II Veterans

Veterans of World War II are dying at the rate of more than one thousand a day. Very soon, we will no longer be able to turn to them for first-hand accounts of life during the war, both on the battlefield and on the home front. Invite one or more World War II veterans (perhaps one from each branch of the service) to talk to the class about their experiences in the war. You might ask them to bring to class some memorabilia from the war. You might also want to invite an elderly person who was on the home front to describe the kinds of sacrifices people made so the soldiers, sailors, and airmen could have war materiel.

Norway or Pas de Calais?

As the Allied invasion of Europe approached, German intelligence worked to determine where it would occur. The Allies planted misinformation in German hands, suggesting that Norway or Pas de Calais in France would be the landing zone.

When Allied efforts to prepare the Norway site stopped, the Germans believed it confirmed that Pas de Calais would be the site of invasion. The belief persisted even while the Normandy invasion was in progress. False information fed to the Germans said that the attack at Normandy was only covering a larger attack that would come at Pas de Calais. Instead of reinforcing their forces at Normandy, the Germans waited at Pas de Calais for an attack that never came.

The Pre-Invasion Attack on France

Several hours before the main D-day amphibious assault on the Normandy coast in France, paratroopers jumped behind enemy lines. Other airborne troops landed using gliders. Both groups had orders to cut the enemy's lines of communication, secure bridges, create confusion, and prepare the way for the main assault. Many of those soldiers were killed or injured when their gliders crashed, and parachutists dropped into water and drowned or were shot. The survivors were widely scattered and had trouble regrouping. But they achieved their goals and made the main invasion a little easier.

In Case the Invasion Failed

The success of the D-day invasion was by no means guaranteed. In fact, much was going against such success. General Dwight Eisenhower, Supreme Allied Commander, prepared two terse notes to be used once the invasion's success or failure

At Casablanca (cahs uh BLAHN kuh) in Morocco in January 1943, the Allies decided to invade Europe through Sicily and Italy.

After Hitler turned against the Soviet Union, that country joined the Allies. Therefore, at the next meeting in Teheran, Iran, Stalin joined the meetings. With the fall of France and the end of the Battle of Britain, most of the fighting was taking place in the east between the Germans and the Soviets. Stalin pressed the Allies to invade northern Europe to take pressure off his troops. The Allies promised Stalin a second European front. In return, Stalin promised that the Soviet Union would help defeat Japan once the Allies had defeated Hitler.

Waging the War in Europe

The United States did not ignore events in the Pacific. But it sent its major forces and equipment into the European theater of the conflict first.

Invading North Africa

Before Germany invaded Russia, Italy launched a major campaign in the deserts of North Africa. The British, however, defeated the Italians and threatened to drive them out of Africa altogether. To prop up his faltering ally, Hitler sent his "Afrika Korps" to Africa. It was under the brilliant command of General Erwin Rommel (RAHM ul), the "Desert Fox." By clever maneuvering and swift movement, Rommel drove back the British. It seemed that he would drive all the way into Egypt and capture the Suez Canal. The battle lines in North Africa shifted back and forth for hundreds of miles in 1941 and 1942, as first Rommel and then the British were victorious.

When U.S. troops stormed ashore in North Africa, they hoped that the Vichy French soldiers there would not resist.

By the middle of 1942, however, American troops began to arrive in Europe. They were commanded by General **Dwight D. Eisenhower**. He guided "Operation Torch," the Americans' invasion in northwestern North Africa, and began to push east toward Libya. Meanwhile, the British drove west from Egypt. The Allies crushed the Axis forces between them. Rommel and some of his men escaped to Europe. But 240,000 Axis troops surrendered to the Allies in Tunisia in May 1943.

Invading Mediterranean Europe

Although Hitler had lost in North Africa, he was determined to keep "Fortress Europe," the lands that the Reich had conquered in Europe. He expected any Allied assault to come across the English Channel into France. But the Allies under American General George Patton launched "Operation Husky." First, they invaded Sicily, the large island off the tip of Italy. American troops under General Mark Clark and British troops under General Bernard Montgomery then invaded Italy at Anzio and Salerno. Working their way up the Italian coast, the Americans captured Naples in October 1943. But the push to take Rome was slowed by Germans who were entrenched in the mountains. It took the Allies four months to travel through Italy's snow-clad mountains.

Japanese American soldiers of the 100th and 442nd battalions proved their worth against the enemy in Italy.

Italian citizens were tired of war. They overthrew Mussolini, surrendered to the Allies, and declared war on Germany. American forces freed Rome on June 4, 1944. Fighting continued against German forces in northern Italy for another year.

🎧 CD: European Theater, 1943–44

Refer to the CD for a map of the European Theater of the war.

▶ U.S. Bombers over Europe

Several videos are available dealing with the U.S. bombers and their crews in the European Theater. "Warplanes" in the *Wings* video series includes World War II planes among its survey of warplanes from the first biplanes used to supersonic jets. "Bombers" in the *Weapons at War* series and "Ball Turrett Gunners" in the *Suicide Missions* series, both by the History Channel, feature riveting photography and explanations of how those war machines worked. Another source

that shows American bombers and fighters in action over Europe is the video *Combat America*, narrated by actor Clark Gable. The story of one crew and its B-17 bomber is *Memphis Belle* (the vintage video, not the more recent Hollywood version). That crew flew—and survived—their full allotment of missions and was then reassigned stateside to promote the sale of war bonds.

💻 From Casablanca to Berlin

An excellent summary of the Allied invasions of North Africa, Sicily, and Italy and the drive to Germany is *From Casablanca to Berlin* by Bruce Bliven. (A part of Random House's Landmark Books series, this book is excellent for slow readers or

students who need a little extra motivation.) Ernie Pyle's *Here Is Your War* covers the common soldier in the war.

European Theater, 1943–44

Scale of Miles

Allied thrusts
Axis & Axis-controlled
Allies & Allied-controlled
Neutral nations

The Allied plan called for opening yet another front. Eisenhower began working in Britain to prepare for a bigger invasion. American generals Omar Bradley and George Patton and British general Bernard Montgomery assisted Eisenhower in the planning. They would invade Germany through northern France in what was called "Operation Overlord." They assembled men and equipment in southern England while bombing Germany around the clock. The British conducted night raids over German cities, destroying two and a half cities per month. The American air force bombed by day, focusing on industrial and military sites.

Invading France

In the predawn hours of June 6, 1944, Allied paratroopers and soldiers in gliders began landing behind German lines in Normandy, France. At the same time, the largest amphibious invasion force in history moved across the English Channel toward the beaches of Normandy, twenty miles away. This was "**D-day**," the day for Operation Overlord to begin. Eisenhower announced by radio, "The tide has turned. The free men of the world are marching together to victory." It marked the beginning of the end of the war in Europe.

The Allied air forces provided air protection. American soldiers landed on beaches code-named Utah and Omaha. The British landed on other nearby beaches code named Juno, Gold, and Sword. German defenses were strong, and Allied losses were heavy. But the

Troops at Normandy faced withering fire from the well-placed German defenders.

was evident. In the one that was not released, Eisenhower accepted full responsibility for the failure of the operation. Thankfully, he did not have to use that note because the invasion was a resounding success.

"Nuts!"

Hitler's last effort to win the war came in 1944 at the Battle of the Bulge counterattack in southern Belgium and the Ardennes Forest in Luxembourg. The Allies were forced to retreat, and the German advance created a bulge in the frontline.

Within the bulge, a pocket of resistance remained. The American 101st Airborne Division still controlled the city of Bastogne. Facing cold weather, low supplies, and a German siege, the Americans stubbornly refused to surrender. On December 22, the Germans sent a message to the Americans demanding their surrender. Brigadier General Anthony McAuliffe replied, "Nuts!"

The Germans were not happy with the reply and continued their attack even through Christmas Day. Allied aircraft dropped provisions and weapons to the Americans inside Bastogne. Finally, on December 26, the Fourth Armored Division of Patton's Third Army reached Bastogne and relieved the 101st Airborne.

Audie Murphy

Born in Texas, one of nine children, Audie Murphy enlisted in the army at age 16 as a private. He was involved in nine major campaigns across the European Theater during his three years of active duty. He was wounded three times. Murphy rose through the ranks to Staff Sergeant. He earned a battlefield promotion to 2nd lieutenant and ended his military career as a major in the Texas National Guard.

▶ D-Day: The Invasion of France

The PBS video "D-Day" from the *Secrets of the Dead* series provides excellent coverage of the events leading up to and during that great invasion.

Activity 5: V-Mail from a Soldier

Use this activity to help the students understand the importance of both mail from home for a soldier and secrecy for the military leaders during World War II.

▶ Audie Murphy Film

The film *To Hell and Back* tells the true story of Audie Murphy, America's most decorated combat soldier.

Murphy became the most decorated combat soldier in U.S. history. He received thirty-three awards—"every decoration for valor that this country had to offer plus five decorations presented to him by France and Belgium." His highest honor was the Congressional Medal of Honor, earned for his actions in France on January 16, 1945. His company was being assaulted by German tanks and infantry. Murphy ordered his men to withdraw to the woods. Murphy stayed behind to hold off the enemy until his men had built defenses. He climbed aboard a knocked-out and burning anti-tank vehicle and for an hour used its .50 caliber machine gun to mow down the advancing enemy. German soldiers crept to within a few yards of him, and he was hit in the leg. He ignored his wound and continued shooting the enemy soldiers. His ammunition exhausted, he returned to his unit and, refusing medical care, organized and led them in a counterattack that halted the enemy assault and saved his unit from almost certain capture or annihilation.

After the war, he made a career in Hollywood, starring in forty-four feature films, the most famous of which was the autobiographical *To Hell and Back*.

Casualties were high in the D-day invasion.

U.S. soldiers battled not only the Germans but also the weather during the Battle of the Bulge.

As the end of the war neared and FDR's health began to fail, he met with Stalin and Churchill in Yalta to plan the final push to crush the Nazi war machine.

Allies had established a beachhead. They pushed inland yard by yard and mile by mile across some of the same ground fought over in World War I.

On August 25, after a grueling, three-month battle, the Allies liberated Paris. German resistance collapsed rapidly after that. By October, the Allies had advanced all the way to the Rhine River. But in mid-December the Germans suddenly launched a huge counterattack into Belgium in an attempt to recapture the strategic port of Antwerp and divide the Allied forces. Although the Germans did not succeed in taking the port, they did succeed in pushing the Allied lines sixty miles westward at one point. That "bulge" in the lines allowed the Germans to surround an American division in the Belgian town of Bastogne. Other Allied forces rushed to rescue the trapped forces, who were fighting desperately in the **Battle of the Bulge**.

After a month of battle in snow and severe cold, the Germans demanded that the Americans surrender. The general of the surrounded American division, Anthony McAuliffe, sent back his response: "Nuts!" The fighting continued, but the German attack began to falter. The American troops reached the beleaguered soldiers in Bastogne and started pushing the Germans back toward Germany again.

German Defeat

While the Allies fought northward from Italy and eastward from the Rhine, the Soviets fought their way westward toward Berlin. The American forces probably could have won the race with the Russians to arrive at Berlin first. But a political decision forced them to delay. The Russians were to be allowed to take Berlin. The Americans and British concentrated on capturing Nazi forces and liberating concentration camps in western Germany.

Another factor that kept the Americans from Berlin was the agreement at the **Yalta Conference** by FDR, Churchill, and Stalin in February 1945. There they recognized Soviet "special interests" in Eastern Europe. In return, Stalin promised to enter the Pacific war. He also promised to hold postwar elections in the Eastern European countries the Soviets liberated. The Soviet promises proved worthless, but Roosevelt thought that the agreement was necessary. Churchill had proposed preventing the Soviets from gaining control of any more of Europe than necessary by launching a British-American operation from the central Mediterranean northward. But he was forced to go along. (His concerns later proved to be valid when Stalin refused to relinquish control of Eastern Europe. At that time, he made his famous declaration that an "iron curtain" had fallen across Europe.) Yalta was the last meeting of Churchill and FDR with Stalin. Within a few months, Roosevelt was dead, and Britain had elected a new prime minister to replace Churchill.

Hitler, seeing his Third Reich crumbling before him, committed suicide. Two days later, on May 2, 1945, Berlin fell to the Russians. On May 7, 1945, the Germans surrendered at a schoolhouse near Rheims (REEMZ). An elated world paused briefly to celebrate "**V-E Day**" ("Victory in Europe") on May 8. American efforts then turned to finishing off the Japanese in the Pacific.

Section Quiz

1. About how many Americans served in the armed forces during World War II?

CD: The Battle of the Bulge

Refer to the CD for photos from the Battle of the Bulge.

Costly Mistakes

No war is fought without mistakes, some of them costly. Do the students recognize any serious mistakes in Allied strategy in World War II? What were the consequences? Many historians criticize the decision to focus on mountainous Italy rather than the "soft underbelly" in the Balkans. They also think that decision allowed the Soviet Union to take over more of Eastern Europe than was necessary.

Another mistake was allowing the Soviets to reach Berlin first, thus dividing Germany in two. Eastern Europe still remembers with bitterness the "ghost of Yalta." The American people must learn from mistakes in the past so that they will be less likely to repeat them.

Another potentially costly mistake occurred during the Casablanca Conference between Roosevelt and Churchill. Roosevelt told the press that he would demand "unconditional surrender." As a result of this controversial announcement, it is certain that the antiwar movement was silenced in Germany and the German government faced utter ruin. The collapse of all German leadership helped the Communists to set up a puppet government there.

Debate Idea

Have your students discuss and/or debate this proposition: The Yalta agreement violated American national security interests in World War II.

Activity 6: Mapping World War II: European Theater

Use this activity to help the students gain an understanding of where the major events in the European Theater occurred.

2. Name three military organizations in which women served. How did women help the cause at home?

3. What had to be done with America's factory production?

4. Where was the first major battleground for American soldiers against the Germans in World War II?

5. What country was liberated from Axis rule under "Operation Husky"?

6. What actions did the RAF and the U.S. Air Force take against Germany so that the Allies could invade it?

7. Where and when did the largest amphibious invasion in history take place? What was this day called?

8. When did Germany finally surrender?

★ How did the conference at Yalta increase the power of the Soviet Union?

★ How were civilians able to aid the war effort?

IV. America Wins in the Pacific

While the war in Europe was being won, events in the Pacific did not come to a standstill. America put men, ships, and planes into the Japanese conflict as it was able, but the early results were discouraging.

Waging the War in the Pacific

The story of the war in the Pacific begins with the Japanese attack on Pearl Harbor. After that critical event, Japan advanced across the Pacific until the Allies found ways to move from the defensive to the offensive. Once they found the right strategy, the days of the Japanese war machine were numbered.

The Japanese Advance

The same day that Japan attacked Pearl Harbor, it also struck other major targets in the Pacific, including the Philippines. Since the Spanish-American War, the Philippines had been administered by the United States. The islands provided an important U.S. base in the Pacific. On Christmas Eve, 1941, the Japanese made a second large-scale landing there. By January, they controlled Manila. The American and Filipino troops, under General **Douglas MacArthur**, held only the Philippine peninsula of Bataan (buh TAN) and the small, nearby island of Corregidor (kuh REHG ih DOR). When FDR realized that American forces could not withstand the Japanese assault on the Philippines, he ordered MacArthur to leave. FDR did not want to risk the capture of a valuable general. MacArthur escaped to Australia by submarine. As he left, he promised the Filipinos, "I shall return."

With the supply lines cut, the American troops who remained in the Philippines ran low on supplies. They suffered from disease and hunger, having been on short rations. They battled to defend Bataan, but it was not enough. On April 9, 1942, most of the troops on the Bataan peninsula surrendered to the Japanese. The Japanese forced them to march in tropical heat, without food or water, for nearly a hundred miles to a prison camp.

Thirteen thousand of the American forces in the Philippines had escaped to Corregidor. By early May, the Japanese were shelling the

---

Bataan Death March

One of the greatest atrocities of the war in the Pacific was the Bataan Death March. The Japanese captured more prisoners (more than 70,000) than they expected. Because the soldiers had been on short rations already, they were not in good condition. Beginning on April 10, 1942, the Japanese forced them to march nearly 100 miles through jungle heat to a prison camp. They denied them food and water for days at a time. They beat and even killed them for little infractions, such as talking, resting, or helping others who had collapsed. Those who fell behind they bayoneted. Many of them drank dirty water from ditches and got sick. A few managed to escape and fight with guerrilla forces. Estimates of those who died on the march range from seven to ten thousand.

Section IV

Objectives

Students should be able to

1. Trace the extent of the Japanese advance.

2. Describe the battles of the Coral Sea and Midway.

3. Explain the American strategy for defeating the Japanese.

4. Explain the success, or lack thereof, of the kamikaze attacks.

5. Explain the need for the Manhattan Project.

6. Name the cities on which atomic bombs were dropped.

7. Describe the cost of World War II to the United States.

Why Did Japan Attack the United States?

To pull Japan out of the Depression, its government greatly expanded its industry. By the mid-1930s, it was well on the road to recovery. But the industrial machine that it had created needed fuel and raw materials that Japan did not naturally possess. Europe and the United States were closely guarding their own industrial and trading positions. Free trade was not a popular economic philosophy at that time. Western nations were imposing high tariffs and dumping their goods on other countries. The Japanese responded with tough protectionist trade measures.

The Japanese determined that if they could not get what they needed by trade, they would take it by force. They built a military machine and, in 1931, invaded Manchuria. In 1937, they attacked China. By then, the warlords controlled the Japanese government, and they acted on their

---

Section Quiz Answers

1. sixteen million

2. WACS, WAVES, and WASP; they became part of the job force, joined the Red Cross, and worked with the United Service Organizations.

3. It had to be retooled for the production of war goods.

4. North Africa

5. Italy

6. The RAF bombed German cities. The U.S. Air Force bombed industrial and military sites.

7. in Normandy on June 6, 1944; D-day

8. May 7, 1945

★ There, with Allied consent, it gained a foothold in Eastern Europe that would lead later to domination.

★ They limited their consumption of certain products; recycled tin cans, paper, aluminum, and iron; and grew gardens to ensure that the soldiers had adequate food and supplies.

CD: World War II in the Pacific

Refer to the CD for a map of the Pacific Theater of Operations during World War II.

The Doolittle Raid

An excellent first-person account of the Doolittle raid on Japan is *Thirty Seconds over Tokyo* by Ted W. Lawson, one of the B-25 pilots who participated in the raid. The journal *Military History* (March 1996) carried an excellent article titled "Interview with Doolittle Raider James Macia." Doolittle shares his memories in his autobiography, *I Could Never Be So Lucky Again*.

Refer to the CD for photos of the Doolittle raiders, their leader (Gen. James Doolittle), and their bomber, the B-25 Mitchell.

"southern strategy," attacking Southeast Asia (1940).

FDR responded to Japanese aggression by imposing an embargo on all oil and steel to Japan. The British were similarly stingy with their rubber in Malaysia.

The Japanese reasoned that with Europe embroiled in a battle for survival against Hitler, only the U.S. Pacific fleet stood in the way of their conquest of Southeast Asia. If Japan could destroy that fleet, it could hold onto and then solidify its control of the resources of Southeast Asia and the entire Pacific Rim. This conclusion led to the attack on Pearl Harbor.

Carrier Warfare Begins

Just as new technology made Hitler's blitzkrieg possible, it played a crucial role in both the Japanese attack on Pearl Harbor and Japan's defeat by the Americans. In 1910, an American stunt pilot named Eugene Ely landed a plane on a ship. By 1941, technology had developed to the point that planes were able to take off from and land on ships routinely. The Japanese airplanes that were used in the attack on Pearl Harbor were launched from Japanese aircraft carriers.

The Japanese carrier task force sailed northward above Hawaii. On December 7, 1941, the Japanese launched their attack. The carriers enabled the Japanese fighters to wreak havoc at the American naval base.

However, the same strategy that helped bring Japanese success also brought them ultimate failure in the war. The Japanese had hoped to find four American aircraft carriers at Pearl Harbor. Instead, they found none. The *Lexington* and the *Enterprise* were delivering marines to Wake and Midway Islands. The *Hornet* and the

American pilots under Lt. Col. James Doolittle launched a surprise bombing raid against Tokyo. For his leadership of the mission, Doolittle received the Congressional Medal of Honor.

Broken Japanese Code Led to Rout in Battle of Midway

American code crackers had broken a new Japanese code, and they learned of an imminent attack on a target they called simply "AF." Naval intelligence officers suspected it might be Midway Island. To test their hunch, they ordered personnel on Midway to send an uncoded message saying that the freshwater distillation plant at Midway was damaged. Then they monitored Japanese transmissions. Soon, they intercepted a Japanese message that said that "AF" was short of fresh water. Now the Americans knew where the attack was going to be made! With the advanced warning, the Americans surprised and defeated the invasion fleet, saving Midway and stopping the Japanese advance.

island constantly. The defenders of Corregidor finally surrendered on May 6. The Japanese now controlled all of the Philippines.

Meanwhile, the Japanese captured most of Southeast Asia and many other Pacific islands. In June, the Japanese turned northward and snatched two of the Aleutian Islands off the tip of southern Alaska. The Japanese seemed to control the entire region of eastern Asia and the western Pacific.

American shipyards and munitions factories were gradually making progress. In just fifteen months they were able to construct and commission new aircraft carriers. A stream of battleships, aircraft carriers, and escort vessels sailed westward to push back the Japanese.

The Allies Strike Back

In the spring and summer of 1942, Americans saw a ray of hope in the Pacific war. On April 8, 1942, the aircraft carrier *Hornet* secretly sailed within seven hundred miles of the Japanese mainland. Sixteen B-25 bombers under the command of Jimmy Doolittle shocked the Japanese by dropping bombs on Tokyo. The Japanese had no idea where the planes had come from. Since the planes could not return to the *Hornet*, they flew west over China. Four of the planes crash landed. Three raiders were killed and eight injured. Eight were captured by the Japanese. Three of those pilots were executed, one died as a prisoner of war, and the other four were liberated in 1945. One plane landed in Russia, and the crew members were imprisoned for thirteen months until they escaped through Iran. Of the eighty raiders, sixty-seven of them were helped by the Chinese. Although the operation did not do great damage, its success was a tremendous boost to American morale and a great blow to the Japanese.

The **Doolittle raid** forced the Japanese to change their war strategy. They did not know the location of the base from which the raiders had flown, so they split their force of aircraft carriers. They sent two to harass Allied naval supply lines near Australia. They moved the other four giant carriers into the middle of the Pacific. Those would be magnets to draw the United States into battle there. Because the Japanese lacked the productive power to fight a long war, they gambled everything on a quick victory.

The Japanese carriers heading for Australia used the Coral Sea as their route. In May 1942, their reconnaissance planes sighted an American naval force led by two aircraft carriers, the *Yorktown* and the *Lexington*. The resulting three-day **Battle of the Coral Sea** was unusual because it was the first sea battle in which all of the fighting was done by airplanes. The naval vessels of the opposing sides never saw each other. The Japanese force turned back, and one of its carriers was sunk. The *Lexington* suffered such extensive damage that it had to be destroyed, but the battle stopped the Japanese advance toward Australia.

The other Japanese carriers headed toward Midway Island, an American island west of Hawaii. The Japanese hoped to attack the island base and then lure American carriers into a battle. But American naval intelligence had cracked the Japanese radio code and had advance warning. Planes from American carriers bombed the Japanese ships before the Japanese could attack Midway. The Americans sank three Japanese carriers in a few minutes, and the fourth went down the next day. The Americans' cost also was high. They lost one aircraft carrier, the *Yorktown*, and most of its planes and pilots.

CD: Pacific Carriers
Refer to the CD for photos of aircraft carriers used during World War II.

CD: Amphibious Assaults
Refer to the CD for photos of some of the amphibious assaults on Japanese-held islands.

Activity 7: Mapping World War II: Pacific Theater
Use this activity to help the students gain an understanding of where the major events of the Pacific Theater of the war occurred.

Activity 8: A Marine's Journal from Guadalcanal
Use this activity to help the students understand the hardships and horrors of war faced by the Marines who fought to capture Guadalcanal.

Early Missions
Two videos that provide excellent insight into the early and lesser-known missions in the Pacific Theater are *Gung Ho!* starring Randolph Scott and *The Stilwell Road*, a documentary on the effort to defeat the Japanese in Indochina and featuring Ronald Reagan as narrator.

However, the Japanese sea offensive was stopped, and the Japanese navy had suffered a major defeat.

The Americans devised a strategy to capture the Japanese-held islands in the Pacific. Starting with the southern islands, American naval forces would work northward until they reached islands that were within bombing distance of Japan. General MacArthur would lead an operation that would push northward from New Guinea to the Philippines. Admiral **Chester Nimitz** (NIM itz) would "island-hop" across the mid-Pacific, taking certain key islands in three chains—the Gilberts, the Marshalls, and the Marianas—and by-passing the others. Then both forces would converge on the Japanese mainland.

MacArthur Moves Northward

The Japanese had almost finished building an airfield on **Guadalcanal** (GWOD ul kuh NAL) in the Solomon Islands near New Guinea. From there, they could bomb Allied convoys at will. So MacArthur began his offensive there in 1942, but it took six months to drive the Japanese out. They fought tenaciously, and American casualties were heavy. Finally, the Marines dynamited the island's caves to force out the last Japanese defenders.

The American attack on New Guinea became bogged down and was saved only when MacArthur airlifted fifteen thousand troops there. By October 1944, U.S. forces were ready to retake the Philippines. They landed first at Leyte (LAY tee). Many liberty-loving Filipino fighters who had hidden in the mountains and jungles now undertook guerrilla warfare to help the Americans free the Philippines. When MacArthur waded ashore, he said, "I have returned. By the grace of Almighty God, our forces stand again on Philippine soil, soil consecrated by the blood of our two peoples." By March 1945, the forces had moved northward and freed the Philippine capital of Manila on the island of Luzon.

Nimitz Moves Westward

The first target of Admiral Nimitz's Pacific operation was Tarawa. It is the largest atoll (a ring-like island of coral) in the Gilbert Islands. After bombing the island for a whole week and pounding it for hours with heavy naval guns, the Americans did not expect much resistance. But they soon learned how well the Japanese held out. American losses soared. The Japanese resisted until only seventeen of more than forty-five hundred defenders remained alive.

From the battle for Tarawa the Americans learned lessons for future attacks. The Japanese did not surrender easily. Two months of bombing before landing troops became normal. Battleships, cruisers, and destroyers hurled thousands of tons of explosives shoreward at Japanese targets.

After launching invasions in the Marshall Islands, the Nimitz forces recaptured Guam in the Marianas. Next, they retook the sea east of the Philippines from the Japanese. The fleet then angled northward toward **Iwo Jima** (EE-woh JEE-muh; "sulfur island"; renamed Iwo To in 2007). That small island, only seven hundred miles from Tokyo, had been a station from which the Japanese could intercept American bombers headed for Japan. If the United States could capture it, Iwo Jima could be an emergency stop for American bombers. It could also provide a takeoff point for shorter-range fighter planes. But Iwo Jima proved to be the costliest chunk of rock and black sand

The invasion of Guadalcanal was one of the first major U.S. offensive actions in the Pacific war.

Jungle fighting in Bougainville, New Guinea, was fierce.

Marines on Iwo Jima seldom saw their enemies and had to use flamethrowers to burn them out of their caves and tunnels.

Yorktown were not even in the Pacific. With their carriers intact, the Americans could still use their air power against the Japanese. And that made the difference in the Pacific War.

The Thach Weave

Compared to the Japanese Zero fighter plane, the American F4F Wildcat lacked maneuverability. The Zero could turn sharper and climb faster, giving it a definite advantage in a dogfight.

Lieutenant Commander J.S. Thach came up with a solution to that problem. He designed a looser, four-plane formation that allowed Wildcats to cover each other. The planes would be a team in battle. If a Wildcat was being chased by a Zero, it would begin a spiraling dive. Another Wildcat would start a similar dive that would intertwine with the first, giving it the opportunity to shoot the pursuing Zero. The Navy soon made the "Thach Weave" a standard tactic for their pilots.

The Stilwell Road

By trucking supplies from the British colony of Burma (known today as Myanmar) to China, the Allies helped the Nationalist Chinese hold out against the Japanese, supplied the American Volunteer Group (Flying Tigers), and forced Japan to keep valuable troops in China rather than in other areas of the Pacific. The British started the route, called the Burma Road, by building a railroad from Rangoon to Lashio in 1937 and 1938. But the Japanese attacked Burma early in the war and cut the road. When the United States entered the war, American pilots flew supplies in C-47 transports over the Himalayas. That route "over the Hump," as the pilots called it, was considered the most dangerous assignment of the war. General Joe Stilwell

The Image of Iwo Jima

Refer to the famous photograph of Marines raising the flag on Mount Suribachi during the battle for Iwo Jima. Ask them to explain how that is a fitting image of America's effort during the war.

Iwo Jima

The video *Iwo Jima* by Timeless Media Group is an excellent (though very graphic) account of battlefield reality. It uses accounts by veterans of the battle and actual war footage.

The Horrors of War

The decision to firebomb Japanese cities was not easy. Debate continues over its morality. Although the Japanese committed many atrocities, was America justified in responding with firebombs? One argument in favor of the decision was to hasten the end of the war and, ultimately, save American lives. One argument against the decision was that it punished civilians.

and his troops drove the Japanese from Burma and performed an engineering miracle in completing a winding road—called the Ledo Road—the rest of the way to China. The combined Burma and Ledo roads were completed in early 1945 and were called the Stilwell Road in honor of the man who had made it happen.

Famous Iwo Jima Photograph

American Marines raised Old Glory atop Mount Suribachi during the Battle of Iwo Jima in 1945. The Marine memorial in Arlington National Cemetery replicates a scene captured on film by Joe Rosenthal, an Associated Press photographer, during the battle. His photograph of the flag-raising on Iwo Jima won him a Pulitzer prize and became the most famous photograph of the war.

Truman's Decision to Drop the Bomb

Truman's decision to drop the atomic bomb on Japan is still debated today. Was dropping the bomb necessary to end the war? Did it prevent a costly American invasion of Japan? Or was the bomb simply used to show America's military superiority?

Traditionally, the rationale given for dropping the bomb was to prevent further loss of American lives. The war in the Pacific had already been costly. To continue the island-hopping campaign, especially to initiate an invasion of the Japanese homeland, would have meant many more deaths—both American and Japanese—and a longer war. Even before the bomb was dropped, some people suggested using it in a test demonstration with U.S. and Japanese officials present. Seeing the force of the blast would have been a powerful deterrent for anyone. However, other

The *Yamato*, Japanese Supership

During World War II, Japan could claim the largest battleship in history. The *Yamato* was so big that a special shipyard had to be built to construct its hull. The ship was 863 feet long and displaced 70,000 tons of water, making it 20 percent heavier than the biggest American battleships. Its sides were made of 25-inch heavy armor weighing 23,000 tons, more than one-third the total weight of the ship. Its hull could survive a direct hit from a 3,000-pound armor-piercing shell. It had 1,150 watertight compartments, leading some Japanese naval officials to claim that it was unsinkable.

Offensively, the *Yamato* was formidable. It boasted nine 18-inch guns with a range of 25 miles, eight 6-inch guns with a range of 17 miles, twenty-four 5-inch guns with a range of 9 miles, and more than 150 machine guns, most in triple-mounted turrets shooting 220 rounds per minute. The tower used state-of-the-art optics in a highly accurate range finder. The ship also carried seven floatplanes, launched from two catapults, for reconnaissance and spotting fire from the big guns. Four steam turbine engines, powered by twelve boilers, produced 150,000 horsepower. At full speed (28 knots, or 32 miles per hour), the *Yamato* burned 70 tons of fuel oil per hour. A crew of 2,800 sailors manned the battleship.

As mighty as the *Yamato*'s potential was, it was used sparingly and spent most of the war in port. It fought Allied ships only once—in the Battle of Samar Gulf—and sank one American escort carrier and one destroyer. Its last confrontation with the Americans was a different story. On April 7, 1945, about fifty miles south of Kyushu, American carrier-based bombers attacked the *Yamato*. In about two hours, the *Yamato* took direct hits by twelve bombs and seven torpedoes. The torpedo planes set their torpedoes so that they hit the ship below the waterline near the bow and stern, where the ship had thinner armor. The resulting fires were the apparent cause of a massive explosion in the aft ammunition magazine, which ripped the vessel in two and sent it to the bottom of the ocean.

Kamikaze attacks, such as this one by a Mitsubishi Zero (circled) on the battleship U.S.S. *Missouri*, plagued the navy in the last months of the war.

More than 12,000 American and 117,000 Japanese soldiers lost their lives in fierce fighting on Okinawa. The shocking death toll made U.S. officials consider using a secret weapon rather than invading Japan directly.

taken by the U.S. Marine Corps in their 168-year history. More than five thousand Marines died during its capture in early 1945.

As war came closer to the Japanese homeland, the fighting intensified. Allied seamen came to fear a new type of Japanese attack: the **kamikaze** (KAH mih KAH zee). Kamikazes were pilots who deliberately tried to crash their planes into an enemy ship. Such attacks were a product of the Japanese belief that the highest gift one could give the emperor was one's life. Furthermore, Japan had already lost its first-rate pilots and its best planes. In kamikaze warfare, the Japanese could load out-of-date or poorly built planes with explosives and let inexperienced pilots fly them. They had only to dive into a ship. The results were devastating. In spite of the kamikaze attacks, the American forces pushed on toward Japan.

Okinawa (OH kih NAH wah) was the last obstacle before reaching the Japanese mainland. The assault on Okinawa began in April 1945 and took eighty-two days to complete. The Japanese fought fiercely. Kamikazes launched 1,465 attacks, sinking 30 U.S. ships and damaging 164 others. Thousands of sailors lost their lives. The Japanese had spread rumors among Okinawan civilians of how inhumanely Americans treated prisoners. The Japanese encouraged (some survivors say ordered) civilians to commit suicide rather than surrender to the Americans. They even distributed hand grenades for that purpose. Many civilians followed their advice and blew up their entire families. Thousands of others jumped from cliffs onto jagged rocks in the sea.

With control of Okinawa, the Americans were just 325 miles from mainland Japan. They were able to attack Japan's military, industrial, and population centers at will. In one ten-day bombing blitz, American planes turned thirty-two square miles of factories into wasteland. Fire bombing of residential areas was especially destructive because the Japanese homes were built close together and were made of highly flammable materials.

Winning the Peace

Japan's cities suffered heavily from Allied bombing raids. The American military had learned, however, how hard the Japanese fought. Many experts feared that to invade and conquer Japan would cost up to a million American lives. To avoid that deadly price, they began to consider using a powerful new weapon that researchers were developing.

The Beginning of the Atomic Era

When Hitler gained power in 1933, he began persecuting German Jews. German physics professor Albert Einstein, a Jew, took refuge in the United States. Einstein wrote to Roosevelt in July 1939 to tell him that the Nazis were trying to develop a powerful uranium bomb. He advised him of the possibilities and dangers of such a weapon. FDR and his advisors decided to set up a secret program to make such a bomb before the Germans could do so. They called the top-secret operation the **Manhattan Project**.

The government bought hundreds of acres of property in a remote area nestled among the high ridges west of Knoxville, Tennessee. They then built an entire "secret city": Oak Ridge. They assembled thousands of laborers and construction specialists and brilliant chemists and engineers. Inside closely guarded plants code-named Y-12, X-10, and K-25, those scientists designed and assembled the materials for the secret weapon. Then they shipped it to the desert at Alamagordo, near Los Alamos, New Mexico. At dawn on July 16, 1945, the first device, an atomic bomb, was tested successfully.

On April 12, 1945, Franklin Roosevelt died suddenly from a stroke. The day after Vice President **Harry Truman** stepped into the presidency, he learned about the Manhattan Project. He thought it would be better to end the war quickly using the new weapon than to waste hundreds of thousands of lives—both American and Japanese—invading Japan. People have debated the wisdom and morality of Truman's decision, but Truman had no doubts. He wrote in his *Memoirs*, "Let there be no mistake about it. I regarded the bomb as a military weapon and never had any doubt that it should be used."

On July 26, Truman met at Potsdam, Germany, for a conference with the other major powers. They issued the **Potsdam Declaration**, demanding that Japan surrender unconditionally or face total destruction.

Although the original military leaders in Japan's war effort were no longer in power, the new premier refused to surrender. Eleven days later, on August 6, 1945, at 8:15 a.m., an American B-29 bomber named the *Enola Gay*, piloted by Paul Tibbets, took off from Tinian, an island with the longest runway in the world at that time. High above the Japanese city of **Hiroshima** (HIR uh SHE muh) the bomb bay doors opened. Out dropped a single uranium bomb nicknamed "Little Boy." Although it was only a little more than two feet in diameter and ten feet long, the bomb's explosive power was equal to twenty thousand tons of dynamite. The blast destroyed the city and killed eighty thousand Japanese civilians. An equal number suffered radiation burns.

On August 9, after the Japanese government ignored another warning to surrender, the United States dropped a single plutonium

Secrecy was a way of life in the "Secret City" of Oak Ridge, Tennessee, during the building of the first atomic bomb.

The *Enola Gay* was the B-29 that was used to drop the first atomic bomb on Japan.

people countered that a test situation was too risky. The bomb had never been used before. If it failed to detonate in a test, it might have had the unintended effect of bolstering Japan's confidence.

Another argument in favor of using the bomb is that it forced Japan to accept "unconditional surrender" terms with the United States.

Many modern historians have focused on the influence of Soviet-American relations in the decision to drop the bomb. Some people argue that the main motivation for the decision was not to force Japan to surrender but to intimidate the Soviet Union. While attending the Potsdam Conference with Churchill and Stalin, Truman learned that the atomic bomb had been successfully tested. He was described as a "changed man" when he next met with Stalin. He had more confidence and determination to resist Stalin's ambitions.

Germany and the Bomb

Germany had nearly perfected the atomic bomb before its armies were defeated; thus, development of the bomb was vital to the United States. Imagine what Hitler could have done if he had gained the atomic bomb first.

The scientists on the Manhattan Project had built only three bombs. One was used in the test in New Mexico, and the other two were dropped on Japan.

 ## CD: Japanese Battleship *Yamato*; The End Approaches

Refer to the CD for artwork of the Japanese superbattleship *Yamato*, photos of the "Big Three" at Potsdam, illustrations of the atomic bombs dropped on Japan, and a photo of Gen. Douglas MacArthur at the surrender of Japan.

 ## CD: Harry Truman, 33rd President

Refer to the CD for information on the life and career of President Harry Truman.

 ## "Living in the Shadow of the Atomic City"

Blue Ridge Country magazine (May/June 1998) includes an interesting article, "Living in the Shadow of the Atomic City," about a young boy who grew up near Oak Ridge, Tennessee, the "Atomic City."

  ## Red Flags—The Decision to Drop the Bomb

The section titled "The Beginning of the Atomic Era" analyzes the controversial decision to drop the atomic bomb. Divide the class into opposing sides on the issue, and ask them to research the arguments given on both sides.

 ## CD: The Cost of America's Wars

Refer to the CD for a table comparing World War II casualties with other major American wars.

 ## Activity 9: Chapter Review

Use this activity as a general review of the main facts of the chapter in preparation for the chapter test.

Adolf Eichmann

The name of Adolf Eichmann continued to surface in the Nuremberg Trials. He and his men hunted down Jews as the Nazis moved into Russia. He was responsible for sending millions of Jews to Nazi death camps.

Eichmann had been captured, but he was using the alias Otto Eckmann. Knowing he would eventually be found out, Eichmann escaped from the American prison near Nuremberg and hid in the mountains of central Germany. He became a chicken farmer and changed his name to Otto Henninger. Later, Eichmann moved to Italy and, with the help of the underground Nazi movement, escaped to Argentina.

Under the name Ricardo Klement, he started a new life as a rabbit farmer and a foreman at a Mercedes-Benz plant. His true identity was concealed until 1959, when the Israelis received a tip regarding his location and his alias. Agents secretly kept him under surveillance, gathering important information to confirm his identity. Undercover agents even asked him for directions while secretly taking pictures of him with a camera hidden in a briefcase.

Finally, the Israelis grabbed Eichmann as he got off a bus. After signing a statement of willingness to stand trial, he was smuggled out of the country to Israel. Eichmann was kept in a high-security prison and charged on fifteen counts of war crimes. He was found guilty of all of them and was hanged. His ashes were spread over the Mediterranean.

Residents of Oak Ridge celebrated the end of World War II.

World War II officially ended with the Japanese signing of the terms of surrender aboard the U.S.S. *Missouri* in Tokyo Bay.

After the war, Nazi war criminals were tried in Nuremberg for crimes against humanity.

bomb nicknamed "Fat Man" on **Nagasaki** (NAH guh SAH kee). That bomb flattened the city and killed about forty thousand people. The next day Japan sued for peace.

Peace

On August 15, 1945, the Japanese people heard the voice of their emperor Hirohito. In a taped radio broadcast, the emperor told his subjects that the war was over. Upon hearing the news, Americans in the States left their work, ran into the streets, and celebrated for joy.

Although a few isolated Japanese in distant, isolated spots—in small groups or individually—continued to fight, the war was really over. On August 21, General MacArthur was in Tokyo. He ordered that the same flag that was flying over the U.S. Capitol on December 7, 1941, be raised over the reopened American embassy. MacArthur said, "Let it wave in full glory as a symbol of hope for the oppressed and as a harbinger of victory."

On September 2, 1945, MacArthur accepted two of the emperor's representatives on board the battleship *Missouri* anchored in Tokyo Bay. There they signed the formal treaty of surrender.

World War II was the costliest war in history. It is estimated that more than fifteen million soldiers and twenty million civilians died in the war. The United States lost nearly three hundred thousand of its military personnel, and many more were wounded. On top of the human effort and loss, the nation spent about $300 billion on the war.

Americans returned to peacetime with great relief. Despite the high price they had paid, Americans had won the war. It then remained for them to take their place in the postwar world.

Section Quiz

1. What American general was forced to evacuate while attempting to hold the Philippines?
2. What two American military leaders took command of much of the action against Japan?
3. An airfield on which of the Solomon Islands took the Americans six months to capture?
4. What small island base had the Japanese used to keep American bombers from Japan? How many marines died in its capture?
5. What was the last American conquest before attacking the Japanese mainland?
6. What was the Manhattan Project?
7. Who became president before the war ended?
8. On what two cities were the atomic bombs dropped?
9. Where, when, and by whom was the Japanese surrender accepted?
10. How many American servicemen died in the war?
★ Why has there been debate over Truman's decision to drop the atomic bomb?

Section Quiz Answers

1. Douglas MacArthur
2. Douglas MacArthur and Chester Nimitz
3. Guadalcanal
4. Iwo Jima; more than five thousand
5. Okinawa
6. research, development, and building of the first atomic bomb
7. Harry Truman
8. Hiroshima and Nagasaki
9. aboard the battleship U.S.S. *Missouri* in Tokyo Bay; September 2, 1945; Douglas MacArthur
10. nearly 300,000
★ People who opposed the bombing argue that targeting civilians with such a destructive weapon is immoral. Some were worried about the dangerous potential of such a weapon if our enemies gained possession of it. Those who supported the bombing argued that the use of the bomb saved both American and Japanese lives that would have been lost in a conventional invasion.

Look Ahead

Point out to the students that at the close of the war, most people, including Truman, hoped that the good relations with the Soviet Union would carry over into the postwar era. The world had only a hint of the coming Cold War. The disappointments of the subsequent years are an essential part of any evaluation of the success of World War II. Like so many other wars, the victory later seemed empty. Christians know that no war can solve mankind's basic problems, and they also know that wars will be fought until Christ's return.

Chapter Review

Review Questions

Identify the best word(s) for each of the following phrases.

1. Italian governing system under Mussolini that stressed nationalism and power
2. giving in to demands in an attempt to avoid confrontation
3. a swift attack of military forces—a "lightning war"
4. young men who were sincerely opposed to war and were allowed to serve in noncombat roles
5. Japanese pilots who flew their planes on suicide missions to destroy American ships

Match each of the following leaders with his country.

6. Franklin Roosevelt
7. Benito Mussolini
8. Joseph Stalin
9. Adolf Hitler
10. Winston Churchill

a. Britain
b. Germany
c. Italy
d. Soviet Union
e. United States

Match each of the following dates with the appropriate event.

11. V-E Day
12. attack on Pearl Harbor
13. Hitler invades Poland
14. bomb dropped on Hiroshima
15. D-day

a. August 6, 1945
b. September 1, 1939
c. May 8, 1945
d. December 7, 1941
e. June 6, 1944

Critical Thinking

1. Should the United States have been better prepared for World War II? Should it be constantly prepared for war? Explain your answers.
2. How does a man like Hitler gain such popularity and power? Could such a man rise to power in the United States? Explain your answer.

People, Places, and Things to Remember:

Benito Mussolini
fascism
Adolf Hitler
Nazi Party
Axis powers
"Good Neighbor Policy"
Winston Churchill
appeasement
Joseph Stalin
blitzkrieg
Allies
Lend-Lease Act
Pearl Harbor
conscientious objectors
rationed
Dwight D. Eisenhower
"D-day"
Battle of the Bulge
Yalta Conference
"V-E Day"
Douglas MacArthur
Doolittle raid
Battle of the Coral Sea
Chester Nimitz
Guadalcanal
Iwo Jima
kamikaze
Okinawa
Manhattan Project
Harry Truman
Potsdam Declaration
Hiroshima
Nagasaki

Chapter Review Answers

Review Questions

1. fascism
2. appeasement
3. *blitzkrieg*
4. conscientious objectors
5. kamikazes
6. e
7. c
8. d
9. b
10. a
11. c
12. d
13. b
14. a
15. e

Critical Thinking

1. Answers will vary. It is easy for us to be "armchair quarterbacks" after the fact; it is different to know what is best at that particular moment. The logical answer to the second question is that we clearly should be prepared in case we have war thrust upon us, but the bigger question is *how* we should do that. Topics that might be discussed include the draft, professional army versus conscripted army, monetary justification, danger of the concept of a military-industrial complex, etc.

2. Answers will vary. He tells the people what they want to hear, and they do not recognize the danger involved. Americans must guard their government to prevent a similar misuse of power.

1946-49: Long-playing (LP) phonograph records were invented.

How much did it cost?

Product	Year	Price
Bread	1950	14¢/loaf
	2004	94¢/loaf
Butter	1950	78¢/lb.
	2004	$2.84/lb.
Coffee	1950	77¢/lb.
	2004	$2.89/lb.
Eggs	1950	57¢/doz.
	2004	$1.57/doz.
Sugar	1950	9¢/lb.
	2004	42¢/lb.

1947 Taft-Hartley Act

1949 Founding of NATO

1950-53 Korean War

1954 Brown v. Board of Education

1959 Alaska and Hawaii statehood

1963 Civil rights march on Washington, D.C.
Assassination of John Kennedy

1964-73 Vietnam War

1973 Roe v. Wade

1947

1965: St. Louis Gateway Arch was completed.

1950-54: Frozen TV dinners first became available.

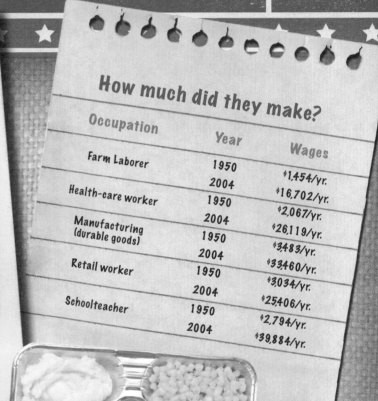

How much did they make?

Occupation	Year	Wages
Farm Laborer	1950	$1,454/yr.
	2004	$16,702/yr.
Health-care worker	1950	$2,067/yr.
	2004	$26,119/yr.
Manufacturing (durable goods)	1950	$3,483/yr.
	2004	$33,460/yr.
Retail worker	1950	$3,034/yr.
	2004	$25,406/yr.
Schoolteacher	1950	$2,794/yr.
	2004	$39,884/yr.

1974 Resignation of Richard Nixon

1979–81 Iranian hostage crisis

1980 Election of Ronald Reagan

1991 Persian Gulf War

1995 Founding of World Trade Organization

1998 Impeachment of Bill Clinton

2000 Disputed election (Bush v. Gore)

2001 (Sept. 11) al-Qaeda attack on United States War on terrorism began

2001

Chapter Goals

Students should be able to

1. Describe the changes in American life after World War II.
2. Explain the effects of the Cold War on United States foreign policy in the fifties and sixties.
3. Define and use the basic terms of the chapter.
4. Understand that the world will never be safe for democracy and that "eternal vigilance is the price of liberty."

Chapter Motivation

Although America had helped other nations win a war for democracy, the next thirty years continued the fight against communism. Remind your students that there are always men and governments that desire to control others and take away their freedoms. Freedom is hard to maintain and is constantly threatened; therefore, free people and societies must always be vigilant against those who would destroy it. Ask the students to look for God's control in the events of the fifties and sixties.

CHAPTER 25

President Harry Truman greets General Dwight Eisenhower following the defeat of Nazi Germany.

Recovery, Cold War, and Coexistence

I. Home from the War

II. The Postwar World

III. Cold War Crises

IV. The Eisenhower Era

Chapter 25 Lesson Plan Chart

Section Title	Main Activity	Pages	Days
I. Home from the War	Activity 1: Jackie Robinson Breaks Baseball's Color Barrier, 1945	473–79	1–2 days
II. The Postwar World	Activity 2: Understanding the United Nations	479–82	1 day
III. Cold War Crises	Activity 4: Two Views of the Firing of General MacArthur	482–87	1–2 days
IV. The Eisenhower Era	Activity 5: Chapter Review	487–90	1 day
TOTAL SUGGESTED DAYS (INCLUDING 1 DAY FOR REVIEW AND TESTING)			5–7 DAYS

MATERIALS LIST

SECTION I
- Special speaker: someone who lived during the fifties
- A prepared wall timeline listing events of the 1950s (optional; see p. 474)
- Video recordings of 1950s television programs (optional; see p. 475)
- CD: Party Platform Summaries, 1948; Electoral College Results, 1948; "Integrated Bus Suggestions" by Rev. M.L. King
- Activity 1 from the *Student Activities* manual

SECTION II
- Activity 2 from the *Student Activities* manual

At 7:00 p.m. (EST) on August 14, 1945, President Harry Truman announced to the nation that Japan had finally accepted the terms of surrender. Church bells rang. Whistles blew. Troop ships halfway across the Pacific turned around and headed home. World War II was over! The United States was at peace.

But the United States faced new challenges that proved to be almost as trying as the war itself. The postwar world was not the same as the prewar world. New problems, new threats, and new fears emerged. But the country would also have new opportunities and new technology that would bring a new prosperity.

I. Home from the War

The end of the war brought nine million men in uniform home to civilian life. It also brought the need to retool industries to produce peacetime goods instead of guns and tanks. It opened the way for new inventions, new styles, and new fads that changed America's way of life.

Changing Times

Many Americans feared that a depression would follow World War II as had happened after World War I. Instead, they found plenty of jobs, and they kept business booming by demanding more and more material goods.

A Material Boom

Americans wanted new things and labor-saving devices. They wanted dishwashers, automatic washers, power lawn mowers, and boats. Easy credit encouraged much spending.

Shortages and rationing of some goods during the war created high demand for them after the war. In 1944, factories had produced 100,000 planes and only 70,000 passenger cars. In 1949, only 6,000 planes were produced, but 3.7 million passenger cars rolled off assembly lines. So many goods were in demand that factories could not produce enough to satisfy the public. Waiting lists for high-demand products such as cars grew. Prices on many goods skyrocketed until the demand was met. But as more factories got in gear to produce needed items, the economy became more stable.

The G.I. Bill

Fearful that soldiers returning from war would be unemployed, as many were after World War I, Congress passed the **G.I. Bill**. It helped veterans move into civilian life. This bill gave veterans benefits in many areas, including help finding jobs and money for education and home purchases. Veterans enrolled in night classes and colleges in record numbers.

The "Baby Boom"

Many young couples had postponed marriage during the war. When the war ended, they got married and many of them started families. The resulting "**baby boom**" created tremendous new demands, which changed over the years as the children grew. A demand for housing was followed by a demand for baby goods such as baby food, diapers, and strollers. When those children started school, an acute shortage of classrooms and teachers became apparent. By the mid-1960s, those children would be young adults, headed for college or the job market. By the turn of the century, they would be nearing

American military personnel returned from the war to face a changed American society.

Former soldiers flooded college admissions offices after the war, taking advantage of the G.I. Bill's educational benefits.

Courtesy: Indiana University Archives (PS4610)

Section I
Objectives
Students should be able to

1. Describe the economic conditions that followed the war.
2. Explain how the places and ways people lived changed in the years after the war, including the baby boom, the growth of suburbs, fads, and technological advances.
3. Describe Truman's Fair Deal, including labor relations and civil rights issues.
4. Trace the development of the civil rights movement.

The Automobile Boom

In 1942, automobile manufacturers stopped making cars and began making tanks and military trucks instead. Tires and gasoline also were rationed during the war. The unsatisfied demand for automobiles and other consumer goods grew throughout the war.

As soon as possible after the war ended, industries shifted to production of consumer goods. People added their names to long waiting lists and paid for cars before they were even built. In addition to new models in the popular prewar brands (e.g., Ford, Oldsmobile, Chevrolet), new brands came out, some to success and others to utter failure. One successful new vehicle was the direct product of the war. The government had contracted the Willys company to build a General Purpose (GP) vehicle for the Army. The soldiers who used it Americanized GP to "Jeep." It was such a successful, popular vehicle that Willys convinced the government to allow it to manufacture consumer versions. One of the failures was the Tucker '48, known as the Tucker Torpedo. Advertised as the

Core Values

In the years following World War II, the United States was guided by its core values. The desire for freedom dominated much of the decision making of this era. Americans saw communism as a threat to freedom and therefore began a long and costly conflict to contain communism across the globe. In order to avoid another global conflict, the leading nations of the world agreed to form the United Nations. By working within an international body, the United States had to sacrifice some of its individualism.

At home, post-war America was characterized by growth. The population exploded, and the economy grew along with it. Suburbs sprang up, and the new interstate highways connected Americans with a network of easily-traveled roads.

In the midst of this growth, many failed to acknowledge that African Americans were denied freedom and equality. Black soldiers had fought for freedom in Europe and the Pacific only to be denied basic freedoms when they returned home.

"Car of Tomorrow," it had a long, low, sleek body style that engineers declared was the most aerodynamic style of its day. It also had multiple safety features, an aluminum block, fuel injection, and an air-cooled engine. It had three headlights, including one in the center of the grill that rotated side to side as the steering wheel turned. It could go from 0 to 60 mph in 10 seconds. The original price was $2,450. Tucker sold $25 million in stock and dealer franchises and built fifty-one of the vehicles before the company folded. More than forty of those fifty-one Tuckers are still in existence, and they are valued at $200,000 to $750,000.

Levittowns

After World War II, many Americans were eager to move from their cramped city apartments. Government measures such as the G.I. Bill had given people the means to move, but builders such as William and Alfred Levitt gave them a destination.

During World War II, the Levitt brothers had obtained a federal contract to build homes for defense workers. During those years, they learned how to build houses cheaply and quickly. They put their skills to good use in 1947 by building a suburban housing development on New York's Long Island.

On 1,200 acres of what had been potato farmland, the Levitts and their workers laid out street after street and built home after home. The Levitts reduced home building to twenty-seven steps. Different materials were dropped off at sites throughout the day, and each worker specialized in one particular task. Trees were laid out exactly twenty-eight feet apart, and houses were built on two models, the Cape Cod and the ranch house.

Subdivisions sprang up, creating a transition zone between cities and rural areas.

retirement and putting great strains on the Social Security system.

The Growth of Suburbs

With housing shortages in the early postwar years and the high cost of land in the cities, more Americans became willing to move to the suburbs. Contractors built homes cheaply and quickly, using the techniques of mass production. Bulldozers graded the lots, and work crews came to lay water, gas, sewer, and electrical lines. They were followed by carpenters, who built row after row of identical houses. Roofers, plumbers, electricians, and painters applied their skills as well. Rolling fields turned into suburbs in a few weeks or months.

About 95 percent of those who moved to homes in the suburbs were younger whites. Cities were left to be occupied by the poor (mostly the elderly and racial minorities). Cities could not collect heavy taxes from the poor. They had to function with less money, so cities began to decay. City governments sought federal government aid for urban renewal projects.

To live in the suburbs, Americans needed more cars. The breadwinner needed a car to drive to work, and the busy family wanted to use another. With more cars came more automotive-related industries like service stations and car washes. Shopping centers were started to cut the travel distance to stores. Cities spread out so much that some people described the situation as "urban sprawl."

Traffic increased, and commuter traffic jams became more common. With more cars, highways, and new jobs, Americans were willing to move from their hometowns to areas of the country that offered new or better jobs. The West, especially California, was the biggest attraction. The South and the Southwest also grew in population. That southwesterly movement was the beginning of the "**sunbelt migrations**," movements toward the areas of the country with warmer climates.

Technological Advances

During the war, scientists had tried to make new materials and inventions that would help the war effort, especially substitutes for materials that were in short supply. With the war over, scientists found peacetime applications for some war inventions and materials. They used new medicines and vaccines to treat diseases. They used synthetic fibers, plastics, and other new materials in consumer industries. New hybrid crops, insecticides, machinery, fertilizers, and better irrigation methods allowed farmers to grow more crops. Those changes in American agriculture have sometimes been called the "**green revolution**."

Such technology also affected leisure time. Although television as a workable invention was known as early as 1927, it was not perfected until after World War II. In 1946, only seven thousand television sets existed. By 1950, there were 4 million; and by 1960, 74 million. Television had many effects on Americans. One effect was to decrease regional differences. People from the North, South, East, and West all watched the same programs.

Firsthand Account of Life in the Fifties

Arrange for a guest speaker who grew up during the 1950s to talk to the class and answer students' questions. In particular, ask the speaker to talk about changes in cars, the interstate highways, fads, sports, the statehood of Alaska and Hawaii, the St. Lawrence Seaway, or the Cold War. Have the students prepare questions. Give the questions to the guest speaker ahead of time.

More on Life in the Fifties

Consider obtaining copies of *Reminisce* magazine to bring to class for the students to examine. That publication quite often has short first-person accounts of

events, people, fads, and other memories of life in the fifties. It also has excellent photographs from that era.

A Timeline of the 1950s

Hang a timeline on the wall and write the foreign and domestic events in their proper places as you discuss them in class. Or have students prepare their own timelines with categories for social, political, literary, and economic events for the 1950s.

As Baby Boomers Age

Discuss the negative repercussions on the Social Security System as baby boomers reach retirement age. The nation will then have more retirees taking money from the system than young workers paying into it.

Old Debates About Internal Improvements

Throughout this unit, help the students to see how modern problems are parallel to problems Americans have faced in the past. When they read about the Federal Aid Highway Act, what similar issues do they remember from the past? (*turnpikes, canals, and railroads; Henry Clay's American System*) Do they remember the issues on both sides

Fads

Crazes were also common in the postwar decade. More than 30 million Americans purchased Hula-Hoops, large plastic rings that could be twirled around the hips for exercise. Never at a loss for ideas, marketers and advertisers seized every opportunity to make a dollar. A Walt Disney television series based on the life of frontier hero Davy Crockett led to a whole series of products. Children carried Davy Crockett lunch boxes and wore coonskin caps and buckskin jackets while singing about the "King of the Wild Frontier."

Materialism

Because of the prosperity of the post-war era, many Americans became **materialistic**, pursuing material possessions over spiritual concerns. Church attendance grew during this period, but many Americans now attended theologically liberal churches that satisfied the new middle class by adding a veneer of religion to their lives.

The Fair Deal

Although the Great Depression was over, many people still wanted the government aid that Roosevelt's New Deal had promised. They wondered if Truman would support such programs. Their answer came in September 1945. At a special session of Congress, Truman presented a twenty-one-point domestic program called the **Fair Deal**. The policies were similar to those of the New Deal. Truman proposed the G.I. Bill, promoted increased aid to science and public education, and advocated subsidized medical insurance. For better or worse, the federal government continued to expand its role in the lives of American citizens.

One issue that did not go Truman's way was the control of labor unions. During the days of high inflation after the war, laborers wanted higher wages without price increases. Auto, steel, coal, and railroad workers resorted to striking to get their way. As the number of strikes grew, some people thought that unions had gained too much power. Truman had a hard time controlling the labor unrest himself, but he did not like the way the Republican Congress dealt with it.

Congress passed the **Taft-Hartley Act** of 1947 over Truman's veto. The act limited union powers by giving employees more freedom to work against unions. The bill outlawed the closed shop, a practice that forced businesses to hire only union members. It allowed states to pass laws prohibiting union shops from requiring workers to join the union within a certain date of their hiring. Unions also had to give a sixty-day notice before changing or ending work contracts. During that time, they could not strike. And if a planned strike threatened national health or safety, a court could issue an eighty-day **injunction**, an order forbidding the strike. During that time the strikers and the management had to settle the dispute through negotiations.

Truman had not been very popular in his first few years as president. The election of 1948 promised to be a hard fight for him. Henry Wallace, FDR's secretary of agriculture, opposed Truman on the Progressive Party ticket. Even conservatives within his own party opposed him. Conservative Southern Democrats especially disliked Truman's efforts to ensure that the civil rights of African Americans were protected. Calling themselves the "Dixiecrats," they bolted the party. They chose South Carolina governor Strom Thurmond to run

Popular TV Shows of the Fifties

Television of the 1950s offered a surprising variety of programming options, from sports to drama to education. One of the earliest sports featured on TV was boxing matches, or "the fights." One of the long-popular drama series was *Lassie* (1954). An early educational series was *You Are There* (1953), in which newsman Walter Cronkite narrated famous historical events as though the viewer were present for them. Early children's programming featured *Howdy Doody* (1947) and *Captain Kangaroo* (1954). Perhaps the most popular variety program was *The Ed Sullivan Show* (1948), which featured everything from musicians to comedians to acrobats. Westerns were also popular with early TV viewers. The top (and longest-running) westerns included *Gunsmoke* (1955) and *Bonanza* (1959). News and discussion programs included *Meet the Press* (1947) and *Today* (1952). But undoubtedly the most popular type of programming for all ages was the comedies. Three of them remain popular as reruns even today: *I Love Lucy* (1951), *The Honeymooners* (1952), and *The Adventures of Ozzie and Harriet* (1952).

The cast of *I Love Lucy*

The Levitts used several cost-cutting measures in their construction. Instead of building basements, the Levitts installed radiant heat coils in the concrete slabs. Sheetrock walls replaced plaster walls. They installed preassembled metal cabinets instead of wooden ones. One of the most distinguishable features was a large wall of windows in the back of the house. That feature not only saved the Levitts from having to build another wall but also made the house seem bigger by giving a broad view of the back yard.

In the first week of sales, they sold more than three hundred homes. Prices started at $6,990, but Levitt soon increased the price by $1,000. Still, it was a good deal, and many people were willing to pay the price. Buyers agreed to follow rules, such as mowing the lawn once a week, not hanging laundry on weekends, and not building fences.

Success in New York inspired the Levitts to build other Levittowns in New Jersey, Pennsylvania, and Florida. Many other suburban developers followed the Levitts' pattern as well. However, some people began to criticize Levittowns as symbols of a growing conformity in American culture. According to them, all of the houses looked the same, and everyone conformed to prescribed social roles. Those criticisms seemed justified at first; but once people got settled, they began to individualize their homes. Many built additions for extra living space or added carports and garages. In fact, Levitt homes were changed so much that the Smithsonian has had difficulty finding an original, unmodified Levitt home for its collection. Only a few now exist, and their owners are not yet willing to give up their homes.

---

of the debate? (*Some opponents say that such expenditures are not the constitutional authority of the federal government. Others say that federal involvement leads to graft and inefficiency. Still others say that it is a misappropriation of funds to take money from one region and spend it in ways that will benefit only people of another region. Proponents say it ultimately benefits the whole nation.*) Have your students express their own opinions, giving historical examples or citations from the Constitution to defend their various positions.

Television in the Fifties

Have the students interview their grandparents (or other older adults in their family) about their favorite TV programs of the 1950s. The students might categorize those favorites, asking their interviewees about their favorite comedy, drama, news/commentary, etc.

Consider obtaining and showing one or more episodes of 1950s television programs.

The "Do Nothing" Congress

Students might have read or heard that Truman called the Republican-controlled Congress of 1947 the "do nothing" Congress. Help the students to recognize the problem

with that evaluation. Would the students have supported Truman's "Fair Deal," which was even more socialistic than the New Deal? By fighting the president's efforts to extend government power and programs, were the Republicans "do nothing" congressmen? What conclusion is implied by that phrase? (*that good leaders introduce more government programs*) You might want to compare the 1947 Republicans to those who withstood President Clinton's efforts to extend government power over health care. Sometimes it is better for Congress to do *nothing* than to do the *wrong* thing.

Recording Industry

New technology in the phonograph industry brought changes for postwar America. The 78 rpm records of the thirties and forties were replaced with 33 ⅓ rpm long-playing (LP) records in stereophonic sound for serious music lovers and with 45 rpm records that became a hit with teenagers. A new type of music, rock-and-roll, gained popularity in the late 1950s. Broadcasted widely by radio stations, it helped encourage teenage rebellion and recklessness. Rock appealed to the emerging teen culture of the 1950s by glamorizing a radical counter-culture that challenged the values and sexual mores of American society.

Wham-O

The Wham-O Manufacturing Company of California launched some of America's greatest postwar fads. Richard Knerr and Arthur "Spud" Melin, two recent college graduates, started the company in 1948 by marketing slingshots and boomerangs. However, their first fad-starting product came ten years later after an Australian friend visited them. He told the two about bamboo hoops used in Australian gym classes. The ancient torso-trimming instrument, called the Hula-Hoop, was used as far back as the fourteenth century in England and even in ancient Greece. Its name came from seventeenth-century missionaries to Hawaii who thought users looked like they were performing the Hawaiian hula. Knerr and Melin made a few changes to satisfy a modern market. Instead of vine, wood, or metal, they made their Hula-Hoop out of another fairly new product—plastic. Sold in a number of bright colors, Hula-Hoops started a craze across America. In the first year alone, between 60,000 and 100,000 hoops sold. Not

Truman proudly displayed the premature headline following his defeat of Dewey.

on their States' Rights ticket. With Wallace and Thurmond pulling votes from the Democrats, political pollsters said that the Republican candidate, Thomas E. Dewey, was a sure winner. Newspapers printed on election night declared the same.

But when all of the ballots were counted, both the pollsters and the papers were wrong. Truman had waged an exhausting campaign, traveling across America making speeches from the end of a railroad car. The public apparently admired his fighting spirit. "I met the people face to face," he explained, "and . . . they voted for me." His tenacity and his idea of giving a "fair deal" to the American people helped him win the election.

The Quest for Civil Rights

The issue of **civil rights** (rights guaranteed by the Constitution to every American citizen) has stirred debate since the Constitutional Convention. The term originally referred to the right of every citizen to receive equal treatment before the law. Despite the guarantees of the Constitution and the brave service of black soldiers in World War II, black Americans were still denied many of their civil rights. Their long struggle for equality became known as the **civil rights movement**.

Religion in the 1940s and 1950s

After World War II, many Americans turned to religion. In 1940, less than half of Americans belonged to a church; by 1960, that number jumped to 65 percent. The government echoed this change. In 1954, Congress added the phrase "under God" to the Pledge of Allegiance. The next year, Congress added the phrase "In God We Trust" to the currency. Even Hollywood gained from the popular interest in religion. In the late 1950s, Charlton Heston starred in two popular movies with religious themes—*The Ten Commandments* (1956) and *Ben Hur* (1959).

In 1942, leaders formed the National Association of Evangelicals, a body designed to unify conservatives. The unity, though, did not last. In the late 1940s, Billy Graham became famous as an evangelist. But in his New York Crusade of 1957, Graham allowed theologically liberal pastors on his platform and sent new converts back to their liberal churches. A minority of conservatives rejected Graham's involvement with liberals and retained the name Fun-

damentalists. But most conservatives embraced Graham. They claimed the name "New Evangelicals." Today, this group refers to themselves simply as Evangelicals.

Liberal Protestants, those who denied key teachings of the Bible and yet continued to call themselves Protestants, grew and prospered. In 1939, the Northern and Southern Methodists reunited to form the United Methodist Church. Between 1940 and 1960, the United Methodist Church was the largest Protestant denomination in the United States. One leader, Norman Vincent Peale, became famous for his message of positive self-esteem. Peale's most popular work was *The Power of Positive Thinking* (1952). Liberals also embraced ecumenism (the merging of all religions into one religion). In 1950, various ecumenical denominations formed the National Council of Churches to further their goals. After this period, however, liberal Protestant denominations began to decline.

Roman Catholicism grew in acceptance among the people. After World War II, anti-Catholic feelings slowly began to erode. In the 1940s and 1950s, the number of Catholics doubled to about 42 million. In the 1950s, Archbishop Fulton J. Sheen had popular radio and television programs. Roman Catholic politicians became more visible too. Senator Joseph McCarthy, a Roman Catholic, was often in the headlines during the 1950s. In 1960, John F. Kennedy, a Roman Catholic, won the presidency. Though some feared that his loyalty would be to the pope rather than to the Constitution, Kennedy calmed those fears by delivering a famous speech to the Greater Houston Ministerial Association in which he endorsed a strong view of the separation of church and state. In the 100 years between 1860 and 1960, many Americans had shifted from the belief that the Bible should be examined for solutions to national problems to the view that religion should be kept out of public life.

 Viewpoints on the Taft-Hartley Act

Divide the class into representatives of big business viewpoints, labor unions, small businessmen, and non-union workers. Have each group present its group's opinion of the Taft-Hartley Act. Note that pro-business Republicans passed the law to curb the special privileges that Roosevelt had granted labor unions. Students' opinions no doubt will be influenced by whether they live in pro-union or right-to-work states, which tend to oppose union involvement in labor.

  CD: Party Platform Summaries, 1948

Refer to the CD for summaries of the major parties' platforms for the 1948 presidential election.

Have the students read the Democrats' 1948 platform and compare and contrast that party in 1948 with the party today.

  CD: Electoral College Results, 1948

Refer to the CD for a map showing the results of the Electoral College vote in the 1948 presidential race.

Let's Make a Deal!

Discuss the monikers that identify various presidential administrations. Theodore Roosevelt promised the American people "a square deal." FDR offered a "New Deal," and Truman promised a "Fair Deal." (One humorist declared that they were all a raw deal.) Continuing the tradition of naming their terms, Kennedy looked forward with his "New Frontier," Johnson with his "Great Society," Nixon with his "New Federalism," and Reagan with his "New Beginning." Have the students speculate what current and future presidents might call their terms in office.

© Elliot Erwitt, Magnum Photos

Jim Crow laws sought to segregate the races not only in public places, such as waiting rooms, but also in public facilities, such as drinking fountains.

Colored Waiting Room, Dallas, R. C. Hickman, Hickman (R. C.) Archive, di_00964

In the years after the war, civil rights for blacks became increasingly important. Congress rejected much of Truman's civil rights legislation, but the president tried to reduce discrimination against blacks through the influence of his position.

Both the North and the South practiced segregation. In the South, **Jim Crow laws** segregated blacks from whites in schools, theaters, restaurants, public buses, and elsewhere. Many stores had separate shopping sections for blacks and whites. Blacks and whites could not drink from the same water fountains. In the North, though not required by law, blacks were still segregated from white neighborhoods, schools, and businesses.

Changes came slowly. During World War II, FDR had issued an executive order for the federal government not to contract its business to any firms that discriminated against minorities. Truman continued that policy. He also formed a committee to investigate instances of alleged discrimination. In 1946, President Truman appointed the President's Committee on Civil Rights.

Truman risked his reelection in 1948 by pushing unpopular racial issues. He called for an investigation of alleged discrimination in the military. He asked Congress to pass laws against lynching and against the poll tax (which was active in seven southern states at the time). He called for an end to discrimination by employers and unions alike and an end to discrimination in transportation (rail, bus, and plane). He also issued an executive order banning segregation in the armed forces. On the advice of Ed Flynn, political boss in the Bronx, he campaigned openly for black votes in Harlem, the first president to do so.

Truman's support for civil rights was limited but quite radical for the time. As the president of all the people, he knew that he had to guarantee equal rights—not for "social equality," he wrote to a friend, but "for equality of opportunity" for all citizens. On election day, Truman got more than two-thirds of the black vote. His position on civil rights cost him three Southern states but gained him Ohio, Illinois, and California and ensured his reelection.

In 1949, Truman made civil rights history. He appointed **William Hastie** to the Third Circuit Court of Appeals, the highest judicial post held by a black person at that time. He also appointed blacks to several high-ranking administrative jobs. One of those was the first

Truman appointed William Hastie, the first black federal appeals court judge.

all were under the name "hula," though. Wham-O was unable to get a patent, and soon "spin-a-hoops" and "hoop-d-dos" also appeared on the market.

Just as the Hula-Hoop fad was dying out, Wham-O introduced another one. Knerr and Melin hired a carpenter and inventor named Fred Morrison to join their company. He had developed a plastic flying disc he called the "Pluto Platter." Wham-O marketed the disk in 1957, but the product's real popularity came after a few changes in 1958. While visiting some Ivy League schools, Knerr saw students throwing pie tins to each other and yelling, "Frisbie." The name came from William Russell Frisbie, a baker who printed his name on the pie plates that came with his pies. Knerr liked the name and changed Wham-O's flying disk to the "Frisbee." Although the Frisbee did not generate the same craze that the Hula-Hoop had, it has been a more permanent part of American culture.

Other Legislation of the Era

Other legislation in 1947 included the establishment of the presidential line of succession. The Speaker of the House and the president pro tempore of the Senate are in line after the vice president. Next are the cabinet secretaries in order of their departments' creation.

The Twenty-second Amendment, passed in 1951, limits a president to two terms of office or, in the case of a vice president who becomes president, a maximum of ten years in office. That amendment was in reaction to the extended presidency of Franklin Roosevelt and represents acknowledgment of the dangers of allowing one man to lead the government for a prolonged time.

The Autobiography of Miss Jane Pittman

A fictionalized but historically accurate account of one black woman's determination to obtain civil rights is the film *The Autobiography of Miss Jane Pittman*.

The Strange Career of Jim Crow

A good teacher resource for more information on the Jim Crow laws that were passed during this time (especially in the South) is the classic work *The Strange Career of Jim Crow* by the dean of Southern historians, C. Vann Woodward.

Jackie Robinson

Jackie Robinson broke the color barrier in baseball in April 1947. In that year, he signed a contract to play second base for the Brooklyn Dodgers in return for $5,000 a year with a $3,500 bonus. In his first game against the Boston Braves, Robinson went hitless, but he scored the winning run. On a sacrifice bunt, the Braves' first baseman fielded the ball but hit Robinson in the back with it. A double by Pete Reiser drove him home and allowed the Dodgers to win 5-3.

Robinson spent his entire ten-year career with the Dodgers. (Although he was traded to the New York Giants late in his career, he refused to report to the new team. The trade was later voided, and he remained a Dodger.) He amassed a career batting average of .311. He played in six World Series, during which he amassed a batting average of .234 and stole six bases. He also played in six All Star games. He was voted Rookie of the Year in 1947. In 1949, he won the batting title with an average of .342 and was voted Most Valuable Player. He led the National League in stolen bases in both 1947 and 1949.

Jackie Robinson

Robinson broke the color barrier in major league baseball in 1947. He signed a contract to play with the Brooklyn Dodgers for $5,000/year with a $3,500 bonus. Owner Branch Rickey warned Robinson that he would face racial prejudice and even violence. He did, but he kept his cool and refused to retaliate. In his first game (against the Boston Braves), Robinson went hitless, but he scored the winning run. On a sacrifice bunt, the Braves' first baseman fielded the ball but hit Robinson in the back with it. A double by the next batter drove Robinson home, giving the Dodgers a 5–3 win. Robinson let his playing speak for him, winning him the respect of both teammates and opponents. He became an accomplished player in a ten-year career with Brooklyn. He batted above .300 in six of those seasons, won the Most Valuable Player award in eight of them, and played in six World Series. He ended his career with a lifetime batting average of .311. In breaking the color barrier, Robinson opened the door for scores of other talented black players who would follow him and build upon his achievements.

White crowds tried to intimidate black students enrolling in Central High School in Little Rock, Ark., September 4, 1957.
Will Counts Collection: Indiana University Archives

black ambassador, Edward Dudley, ambassador to Liberia. He also appointed the first female district judge, Burnita Shelton Matthews.

Other societal changes helped blacks integrate into more areas. In 1947, **Jackie Robinson** became the first African American to play major league baseball. Brooklyn Dodgers general manager Branch Rickey signed him as their second baseman. Higher education also began to open to blacks. The University of Oklahoma admitted blacks to its graduate school in 1948.

Jackie Robinson and Branch Rickey confer as Robinson signs his contract with the Dodgers.

The Courts Intervene in Civil Rights

The Supreme Court case *Plessy v. Ferguson* (1896) had allowed blacks to be separated from whites as long as their facilities were equal. For many years, the National Association for the Advancement of Colored People (NAACP), which had been formed in 1910, worked to get judges to end inequalities. Lawyers for the NAACP challenged segregation in the courts, winning small victories here and there over the decades.

Lawyers also challenged the concept of "separate but equal." The big victory came in 1954 in *Brown v. Board of Education*. The Supreme Court ruled that racial segregation in public schools violated the equal treatment guaranteed under the Fourteenth Amendment (see Chap. 16). The *Brown* case applied to schools in seventeen states. Schools there were told to integrate "with all deliberate speed." But some school districts did not start to integrate until 1969 or later.

Truman's successor, Dwight Eisenhower, did not pressure the states to integrate. He hoped that they would follow the court's instructions on their own. He believed that racial attitudes had to change slowly from below, not be imposed by the courts from above. He was furious over the Supreme Court ruling in *Brown*. After all, he had appointed Earl Warren as Chief Justice and thought he should have ruled otherwise. But Eisenhower was also determined to enforce the law. When the governor of Arkansas challenged the ruling in 1957, Eisenhower federalized the Arkansas National Guard to

Activity 1: Jackie Robinson Breaks Baseball's Color Barrier, 1945

Use this activity to help the students understand both the boldness of Branch Rickey and the Dodgers in signing Robinson to a major league baseball contract and the courage that Robinson exhibited as the first black baseball player in the major leagues. He endured verbal and physical abuse by players from opposing teams and refused to allow their intimidation to prevent him from breaking the racial barrier in baseball.

 ### CD: "Integrated Bus Suggestions" by Rev. M.L. King

Refer to the CD for a photo of a document written by Martin Luther King during the bus boycott.

ensure the safe enrollment of black students at Little Rock's Central High School.

Early Civil Rights Protests

Black activists did not rely on the courts alone. In 1955, **Rosa Parks**, a seamstress and civil rights activist in Montgomery, Alabama, rode a city bus home after a hard day at work. Tradition and the law divided the bus into two sections, with blacks sitting in the back. But Mrs. Parks sat in the white section in one of the few empty seats on the bus. When the bus driver told her to give up her seat, she refused and was arrested. To show support for her action, other blacks, led by Rev. Martin Luther King Jr., started a bus boycott. They refused to ride city buses for more than a year, depriving the bus company of desperately needed money. Finally, the city ended the practice of segregation on buses. When civil rights activists saw the results that protests and boycotts could get, they expanded their efforts to other areas and issues.

King's leadership in the Montgomery bus boycott marked a shift to other strategies to accomplish the goals of the civil rights movement. He appealed to middle class whites through the media. He also used the power and influence of black churches and their ministers. They provided the "foot soldiers" and organized the events. These efforts in the mid-1950s developed into the civil rights movement of the 1960s.

Rosa Parks became a symbol of efforts to secure black civil rights when she refused to give up her seat on a bus, sparking the Montgomery bus boycott.

Section Quiz

1. How did the G.I. Bill help veterans?
2. To what parts of the country did many Americans move in the postwar years?
3. What was Truman's domestic plan called?
4. What act limited the powers of labor unions?
5. Which person broke the color barrier of major league baseball, and for which team did he play?
6. Which Supreme Court case mandated that public schools in America integrate "with all deliberate speed"?
7. Name the civil rights leaders—one man and one woman—who were instrumental in ending segregation on public transportation in Montgomery, Alabama.
★ How did the "baby boom" and suburban life affect the American economy?

II. The Postwar World

The end of the war presented both opportunities and problems. The war effort had given the Allies an organization. Perhaps they could use it to ensure peace. The Allies had held eleven conferences during the war to plot strategy and deal with problems. The idea of a postwar peace-keeping organization arose at the Teheran Conference late in 1943. The topic was revisited at Yalta in February 1945. The Big Three—the United States, Britain, and the Soviet Union—called for a meeting of nations at San Francisco to write a charter for another world peace-keeping organization.

Section II
Objectives

Students should be able to

1. Describe the founding and organization of the United Nations, including its three parts.
2. Evaluate the activities of the United Nations.
3. Describe how the Allies dealt with Germany after the war.
4. Describe how the Allies dealt with Japan after the war.
5. Explain the Marshall Plan.

Section Quiz Answers

1. It gave them benefits in finding jobs, getting an education, and purchasing homes.
2. the West, the South, and the Southwest
3. "Fair Deal"
4. Taft-Hartley Act
5. Jackie Robinson; Brooklyn Dodgers
6. *Brown v. Board of Education*
7. Martin Luther King Jr. and Rosa Parks
★ They created greater demands for baby goods, housing, and transportation. Related industries also grew.

Learning from Past Victories

Ask the students to put themselves in the position of the victors at the end of World War II. List the international problems that had to be solved; then discuss alternative solutions. Americans were deeply concerned about the possibility of another world depression, the rise of radicalism among the dispossessed poor, and the potential for a new war.

After having won the biggest and costliest war in history, Americans had many options in their treatment of their vanquished foes. The United States wanted to demilitarize and democratize Germany and Japan; it feared that the industries of those countries might be used for war again. Once the students consider the options that the United States had, they will better appreciate the generous choices it made. Perhaps never before has a victor been so good to its enemies and converted them into lasting allies. Ironically, the Soviet ally became America's great enemy.

The United Nations

The United Nations' organizational meeting at San Francisco was preceded by a planning meeting at Dumbarton Oaks in Washington on August 21, 1944. Roosevelt had promised the Soviet Union advantages in the United Nations when the topic was discussed at Yalta. The difficulty of dealing with the Soviet Union on the formation of the UN became increasingly evident through the Dumbarton Oaks and San Francisco meetings.

The UN has been ineffective since those who do wrong are also part of the organization. They use their influence to prevent the UN from holding them accountable for their actions.

Delegations of the major world powers met in San Francisco in 1945 to discuss the organization of the future United Nations.

The Formation of the United Nations

On April 25, 1945, Truman welcomed delegates from fifty nations to San Francisco. They spent two months talking and arguing. Some threatened to leave because the Soviet demands were too selfish. Finally, the delegates made enough concessions to forge a charter for the new **United Nations** organization.

New York City gave the United Nations land for a permanent world headquarters in 1947. John D. Rockefeller Jr. gave $8.5 million to construct a building. The United States loaned the U.N. another $65 million. The new headquarters opened in 1952.

The General Assembly

The organization has three main parts. The **General Assembly** is like a legislature. Every member nation sends a representative. It is designed to permit the nations of the world to discuss their problems peacefully and reach nonviolent agreements. By 2007, membership consisted of 192 countries. But the General Assembly really has little power because the member nations are not forced to abide by its decisions.

The Security Council

The **Security Council** has five permanent member nations and ten nonpermanent members. The latter are elected by the General Assembly for two-year terms and are usually drawn from the smaller countries. The Security Council is the strongest part of the U.N. because it has the power to enforce U.N. policy with military action. But because any one of the five permanent members (the United

A Christian Perspective of the United Nations

The potential consequences of atomic weapons caused many people to look for ways to avoid war. In more recent times, people have looked for ways to prevent atrocities like the genocides in Rwanda or Darfur or to stop health scourges like malaria and AIDS in Africa. An international body that tries to address these issues could be a very good thing.

Sadly, the record of the U.N. reveals ineffectiveness. Since its founding, at least seventy-five wars have erupted in the world. There are several reasons for these failures.

First, issues like human rights, health care, and war all have moral issues at their core. For instance, should programs designed to stop the spread of AIDS take an abstinence-only approach? Is it ever right for one nation to begin a preemptive war to defend itself? To answer these questions Christians turn to the Bible as the ultimate standard that governs what is right and wrong.

Without the Bible as its governing authority, the United Nations is left to try to unite nations—many with contradictory moral views—around common causes.

Second, the United Nations is unable to address the underlying cause for the world's problems: sin. Nations that sin against other nations are still given a place at the United Nations table. During the Cold War, Communist nations tended to honor an agreement only when it benefited them. More recently, Libya, a human rights violator, was voted to chair the United Nations Human Rights Commission for the year of 2003.

Third, the United Nations often is unable to enforce its own resolutions. Since offending nations are members of the organization, they are able to block U.N. resolutions. This was especially true during the Cold War, when the Soviet Union and China could veto U.N. actions against Communist aggression.

The words of Isaiah 2:4—"They shall beat their swords into plowshares, and their spears into pruninghooks: nation shall not lift up sword against nation, neither shall they learn war any more"—appear in the U.N. headquarters. These verses reveal the ideal world that will be ruled over by Christ in the future. Christians today can support just efforts to bring peace to nations around the world, but the history of the United Nations demonstrates that to truly bring peace to the world will require the reign of God Himself.

Comparing the UN with the League of Nations

Have the students research and compare the League of Nations and the United Nations. Make a chart to show the similarities and the differences.

The UN in the News

Ask the students to find an article on some issue related to the UN today, or bring in an article and discuss it with the class. How have the issues changed, and how are they similar to the issues after World War II?

Activity 2: Understanding the United Nations

Use this activity to reinforce student understanding of the United Nations while encouraging the use of outside resources.

States, the United Kingdom, France, China, and the Russian Federation) can veto any decision, the council's power is often curtailed. It has acted successfully only in minor disputes or when the Big Five decided to use force. During the Cold War, the Soviet Union vetoed more than a hundred decisions of the council—more than all of the other members combined. Moreover, when the seat of Free China was given to Communist China, the chance of a veto by a Communist power increased.

The Secretariat

The **Secretariat** is a type of executive branch. It is composed of U.N. agencies and administrators that handle the daily affairs of the organization. It is headed by a secretary-general elected by the General Assembly. Two of the most well known U.N. agencies in the Secretariat are the United Nations Children's Fund (UNICEF) and the United Nations Educational, Social, and Cultural Organization (UNESCO).

Postwar Europe

The United States emerged from World War II as the most powerful nation in the world. After the war, it had only one strong rival—the Soviet Union. They had fought as allies in the war, but the differences between the two postwar superpowers led to great tensions. Europe and Eastern Asia, lying in ruins after the havoc of war, needed the help of the superpowers to rebuild. But American ideas about how that should be done usually conflicted with the demands of the Soviet Union.

When the Allies defeated the Nazis, the Germans were left without a government. To fill this power vacuum, the Allies divided Germany into four sectors. American, British, and French troops occupied the three western sectors. The Soviets occupied the fourth sector—the eastern part of Germany closest to the Russian border. The Soviet Union quickly showed that it would have its way in that sector. It ensured that the East German economy and politics would be Communist. Tensions developed in Germany, resulting in major conflicts between the United States and the Soviet Union.

Europeans, who had seen World War II fought on their own lands, had suffered more than Americans. Millions of their soldiers and civilians had been killed. Millions of the survivors were homeless, wandering from place to place seeking shelter and food. To many of these "displaced persons," life seemed hopeless. There were no jobs. The war-time governments of the defeated countries no longer existed, and the winners were so deeply in debt from their own war efforts that they could do little to help. Bombing and fighting had destroyed most industries. Railroads and roads were in ruins. Farmlands did not produce, and near-famine conditions existed in Europe.

The United States helped Europe recover. First, it furnished aid through the United Nations Relief and Recovery Administration (UNRRA). They met immediate needs by shipping tons of food, clothing, and medicine. Communists could make easy inroads among the discontented and downtrodden, so the United States showed special concern for such people to keep them from falling under Communist influence.

On June 5, 1947, Secretary of State **George Marshall** proposed a vast new aid program for Europe. He asked Congress for huge sums

Trygve Lie of Norway was the first secretary-general of the United Nations.

Ban Ki-moon of South Korea, the eighth U.N. secretary-general, took office in January 2007.

General George C. Marshall was the mastermind behind the plan to rebuild Europe after World War II.

Section III
Objectives

Students should be able to

1. Define the Cold War and containment.

2. Describe the circumstances that led to the Berlin airlift.

3. Describe the relationship of the United States to China since World War II.

4. Explain the circumstances and results of the Korean War.

Problems with the Soviet Union

Remember that the Soviet Union had begun World War II as Hitler's friend under the nonaggression pact. The Soviets had rushed into Poland to collect the spoils alongside the Nazis. Only when Hitler turned against the Soviet Union did that country join the Allied cause. Also, Stalin had agreed at Teheran and Yalta to help defeat Japan once Hitler was defeated. That help did not come until three months after V-E Day, however. The Soviets waited until August 9, the day the second atomic bomb was dropped on Japan, to declare war on Japan. By then, Japan was, for all practical purposes, already defeated. So the Soviet declaration only allowed the Communists to rush into Japanese-held areas on the Pacific coast and gain control for themselves. In addition, the Soviets did not allow free elections in the lands they had "freed" in Eastern Europe. All of those deplorable actions appalled the United States, but no one wanted to risk further war.

Origins of the Cold War

The Cold War technically began in 1945 with a state of hostility between the

MacArthur spared Hirohito's life because he thought the figurehead emperor could help ease the transition to a peaceful postwar Japan.

of money to rebuild the European countries ravaged by war. The **Marshall Plan** offered aid even to Eastern European countries already subjected to Soviet control. But the Soviet Union rejected the offer. It would not allow its satellites (Soviet-dominated countries) to take advantage of the offer.

Although the Marshall Plan cost a great deal (more than $12 billion), it greatly aided European recovery. The Western European countries that received American help rebuilt quickly and soon surpassed their prewar production. The Soviet-dominated countries remained mired in economic despair for decades and never matched the progress of the free countries.

Postwar Japan

Japan had been destroyed by the war. Her cities and harbors lay in ruins. Her merchant fleet had been sunk. The United States took sole responsibility for helping Japan rebuild. Truman appointed General Douglas MacArthur to head a military government to supervise the recovery efforts. One of MacArthur's first priorities involved religion. He met with a group of American Christian missionaries. "Japan is a spiritual vacuum," he told them. "If you do not fill it with Christianity, it will be filled with communism." He then called on them to send a thousand missionaries to Japan. Between 1946 and 1950, more than two thousand missionaries, teachers, and social workers went to Japan to help the country recover both economically and spiritually. The door to Japan was opened to the gospel.

The United States helped the Japanese write a new constitution. The Japanese elected a legislative body and gave rights to all citizens. Women received the right to vote. As in Germany, war criminals went to trial.

The UNRRA sent aid to Japan from 1945 to 1948. It provided food, clothing, and medicine to meet immediate needs. The United States was the chief donor to that organization. Japan quickly rebuilt and soon became a thriving industrial nation. In 1951, the United States ended its military occupation of Japan. The United States had helped Japan to rebuild and had gained a powerful ally for the free world.

Section Quiz

1. What are the three bodies of the United Nations? Which body is the strongest?

2. Which section of Germany came under Communist control?

3. What changes occurred in Japan under U.S. supervision?

4. What plan was developed for giving aid to Europe after the war?

★ Why has the United Nations been unable to achieve its goal of international peace and security?

III. Cold War Crises

After Word War II the Soviet Union imposed the Soviet system on its sector of Germany. The Soviets also sought to bring as much of Europe as it could within its sphere of influence. As a result, the **Cold War** developed between the United States and the Soviet

---

Debate Ideas

Have your students discuss and/or debate one of the following propositions:

• The United States received significant benefits from joining the United Nations.

• General Douglas MacArthur should have been permitted to bomb China and cross the Yalu River in pursuit of North Korean forces.

• The Nuremberg Trials were an illegitimate means of assessing and punishing Germany for its World War II crimes.

• The United States should withdraw its support from the United Nations.

Section Quiz Answers

1. General Assembly, Security Council, and the Secretariat; the Security Council is the most powerful.

2. East Germany

3. Japan wrote a new constitution, elected a legislative body, gave the vote to all citizens, tried its war criminals, opened its doors to missionaries, and through aid became a strong industrial nation.

4. Marshall Plan

★ The United Nations has failed in its mission because of man's sinful nature. Not until Christ returns to this earth will there be lasting peace.

Union. The two superpowers avoided direct military conflict, but they often were involved in disputes that sprang from the tensions between them. Fear that a war might erupt and lead to a third world war was often present.

At Yalta, Stalin had pledged to hold free elections in the countries that the Soviets captured. But he had no intention of doing that. Even before the war began, the Soviets had organized Communist parties in the countries of Eastern Europe. They already had the groundwork for a Communist takeover. As Soviet troops occupied Eastern Europe, they placed Communists in power, taking over Bulgaria, Yugoslavia, Albania, Rumania, Poland, Hungary, and Czechoslovakia. To ensure that those countries stayed in the Communist camp, Red Army units remained in each nation and kept pro-Soviet leaders in control despite opposition from the people.

On March 5, 1946, Winston Churchill spoke at Westminster College in Fulton, Missouri. He described in graphic language the situation in Eastern Europe: "From Stettin in the Baltic to Trieste in the Adriatic, an iron curtain has descended across the Continent." From that time, countries under Communist control were said to be "behind the **Iron Curtain**." That barrier represented the differences in beliefs between the two sides. Churchill believed that the West would have to take firm action to halt future Communist expansion.

The Truman Doctrine: Containing Communism

The Soviets soon proved Churchill's point by showing that they were not content to control only Eastern Europe. Their next goal was to claim the oil-rich Middle East.

During the war, Allied troops had occupied Iran to keep open its vital oil supply. After the war, American and British troops withdrew, but Soviet troops remained. Soviet-inspired rioting took place, and Iranian troops who sought to restore order were kept from doing so. When Iran, with American backing, complained to the U.N., the Soviet troops left.

Communist-led guerrillas also were trying to take over Greece. And Turkey seemed to be on the brink of falling to communism. Truman realized that the United States had to "contain" communism. Someone had to stop the Soviets from taking over any more governments. To fund his **containment** policy, Truman asked Congress for $400 million for military aid to Greece and Turkey. The use of military aid to support pro-Western, anti-Communist governments was known as the **Truman Doctrine**.

Confrontation in Germany

Germany was divided among the Allies after the war. But the country's old capital, Berlin, was in the middle of Soviet-controlled East Germany. Because Berlin was such an important city, the Allies agreed to divide it among themselves, just as they had divided the country. France, Britain, and the United States controlled three zones on the western half of the city, and the Soviet Union controlled the eastern half. The French, British, and American zones of Berlin received supplies from West Germany by truck or train across Soviet-held lands.

The United States, Britain, and France decided to combine their sectors of Germany. The Soviet Union responded by denying all road, rail, and river access across East Germany to Berlin, beginning

Churchill's "iron curtain" speech marked the symbolic beginning of the Cold War.

United States and the Soviet Union. Understanding the animosities between the two superpowers, however, requires looking back over the preceding one hundred years. The United States was suspicious of czarist Russia in the nineteenth century.

The Bolshevik Revolution of 1917 further alienated Russia from the West. Communism was not only totalitarian but also antireligion and aggressive, threatening to initiate revolutionary movements elsewhere in the world. Mistrust was so strong between America and the Soviet Union that the United States did not give diplomatic recognition to that nation until 1933. The Soviet Union was an ally in World War II, and U.S. relations with Stalin became more complicated. President Roosevelt and British prime minister Churchill believed that an alliance with the Soviet Union against Hitler was the best, though not a perfect, way to defeat Nazi Germany. This "marriage of convenience" forced Hitler to fight a two-front war, thus placing him in a serious strategic disadvantage. Curiously, American propaganda during the war revamped the images of Stalin and the Soviet Union, making the Russians "good guys." During this wartime alliance, the Soviet Union received Lend-Lease assistance from the United States.

But even with the wartime cooperation, serious divisions existed between the Soviet Union and the other Allies over the timing and location of the second front, the one from the west, against Hitler. Stalin wanted it soon and in Western Europe. Churchill wanted the attack to be made in southeastern Europe, closer to the Soviet Union, thereby giving the Communists less of a free hand in Eastern Europe after they liberated it from the Nazis. Roosevelt convinced Churchill that the invasion should take place in France.

Activity 3: The Berlin Candy Bomber

Use this activity to help the students understand the human element amid the events of the Berlin Airlift.

In the spring of 1945, when the common enemy that bound them together was defeated, the United States and the Soviet Union reverted to a familiar pattern of hostility. The Cold War was under way.

China and the Cold War

The role of China in the Cold War is often overlooked. China is important, if for no other reason, as the most populous nation in the world. It played a role in both intensifying the Cold War and helping to end it.

Mao Zedong rose to power after the United States forced the Chinese to grant special rights to U.S. businesses. He mixed communism with Chinese nationalism, which made him popular with the masses.

In 1927, Chiang Kai-shek, Sun Yat-sen's successor, kicked the Communists out of his "nationalist" party (the Kuomintang). A civil war between Chiang and Mao raged for the next twenty years. During the World War II era, they agreed to unite their forces against the Japanese threat, but in 1945, with that threat removed, they resumed their civil war. Chiang, a non-Communist, had the support of the United States, but by 1949 Mao had defeated his opponent and claimed the Chinese mainland for communism. Chiang's Nationalists fled to the small island of Formosa, which they renamed Taiwan.

With China's fall to communism and the Soviet Union's production of its first atomic bomb, 1949 was one of the worst years during the Cold War. Communism presented an impressive geographical, military, and ideological front.

China played pivotal roles in two of the Cold War's worst episodes—the Korean and Vietnam wars. President Nixon, in a bold strategic move to help end the Vietnam War, opened relations with China in

The Berlin airlift prevented the starvation of thousands of Germans and ensured their freedom from Soviet domination.

The Berlin Airlift Statistical Summary

Food delivered: 537,000 tons

Coal delivered: 1,586,000 tons

Other goods delivered: 202,775 tons

Total tonnage: 2,325,775 tons

Sorties flown: 277,569

U.S. fatalities: 32

Record deliveries on Easter Sunday, 1949—Sorties: 1,398

Total miles flown: 78,954,500

Occupation of Germany After WWII

June 24, 1948. This was a violation of the Yalta agreement. It left two million residents of West Berlin without food and other supplies. The Soviet Union thought that its blockade would force the Allies out of Berlin. Stalin also believed that his action would undermine the confidence of the European Allies in the United States.

Truman responded quickly. He announced that the United States would conduct a massive airlift to West Berlin. For the next 321 days, more than 250,000 flights carried supplies into West Berlin. Nearly 2.5 million tons of supplies were airlifted to the blockaded city. The Soviets did not attack the planes, as some people had predicted. When the Soviets realized that the United States would keep the **Berlin airlift** going indefinitely, it lifted the blockade in May 1949.

The Soviet Union had taken such a strong grip on East Germany that attempts to unify Germany seemed futile. In September 1949, the United States, Britain, and France allowed their sectors of Germany to become the independent Federal Republic of Germany (West Germany). Bonn became its capital.

Alliances and Aid

Truman believed that the free European countries needed more than financial aid. He asked Congress for military support and the formation of a joint alliance, with the United States as a member. The alliance was called the **North Atlantic Treaty Organization (NATO)**. Charter members were Great Britain, France, Italy, Portugal, the Netherlands, Denmark, Norway, Belgium, Luxembourg, Canada, Iceland, and the United States. In 1952, Greece and Turkey joined. In 1959, West Germany joined. Member nations agreed to provide money, troops, and military equipment for mutual protection. General Dwight D. Eisenhower became the first supreme

Unprecedented NATO

Stress that NATO—the first peacetime defensive alliance in U.S. history—had no precedent in the country's history. Can the students find any period in America's past similar to the one that led to the formation of NATO? Did the circumstances warrant that change in U.S. policy? Since the Cold War has ended, some have wondered whether any circumstances would justify an end to NATO and a return to isolationism. Has the United States entered such a period? Is isolation really even possible given the war against terrorism?

Changing NATO

Discuss how the role of NATO in Europe has changed since the fall of the Soviet Empire. Possible issues to include in the discussion are efforts by former Soviet republics and satellites to gain NATO membership and NATO involvement in the war in Afghanistan.

commander of NATO forces. America's membership in NATO was a departure from its long-standing policy of isolationism. NATO became the first peace-time defense alliance that the United States had ever joined.

In response, the Soviets formed their own alliance. Called the **Warsaw Pact**, it included Poland, Albania, East Germany, Bulgaria, Rumania, Czechoslovakia, Hungary, and the Soviet Union.

The China Question

At the same time that postwar Europe was undergoing change, so was the Far East. China, the most populous nation in the world, became a special concern. The Communists had been trying to take over China when the Japanese invaded Manchuria. The Chinese agreed to end their civil war and join forces against the Japanese. As World War II neared its end, the Communists were poised to gain control of China.

China had suffered from fighting warlords and domineering foreign countries in the decades before the war. Generalissimo **Chiang Kai-shek** had emerged as leader of the strong Nationalist party. He supported a free government and a free economy. The United States had made trade agreements with Chiang and had aided the Chinese against Japan during the war. But corruption and conflicts within his party had hurt Chiang's efforts to defeat the Japanese and control China. Some American troops were sent to aid Chiang, but they were pulled out in 1947.

Almost immediately China was again engulfed in war between the Communists, led by **Mao Zedong**, and the Nationalists, led by Chiang. Mao's forces were highly motivated. The Communists had promised to give land to the poor. By 1949, the Communists gained control of the mainland. They forced Chiang to flee with his army to the coastal island of Taiwan. There he set up the Republic of China (also called Nationalist China or Free China). Mainland China became the People's Republic of China.

Communism in China posed a new threat. China and the Soviet Union signed the Sino-Soviet Pact in February 1950. That confirmed American fears that the Communists might try to work together against the free world. Truman and several presidents after him supported Chiang and his government on Taiwan. (In spite of the fact the Chinese Communists were suppressing free ideas, killing or imprisoning those who opposed Mao, and persecuting Christians, the U.S. government finally recognized the People's Republic as the one legitimate government of China in 1979.)

The Korean Conflict

China was not the only Communist target in Eastern Asia. The Soviet Union had begun to take a grip on part of Korea before World War II ended. While the United States defeated Japan, the Soviet Union poured troops into Korea. The Yalta agreement allowed the Soviets to occupy Korea north of the 38th parallel. The Soviets again promised that at the proper time, free elections would be held. Of course, the Communists established their style of government in North Korea instead. South Korea held its own elections and formed the free Republic of Korea with Seoul as its capital. Korea, like Germany, was thus divided—the north Communist, the south free.

Diplomats held talks in hopes of unifying the country, but the talks broke down. Then North Korea invaded South Korea on

The Nationalist Chinese under Chiang Kai-shek (left) were unable to defeat the Communists led by Mao Zedong (right) and were forced to flee to Taiwan.

a 1972 visit to that country. The United States had not extended diplomatic recognition to mainland China following the end of the civil war. Instead, America had recognized Taiwan as the real China. Taiwan also held China's seat in the UN. Nixon sought to play China against the Soviet Union, hoping that Soviet fears of a U.S.-China relationship would cause the Soviet Union to be more cooperative in seeking peace in Vietnam and nuclear arms reductions.

By the late 1970s, China had gained U.S. diplomatic recognition and replaced Taiwan on the UN Security Council. With the collapse of the Soviet Union, Communist China looked less threatening, and most Americans saw it merely as a huge market for American goods.

Did the United States Do Enough?

Guide the class in debating whether the United States did enough to prevent the fall of China to the Communists. Expand this discussion to include whether the United States should continue to recognize only Communist China or move toward recognition of *both* Chinas as sovereign nations. Note the pros and cons of each position.

China Policy

Review U.S. policies toward China over the years. China is potentially one of the great powers of the world. When have the two countries been friends? When were they foes? Note the immigration restrictions, the Open Door policy, the Boxer Rebellion, U.S.

support of Chiang Kai-shek, the World War II alliance, and the modern split between Taiwan and the mainland. Emphasize that finding the right policy toward China has never been easy.

After the loss of China to the Communists, political parties in the United States did a lot of finger pointing, asking, "Who lost China?" But in reality, the level of U.S. responsibility for the outcome of internal conflicts in other countries is debatable. The United States felt compelled to withdraw its military support from China's corrupt nationalist government. The same question can be asked in relation to many other countries: "Should the United States support a corrupt democracy that does not enjoy the

support of its people?" This question has arisen concerning South Korea, South Vietnam, Pakistan, and various Latin American and African countries. Bring up other recent examples in the news.

Korean War Veteran

Invite a veteran of the Korean War to speak to the class concerning his experiences/remembrances of that era. (Like veterans of World War II, Korean War veterans are a fast-vanishing breed, so we need to take advantage of their expertise while they are with us.) Consider also having someone who was an adult and remembers Truman's firing of MacArthur to share his or her memories of that event as well.

Anti-Communism at Home

Communism was gaining ground around the world, and one popular explanation—real or imagined—was that traitors and spies inside the U.S. government were helping the enemy. The most famous episode of anti-Communist suspicion was the Hiss case. In 1948, Congressman Richard Nixon of the House Un-American Activities Committee was investigating subversives in government. He discovered through the testimony of a former Communist, Whittaker Chambers, that Alger Hiss, a former New Dealer and a State Department official, had been a Communist in the 1930s and had arranged for secret documents to be transferred to the Soviets. Hiss denied the charges under oath. In 1950, he was convicted of perjury; the statute of limitations had expired for the crime of spying. Hiss was sentenced to five years in prison. More importantly, however, he became a symbol for both right-wing and left-wing attitudes about the Cold War. Conservatives looked at Hiss as a symbol of big government and weak policies toward communism. The episode also catapulted Nixon into national politics.

The Alger Hiss case also gave credibility to later charges by Senator Joseph McCarthy that Communists inside the U.S. government were helping the enemy. Other factors reinforced the suspicion. In 1950, the Rosenburgs, spies who had given atomic secrets to the Soviets, were exposed. Communist North Korea invaded South Korea the same year. McCarthy exploited the issue with speeches and congressional hearings. Democrats and liberals were on the defensive; they did not want to seem sympathetic to the Communists. In 1950, Congress passed the McCarran Act, which required Communists to register with the government. McCarthy and the Re-

The Korean War, 1950–53

Eisenhower fulfilled a campaign pledge when he went to Korea to revive peace talks.

June 25, 1950. The U.N. Security Council called an emergency session to deal with the crisis. It demanded North Korea's immediate withdrawal. When the troops were still there two days later, the Council suggested that the U.N. provide military aid to South Korea. The Security Council avoided a Soviet veto and approved the request because the Soviet Union was boycotting sessions at the time. Once again, America mobilized for war.

That same day Truman committed American planes and ships to support the South Koreans. On June 30, he ordered American troops to Korea. Within a week, the U.N. voted to send a peace-keeping force to Korea to seek an end to the conflict. Since four-fifths of the force's soldiers were Americans, Truman was allowed to name its commander. He chose General Douglas MacArthur, the U.S. general most experienced in Asian matters.

Truman hoped that U.N. troops could drive Communist troops out of South Korea. But a shortage of equipment and American lack of readiness produced a shabby start for the **Korean War**. North Korean troops, well equipped by the Soviets, continued to push their way south. By the end of August, U.N. forces held only the tiny southeastern corner of Korea near Pusan. But MacArthur surprised the North Koreans by going behind their lines in amphibious landings at Inchon near Seoul. In two weeks, they regained all of the ground they had lost and were pushing the enemy back into North Korea.

On October 26, 1950, MacArthur's advancing armies reached the Yalu River, the border between North Korea and China. Suddenly, China threw more than two hundred thousand "volunteers" across the Yalu River into North Korea to stop the U.N. forces.

In fierce fighting, the Chinese drove U.N. troops back to the 38th parallel and into South Korea. MacArthur believed that winning a land war in Korea required full-scale war. The Chinese bases and supply lines from China must be bombed—using nuclear weapons if necessary. In making his case, he declared, "There is no substitute for victory."

But Truman and his advisors were content simply to restore the boundary to where it was before the North Koreans invaded. Truman decided to wage a limited war with very specific aims. He did not want to risk the use of nuclear weapons in Korea. Neither did he want to risk all-out war with Communist China or possibly even the Soviet Union. When an angry MacArthur publicly denounced the president's policy of limited war, Truman fired him.

In July 1951, cease-fire talks started, but the fighting continued. The talks stalled. Campaigning for president in 1952, Dwight Eisenhower pledged that he, if elected, would go to Korea personally to end the war. Upon his election, he did travel to Korea and revived the stalled talks. A cease-fire was signed on July 27, 1953. It restored the 38th parallel as the boundary. It also established a demilitarized zone (an unfortified "no man's land") between Communist North Korea and free South Korea.

Domestic Communism

America also faced growing communism within its own borders. During the late 1940s and early 1950s, a second "Red Scare" swept the country. Many Americans suspected that Communists had infiltrated the U.S. government. They were especially concerned about the State Department and the military. In response, Truman

Contrast the Korean War with Previous Wars

The Korean War was unlike anything the United States had ever fought. Ask the students to find those differences and draw conclusions about the wisdom of wars for the current generation. The Korean War was never officially declared; the United States military sought authorization from an international organization; and the president was content with a stalemate rather than unconditional victory. The national interests we fought to achieve were different from those in any previous war. As a result of that new type of war, the basic issues were never settled, and the United States was forced to maintain a military force in South Korea for the next fifty years. Extend this issue to a discussion of the wars in Iraq and Afghanistan and the war on terror.

Activity 4: Two Views of the Firing of General MacArthur

Use this activity to help the students understand both sides in the controversy between Truman and MacArthur and to form opinions concerning MacArthur's firing.

CD: The Korean War
Refer to the CD for photos of the Korean War and the Korean War Memorial.

set up a loyalty program to investigate government employees and ensure internal security.

In 1948, Whittaker Chambers, a former Communist spy, testified before Congress that Alger Hiss, a State Department official, had passed secret documents to him while he was a Communist spy in the 1930s. Hiss was later convicted of lying under oath but not of spying (the statute of limitations had expired on the spying accusation).

In 1950, two members of another spy ring, **Julius and Ethel Rosenberg**, were convicted of giving atomic secrets to the Soviets. They were executed in 1953 for treason.

These incidents prompted congressional investigations, including those of the House Un-American Activities Committee. Congress passed in 1950 (over Truman's veto) the McCarran Internal Security Act, making it easier for government to combat spying and requiring Communists and their organizations to register with the Justice Department.

In 1951, Senator **Joseph McCarthy** accused the State Department of harboring Communists. He conducted hearings on Communists in the government. But by 1954, McCarthy was making reckless accusations, and the Senate censured him. His opponents coined a new word, *McCarthyism*, to describe McCarthy's tactics of attacking someone by distorting facts, casting suspicion, and making outright false accusations. Although McCarthy's initial attempts to root out any Communists who might have been in the government were praiseworthy, he set back the efforts of legitimate anti-Communists with his reckless accusations.

Sen. Joseph McCarthy brought attention to the dangers of Communists within the U.S. government but discredited himself by making outlandish accusations.

Section Quiz

1. What did Winston Churchill call the barrier between Communist-controlled countries and the West?

2. What idea promoted the use of military aid to carry out the United States' containment policy?

3. How did the United States keep West Berlin from falling into Communist hands?

4. What military alliance was formed to halt the threat of Soviet aggression in Europe?

5. What alliance did the Soviet Union form to challenge the organization in the preceding question?

6. Who was the leader of Free China? Who led the Communist takeover of China?

7. Whom did Truman choose to lead the U.N. forces in Korea?

★ How was the Cold War a different type of war from World Wars I and II? Why?

IV. The Eisenhower Era

Both the Republicans and the Democrats would have been happy to have war hero Dwight D. Eisenhower as their candidate in 1952. He chose to be a Republican and ran against Democrat Adlai E. Stevenson, the governor of Illinois. The public decided that they "liked Ike" (as he was called), because his grandfatherly image made many

publicans used the anti-Communist issue effectively in the 1952 elections, in which Eisenhower was elected president and Republicans dominated Congress. With Republicans in charge of the government, the dynamic shifted for McCarthy. His attacks on the State Department and the U.S. Army were less successful. In the long run, Richard Nixon was more effective than McCarthy as an anti-Communist crusader. McCarthy, despite lack of evidence, used his anti-Communism crusade as a political weapon, and in 1954 his Senate colleagues censured him. He died three years later.

Section IV

Objectives

Students should be able to

1. Describe the circumstances in Vietnam during the 1950s.

2. Name the new Soviet leader and the new policy that developed between the Soviet Union and the United States.

3. Explain how Fidel Castro turned Cuba to Communism.

4. Name the two states that joined the Union in 1959.

Washington Dulles International Airport

In 1962, President Kennedy dedicated a new airport to be named for Eisenhower's Secretary of State, John Foster Dulles. Located about twenty-six miles from downtown Washington, D.C., Dulles airport was noted for its modern architecture and its "mobile lounges," huge bus-like vehicles used to shuttle passengers to and from the terminal and their planes. The vehicles had two front ends and could be driven

---

either direction right up to the terminal gate and right to the airplanes' doors so that passengers never had to go outside. The mobile lounges are slated to be replaced by an underground "people mover" system.

Communist Expansion

The United States met problems with Soviet-inspired Communist expansion attempts in other places besides those mentioned in the text. For example, a pro-Soviet government in Guatemala was unseated through the influence of Eisenhower's secretary of state, John Foster Dulles. Communists also tried to foment revolutions in numerous other Third World countries.

Eisenhower's Foreign Policy

In the campaign of 1952, Republicans preached change in Cold War foreign policy. Truman's principles of limited war, containment, and coexistence with communism, they argued, had failed. Eisenhower proclaimed, "I will go to Korea," implying that he had a plan for victory. The rhetoric of Eisenhower and Secretary of State Dulles was strongly anti-Communist, but their actual record, according to historians, is otherwise. Some people look at the 1950s and see problems that were unresolved and passed on to the 1960s. Others admire Eisenhower for his unwillingness to use force to deal with military crises.

Several incidents indicate that Eisenhower did not really solve diplomatic and military problems but only postponed them and passed them on to John F. Kennedy. In Korea, he negotiated an armistice that ended the fighting but did not resolve the problem of a divided Korea. The military tension and American troops remain in that country to this day. A policy of

The American Automobile Association led a campaign to encourage Congress to pass a bill to improve U.S. highways.

The Pennsylvania Turnpike was a forerunner of the federal interstate highway system.

The National Interstate and Defense Highways Act greatly improved motor transportation across the country.

Americans feel comfortable. Eisenhower won handily. For the first time in nearly twenty years, the nation had a Republican president.

His Domestic Agenda

The United States became involved in some important activities at home during the Eisenhower era. Three of the most significant accomplishments during the Eisenhower era were the completion of the St. Lawrence Seaway, the beginning of the interstate highway system, and the addition of two new states.

In 1954, the United States and Canada undertook a joint project called the **St. Lawrence Seaway**. The two countries cooperated to deepen the St. Lawrence River and build canals and locks where necessary. The completed seaway allowed ocean-going vessels to sail from the Atlantic Ocean to the Great Lakes. It helped the economies of both nations and turned cities along the Great Lakes into major inland seaports. The water that moved through the seaway was also used to provide electrical power.

But Eisenhower also faced problems that the postwar economic boom created. The increased traffic of cars and trucks pressed the nation's infrastructure to the limit. To solve those problems and at the same time provide a way to move troops and equipment in case of war, he pushed for more and better highways. In 1956, Congress passed the **Federal Aid Highway Act** (also called the **National Interstate and Defense Highways Act**). That law approved construction of 41,000 miles of interstate highways at a cost of $28 million over thirteen years. As use of auto, truck, and air transportation increased, use of railroads, especially passenger service, declined.

In 1959, Congress admitted two states to the Union: Alaska and Hawaii, the forty-ninth and fiftieth states. These states differ from the other states because they are noncontiguous territories (i.e., not physically connected to the other forty-eight states). They are also unique because of their populations. About one-fifth of Alaskan citizens are Indian (Eskimo, Aleut, or other tribes). Half of Hawaii's citizens are of Asian descent—Japanese, Chinese, Filipino, or Korean. The addition of Alaska and Hawaii to the Union gave the United States an even wider cultural heritage.

His Foreign Policies

During World War II, Eisenhower had led the Allies to victory over tyranny in Europe. When he became president, he faced a different kind of tyranny—the threat of Communist expansion in not only Europe but also Southeast Asia, China, and Cuba.

Southeast Asia

The Southeast Asian area known as Indochina (Vietnam, Cambodia, and Laos) became a target of Communists. It had been a French colony, but after World War II French control in the land deteriorated. **Ho Chi Minh**, a Communist, tried to gain independence for Vietnam. His forces defeated the French at Dien Bien Phu in May 1954. The United States did not intervene with troops at that time because it did not want to risk another land war in Asia.

An international conference in Geneva, Switzerland, tried to resolve the conflict. As the U.N. had decided in the cases of Germany and Korea, the conference decided to create two Vietnams. North Vietnam under Ho Chi Minh would be Communist. South Vietnam would be non-Communist and would receive American support. But

What Did Alaska and Hawaii Offer the United States?

Discuss the benefits that Alaska and Hawaii brought to the United States when they were admitted to the Union. Ask the students if they think the United States will ever add another state? If so, which territory? *(Their most likely answer will be Puerto Rico.)* What benefits would that area offer the United States?

Modern Foreign Affairs

Why did the United States care about politics in Eastern Europe, Greece, Turkey, Germany, Japan, China, Korea, Southeast Asia, the Soviet Union, and Cuba?

The world changed greatly after World War II. Democracy was engaged in a worldwide struggle against a foe whose primary purpose was to wipe out democracy and free enterprise. The whole free world looked to America for help and guidance; the rest of the world plotted against her.

What lessons does the Cold War hold for us today? The whole world still looks to the United States as either a friend or a foe. This is especially true among the Islamic countries of the world, which see the United States as the "great Satan" and are willing to support terrorism to defeat the entire Western world. Christian teachers must challenge students to be responsible U.S. citizens and leaders.

John Foster Dulles

The architect and key figure in the implementation of Eisenhower's foreign policy was Secretary of State John Foster Dulles. A good biography on Dulles is John Beal's *John Foster Dulles: 1888–1959*.

North Vietnam was not content. The Communists wanted control of all Vietnam. It attacked South Vietnam with both conventional armies and guerrilla forces known as the Viet Cong. Before long, the United States discovered that both China and the Soviet Union were supplying military aid to the North Vietnamese.

Events in Korea and Indochina not only made the United States tense but also alarmed other free countries in the Far East. In 1954, eight countries—Australia, New Zealand, Thailand, Pakistan, the Philippines, Britain, France, and the United States—formed an alliance to contain the spread of communism in Southeast Asia. The **Southeast Asia Treaty Organization (SEATO)** pledged mutual aid to any member nation that was threatened by an aggressor. By the end of 1955, America was sending military advisors to South Vietnam to train Vietnamese forces. The United States also pledged to aid Taiwan if it was attacked by mainland China.

The Soviet Union

The United States was the leading nation of the free world. It could no longer remain isolated from international affairs as it once had done. Because its interests were affected by conditions abroad, the United States became involved in international problems. The greatest problems lay in the Cold War tensions with the Soviet Union, which always seemed to have the world's attention.

In July 1955, Britain, France, the Soviet Union, and the United States met in Geneva, Switzerland. They sought to relieve some of the Cold War tensions. But about the only thing they agreed on was that they would not resort to war to resolve differences. Eisenhower suggested that the United States and the Soviet Union allow aerial inspections of each other's military installations to check for the presence of missiles. But the Soviets rejected the idea.

The Soviet Union was struggling to project a new image. Stalin had died in 1953, and his successor, **Nikita Khrushchev** (KROOSH chef), claimed to be critical of the former leader's terror tactics. He once declared that the Soviets wanted to be friends and promote peace with the United States. Yet Soviet intentions had not really changed. On another occasion, Khrushchev threatened, "We will bury you."

The United States and the Soviet Union settled into a "**peaceful coexistence**." The two countries agreed to try settling tensions between them without hostility. They also arranged events to promote goodwill between them. In 1959, Khrushchev became the first Soviet leader to visit the United States. Unfortunately, the policy of peaceful coexistence committed the United States to settle each issue peacefully, even if Soviet wrongs were not stopped or punished.

Europe

Further examples of Soviet oppression came in Eastern Europe. People in the Soviet satellites were unhappy under Communist rule. In October 1956, freedom fighters in Hungary, interpreting comments by Eisenhower to be a promise of U.S. aid, revolted against Soviet control. Using short-wave radio broadcasts, they pleaded for help from the West, but none came. For four days, the Hungarians continued to hope. Soviet troops with tanks invaded Hungary and crushed the revolt. The freedom fighters were brave, but they could not stop tanks with only homemade grenades and their bare hands.

The United Nations debated the Soviet invasion of Hungary and voted to condemn it. But when the Soviets ignored the U.N. vote,

Eisenhower and Soviet dictator Nikita Khrushchev met at Camp David, Maryland, in 1959.

Khrushchev's Visit to the Farm

During Khrushchev's visit to the United States, he toured the farm of Roswell Garst in Coon Rapids, Iowa. Garst was a highly successful corn farmer who managed more than 5,000 acres. He touted the benefits of growing hybrid corn and using fertilizers to increase yield. Reporters called Garst "a master salesman with evangelical enthusiasm." Khrushchev listened to Garst, but the Russians failed to follow his advice. Garst concluded that the Soviet system was rotten on the inside, something U.S. officials did not realize until Ronald Reagan became president and set in motion the program that led to the fall of Soviet communism in 1991.

Soviet tanks crushed the 1956 Hungarian Revolt.

---

nonrecognition toward mainland China remained the same as it did under Truman. When protests against Communist rule broke out in Hungary in 1956, Eisenhower offered only rhetorical support. (The Hungarian freedom fighters, buoyed by the hope of American help, proceeded with their revolution but were cruelly suppressed by the Soviets when American help was not forthcoming.) Policy toward Communist Eastern Europe continued as it had under Truman. When Castro, a Communist, took over Cuba in 1959, Eisenhower took no military action to reverse it.

Liberal historians tend to look more positively at Eisenhower's foreign policy record. He was a peace president, a strong leader who avoided war whenever possible. Perhaps his military background made him more cautious about military intervention. Instead of expanding the Korean War, as some conservatives wanted to do, Ike stopped the fighting through negotiations. He did not sanction an invasion of mainland China to satisfy either Taiwan or American anti-Communists.

Even Eisenhower's harshest conservative critics would concede, however, that he was wise in staying out of the Vietnam War, which escalated in 1954 when the defeated French left and the Geneva Accords divided the country into a Communist north and a non-Communist south. Ho Chi Minh continued his fight for a united Communist Vietnam, but Eisenhower gave only material aid to the South Vietnamese, not large numbers of American troops, as did Kennedy and Johnson later. Ike's intervention with Khrushchev in the 1956 Suez crisis and his failure to intervene in Hungary that year or in Cuba in 1959 solidified, for some people, his credentials as a peacemaker. Khrushchev's visit to the

---

The Threat of "the Bomb"

Have the students imagine what life was like under the constant threat of nuclear attack. (You might also refer them to an article titled "Living in the Shadow of the Atomic City" in *Blue Ridge Country* magazine of May-June 1998, which gives such a description.) Students would enjoy hearing human-interest stories from someone who lived during that time. Or you could show clips from training films produced by the government during the Cold War. Interestingly, fear of world destruction even influenced movies, as horror movies spawned new powerful creatures, such as Godzilla, that threatened the world.

Did fears of world destruction lead to religious revival. Why or why not? (*It did not. Again, man trusted in his own ability to save himself.*) What current dangers could again bring the world into such a state of fear? (*terrorism, biological disaster*) Those dangers have the advantage of keeping people focused on issues beyond self-gratification.

Is Peaceful Coexistence Always Possible?

Ask the students how two countries can peacefully coexist when one of them is constantly making statements about burying or defeating the other. Discuss the different meanings that each country's leaders had for *peace* and *coexistence*.

Soviet Views on the Cold War

Ask the students to consider what the Soviet people during the Cold War must have thought about U.S./NATO activities and threats of future war. Note that the Russian people had suffered greatly from foreign invasion twice during the century, and they had a natural suspicion of military forces near their border. Also, it was easy for them to find flaws in American society.

Interestingly, some liberal historians actually blame the United States for starting the Cold War. Why might they reach that conclusion, and why is it so outrageous? (*They argue that America's strong military and nuclear power made the Soviet Union feel insecure. But the United States had never expressed a*

United States in 1959 and the resulting partial thaw enhanced Ike's pacifist image.

Fidel Castro quickly aligned himself with Nikita Khrushchev and the Russians once his revolution in Cuba was complete.

the U.N. took no real action. The nations feared that aiding Hungary might start a third world war, so the Soviets felt secure in ruthlessly crushing the revolution without fear of interference by the free world.

Cuba

Latin America became another source of Cold War tension. Communism was winning support in the region. Many of the poor and uneducated people believed the Communists' promises. The growth of communism in Latin America alarmed Americans because it brought the Soviet threat closer to home.

The most disturbing gain for the Communists was the victory of **Fidel Castro** in Cuba. In 1959, Castro's forces defeated Fulgencio Batista, the long-time dictator of Cuba. State Department officials knew about Castro's Communist leanings, but the American people did not. They believed that conditions might get better in Cuba under Castro. Instead, conditions got worse.

Castro was a cruel dictator. He jailed thousands of his political enemies. He seized private property, including that of Americans, American businesses in Cuba, and even his own mother. He declared openly that he was a Communist. Cuban refugees tried to escape Castro's regime by fleeing to Florida any way they could. Some flew; more floated on rickety boats. Soon, Soviet aid was on its way to Cuba. The Caribbean was no longer an American lake. Ninety miles from Florida lay a Communist threat to American freedom.

Section Quiz

1. Who was elected president in 1952? What party did he represent?

2. What were that president's three great domestic accomplishments?

3. How did the St. Lawrence Seaway benefit the United States and Canada?

4. What alliance was started to contain communism in Southeast Asia?

5. What Latin American country turned Communist in 1959? Who became its leader?

☆ Why was it dangerous for the United States to agree to a policy of "peaceful coexistence" with the Soviet Union?

---

desire or taken any actions that might be inferred to indicate a desire to take over foreign countries. Communists, on the other hand, never hid their hatred of capitalism or their desire to take over the world.)

You might want to examine John Lewis Gaddis's *The Cold War: A New History* for a useful response to liberal revisionists.

Cuba's Future

Discuss the current (as of 2009) situation in Cuba with Fidel Castro in failing health and his brother Raul serving as president. What do the students think will happen when Fidel dies? Will Cuba continue under communism, or will the people insist on a

democratic government? How will the U.S. respond?

Section Quiz Answers

1. Dwight D. Eisenhower; Republican

2. the St. Lawrence Seaway, the interstate highway system, and the addition of two new states (Alaska and Hawaii) to the Union

3. It opened the Great Lakes to ocean-going vessels and allowed the water to be used for electrical power.

4. Southeast Asia Treaty Organization (SEATO)

5. Cuba; Fidel Castro

☆ It sometimes committed the United States to peaceful solutions that did not punish Soviet wrongdoings. Without fear of United States retaliation, the Soviets could continue to spread communism.

Activity 5: Chapter Review

Use this activity to help the students prepare for the chapter test.

Chapter Review 25

Review Questions

Answer each of the following questions.

1. What did President Truman call his domestic program?
2. Who devised a plan for helping the war-torn countries of Europe?
3. What are the three important divisions of the United Nations?
4. What legislation initiated the interstate highway system?
5. What two states entered the Union in 1959?

Explain the meaning of each of the following terms.

6. baby boom
7. green revolution
8. McCarthyism
9. Cold War
10. peaceful coexistence

Match each of the following men with his country.

11. Fidel Castro
12. Chiang Kai-shek
13. Ho Chi Minh
14. Nikita Khrushchev
15. Mao Zedong

a. Communist China
b. Free China
c. Cuba
d. Soviet Union
e. Vietnam

Critical Thinking

1. Why should Christians oppose Communism?
2. What would have happened if the United States had taken an isolationist position after World War II?

People, Places, and Things to Remember:

G.I. Bill
"baby boom"
"sunbelt migrations"
"green revolution"
materialistic
Fair Deal
Taft-Hartley Act
injunction
civil rights
civil rights movement
Jim Crow laws
William Hastie
Jackie Robinson
Brown v. Board of Education
Rosa Parks
United Nations
General Assembly
Security Council
Secretariat
George Marshall
Marshall Plan
Cold War
Iron Curtain
containment
Truman Doctrine
Berlin airlift
North Atlantic Treaty Organization (NATO)
Warsaw Pact
Chiang Kai-shek
Mao Zedong
Korean War
Julius and Ethel Rosenberg
Joseph McCarthy
St. Lawrence Seaway
Federal Aid Highway Act (National Interstate and Defense Highways Act)
Ho Chi Minh
Southeast Asia Treaty Organization (SEATO)
Nikita Khrushchev
"peaceful coexistence"
Fidel Castro

CHAPTER REVIEW ANSWERS

Review Questions

1. Fair Deal
2. Secretary of State George Marshall
3. General Assembly, Security Council, Secretariat
4. Federal Aid Highway Act (commonly called the National Interstate and Defense Highways Act)
5. Alaska and Hawaii
6. the large number of babies born in the years following World War II
7. new developments in seeds, machinery, chemicals, and production techniques that helped farmers increase their production dramatically
8. the tactic of attacking someone by distorting facts, casting suspicion, and making outright false accusations
9. a time of high tension between the Soviet Union and the United States but without direct military conflict between the two nations
10. the U.S./Soviet agreement to settle disputes peacefully and to promote good will between themselves rather than to increase hostilities
11. c
12. b
13. e
14. d
15. a

Critical Thinking

1. Twentieth-century communism promoted atheism and persecuted Christians. It also denied the legitimacy of private property, which the Bible affirms. Communism has failed to work. Despite claiming to help the poor, it actually harms them.
2. Communism would probably have expanded over far more lands than it did.

Chapter Goals

Students should be able to

1. Summarize the presidencies of Kennedy, Johnson, and Nixon.
2. Identify the important civil rights changes in the decades covered by this chapter.
3. Summarize the background, causes, and consequences of the Vietnam War.
4. Define and use the basic terms of the chapter.
5. Identify the internal battles for democracy being waged during the era covered by the chapter.

Chapter Motivation

In this chapter, the students will learn about the continued problems of big government and threats to democracy. Challenge the students to see both the internal and the external threats to democracy in this chapter.

The Vietnam War sharply divided the United States during the late 1960s and early-to-mid 1970s.

The Sixties—Nation in Crisis

I. The Kennedy Administration

II. The Johnson Administration

III. The Vietnam War

IV. The Nixon Administration

Chapter 26 Lesson Plan Chart

Section Title	Main Activity	Pages	Days
I. The Kennedy Administration	Activity 1: Kennedy's Inaugural Address, 1961	493–98	1–2 days
II. The Johnson Administration	King's "I Have a Dream" Speech	499–503	1 day
III. The Vietnam War	Activity 4: One Soldier's Experience in Vietnam	503–9	2–3 days
IV. The Nixon Administration	Activity 5: The Resignation of Richard Nixon	509–17	2–3 days
TOTAL SUGGESTED DAYS (INCLUDING 1 DAY FOR REVIEW AND TESTING)		7–9 DAYS	

MATERIALS LIST

SECTION I
- CD: Party Platform Summaries, 1960; Electoral College Results, 1960; John F. Kennedy, 35th President; The U.S. Space Program
- A copy of JFK's inaugural address
- Activity 1 from the *Student Activities* manual
- Articles on the current space program, including a new space station and a manned flight to Mars
- Picture books and magazines as resources for a collage, mural, or display

The decade of the Sixties was a turbulent era in American history. Various challenges forced the nation to realize that the values of American culture had declined, and as a result the nation was being pulled apart.

First, African Americans began to insist that white Americans take seriously the American declaration that "all men are created equal." They knew from painful experience that claims of "separate but equal" were hollow. During this decade blacks and a growing number of whites insisted that equality meant that all Americans should enjoy the same civil rights. Second, Americans began to reconsider the impact of growth. Industrial growth was good, but not at the expense of clean air and water. Third, the youth culture of the Sixties distorted the American concept of liberty. No longer did liberty mean freedom from totalitarian government. It now meant freedom from all constraints.

At the same time the American court system redefined freedom as secularism—freedom from religion. A few landmark decisions of the Supreme Court reordered American society, making life in the United States far more secular than it had been. In order to reduce religious influence on American society, judges removed prayer and Bible reading from public schools, struck down laws against pornography, and made abortion-on-demand legal.

I. The Kennedy Administration

The Sixties began with the bright hopes of a young senator who challenged America with a dream of conquering a "New Frontier."

The Election of 1960

The Republicans chose Eisenhower's vice president, Richard Nixon, as their candidate in 1960. The Democrats chose Massachusetts senator **John F. Kennedy** (JFK). Kennedy's running mate, Texan Lyndon B. Johnson, was the well-known Senate majority leader. With that ticket, the party hoped to win the votes of both Northern and Southern Democrats. Kennedy was young (only 43) and a Roman Catholic.

For the first time in history, the candidates engaged in a series of television debates. Kennedy entered the debates as an underdog, but his youthful appearance and charm had good effect. In contrast, Nixon seemed to lack energy and appeal. He also refused to use studio makeup and looked unshaven. The election was close. Of 68.3 million votes cast, Kennedy won by only 120,000—a difference of less than one vote per precinct (local voting place). The election highlighted the importance of individual votes even in a large country.

Nixon and Kennedy engaged in the first televised presidential debate in the 1960 election campaign.

Kennedy's Domestic Program: The "New Frontier"

Kennedy's campaign had promised a new program, what he called the **New Frontier**. Kennedy pressed for measures similar to those of the New Deal—economic aid to poor areas, medical insurance (called Medicare) for the aged, aid for college students, and an ambitious space program. In his inaugural address, Kennedy challenged Americans, "Ask not what your country can do for you; ask what you can do for your country." He also asked America's enemies to join the United States in a quest for lasting peace.

Kennedy used tax policy to stimulate the nation's economy. He pushed Congress to cut taxes. As a result, spending and investing

Section I
Objectives

Students should be able to

1. Name the candidates in the 1960 election.
2. Describe advances in civil rights during the Kennedy administration.
3. Identify the Peace Corps and the Alliance for Progress as two of Kennedy's foreign programs.
4. Explain the significance of the construction of the Berlin Wall.
5. Explain the significance of the Cuban Missile Crisis and the Bay of Pigs.
6. Describe Kennedy's assassination and America's reaction to it.

Presidential Press Conferences on TV

President Eisenhower was the first president to use television, conducting press conferences for both radio and television.

The U-2 Incident

Relations between the United States and the Soviet Union cooled even further before the election of 1960. The Soviets shot down an American U-2 spy plane over Soviet air space. The pilot, Frances Gary Powers, parachuted to safety but was captured. The Soviets accused the Americans of spying and used the incident as an excuse to cancel a scheduled summit with Eisenhower in Paris.

SECTION II

- CD: Party Platform Summaries, 1964; Electoral College Results, 1964; Lyndon B. Johnson, 36th President
- February 1993 issue of *National Geographic* magazine
- A copy of "Letter from a Birmingham Jail" by Martin Luther King Jr.
- Documentary video on the civil rights movement

SECTION III

- CD: The Weaponry of the Vietnam War; Party Platform Summaries, 1968; Electoral College Results, 1968
- Activities 2–4 from the *Student Activities* manual

SECTION IV

- CD: Richard M. Nixon, 37th President; Party Platform Summaries, 1972; Electoral College Results, 1972
- A recording of Nixon's resignation speech
- Activities 5 and 6 from the *Student Activities* manual

Core Values

Many of America's core values changed in the 1960s. Conservatives often think of these changes negatively due to the changes in the youth culture. Young people wanted to be free from all restraints: moral, social, or legal. In the courts freedom was interpreted as secularism. In terms of civil rights, however, the changes were positive. Freedom for

African Americans meant they could now eat at lunch counters, sleep in motels, and participate in activities just as white Americans were able to do. African Americans in this decade began to see successes in their struggle to be treated as equals.

Anything New under the Sun?

As the students read through each section, ask them to look for issues and situations they have seen before. Very few of the themes in this chapter are new. JFK and LBJ merely sought to extend the New Deal in new ways. Even moral decay is an old theme, reaching back before the Roaring Twenties and the Gilded Age.

The Mercury 7 Astronauts

- Scott Carpenter
- Gordon Cooper
- John Glenn
- Virgil "Gus" Grissom
- Walter "Wally" Schirra
- Alan Shepard
- Donald "Deke" Slayton

The Gemini Astronauts

- Gordon Cooper
- Gus Grissom*
- Wally Schirra*
- Neil Armstrong*
- Frank Borman*
- Charles "Pete" Conrad*
- Jim Lovell*
- James McDivitt*
- Tom Stafford*
- Edward White*
- John Young*
- Edwin "Buzz" Aldrin*
- Eugene Cernan*
- Michael Collins*
- Richard Gordon*
- David Scott*

*Also on the Apollo projects.

The Space Race

The Soviets dropped a "bomb" on the United States on October 4, 1957: the Russians had successfully launched *Sputnik I* into space orbit. Americans were shocked. How could the Communists be the first to develop the technology to launch a satellite into space? The United States would never be the same.

But Americans rose to the challenge and jumped into the space race. They had a long way to go. A month after the launch of *Sputnik*, another Soviet rocket carried a dog into space. In April 1961, the Russians dropped another bomb: the cosmonaut Yuri Gagarin had orbited the earth.

Alan Shepard

In response, President Kennedy committed the nation to the most ambitious science project in its history: landing a man on the moon by the end of the decade. Congress established the National Aeronautics and Space Administration (**NASA**) to run the new space program. It put aside money to promote science and math education from which future astronauts would come. Many tense years passed, but the United States pulled ahead in the space race. One by one, NASA scientists overcame the complex problems of space travel in a series of space projects.

John Glenn

The *Mercury* astronauts were the first Americans to enter space (Alan Shepard) and to orbit the earth (John Glenn). The *Gemini* missions tested the technology to dock two craft in outer space. The *Apollo* project blasted astronauts 385,000 miles to and around the moon and back.

On July 20, 1969, the radios in NASA's Houston command center crackled a transmission from *Apollo 11*: "The Eagle has landed." Neil Armstrong, the commander of *Apollo 11*, stepped from the ladder of the Eagle lunar module (LM) and became the first person to set foot on the moon. The world listened in awe as he declared, "That's one small step for man, one giant leap for mankind." President Kennedy's goal had been achieved.

Overshadowed and virtually unpublicized during the *Apollo 11* moon landing was the first communion service conducted in space. The pilot of the LM, Buzz Aldrin, was an elder in his Presbyterian church in Texas. Just before Armstrong stepped out of the LM and made his famous statement, Aldrin transmitted the following message to the command center: "Houston, this is Eagle. This is the LM Pilot speaking. I would like to request a few moments of silence. I would like to invite each person listening in . . . to contemplate for a moment the events of the past few hours and to give thanks. . . ." He then quietly opened a kit that his church had provided and partook of the communion elements. "I read the words which I had chosen to indicate our trust that as man probes into space we are in fact acting in Christ." He then read John 15:5: "I am the vine, you are the branches. Whoever remains in me, and I in him, will bear much fruit; for you can do nothing without me."

But the American space program did not stop with the moon landing. It continued with other projects: *Skylab*, the space shuttle, the international space station, the Hubble telescope, and others.

Neither has the program been without its tragedies. In 1967, three astronauts were killed during a simulated launch of *Apollo I*. In 1986, the space shuttle *Challenger* exploded seventy-three seconds after liftoff, killing the seven-person crew. And

Buzz Aldrin

in 2003, the space shuttle *Columbia* burst into flames upon reentry, killing all seven people in that crew. Despite the dangers, NASA continues to chase the unknowns in space, going far beyond Kennedy's wildest dreams.

 CD: Party Platform Summaries, 1960

Refer to the CD for summaries of the major party platforms in the presidential campaign of 1960.

 CD: Electoral College Results, 1960

Refer to the CD for a map showing the results of the Electoral College in the presidential election of 1960.

 CD: John F. Kennedy, 35th President

Refer to the CD for information on President Kennedy.

JFK's Inaugural Address

Read from JFK's inaugural address or play a recorded clip of it so that the students can get a sense of the optimism he conveyed. The two key statements are his request for service of country and his claim that America would make any sacrifice during the Cold War in the defense of liberty. Evaluate the rhetoric of the speech. What other more recent president was known for his attitude of optimism?

Activity 1: JFK's Inaugural Address

Use this activity to help the students better understand the principles included in Kennedy's inaugural address.

 CD: The U.S. Space Program

Refer to the CD for photos of the first astronauts (Mercury, Gemini, and Apollo projects) and their spacecraft.

Discuss the Modern Space Program

Find articles on the current space program, including a new space station and a manned flight to Mars. Why does the space program generate so little excitement today compared to the Space Race of the 1960s? Discuss the legitimate reasons for space exploration, then and now. Is it appropriate for the federal government in a free republic to fund science?

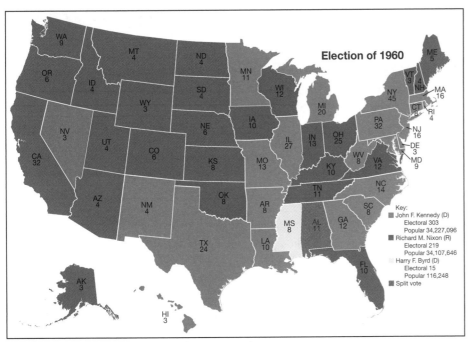

Election of 1960

Key:
■ John F. Kennedy (D)
Electoral 303
Popular 34,227,096
■ Richard M. Nixon (R)
Electoral 219
Popular 34,107,646
□ Harry F. Byrd (D)
Electoral 15
Popular 116,248
■ Split vote

increased and the economy rebounded. Nearly twenty years later, President Ronald Reagan got a sluggish economy rolling again by doing the same thing.

Struggles with Congress

Because Kennedy's victory was so narrow, and because conservative Southern Democrats often voted with House and Senate Republicans, Kennedy's "New Frontier" met opposition in Congress. Congress did agree to a few of Kennedy's goals. It raised the minimum wage to $1.25 per hour, passed the Trade Expansion Act, and expanded the Social Security system. But Congress rejected Medicare, aid to college education, and a bill that would have created a department of urban affairs.

Struggles for Civil Rights

Blacks had used the boycott in Montgomery, but they tried other forms of protest too. In 1960 four black college students sat down at a "white's only" lunch counter at a Woolworth's in Greensboro, North Carolina. They refused to leave unless they were served. This sit-in launched sit-ins at white lunch counters around the country, kneel-ins at churches, and wade-ins at schools. "Freedom riders" rode from place to place in the South, seeking to integrate the buses and to encourage blacks to register to vote.

Almost everywhere civil rights demonstrators went they faced angry mobs of whites, who mocked and beat them. Some blacks were murdered. A bomb destroyed a black church in Birmingham, Alabama, killing four girls. In 1963, civil rights activist Medgar

Debate Topic Idea

Have your students discuss and/or debate the following:

The space program is profitable.

Collage of the Sixties

Bring in picture books and magazines from which your students can choose materials to make a collage, mural, or display that reflects life in this time period. (You could make photocopies of the book and magazine photos.) Include works of art, musical titles (patriotic, religious, classical, and popular), painters, books (authors), entertainers, and sports figures of this decade. Students should write a synopsis of their findings and should include a description or explanation of their collage, mural, or display.

Berlin Wall

The Soviet Union wanted the West out of Berlin so the Communists could control the whole city. Nikita Khrushchev demanded that all Western troops withdraw and allow Berlin to become a "free" city. Khrushchev threatened that if his demand was not met, he would make a new treaty with the East Germans that would sever Western access to Berlin. President Kennedy and other Western leaders would not back down from their determination to hold on to West Berlin, but East Germans were fearful of the consequences of a Western withdrawal. Many East Berliners migrated to the West, causing great consternation among Soviet and East German leaders. The Communists erected a wall in August 1961 to stop the outflow of frightened refugees to the West.

The main portion of the barricade ran approximately twenty-six miles through the center of Berlin. The primary barrier was a wall constructed of huge slabs of concrete and varying in height from twelve to fifteen feet. The top of the wall was covered with concrete tubes, barbed wire, or other impediments. Beyond the wall (in East Berlin), a "no man's land" was secured by land mines, barbed wire, watchtowers, and armed guards with dogs and orders to shoot anyone who tried to escape. A second wall enclosed that neutral area. All citizens of East Berlin who lived within one hundred meters of the Wall were required to register with the government, and some of them had to leave their homes. (Upper-story windows or rooftops provided too much potential as escape routes over the wall.) The rest of West Berlin (the part that was not bordered by East Berlin) was also isolated from East Germany by guarded barriers. In all, approximately 110 miles of barricades surrounded the city.

"Letter from a Birmingham Jail"

Read from the student text the excerpt of Martin Luther King Jr.'s influential "Letter from a Birmingham Jail," which reveals the plight of black Americans in the 1960s.

Letter from Birmingham Jail (Excerpt)

We have waited for more than 340 years for our constitutional and God-given rights. The nations of Asia and Africa are moving with jet-like speed toward gaining political independence, but we still creep at horse-and-buggy pace toward gaining a cup of coffee at a lunch counter. Perhaps it is easy for those who have never felt the stinging darts of segregation to say, "Wait." But when you have seen vicious mobs lynch your mothers and fathers at will and drown your sisters and brothers at whim; when you have seen hate-filled policemen curse, kick, and even kill your black brothers and sisters; when you see the vast majority of your twenty million Negro brothers smothering in an airtight cage of poverty in the midst of an affluent society; when you suddenly find your tongue twisted and your speech stammering as you seek to explain to your six-your-old daughter why she can't go to the public amusement park that has just been advertised on television, and see tears welling up in her eyes when she is told that Fun-town is closed to colored children, and see ominous clouds of inferiority beginning to form in her little mental sky, and see her beginning to distort her personality by developing an unconscious bitterness toward white people; when you have to concoct an answer for a five-year-old son who is asking: "Daddy, why do white people treat colored people so mean?"; when you take a cross-country drive and find it necessary to sleep night after night in the uncomfortable corners of your automobile because no motel will accept you; when you are humiliated day in and day out by nagging signs reading "white" and "colored"; when your first name becomes "nigger," your middle name becomes "boy" (however old you are) and your last name becomes "John," and your wife and mother are never given the respected title "Mrs."; when you are harried by day and haunted by night by the fact that you are a Negro, living constantly at tiptoe stance, never quite knowing what to expect next, and are plagued with inner fears and outer resentments, when you are forever fighting a degenerating sense of "nobodiness"—then you will understand why we find it difficult to wait. There comes a time when the cup of endurance runs over, and men are no longer willing to be plunged into the abyss of despair. I hope, sirs, you understand our legitimate and unavoidable impatience.

Martin Luther King Jr. and other black leaders led the 1963 March on Washington at which King delivered his now-famous "I Have A Dream" speech.

Evers was killed. Black activists who promoted nonviolent protest restrained revenge for such attacks only with great effort.

A Baptist minister, **Martin Luther King Jr.**, was the first black leader to win national prominence after he helped to organize the bus boycott in Montgomery. King also founded the Southern Christian Leadership Conference. That group sought to liberate the poor and underprivileged through social action.

In April 1963, Martin Luther King Jr. led a nonviolent demonstration against segregation in Birmingham, Alabama. The protesters were met by police who used tear gas, cattle prods, attack dogs, and high-powered water hoses to break up their protests. King was arrested on April 12. On April 16, he penned his famous **Letter from Birmingham Jail**, which justified his acts of civil disobedience to local clergymen.

The **Twenty-third Amendment** passed during the Kennedy administration. It gave the residents of the District of Columbia the right to vote in national elections. Because the district's population was heavily black, the amendment was regarded as a step forward in civil rights.

The biggest civil rights event of the Sixties took place in Washington, D.C., in August 1963. Martin Luther King Jr. organized it. Its purpose was to rally support for proposed civil rights legislation. About 250,000 blacks and whites participated in the **March on Washington**. There, on the steps of the Lincoln Memorial, King delivered a memorable address. Repeating the phrase "I have a dream,"

King spoke of an ideal America where liberty and equality would be a reality for all—both black and white.

Kennedy's Foreign Policies

Kennedy entered the presidency with several ideas for helping needy countries and spreading peace. As he was beginning to implement these plans, however, they were cut short by the escalation of the Cold War.

The Peace Corps

Kennedy introduced the Peace Corps in 1961. The "best and brightest" Americans—teachers, engineers, technicians, and businessmen—agreed to volunteer two years of their lives to work in poverty-stricken countries. They improved schools, medical care, and conservation in more than sixty countries.

The Alliance for Progress

Kennedy knew that Cuba was training soldiers to spread communism throughout the region. He announced a program called the **Alliance for Progress**. Under that plan, the United States provided almost $12 billion to Latin American nations in the 1960s. The funds were used for housing, schools, and health clinics or hospitals. JFK hoped that easing poverty would reduce the unrest that allowed communism to spread. Critics said that the large expenses of the program did more to encourage corruption than to benefit the poor.

The Berlin Wall

Kennedy had several dangerous confrontations with the Soviets. Thousands of East Germans—mostly professionals—were escaping into the free city of West Berlin. As a result, in 1961 the Soviet dictator, Khrushchev, ordered a wall to be built around West Berlin. Armed guards had orders to shoot anyone who tried to escape across the **Berlin Wall**.

Kennedy responded by sending more troops to West Berlin. In 1963, he made a dramatic visit to the Berlin Wall. Thousands of Berliners lit candles to show their support of freedom. Kennedy expressed his support by saying in German, "Ich bin ein Berliner." ("I am a Berliner.") Despite Kennedy's actions, the wall remained a blow to the free world.

On the Brink of War with Cuba

Under Communist Fidel Castro, Cuba's problems worsened. His economic policies hurt the people greatly. He also seized all privately owned American property in Cuba. In response, President Eisenhower ended Cuban sugar imports and later severed diplomatic relations with Cuba.

As life in Cuba worsened, many Cubans fled to the United States. A large pro-democracy Cuban community developed in Florida. The Central Intelligence Agency (CIA) trained fifteen hundred of them to overthrow Castro. Soon after JFK took office, he allowed the plan to proceed. The CIA believed that when the Cubans heard about the invasion, they would rise up to overthrow Castro.

But nothing went as planned. On April 17, 1961, the force landed at the **Bay of Pigs**. At the last minute and without informing the invaders, Kennedy withheld promised air support. Castro's forces crushed the invasion and killed more than four hundred of the attackers. The rest were captured. Castro used the unsuccessful invasion to embarrass the United States in front of the world.

The Communist East Germans built the Berlin Wall during the Kennedy administration.

In spite of these formidable obstacles, the desire for freedom proved too strong for many people, who attempted to escape in a variety of ways. Some people tried to climb over, jump over from nearby multi-storied buildings, tunnel under, or even sail over in a homemade hot-air balloon. An estimated 400 to 800 people died in such attempts.

Camelot

The term *Camelot* was first applied to JFK and his family in an essay written after his assassination.

On November 29, 1963, just a week after the assassination, Jackie Kennedy was interviewed by veteran journalist Theodore White. During that interview, she revealed that her and John's favorite Broadway show was *Camelot,* a musical about King Arthur and his knights of the Round Table in the fictional land of Camelot. The show starred Richard Burton and Julie Andrews, and the Kennedys listened to a record of it before retiring every night. JFK's favorite lines from the musical were these:

"Don't let it be forgot,

that once there was a spot,

for one brief shining moment,

that was known as Camelot."

This information became the basis of White's article "For President Kennedy: An Epilogue," which was published in the December 6, 1963, issue of *Life* magazine. Thereafter, the Kennedy years were known as Camelot.

National Mourning

For four days after the assassination, the nation watched almost continuous television coverage of the events surrounding

---

Media Reports in the Sixties

Have your class research how reporters, photographers, and war correspondents treated and influenced a war, an important issue, or a famous event during the sixties.

Lessons from Latin American Policy

Ask the students to compare the Alliance for Progress with past policies toward the nations in Latin America. Note the similarity to Taft's dollar diplomacy and the difference from Teddy Roosevelt's "big stick" policy. Neither money nor force has solved the region's problems. What can students conclude from this experience? Give enough information to prepare the students for Reagan's new approach in the 1980s. Also, look for reports on Latin American policy today, such as the growing tensions between the United States and Venezuela's Cesar Chavez.

Recent Events in Cuba

Discuss recent issues involving Cuba. In 1999 Fidel Castro was the only remaining Cold War warrior still in power. Failures such as the Cuban Missile Crisis had long-term consequences for millions of people. The trade embargo lasted more than thirty years. Discuss Castro's poor health and his recent election of his brother, Raul, as president of Cuba. What are the prospects for freedom in Cuba once Fidel Castro dies? Will the people overthrow Raul, or will communist domination of the island nation continue?

Kennedy's assassination and his funeral. Scenes of mourners filing through the Capitol Rotunda, where the body lay in state, and of his flag-draped coffin moving through the streets of Washington, D.C., on a horse-drawn caisson created great emotion for the nation. Perhaps one of the most memorable photos of the funeral was that of little John ("John-John") Kennedy saluting his father's casket as it passed.

Scene of the Assassination

Vice President Lyndon Johnson was in Dallas with Kennedy, riding two cars behind the president, when the assassination occurred. Texas governor John Connally was riding in the front seat of the car bearing President and Mrs. Kennedy, and he was wounded in the shooting.

The Aftermath of Assassination

Compare and contrast the aftermaths of Lincoln's assassination and JFK's assassination. Both men became heroes, and their failures were easily forgotten. But in Kennedy's case, his program succeeded better after his death than it had before, whereas Lincoln's program for Reconstruction died on the vine. Ask the students to explain why. *(Factors include the skills of the vice presidents, the political views of the leaders in Congress, and the bitter disputes over the Civil War.)*

 More on the Assassination of Kennedy

The official source of information on the assassination of President Kennedy is the *Warren Commission Report*, the report of the investigation by the committee headed by Supreme Court Chief Justice Earl Warren. Another good source of information is *The Day Kennedy Was Shot* by Jim Bishop (who also wrote the books *The Day Lincoln Was Shot* and *The Day Christ Died*).

Kennedy addressed the nation on radio and television about the discovery of Russian missiles in Cuba on October 22, 1962.

Moments after this photograph was taken, the assassin's bullets hit Texas governor John Connally (far left) and the president.

Jack Ruby shot and killed Lee Harvey Oswald before Oswald could be brought to trial.

Problems with Cuba grew worse. Cut off from the United States, Castro turned to the Soviet Union for aid. On October 14, 1962, American U-2 spy planes flew over Cuba. They returned with photographic proof that the Russians were shipping missiles to Cuba that could carry nuclear warheads capable of destroying American cities. The nation was horrified when Kennedy announced the presence of the missiles and his decision to blockade Cuba. U.S. warships surrounded the island. They were ready to stop and search any Soviet vessels that tried to violate the blockade. Kennedy also demanded that the Soviets remove the missiles. He put the nation's armed forces on full alert.

Khrushchev was enraged. He blamed Kennedy for pushing mankind to the brink of nuclear war. After a tense, week-long standoff, he sent Kennedy a message on October 28 offering to remove the missiles if the United States promised not to invade Cuba. As suddenly as it had begun, the **Cuban Missile Crisis** was over. Kennedy's secretary of state, Dean Rusk, boasted, "We're eyeball to eyeball, and I think the other fellow just blinked." But he said nothing about the U.S. side of the bargain. In return for Soviet compromise, the U.S. agreed not to invade Cuba or monitor the removal of the missiles.

The Hot Line in the Cold War

In the wake of the Cuban Missile Crisis, the United States and the Soviet Union wanted to ease tensions. A "hot line"—a direct telephone line between the White House and the Kremlin in Moscow, the Soviet capital—was installed in 1963. The same year at Geneva, Switzerland, the United States, Britain, and the Soviet Union signed a Limited Test Ban Treaty. They agreed that they would not test nuclear weapons above ground. Each nation would tell the others of any underground tests it conducted and would police itself. But France and China, who also had nuclear weapons, refused to sign the treaty.

Kennedy's Assassination

When JFK came to office, the musical *Camelot* was popular on Broadway. The play retold the story of King Arthur's Round Table and his dream of creating a new England where truth, justice, and equality reigned. Some journalists, seeing a parallel between King Arthur's dream and that of Kennedy, began to refer to JFK's administration as "Camelot." But the dreams of the American Camelot came to an abrupt end on November 22, 1963. Lee Harvey Oswald shot and killed the forty-six-year-old president while JFK rode in an open car down a street in Dallas, Texas. Texas governor John Connally was also hit. Vice President Johnson, riding in a separate car, was not hurt.

The reasons for the assassination remain a mystery. Conspiracy theories abound in spite of official conclusions that Oswald acted alone. The mystery deepened when Jack Ruby, a local nightclub owner, shot and killed Oswald before he could be tried.

Like Lincoln, JFK became a hero after his death. Most Americans remembered things they liked about him—his youth, idealism, and vitality. He had symbolized optimism for America's future. Congress quickly passed many of Kennedy's New Frontier programs, which had been stalled in Congress, as memorials to the late president. Kennedy's vice president, Lyndon Baines Johnson, became the new president.

Section Quiz

1. What name did Kennedy give to the domestic program of his administration?

2. What was the purpose of the Peace Corps?

3. In what city did the Soviets build a wall to stop escapes from the Communist-controlled area?

4. What two situations in Cuba created problems for the United States?

5. What was the primary evil that African Americans sought to overcome through the civil rights movement? Why was this an evil?

★ Considering the election of 1960 and more recent ones, do you think television has had a positive or a negative impact on the political process? Explain and support your answer.

Lyndon Johnson took the oath of office aboard *Air Force One*.

II. The Johnson Administration

Lyndon B. Johnson (LBJ) took the oath of office on the presidential airplane, *Air Force One*, on the way back to Washington after Kennedy's death. Since Johnson had been on Capitol Hill for thirty-two years, serving in both the House and the Senate, he knew how to work the political system. A powerful and persuasive man, he was able to get bills passed.

Johnson called his legislative program the **Great Society**. It was supposed to help America bring "an end to poverty and racial injustice . . . in our time."

The Election of 1964

Johnson was just putting his program into place. Before he could achieve all of his goals, he had to win the election of 1964. His Republican challenger was **Barry Goldwater**, a conservative senator from Arizona.

Goldwater represented a small but growing branch of the Republican Party that openly denounced big-government programs. These conservative Republicans saw big-government liberalism as very similar to the communism America opposed. Religious conservatives feared the federal government was undermining traditional values. Southern segregationists supported the movement because its emphasis on states' rights meant less imposition of racial integration by the federal government.

Johnson ran anti-Goldwater ads that frightened voters with the threat of nuclear destruction. One TV ad showed a little girl counting the petals of a daisy while pulling them off. When she pulled the last petal a man's voice began the countdown for a nuclear missile launch. The ad ended with a bright flash of light and a mushroom cloud. It implied that Goldwater would bring about a nuclear war and encouraged viewers to cast their vote for Johnson.

Other ads called Goldwater an extremist. Goldwater responded by declaring that extremism in the defense of liberty is no vice. The Republicans declared, "In your heart you know he's right—vote for Barry Goldwater." The Democrats retorted, "In your guts you know he's nuts—vote for Lyndon Johnson." LBJ won the contest by a landslide, receiving 61 percent of the vote.

Senator Barry Goldwater's 1964 campaign ended in a landslide loss to Lyndon Johnson, but it marked the beginning of the conservative movement within the Republican Party.

Section II
Objectives

Students should be able to

1. Describe the presidential election of 1964.

2. Describe Johnson's "Great Society" program.

3. Explain the significance of the *Brown v. Board of Education* case.

4. List and describe the major civil rights legislation and amendments of the 1960s.

5. Name the most prominent black civil rights leader of the 1960s.

Separate but Equal

The 1896 case that established the "separate but equal" principle was *Plessy v. Ferguson*. In practice, however, few black schools were equal to white schools, not just in the South but anywhere in the country. It was these discriminatory practices that the civil rights movement sought to correct.

Civil Rights Act of 1964

Note that the Civil Rights Act of 1964 empowered officials to cut off federal funds and contracts to companies and institutions that discriminated in their hiring and admissions practices. That authority was significant because of increased dependence on government funding.

Twenty-third Amendment

The Twenty-third Amendment granted the District of Columbia three electoral votes, the same as the least populous states, in presidential elections.

Section Quiz Answers

1. "New Frontier"

2. to help improve conditions in poverty-stricken countries

3. Berlin

4. the failed invasion at the Bay of Pigs and the Cuban Missile Crisis

5. segregation; segregation was evil because it in practice denied that black people were created in the image of God in the same way as white people. It also facilitated the oppression of a whole class of people simply on the basis of their skin color.

★ Answers will vary. Appearance or charisma might become more important than the substance of a candidate's positions when television becomes the primary medium of information for most people. On the other hand, greater exposure of candidates might allow citizens to be more informed politically, especially those who are not readers.

Was It a Mistake to Choose Goldwater?

Goldwater lost by a landslide. Should the Republicans have concluded that they made a mistake in choosing him as their nominee?

Students need to recognize that presidential elections have a value that goes far beyond the current winner or loser. Candidates are positioning themselves for future elections, and different wings of the party are struggling to present their ideas to the American people, hoping that their ideas will eventually take root. As we look back, Goldwater's nomination is considered a watershed in the rise of the Republican Right, which swept Reagan into office in 1980. In fact, Reagan won national recognition because of his spellbinding speech during Goldwater's nomination. Make parallels to the most recent presidential election so that students can see the long-term goals of the participants.

Changing Strategies

Many civil rights activists began with legal steps and then progressed to nonviolent protests if their goals were not met. The legal and nonviolent methods produced some results but not at a pace fast enough to satisfy radical elements within the movement. Those disgruntled activists often turned to violence in an attempt to hasten equal treatment.

The founding of the NAACP in 1910 began a legal strategy to end racial segregation. Lawyers for the organization challenged segregation in the courts, winning small victories over the decades until the big victory came in 1954 with the decision in *Brown v. Board of Education*. Although it took two more decades to implement school desegregation, the *Brown* decision marked a high point in the legal battle for black civil rights. This struggle was necessary in light of the inferior education made available to black children.

The following year, 1955, Martin Luther King Jr. launched a bus boycott in Montgomery, Alabama, to end discrimination in that city's bus system. King's success led to more protests. In 1960, the Student Non violent Coordinating Committee organized sit-ins at the segregated lunch counter of the Woolworth's store in Greensboro, North Carolina, to protest the segregation practice. The following year, the Congress of Racial Equality sponsored "freedom rides" into the Deep South to dramatize racial discrimination in public facilities. The 1964 Civil Rights Act ended racial segregation in public accommodations; the 1965 Voting Rights Act empowered federal officials to register blacks for voting; and the 1968 Open Housing Act ended legal segregation in housing.

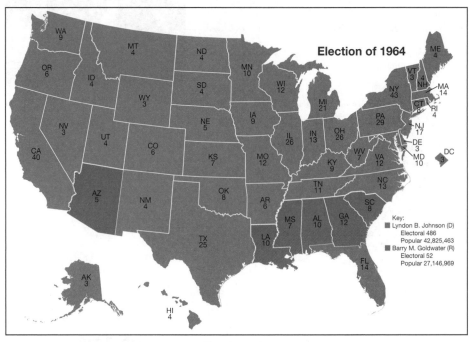

Johnson's Domestic Policies

Forty million Americans did not share in the nation's rising wealth during the 1950s. That hidden minority, according to Michael Harrington in his book *The Other America* (1962), was stuck in a "culture of poverty."

The War on Poverty

Johnson took up the cause of the poor in his Great Society, declaring a "War on Poverty." He created the Job Corps. It was similar to the Peace Corps, but it focused on the needs at home. Other Great Society programs included aid to poor areas of the eleven states of Appalachia and a food stamp program for poor families. He also started the Head Start Program for underprivileged children who needed a "head start" in education before they started regular school.

In 1965, Johnson pushed through several more Great Society programs. Medicare and Medicaid gave qualifying Americans two months of low-cost hospital care and allowances for other medical costs. The Johnson Administration also added two new cabinet positions—the Department of Transportation and the Department of Housing and Urban Development.

All of those programs were expensive. Combined, they cost more money than the government took in. Overspending put the nation in debt. That problem would plague America for the next thirty years. The Great Society made Americans more dependent on government programs and "entitlements" (benefits to which the recipients were "entitled" or had a right). It also gave the federal government more

Johnson's social programs, such as the Medicare bill he is shown signing here, greatly expanded the role of government in society.

 CD: Party Platform Summaries, 1964

Refer to the CD for summaries of the major party platforms in the election of 1964.

 CD: Electoral College Results, 1964

Refer to the CD for a map showing the results of the Electoral College in the 1964 presidential election.

 CD: Lyndon B. Johnson, 36th President

Refer to the CD for a summary of the life and career of Lyndon Johnson.

 Nuggets from *National Geographic*

Poverty grips the part of the nation known as Appalachia. "In the Hearts of Appalachia" in the February 1993 issue of *National Geographic* magazine describes the lifestyles and culture of Appalachia.

Why Do Many Americans Like Government?

Ask the students to explain why many Americans were so supportive of the massive government programs that LBJ pushed through Congress. What had caused such a dramatic change in America's fundamental dislike of a strong central government and high taxes? After all, the country was

founded because of this issue. It can be argued that the schools no longer instilled traditional values. But another explanation is the reform tradition and the philanthropy tradition in America. If the government truly could help the poor, Americans were willing to sacrifice for them. But, as students will see in their study of the 1990s, many Americans were disillusioned by their bad investment. It is never easy to explain the motives behind voters' choices.

power over people's lives. Critics claimed that such programs were "buying" the votes of those who benefited from the programs. If an opposing party threatened to reduce government spending by cutting back on such programs, the recipients would surely vote for the party that protected their "rights."

Despite Johnson's skill in passing legislation, he soon came face to face with two major issues that would drastically reduce his popularity during his remaining years in office. One was civil rights. The other was the Vietnam War.

The Civil Rights Movement

Following the March on Washington and Kennedy's assassination, Congress rallied to pass new civil rights legislation. The **Civil Rights Act of 1964** forbade racial segregation and discrimination in schools and public places, such as motels. The federal government would no longer make contracts with private companies that discriminated, and it would no longer give money to institutions that discriminated in their hiring practices.

The **Twenty-fourth Amendment** (see Chap. 7), ratified in 1964, forbade states from levying poll taxes. The poll tax required voters to

A major focus of Johnson's Great Society dealt with improving race relations by ensuring civil rights.

Negative Aspects of the Civil Rights Movement

With the successes, however, came problems. In 1965, in the Watts section of Los Angeles, one of the worst race riots in American history occurred. For the next few summers blacks continued to riot, loot, and burn their neighborhoods in major cities. King's death in 1968 encouraged black radicals, such as the Black Panther Party, to turn more frequently to violence in their struggle. Calls for "black power" replaced the cries for integration. Many blacks rejected even the white liberals who had been their allies during the 1950s and 1960s. Black militancy and violence ultimately alienated whites in politics and even some of the media, bringing an end to much of the civil rights movement and helping to usher in a conservative backlash in the 1970s.

The Nation of Islam

In 1930, W. D. Fard, a silk salesman in Detroit, founded the Nation of Islam. His followers were commonly known as Black Muslims. He believed that Islam was the true religion of the black man because it had supposedly started with the "blacks" of Asia and Africa. He combined Muslim teachings with a quest for black autonomy. One of his goals was to have a separate nation within the United States for blacks.

Later leaders included Elijah Poole (changed his name to Elijah Muhammad), and Malcolm X. Malcolm was a charismatic leader, but after a pilgrimage to Mecca, he became a Sunni Muslim in 1964 and was gunned down while giving a speech in 1965.

Upon Elijah Muhammad's death in 1975, his son Warith Deen Muhammad took

King's "I Have a Dream" Speech

Rev. Martin Luther King used his gifts as a speaker to rally support for civil rights legislation. The following text is the conclusion of his powerful speech.

ooo

I say to you today, my friends, that in spite of the difficulties and frustrations of the moment, I still have a dream. It is a dream rooted in the American dream.

I have a dream that one day this nation will rise up and live out the true meaning of its creed: "We hold these truths to be self-evident, that all men are created equal."

I have a dream that one day on the red hills of Georgia the sons of former slaves and the sons of former slaveowners will be able to sit down together at the table of brotherhood.

I have a dream that one day even the state of Mississippi, a desert state sweltering with the heat of injustice and oppression, will be transformed into an oasis of freedom and justice.

I have a dream that my four little children will one day live in a nation where they will not be judged by the color of their skin but by the content of their character.

I have a dream today.

I have a dream that one day the state of Alabama, whose governor's lips are presently dripping with the words of interposition and nullification, will be transformed into a situation where little black boys and black girls will be able to join hands with little white boys and white girls and walk together as sisters and brothers.

I have a dream today.

I have a dream that one day every valley shall be exalted, every hill and mountain shall be made low, the rough places will be made plain, and the crooked places will be made straight, and the glory of the Lord shall be revealed, and all flesh shall see it together.

This is our hope. This is the faith with which I return to the South. With this faith we will be able to transform the jangling discords of our nation into a beautiful symphony of brotherhood. With this faith we will be able to work together, to pray together, to struggle together, to go to jail together, to stand up for freedom together, knowing that we will be free one day.

This will be the day when all of God's children will be able to sing with new meaning: "My country, 'tis

of thee, sweet land of liberty, of thee I sing. Land where my fathers died, land of the pilgrim's pride, from every mountainside, let freedom ring."

And if America is to be a great nation, this must become true. So let freedom ring from the prodigious hilltops of New Hampshire. Let freedom ring from the mountains of New York. Let freedom ring from the heightening Alleghenies of Pennsylvania!

Let freedom ring from every hill and molehill of Mississippi! From every mountainside, let freedom ring!

When we let freedom ring, when we let it ring from every village and every hamlet, from every state and every city, we will be able to speed up that day when all of God's children, black men and white men, Jews and Gentiles, Protestants and Catholics, will be able to join hands and sing in the words of the old Negro spiritual, "Free at last! Free at last! Thank God Almighty, we are free at last!"

Reprinted by arrangement with The Heirs to the Estate of Martin Luther King Jr., c/o Writers House as agent for the proprietor New York, NY.

Copyright 1963 Dr. Martin Luther King Jr; copyright renewed 1991 Coretta Scott King

King's "I Have a Dream" Speech

Have the students read King's "I Have a Dream Speech" in the student text. Discuss the original meaning of the statements that King quotes. Ask the students what King means by brotherhood among "all of God's children." King looked forward to an event on earth among people of many faiths. It must be said that this vision contradicts the Bible, which defines God's children as those who place faith in Christ (Gal. 3:26-28), and it says that they look forward to unity in heaven (Rev. 7:9). However, we must avoid the temptation to cast aside this historic oration.

King's speech effectively used poignant language to portray a people who were still not

being treated as free men and women one hundred years after their ancestors had been freed from slavery.

Video on the Civil Rights Movement

Watch a documentary video on the civil rights movement. Make sure that your students view the video with scriptural principles in mind. Preview the video carefully for sections that may be too violent.

Viewpoints on Civil Rights

Since the Civil War, Americans held various views on ways to guarantee equality for blacks in society. Note the fundamental

difference between Booker T. Washington and the NAACP. Washington believed that blacks should earn an equal place by their own hard work, while the NAACP concluded that there were too many political hindrances for blacks ever to have a chance. At first the NAACP worked through the courts, but the 1960s saw the rise of civil disobedience, which refrained from violence, and more radical approaches that sometimes led to violence. Both were designed to advance the goal of equality.

Divide the class into different groups and have them research some of the arguments that each group gave. Ask the students to explain how a Christian should decide on the best alternative. Christians need to make

over the leadership of the Nation of Islam, and significant changes followed that included opening membership to non-blacks and changing the organization's name to American Muslim Mission.

There is a Nation of Islam today, but it is separate from the American Muslim Mission. Louis Farrakhan led a group of people away from the main movement in 1978. His group holds to the black separatist teachings of Elijah Muhammad, and members call themselves Black Muslims.

The Black Panthers

One of the most militant and radical organizations in the black civil rights movement was the Black Panther Party for Self-Defense (better known as the Black Panthers), which was founded in 1966 by Bobby Seale and Huey Newton. It was based for the most part on the ideas of Karl Marx, Lenin, and Mao Zedong and sought to abolish all nations and states and to set up interdependent socialist communities.

Rosa Parks

Rosa Parks became a catalyst for change in the civil rights movement. On December 1, 1955, Mrs. Parks refused to give up her seat to a white passenger on a bus in Montgomery, Alabama. For this offense, she was arrested. The attention brought on the city by this action and the reaction by the African American community resulted in the Montgomery Bus Boycott. Martin Luther King Jr. led the boycott and was catapulted to national standing as a leader of the civil rights movement. The boycott lasted for one year, and the financial and public pressure led the city of Montgomery to capitulate. Mrs. Parks's actions resulted in the loss of her job as a

choices based on principles, not on whatever "works."

Rev. Martin Luther King Jr. delivered perhaps his most famous speech on the steps of the Lincoln Memorial during the March on Washington.

pay a fee and show the receipt before they could vote. Poll taxes were popular in the South because they kept both poor blacks and poor whites from voting.

The **Voting Rights Act of 1965** ended long-standing injustices in federal elections. Although the Fifteenth Amendment (1870) kept the states from denying any race the right to vote, Southern states had gotten around the law in a variety of ways. Many states had literacy tests. Often, those laws required not only reading ability but also understanding of difficult parts of state constitutions. Often, blacks who sought to register were harassed. The new act gave the national government the power to register blacks in states where the number of black voters was significantly lower than the census population. Federal officials also had the authority to check any complaints of discrimination.

Divisions Among Civil Rights Leaders

Martin Luther King Jr., who was recognized as a key leader of the civil rights movement, advocated nonviolent resistance to bring political pressure on cities and on the nation to change unjust laws and practices. But some black leaders rejected King's nonviolent views. Among them was **Malcolm X**, a convert to the Nation of Islam (also known as the Black Muslims). That group preached black supremacy and the need to create a separate black nation to keep the black race pure. Malcolm X's preaching won a large audience, especially in the North. But he also had many enemies, especially after he visited Mecca in 1964. While there, he embraced racial harmony and denounced the "black racism" of the Nation of Islam. Gunmen killed Malcolm X at a rally in New York City the following year.

Radical young blacks were also attracted to Stokely Carmichael, who advocated "black power." The emphasis on violence frightened many whites and angered conservative blacks. They feared the effects it might have on the progress of the civil rights movement.

Malcom X (1925–65)

Malcolm Little was reared in Omaha, Nebraska, in an environment of turmoil. The KKK burned his home. His father, a black Baptist minister, was killed by racists when Malcolm was six. At fifteen, Malcolm dropped out of school and got involved in crime. In 1946, he was convicted of petty burglary and sent to prison.

While there, he joined the Black Muslim faith (Nation of Islam). Upon his release, he dedicated himself to his faith and became one of its leading spokesmen. He also changed his last name to "X," rejecting "Little" because the name was given to his ancestors by their slave master.

Malcolm skillfully described the racial conditions of the United States and denounced the white race. He seemed likely to become a major leader in the Nation of Islam. But disagreements with the leader, Elijah Muhammad, led Malcolm to form his own religious group—the Muslim Mosque.

He made a pilgrimage to Mecca in 1964. Later, he publicly denounced racism and envisioned a world brotherhood. But he still promoted the use of violence. Other groups soon attacked Malcolm. While he was delivering a speech in New York, three Black Muslims assassinated him. He has continued to be a powerful symbol of the civil rights movement.

While the nation's attention was drawn to the segregation laws of the South, it overlooked the social prejudice that had segregated black communities in the North and on the west coast. Riots broke out in several cities in those regions. Just days after the passage of the Voting Rights Act in 1965, rioters burned a black community in Los Angeles known as Watts. Thirty-four people died, and property damage exceeded $35 million. The next year rioters burned parts of Detroit and Newark, and dozens more were killed. The looting and destruction shocked Americans.

Another blow to the civil rights movement came in April 1968. A white man, James Earl Ray, shot and killed Martin Luther King Jr. while he was standing on a hotel balcony in Memphis, Tennessee. King's murder set off a wave of violence in black neighborhoods across America. In spite of government efforts to improve civil rights, the dream of racial harmony seemed far away.

Violence in America continued when Martin Luther King Jr. was gunned down in Memphis on April 4, 1968.

Section Quiz

1. What name was given to Lyndon Johnson's legislative program?

2. What conservative senator from Arizona lost to Johnson in the election of 1964?

3. Who was the most prominent black civil rights leader? What strategy did he adopt?

4. What three pieces of civil rights legislation were passed after President Kennedy's assassination? What did each accomplish?

★ Evaluate Johnson's War on Poverty in light of Scripture passages such as Proverbs 14:31.

III. The Vietnam War

The biggest single issue in foreign affairs in the 1960s was the **Vietnam War**. LBJ inherited a conflict that had been brewing in Southeast Asia for nearly a decade. (The first American combat death in Vietnam occurred on December 22, 1961, when Army Specialist 4 James Thomas Davis of Tennessee was killed.) During Johnson's administration, Vietnam became the raging issue as American involvement increased. By the time the war was over in the mid-1970s, about 55,000 Americans had been killed and $150 billion had been drained from the U.S. economy. Yet despite these sacrifices, the war's outcome was a tragic disappointment. The United States government restricted the military to fighting a limited war to contain the Communists. The Communists fought a total war for total victory. This legacy of the Vietnam War would haunt and hinder U.S. policies for the next thirty years.

America Inherits a War

Eisenhower had pledged that he would not allow South Vietnam to fall to the Communists and had supplied financial aid to that country. But Kennedy was the first president to send large numbers of Americans to Vietnam. By November 1963, the United States had 16,000 troops in Vietnam. Most of them were advisors who trained the South Vietnamese to fight their own war.

The Vietnam War

0   100   200   300
Scale of Miles

---

seamstress, but she became known as the "Mother of the Modern-Day Civil Rights Movement."

Section III
Objectives

Students should be able to

1. Name the resolution that gave the president authority to send troops into conflict in Vietnam.

2. Describe the difficulties of fighting the war in Vietnam.

3. Describe American opinions toward the war in Vietnam.

4. Explain the significance of the Tet Offensive.

5. Explain the circumstances and results of the election of 1968.

6. Define *Vietnamization*.

Tonkin Gulf Resolution

The Tonkin Gulf Resolution was the statement by which both Presidents Johnson and Nixon gained congressional support for their military actions in Vietnam. The resolution received overwhelming support, passing the House by a vote of 416 to 0 and the Senate by a vote of 88 to 2. In intervening years, however, the incident that provoked the resolution has been called into question.

The U.S.S. *Maddox* was conducting electronic espionage in the region of the Gulf of Tonkin in August 1964. On August 2, three North Vietnamese patrol boats attacked the *Maddox*. In the fighting that followed, one of the patrol boats was sunk and the others retreated. Although that attack caused concern over future North

---

Section Quiz Answers

1. Great Society

2. Barry Goldwater

3. Martin Luther King Jr.; nonviolent resistance

4. The Civil Rights Act of 1964—forbade racial segregation and discrimination in schools and public places; Twenty-fourth Amendment (ratified)—forbade states from levying poll taxes; the Voting Rights Act of 1965—gave the national government power to register blacks in states where the registered black vote was lower than the census population indicated it should be

★ Assisting the poor is a biblical goal. The question then becomes, What is the most effective way to achieve this? Those who advocate a large government role might use Proverbs 14:31 to support their position. Others believe government programs are often ineffective and perpetuate cycles of poverty. They advocate independent action by charities and churches. They also note that verses such as Proverbs 14:31 are given to individuals, not governments.

Contrast Korea and Vietnam

After they read the section on Vietnam, the students should be able to explain why the Vietnam War turned out so differently from the Korean War. Make comparisons and contrasts as you look for the answer. *(Both were police actions; both propped up corrupt regimes; both were fought to contain Communism; and both enemies were supported by powerful Communist countries. Unlike the Vietnam War, the Korean War was short; America had allies in Korea; the Korean War followed on the heels of victory during World War II; and the Koreans started the war with a direct assault by a conventional army.)*

Vietnamese actions, the *Maddox* was not violating international law by its presence in the region and so was ordered to continue its operations. Two days later, the *Maddox* was sailing with another destroyer, the U.S.S. *Turner Joy*, when sonar readings seemed to indicate the presence of enemy torpedoes. Both ships opened fire, and one of them reported sinking two enemy vessels. Yet no personnel on either boat had actually seen any ships or heard any gunfire. Later, a commander on the *Maddox* acknowledged the possibility that they were mistaken in their belief of an attack. Nevertheless, President Johnson, without getting a firm confirmation of the facts, used the incident to promote the escalation of war with North Vietnam.

Understanding the Student Protests of the Sixties

Among the most important movements to shape American society in the late twentieth century were the student protests and hippie movement of the sixties. Their opposition to the Vietnam War helped end that war and thereby change the nation's foreign policy. Furthermore, they revolutionized American colleges and universities by insisting on easier academic and moral standards; and their counterculture, with its rock music, drugs, immorality, shabby dress, and long hair, changed American culture. Families were divided and lives were destroyed, in part, by the negative results of these expressions of rebellion. The generation of the sixties, in large part, self-destructed.

A major question for historians is why young people at that particular time became so rebellious. One cause was demographic. The postwar baby boom population became college students by

Senator Eugene McCarthy was one major antiwar politician, or "dove," in Washington.

The Viet Cong were elusive and formidable opponents, and they were hard to distinguish from the civilian population.

North Vietnamese prisoners repeatedly admitted that the B-52 was the weapon they feared most in the U.S. arsenal.

Johnson had campaigned on the promise not to send American boys "to do what Asian boys ought to be doing for themselves." But he became increasingly concerned that Southeast Asia would be conquered by the Communists as China had been in 1949. If that happened, he feared that the other countries of Southeast Asia would fall in turn to the Communists. That bleak scenario was called the "domino theory."

In August 1964, North Vietnamese patrol boats attacked two American destroyers in international waters in the Gulf of Tonkin off the coast of Vietnam. The president reported this incident to the American people in a televised address. He asked Congress for power to act. Congress passed the **Gulf of Tonkin Resolution**. It authorized the president "to take all necessary steps, including the use of armed forces" against the North Vietnamese. The resolution was not a declaration of war, but it gave the president broad powers to increase American activity in Vietnam.

The topic was hotly debated in the United States. Leaders who favored increased American presence in Vietnam, or an "escalation" of the war, were called **hawks**. Those who wanted the United States to pull out completely were called **doves**. Under Johnson, the number of troops in Vietnam escalated rapidly. By May 1965, more than half a million Americans were on Vietnamese soil.

A Two-Front War

The United States was committed to protecting the government of South Vietnam. The United States might have had a better opportunity for success had Vietnamese politics been free of corruption and had the South Vietnamese people consistently backed their own government. The United States had to fight not only the Communists from the North but also Communist supporters in the South. The **Viet Cong**, Vietnamese Communists who had stayed in South Vietnam after the division of the country, carried out guerrilla warfare against American and South Vietnamese troops.

Challenges on the Foreign Front

The United States entered the conflict with other disadvantages. Because Congress had never officially declared war, technically the country was engaged in only a "police action." The United States feared that if it declared war, many more countries would join the fight, leading even to world war. Yet thousands of Americans were dying in Vietnam for a cause that politicians were still debating. As the war dragged on, it seemed that the United States was not fighting to win anything. There seemed to be no clear objective to rally public support.

Although the United States had modern high-tech weapons, it could not use them easily in Vietnam. In World War II the United States had defeated Germany, in part, by bombing its industrial cities. But North Vietnam had no large industrial plants. Rather, it had thousands of little shops scattered across the land. The jungle terrain also made bombing difficult. American bombers found it difficult to identify targets on the **Ho Chi Minh Trail**, the route that the Viet Cong forces used to move their men and goods. Even when they identified specific targets, success was not guaranteed. For example, one log bridge was destroyed at least twenty times, but the North Vietnamese kept rebuilding it in only a few days. The North

CD: The Weaponry of the Vietnam War

Refer to the CD for photos and illustrations of the various weaponry (tanks, planes, artillery, helicopters, and various small arms) used by the United States during the Vietnam War.

Background and Analysis of the Vietnam War

An excellent teacher resource for valuable background information and analysis of the Vietnam War is *The War Everyone Lost—And Won: America's Intervention in Vietnam's Twin Struggle* by Timothy Lomperis. Richard Tregaskis, author of the acclaimed *Guadalcanal Diary*, also wrote *Vietnam Diary* about the early years of American involvement in the Vietnam War.

Promises, Promises

Ask the students to recall another president who campaigned on the slogan "He Kept Us Out of War." *(Woodrow Wilson)* Discuss the difficulties of presidents in keeping their campaign promises. What reasons might prevent their doing so? *(unpredictability of economic conditions and foreign affairs; weather; tactics of political opponents; the fact that the Congress acts to pass laws whereas the president can only suggest or request legislation)*

Activity 2: Gulf of Tonkin Resolution

Use this activity (the full text of the Tonkin Gulf Resolution) to help the students understand the incident (whether real or exaggerated) that prompted full-scale U.S. involvement in the Vietnam War.

Hawks and Doves

Ask the students to guess the origins of these two terms—*hawks* and *doves*. *(Hawks hunt for their prey and are often ruthless in obtaining their food; doves are harmless birds who have become the symbol of peace.)*

Vietnamese received a steady stream of military supplies from both China and the Soviet Union.

United States servicemen often could not identify the enemy. To the servicemen, the Viet Cong looked just like South Vietnamese civilians. People in the cities usually supported the Americans. In rural areas, no one knew whom to trust. The Viet Cong even used children to lob hand grenades at American soldiers. Children killed many soldiers; yet when children were killed in the war, the American public was appalled.

Challenges on the Home Front

A greater threat than the enemy in Vietnam was the lack of unity at home. As the war continued, political activists who strongly opposed the war gained increasing public attention. A **"New Left"** movement, often led by Communist sympathizers, grew among disenchanted Americans and civil rights workers looking for a new cause. Many college students, who were subject to the draft, joined the protests. A few defiant ones burned their draft cards and the American flag. Some young men fled to Sweden or Canada. In October 1965, more than ninety cities had antiwar demonstrations. The Students for a Democratic Society, a left-wing organization, was at the fore. In April 1967, antiwar marches in New York and San Francisco attracted up to 300,000 people.

The antiwar movement was the most visible outpouring of a radical change in thinking and morals among American young people. For years, schools and liberal churches had been teaching that mankind is evolving and that there are no absolute standards of right and wrong. Young people took that teaching to heart. Radical youths rejected their parents' vain search for happiness through hard work and material wealth. The youth **counterculture** toppled accepted standards of morality and rejected authority. They adopted standards completely different from their parents' "old-fashioned" culture. Many of them indulged in drugs and sexual immorality in an effort to achieve complete freedom and happiness. They believed that the world could solve its problems if everyone just started loving each other as innocent children. "All we need is love," claimed one popular song by the Beatles.

The Tet Offensive

By clever use of guerrilla warfare and supplies from the Soviet Union and China, the North Vietnamese, led by Ho Chi Minh, made headway against the South. They believed that if they could just prolong the war, they would win. The Americans would give up and pull out.

To slow the stream of supplies flowing into North Vietnam, the United States began bombing the North Vietnamese port of Haiphong and the capital, Hanoi. The bombings were extremely effective. But every time the United States increased the bombing, the wily Ho Chi Minh hinted that he might go to the peace table if they stopped bombing. Liberal politicians convinced LBJ to reduce the bombings. But that only allowed the Communists time to move in more troops and supplies.

Despite setbacks, the president and General William Westmoreland, the U.S. military leader in Vietnam, were publicly optimistic in 1967. They expanded the air war and sent more American

General William Westmoreland developed a three-phase plan for winning the war in Vietnam, but civilian politicians refused to leave the fighting of the war to the professional warriors.

the mid-sixties, and universities became unbelievably overcrowded. With more students the competition became fiercer. Also, before the mid-sixties, colleges were strict, with high academic and moral standards. Colleges were seen as part of the establishment, which, according to the students, was responsible for problems such as the Vietnam War. By the late sixties, therefore, colleges became tense places, and many students resorted to protests—demonstrations, sit-ins, and walk-outs—and violence against college administrations.

Another factor was the post-World War II generation's failure to discipline their children. Parents followed Dr. Benjamin Spock's theories of childrearing, which discouraged any form of discipline in favor of letting children "express themselves." A third factor was the baby-boom generation's rejection of their parents' materialism. The "affluent society" of the postwar era placed a premium on hard work and the accumulation of wealth. Young people in the sixties were correct in discovering that middle-class materialism did not satisfy. They were wrong, however, in their remedy. Instead of searching for spiritual fulfillment, they sought refuge in drugs, rebellion, immorality, rock music, and unrestrained "self-expression."

Prisoners of War

Four hundred sixty-nine American servicemen and one civilian were held as prisoners of war (POW) by North Vietnam. The majority of those POWs were Navy and Air Force personnel, and most of those were pilots who were shot down over North Vietnam and captured.

One of those POWs was Jeremiah Denton, the pilot of a Navy A6 Intruder. He was on his twelfth mission when he was shot down on July 18, 1965. He was captured, imprisoned, and mercilessly tortured until his release on February 12, 1973.

While in prison, Denton became one of the leaders of the POW resistance. His determination not only to survive the prison ordeal but also to do everything possible to prevent the enemy from achieving any victory over them, no matter how small, encouraged his fellow prisoners not to give up but to survive and "return with honor." The prisoners communicated with each other by tapping and scratching out Morse code on the prison walls.

Denton remained in the service after his release until his retirement as a rear admiral. He was elected to the U.S. Senate as a Republican from Alabama in 1980 and served until January 1987. He wrote a moving account of his POW experience, *When Hell Was in Session*. It was later made into a movie starring actor Hal Holbrook.

Assassination of Robert Kennedy

In the early hours of June 5, 1968, Robert Kennedy finished speaking to an enthusiastic crowd of supporters in a ballroom in Los Angeles's Ambassador Hotel after winning the California Democratic presidential primary. He left the ballroom to hold a press conference in another room. His escorts took him on a shortcut through the hotel kitchen. There, a twenty-five-year-old Palestinian immigrant, Sirhan Sirhan, fired a .22-caliber revolver at the candidate, hitting Kennedy three times. Five other people were also wounded, but only Kennedy's wounds were fatal. He died the next day. Sirhan was tried and convicted of first-degree murder. He was sentenced to death, but his sentence was later reduced to life in prison when Califor-

U.S. troops used the base at Khe Sanh to draw Communist forces into the open and defeat them. The North Vietnamese hoped to make it America's Dien Bien Phu.

The Twenty-sixth Amendment

Because eighteen-year-olds were eligible to be drafted for military duty but were not able to vote, many Americans argued that the voting age should be lowered. The **Twenty-sixth Amendment** was passed in 1971 to lower the voting age from twenty-one to eighteen. Supporters said that an American who is old enough to die for his country is old enough to vote.

Robert Kennedy was leading the field of Democrats in the race for the 1968 nomination when he was killed by an assassin on June 5, 1968.

soldiers into battle. Some people believed the fight would be over in two to three years.

The United States called for a ceasefire during the 1967 Christmas holidays. The Communists used the lull to their advantage. They moved huge quantities of supplies and troops into South Vietnam. Large numbers of disguised soldiers walked or rode into South Vietnam's cities. They smuggled in weapons hidden in coffins.

Then, when their troops were in position, the North Vietnamese and the Viet Cong unleashed multiple surprise attacks on January 30, 1968, the Chinese New Year (Tet). From one end of the country to the other, they attacked police stations, military bases, government buildings, radio and power stations, and foreign embassies. In the first few hours of the attack, they destroyed one thousand U.S. planes on the ground. In the first week, the Communists attacked every major city, including 34 provincial cities and 64 district towns. They captured the old imperial city of Hue (HWAY) and assaulted Saigon, the capital. They surrounded the U.S. base at Khe Sanh, hoping to make it another Dien Bien Phu (see p. 488).

American and South Vietnamese forces counterattacked. Within a few weeks, they regained what had been lost. By March 31, huge numbers of people had been killed: Americans—3,845; South Vietnamese—4,954; and civilians—14,300. But 58,373 North Vietnamese and Viet Cong had been killed. By mid-May, the Communist losses were 92,000. Numerically, the Tet offensive was a crushing defeat for the Communists.

However, the media convinced the American people the Tet offensive was a miserable defeat for American forces. News magazines ran articles urging withdrawal. Walter Cronkite, the respected news anchor from CBS, said with dismay during a newscast, "I thought we were winning this war." LBJ later remarked, "If I've lost Walter, then it's over. I've lost Mr. Average Citizen."

Johnson responded to the antiwar surge by doing four things.

★ He stopped the bombing of North Vietnam.

★ He showed a willingness to negotiate.

★ He increased U.S. troop strength modestly.

★ He announced that he would not run for reelection in 1968.

The Election of 1968

The 1968 election occurred in the midst of the turmoil over Vietnam. Most Americans had expected Johnson to win reelection easily. But Johnson, a shrewd politician, knew he could not win. The campaign of Democrat Eugene McCarthy, an antiwar senator from Minnesota, gained momentum. With Johnson's withdrawal from the race, **Robert Kennedy** (the brother of the late president and a senator from New York) threw his hat into the ring. He counted on the popularity of his name and support from minorities and labor unions. Also, immediately upon Johnson's announcement that he would not run, the vice president, **Hubert Humphrey**, declared his candidacy.

Kennedy became the front-runner among the Democrats. But on the night of his victory in the California primary, Sirhan Sirhan, an Arab radical, killed him in a Los Angeles hotel. The loss of Kennedy was a blow from which the Democrats could not recover. They held their party convention in Chicago and nominated Humphrey as their candidate. But the convention was marred by a wave of antiwar

---

CD: Party Platform Summaries, 1968

Refer to the CD for a summary of the major parties' platforms for the 1968 presidential election.

CD: Electoral College Results, 1968

Refer to the CD for a map showing the results of the Electoral College in the 1968 presidential election.

Third Parties—What Good Are They?

Discuss the students' opinions concerning the value—if any—of third parties in American presidential politics. Because they sel-

dom seem to stand a chance of succeeding in America's entrenched two-party system, what good are they? *(They often serve as "spoilers" for one of the major parties, taking enough votes from it to prevent its candidate from winning. So they tend to force one party or the other to either moderate or stiffen their views on issues pertinent to that election. They also influence the topics being debated.)* Ask the students if they see any danger in the presence of third parties. *(Too many parties in a race can so dilute the vote that a candidate might win without a majority. For example, Lincoln was a minority president who had the support of less than half of the country.)*

riots and demonstrations. Young demonstrators protested the war. Police responded firmly to the protests. Critics of the police said they overreacted. Much of the American public became convinced the nation was out of control.

The Republicans revived the hopes of Richard Nixon and put him on their ticket with Maryland governor Spiro T. Agnew. A third party, the American Party, ran Alabama governor George C. Wallace. Wallace was noted for his opposition to integration. He appealed to voters who were tired of high taxes, liberal court decisions, and federal interference in the lives of citizens. But he had little chance of winning outright. His only hope was to prevent either major candidate from winning a majority and thereby to throw the election into the House of Representatives. There he would have a better chance of winning. In the election, he captured five Deep South states and garnered 46 electoral votes. The election was close, but Nixon won.

America Gets Out of the War

Nixon inherited a war and a "no-win" policy in Vietnam, a huge national debt, and an economy that was nearly out of control. Johnson had ignored the advice of his Council of Economic Advisors. He thought he could fight a war, keep his Great Society programs, and limit inflation without a tax increase. Since he was already unpopular, Johnson had no desire to raise taxes. But he did not want to cut programs either. The consequences were disastrous.

Not wanting to repeat the failures that had ended Johnson's career, Nixon made his priority ending American involvement in Vietnam "with dignity." He intended to pull large numbers of ground troops out of Vietnam while continuing intensive bombing raids. Yet he did not want it to seem as though the United States had lost the war.

Vietnamization

In the fall of 1969, President Nixon announced his proposal for the **Vietnamization** of the war. The United States would gradually turn over responsibility for the fighting to the South Vietnamese. The United States would continue to provide supplies and air support to the South Vietnamese. As Vietnamization proceeded, more American troops came home. When Nixon took office, 543,400 U.S. troops were in Vietnam. By December 1971, there were 157,000. And by the end of 1972, only 24,000 were left.

The success of Nixon's policy depended on continued U.S. support for the South Vietnamese and American determination to force North Vietnam to honor its agreements. But as Americans pulled out of Vietnam, the Communists increased their forces and stockpiled supplies.

The Communists withdrew to supply bases in Cambodia between attacks on Americans in South Vietnam. Without seeking congressional approval, Nixon ordered the Cambodian bases bombed. On March 18, 1969, the United States began secret B-52 bombing raids over Cambodia. During the next fourteen months, the B-52s made 3,600 strikes inside Cambodia. In April 1970, Nixon announced a temporary expansion of the war into Cambodia. In 1971, the United States also attacked Vietnamese forces and supply convoys along the Ho Chi Minh Trail in Laos.

In response to the move into Cambodia, demonstrations erupted on college campuses. At **Kent State University** in Ohio, students

Richard Nixon and Spiro Agnew were on the Republican ticket in 1958.

Alabama governor George Wallace ran a strong third-party race, hoping either to force a more conservative stand by the Democrats or to throw the election into the House of Representatives.

> ### Unanswered Questions from the Vietnam War
> - To what extent should the press be allowed to report the actions of the military?
> - How much power should the president have to wage war?
> - Should Americans entangle themselves in foreign conflicts that might end without victory?
> - Nearly six hundred U.S. prisoners of war (POWs) were released in 1973, but what about the more than two thousand soldiers who were listed as missing in action (MIA) and are still unaccounted for?

nia's death penalty was declared unconstitutional in 1972. Sirhan's alleged motive was anger over Kennedy's support for the sale of U.S. fighter jets to Israel. As was true after JFK's assassination, some people questioned whether the man caught was the real and only assassin.

Evaluate Vietnamization

Given the difficulties in Vietnam, what would the students have done if they had been president in 1969? The results of Vietnamization were disappointing and predictable, but did the United States have a better option? Ever since America's loss in Vietnam, the Pentagon and the State Department have tried to learn the lessons of that loss so that the nation would never lose another war. The United States applied these lessons when it entered the Persian Gulf War. One of the keys to success was a clear set of achievable objectives. Discuss any recent debates about new military conflicts. Show the students any evidence of the current president's fear of the "ghost of Vietnam."

How the Vietnam War Came To Be

To properly understand how the United States became involved in Vietnam requires knowledge of some history of the Vietnamese people. One of their traditions is a concept called the Mandate of Heaven. That belief commits them to preserving the Vietnamese identity and ridding their country of foreign "invaders and meddlers." The loyalties of the people were to their tribal leaders more than to their national leaders.

The first contact of the Vietnamese with Europeans was with Portuguese traders. Portuguese (and later French) missionaries tried to convert the Vietnamese to Roman Catholicism. By the mid-1700s they had gained more than 300,000 converts, mostly in the southern end of the country.

By 1862, the French had seized three provinces. They eventually colonized all of Indochina. They succeeded in destroying the old Vietnamese order but failed to replace it with a successful new one. The main government was one of French oversight of a Vietnamese "mandarin bureaucracy." In the 1920s, the French began to take more direct control of village government and tried to suppress all nationalistic sentiments.

When the Japanese took over during World War II, the Vietnamese joined with the French to drive them out. A Communist-dominated group called the Viet Minh united the various tribal groups to oppose the Japanese. The Viet Minh in the south conducted a premature uprising and were totally suppressed. The Viet Minh in the north were more patient. They gathered strength under the leadership of Vo Nguyen Giap and awaited a time when they were assured of success.

The U.S. Office of Strategic Services [the forerunner of the modern Central Intelligence Agency (CIA)] and the French government provided the Viet Minh arms and equipment for fighting the Japanese. Little did they know that they were arming a potential enemy.

As the war wound down, the Viet Minh, realizing that the weakened Japanese would soon be defeated, acted. They divided the country into military zones and formed the Vietnam Liberation Army. On August 17, 1945, they staged demonstrations of force in multiple cities, including Hanoi, Hue, and Saigon. The Japanese offered no resistance. The puppet emperor, Bao Dai, resigned and handed over power to the Communists with Ho Chi Minh as their head.

Elections were held on January 6, 1946, and the Communists won 310 of the 380 seats in the legislative assembly. No elections were held in the south or in provinces controlled by other political parties, but Viet Minh representatives were appointed to fill those seats.

In December 1946, the Viet Minh began attacking the French in the cities. The French pushed the Viet Minh into the hills, where the Communists began fighting a guerrilla war of attack, attrition, and movement. The French tried to negotiate and fight at the same time, but neither tactic worked. They sought U.S. help, and America responded by supplying arms and ammunition. Communist China shipped arms to the Viet Minh.

In March 1953, Giap's 40,000 Viet Minh surrounded the 16,000 French troops at Dien Bien Phu and besieged them for 55 days. The French finally surrendered. They agreed to divide the country at the seventeenth parallel, with the north controlled by the Communists and the south by a democratic government. Between 1954 and 1960, one million refugees fled south. Free elections were not held, despite Viet Minh promises. Sixty countries recognized the legitimacy of South Vietnam. But the Viet Minh refused to do so. Instead, they established the National Liberation Front and the Viet Cong military force to conduct guerrilla warfare against the South.

In an effort to save South Vietnam, America began to send troops, supplies, and equipment to the South Vietnamese. U.S. troop strength there escalated: 875 in 1960, 3,164 in 1961, 11,326 in 1962, 16,263 in 1963, and 23,210 in 1964. The Communists escalated in turn. After the Tonkin Gulf incident, the United States was committed to a full-scale war. It turned into the longest and most controversial war in American history.

disregarded the instructions of the Ohio National Guard to disperse. When the soldiers felt threatened, they panicked and fired into the crowd, killing four students. A similar riot at Jackson State University in Mississippi led to two more deaths.

The Paris Peace Talks

At the same time, Nixon sought to get the North Vietnamese to the peace table. It took six weeks to get the two sides into the same room in Paris because the Communists argued about the shape of the table and the seating order. The talks broke up when the

Activity 3: Summary of the Vietnam War

Use this activity to help the students better understand the chronology of the Vietnam War.

secretary of the Communist Party left in anger. Nixon responded with air strikes and heavy bombing of Hanoi and Haiphong. The U.S. Navy also mined Haiphong Harbor. "The Christmas blitz" was heavy enough that North Vietnam came back to the peace talks and signed a ceasefire on January 24, 1973.

North Vietnam again used the lull to rebuild its forces. When the Communists attacked Saigon in 1975, Nixon's successor, Gerald Ford, asked Congress to increase aid to South Vietnam, but it refused. The cause of South Vietnam was lost. The last American troops left Saigon in the spring of 1975. Within two weeks of the American departure, Saigon fell to the North Vietnamese. In the years following, reports of Communist massacres and inhumanity regularly found their way out of Southeast Asia. Hundreds of thousands of Vietnamese fled the country.

The Cost of the War

The cost of the Vietnam War was high: more than 58,000 Americans killed; 300,000 wounded; and about $150 billion spent. But the war cost far more. War veterans came back to a disillusioned country. Few were welcomed as heroes; most were ignored. Not until 1982 was a national memorial created and dedicated to the Vietnam War dead.

Congress reacted to the cost and controversy of the Vietnam War by limiting the president's power to fight such wars in the future. The **War Powers Act** (1973), vetoed by Nixon but overridden by Congress, defined the circumstances necessary before the president could go to war. It also required that all action be ended in thirty days unless Congress authorized action beyond that.

An antiwar demonstration at Kent State turned deadly when National Guardsmen fired into a crowd of protesting students, killing four, on May 4, 1970.

The Paris peace agreement ended U.S. involvement in the Vietnam War.

Section Quiz

1. What action of Congress gave President Johnson the authority to increase American involvement in Vietnam?

2. What were the South Vietnamese Communists called?

3. Name three disadvantages the United States military faced on the foreign front of the Vietnam War.

4. How did American young people respond to the Vietnam War?

5. What was "Vietnamization"?

6. When did the last American troops leave Vietnam? What was the result of their departure?

★ How was Vietnam different from American wars before that time? How did these differences affect public reaction?

IV. The Nixon Administration

Richard Nixon appealed to people he believed were decent, law-abiding, tax-paying Americans. He called these people "the silent majority." Although antiwar protests continued for a while, unrest seemed to be disappearing. Americans approached the next decade with hopes for an end to the turmoil. President Nixon's leadership had given the country a new confidence.

"Chappie" James: American Hero

As the Commander of the North American Air Defense Command (NORAD), Gen. Daniel "Chappie" James was the first black to attain the rank of full general. James was a veteran of World War II (training the famed Tuskegee Airmen) and the Korean and Vietnam Wars. He was much in demand as a motivational speaker, especially for minority youth. He died on May 2, 2000, and is buried in Arlington National Cemetery.

Section IV
Objectives

Students should be able to

1. Describe Nixon's foreign affairs activities.

2. Explain Nixon's failures with the economy and the federal courts.

3. Identify and describe the three new rights movements of the Nixon era.

4. Explain the circumstances that led to Nixon's resignation.

Activity 4: One Soldier's Experience in Vietnam

Use this activity to give the students a better feel for what the life of a combat soldier in the Vietnam War was like by reading a first-hand account of typical military actions in that conflict.

Class Debate

Have the students debate whether the War Powers Act is necessary or constitutional, considering the fact that the Constitution makes the president the commander in chief and gives Congress power to declare war.

Section Quiz Answers

1. Tonkin Gulf Resolution

2. Viet Cong

3. With no official declaration of war, the conflict seemed to lack purpose. America's technology was not a great advantage in the jungles of Vietnam. And U.S. troops had trouble distinguishing between the Viet Cong and loyal or innocent South Vietnamese civilians.

4. Many of them participated in antiwar demonstrations; some young men avoided the draft; many were obedient to the draft and served honorably, more than 50,000 giving their lives.

5. gradually returning the responsibility for fighting the war to the South Vietnamese

6. spring 1975; the fall of Saigon to the North Vietnamese within two weeks

★ The Vietnam conflict was not even a war officially. It lacked clear direction and seemed to make no progress toward a satisfying conclusion. As a result, Americans at home did not rally to support the action or the soldiers as they had in previous wars. Vietnam was the first military action to be covered extensively by television. Constant images of death and destruction aroused strong animosity toward the conflict.

Nixon's Rise to the Presidency

Judging by his early political career, Richard Nixon was an unlikely person to reach out to the Communists in the Soviet Union and China. During the late 1940s and early 1950s, Nixon was a member of the House Un-American Activities Committee. He was instrumental in securing the conviction of Alger Hiss for perjury. (Hiss was a former State Department official suspected of spying for the Communists in the 1930s.) Nixon was also elected to the Senate from California in 1950 on a platform of rooting out Communist and socialist influence. His campaign made much use of anti-Communist propaganda.

Eisenhower chose Nixon to be his running mate in 1952, and Nixon served as vice president for Ike's two terms. He lost his first bid for the presidency to JFK in 1960 but came back to win in 1968 and 1972. In foreign affairs, he was active in seeking better relations with both China and the Soviet Union.

Progress in the Space Race

After the successful completion of the Apollo moon landing, NASA began to flounder. The Soviets launched the first manned space station, Salyut I, in 1971. The United States followed two years later with Skylab, launched on May 14, 1973. The U.S. space shuttle program seemed to be a phenomenal success, but then it suffered setbacks in the *Challenger* and *Columbia* disasters. Other successes were the positioning of the Hubble space telescope in space and the unmanned Mars expeditions. NASA has begun planning for Project Constellation, which, by the end of the 2020s, aims to return man to the moon to establish a permanent human presence there.

 CD: Richard M. Nixon, 37th President

Refer to the CD for information on President Richard Nixon.

Was Nixon Conservative?

Nixon nourished a reputation as a conservative, but his policies as president belie his reputation. Modern (and early) conservatives would have attacked many of President Nixon's policies as liberal if a Democratic president had proposed them. Ask students to look for hints in their reading that Nixon was no conservative. *(appealed to the middle-of-the-road "silent majority," signed an arms treaty with the Soviets, opened diplomatic relations with Communist China,*

Henry Kissinger was a trusted advisor to Nixon on foreign policy.

Foreign Affairs

Unlike LBJ, whose interest had been in domestic matters, Nixon's emphasis was on foreign affairs. He dealt with the problem of Vietnam. He also developed friendlier relations with Communist China and the Soviet Union. In the Senate, Nixon had earned a reputation as a "cold warrior" against communism. But as president he brought in a new era of **détente** (an easing of tensions) with the Soviet Union. Nixon relied heavily on Dr. **Henry Kissinger**, a Harvard professor born in Germany, who became his special advisor. In 1973, Kissinger became Nixon's secretary of state.

The Soviet Union

In May 1972, Nixon went to the Soviet Union to discuss the Strategic Arms Limitations Treaty (**SALT**). Both nations agreed to limit the types and number of nuclear warheads and missiles. They also agreed on trade issues and cooperative scientific and space projects. Conservative opponents of those agreements said they were not worth the paper on which they were written. The Soviet Union had a history of ignoring treaties. But the agreements did have considerable political value at home.

Communist China

China closed its doors to the West when the Communists took over in 1949. Americans feared that China might join forces with the Soviet Union, although the two countries were bitter rivals. In 1971, Kissinger seized an opportunity to open relations, making a secret trip to China. While there, he arranged for a presidential visit in February 1972. Accompanied by American reporters and camera crews, Nixon toured the Great Wall, attended banquets, and met with Chinese leader Mao Zedong.

Many historians view this feat as Nixon's greatest achievement. By opening diplomatic relations with the People's Republic of China, Nixon drove a wedge between the world's two largest Communist countries. This wedge led the Soviets to seek arms negotiations with the United States. It also opened the door to China's economic and industrial transformation. However, Nixon's diplomatic achievement also had negative consequences. Opening diplomatic relations with the People's Republic of China hurt America's support of "Free

Efforts at détente eased Chinese-American relations enough for Nixon to visit China in 1972.

Ping-Pong Diplomacy

In April 1971, Secretary of State Henry Kissinger conducted secret negotiations with China in an effort to ease tensions between the countries. But the two nations needed something more to break the ice. Ping-Pong was the answer. Chinese prime minister Zhou Enlai invited the American Ping-Pong team to visit Communist China for a tournament. They accepted, becoming the first American delegation to visit China in twenty-two years.

Eighteen thousand eager fans crowded into Beijing's Indoor Stadium for the tournament. The American and Chinese players engaged in a close but friendly competition. The Chinese, who were world-class Ping-Pong champions, narrowly won both the men's (5–3) and the women's games (5–4). The Chinese players admitted that they had been easy on the Americans.

Although the Americans lost in Ping-Pong, they won in diplomacy. The stage was set for formal talks. Three months later, Kissinger made a formal visit of his own. He arranged for President Nixon to make his historic visit the next year. The success in Beijing opened the door for similar "sports diplomacy" around the world.

imposed wage and price controls, and signed new environmental regulations) How might Goldwater or Reagan have responded differently?

China," its former ally during World War II, which had fled to the island of Taiwan. When the United States recognized Communist China, the U.N. removed Taiwan from the Security Council and gave its seat to Communist China, giving the mainland country veto power over every issue brought before the Security Council.

The Middle East

The Middle East was a constant source of worry. In October 1973, Egypt and Syria, armed with modern weapons from the Soviet Union, launched a surprise attack against Israel, America's ally. The first week of the Yom Kippur War devastated Israel's army, but in the second week Israel took the offensive. A brilliant thrust across the Suez Canal threatened the rear of Egypt's army. The Soviet Union prepared to send troops to assist the Arab states, but it held back after Nixon put America's nuclear forces on alert. Nixon also flew in military hardware worth nearly two billion dollars to strengthen Israel.

Secretary of State Henry Kissinger became the go-between to help restore peace. Over several months, planes shuttled him back and forth from the United States to Damascus, Syria; to Cairo, Egypt; on to Tel Aviv, Israel; and back home again. This **shuttle diplomacy** ended the bloodshed but yielded no permanent peace agreement.

Domestic Issues

During the Vietnam War, the government spent money for not only the war but also new domestic programs. When Nixon came to office, he inherited both a war debt and runaway inflation.

Economic Problems

Nixon had his hands full dealing with foreign affairs, but he also had a number of important and perplexing domestic problems. The economy and an energy crisis were only two of those problems.

Recession—Nixon tried to curb inflation by slowing government spending and increasing taxes. With less money in circulation, people would not be able to buy as much. But such action often results in a **recession**. (A recession is a slowdown in the economy, not as severe as a depression but a time when businesses produce fewer products and must lay off some of their workers.) This was the result of Nixon's action. To make the recession less painful to the average American—and to help his own chances of reelection—Nixon raised government spending to create new jobs. But that only increased the national debt.

Conservatives objected, but Nixon decided to use government power to curb inflation. In August 1971, he imposed wage and price controls. All wages and prices were frozen at August levels for ninety days. At the end of ninety days, the newly organized Cost of Living Council set guidelines that allowed some increases. But Nixon's wage and price controls did not deal with the causes of inflation—excessive government spending and a growing national debt. They only temporarily controlled some of its symptoms. The controls artificially slowed inflation to about 3 percent annually. When those controls ended in 1973, inflation doubled. In 1974, it almost doubled again to 12.2 percent.

Energy Crisis—Another problem arose in October 1973. The Organization of Petroleum Exporting Countries (OPEC), made up mostly of Arab nations, was angry over American support of

Causes of Stagflation

Stagflation refers to a stagnant economy in recession with high inflation. Some economists blame inflation and depression on government interference with the money supply. They criticized Nixon's decision to devalue the dollar during his first term. To gain the short-term benefits of higher economic growth rates and lower unemployment, Nixon separated the U.S. dollar from the gold standard, and the U.S. Federal Reserve (Fed) cranked up the printing presses. Too much money in circulation always leads to higher prices. The short-term benefits gave way to a long-term economic crisis that endured through the rest of the decade. Not until the Fed reined in the money supply under Reagan did the government kill the beast of stagflation.

Oil Embargo

The Arab oil embargo was a reaction against America's support for Israel in the Yom Kippur War (1973–74). Since that time, the Oil Producing and Exporting Countries of the world (OPEC) has periodically tried to influence world affairs by increasing or decreasing their production of oil.

The Arab oil embargo led to long lines at gasoline stations in the United States.

Israel. They ordered an embargo (complete ban) on American oil shipments. The United States imported one-quarter of its oil from Middle Eastern countries, so the **oil embargo** hurt Americans. To compound the problem, price controls kept gas stations from raising prices. Complex government regulations limited how businesses could adapt. Some gas stations were forced to close. Others limited how much gasoline each customer could buy. Motorists waited in long lines for gasoline. When price controls were lifted, the prices of gasoline, fuel oil, plastics, and other petroleum-based products skyrocketed as the market sorted things out according to the law of supply and demand.

Nixon asked Americans to conserve energy. Some people bought smaller cars that got better gas mileage. Many people in big cities began car-pooling or "ride-sharing." Many Americans vacationed closer to home. Congress lowered the speed limit to 55 mph. It also approved a pipeline across Alaska to gain access to oil reserves above the Arctic Circle. The oil embargo also encouraged Congress to spend money on new programs to develop alternative sources of energy.

OPEC lifted the embargo in March 1974, and the **energy crisis** eased a little. But OPEC steadily raised crude oil prices. Some extremist Muslim countries hoped to destroy America with high prices. Moderate OPEC members, such as Saudi Arabia, argued that ruining the economies of Western industrialized countries would only hinder their buying oil. Unable to agree on prices and production limits, OPEC members split. Oil again flowed.

Conflicts with the Courts

President Nixon had the rare opportunity to appoint four justices to the Supreme Court, including a new chief justice.

Nixon's Court Appointments—The Warren Court was unpopular with conservative Americans. Many were outraged at its rulings against prayer and Bible reading in the nation's public schools. The Court also struck down laws prohibiting pornography. When Chief Justice Earl Warren retired in 1969, many Republicans hoped that Nixon would replace him with a conservative justice. Nixon chose **Warren Burger**. He also nominated Harry Blackmun, Lewis F. Powell, and William H. Rehnquist to fill later vacancies.

Burger proved to be a disappointment to conservatives. His Court limited the scope of some landmark decisions of the Warren Court, but it did not reverse them. Rehnquist, however, was a conservative justice who would serve into the twenty-first century and would eventually become the chief justice.

Roe v. Wade—Too few conservatives were on the court to prevent a liberal decision on abortion in 1973. In *Roe v. Wade*, the court decided that a woman had the right to abort her unborn child within the first three months of pregnancy. The ruling overturned the abortion laws of all fifty states. Since then, the annual average number of abortions performed is nearly 1.5 million. These abortions kill nearly one third of all babies in America each year. Conservatives saw *Roe v. Wade* as the climactic decision in a series of extreme rulings. Conservative Americans across the country began to get involved in politics in order to change the moral direction of the nation. *Roe v. Wade* became a key catalyst for the conservative resurgence of the 1980s.

Warren Burger was a disappointment to conservatives when he proved to be quite liberal in his Supreme Court rulings.

The United States and the Middle East

Discuss the ongoing problems that the United States has had with the Middle Eastern nations and the problems created by the disruption of the oil supply. Discuss the desirability and wisdom of becoming energy self-sufficient. Is it desirable—or even possible—to be energy self-sufficient in a global economy? Discuss also the environmental issues that are raised over efforts to achieve energy independence. Are they legitimate concerns or a threat to national security?

A Problem with Supreme Court Nominations

Discuss with the students the difficulty of selecting Supreme Court justices. What lessons do these difficulties hold for presidents who have the opportunity to nominate justices?

Growth of Federal Power

In the 1960s, a number of issues led activists to start new movements to deal with the abuses of industry and the denial of certain human rights. These movements contributed to the unrest of the decade, since the American people often disagreed over how to deal with these issues.

The Search for Clean Air and Water—The publication of Rachel Carson's book *Silent Spring* (1962) launched the modern environmentalist movement, a concern about man's relationship to his environment. That book contained inaccurate information and alarmed Americans by exaggerating the harmful effects of pesticides, such as DDT. Nevertheless, there were real environmental problems that needed to be addressed. Under LBJ, the government spent billions of dollars to clean up lakes and rivers. The first lady, Lady Bird Johnson, led a crusade to beautify America. However, cities and states retained primary responsibility for regulating their own industries and pollution.

April 22, 1970, witnessed a nationwide protest called Earth Day. It encouraged the federal government to step in and work for clean air and water. That year, Congress established the Environmental Protection Agency (EPA) to oversee environmental regulations. The Clean Air Act of 1970 (amended in 1977 and 1990) regulated air pollution. The Water Pollution Control Act (1972) and the Clean Water Act (1977) regulated water pollution.

Nixon signed the Endangered Species Act (1973), granting bureaucrats power to decide which species are threatened and how to protect them. Environmentalists complained that the law was too weak. Conservatives complained that it was too arbitrary. Bureaucrats could limit industry and construction, such as logging and dam building, without weighing the costs and benefits. For example,

According to National Right to Life:

Since the decision in *Roe v. Wade* in 1973, at least 43 million—and perhaps as many as 50 million—abortions have been performed in the United States. Approximately 3,500 abortions are performed each day in the United States. That is about 146 an hour or one every 25 seconds. "In 2003, more children died from abortion than Americans died in the Revolutionary War, the Civil War, World Wars I and II, the Korean, Vietnam, and Gulf Wars combined." Abortion is a $400 million a year industry in America.

César Chavez (1927–93)

César Chavez was born near Yuma, Arizona, and grew up migrating across the Southwest with his family. Like other Hispanic migrant workers, he made less than minimum wage and had to endure life in work camps.

After serving in World War II, Chavez began working in an apricot field near San Jose. There, he became involved with the Community Service Organization. Chavez eventually became its general director. He dreamed of uniting farm workers and helping them fight against poor working conditions, so he later resigned and formed his own group—the National Farm Workers. In 1966, he merged his organization with another union to form the United Farm Workers (UFW).

To fight for higher pay, family health coverage, and pension benefits, Chavez used the nonviolent tactics of Gandhi and Martin Luther King Jr. One of his most successful methods was the boycott—encouraging people not to buy from, sell to, or deal with a company.

In 1965, he organized a boycott against grape growers around Delano, California. By 1970, most growers had signed contracts with the UFW. He also conducted a boycott of lettuce producers.

Another method he used was the fast. He held a thirty-six-day fast in 1988 to protest the use of poisonous pesticides where grape workers worked. He died in 1993, but the UFW has continued fighting on behalf of Hispanic workers.

Modern Environmentalism and Other Issues

Students are reading in their textbook about issues that remain in the news today. Discuss recent legislation dealing with environmentalism and have the students summarize both sides of the issue. Conservatives do not want to see America's resources trampled, but they argue that a free society, unfettered by excessive regulations, will do a better job of developing resources than government officials. Liberals, on the other hand, do not believe that free men can be trusted to act in the "public interest." Since Christians know that mankind has a sinful nature, they should realize that a God-established government can serve a role in protecting the environment. The key is to work toward proper stewardship as commanded in Genesis 1:26–28.

Discuss other issues in this section to guide your students in thinking scripturally about them.

Roe v. Wade

The "Roe" of *Roe v. Wade* was Norma McGorvey of Texas. Because she was denied her desire to have an abortion, she sued the state of Texas. The Supreme Court decided in a 7–2 ruling that a woman had an unrestricted right to an abortion within the first three months of pregnancy. That unrestricted "right" was applied essentially to the time when the baby would be unable to survive outside the mother's womb, and the court justified its decision by citing a woman's right to privacy. They also cited the First, Ninth, and Fourteenth Amendments to support that right to privacy.

Indian Rights

Indians became more vocal about their rights during the 1960s. Indian leaders demanded repayment for the many treaties that the federal government had made with them but then broken or ignored. Some protests became violent. For example, a group of Indians seized a government trading post at Wounded Knee, South Dakota, in 1973. Leonard Peltier, a member of the radical American Indian Movement, killed two FBI agents at the Pine Ridge reservation in 1975. Although the violence was regrettable, it drew attention to legitimate complaints about mismanagement of the Bureau of Indian Affairs. In a sense, that program was the United States' first experiment in socialism, and it had proved to be a disaster. The federal government provided a financial subsidy to the Indians that diminished or removed their incentive to labor to support their families. This misguided aid, along with chronic alcoholism among the Indians, reduced the once noble Indians to mere dependents of the state and has

a tiny fish called the snail darter stopped the construction of a much-needed nuclear reactor in Tennessee.

Some Christians initially reacted to the extremes of the environmentalist movement. However, others argued that Christians should be concerned to protect the environment for biblical reasons. They noted that nature is precious, not because it is our mother but because it is God's creation. A growing number of Christians observed that man has been called by God not to exploit but to exercise dominion as a steward of God's work.

New Rights Movements—During this time many groups began pressuring the government to intervene on their behalf. They demanded changes such as forcing employers to provide better working conditions and higher wages. Those groups included low-paid Hispanic grape pickers in California, led by César Chavez of the United Farm Workers. Another group, the American Indian Movement (AIM), gained strength among militant Indians who sought financial compensation for past treatment of Indians. AIM won notoriety when members seized a government trading post at Wounded Knee, South Dakota, in 1973.

The most prominent of the new civil rights movements was the women's rights movement. Betty Friedan's book *The Feminine Mystique* (1963) sparked the movement. Friedan mocked the lives of moms who stayed at home and raised kids in "a comfortable concentration camp." Some people joined the women's rights movement to earn equal pay. Others sought far more.

The radical National Organization for Women (NOW), co-founded by Friedan, pushed for legal abortions and easy divorce laws. NOW also supported the **Equal Rights Amendment** (**ERA**). Conservative women denounced the ERA. They said that its vague language would give the federal government virtually unlimited power over daily life. Critics also warned that feminists would use

Russell Means (1939–)

Russell Means grew up on the Pine Ridge Indian Reservation near the Black Hills of South Dakota. He joined an Indian rights group in Minnesota called the American Indian Movement (AIM). Means was part of an AIM-led band of activists who took over and occupied Alcatraz Island for 19 months. He soon became the organization's first national director.

In February 1973, Means led two hundred AIM members to declare their own nation at Wounded Knee, South Dakota, the site of the 1890 massacre of Indians by the U.S. Cavalry. Federal marshals arrived, and an armed standoff began. By the end of the confrontation on May 3, two Indians had been killed and one marshal seriously injured. Means and the other protesters surrendered after the government promised to discuss the Indians' grievances.

The Wounded Knee standoff marked a high point in Means's career. He continued working with AIM, ran for president, and launched a Hollywood career, taking part in such movies as *The Last of the Mohicans*. But some members of AIM sought to distance the organization from Means. They believed he was portraying Indians falsely in the movies.

The differences between AIM and Means became greater when he was charged with battery against his father-in-law. The Indian community highly values respecting one's elders, and Means had gone too far. AIM repudiated Means and continued to work for Indian rights without him.

led to the collapse of family life among many tribes.

Betty Friedan (1921–2006)

Betty Friedan was born in Peoria, Illinois, and grew up in a Jewish family. She attended Smith College, majored in psychology, and edited a campus magazine covering social issues. Although offered a scholarship to get a Ph.D. at Berkley, she turned it down, believing that if she accepted it, she wouldn't have time to get married and start a family. Instead, she became a reporter for the *Worker's Press* in New York. While working there, she noticed discrimination against women in the workplace.

Friedan married in 1947 and started a family. After she requested time off to have her second baby, the newspaper fired her. Friedan became a housewife, but she was never content. She talked to some of her college friends and found that many of them were also dissatisfied. They wanted to have both families and careers outside the home.

Friedan expressed her ideas in a book titled *The Feminine Mystique*. The book was an instant success among liberals. Friedan soon became a leading spokesperson for women's rights. In 1966, she helped found the National Organization for Women (NOW) and was named its first president. Friedan fought for changes such as equal pay for women in the work force and legalized abortions. But not all women in NOW supported Friedan. Some of them believed that she was going too far. Others thought that she was not going far enough.

Friedan divorced in 1969 and retired from NOW's presidency the following year. She continued to focus on political reform and became an active member in the women's liberation movement. She died of congestive heart failure at the age of 85.

---

the ERA to abolish time-honored traditions that respect the obvious differences between the sexes. It could be used to nullify everything from separate bathrooms for women to the ban on women in combat. Congress passed the ERA in 1972. But its supporters could not get enough states to ratify the amendment, even after liberals in Congress granted extra time.

Political Scandals

In 1972, Nixon was reelected. He defeated liberal Democrat George McGovern of South Dakota in a landslide. Pleased with détente, a stable economy, and favorable developments in Vietnam, the people were confident of Nixon's leadership. But cracks soon appeared in the Nixon image.

Resignation of the Vice President—Nixon's vice president, **Spiro T. Agnew**, was charged with accepting bribes from construction companies when he was governor of Maryland. He was also charged with income tax evasion. To the latter charge he pleaded no contest (almost but not completely admitting guilt). Facing a possible prison sentence, Agnew resigned the vice-presidency on October 10, 1973. He was the first vice president to resign since 1833 (when Calhoun resigned) and the first one to resign because of a criminal charge.

For the first time since its ratification in 1967, the Twenty-fifth Amendment was used to pick a new vice president. Following the guidelines in the amendment, Nixon selected Gerald R. Ford, a Michigan congressman. Ford was sworn in on December 6, 1973.

The Watergate Coverup—In 1972, Nixon himself got into trouble. Five men were arrested for breaking into the Democratic Party's National Campaign Headquarters in a Washington office complex named the **Watergate** during the campaign. They planted electronic listening devices in the office. The press learned that the

> ### Harmless Sounding but Dangerous: The Proposed Equal Rights Amendment
>
> "Equality of rights under the law shall not be denied or abridged by the United States or by any state on account of sex."

Meaning of the Watergate Scandal

According to some historians, the sheer magnitude of the Watergate scandal dwarfs other presidential scandals—Grant's, Harding's, and even Clinton's. It involved more than just an illegal break-in at the Democratic Party headquarters in the Watergate complex. It also included illegal campaign contributions, political sabotage or "dirty tricks," and the break-in at Daniel Ellsberg's psychiatrist's office. Two attorney generals, several presidential aides, the IRS, the FBI, and the CIA were all tainted by the scandal. And most dramatically, a president resigned, an unprecedented event in American history.

The question that still haunts students of the scandal is why someone as smart as Nixon would do something so foolish. We will never know fully what went on in his mind, but we can give a general answer to that question: Nixon's overwhelming desire to win reelection in 1972. Nixon

---

CD: Party Platform Summaries, 1972

Refer to the CD for summaries of the major parties' platforms from the presidential campaign of 1972.

CD: Electoral College Results, 1972

Refer to the CD for a map showing the results of the Electoral College results in the 1972 presidential campaign.

Additional Information on the Watergate Scandal

The following books are good sources of information on the Watergate scandal:

- *The Whole Truth: The Watergate Conspiracy* by Sam Ervin Jr. (N.C. senator who headed the committee investigating Watergate, noted for his frequent quoting of the Bible and Shakespeare during the hearings)
- *All the President's Men* by Carl Bernstein and Bob Woodward (the two reporters who first investigated the story and knew that it was more than a botched robbery)

Why Gerald Ford?

Ask the students to speculate on why Nixon chose Ford to succeed Agnew as vice president. (*Answers might include his reputation as an honest and fair, gregarious, easy-going man who was liked by members of both parties; he knew the workings of Congress and could get things done there; he was considered a conservative; etc.*)

and his aides were desperate to know the Democrats' strategy for the fall campaign. Nixon also wanted to know if the Democrats had any "dirt" that they might use against him.

Watergate proved to be a threat to democracy. It is clear now that Nixon did not trust the democratic electoral process. If he had, he would not have resorted to illegal campaign contributions or sabotage of political enemies. Perhaps the most dangerous aspect to the scandal was Nixon's use of "spies" to accomplish his ends. He was attempting to do on the domestic level what the CIA had been doing in foreign lands—subvert the natural processes of government.

To this day, Americans mistrust governmental institutions, from the White House on down. Also, Watergate changed the nature of the press. Investigative reporting, or finding the next scandal, drives the media and only intensifies Americans' cynicism about public officials.

arrested men were members of the Committee to Reelect the President (CREEP). No evidence turned up to link Nixon to the break-in, but suspicions grew that he had tried to cover up the crime after he learned about it.

The trial of the Watergate burglars and two other Nixon officials began in January 1973. One of the burglars claimed that the witnesses had committed perjury (lied in court). He also said that someone higher in the administration had told the men to plead guilty.

In May 1973, the Senate began its own independent investigation of the scandal. The committee discovered that the White House had secretly tape-recorded all of Nixon's office conversations. By listening to the tapes, the committee would be able to determine if the president had been involved in the cover-up. But when the courts ordered Nixon to turn over the tapes, he refused. He argued that he had executive privilege and that turning the tapes over would endanger national security.

Nixon's Resignation—The American people were outraged. Many people called for Nixon's impeachment. The House Judiciary Committee began hearings on fifteen charges. The president responded by turning over the tapes to a new special prosecutor. But some of the tapes were missing. An eighteen-and-a-half minute section had been erased on one tape. Nixon claimed that it was a secretary's error. When a court order asked for more tapes, the president refused to comply. But he did supply a transcript (written version). The transcript showed that the president had known about the efforts to cover up the scandal, but he was not necessarily the instigator.

The Nixons and the Fords walk to the Marine helicopter that will fly resigning President Nixon to California.

At this point Republicans also agreed that Nixon needed to face consequences for his actions. No one, not even a president, is above the law. At the end of July, the House Judiciary Committee voted to recommend impeaching the president. Charges included obstruction of justice, misuse of presidential powers, and refusal to comply with Congress's requests for evidence. When the committee proved determined to examine additional charges, the president's lawyers persuaded him to release more transcripts.

The new transcripts showed that the president not only had known of the burglary but also had acted to stop an FBI investigation of it. The president's position was then hopeless. Rather than be impeached and face a trial before the Senate that would lead to his removal, Nixon resigned on August 9, 1974, the only president ever to do so.

The Watergate conspiracy troubled the public, not only because of the political corruption but also because of the president's virtually unlimited power. The power of the president had been increasing steadily since the time of Franklin Roosevelt. Congress acted to prevent similar scandals. It forbade the president from refusing to release budget funds that Congress had earmarked for a specific program or action. It strengthened the Freedom of Information Act, allowing the public more access to government documents. A Fed-

Nixon's Resignation Speech

Obtain an audio or video tape of Nixon's resignation speech and play it for the class. Discuss its points in class.

Discuss the Meaning of the Watergate Scandal

Ask the students to contrast the Watergate Scandal with the other presidential scandals in U.S. history. Why was it worse than any other? (See margin note above.) Ask the students to share examples of political cynicism that they have heard. Discuss the basis for this cynicism and the proper Christian response.

Activity 5: The Resignation of Richard Nixon

Use this activity to help the students understand Richard Nixon's reasons for resigning and to give them insight into the mind and life of that president.

eral Campaign Reform Act in 1974 placed a limit on the amount of money private individuals can give to candidates. This restriction was intended to limit the use of contributions to "bribe" candidates.

The American political system successfully exposed and dealt with the Watergate conspiracy rather than push it under a rug. It showed that the president was not above the law. The Constitution's system of checks and balances worked. Yet Nixon's corruption seriously damaged the prestige of his office, and he undermined the faith of the American people in their political leaders. After 1974, the percentage of Americans who exercised their right to vote declined dramatically. Many people wondered whether America would ever recover.

Section Quiz

1. What two Communist countries did Nixon visit?

2. Who conducted shuttle diplomacy to help stop the bloodshed in the Middle East?

3. Whom did Nixon appoint as chief justice? What landmark decision was passed under his court?

4. What group of Americans made a special push for civil rights at this time? What piece of legislation did they unsuccessfully champion?

5. Who was Nixon's first vice president? Why did he leave office?

6. What was the crime that Nixon was accused of trying to cover up?

7. How did the Supreme Court decision on *Roe v. Wade* impact conservatives?

★ Was it necessary to include an impeachment clause in the Constitution? Defend your answer.

Section Quiz Answers

1. China and the Soviet Union

2. Secretary of State Henry Kissinger

3. Warren Burger; *Roe v. Wade*

4. women; Equal Rights Amendment (ERA)

5. Spiro Agnew; because of criminal charges of income tax evasion and accepting bribes

6. a break-in at the Democratic Party's National Campaign Headquarters at Watergate and planting of electronic listening devices during the 1972 election campaign

7. The decision shocked conservatives and played a role in the rise of the Right.

★ Answers will vary. If there is to be equal justice, the innocent must be cleared and the guilty must be punished. If one person is placed above the law, the judicial system is threatened.

Chapter Review 26

People, Places, and Things to Remember:

John F. Kennedy
New Frontier
Sputnik I
NASA
Martin Luther King Jr.
Letter from Birmingham Jail
Twenty-third Amendment
March on Washington
Alliance for Progress
Berlin Wall
Bay of Pigs
Cuban Missile Crisis
Lyndon B. Johnson
Great Society
Barry Goldwater
Civil Rights Act of 1964
Twenty-fourth Amendment
Voting Rights Act of 1965
Malcolm X
Vietnam War
Gulf of Tonkin Resolution
hawks
doves
Viet Cong
Ho Chi Minh Trail
"New Left"
counterculture
Twenty-sixth Amendment
Robert Kennedy
Hubert Humphrey
Vietnamization
Kent State University
War Powers Act
Richard Nixon
détente
Henry Kissinger
SALT
shuttle diplomacy
recession
oil embargo
energy crisis
Warren Burger
Roe v. Wade
Equal Rights Amendment (ERA)
Spiro T. Agnew
Watergate

Review Questions

Indicate whether each of the following items is most closely associated with (A) President Kennedy, (B) President Johnson, or (C) President Nixon.

1. Watergate
2. the Great Society
3. Vietnamization
4. Gulf of Tonkin Resolution
5. the New Frontier
6. Cuban Missile Crisis

Match each of the following items with its description.

7. Berlin Wall
8. Peace Corps
9. *Roe v. Wade*
10. Tet Offensive

a. Communist attack on South Vietnam
b. barrier between East and West Germany
c. legalized abortion
d. sent American volunteers to needy places

Answer these questions about the 1960s.

11. Whose shuttle diplomacy temporarily ended Middle Eastern bloodshed?
12. Who was the first man to walk on the moon?
13. What black preacher led much of the civil rights activity of the 1960s?
14. What three Democrats ran for the presidential nomination in 1968?

Critical Thinking

1. Was the civil rights movement of the 1960s necessary? Why or why not?
2. Should the United States have entered the Vietnam War? Why or why not?

Activity 6: Chapter Review

Use this activity to help the students prepare for the chapter test.

Chapter Review Answers

Review Questions

1. C
2. B
3. C
4. B
5. A
6. A
7. b
8. d
9. c
10. a
11. Henry Kissinger's
12. Neil Armstrong
13. Martin Luther King Jr.
14. Eugene McCarthy, Robert Kennedy, Hubert Humphrey

Critical Thinking

1. Answers will vary but might include such ideas as the civil rights laws were not fairly or consistently enforced and needed to be strengthened or that more needed to be done to ensure the civil rights of all people regardless of race.

2. Answers will vary.

CHAPTER

27

Ronald Reagan became the face of the conservative movement and served as president from 1981 till 1989.

The Conservative Surge

I. The Ford Administration

II. The Carter Administration

III. The Reagan Administration

IV. The Bush Administration

Chapter 27 Lesson Plan Chart

Section Title	Main Activity	Pages	Days
I. The Ford Administration	Activity 1: Ford's Dilemma: The Nixon Pardon	520–22	½–1 day
II. The Carter Administration	Activity 2: The Story Behind the Camp David Accords	522–26	2 days
III. The Reagan Administration	Activity 4: The Attempted Assassination of Reagan— in His Own Words	526–32	2 days
IV. The Bush Administration	Activity 5: Federal Spending Under Recent Presidents	532–36	2 days
TOTAL SUGGESTED DAYS (INCLUDING 1 DAY FOR REVIEW AND TESTING)			7½–8 DAYS

Section I

Objectives

Students should be able to

1. Define the "strike" that Ford had against him from the beginning of his administration.

2. Name and describe the controversy that Ford ignited in his first month in office.

3. Describe Ford's plan to "whip" inflation and explain how it failed.

How Media Portrayed Ford

The press afforded Ford a very short "honeymoon" period after he became president. After he stumbled while leaving a plane and later bumped his head exiting another time, the press began to portray him as a clumsy, bumbling figurehead who was anything but a capable president. The media's image seemed to stick in the minds of the people. They forgot Ford's plea that they should remember he was a Ford, not a Lincoln.

The *Mayaguez* Incident

On May 12, 1975, a week after the fall of South Vietnam, the Khmer Rouge, using former U.S. Navy swiftboats, captured the S.S. *Mayaguez*, a merchant ship, in international waters near the border between Cambodia and Vietnam. The Khmer Rouge removed the crew from the ship and took both them and the *Mayaguez* to an island off the coast of Cambodia. They later tried to move the crew to the mainland. The United States had no diplomatic relations with the Khmer Rouge, so negotiations were not an option. President Ford believed that he had to act to restore U.S. prestige, which had been severely

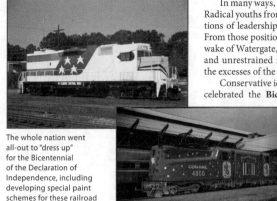

The whole nation went all-out to "dress up" for the Bicentennial of the Declaration of Independence, including developing special paint schemes for these railroad locomotives.

Neither Ford nor Rockefeller had been elected to office by the people.

In many ways, the crises of the 1960s still haunt the United States. Radical youths from the "hippie" generation eventually entered positions of leadership. They became writers, teachers, and politicians. From those positions, they proclaimed their radical ideas. Yet, in the wake of Watergate, Americans saw the bad results of big government and unrestrained morals. The resulting politics were a reaction to the excesses of the Sixties.

Conservative ideas were reemerging. On July 4, 1976, Americans celebrated the **Bicentennial** (two-hundredth anniversary) of the Declaration of Independence. It brought back memories of the values that had made America great. Because it followed the national defeat in Vietnam and the embarrassment of Watergate, the Bicentennial was a welcome reason for a return of patriotism.

The drive to restore traditional values climaxed in the election of Ronald Reagan. A conservative Republican, he promised to restore America's greatness. By 1986, the country was again enjoying a booming economy and new pride. In that year, the nation also celebrated the one-hundredth birthday of the Statue of Liberty. The next year, it celebrated the bicentennial of the Constitution.

I. The Ford Administration

Vice President Gerald R. Ford took the oath of office the day Nixon left. Ford's position was difficult. He had been named vice president when Agnew resigned and became president when Nixon resigned. He was the first person to hold either of those positions without having been elected to them.

Ford saw the need to restore the public's confidence in the presidency. He promised "openness and candor" in contrast to Nixon's secrecy and dishonesty. Ford tried to lower people's expectations. "Remember," he told them, "I'm a Ford, not a Lincoln." He emphasized that he was only an ordinary man who would try to do his best. Ford also promised regular news conferences so that the public would be informed of his actions. He chose as his vice president a former New York governor from the liberal wing of the Republican Party, Nelson Rockefeller. (This was the first time in history that both the president and the vice president were unelected.) He kept Henry Kissinger as secretary of state and said that he would pursue a Nixonian foreign policy.

Ford's Pardon of Nixon

One month after he became president, Ford ignited a controversy that may have cost him his reelection. He pardoned Richard Nixon. By pardoning Nixon for any crimes he "may have committed" while in office, Ford angered many of his own supporters. Some Democrats accused him of making a "buddy deal" with the president in exchange for his nomination as vice president. Many Americans were dismayed that the former president could go free while other men serving under him remained in jail for their Watergate crimes. However, Ford insisted that putting the former president on trial would only prolong the country's agony.

SECTION III
- CD: Ronald Reagan, 40th President; Reagan Delivering the State of the Union Address; Electoral College Results, 1984
- A copy of Reagan's first inaugural address
- Activity 4 from the *Student Activities* manual

SECTION IV
- CD: George H.W. Bush, 41st President; Five Presidents; Growth in Federal Spending Under the Elementary and Secondary Education Act; Growth in Total Government Spending
- Activities 5 and 6 from the *Student Activities* manual

Core Values

Corruption in Washington and a general disillusionment with the excesses of the counter-culture paved the way for a resurgence of conservatism in the 1980s. Christians became more politically involved, and the Religious Right became a force in American politics. Freedom was emphasized as the world emerged from the threat of communism. Conservatives also promoted freedom from governmental regulation.

During these years growth was valued but not always experienced. The era of growth in the 1980s was bounded by severe economic hardship in the late 1970s and a less severe recession in the early 1990s.

Chapter Project: Checklist of Presidents' Strengths

Create and distribute a checklist of qualities that you believe a good U.S. president should have. As the students read through the chapter, have them write beside each quality the names of the presidents who exhibited that quality. Consider personal qualities and leadership in both foreign and domestic affairs. Assign each quality a numeric value based on what you believe to be its importance relative to the other qualities. Grade the presidents in this chapter numerically based on their presidential qualities. Make a profile sheet for each president. Keep track of why each president scored the way he did in each category. After the

Ford's Effort to Whip Inflation

When Gerald Ford took office, Nixon's wage and price controls had failed to check inflation. In 1974, inflation reached a record 12.2 percent.

Ford could do little directly to solve the main cause of the problem. The Federal Reserve, an independent government agency created in 1913, controlled the supply of money in the country. (When more money is in circulation, prices rise.)

At first, Ford pushed for a voluntary anti-inflation crusade. Called WIN ("Whip Inflation Now"), the plan urged consumers to stop buying high-priced goods. It asked workers not to seek wage increases. But workers and businesses believed that they were the *victims* of inflation rather than the *cause* of it, so they ignored WIN. The economic recession grew even worse when the Federal Reserve raised interest rates (one of the tools it uses to limit the amount of money in circulation). Sales of new products fell. The number of people out of work climbed above 9 percent.

Ford then asked Congress for a tax cut and spending cuts. Liberal Democrats, who controlled Congress, approved the tax cut, but they spent more and more money on new programs. Ford vetoed sixty-six bills in an effort to hold down the growth of government. But inflation continued to spiral upward.

The Election of 1976

Ford decided to run for president in 1976. Because he had not been in office long, he had not made many of his own policies. The Republican Party was also still recovering from the shame of Watergate. Ford's inability to solve the nation's problems gave Democrats confidence that they "could run an aardvark this year and win."

From the many candidates competing for the nomination, the Democrats picked little-known **Jimmy Carter**. He was a wealthy peanut farmer and former one-term governor of Georgia. During the campaign, Carter stressed his honesty and the fact that he was an outsider to Washington politics. He had taken a strong stand on civil rights in Georgia, so he appealed to black voters. Labor unions also supported him.

Carter ran openly as a "born-again" Christian. This appealed to conservative evangelicals and opened the way for other Christians to enter the political arena. After 1976 it was easier for Christians to be politically involved without hiding their religious convictions. Carter's moral image and broad smile seemed to be the perfect answer to the shame and scandals of the Nixon years. In spite of those advantages, Carter ran a lackluster campaign. He defeated Ford by only a narrow margin, 51 to 48 percent.

Although the Republicans lost in 1976, they laid the groundwork for a major political revolution. One of their major candidates was a former actor and two-term California governor. **Ronald Reagan** had once been a Democrat. He became a Republican in 1962 and campaigned for Nixon in the California governor's race. In 1964, he campaigned nationally for Barry Goldwater for president. Reagan quickly became the spokesman for the conservative wing of the party.

Reagan was elected governor of California in 1966 and 1970. That feat was impressive because California Democrats outnumbered Republicans 3 to 2. In 1976, Reagan and Ford both went into the national convention just short of the support needed to gain

Ford appeared to trivialize the economic problems of the country when he encouraged people to wear buttons promoting his "WIN" program to fight inflation.

Presidents Who Used the Veto Most	
Franklin Roosevelt	635[1]
Grover Cleveland	584[2]
Harry Truman	250
Dwight Eisenhower	181
Ulysses S. Grant	93

[1] 497 of these were private bills (i.e., for the relief or benefit of an individual).

[2] 482 of these were private bills.

Presidents Who Never Used the Veto
John Adams
Thomas Jefferson
John Quincy Adams
William Henry Harrison
Zachary Taylor
Millard Fillmore
James Garfield

Presidents Who Had the Most Vetoes Overridden by Congress	
Andrew Johnson	15
Harry Truman	12
Gerald Ford	12
Franklin Roosevelt	9
Ronald Reagan	9

(Thirteen presidents had *no* vetoes overridden.)

damaged by its loss of the Vietnam War, so he ordered a rescue operation to free the crew and retrieve the *Mayaguez*. In preparations for the operation, a helicopter crashed, killing twenty-three U.S. army personnel. U.S. planes, helicopters, and marines then rescued the ship's crew. Thirty-eight Americans were killed (fifteen of them in actual combat) three were missing and presumed captured and killed by the Khmer Rouge, and forty-one were wounded.

Carter as a Candidate in 1976

Jimmy Carter was an ideal candidate for the post-Watergate era. He presented himself as an outsider, someone who was uncorrupted by the failures in Washington. He was not a lawyer or a Washington Beltway politician. He was a one-term governor of Georgia and a peanut farmer. He did not campaign in an expensive suit but rather flannel shirts and blue jeans. In stark contrast to the dour Nixon, Carter made his broad grin a trademark. Through clever advertising and public speaking, he was able to craft his own image.

Another major element of Carter's persona during the 1976 campaign and later his presidency was his religious faith. He was the first serious presidential candidate to talk openly about being a "born-again Christian," and he was a Southern Baptist, the largest Protestant denomination in America. It was politically advantageous in the post-Watergate environment to be seen as wholesome and uncorrupted. Carter even told audiences that he would never tell a lie.

---

students have finished reading the chapter, tally the class scores to find out whom they consider to have been the best president of the period.

 CD: Gerald Ford, 38th President
Refer to the CD for information on President Gerald Ford.

From Vice Presidency to Presidency

How many vice presidents during the twentieth century became presidents? *(six— Theodore Roosevelt, Harry Truman, Lyndon Johnson, Richard Nixon, Gerald Ford, and George H.W. Bush)* How many of them served two terms? *(only Nixon, but he lost*

his first election at the end of his vice presidency) Why is it so difficult for vice presidents to win and keep the presidency? *(They are held responsible for their predecessor's legacy and/or saddled with his failures.)*

Activity 1: Ford's Dilemma: The Nixon Pardon

Use this activity to help the students gain a greater appreciation for Ford's reasons for pardoning Nixon. As you discuss the answers to the questions, you might consider having the students debate whether Ford was right or wrong to offer the pardon.

CD: Electoral College Results, 1976
Refer to the CD for a map showing the results of the Electoral College voting for the 1976 presidential election.

The Religious Right

The media derisively applied this term to describe a conservative response to the growing liberalism in political and educational circles. Those who were so labeled came from a broad spectrum of religious beliefs including Lutherans, Catholics, Mormons, Pentecostals, Baptists, and others. Well-known leaders such as Jerry Falwell, James Dobson, and Pat Robertson often became the face and voice of this movement, although it was actually a grass-roots movement with broad conservative participation. Issues included opposition to abortion, limiting the growth of government and its resulting slide toward socialism, and fundamental reforms in education. Educational issues included allowing prayer in public schools, the teaching of creation alongside evolution, the right to homeschool one's children, and school vouchers to allow parents to determine which school their children attended.

Section II
Objectives

Students should be able to

1. Identify Carter's domestic and foreign policy failures.

2. List the leaders involved in the Camp David Accords and the countries they represented.

3. Identify the Muslim ruler who encouraged the taking of hostages at the American embassy in Iran.

Carter's presidency anticipated stability and a restoration of morality to the White House, but it brought instead indecision, economic stagnation, and a sense of inability to deal with the nation's problems.

Inflation Rates (1960–1992)

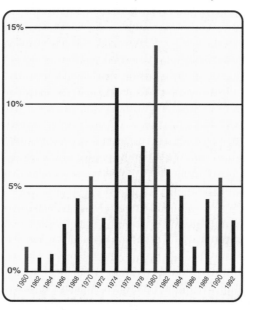

the nomination. In an effort to gain moderate delegates, Reagan announced that if nominated he would tap liberal senator Richard Schweiker to be his running mate. The ploy backfired, costing him conservative delegates. Ford won the nomination. Reagan spent the next four years preparing for the 1980 race.

Section Quiz

1. Whom did Ford choose for his vice president?

2. What controversial step did Ford take shortly after becoming president?

3. What was Ford's plan to lower inflation? Why did it fail?

4. What was Jimmy Carter's political background?

★ Do you agree with Ford's decision to pardon Nixon? Why or why not?

II. The Carter Administration

Jimmy Carter entered the presidency with high hopes. Democrats controlled both houses of Congress by large margins. Americans were looking for someone to solve the problems of the day. Carter wanted to bring new faces to Washington and to use the same simple, down-home style he had used in Georgia.

But Carter's inexperience greatly hindered his effectiveness in office. He failed to make efforts to win support for his programs. He also got bogged down in the details of governing and failed to spell out the principles that guided his administration. Few people, even in his own party, really knew the president's long-term goals. To make matters worse, Carter did not have a solid grasp of foreign affairs.

Domestic Affairs

Amnesty

One of President Carter's first acts was to offer **amnesty**, or a group pardon, to those who had dodged the draft during the Vietnam conflict. The president wanted to heal the rifts left by the war. However, Americans who had complied with the law and lost family members in the war saw the pardon as an insult. The number of people who took advantage of the amnesty was smaller than expected. Some draft dodgers snubbed the offer because they believed accepting it was an admission that their actions had been wrong.

Inflation

Economic troubles mushroomed under Carter. To escape inflation, consumers were borrowing money to get what they wanted before prices went up. The increase in the money supply caused prices to rise rapidly. The annual inflation rate rose to double digits—more than 10 percent. Workers were unable to afford the higher prices. They demanded higher wages. At the same time, interest rates on loans

its government. But if President Nixon was guilty of a crime, he should have been punished to uphold the integrity of the judicial system.

CD: Jimmy Carter, 39th President

Refer to the CD for information on President Jimmy Carter.

Compare the Weaknesses of Ford and Carter

Both Ford and Carter are considered weak presidents. Compare and contrast their circumstances and legacy to understand the different ways they were weak. The Republican Ford stood up against a liberal Democratic Congress, but he was hampered by the aftermath of Watergate. Carter enjoyed the advantage of a Democrat-controlled Congress, but he lacked the political skill to pass legislation. Both presidents were helpless in the face of inflation and the congressional spending spree.

Ask the students what makes a president great. Do circumstances make the man, or does the man create the circumstances? Note that circumstances are almost as important as the person. Even good people can accomplish little unless circumstances are in their favor.

reached record levels. People could not afford home mortgages. Builders found themselves out of work. Related businesses suffered. Unemployment rose.

Like Ford, Carter sought to curb inflation by slowing the growth of federal spending and revising the tax system. He asked people to accept voluntary wage and price controls but had little success. His tax bill was supposed to cut taxes for the poor by closing loopholes open to the rich. But by the time Congress finished with the bill, it had reduced some taxes for the wealthy while raising Social Security taxes on everyone.

Energy

From 1973 to 1977, the cost of imported oil for the nation skyrocketed from $8 billion to $40 billion a year. Carter devised a program that he believed would end dependence on foreign oil.

1. He called for nationwide conservation.

2. He created the Department of Energy. It would help American companies find new oil fields and develop alternative energy sources.

3. He proposed **deregulation** and an end to price controls on gas and oil. Higher prices would encourage conservation and boost the search for oil at home.

4. He wanted to tax profits on oil and use that revenue to fund his government programs.

These plans were set back when Muslim radicals took over Iran. They cut oil production in 1979. This created an energy crisis similar to the 1973 oil embargo.

Carter believed that using nuclear power might help solve the energy crisis. But he faced opposition on all sides. Conservatives complained that nuclear power required a massive monopoly run by the central government. Liberals complained about the potential hazards of nuclear waste and nuclear accidents.

Those fears seemed to be justified on March 28, 1979. At the **Three Mile Island** nuclear power plant near Harrisburg, Pennsylvania, the cooling system failed. Before the reactor could be shut down, radioactive steam was released. It contaminated the water in a nearby stream. The back-up system worked and the immediate crisis passed, but the accident prompted increased antinuclear protests and hampered the building of more nuclear power plants.

Safety systems at the Three Mile Island nuclear station narrowly prevented a nuclear disaster.

Foreign Affairs

In his inaugural address, Carter had declared that human rights would be central in his foreign policy. "Because we are free, we can never be indifferent to the fate of freedom elsewhere," he said. "Thus people everywhere should have freedom to make political choices, exercise their ideas free of intimidation or persecution, and to own property." Such ideas are wonderful. But they require wisdom to implement, and they cannot be imposed on countries where the United

Carter's Three Mile Scare

In an attempt to calm and reassure the nation following the disaster at the Three Mile Island nuclear power plant, President Carter decided to visit the plant. Even as the president made his way to the site, workers were still trying to determine whether the reactor was going to blow up. One theory, later disproved, suggested that a hydrogen bubble was building and that it was only a matter of time before a huge explosion occurred.

On arriving in Harrisburg, Pennsylvania, Carter was informed about the hydrogen bubble theory. Despite the danger, Carter could not turn back without creating greater fear among the public. He continued to Three Mile Island. Wearing special boots to protect them from radioactive water on the floor, the members of the tour group made their way through the plant.

Once he was outside the accident area, Carter and the others checked their dosimeters—tools that measure radiation. Carter's read seventy-eight millirems. It should have been at zero. For a few minutes there was a panic because the president seemed to have been exposed to dangerous levels of radiation. Finally, however, the workers realized that some of the dosimeters had not been recharged and reset at zero. Carter was fine.

Human Rights in Foreign Policy?

Discuss the pros and cons of Carter's desire to base foreign policy on the promotion of human rights. Note that his idealism resembles that of Woodrow Wilson. Contrast his approach with the pragmatism of Henry Kissinger, who was willing to overlook the evils of dictatorships if doing so furthered U.S. interests in the Cold War.

The place of human rights in U.S. foreign policy fluctuates with each administration. Leaders of other nations have acknowledged that they are careful not to offend the United States because of the potential ramifications. However, if a president shows no concern about human rights abuses, then he emboldens totalitarian leaders to repress dissidents.

Carter's Response to the Soviet Invasion of Afghanistan

When the Soviet Union invaded Afghanistan, Carter responded with several actions. He first strongly condemned the invasion. He prohibited U.S. involvement in the Summer Olympics, which were to be held in Moscow. He stopped a deal to sell wheat to the Soviet Union. He sought covert ways to aid the Afghans (Mujahideen) in opposing the Soviet troops. Eventually, these actions led to internal cracks in the Soviet wall, contributing to the failure of the invasion and the fall of the Soviet Empire.

The Soviet Union's invasion in 1979 and the U.S. invasion in 2001 are very different. The Soviets were trying to support and strengthen a Communist puppet government in Afghanistan. The United States was fighting terrorists and their supporters who were using Afghanistan as a training and staging area for attacks against the United States. The broader U.S. goal is to bring freedom and democracy to Afghaninstan.

States has little influence. The test for Carter was whether or not he could convince other nations to implement these ideas.

The Panama Canal Controversy

But the United States had signed a ninety-nine-year lease on the Panama Canal, beginning in 1903. But Panamanian nationalists demanded that it be put under their control immediately. Carter entered negotiations. In 1977, he signed the **Panama Canal Treaty**. The United States agreed to transfer control of the canal to Panama by 1999. The United States, however, kept the right to intervene with military force if the canal's neutrality were ever threatened.

After heated debate, the Senate approved the treaty. Those who supported the treaty believed that the United States was imposing itself on Panama, another sovereign state. But many Americans opposed the "surrender" of a canal that Americans had built. They also feared that under Panamanian rule American access to the canal might be threatened.

The Camp David Accords

In foreign affairs Carter brought to a successful conclusion talks begun under the previous two Republican administrations. Kissinger's shuttle diplomacy had helped to persuade Egypt and Israel to end their fighting. Egyptian leader Anwar Sadat visited Israel's Prime Minister Menachem Begin (BAY gin) in Tel Aviv. Carter then invited Sadat and Begin to Camp David, a presidential retreat in Maryland. There, with Carter as mediator, they reached a historic accord, or agreement. In September 1978, Sadat and Begin signed the **Camp David Accords**. Israel agreed to return the Sinai Peninsula to Egypt, and Egypt agreed to recognize Israel's right to exist. Egypt was the first Arab nation to recognize that right.

Carter is credited with mediating the Camp David Accords that brought peace between Israel and Egypt.

SALT II

Carter also continued negotiations with the Soviets for another Strategic Arms Limitations Treaty. But he offered the Soviets a new set of proposals. One of his aims was to guarantee equality in bombers and nuclear missiles. His insistence on that point slowed the talks. The treaty, called SALT II, was not signed until March 1979. When Carter submitted the treaty for Senate approval, both the Senate and the press reacted negatively. Opposition grew when the Soviet Union invaded Afghanistan in 1979. The disappointed president withdrew the treaty.

The Soviet Invasion of Afghanistan

The Soviet invasion of Afghanistan deeply angered Americans. Claiming that they had been invited into Afghanistan, the Soviets executed the Afghan president soon after they arrived. Their plans to set up a puppet regime were hindered by Afghan guerillas. Although Carter had earlier stated his opposition to secret military operations, he let the Central Intelligence Agency (CIA) aid Afghan freedom fighters. But Carter's overall reaction to the Soviets was weak. He limited his response to preventing U.S. teams from taking part in the 1980 Olympic Games, which were held in Moscow.

The Iranian Hostage Crisis

During the Cold War, Iran was an ally of the United States. In turn, the United States helped the ruler of Iran, the shah. Many Iranians were unhappy with the shah's self-serving rule, the country's deep economic problems, and widespread unemployment. They re-

The Iranians paraded blindfolded American hostages before cameras to humiliate "the great Satan," as they called the United States.

Activity 2: The Story Behind the Camp David Accords

Use this activity to help the students understand Carter's determination to guide Israel and Egypt into making a lasting peace agreement at Camp David and the frustrations he encountered in that quest.

volted, and the shah was forced to flee the country. A Muslim leader, the **Ayatollah Khomeini**, emerged as the most powerful figure in Iran's new government. In October 1979, Carter allowed the shah, who was ill with cancer, to enter the United States for medical treatment. Carter made his decision on humanitarian grounds, ignoring his advisors' warnings that the Iranians would retaliate.

On November 4, 1979, a group of radical students with connections to Khomeini stormed the U.S. embassy in Iran and took sixty-six Americans hostage. Though American leaders should have known that many Iranians were upset with the United States because of its support for the shah, the **Iranian hostage crisis** caught most Americans by surprise.

Carter responded by freezing Iran's assets (investment money) in America. Then he stopped the importation of Iranian oil to the United States. He made some attempts at some secret talks, but the Iranians demanded conditions that the United States could not accept. He set no deadlines, nor did he authorize any military actions. By Christmas, Carter was considering a rescue attempt, and the attempt took place in April of 1980. But a dust storm damaged several of the rescue helicopters and the mission was canceled. In returning from the staging ground in Iran, a helicopter collided with a transport plane, killing eight soldiers. This failure only added to America's feelings of frustration and humiliation.

The situation changed when neighboring Iraq invaded Iran in September 1980. The ancient foes locked horns in a deadly eight-year war. More than three hundred thousand Muslims were killed. Khomeini offered to release the American hostages on three conditions. Carter must free Iranian assets, promise never to interfere in Iranian affairs, and return the shah's wealth. Since the United States had no legal access to the shah's money, it refused. The crisis did not end until the day of President Reagan's inauguration. On January 21, 1981, after 444 days in captivity, the American hostages were set free.

The failure of the secret rescue operation further embarrassed the American government.

The Election of 1980

Carter entered the 1980 election campaign with an approval rating of 23 percent. That was lower than Nixon had had at the height of the Watergate scandal. Carter faced two major opponents. One was an independent, John Anderson, who had once been a Republican. He also faced a formidable opponent in California's former governor Ronald Reagan.

Reagan's speeches were direct, sincere, and stirring. Americans were tired of the failures under Carter. Reagan was optimistic and offered hope. Americans were ready to listen to Reagan's conservative proposals. Reagan promised to strengthen the national defense, cut the size of the federal bureaucracy, and get big government "off the backs of the people." Government is not the solution to the problems, he said, it is the problem. He offered to restore American strength and pride. The people were ready for his message.

Although Reagan generally ran a positive campaign of hope and national pride, he also pointed out some unpleasant facts. He referred repeatedly to the "misery index," a combination of the inflation rate and the unemployment rate. He told the voters that if they were better off then than they had been when Carter first took office, to vote for Carter. If they were not better off, they should vote for Reagan.

Independent candidate John Anderson received more than 5.5 million popular votes but none in the Electoral College.

Credible Sport

Operation Eagle Claw was a disastrous attempt to free the Iranian hostages. However, few people know that just before the actual release of the hostages, a second rescue attempt was being planned. Operation Credible Sport centered on a high-tech rescue plane. The military planned to use a C-130 with rockets on its sides to allow it to land and take off quickly at the rescue zone.

The plan called for Delta Force commandos to escort the hostages to a Teheran soccer field, where the plane would meet them. According to CNN, the plane would then ignite its rockets, sending everyone on a "leap to liberty." Thankfully, the crisis ended and the hostages were released before the plan was put into action. In its first test, the modified C-130 crashed after one rocket ignited early and ripped off a wing.

The Misery Index by President

One can gain a greater appreciation for the "misery index" Reagan referred to in the 1980 election campaign by seeing how it had increased during the previous administrations.

President	Index
Johnson	6.78
Nixon	9.98
Ford	15.93
Carter	16.27

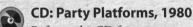

CD: Party Platforms, 1980

Refer to the CD for a summary of the major parties' platforms for the presidential election of 1980.

CD: Electoral College Results, 1980

Refer to the CD for a map showing the results of Electoral College voting for the presidential election of 1980.

Activity 3: Interpreting Editorial Cartoons

Use this activity to help the students look beyond the obvious to interpret editorial cartoons during the election of 1980.

Section III

Objectives

Students should be able to

1. Define *supply-side economics*.
2. Describe the changes in the Supreme Court during the Nixon and Reagan administrations.
3. Describe Reagan's policy toward the Soviet Union.
4. Name the two groups involved in the revolution in Nicaragua.
5. Identify the event that hampered Reagan's effectiveness at the end of his second term of office.

Ronald Reagan's Background

Ronald Reagan was the most successful president of the second half of the twentieth century and a conservative icon whose legacy is still influencing government and politics today. He brought a diverse background to the White House. Ironically, many things about his early life were at odds with the conservative views he espoused later.

Before the 1950s, Reagan was a Democrat, even a liberal. He had supported Franklin Roosevelt and the New Deal and its continuation under Harry Truman. As president of the Screen Actors Guild, Reagan was popular among Hollywood liberals and leftists. In 1950, when Richard Nixon ran against the very liberal Helen Douglas for the U.S. Senate in California, Reagan endorsed Douglas, but she did not want the endorsement publicized for fear it would reinforce her leftist image.

In the 1950s, Reagan slowly shifted to the right. He supported Eisenhower over Stevenson in both 1952 and 1956. In 1962, he switched his party registration

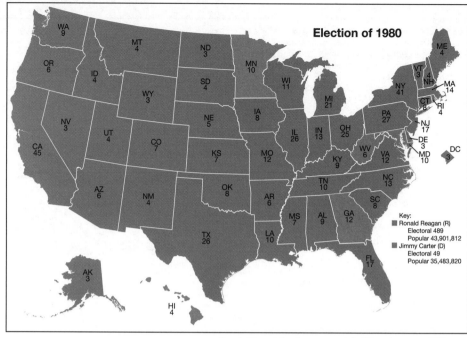

Election of 1980

Key:
- Ronald Reagan (R)
  Electoral 489
  Popular 43,901,812
- Jimmy Carter (D)
  Electoral 49
  Popular 35,483,820

On election night, Reagan carried all but six states. Riding on Reagan's "coattails," Republicans won enough seats to take control of the Senate for the first time since 1954.

Section Quiz

1. What did Carter do for those who had illegally escaped service in Vietnam?
2. How high did inflation go during Carter's term of office?
3. What alternative source of energy did Carter push? What event seriously damaged support for his program?
4. The Camp David Accords brought peace between what two Middle Eastern nations?
★ In 2000 and 2005, the *Wall Street Journal* asked prominent professors to rank the presidents of the United States. President Carter ranked in the bottom ten United States presidents. Is this ranking fair? Why or why not?

III. The Reagan Administration

Reagan worked to restore national pride after the devastating years of Nixon, Ford, and Carter. Determined to "make America great again," Reagan opposed communism abroad and supported smaller government at home. He also supported conservative social

Ronald Reagan was sworn in as president by Warren Burger, chief justice of the Supreme Court.

Section Quiz Answers

1. He offered amnesty, or a group pardon, to them.
2. double-digit—more than 10 percent
3. nuclear power; the accident at Three Mile Island nuclear power plant
4. Israel and Egypt
★ It is a fair ranking. A president's effectiveness is judged by the success of his domestic and foreign policies. None of Carter's domestic policies were successful. In foreign policy, only the Camp David Accords were a success.

 CD: Ronald Reagan, 40th President

Refer to the CD for information on President Ronald Reagan.

Reagan's First Inaugural Address

Read portions of Reagan's first inaugural address and ask the students to cite the main goals of his administration. Discuss how well he reached his goals.

CD: Ronald Reagan Delivering State of the Union Address

Refer to the CD for a color photo of Reagan delivering the State of the Union Address to Congress.

values. Despite a Democratic majority in the House, Reagan was able to get much legislation passed with the help of southern Democrats.

Domestic Policies

Reagan's first priority was to solve the problems at home. He offered a new approach to the economy, and he promised to restrain the liberal courts.

Supply-side Economics

The causes of inflation are complicated. An easy way to explain it is that the supply of money is greater than the supply of products that people can buy. (Too much money is chasing too few goods.) Under these circumstances, businesses must raise prices. The government can stop businesses from raising prices in several ways. One option is to take money away from buyers through taxes and high interest rates. But Reagan suggested another way. He focused on the other side of the equation: make more products available by lowering taxes and reducing regulations on businesses and investors. Businesses would then have more money to make products and individuals would have more money to invest. The improved economic benefits would then "trickle down" to the average consumer.

Reagan called his solution **supply-side economics**. He argued that tax cuts actually increased tax revenues. During the primary races, George Bush, one of Reagan's chief opponents and later his vice president, called Reagan's idea "voodoo economics." Other critics called it "Reaganomics" or "trickle-down economics."

In 1981, Congress passed the first part of Reagan's plan. It cut inheritance and gift taxes, corporate taxes, and income taxes. The Economic Recovery Tax Act of 1981 included the largest income tax cut in American history—25 percent reduction over three years for each taxpayer. To help balance the budget, the president hoped to cut the size of the government bureaucracy. He also wanted to reduce increases in federal spending in almost every area except the military. But the House of Representatives was not interested in reducing spending. When Reagan pushed for cuts, Democrats accused him of being hard-hearted and wanting to hurt the poor.

Before tax reforms passed, the country fell into a deep recession. Reagan agreed to tax increases on some products, such as cigarettes and airline tickets, to ease worries that the government was not earning enough money. Otherwise, he called on Americans to "stay the course" he had proposed. The recession lifted.

In 1983, the United States entered its longest period of continuous economic growth. Inflation almost disappeared. Jobs were abundant. Tax revenues almost doubled, just as Reagan had predicted. But Congress continued to spend money faster than it came in. Government debt mounted to record levels. America's long-term prosperity was threatened.

The Reagan Court

Reagan realized that the court system had become characterized by judicial activism, the misuse of judicial power to obtain decisions without regard to written law. He desired to appoint judges characterized by judicial restraint. That required more conservative judges. Reagan's first appointment to the Supreme Court was **Sandra Day O'Connor**. She was the first female Supreme Court justice. Later, when Chief Justice Warren Burger retired, Reagan named Justice **William H.**

Reagan's "whiz kid" budget director was David Stockman.

One target of Reagan's domestic program was overregulation by government, as he illustrated during his State of the Union address by holding up thousands of pages of government regulations.

Chief Justice Warren Burger administers the oath to Sandra Day O'Connor, the first female justice on the Supreme Court.

to Republican. Why did Reagan change so dramatically? He cited his years as leader of the Screen Actors Guild, during which he saw the destructive influence of the left and of communism in Hollywood. Also his success in television, first as the host of *GE Theater* and later as host of the *Death Valley Days* series, made him wealthier. As he saw the negative effect of government-imposed social policies, he became more conservative politically. Some people also credit the influence of his wife Nancy, whom he married in 1952.

Laffer Curve

As part of his "supply-side economics" approach, Reagan adopted the Laffer curve theory. That theory was proposed by Dr. Arthur Laffer of Reagan's Economic Policy Advisory Board. It was based on two assumptions. First, it said that if there was a zero percent income tax, then obviously there would be zero income tax revenue generated. Second, it said that a one hundred percent income tax would also generate zero revenue. In other words, the government would not get any money by taxing nothing, but it also would not get any money by one hundred percent taxes because people would find it pointless to generate income if it was simply all taxed away. With these facts in mind, proponents of the theory suggested that there must be a point between those extremes at which the most revenue could be generated. The trick was to find that point.

Some critics claim that the Laffer curve theory was a failure because Reagan failed to balance the budget. However, the claim is unfair considering the evidence. Reagan and his economic advisors estimated that income taxes were too high. According to the Laffer curve, lowering taxes would result in higher revenue because people

Activity 4: The Attempted Assassination of Reagan—In His Own Words

Use this activity to help the students understand the events leading up to and immediately after the attempted assassination of President Reagan. Help the students focus especially on the qualities of leadership evident in Reagan's response to the attempt on his life.

Was This a Revolution?

Ask the students to consider the expression "the Reagan Revolution." First, ask them to define *revolution*. Then discuss the sense in which the nation might go through a revolution. Historians question whether

the changes were mistakenly labeled as a "revolution." Give both sides of this debate. No one can deny that Reagan failed to accomplish everything he wanted, primarily because Republicans did not control the House. The Republican takeover of the House in 1994 was also called a revolution. In the sense that they had been barred from the seats of power for nearly sixty years, that election was a revolution. But they found themselves just as hamstrung as Reagan because the president at the time was a Democrat, and he vetoed almost everything they tried to pass.

The most valuable lesson from this discussion is that the founders intentionally set up checks and balances to prevent a revolu-

tion. The lingering effects of the progressive liberalism in the early 1900s would take at least two decades (the 1980s and 1990s) to change. Any presidential candidate who promises to revolutionize America during his administration is either deceived or lying. Some changes do occur quickly. For example, the nation is still affected by many of the laws passed during the first one hundred days of the New Deal. Most changes, however, come much more slowly.

Illustrate the Laffer Curve

Make a simple illustration of taxes and revenue to show the logic of the Laffer curve (i.e., the theory that when taxes are too high, reducing them will actually increase

would invest the increase in available money in money-producing activities, thereby increasing taxable income. Reagan tested the theory in 1981 with the Economic Recovery Act, which included a large cut in the income tax. The result was a doubling of government income. The Laffer curve worked. Unfortunately, government spending counteracted any gains the tax cut produced.

Time Delay in Government Actions

History shows that government actions regarding the national economy rarely have immediate results. It generally takes several months for government actions to be reflected in the broader economy. By the time government acts to resolve a particular "problem," the problem has solved itself or gone away. Therefore, one administration might take credit—or get blamed—for the actions or inactions of a previous administration.

Reagan's Consideration for Others

On March 30, 1981, Reagan was shot by a would-be assassin. By the grace of God and the quick actions of Secret Service agents and medical personnel at George Washington University Hospital, he survived. During his days in the hospital, Reagan exhibited consideration for others many times. Reporter and Reagan biographer Lou Cannon recorded one such instance in his book *Reagan*.

"He had always been a considerate man, but he was even more considerate after the shooting. For several days in the hospital Reagan ran a fever, and doctors refused him permission to shower or bathe. One night, drenched with perspiration, Reagan decided to clean himself anyway. He went into the bathroom, filled the basin with water and gave himself a sponge bath. When he had finished, he noticed that the bath-

room floor was covered with water. Reagan went down on his hands and knees to mop it up. 'What did you do that for?' George Bush wanted to know when he visited Reagan at the hospital. Reagan told the Vice-President that he knew the nurse on duty would be blamed if the doctors found out that he had bathed. 'I didn't want her to get in trouble,' he said."

Rehnquist, a conservative justice already on the court, to replace Burger. Another conservative appointment, Antonin Scalia, helped to tilt the high court away from the liberals. But O'Connor and a later appointment, Anthony Kennedy, disappointed conservatives. Though they ruled in favor of strong criminal laws and police powers, they refused to overturn the *Roe v. Wade* decision legalizing abortion.

The 1984 Election

The Democrats nominated former vice president Walter Mondale to challenge Reagan in the 1984 elections. He surprised people by promising to raise taxes. He also chose the first woman presidential running mate—Geraldine Ferraro, a liberal congresswoman from New York. The Democrats attacked the high debt, the military buildup, and the reductions in social spending. But Americans trusted Reagan, and he led in the polls the entire campaign. On election night, he carried every state but Mondale's home state of Minnesota. It was one of the biggest landslides in American history. The American voters liked Reagan, and they liked his policies.

The Mondale-Ferraro ticket did nothing to change the image of Democrats as "tax-and-spend liberals."

Foreign Affairs

Reagan believed that previous presidents had taken the wrong approach in dealing with the Cold War. He was not interested in achieving a stalemate. He intended to defeat the Soviets. He also attempted to contain the spread of communism in Latin America.

The Soviet Union

Reagan had long been a vocal opponent of communism. Carter's friendliness with the Soviets had turned to frost—if not ice—before Reagan took office. The Soviets had invaded Afghanistan. Soviet-equipped Cuban troops were fighting America's ally in Angola, Africa. The Soviets also were installing long-range missiles in Eastern Europe.

tax revenue). (You might want to refer to economics textbooks and/or the Foundation for Economic Education website for more information about this theory.)

 CD: Electoral College Results, 1984

Refer to the CD for a map showing the Electoral College results for the 1984 presidential election.

Tensions increased in 1983 when the Soviets shot down a Korean airliner. Of the 269 people on board, 61 were Americans, including conservative U.S. Congressman Larry McDonald of Georgia. (The Soviet Union claimed that the plane had crossed into its air space and was spying.) The Soviets also backed Poland's crackdown on workers demanding greater freedom. Reagan boldly condemned the Soviet Union as an "evil empire."

Reagan wanted to negotiate limits on nuclear arms, but he took a different approach than Carter. Rather than voluntarily reducing the U.S. military with the hope of calming Soviet fears of American aggression, Reagan believed that the best way to achieve peace was to build a strong military. He set aside money to develop the B-1 bomber. He supported further research on nuclear and chemical weapons. By outspending the Soviets on defense, he hoped to dash Soviet hopes of defeating the United States. He believed the Soviets would have no choice but to negotiate a better peace agreement. When the Soviets balked during talks in 1982, Reagan placed more nuclear missiles in Western Europe. Reagan's tough stand made American allies nervous, but he stuck to his policies.

Reagan also encouraged the development of a defense system that could knock out nuclear missiles aimed at American cities before they could reach their targets. Liberals in Congress and many in the media mockingly called the Strategic Defense Initiative (SDI) the "**Star Wars**" program. They also claimed SDI was dangerous because it would destabilize the situation with the Soviets. The Soviets opposed SDI because they realized the Soviet Union could not keep up with America's dynamic economy and sophisticated technology. If the United States could defend itself from a Soviet nuclear launch, the Soviet Union would lose its ability to threaten a nuclear war.

The Soviet Union also suffered during this time due to a rapid turnover in leaders. Three Soviet leaders died within a three-year span. Finally, **Mikhail Gorbachev** came to power in the Soviet Union in 1985. He was a young leader brimming with new ideas. That same year, he became the first Soviet leader to meet with Reagan. They had a second meeting on arms limitations two years later in Reykjavik, Iceland. But the talks collapsed because Reagan refused to give up SDI. Many criticized Reagan for not conceding on SDI, but Americans later discovered that Reagan's push for a defense against a nuclear attack had disturbed the Soviets more than anything else he proposed. The Soviets knew they would not be able to respond with a similar defense.

Meanwhile, discontent was growing within the Soviet Union. A desperate Gorbachev finally gave in to Reagan's demands. On December 9, 1987, the two leaders signed the historic Intermediate Nuclear Forces (INF) Treaty. It got rid of most of Europe's medium-range nuclear missiles. It was a first step toward further reductions.

The Middle East

Early in Reagan's first term, civil war and foreign intervention in Lebanon led the U.N. to send in peacekeepers. U.S. Marines were stationed in Lebanon as part of that force. But on October 23, 1983, a truck loaded with heavy explosives ran through a series of barricades and slammed into the marine headquarters on the outskirts of Beirut. The suicide attack killed more than two hundred Marines. Reagan pulled the remaining force out of the country.

U.S. Rep. Larry McDonald was killed when Soviet planes shot down Korean Air Lines flight 007.

Reagan's Frustrations with the Soviet Leadership

Liberal reporters criticized Reagan for his failure to achieve a peace agreement with the Soviets. In response to one reporter's question about the problem, Reagan quipped in frustration, "Well, they keep dying on me!"

Reagan's disappointment at not achieving an agreement with Gorbachev at Reykjavik is apparent, but it was his insistence on SDI that brought about the downfall of the Soviet Empire.

Star Wars II

When Reagan first proposed his Strategic Defense Initiative (SDI), he faced severe criticism from both inside and outside the country. Many critics said that it would upset the delicate balance of power between the United States and the Soviet Union. Once Reagan left office, Congress cut the budget for the program (derisively dubbed "Star Wars") drastically, and some programs were even canceled. The need for the program seemed outdated when the Soviet Union collapsed in 1991. But Star Wars was not dead.

By the end of the nineties, both Republicans and Democrats were calling for missile defense for the nation. The Soviet Union might have been gone, but many of its nuclear warheads were still around and unaccounted for. Now they were in the hands of smaller nations, many of them former Soviet republics and many with unstable governments. Nuclear technology was not a well-kept secret either. Unsettling evidence showed that Chinese spies working in the United States had been stealing nuclear information. Up to thirty nations also had ballistic missile technology that would allow them to fire warheads over long distances. When North Korea test fired a three-stage missile over northern Japan in 1998, the call for security intensified.

In 1999, both the House and the Senate passed bills to construct a national missile defense system. It was Reagan's SDI all over again but with a new name: the "Ballistic Missile Defense Organization." Clinton reversed Democratic policy and set aside $10.5 billion dollars over five years to build the system. The new Star Wars plan has less to do with space though. Whereas Reagan's SDI included X-ray lasers fired from space satellites, the sequel

More on Reagan

For more information on Ronald Raegan, his life and philosophy, and his dealings with Gorbachev, consider the following books:

- Peggy Noonam, *When Character Was King*
- Ronald Reagan, *An American Life*
- James Strock, *Reagan on Leadership*

focuses on land- and sea-based defense rockets. U.S. tests of these rockets, both from Kwajalein in the Pacific Ocean and from naval vessels, have proven that they are capable of shooting down incoming enemy missiles.

Space Shuttle Setbacks

During Reagan's second term of office, one of America's most memorable disasters occurred. On January 28, 1986, people across the nation watched their televisions as the *Challenger* space shuttle lifted off from Kennedy Space Center on its tenth mission. Among the seven crew members was Christa McAuliffe, a high school teacher from New Hampshire. She was to be the first teacher in space.

After five launch delays, NASA officials decided to continue with the launch despite the cold (28.5°F) temperature.

Approximately sixty seconds into the launch, flames appeared near the base of the solid rocket booster (SRB). At seventy-three seconds, a huge explosion destroyed the shuttle and killed all seven crew members.

An investigation showed that the disaster was caused by a faulty "O-ring" in the right SRB. Its ability to seal properly might have been lessened by the cold temperatures. For the space program, the explosion was a major setback. Shuttle operations did not resume for another two years. For the nation, the event was a horrible tragedy.

About seventeen years later, on February 1, 2003, the space shuttle *Columbia* suffered its own disaster. After a normal launch and a successful mission, the *Columbia* was making its reentry when it burned and broke into pieces, killing all seven crew members. Investigation showed that a briefcase-size chunk of the

U.S. F/A-18s escorted this Libyan MiG-23MS away from a U.S. carrier task force. After repeated Libyan threats and evidence linking Libya to terrorism, U.S. planes attacked Libyan bases.

This is just some of the damage caused by U.S. attacks on Libyan targets.

Lt. Col. Oliver North testified before Congress concerning his involvement in the Iran-Contra affair.

Elsewhere in the Middle East, Muslim terrorists launched a series of attacks on Westerners. Intelligence officials in the United States learned that Libya's leader, **Muammar Qaddafi**, was behind some of the terrorism. He then made new threats against the United States. His jets even threatened U.S. naval exercises in the Mediterranean. Reagan responded with a surprise bombing raid on March 31, 1986. The attack was brief, but it got Qaddafi's attention. The terrorist rampage stopped.

Latin America

Ever since Castro's rise to power in Cuba in 1959, the United States had been concerned about the spread of communism in Latin America. Struggles with poverty, inequality, and dictatorship made the region a breeding ground for revolution. Grenada, a small island in the Caribbean, became a focus of Reagan's concern. An anti-American government had ruled Grenada since the 1970s. It allowed Cuba to build a major runway there. The Cubans could use the runway to support Communist rebels throughout the region. The threat increased after rebels overthrew and executed Grenada's president in 1983.

A civil war erupted, threatening the lives of about seven hundred American students enrolled in a medical school there. Fearing for their own security, several Caribbean nations asked the United States to intervene. In a surprise attack, American paratroopers, joined by forces from five Caribbean nations, restored peace to Grenada. The United States finished the airstrip and oversaw a free election in 1984. American troops remained in Grenada only a matter of weeks.

Another revolution had taken place in Latin America before Reagan took office. With the help of Cuban advisors, a group called the **Sandinistas** set up a Communist government in Nicaragua. The CIA had begun channeling aid to anticommunist rebels called **Contras** (a shortened form of the Spanish *contrarevolucionarios*). Reagan feared that revolution would spread to Nicaragua's neighbors. He was especially concerned about El Salvador, the most crowded nation in Central America.

At first, Congress went along with Reagan's plans to aid the Contras and El Salvador. But the unstable conditions led to fears that America might be pulled into another Vietnam-like conflict. Investigators also found that some Contras had violated human rights.

Iran-Contra Affair

A 1987 incident hindered Reagan's success in the final years of his presidency. His administration had arranged the sale of weapons to Iran. In exchange, Iran helped free some Americans who had been captured and were being held hostage in Lebanon. Although Reagan had a policy that forbade bargaining with terrorists, he wanted to see the hostages freed and approved the deal. To complicate matters, some of the profits from the sale of the weapons went to aid the Contras in Nicaragua.

Congress had ended aid to the Contras before the transactions with Iran because of reported human rights abuses by the Contras. Though members of Reagan's administration believed the transfer of money from the arms sale to the Contras avoided Congress's ban, opponents charged that he had violated the law. Reagan said that he knew nothing of the diversion of funds to the Contras. His opponents claimed this revealed Reagan could not control his own administration. Congress hired an independent counsel (lawyer) to investigate. The independent counsel spent almost seven years and $37 million on the investigation of the **Iran-Contra affair**. Six members of Reagan's administration were indicted and convicted of wrongdoing, but the Supreme Court reversed several of these convictions. The counsel's report concluded, "President Reagan's conduct fell well short of criminality which could be successfully prosecuted."

Conservative Consolidation and the End of the Cold War

The "Reagan Revolution" extended to social issues as well as foreign affairs and economics. Reagan attempted to apply the moral values of religious conservatives to the issues of his day. Symbolic of his concern for morality was his appointment of C. Everett Koop as the Surgeon General. Koop became the most famous person to hold that office. He opposed abortion and also used his considerable influence to educate the public regarding the serious health risks that result from an immoral lifestyle. In addition, he alerted Americans to the fact that the nicotine in tobacco was addictive.

Reagan's concern for social issues allowed conservatives to consolidate their gains. Many organizations on the "Religious Right" were born during his administration. The Christian Coalition and Concerned Women for America were two such organizations. Conservative "think tanks" (groups of intellectuals who studied and presented position papers on various issues in the hope of influencing public policy) also developed. Two of the major think tanks were the Heritage Foundation and the American Enterprise Institute.

In addition, conservative media outlets arose to compete with liberal media for influence among the voting public. Fox News, the *Weekly Standard*, columnist George Will, and radio talk-show host Rush Limbaugh gained widespread respectability during the Reagan years. Before, only liberals had enjoyed such widespread cultural influence.

The Reagan administration also marked a turning point in the history of the world. The year after Reagan left office, communism collapsed in Eastern Europe. Two years later, the Communist leader of the Soviet Union stepped down, and fifteen new countries rose from the ashes of the former Soviet Empire. The American system of government and free enterprise had proved victorious. The Cold War that had dominated the last half of the twentieth century was finally over.

All eyes now turned to the president of the United States to guide the free world into the next century. Americans were ready for sweeping changes at home, now that the specter of communism had stopped haunting Europe. Who was the right man to lead the nation?

The Election of 1988

Reagan proposed that his vice president, **George Bush**, would be the best man to carry on his vision. He could, in effect, give the Reagan Revolution a "third term" (and possibly even a fourth) by continuing Reagan's policies. But, unlike Reagan, Bush did not have a moral vision for the nation. He accepted many of the traditional values in which he had been reared, but he rarely spoke of right and wrong. Instead, he spoke of the views of "my generation" and "your generation." He supported many of Reagan's policies, not on principle but because he thought they worked well at the moment. He

insulating foam had broken off the external fuel tank and damaged the leading edge of the left wing's thermal protection system. The hot gasses penetrated the wing, causing it to burn and detach from the shuttle body. The shuttle program was set back another two years. Other shuttle flights have been launched and returned since those disasters, but NASA has struggled to regain the confidence of the public. NASA is considering retiring the shuttles as early as 2010.

Half-hearted Gorbachev

Mikhail Gorbachev was ultimately replaced by Boris Yeltsin, partly because Gorbachev was unwilling to trust a free enterprise economy in a free, representative government. Although he was eager to relax tensions with the West by helping the Soviet Union become a more open society, he resisted pressure to abandon the principle of government control. He sought to retain control over the people and the economy. But allowing a little bit of openness and a little bit of free enterprise capitalism was like letting the nose of the proverbial camel into the tent. Hard-liners, fearing the change that Gorbachev condoned, attempted to stage a coup and briefly detained Gorbachev. A new generation of leaders such as Boris Yeltsin insisted on Gorbachev's release, and the coup failed. Shortly thereafter, Yeltsin came to power and led Russia to become a truly free society.

Section IV

Objectives

Students should be able to

1. Note the differences between Ronald Reagan's and George H.W. Bush's leadership philosophies.
2. Identify the high point of the Bush administration.
3. Describe and explain the reasons for Bush's domestic failures.

SALT vs. START

The Strategic Arms Limitation Talks (SALT) and Strategic Arms Reduction Treaty (START) agreements both dealt with the modern arms race but in different ways. SALT I and II set the upper limits on the number of select nuclear weapons that both countries could possess. However, those agreements said little about new nuclear technology, and they lacked any real power without surveillance to ensure enforcement.

Under the Reagan administration, the START agreements were launched. They focused on an actual reduction of nuclear arms by both sides. In total, START I called for a 30 percent reduction of U.S. and Soviet nuclear arsenals. Under START II, the arsenals were not to exceed 3,000–3,500 warheads by 2003. The agreements also included on-site inspections, satellite surveys, and an exchange of data that would ensure that measures were being enforced.

War over an Insult?

In January 2008, George Piro, a Lebanese-born FBI agent, revealed his experiences in interrogating Iraqi dictator Saddam Hussein. He questioned Saddam for

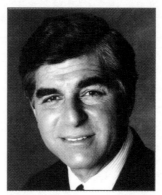

Michael Dukakis ran a lackluster campaign against George Bush.

was an uninspiring speaker. He also admitted that he lacked "the vision thing."

The 1988 election pitted Bush against liberal Massachusetts governor Michael Dukakis. When Reagan picked Bush to be his running mate in 1979, Bush had been a "moderate" Republican. He had a lifetime of experience in public service and foreign affairs. During his eight years as vice president, serving in Reagan's shadow, Bush had remained a mystery. Now he struggled to establish a separate identity. He wanted to soften Reagan's strictly conservative message. "I want a kinder, gentler nation," Bush said in his acceptance speech. He spoke of solving social ills by kindling the vast resources of the American people as "a thousand points of light."

After a shaky start, Bush rallied support largely by returning to Reagan's popular positions: American strength at home and abroad. His running mate, Dan Quayle, was a young and solidly conservative senator. That formidable ticket gained a solid win on Election Day. In a sense, Bush's election was a vote of approval of Ronald Reagan.

Section Quiz

1. How did "supply-side economics" propose to lower inflation?
2. Who was the first woman appointed to the Supreme Court?
3. Which Soviet leader agreed to come to the bargaining table with Reagan?
4. One of the complaints in the Iran-Contra affair was that weapons were sold to Iran. What was the other complaint?
5. How did Reagan's strategy of dealing with communism differ from that of détente?
⋆ Explain how the Reagan administration influenced the moral tone of American culture.

IV. The Bush Administration

Bush was the first vice president since 1836 to be elected to replace the president under whom he served. (Van Buren had succeeded Jackson in 1836.) He was a World War II veteran, a Texas oil man, a former congressman, former ambassador, and former head of the CIA. Bush was inclined to focus on foreign affairs. In domestic matters he indicated that he would both follow Reagan's agenda and work in a bipartisan manner with Democrats.

Foreign Affairs

Bush brought to foreign affairs the same resolve as Reagan. Bush faced several international crises with amazing success. His experience and skill led to major triumphs in Panama and the Persian Gulf. He also cautiously observed and privately encouraged sweeping changes in China and the Soviet Union.

Panama

Panama's drug-dealing leader, General Manuel Noriega, had become an embarrassment to the U.S. government. Reagan had tried unsuccessfully to remove him peacefully. In December 1989, Noriega

George H. W. Bush, Reagan's vice president, tried to continue the "Reagan Revolution," but he never matched Reagan's charisma.

Sen. Dan Quayle became George Bush's vice president.

Section Quiz Answers

1. by reducing taxes and regulations on businesses and investors to ensure the availability of more products
2. Sandra Day O'Connor
3. Mikhail Gorbachev
4. that some of the profits had been used to aid the Contras in Nicaragua
5. By engaging the Communists in an arms race that challenged them both militarily and economically, Reagan planned to defeat communism rather than coexist with it.
⋆ By appointing people with Christian values to significant public offices,

Reagan confronted the American people with important moral questions and challenged them to consider the answers offered by his conservative appointees. This influence led many conservative Christians to gain a stronger voice in the public square.

💿 CD: George H. W. Bush, 41st President

Refer to the CD for information on President George H.W. Bush.

🖥 Understanding Quayle

For your own better understanding of Vice President Dan Quayle, consider reading his memoirs, *Standing Firm: A Vice Presidential Memoir* (1999) and *The American Family: Discovering the Values that Make Us Strong* (1996).

went too far. His troops killed a U.S. Marine and attacked an American couple. Then he declared war on the United States.

In the early morning hours of December 20, Bush launched Operation Just Cause. Within days, American troops had crushed Noriega's forces and captured Noriega at a cost of only twenty-three American lives. Noriega was the first foreign head of state to be captured and tried in a U.S. court. He was convicted in 1992 of drug trafficking and sentenced to forty years in prison.

China, Germany, and the End of the Soviet Union

Meanwhile, there were rumblings on the other side of the globe. The Cold War was coming to an end. Chinese students led a massive protest at Beijing's Tiananmen Square in 1989, hoping to spread democracy to the Communist country. Tanks crushed the protest, killing more than two thousand people. Bush refused to take any action aside from issuing a condemnation of the Chinese government's action. When it came time to renew China's "most-favored-nation" trade status, Bush did so.

However, many of the changes in the late 1980s were more lasting. At this time, East Germans were urging reunification, and the West German government was open to the idea. Although many Europeans feared a reunified Germany, Bush supported this movement. He quietly supported the reunification and worked with key leaders to bring it about in a peaceful manner. Though many in the United States desired for Bush to travel to Germany and make a triumphant statement, he was concerned that the Soviet Union not appear humiliated on the international stage.

Changes similar to those in East Germany were taking place in the Soviet Union. As the "evil empire" began to break apart, Bush continued to support Gorbachev. Bush spoke with Gorbachev about creating a "new world order." They negotiated a strategic arms reduction treaty (START). Shortly after this, members of the Red Army, KGB, and Communist party attempted to remove Gorbachev from power. The revolt did not succeed, but it did seriously damage Gorbachev's reputation as a capable leader. Soon he was replaced by Boris Yeltsin, who favored dissolving the Soviet Union. Over the next several months, Bush cautiously observed these events from a distance. He did communicate to Gorbachev and then Yeltsin that the United States would support the nation's democratic movement. This move was made final on Christmas Day 1991. On that day the Soviet Union ceased to exist.

The Persian Gulf

A high point of Bush's presidency occurred when he put together an international coalition to force Iraqi troops from Kuwait in 1990. Iraqi dictator **Saddam Hussein** had invaded that tiny, oil-rich neighbor. He hoped to win glory for himself and easy wealth for his nation. But Bush vowed, "This will not stand."

A U.N. directive (order) told Hussein to withdraw by January 15, 1991. It authorized the U.N. to use "all necessary means" to liberate Kuwait if Hussein did not comply. The U.S. Congress also approved

Panamanian dictator Manuel Noriega was ousted from power, arrested, tried, and imprisoned in the United States on drug trafficking charges.

President and Mrs. Bush meet with troops stationed in Saudi Arabia before the beginning of Operation Desert Storm.

seven months after his capture during the second Gulf War, slowly gaining his confidence and getting him to reveal many secrets concerning events leading up to and during the Persian Gulf War and the subsequent invasion of Iraq by Coalition forces. He said that when asked for a reason for Iraq's invasion of Kuwait, Saddam revealed that he interpreted as an insult something the emir of Kuwait said to Iraq's foreign minister. History turned, in that instance, on a personal insult.

Stealth Technology

In Operation Just Cause (the U.S. invasion of Panama) and Operation Desert Storm, a new form of technology was used. Since the seventies, American engineers had been secretly designing a jet that was undetectable to radar defenses. The strategy was to design the jet's body to reflect as little energy as possible. To achieve that, engineers limited the angles of the jet to give it a flat design. In a prototype design, the back tail fins were pointed inward, but this caused another problem. Heat from the exhaust reflected off the fins. The final design had the fins pointing outward.

To keep the jet invisible on radar, every precaution was taken. Mesh covers over the engine intakes protected against internal reflections. The skin of the plane was made of radar-absorbent material. The canopy was coated with a substance to make it impenetrable to radar. Even screw heads were redesigned to ensure they would not cause reflections. To reduce the jet's noise, exhausts were soundproofed, and the turbine was made to give off a high-pitched whine instead of a loud scream.

At the time of the Panama invasion, the stealth fighter jet, called the F-117

Discuss Term Limits

Discuss the pros and cons of term limits. The arguments are strong on both sides of the issue. Supporters point to the tendency of power to corrupt and the tendency of those in power to abuse their power in order to stay in office. They also mention that the Founding Fathers envisioned statesmen who would serve a short time and then return to private life. Opponents of term limits believe that the people should be free to vote as they choose. They say that the electoral process is itself a form of term limits. They also are wary of any fundamental changes in the basic structure of the republic because such changes usually have unintended consequences. For example, they fear that term

limits would weaken the power of elected officials and actually strengthen the power of unelected experts from each party who run the offices and seem to do the real work of the representatives.

Though sinful people find ways around restrictions, we should still try to stem the effects of sinful humans.

Nighthawk, was ready for service. Six jets were sent on missions, but two returned unneeded and another two had their mission canceled. The final two completed their bombing mission undetected by enemy radar.

During the Persian Gulf War, the F-117 saw more action. In the first twenty-four hours of the war, the jets accounted for 31 percent of the targets attacked. One target was particularly memorable for CNN viewers. A bomb from an F-117 destroyed the AlKark Communications Tower. CNN's television signal was transmitted from there. When the bomb hit, the station suddenly went blank. Reporters Peter Arnett and Bernard Shaw had to continue the broadcast without the aid of video.

Stealth technology continued with the development of the Stealth B-2 bomber. These and other high-tech weapons reveal what war may be like in the twenty-first century. The F-117 is slated for retirement and is being replaced by an even stealthier plane, the F-22 Raptor.

Perspectives on Corruption

Because human graft and corruption often occur in government as well as industry, America's founders wanted a small government that stayed out of business, except to enforce and defend the law. Lawmakers were supposed to be regular citizens—not professional politicians—who met for a few weeks each year to pass laws and then went back to their normal lives. They believed that big government would promote abuse of taxpayer money, whether by greedy politicians or crooked businessmen.

The F-117 Nighthawk Stealth fighter opened the air strikes against Iraq in the Gulf War.

Gen. Norman Schwarzkopf drove Iraqi forces out of Kuwait and defeated them in one hundred hours.

Riots in Los Angeles complicated domestic issues during this period.

war, if necessary. It was America's first official declaration of war since World War II.

The brief **Persian Gulf War** (January 16–February 27, 1991) began with five weeks of massive, around-the-clock bombing. That was followed by a surprise ground attack. General Norman Schwarzkopf's forces encircled the Iraqi army and almost trapped it in Kuwait. As the Iraqi army escaped northward, U.S. planes attacked it along the "highway of death." The Iraqis surrendered en masse.

The ground war was over within one hundred hours, and Americans rejoiced that the ghosts of the Vietnam War had vanished. Yet, the cream of Hussein's army, the Republican Guard, remained safe at home in Iraq. Schwarzkopf did not move north to capture Hussein because the United States had achieved its stated goal. Bush's advisors were concerned that removing Hussein would leave American troops as occupiers in a hostile country. They also desired that Iraq continue to serve as a restraint against Iran.

In the wake of victory, Bush's popularity ratings soared to an unprecedented 89 percent. No leading Democrat wanted to run against him in the next election.

Domestic Affairs

When Bush came to office, he was confronted by a number of challenges that demanded immediate attention. Congressional scandals, a high deficit, and a growing drug problem combined to challenge Bush's leadership ability at home. Bush took decisive action, but some of these actions were very unpopular.

Savings and Loan Bankruptcies

Bush inherited a large federal deficit. (A deficit occurs when government spends more money than it receives in taxes.) He planned to reduce the deficit by cutting the budget. This plan was complicated by the Savings and Loan crisis. The savings and loan (S&L) banks had begun to go bankrupt because of unsound investments. Recognizing that thousands of citizens were about to lose their savings, Bush worked with Congress to rescue the S&Ls. The decision was costly. Experts estimated that the bailout would cost taxpayers more than $300 billion over thirty years.

The 1990 Budget Deal and Economic Recession

At the 1988 Republican National Convention, Bush had attempted to prove that he was a Reagan conservative by promising not to raise taxes. He famously said that he would tell Congress, "Read my lips: No new taxes." However, the deficit and the S&L crisis made this promise very difficult—if not impossible—to keep. The White House entered into a discussion with Congressional leaders. Congress promised to cut spending, and Bush chose to go back on his campaign pledge of "no new taxes." After the **1990 budget deal** (and continued spending by Congress), the country entered a recession. As a result, tax revenues declined and the deficit increased. In the end, Bush was blamed and his credibility suffered.

Congressional Scandals

During these years, Congress was embarrassed by several scandals. In 1989, congressmen gave themselves a pay raise and established automatic annual cost-of-living adjustments (COLAs). Taxpayers were furious. States responded by ratifying the Twenty-seventh Amendment on May 7, 1992. Nonetheless, COLAs contin-

CD: Growth in Federal Spending Under the Elementary and Secondary Education Act

Refer to the CD for a table showing the growth of federal spending for education under the Elementary and Secondary Education Act.

CD: Growth in Total Government Spending

Refer to the CD for a table showing the growth in overall total government spending in recent years.

Economics 101

Review the difference between national debt, deficit, recession, and depression.

Activity 5: Federal Spending Under Recent Presidents

Use this activity to help the students develop a picture of the growth of federal spending under recent presidents.

ued. (For example, in 1993, COLAs gave each congressman an extra $4,100.)

In 1992, news leaked that some congressmen had serious House Bank overdrafts. These congressmen could overdraw on their checking accounts without penalty, while taxpayers paid the interest. The House Ethics Committee released the names of 247 congressmen who had overdrafts.

A more serious scandal involved the House Post Office. Investigators found that congressmen were abusing their privileges to pay office expenses and to buy stamps. The most infamous case involved Dan Rostenkowski, the chairman of the Ways and Means Committee. He pocketed more than ten thousand dollars in money for stamps, hired employees who were paid for work they never did, and used his congressional staff for private work. These abuses cost taxpayers half a million dollars. He was found guilty and sentenced to jail.

Many Americans thought that incumbents (officeholders who sought reelection) had lost touch with the people. Support grew for **term limits** (limiting the number of years an elected official can stay in office). During 1992, fourteen states passed laws to limit senators to two terms (twelve years) and House members to anywhere from three to six terms (six to twelve years). The number of states with term limits increased to twenty-two after 1994.

Bush and the Reagan Revolution

George Bush was the heir to Ronald Reagan's conservative revolution. However, he was also the son of a moderate Republican senator, Preston Bush. George Bush had gained his office on the momentum created by Reagan, but he had entered politics because of the beliefs he had received from his father. Consequently, Bush's domestic policies were a mix of moderate conservatism and Reagan conservatism.

Unlike Reagan, Bush favored increasing the power of the federal government in order to deal with social issues. Reagan opposed many environmental initiatives because they were too expensive and required too much governmental control. But Bush, who wanted to be known as the "environment president," worked with Congress to pass the Clean Air Act. This legislation required the states to develop programs for keeping air pollution below certain levels.

One of Bush's most important domestic achievements was the **Americans with Disabilities Act**. The act outlawed job discrimination based on disabilities. It also made local governments and businesses provide better working conditions for the disabled. But Bush did not see this act as a large government program. The act provided guidance to the private sector, demanding they make just and wise choices that they were unlikely to make on their own. Conservatives objected to this legislation. They said these **unfunded federal mandates** (federal requirements that the federal government does not pay for) were still government interference in the private sector and a heavy burden on small businesses.

Twenty-seventh Amendment

No law, varying the compensation for the services of the Senators and Representatives, shall take effect, until an election of Representatives shall have intervened.

House Ways and Means Committee chairman Rep. Dan Rostenkowski (D-Ill.) was found guilty of misusing his congressional mailing privileges.

Supporters look on as President Bush signs the Americans with Disabilities Act of 1990.

Confirmation Hearings for Clarence Thomas

Except for the Senate hearings for Robert Bork in 1987, the confirmation hearings for Clarence Thomas in 1991 were the most controversial in modern history. George H.W. Bush appointed Thomas, a conservative, pro-life black, to replace the outgoing liberal Supreme Court justice Thurgood Marshall. At the last minute, Anita Hill, who had worked for Thomas at the Equal Opportunity Employment Office ten years earlier, came forward and accused Thomas of making lewd advances toward her. The senators at first praised her for her bravery, but their search for the truth became confused when Thomas categorically denied all of the accusations. He accused the liberal senators of a "high-tech lynching." Someone was lying, but the senators described both of them as exemplary Americans. The media portrayed Hill as an innocent, mainstream lawyer. They ignored reports of her close connections with leading feminists. Only after the trial did the public become aware of Hill's potential motives for lying. Thomas was confirmed after a close vote. During his first year, he proved to be one of the Court's most conservative justices.

Iran-Contra Conclusion

One of Bush's last acts as president was to pardon several government officials involved in the Iran-Contra affair. The charge against most of them was that they had withheld information or otherwise obstructed the congressional investigation. Former secretary of defense Caspar Weinberger was one of the highest profiled to receive a pardon. His pardon was controversial to some people because he had not even been found guilty of any crime, although he had been indicted.

🔘 **CD: Five Presidents**

Refer to the CD for a photo of the historic moment when, for the first time, five U.S. presidents were together.

One way in which Bush showed himself to be Reagan's heir was in his aggressive approach to America's growing drug problem. Bush expanded the Reagan administration's efforts to combat drug abuse by appointing William Bennett to be the "drug czar." Under Bennett, the Office of National Drug Control Policy emphasized intercepting drug shipments and local law enforcement in drug matters. Liberals criticized Bush's approach. They believed he should have focused on prevention and rehabilitation rather than on law enforcement.

Another similarity between Bush and Reagan was Bush's choice of Supreme Court justices. Like Reagan, Bush desired to move the court in a more conservative direction. And, like Reagan, Bush met with success and failure. David Souter, George Bush's first appointment to the Supreme Court, was a relatively unknown New Hampshire judge. Bush chose him hoping to avoid the kind of confirmation hearings that Robert Bork had faced. Once on the court, Souter moved to support increasingly liberal positions. Bush's second Supreme Court nominee, Clarence Thomas, faced a much tougher confirmation. He had already stated his opposition to abortion and affirmative action. Democrats in the Senate went to great lengths to prevent his appointment. In the end, Thomas was confirmed, and he has proved to be one of the most conservative justices.

The mixed success of the Reagan-Bush appointments became clear in the 1992 case *Planned Parenthood v. Casey*. The case concerned what sort of restrictions a state could place on abortion, and it was seen as an opportunity to overturn *Roe v. Wade*. Americans certainly had reason to think that the Court might do this. Eight of the nine justices had been nominated by Republican presidents, and five had been nominated by Reagan and Bush. But after hearing the case, Souter surprised his colleagues by siding with those who wanted to uphold *Roe v. Wade*. It then appeared that the Court would narrowly overturn *Roe* by a 5 to 4 vote. At the last minute, however, Anthony Kennedy (a Reagan appointee to the Court) changed his decision and announced he was siding with Souter. The famous landmark decision of *Roe v. Wade* had barely survived, but it had survived.

Section Quiz

1. What was Bush's position on the reunification of Germany? Why was his position important?

2. What action caused the United States to declare war on Iraq?

3. What congressional scandal led to the Twenty-seventh Amendment?

4. What campaign pledge did Bush go back on during the 1990 budget deal?

★ What do you consider to be Bush's greatest accomplishment? What do you think was his greatest failure?

Section Quiz Answers

1. Bush supported the reunification of Germany; his support hastened the reunification.

2. Iraq's invasion of Kuwait

3. Congress gave itself a payraise and established automatic annual cost-of-living raises.

4. "Read my lips. No new taxes."

★ Answers will vary. His greatest accomplishment was either helping end the Cold War or successfully prosecuting the Gulf War. Answers for his greatest failure might include failing to keep his word about taxes, to appoint truly conservative judges, or to punish China after Tiananmen Square.

Activity 6: Chapter Review

Use this activity to help the students prepare for the chapter test.

Chapter Review

Review Questions

Answer these questions.

1. What two bicentennial celebrations did America have during the 1970s and 1980s?

2. What was President Carter's greatest foreign relations triumph?

3. What two groups were fighting against each other in Nicaragua in the 1980s?

4. Who was the first woman appointed to the Supreme Court?

5. Name one of the most significant domestic crises during the Bush administration.

Match these men with their descriptions.

6. Mikhail Gorbachev
7. Saddam Hussein
8. Ayatollah Khomeini
9. Muammar Qaddafi
10. William Rehnquist

a. Iranian Muslim ruler
b. Libyan leader
c. Soviet leader
d. Iraqi leader
e. chief justice appointed by Reagan

Indicate whether each of the following items is most closely associated with (A) President Ford, (B) President Carter, (C) President Reagan, or (D) President Bush.

11. pardon of Richard Nixon
12. Persian Gulf War
13. supply-side economics
14. Grenada invasion
15. Iranian hostage crisis

Critical Thinking

1. Compare and contrast Reagan and Bush.

2. Should the United States have become involved in the Persian Gulf War? Would it have been better to remove Saddam Hussein from power?

People, Places, and Things to Remember:

Bicentennial
Jimmy Carter
Ronald Reagan
amnesty
deregulation
Three Mile Island
Panama Canal Treaty
Camp David Accords
Ayatollah Khomeini
Iranian hostage crisis
supply-side economics
Sandra Day O'Connor
William H. Rehnquist
"Star Wars"
Mikhail Gorbachev
Muammar Qaddafi
Sandinistas
Contras
Iran-Contra affair
George Bush
Saddam Hussein
Persian Gulf War
1990 budget deal
term limits
Americans with Disabilities Act
unfunded federal mandates

CHAPTER REVIEW QUESTIONS

Review Questions

1. Declaration of Independence, Constitution
2. Camp David Accords
3. Sandinistas and Contras
4. Sandra Day O'Connor
5. one of the following: the L.A. riots, savings and loan bankruptcies, 1990 budget crisis, congressional scandals, unfunded mandates
6. c
7. d
8. a
9. b
10. e
11. A
12. D
13. C
14. C
15. B

Critical Thinking

1. Answers will vary. Both could claim foreign policy triumphs, though Bush gave too much control to the UN in the Gulf War. In domestic affairs, Reagan wanted less government involvement while Bush's policies tended to promote more.

2. Answers will vary.

Chapter Goals

Students should be able to

1. Define and use the basic terms of the chapter.
2. Analyze the effect of social changes under the Clinton administration.
3. Evaluate the foreign policy changes under the Clinton administration.
4. Analyze the effectiveness of the "Republican Revolution."
5. Analyze the causes of the cultural changes in the 1990s and assess the impact of these changes on American society.

Chapter Motivation

In this chapter, your students should note the unintended consequences of electing Bill Clinton. (The public did not approve of his loose morals or his social reengineering of American society, but these became his main legacy.)

The inauguration of Bill Clinton and his vice president Al Gore began eight years of Democrats' attempts to undo the Reagan Revolution.

Bridge to the 21st Century

I.   A New Face in Washington

II. The Republican Revolution of 1994

III. Culture Wars

IV. Domestic Difficulties of the Second Term

V.   Foreign Policy in the Clinton Administration

Chapter 28 Lesson Plan Chart

Section Title	Main Activity	Pages	Days
I. A New Face in Washington	Activity 1: Hillary Clinton and the Health-Care Debate	539–42	1 day
II. The Republican Revolution of 1994	Activity 2: Contract with America!	542–44	½–1 day
III. Culture Wars	Activity 3: What the Bible Says About Modern Issues	545–48	½–1 day
IV. Domestic Difficulties of the Second Term	Activity 4: Ending the Welfare State Through the Power of Private Action	549–52	1 day
V. Foreign Policy in the Clinton Administration	Activity 6: Chapter Review	552–56	1–2 days
TOTAL SUGGESTED DAYS (INCLUDING **1** DAY FOR REVIEW AND TESTING)		5–7 DAYS	

MATERIALS LIST

SECTION I
- CD: Electoral College Results, 1992; Bill Clinton, 42nd President
- Activity 1 from the *Student Activities* manual

SECTION II
- Activity 2 from the Student Activities manual

SECTION III
- Activity 3 from the *Student Activities* manual

SECTION IV
- Activities 4 and 5 from the *Student Activities* manual

The 1990s brought a new era in American life. The Cold War was over. The biggest issues in this decade did not concern foreign policy. The troubles in foreign policy that would dominate in later years seemed small and unimportant. The leading events of the 1900s concerned social issues. During this decade, American public opinion changed on several important moral issues, and Christians worried about the direction of the nation.

I. A New Face in Washington

In 1992, the nation was ready for change. Many believed that President Bush was not doing enough to stimulate the economy. This broad dissatisfaction opened the way for a new personality in the nation's capital. Although this politician did bring change, the greatest change he brought was social, not economic. His support for causes like gay rights transformed American society.

The 1992 Election

Three successive Republican victories showed that Americans did not trust liberalism. The Democrats needed a way to change their liberal image. Governor **Bill Clinton** of Arkansas and other young Democrats met to discuss new ideas. They called their forum the **Democratic Leadership Council**. They tested their ideas in the election of 1992 by running Clinton as a moderate "New Democrat."

Clinton had many strengths that helped him win the Democratic nomination. He was a Rhodes scholar and a graduate of Yale Law School. He was the governor of Arkansas. He also demonstrated remarkable skill for reading public opinion and shaping his message to fit that opinion. Clinton succeeded in convincing many Americans that he was no liberal politician by expressing support for the death penalty, free trade, a balanced budget, and lower taxes for the middle class.

But Clinton also had several weaknesses. For many years he had faced accusations of adultery. It was also rumored that he had used marijuana, and when he was questioned about this illegal activity, he admitted that he had smoked the drug but insisted he had never inhaled. And for someone who aspired to be the commander-in-chief of the nation's military, his record was particularly problematic. While in college he had opposed the Vietnam War and had dodged the draft.

But President Bush had serious problems as well. Even many in his own party were not supporting him. Conservatives attacked Bush's mixed record. Bush apologized for breaking his "no new taxes" pledge in 1990, promising to fight taxes in the future. But he never convinced voters of his sincerity. Democrats added to Bush's problems by responding to attacks on Clinton's character with attacks on Bush's economic policy. When faced with charges of scandal, Clinton's campaign headquarters reminded themselves, "It's the economy, stupid."

Clinton's weaknesses and Bush's apparent failure to address the country's economic troubles opened the way for a billionaire named **Ross Perot** to enter the race as an independent candidate. He promised drastic measures to wipe out the deficit. Many voters turned to him as an outsider. He even took a temporary lead in opinion polls.

On Election Day, Clinton won by a large margin in the Electoral College (370 to 168). Democrats credited their win to Clinton's

The presidential debates of 1992 were three-way contests between President Bush, Bill Clinton, and third-party candidate Ross Perot.

Third-party candidate Ross Perot took his message to the people via television, complete with an array of charts.

Section I
Objectives
Students should be able to
1. Identify the Democrats' strategy for the 1992 election.
2. Explain how Clinton used his mandate to change social policy.
3. Evaluate the social changes advocated by Clinton in his first term.

H. Ross Perot

Henry Ross Perot was born in 1930 in Texarkana, Texas. He graduated from the U.S. Naval Academy in 1953. After serving his tour of duty, he resigned his navy commission and became a salesman for IBM. In 1962, he founded Electronic Data Systems (EDS) and grew it into a multibillion-dollar business and himself into one of the richest people in the nation. In 1984, he sold the company to General Motors. In 1988, he founded Perot Systems.

Between 1969 and 1972, Perot worked in cooperation with the Department of Defense to gain release of Vietnam prisoners of war. In 1978 he financed and planned a commando raid into Iran to rescue two jailed EDS employees.

Perot ran for president of the United States twice. In 1992 he was the standard-bearer of United We Stand America, with retired Vice Admiral and former Vietnam POW James Stockdale as his running mate. They ran against George H.W. Bush and Bill Clinton. Perot attracted people with his "folksy, straight-talking" style and got 19 percent of the popular vote but no electoral votes. Some blamed him for Bush's loss. He ran again in 1996 on the Reform Party ticket, that time with economist Pat Choate as his running mate, but he gained only 8 percent of the vote.

- Special speaker: an expert on computer technology
- CD: Electoral College Results, 1996; Key Figures in the Clinton Impeachment

SECTION V
- Activity 6 from the *Student Activities* manual

Core Values

Since the beginning of the Republic, Americans have shared the core values of freedom, equality, individualism, and growth. The ways these values have been worked out have changed over the centuries. Growth has been important throughout American history, but in earlier times economic growth would not have been sufficient for the nation to overlook the immorality and perjury of a sitting president. Individualism has also changed over time. In many ways community has taken a more prominent place in American thought. Yet this coincides with increasing isolation as small towns and neighborhoods give way to more isolated suburban settings and socialization moves online. Individualism is also used to defend abortion ("It's my body"), which earlier generations would have found incredible. More positively, the early rhetoric of all men being created equal has become a greater and greater reality in the United States as African Americans and other minority groups have gained equal standing with all other Americans. Unfortunately, homosexual activists have appealed to equality in an effort to gain acceptance in the broader culture. They have also appealed to freedom, as have those who support abortion. Freedom has been transposed from the freedom to obey God, which was sought by the Pilgrims, to the freedom to do what one pleases—the autonomous freedom sought by Adam and Eve in the Fall.

These values are picked up unconsciously by students simply because they live within the American culture. Therefore, they must be taught to evaluate these values and their application by the standard of God's Word.

Homosexuality and the Bible

Clinton's attempt to lift the ban on homosexuals in the military resulted in the "Don't ask, don't tell" compromise. Even though this compromise satisfied no one, Clinton's efforts did make homosexuality far more accepted in American society. Because of this growing acceptance, Christians need to understand this issue from the perspective of Scripture.

Many who support homosexuality today make comparisons between the civil rights movement and homosexual activism. Some also claim that Christian opposition to homosexuality is similar to Christian support of slavery and segregation. However, these comparisons are not valid. Those who support homosexual practice argue that Old Testament condemnations of homosexual behavior can be ignored because Christians today no longer obey the Old Testament dietary regulations or laws about not wearing clothing of mixed fabrics. But this argument fails to note what Bible scholars have long known. Although the Old Testament contains some laws that were given specifically to ancient Israel and that no longer apply to God's people, it also contains moral laws that transcend the testaments. Sexual practices, including regulations about homosexuality, fall into the moral category. This condemnation is confirmed by New Testament passages such as Romans 1:26–28. Those supporting homosexual practice claim that Paul was speaking about homosexual lust, not loving homosexual behaviors. But Paul says clearly that homosexuality is "against nature" (Rom. 1:26); that is, against God's intention for human sexuality.

Election of 1992

(Map of the United States showing the Election of 1992)

WA 11, MT 3, ND 3, MN 10, OR 7, ID 4, SD 3, WI 11, ME 4, VT 3, NH 4, NY 33, MA 12, MI 18, CT 8, RI 4, NV 4, UT 5, WY 3, NE 5, IA 7, IL 22, IN 12, OH 21, PA 23, NJ 15, DE 3, DC 3, CA 54, CO 8, KS 6, MO 11, KY 8, WV 5, VA 13, MD 10, AZ 8, NM 5, OK 8, AR 6, TN 11, NC 14, SC 8, MS 7, AL 9, GA 13, TX 32, LA 9, FL 25, AK 3, HI 4

Key:
■ William J. Clinton (D)
Electoral 370
Popular 44,908,254
■ George Bush (R)
Electoral 168
Popular 39,102,343

campaign skills and the country's anger against the "failed trickle-down policies of the 1980s." Republicans blamed a weak economy, bad press, and Bush. But Clinton failed to attract a majority of the popular vote (43% Clinton, 37% Bush, 19% Perot). Perot gained the largest number of votes by a third-party candidate since Teddy Roosevelt ran in 1912. Democrats won no seats in the Senate but lost nine in the House.

Early Controversies

Clinton appealed to many Americans because, though he was a Democrat, he also portrayed himself as a **centrist**, a politician who favored some Democratic policies and some Republican policies. But the first two years of Clinton's presidency were mired in controversy. The centrist Clinton of the campaign seemed to be replaced by the liberal Clinton of the White House. The new president failed to implement the Republican economic policies he claimed to favor, but he vigorously promoted a liberal social agenda.

Homosexuality

The day after the inauguration, Clinton began discussions about lifting the ban on homosexuals in the military. This angered many Americans, including most military leaders, who opposed homosexuality. Clinton responded to the opposition by proposing a compromise called "Don't ask, don't tell." Military personnel were not allowed to ask if someone was homosexual. But those who were open about their homosexuality could be discharged. This compromise pleased no one. Conservatives were not happy that the ban was

Bill Clinton took office claiming to be a "New Democrat."

Compare Intraparty Conflicts During Recent Elections

Point out some of the issues during the most recent election and show how they are a continuation of issues raised by the Democratic Leadership Council during the 1992 election. Note how both major parties are divided on the best way to define themselves. The debate concerns the level of government intervention in social issues (such as abortion and homosexuality) and economic issues (such as welfare and pork-barrel spending).

Does Character Matter?

Ask the question that was raised during the 1992 election: "Does character matter?" Why would anyone say no? The Bible teaches that all of our actions are products of our inner character (Prov. 4:23).

Use the profile list that the students developed during the previous chapter to check whether President Clinton had the character qualities that make a good president.

CD: Electoral College Results, 1992

Refer to the CD for a map showing the results of the Electoral College voting for the election of 1992.

CD: Bill Clinton, 42nd President

Refer to the CD for information on President Bill Clinton.

UN Convention on the Rights of the Child

The UN Convention on the Rights of the Child is easily accessible on the Internet. Read some of its provisions and discuss them with your class so that they understand the dangers of children's rights. Of particular interest are the freedom of speech (Article 12), the right to receive information of all kinds through any media of the child's choice (13), freedom of conscience and religion (14), freedom of association (15), the right to privacy (16), the right to fam-

lifted, and supporters of gay rights were angered that homosexuals were forced to be silent.

Clinton extended his pro-homosexual agenda into his administrative appointments. He said that he wanted to create a diverse cabinet that reflected the mix in American society. In his first year, he appointed almost thirty open homosexuals to key posts.

Abortion

Two days after assuming office, he removed several limits that Reagan had placed on using government money for abortions. These limits had banned abortions from taking place in clinics that received federal money. The limits also included military hospitals. Clinton then began to contribute to United Nations health programs that promoted abortion. Both Reagan and Bush had refused to fund such programs.

Clinton's support for abortion was also evident by the people he nominated. He appointed Joycelyn Elders as surgeon general. She attacked what she called the pro-life movement's "love affair with the fetus." She also promoted controversial views, such as sex education in kindergarten. Clinton later fired Elders when her public statements proved too embarrassing.

Janet Reno, the nation's first female attorney general, made clamping down on pro-life protests at abortion clinics her first priority. With her backing, Democrats in Congress passed the **Freedom of Access to Clinic Entrances** law. This act made activities such as obstructing abortion clinics a federal crime.

Healthcare

Hillary Rodham Clinton, the First Lady, led the new president's first policy proposal. The Clintons proposed to create a government agency to regulate all healthcare in the United States. In November 1993, following secret meetings, she introduced her massive 1,342-page plan to Congress. The proposal guaranteed healthcare coverage for all Americans and legal immigrants. It also mandated that businesses contribute to the program. Critics of the program objected that the White House was proposing to take over one-seventh of the U.S. economy. They also argued the plan would be enormously expensive for the taxpayer. The healthcare plan never gained broad public support, and President Clinton's refusal to compromise doomed the plan.

Environmentalism

The Democrats had long supported environmental initiatives, but Presidents Reagan and Bush had often blocked their progress because these proposals hurt the economy and required too much government intrusion into people's lives. President Clinton tasked his vice president, Al Gore, to oversee the administration's environmental policies.

Perhaps the most controversial environmental actions involved efforts to save the spotted owl. Clinton's secretary of the interior imposed stiff restrictions on the use of government lands in the West. These actions along with others shut down logging in federal forests and cost thirty thousand loggers their jobs.

Waco and Oklahoma City

Concerns about an increasingly intrusive government were only heightened by a confrontation between the Bureau of Alcohol, Tobacco, and Firearms (ATF) and a cult group known as the Branch

Among Clinton's controversial appointments was Janet Reno, the first female attorney general.

Hillary Clinton proposed health-care reforms that would have given the federal government unprecedented control over the nation's health care profession.

Clinton's Nominees

The first lesbian ever confirmed by the Senate was Clinton appointee Roberta Achtenberg, an outspoken homosexual activist. She once tried to force Boy Scouts in San Francisco to approve homosexual scoutmasters. Her job as assistant secretary in the Department of Housing and Urban Development was to ensure fair housing and equal opportunity.

Other Clinton nominees, including Zoë Baird, Kimba Wood, and Ron Brown also had legal problems.

The Clinton Health Care Plan

Under the Clinton health care plan, one-seventh of American businesses would have been brought directly under government supervision. In addition, all Americans would have been required to pay insurance premiums that would cover abortions.

Hillary Clinton

Hillary Clinton graduated from Wellesley College with a degree in political science in 1969 and entered Yale Law School the same year. She met her future husband, Bill, there and graduated in 1973. They married in 1975 and moved to Arkansas, where Bill began his political career. Their only child, Chelsea, was born in 1980.

Hillary taught at the University of Arkansas Law School and joined the Rose Law Firm. President Jimmy Carter named her to the board of the Legal Services Corporation. She was the First Lady during Bill's presidency. During the White House years, she wrote *It Takes a Village and Other Lessons Children Teach Us*.

Clinton was elected to the U.S. Senate in 2000, making her the first former First

---

ily planning (24), the right to use his own language (30), and the right to have "rest and leisure" (31). Note that Article 19 could be used to prohibit corporal punishment or teaching certain Christian doctrines, such as those about hell. Though the government has the responsibility to punish evildoers, including those who do wrong to children, Christians are skeptical of the Convention because the United Nations rarely judges moral issues from a biblical perspective. Often it is openly hostile to the Christian worldview.

Discuss the Wisdom or Folly of Federal Crimes

Discuss the wisdom or folly of making so many crimes federal issues rather than state

issues. The Founders feared a powerful "police state" run by the central government because of the potential for abuse. On the other hand, crimes such as kidnapping, tax evasion, and counterfeiting are federal crimes and may offer citizens greater protection on the federal level than is possible on the state level.

The Bible and Homosexuality

Robert A. J. Gagnon's, *The Bible and Homosexual Practice: Texts and Hermeneutics* (Abingdon, 2002) is a helpful resource for dealing with homosexual practice from a biblical perspective.

Koresh and the Branch Davidians

Vernon Howell was a high school dropout from a dysfunctional family. He claimed to have been converted in a Southern Baptist church but soon joined the Seventh Day Adventists. He later joined the more radical Branch Davidian faction of that church and eventually became its leader. He changed his name to David Koresh and believed that he was the head of the house of David and a latter-day Cyrus the Great. He claimed that the name *Koresh* meant "Cyrus," but he later told an FBI negotiator that it meant "death."

Koresh taught polygamy and total allegiance to himself over all other relationships. He even taught the children in the compound to think of him as God. His followers believe that he was the Chosen One who would die, be buried, and then come back from the dead to save the true believers.

Koresh had been suspected of a variety of crimes, including attempted murder, child abuse, sexual abuse of minors, and various firearms violations. He swore his followers, especially the children, to silence about what went on at the compound, explaining that outsiders, or "unbelievers," "would not understand."

The Branch Davidians still function today, claiming about six hundred members. They still believe that Koresh will be resurrected. In fact, they have set several dates

The compound of the Branch Davidian cult led by David Koresh went up in flames when federal officials tried to force their way in. More than seventy people, including many women and children, died.

Timothy McVeigh was found guilty of bombing the Alfred P. Murrah Federal Building in Oklahoma City.

Davidians. On February 28, 1993, the ATF raided the Davidian's seventy-seven-acre compound in Waco, Texas. Agents believed that cult leader **David Koresh** was stockpiling illegal arms. The poorly organized raid failed. Four agents were killed. After a fifty-one-day standoff, Reno ordered tanks to break into the compound and fire tear gas. When they did, the compound erupted in flames and seventy-five Davidians died.

On the second anniversary of the raid on the Branch Davidians, a radical named Timothy McVeigh bombed a federal office building in Oklahoma City. The blast destroyed the building and killed 168 people. It was the largest act of domestic terrorism in American history to that point.

Bigger Government

Clinton had campaigned against government waste and inefficiency. But under him bureaucracy increased. He signed into law much big-government legislation that Reagan and Bush had vetoed. The Family and Medical Leave Act forced businesses to give employees twelve weeks of unpaid leave to care for newborn babies or seriously ill family members. The Brady Bill required states to conduct background checks on people who wanted to buy guns.

One of Clinton's most popular campaign pledges was designed to promote community service. Similar to Kennedy's Peace Corps, **AmeriCorps** offered federal money to students who wanted money for school bills. In return for two years of full-time community service work, volunteers received $14,800 in living expenses, a $9,500 credit toward higher education, and free health- and child-care benefits. Their hourly wage, excluding benefits, was $7.27. AmeriCorps "brought the taxpayer the $30,000 'volunteer,'" complained one senator.

Clinton's first budget called for new government programs, higher taxes on everyone, and few spending cuts (except in the military). He proposed a record-breaking $496 billion increase in taxes. The budget barely passed Congress. It did not get any Republican votes.

Section Quiz

1. What were Bill Clinton's weaknesses in the 1992 election?
2. What did Clinton indicate would be his priority if elected?
3. List four causes promoted by President Clinton in his first year in office.
4. Who led President Clinton's task force on health-care reform?
★ What are the advantages and disadvantages of having health care paid for by the government?
★ How did Clinton's social agenda change American culture? Compare what is accepted today with what was controversial when Clinton first proposed it.

II. The Republican Revolution of 1994

Clinton faced many problems in his first two years. Voters were most bothered by his failure to keep campaign pledges, including a middle-class tax cut. Smoking and drug use were on the rise. Crime

---

Activity 1: Hillary Clinton and the Health-Care Debate

Use this activity to help the students understand reasons for the defeat of Hillary Clinton's health care plan.

Section Quiz Answers

1. accusations of adultery, marijuana use, opposition to the Vietnam War, and draft dodging
2. the economy
3. homosexual rights, abortion, government healthcare, and environmentalism
4. Hillary Rodham Clinton

★ Answers will vary. Government intervention does enable everyone to get some care no matter what their financial condition. However, government interference in the free market dampens the profit motive to find new cures and techniques, and it encourages waste and graft.

★ Homosexual rights are more accepted by some today than they were when Clinton first proposed raising the ban on homosexuals in the military. Nationalized healthcare has also recently become popular within a segment of the American populace. Environmentalism, especially concern over global warming, has also increased in popularity.

Lady to be elected to the Senate. She was assigned to the following committees: Budget, Armed Services; Environment and Public Works; and Health, Education, Labor, and Pensions. In 2008 she lost her bid to become president. However, President Obama appointed her to serve as Secretary of State.

was so bad that it moved ahead of the economy as Americans' greatest concern. The country wanted action.

The Contract with America

Newt Gingrich, an outspoken Republican representative from Georgia, came up with a plan to help his party win in the 1994 midterm elections. House Republicans united to sign a **Contract with America**. They promised that, if elected, they would introduce ten popular bills in the first one hundred days of the next Congress.

As the numbers came in on election night, analysts were astounded. For the first time in forty years, voters handed control of the House to the Republicans. The margin was a comfortable 230–204 (with one independent). The GOP also won control of the Senate (52–48) and most governorships.

The newly elected Republicans knew that voters wanted results. Gingrich was elected Speaker of the House. He moved quickly to put his supporters in positions of power. By overlooking senior congressmen, he proved his dedication to renew Congress and to push through his conservative program.

New Senate majority leader Bob Dole, like his colleagues in the Senate, had not signed the Contract with America. He did not feel obligated to support it.

Realizing that his first actions would set the tone of the next two years, Gingrich set to work right away fulfilling the Contract. On the very first day, the congressmen passed all eight of the promised reforms in the way the House ran. For example, one reform required Congress to obey the regulations that it had imposed on the rest of the nation.

The rest of the session was no less hectic because, in addition to the operational reforms, the Contract promised that representatives would bring up for a vote ten specific bills in the first hundred days. The three most important bills would have radically changed the balance of power established by the Constitution. Two were amendments to the Constitution. The **balanced budget amendment** would make Congress balance the budget by 2002. The term limits amendment would limit congressmen to twelve years of office in each house of Congress. The third major bill instituted the **line-item veto**. It gave the president the right to cut individual items in the federal budget without approval from Congress.

The House pushed the Contract energetically. The line-item veto passed the House and Senate with ease. (The Supreme Court later declared the law unconstitutional.) The term limits bill got a majority of votes but not the two-thirds it needed. The balanced budget amendment passed in the House but failed in the Senate by only one vote. All of the other bills in the Contract passed the House in some form.

But the initial success of the House was mostly symbolic. The bills still had to go to the Senate and be signed by the president. The only bill that actually became law was a restriction on future unfunded mandates. The greatest test of the Republican Congress was its effort to prepare a serious plan to balance the budget. Gingrich acknowledged that every other issue was secondary to balancing the budget by 2002.

Georgia congressman Newt Gingrich masterminded a powerful conservative movement by promoting the Contract with America.

for his return, none of which have materialized, forcing them to change the date repeatedly.

Section II
Objectives

Students should be able to

1. Identify Newt Gingrich and describe the Contract with America.
2. Identify the budget battle that shut down the government.
3. Analyze the effectiveness of the "Republican Revolution."

Election Overturn

As a result of the 1994 elections, Republican governors headed eight of the nine largest states. (Florida was the only exception.) One closely watched shift in American politics was the breakdown of the Democrats' "Solid South." For the first time since Reconstruction, southerners elected a Republican majority to Congress.

This breakdown of the Solid South had begun during the early sixties as southerners became increasingly disgruntled with the spread of liberalism among the Democrats. George Wallace's third party campaign for president in 1968 accentuated that conservative bent. Nixon's "Southern Strategy" turned it to the advantage of the Republicans in 1968 and 1972. Reagan solidified the South behind Republicans.

Newt Gingrich

Gingrich's political career began in 1989, when he was elected to the U.S. House of Representatives. He served in the House for the next twenty years. From 1989 to 1995, he was the Minority Whip. In 1995, he became the first Republican Speaker

Debate Idea

Have your students discuss and/or debate the following proposition: Resolved, that Congress should be required to run the country on a balanced budget.

Can Congress Lead a Revolution?

Throughout this chapter, ask the students to recall parallels from U.S. history to help them understand the dynamics of recent events. Can they think of other times that Congress and the president were at odds over the future direction of the country? Was Congress ever able to overcome presidential opposition and take control of the direction of the nation? (*Consider the Radical Republicans of the middle-to-late 1860s,*

who eventually won a two-thirds majority in Congress because of Johnson's obstinacy.)

Activity 2: Contract with America

Use this activity to help the students understand the contents of the Contract with America and how the newly elected Republicans in Congress went about their "revolution" by addressing each of their pledges in that contract during their first one hundred days in office.

of the House since 1928, and he served in that position until he retired in 1999. He was famous for his firmly conservative views and his straightforward, often blunt, speaking. He was fined $300,000 in 1997 for ethics violations concerning the proceeds of one of his books. He has written numerous books, including several novels.

Welfare Reform Act

The Welfare Reform Act changed the welfare system in six ways.

1. Aid to Families with Dependent Children would no longer be an entitlement. Instead, states would have the freedom to set their own eligibility standards and the level of assistance.

2. Welfare recipients would have a five-year lifetime limit on assistance (with exceptions for "severe hardship").

3. Over a seven-year period, states were to require at least half of their single-parent recipients to work at least thirty hours a week.

4. States would be awarded additional funds for reducing illegitimacy. Underage mothers could receive benefits only if they lived in an adult-supervised household and attended high school.

5. The definition of "disabled" children whose parents would qualify for additional cash payments was tightened.

6. Immigrants would not receive welfare assistance until they had been five years in residence. In addition, states would have the option of reforming the way in which Medicaid benefits were given to noncitizens.

Budget Battles

In February 1995, Clinton presented a $1.6 trillion budget. The House drafted an alternative plan that balanced the budget. The Democrats condemned the Republicans as "extremists" who wanted to balance the budget at the expense of the elderly and the poor.

Clinton vetoed the thirteen Republican spending bills passed by Congress. The summer wore on without a budget agreement. Under the Constitution, the federal government can spend money only when Congress has approved it by law. If the government failed to pay its debts, it would wreak havoc on world finances. Both the president and Congress hoped that the other side would accept a compromise before a shutdown was necessary.

As a shutdown loomed in November 1995, the Senate leaders passed a "continuing resolution" to keep the government running under the old budget. The House demanded some cuts first, and the president vetoed the resolution. As a result, all nonessential government services, such as parks, shut down. For six days, the Treasury Department juggled money to pay the government's bills, but it could not keep up for long. The House finally agreed to a compromise, but not until the president signed a pledge to seek a balanced budget in seven years.

The House rejected Clinton's next budget proposal, and the government shut down again just before Christmas. The Senate agreed to a compromise that ended the shutdown and undercut the conservative Republicans in the House. Clinton won the battle for popular opinion, and the Republican Revolution never recovered.

Clinton Moves Toward the Center

Though the Republican Revolution failed to enact most of its policy initiatives, it did force President Clinton to move toward the center on several issues. Republicans also managed to get some of what they wanted through compromise. They agreed to an increase in the minimum wage in exchange for $21 billion in tax cuts over the next decade.

The Republican Congress wanted to overhaul the federal welfare system. Clinton had made a campaign pledge in 1992 to "end welfare as we know it." With the 1996 election looming, he was finally ready to work with Republicans. He signed the **Welfare Reform Act** in 1995. For the first time since FDR's New Deal, the government rolled back its financial aid for the poor. The law required welfare recipients to go back to work within two years and set a lifetime cap of five years for assistance. The law also gave states greater freedom to spend the federal welfare money as they chose. Democrats attacked Clinton for abandoning core principles of the party, but a decade later even liberals acknowledged the success of this reform.

During this time Republicans pushed for tougher sentencing of criminals and a stricter enforcement of the death penalty. Efforts on the state and local levels were successful in reducing crime in the late 1990s.

Section Quiz

1. What did the Contract with America promise?

2. What were the three most important bills of the Contract? Name one that passed both the House and the Senate.

Section Quiz Answers

1. to bring up ten popular bills for a vote in the first one hundred days of the next Congress

2. balanced budget amendment, term limits amendment, line-item veto; line-item veto

3. How did President Clinton respond to the Republican Revolution?

★ Why was the Welfare Reform Act in 1995 a significant victory for reducing big government?

III. Culture Wars

The conflicts that Clinton faced in his first term indicated a much deeper conflict going on in the nation. For decades the United States had been increasing in diversity. By 1990, 32 million Americans lived in homes where something other than English was spoken. It was also remarkable how many citizens considered themselves "hyphenated Americans." Many Arab-Americans, Asian-Americans, and Latino-Americans insisted that being American did not alter what they had been before coming to the United States. Diversity was not new to American culture. What was different was how the diversity was viewed.

The American Salad Bowl

In the past America had been known as a melting pot of nations. People from around the world would come to America, conform themselves to an American way of thinking about life, and then would take part in American culture. Now, however, the conforming was cut out of the process. The result, as many people noted, was that the American melting pot had become the American salad bowl. No longer did it seem best to have a single American culture. Very different people (with very different views) should work side by side in American culture and society.

The difficulty of making this grand dream work became obvious in the 1990s. The problem was not that some Americans came from other parts of the world. The problem had to do with worldviews. A **worldview** is a set of beliefs that a person uses to look at the world and interpret it. Worldviews are used to answer questions like Where did the world come from?, Is there a God?, What is good?, and What happens to humans when they die? Different worldviews answer these questions differently. People with different worldviews have great difficulty working together on addressing the problems of a society because they cannot agree on what is good for that society.

Even though the salad bowl imagery was used to describe this new diversity, the reality was more like salad dressing. American culture was not divided among six or seven competing viewpoints. America instead became a "fifty-fifty nation"—an oil and vinegar mixture of multiculturalists and cultural conservatives.

Multiculturalism

The belief that different cultures should exist side by side without one leading the others is called **multiculturalism**. Many Americans insisted that because the nation was very diverse, multiculturalism was the only belief that could protect the liberties of all. For such people, the ethnic, religious, and moral diversity of America was not a difficulty to be managed. It was a strength to be celebrated.

Some of the leading supporters of this viewpoint were teachers on college campuses. These teachers attacked Western culture (the culture produced by the nations of Europe over the past two thousand years). They believed that Western culture had been poisoned

House Reforms

These are the eight reforms that the 104th Congress passed on its first day:

1. Require Congress to obey the laws and regulations that it has imposed on the rest of the nation.

2. Hire an independent auditor to uncover waste, fraud, or abuse in Congress.

3. Cut committee staffs by one-third and eliminate three full committees and twenty-five subcommittees.

4. Limit the terms of committee chairmen to six years; limit the term of the Speaker to eight years.

5. Ban proxy votes by absent committee members.

6. Open committee meetings to the public.

7. Require a three-fifths majority to increase taxes.

8. Use honest budget figures that do not adjust for inflation (zero base-line budgeting).

Section III
Objectives

Students should be able to

1. Assess the impact of diversity in American culture in the 1990s.

2. Analyze the multiculturalist worldview and illustrate the impact of this viewpoint on American culture.

3. Analyze the conservative worldview and illustrate the impact of this viewpoint on American culture.

4. Evaluate the multiculturalism and cultural conservatism of the 1990s.

---

3. At first he opposed the legislation in the Contract with America, but later he moved toward the center on a number of issues in order to improve his chances of being reelected in 1996.

★ It was the first time since the New Deal that government aid to the poor had been rolled back.

Christian Worldview

Teachers who wish to learn more about worldview should consult David K. Naugle's *Worldview: The History of a Concept.* Helpful treatments of the Christian worldview include *Creation Regained* by Al Wolters and *The Transforming Vision* by Brian J. Walsh and J. Richard Middleton.

Discuss Parallels with the Twenties

Discuss parallels between the nineties and the Roaring Twenties. Note that evil is not a new thing, and in some ways things might have been worse then than they are now.

Time Travel

Have the students imagine that politicians during the 1960s could go forward in time to the 1990s to see the results of their programs. What might have happened to the War on Poverty and other programs if Congress and the president had enjoyed such an opportunity?

Politicians should try to anticipate or forecast the long-term results of their policies. (After all, construction companies are required to prepare environmental impact statements for construction projects to determine how their work will affect the physical environment. Why not have politicians do a similar assessment of how their policies will affect the economic and social environment?) How does knowledge of history help politicians make wise forecasts? Should the politicians in the 1960s have been able to forecast the failure of their programs? If so, how?

What is a Worldview?

The *American Heritage Dictionary* defines a worldview as "the overall perspective from which one sees and interprets the world; a collection of beliefs about life and the universe held by an individual or group." To this definition should be added the idea of narrative. According to David Naugle, a worldview is made up of stories that give meaning to human experience and enable people to interpret the world around them (*Worldview, the History of a Concept*, 229-230). A secular humanist orients his thinking by the story of evolution. A Christian orients himself by Scripture: (1) God made the world for His own glory; (2) God has allowed this world to fall into a broken condition because of human sin; and (3) God is working to redeem this world to Himself through His Son.

In reflecting on this concept, three observations become apparent. First, all human thinking is ultimately based on faith. The difference between the secularist and the Christian is not that the secularist lives by evidence and the Christian lives by faith. Both live by faith. The secularist has his faith ultimately in human reason and science. The Christian has his faith ultimately in God and His Word.

Second, competing worldviews drive humans apart. An evolutionary worldview cannot be harmonized with a Christian worldview. If one attempts to make these worldviews agree, the result is something that is not evolutionary, or is not Christian, or is not a worldview. So long as human communities are committed to being defined by their worldviews, these communities will not be able to join together.

Third, it is difficult for people with different worldviews to talk to one another. Equally intelligent and informed people

Rush Limbaugh's no-nonsense conservative message propelled him to become the most popular talk-show host in America.

Preachers Jerry Falwell and Pat Robertson were not only leaders of the "Religious Right" but also lightning rods for liberal criticism.

Government programs for public education increased under Clinton, especially those associated with the Goals 2000 initiative.

by ideas and values taken from the Christian religion. These ideas and values, they insisted, had been used by white males to oppress the rest of the world. In order to encourage tolerance, these teachers deemphasized the literature and history of the West and emphasized instead the cultures of Africa, Asia, and South America.

Much of what the multiculturalists said did not become popular away from college campuses. However, their emphasis on tolerance did become very popular, especially among public-school teachers and liberal Democrats. In the 1990s, history and literature classes in public schools changed to reflect some of the thinking of this philosophy. Also, liberal Democrats became very vocal about certain controversial issues. In the interest of encouraging tolerance, they supported homosexual rights, abortion, feminism, and environmentalism. They also sought fewer restrictions on pornography, more restrictive gun-control laws, and more laws that excluded participation between church and state.

Cultural Conservatism

As multiculturalism grew in influence, economic conservatives joined forces with religious conservatives and together became active in the Republican Party. These cultural conservatives believed that the United States was in decline and needed to be restored to its traditional values. Economic conservatives saw government funding of abortion and environmentalism to be a waste of the taxpayers' money. Religious conservatives saw the liberal agenda as government promotion of wickedness.

A major factor in spreading the conservative message was conservative talk radio. Rush Limbaugh led the way. His message connected with cultural conservatives, and they were active politically. His success encouraged other conservative talk show hosts, both nationally and locally. Liberals did not like having competition for the traditional media, which tended to support the liberal agenda.

The religious conservatives were called the **Religious Right**. Its Christian leaders and organizations believed that the country should return to the Judeo-Christian principles that had guided the nation in the past. The Religious Right became a significant force in the 1970s, when religious conservatives were seeking a way to respond to the *Roe v. Wade* decision of the Supreme Court. At that time, its best-known organization was the Moral Majority, headed by Baptist preacher Jerry Falwell.

The Religious Right faded somewhat during the 1980s. But it was rejuvenated in the 1990s. Clinton's liberal social policies and the aggressive agenda of multiculturalism together drove many Christians into political involvement. Pat Robertson, the host of television's *700 Club* started a grassroots organization called the **Christian Coalition**. Under the leadership of Ralph Reed, the organization was very successful. Members sought to elect conservatives to local offices and school boards. They wanted to restore America from the ground up.

Specific Issues

One specific issue during the culture war of the 1990s concerned public education. While costs increased, student performance declined. In his 1997 State of the Union Address, Clinton said, "My number one priority as president for the next four years is to ensure that Americans have the best education in the world." One of his

Religion and Politics

Explain the impact of the new wave of immigration—newcomers from Asia and Latin America—on religious diversity in America. It is interesting to note that religious differences usually carry over into political differences. Help the students to identify the major religious groups in your region (and across the country), and explain the diversity of political views evident among them.

Discuss the Modern Generation

Ask the students to summarize the features of "modern culture" that differ from any period in America's past. Challenge them to explain events and trends that gave rise to those features of modern culture. (*Possible*

answers include the corrupting power of "pop culture" [such as MTV], the commercialization of professional sports, and the rising power of the media.)

Your students may not realize that the modern television ratings were a direct result of the culture wars in the 1990s. Conservatives complained about sex and violence on television, and Clinton responded by supporting government oversight of the industry. In fear of losing their freedom, television executives decided to regulate themselves. Ironically, many conservatives scoffed at the value of their new ratings, arguing that they would actually worsen the situation. Their warning proved true. The television producers believed that as long as they labeled the of-

fensive elements in their programs they had no more restraints or responsibility.

primary initiatives was **Goals 2000**. It set up a new program of voluntary standards that states must meet to get federal funds.

Conservative Republicans believed that states and local communities should handle education and most other social issues, as they had since the founding of our nation. Religious conservatives were concerned that Goals 2000 would require all schools to accept the agenda of multiculturalism. Because of these concerns, Congress took out some parts of Goals 2000 before passing it into law.

Through the efforts of cultural conservatives, support grew for different solutions to the problems in education. One of the most popular ideas was **educational vouchers**. Instead of dictating where students would attend school, the government would give parents vouchers (or scholarships). They could use them at any school of their choice. But leaders in public education fought the voucher system. They saw it as a threat to the monopoly that public schools had over education.

Abortion was another key issue in the culture war. Republicans passed a series of bills on serious social issues. Perhaps the most important was a ban on **partial birth abortions**. President Clinton, however, vetoed the bill.

A third issue concerned homosexuality. Liberals argued that not letting homosexuals marry violated homosexuals' civil rights. But cultural conservatives still found homosexual behavior immoral, and conservative Christians believed it was sinful. Republicans in Congress responded by producing a bill called the **Defense of Marriage Act**. The bill stated that the federal government would not recognize any homosexual union as a marriage. It further said that even if one state recognized homosexual marriage, the other states were not required to do so. The bill moved easily through both houses of Congress. On September 21, 1996, the president signed it into law. This issue, however, was far from over.

Evaluating the Culture Wars

Both sides in the culture wars of the 1990s had significant flaws. The multiculturalists believed that their view of tolerance was just another way of talking about the American value of liberty. But hidden in their tolerance talk was an agenda of oppression. They said that women must be free to choose what to do with their unborn children. But this meant that some Americans should die for the convenience of other Americans. They insisted that homosexuals should be treated the same way as heterosexuals. But this meant that those who believed homosexuality was a sin would need to give up many of their liberties so that the liberties of homosexuals might be protected. They also insisted that the role of women in society must be radically altered so that men and women would both have the same opportunities. But this meant that many children would not have the care and concern of their mothers.

Multiculturalists made freedom the most important American value. However, if freedom is the liberty to pursue one's own desires without fear of disapproval or rejection, then a free society is a shattered society. Such a society will fall apart when faced with a major hardship. For a nation to be unified and strong, it must value goodness above liberty.

Conservatives also had several problems. Some of the leaders did not live up to the values they proclaimed. Some got caught up in Washington politics and compromised their principles. Voters were

As problems in public schools multiplied, the popularity of homeschooling increased.

President Clinton had promised to make abortions safe and rare, but he vetoed the bill banning partial-birth abortions.

can talk for hours without making progress. For progress to be made, people have to agree to change their perspective and look at the evidence and the arguments through someone else's worldview. Few people are willing to do this, and many who are willing still have difficulty learning from the experience.

Goals 2000

Under Goals 2000, nineteen secular educators, appointed by the president, would run the powerful new National Educational Standards and Improvement Council (NESIC). Like a national school board, NESIC began developing national standards for curriculum and testing. After the NESIC released the first series of curriculum standards, critics noted that the U.S. history standards contained nineteen negative references to the anti-Communist Joseph McCarthy but did not mention such figures as Paul Revere and Thomas Edison. "They make it sound as if everything in America is wrong and grim," complained Lynne Cheney. The Senate voted 99-1 to condemn the standards. The new Republican Congress dismantled NESIC and other controversial elements of Goals 2000.

Even without the biases of Goals 2000, public school students are still being influenced by the politically correct information their schools are teaching. For example, the February 4, 2008, *USA Today* reported the results of a survey of 2,000 high school juniors and seniors, who were asked to name the ten most famous Americans. Their list included such people as Marilyn Monroe and Oprah Winfrey but *no* presidents, not even George Washington. Benjamin Franklin and Martin Luther King Jr. were the only political figures named.

quick to replace them at the next election when promises were not kept. Others became involved in financial and moral scandals. Conservative voters lost no time punishing those who failed in these and other areas.

Communications Technology

Communication became an obsession in the last part of the twentieth century. More people were exchanging more information at faster rates than ever before. Drivers took their phones with them in their cars. Important documents crossed the country instantly through fax machines. Cable and satellite subscribers had hundreds of television channels to watch. And people carried pagers for both business and personal use.

Possibly the greatest change in communications was the introduction of the Internet, a system that allows computers to share information over phone lines or cables. Government researchers developed the Internet in 1969 to connect computer scientists and engineers working on military projects. Large universities and research companies soon joined up. For several years, government and education kept the Internet to themselves, and the system was difficult to use. But two developments changed the Internet into an information highway for the entire nation.

The first development was the creation of tools for finding information. Regardless of how much data it held, the Internet would not be valuable without a practical way to look up a topic. Two tools helped organize the Internet. Browsers allowed users to view documents easily, and hypertext joined together documents on related topics through underlined words or phrases. (The researcher could use his mouse to click on one of the underlined portions and be taken to a document on that subject.)

The second development was a change of control. Though the government had developed the concept of the Internet, it gradually stepped back and let private companies take leadership. The Internet developed from a center for professional research and communication into a marketplace and a high-tech post office. Advertisements popped up along with information; consumers made on-line purchases with their credit cards (yearly sales were estimated to grow from $272 million in 1993 to $108 billion ten years later); and people from all over sent personal notes via e-mail or joined strangers in "chat room" discussions.

The Internet has become a growing part of American life, and Christians, like others, are trying to determine how to deal with it. They do not want to miss the opportunity to influence large numbers of people easily. At the same time the Internet can be dangerous. Large amounts of ungodly material confront the user (though tools to block objectionable sites are available), and Internet browsing can waste a great deal of time. So how should a Christian handle the Internet? Whether on the Internet or off, the key is to follow Ephesians 5:15-16: "See then that ye walk circumspectly, not as fools, but as wise, Redeeming the time, because the days are evil."

Section Quiz

1. How was American diversity different in the 1990s?
2. Why did multiculturists on college campuses oppose Western culture?

Special Speaker on Computer Technology

Have a special speaker talk about advances in computer technology. He or she could also discuss ways that computers might be used in the future and how those advances will change our lives.

The Information Age

Many sociologists have begun comparing the impact of the computer age (or "Information Age") to the impact of the Industrial Revolution. Review the changes to American culture that followed the rise of industry and cities. Is it likely that computers could have a similar impact on daily life? Discuss how computers could one day change everyday patterns at home and work. Computers are even changing politics; politicians are able to make direct contact with more of their constituents and supporters. You may want to refer to Neil Postman's *Technopoly* as a thoughtful approach to using technology.

Activity 3: What the Bible Says About Modern Issues

Use this activity to help the students examine current issues in the "culture wars" from a biblical perspective. Help the students understand that although government cannot change hearts, laws should still be designed to reward the good and punish evildoers (Romans 13:1–4).

Section Quiz Answers

1. Instead of a nation of diverse peoples who shared common values, America became a nation of many peoples with many different value systems.

2. They believed that Western culture had been poisoned by ideas and values taken from the Christian religion. These ideas and values, they insisted, had been used by white males to oppress the rest of the world.

3. What U.S. Supreme Court case played a key role in the formation of the Religious Right?

4. What are three specific issues that were key in the culture wars?

5. What two problems hindered conservatives in the culture wars?

★ How did the agenda of multiculturalism demonstrate the problem of making freedom the most important American value?

IV. Domestic Difficulties of the Second Term

After the Democrats lost the 1994 midterm elections, Clinton began raising money to win in 1996. His party covered the nation with costly television ads. During the campaign, he spent more money on advertising than any other candidate in history. But his reelection did not end his problems.

The 1996 Election

Clinton ran a brilliant campaign. He focused on a few important ideas and avoided controversies. He presented himself as a New Democrat. "The era of big government is over," he said. Rather than present his own programs, he let others attack him on both sides—the liberals on the left and the "radical" Republicans on the right.

Bob Dole ran as a moderate Republican but failed to convince the voters that he would change things for the better.

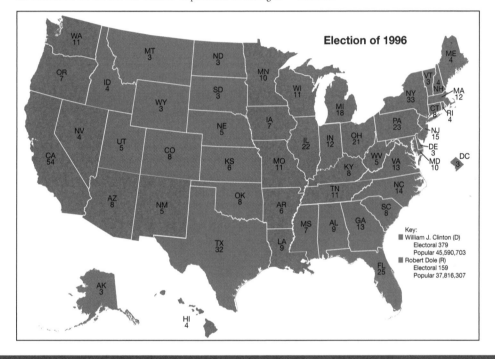

Election of 1996

Key:
■ William J. Clinton (D)
Electoral 379
Popular 45,590,703
■ Robert Dole (R)
Electoral 159
Popular 37,816,307

Section IV
Objectives
Students should be able to

1. Evaluate the budget deal of 1997.

2. List the scandals of the Clinton administration.

3. Analyze the results of the impeachment proceedings.

4. Compare and contrast the impeachments of Johnson and Clinton.

Balanced Budgets

A national budget is said to be balanced when its government expenditures equal its revenues. A surplus occurs when the government receives in tax revenues more than it spends (which means that it is taxing the people too much). A deficit (debt) occurs when the government either spends too much or the country experiences a sharp economic decline that reduces tax revenues.

The "budget battles" actually began with the first presidential administration. Alexander Hamilton, the first secretary of the treasury, thought that having a national debt was good for the country. Thomas Jefferson, on the other hand, thought it was bad.

According to the Heritage Foundation, the annual federal budget in 1997 was eighteen times larger than that in 1960. Government spending (adjusted for inflation) is now three times greater than in 1960. In that year, the per capita expenditure was $510; today it is $1,600. Between 1960 and 1998, the budget was balanced only twice. The national debt rocketed from $237 billion in 1960 to $3.9 trillion. The share of the national debt for each person is

3. *Roe v. Wade*

4. education reform, abortion, and the definition of marriage

5. Their leaders did not always live up to the values they said they supported. They often got caught up in Washington politics and compromised their principles.

★ If freedom is the liberty to pursue one's own desires without fear of disapproval or rejection, then a free society is a shattered society. For a society to function, humans must work together. And for humans to work together, they must agree on what is good, just, and right.

Debate Ideas

Have your students discuss and/or debate the following propositions:

• The Social Security system should be abolished.

• The welfare state undermines the work ethic.

• Education vouchers would improve education in America.

CD: Electoral College Results, 1996

Refer to the CD for a map showing the results of Electoral College voting in the 1996 presidential election.

$14,450. The interest alone on the national debt today is $240 billion a year.

Most Investigated President in History

At least eleven committees in Congress planned to investigate some aspect of President Clinton's scandals during the first year of his second term. He earned the dubious distinction of being "the most investigated president in history."

The Reform Party's First Governor

Ross Perot converted his campaign organization into a third party known as the Reform Party. In 1998, a Reform Party gubernatorial candidate won an upset victory in Minnesota, defeating strong candidates from both major parties. Jesse "the Body" Ventura was a former pro wrestler who liked to wear outlandish clothes and to speak his mind on his libertarian social policies, such as the legalization of drugs and prostitution. He also made disparaging remarks about organized religion.

More on Impeachment

Some people thought that the honorable thing for the president to do during the impeachment trial was to resign, as Nixon had done. More than a third of the newspapers in the country called for his resignation, realizing that it was dangerous for the nation to be led by a dishonest man that neither allies nor enemies of the nation could respect. But Clinton vowed to remain in office to the last day of his term.

Clinton's own friends in the Senate prepared a censure statement that described his relationship with Lewinsky as "shameful, reckless, and indefensible." Democrats further warned that his conduct "creates

Super Tuesday

The term Super Tuesday is used to refer to the day in February or March in presidential years when the greatest number of states hold their presidential preference primaries or party caucuses. In 2008, Super Tuesday was February 5, when 24 states had primaries or caucuses. Fifty-two percent of the pledged Democrat delegates were selected that day; 41 percent of the Republican delegates were at stake.

Susan McDougal chose to go to prison for contempt of court rather than testify against the Clintons in the Whitewater scandal.

He wanted Americans to see him as a moderate they could trust. He also used the "bully pulpit" of the presidency to push small, popular reforms. Those included recommending school uniforms and reducing smoking by teens.

Republicans had no clear candidate to run against Clinton. President George H. W. Bush was not interested in running again. Pat Buchanan ran from the conservative side of the Republican party and won early primaries in several states. Senate Majority Leader **Bob Dole** of Kansas also ran. He was a pragmatist like George Bush. During Dole's many years in the Senate, he had made many friends. His political connections made it easy for him to raise money and to win the nomination. He quickly overtook Buchanan and swept every state from Super Tuesday on.

Despite his Senate experience and political connections, Dole also had several disadvantages. His sharp tongue alienated some voters. His age (over seventy) counted against him. More importantly, Dole failed to express a clear vision for America's future. Dole focused the campaign on concerns about Clinton's character. Republicans highlighted reports of Clinton's moral failings and allegations of improper fund-raising (including illegal contributions from China). This focus failed to resonate with the majority of Americans.

For months, the media had predicted that Clinton would win by a landslide. But when the votes were finally tallied, Clinton received 49 percent to Dole's 41 percent. Ross Perot, who again ran as an independent, got 8 percent. The races for Congress were close, but the Republicans held on to their majority.

Balanced Budget

Both the Republican Congress and President Clinton desired to balance the federal budget. After weeks of talks, the president and Congress hammered out a compromise. Unlike the 104th Congress, the new Congress did not propose to eliminate any major government programs or departments. In fact, spending for the Department of Education jumped 34 percent in the first year of the new budget plan.

The booming economy made the budget deal possible. At the last moment, the Congressional Budget Office found $225 billion in unexpected money.

The budget deal created the first surplus in thirty years. However, this surplus was possible only because the government included income from Social Security taxes, although that money was supposed to be set aside to pay future retirement costs. The "surplus" completely changed the debates in Washington. No longer did representatives argue about spending cuts; the question became how to spend the extra money.

Scandals of the Clinton Presidency

In 1992, Clinton had promised that his presidency would be "the most ethical administration in the history of the Republic." But scandals hurt his party in both the 1994 and 1996 elections. These scandals only grew during Clinton's second term.

One scandal involved his past investment in a resort in northeastern Arkansas, called Whitewater Development Corporation. The **Whitewater scandal** was a complicated web of questionable relationships between politicians, law firms, and businessmen while Clinton was governor of Arkansas. More than a dozen people pleaded guilty

Budget Battles Today

Update the students on the latest budget battles in Congress. (Or ask them to bring in articles concerning the budget.) Ask them to find the periods in American history when the budget was the focus of national politics. Although economic issues might loom large in our day, we know that other issues are likely to take their place in the future, just as they have in the past. What issues do the students foresee replacing the economy and the budget? (*Answers might include various aspects of the war on terror, privacy issues, and moral and cultural decline.*)

Compare Clinton's Scandals to Scandals of the Past

Compare and contrast the social conditions in America during past scandals and the social conditions surrounding Clinton's scandals. Note that the Grant scandals occurred during the Gilded Age, and the Harding scandals occurred during the Roaring Twenties, both periods that were characterized by great moral declension. Is it true that the president is often a reflection of the times? Evaluate how other presidents, beginning with Washington, reflected the strengths and weaknesses of their generations.

to various crimes in the scandal. The most embarrassing confession came from Webster Hubbell, a former law partner with Hillary Clinton and a Clinton appointee to a high position in the Justice Department.

Another scandal surfaced in 1996. The White House had obtained confidential files from the FBI on hundreds of Republicans. The president called the incident an innocent mistake, but Filegate embarrassed the administration.

Another scandal involved the way Democrats—and the president in particular—had raised funds for the 1996 campaign. For instance, Clinton rewarded big donors to his campaign with meals and coffees at the White House as well as overnight stays in the Lincoln Bedroom.

Clinton was also damaged by reports that some of the campaign money had come from questionable sources. The Democratic Party promised to return more than $1.5 million. One of the fundraisers, John Huang, later told investigators that China had contributed to the president's campaign indirectly through Asian companies. The Clinton administration was further embarrassed by reports that China had bought American computer and missile technology that they used to improve the accuracy of their long-range nuclear missiles.

Impeachment of the President

One scandal led to Clinton's impeachment. It came from an unexpected source. Paula Jones, a former beauty queen from Arkansas, sued him in 1994 for sexual harassment—and she had witnesses. The president raised more than a million dollars for a legal defense fund. He used the money to delay the case until after his 1996 reelection. He appealed to the Supreme Court, claiming that his duties as president gave him special privileges to avoid such trials while in office. But he lost his appeal in 1997.

The trial attracted much publicity. Defense attorneys called many witnesses to testify about the president's character. During the trial investigators discovered that Clinton may have committed adultery with White House intern Monica Lewinsky and that he may have

Clinton's entire political career had been clouded by alleged affairs, and they almost ended his presidency when affairs with Paula Jones and Monica Lewinsky were made public.

Kenneth Starr's investigation produced evidence that led to the impeachment of the president.

disrespect for laws of the land; ... brought shame and dishonor to himself and to the office of the president; [and] violated the trust of the American people."

"High Crimes and Misdemeanors"

Representatives in Congress never resolved the most fundamental question related to the Clinton trial: Did his conduct fall under the definition of "impeachable offenses" given in the Constitution? Conservative constitutional scholars explained the terms based on the context of the day in which they were written. In British legal tradition (from which the United States got the concept of impeachment), "high crimes" refers to crimes in high office, not to "big" crimes as opposed to "little" crimes. The word *misdemeanors* refers to "bad behavior," not to the modern concept of lesser crimes. Liberals defined the terms as they might be used in modern usage.

Republicans Vindicated

The Republicans were vindicated in their actions in the impeachment when the judge in the Paula Jones case held the president in contempt of court for lying and obstructing justice, fining him a large sum of money. Clinton was later disbarred. The judge's decision was the first of its kind against a president.

 CD: Key Figures in the Clinton Impeachment

Refer to the CD for photos of the key figures in the Clinton impeachment.

America's Two Impeachments

With the students, contrast America's two impeachments. Unlike Clinton, Andrew Johnson was not elected president—he succeeded to the presidency when Lincoln was assassinated. Johnson's subsequent impeachment resulted from a political power struggle rather than any criminal conduct or moral misbehavior.

Is the Constitution Working Properly?

A popular question during the impeachment and trial was "Is the Constitution working?" Supporters of the president argued that the Constitution was never meant to be used as a political weapon to bring down an opponent. Others said that the process was successful because the embarrassment would force future presidents to avoid conduct similar to that of President Clinton, regardless of whether such conduct leads to removal from office.

It is interesting to note that the founders' original design for impeachment was ruined by the direct election of senators. The founders intended that the trial be held by

men who were not influenced by the whims of public opinion. Originally, senators were elected by the state legislatures and were therefore insulated from much of the public pressure that assails modern senators.

Activity 4: Ending the Welfare State Through the Power of Private Action

Use this reading activity to help the students understand the position that the best solution to the problem of poverty is not government welfare programs but private charitable efforts.

encouraged her to lie under oath about the matter. Clinton himself appeared on national television declaring his innocence.

A judge eventually dismissed the Jones case. But **Kenneth Starr**, the **independent counsel** who was investigating the Whitewater scandal for the Justice Department, received court approval to investigate the president. Secret audio tape recordings by a friend of Lewinsky later showed that she had lied and was covering up. After months of stalling, Clinton agreed to testify to the grand jury that was investigating him. During his testimony he admitted to wrongdoing with Lewinsky. Nonetheless, he maintained that nothing he had done was illegal.

Starr continued the investigation to determine whether Clinton had encouraged Lewinsky to lie. He sent the evidence to the House, listing thirteen impeachable offenses. Four articles of impeachment came to the floor of the House for a vote on December 19, 1998. Two of them passed. They claimed that the president had committed perjury (lied under oath) and obstructed justice (hidden evidence from a court). Clinton became only the second president to be impeached.

The Senate then tried the case. When it came time to vote, no Democrats voted in favor of the articles of impeachment. Robert Byrd, a senator from West Virginia, admitted on television that the evidence was clear, but he voted against conviction anyway. The Democrats argued that removal from office was too extreme a punishment. Several moderate Republican senators voted with the Democrats. But the majority of Republicans voted for conviction. The number of senators voting in favor of conviction fell below even a simple majority of 50. (The Constitution requires a two-thirds majority—67 of 100—to remove the president from office.)

During this time polls showed that 70 percent of Americans approved of the president's performance. However, polls also showed that respect for his character had fallen lower than respect for Nixon's during the Watergate scandal.

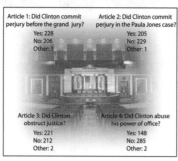

How the House of Representatives voted on the Articles of Impeachment

Section Quiz

1. What strategy did President Clinton use to win the 1996 election?

2. What scandal involved Bill Clinton's business investment in northeastern Arkansas?

3. What independent counsel presented evidence for Clinton's impeachment?

4. On what two counts was President Clinton impeached?

★ Why do you think so many people supported Clinton during his scandals?

V. Foreign Policy in the Clinton Administration

Clinton ran for office primarily on domestic policy. Though he initially had little interest in foreign policy, Clinton found avoiding international concerns impossible.

He hoped his foreign policy would shine during his second term. He selected a whole new team of foreign advisors. **Madeleine**

Madeleine Albright became the first female secretary of state under Clinton.

Section V

Objectives

Students should be able to

1. Identify the first female secretary of state.

2. Discuss Clinton's dealings with Communist countries.

3. Define *multilateralism*.

4. Explain changes to free trade under the Clinton administration.

Section Quiz Answers

1. Clinton let others attack him from both sides so that he could appear as someone in the middle whom Americans could trust.

2. Whitewater

3. Kenneth Starr

4. perjury and obstruction of justice

★ Answers will vary. Most Americans seem to have accepted the philosophy of moral relativism. Perhaps they also felt that it would be hypocritical to expect more of their leaders than they did of themselves. Others may have supported him for purely partisan political reasons (to keep the Republicans from winning a victory over a Democrat).

The Ripple Effect of Dishonesty

Explain to the students that all of the nations of the world closely follow events in the United States. Foreign leaders are constantly assessing the president of the United States to comprehend his personality, principles, and goals. Whenever a president makes a threat and keeps his word, as President Reagan did when he fired the air traffic controllers, it has a direct impact on foreign relations because foreigners know that president will keep his word and carry out his threats.

As the students read about President Clinton's administration, however, they should be alert to instances in which Clinton blustered and threatened but never acted consistently with those strong words. Ask them to consider how that influenced foreigners in their relations with the United States. Character *does* matter. Discuss also the current situation in America to find examples of leaders who keep their word or of those who cannot be trusted.

Albright, the first woman to serve as secretary of state, made an aggressive effort to solve the world's problems with the help of the U.S. military.

Challenges at the End of the Cold War

When Clinton assumed office, communism appeared to be in its death throes. Only five countries remained under its shadow. Two of these countries remained a potential military threat. But by failing to adopt a clear policy toward regions once dominated by communism, the president allowed a host of new dangers to take root.

Chinese Resurgence

After the fall of the Soviet Union, mainland China became the dominant Communist power in the world. During the 1992 election campaign, Clinton attacked Bush for keeping the Most Favored Nation (MFN) trade status with China despite its human rights abuses at Tiananmen Square and against Christians and dissenters. Once in office, however, Clinton renewed MFN status because of the prospects for enormous profits for American businesses in one of the world's fastest growing markets.

Though China was opening economically, it continued a massive buildup of arms and began to make threatening gestures toward America's friends in the Far East. One of the touchiest issues was the status of Taiwan. (China considers it a rebel province.) Clinton responded with a policy of "strategic ambiguity." Previous to this, the United States typically had made plain its intention to protect Taiwan, by force if necessary.

Nuclear Threats and North Korea

North Korea proved to be troublesome during the Clinton administration. In 1993, it threatened to withdraw from the **Non-Proliferation of Nuclear Weapons Treaty (NPT)**. Under that treaty, the five nations with nuclear weapons agreed to prevent any new countries from developing or buying such weapons. The other nations of the world agreed to the treaty only as long as they felt relatively safe. The development of a nuclear bomb in North Korea could touch off a nuclear arms race in Southeast Asia.

Clinton was urged by some to end North Korea's nuclear capabilities by a pre-emptive strike. However, Clinton chose a diplomatic route. The United States agreed to help North Korea build two nuclear power plants. In return, North Korea promised to stop trying to make nuclear weapons. Critics noted that the delay caused by the negotiations gave the North Koreans extra time to collect material to build nuclear weapons without giving any proof that the weapons program had stopped. These concerns proved to be justified when North Korea tested a nuclear device in 2006.

The NPT, first signed in 1968, came up for renewal in 1995. Fearing a new arms race, Clinton convinced many countries to make the treaty permanent. In return, the five declared nuclear powers—Russia, the United States, China, Britain, and France—promised to work harder to reduce their stockpiles. But some of the most dangerous countries in the world, such as Iran and Pakistan, refused to sign.

The United States around the World

When Clinton took office he adopted a policy of **multilateralism**—listening to many nations before making decisions with which every side could agree. Conservative Republicans accused him of

Clinton often met with Russia's president Boris Yeltsin to discuss the future of democracy in Russia.

Dangerous Changes in Taiwan

Taiwan created a furor when it held presidential elections in 1996, its first since the Nationalist government fled to the island after World War II. Hoping to intimidate Taiwan, China held war games in the Taiwan Strait, shooting test missiles toward the island.

Defense Secretary William Perry said the U.S. response "would depend on the circumstances." Former Reagan Defense Secretary Caspar Weinberger warned, "That kind of comment is an invitation to aggression." Since that time, the Communist Chinese have sought to influence Taiwanese elections, especially discouraging election of politicians who favor a hard line position regarding official independence of Taiwan from mainland China.

Identifying World Hot Spots

Point to a world map and ask the students to name the countries that are most often in the news and to explain why they are newsworthy. An alternative activity is to have students bring in newspaper pictures portraying American involvement in other countries. Post those pictures on the map beside the appropriate countries. Perhaps you can do some research and put a star over all the countries in which at least one thousand American troops are stationed.

Ask the students to explain why Christian citizens of this country should know about world geography and world history. (*They especially should know about the hot spots where the United States might become in-*volved *in the future.*) This activity helps to prepare the students for their study of geography in ninth grade.

Rise in Worldwide Terrorism

One positive development following the end of the Cold War was the release of the last Muslim-held hostages. Muslim extremists could no longer play superpower against superpower. Yet Islamic extremism remained a threat to international peace and security. Following the example of Iran, radical Muslims in every country hoped to win popular support and to take over their governments.

The United States and its friends became the focus of this terrorism. The worst Islamic attack on American soil to that point came on February 26, 1993, at the World Trade Center in New York City. Muslim radicals planted fifteen hundred pounds of explosives in a van parked in the complex's underground parking garage. The blast killed six, wounded one thousand others, and destroyed millions of dollars of property. The FBI moved swiftly to arrest the four men directly involved and indicted in absentia the ringleader, Ramzi Ahmed Yousef. Investigators uncovered another plot to bomb several other buildings and landmarks around New York City and to assassinate several political leaders. The men involved in both bombing conspiracies were followers of a religious leader named Sheik Omar Abdel Rahman. Years earlier, that radical cleric had been tried and acquitted in Egypt as a supporter of Anwar Sadat's assassination. Abdel Rahman surrendered to authorities in 1993 and was convicted in U.S. federal court in 1996.

Terrorists have attacked American forces in the Middle East also. On November 13, 1995, terrorists blew up a U.S. military building in Riyadh, Saudi Arabia, killing five Americans and two others. In May 1996, the Saudis beheaded the four men who confessed to the crime without let-

shirking his responsibilities. They preferred a policy of unilateralism—making decisions, alone if necessary, that were in America's national interest. With so many conflicting voices, the UN could not take timely action.

Somalia

In December 1992 President Bush had sent American troops to Somalia to help the UN protect aid shipments and to restore order. When the UN decided to disarm the warring factions, the most powerful "warlord," General Aidid, fought back. As more UN troops were killed, the UN and the United States began an unsuccessful effort to capture Aidid. Chief of Staff General Colin Powell requested tanks and heavy armament to protect his troops, but Secretary of Defense Les Aspin turned him down, fearing that it would be too provocative.

Clinton eventually sent U.S. Rangers (army specialists) to track down Aidid. But a raid that was to last only an hour turned into the largest firefight since Vietnam. The Somalians shot down a helicopter, captured the pilot, and dragged a soldier's body through the streets. The failed raid cost eighteen lives. As a result, Clinton ordered the withdrawal of American forces from the country.

From this point forward, Clinton was unwilling to commit U.S. troops to situations that could result in casualties. He preferred to use them in peacekeeping situations in which the fighting had already ceased. Muslim terrorists noted that America retreated quickly after sustaining casualties.

The Rise of Islamic Terrorism

Radical Islamic terrorists began expanding beyond the Middle East. In the 1990s, they made that painfully clear to the United States. Their targets were no longer just Israelis but also Americans. For example, on February 26, 1993, terrorists set off a car bomb on the lower level of Tower One of the World Trade Center in New York City. They wanted to make the tower collapse into Tower Two but failed. Nonetheless, six people were killed and more than one thousand were injured. In 1998, Muslim terrorists bombed the U.S. embassies in Tanzania and Kenya, killing more than four hundred people and injuring about four thousand. And on October 12, 2000, terrorists in a small boat approached the destroyer U.S.S. *Cole* as it refueled in Yemen. When they got alongside, they set off a bomb, killing seventeen sailors and injuring thirty-nine others. These attacks were only a foretaste of a much larger attack they would soon make on the United States. All of the attacks were connected to a new international terrorist group called **al-Qaeda**. It was led by a wealthy Saudi named **Osama bin Laden**.

Haiti

Haiti, a poverty-stricken Caribbean island, was another nation that concerned the Clinton administration. Haiti's military leaders decided to back out of negotiations to reinstate President **Jean-Bertrand Aristide**. They had overthrown him in a 1991 coup. For a year, Clinton repeatedly threatened armed intervention if the regime did not return to negotiations.

In the fall of 1994, Clinton ordered an invasion to put an end to the "most violent regime in our hemisphere." To minimize the necessity of military force, Clinton allowed a three-man team to negotiate with the head of Haiti's military rulers, Raoul Cedras. The

Jean-Bertrand Aristide returned to Haiti under U.S. protection in 1994, but he later was forced into exile.

Debate Isolationism and Interventionism

Christians should realize that America's well-being depends on the blessing of the Lord, not the devices of men (Isa. 31:1, 3). Honoring the Lord is the best foreign policy. Nevertheless, the students should choose sides on the issue of America's role in world affairs. Some debates about government are not necessarily issues of "right or wrong" but "strong or weak." Put the following list of arguments on the overhead. Then debate which is the strongest argument.

Arguments for isolationism:

1. "Entangling alliances" go against tradition.

2. Each country needs to defend itself.

3. America does not have the power to right every wrong.

4. Many of the countries America supports are corrupt and undemocratic.

5. America's involvement with NATO and the UN has not prevented wars.

6. Americans cannot impose their will on the rest of the world.

Arguments for interventionism:

1. America has close cultural ties to Europe.

2. The United States has an obligation to honor commitments made during the Cold War.

3. As the most powerful country, the United States is obligated to help the weak nations of the world.

4. America's businesses depend on open markets and free commerce.

5. Isolationism failed to prevent the United States from entering two world wars.

6. The spread of peace and free trade will help everyone.

negotiators—including former president Jimmy Carter—convinced Cedras to resign after assuring him of a generous reward.

Later, American troops handed the mission over to the UN. Clinton declared the mission a "remarkable success." Tragically, after the operation (which cost more than one billion dollars), Haiti remained a violent, poverty-stricken land.

NATO and Eastern Europe

The countries of Eastern Europe, fearing new Russian aggression, looked to the West for help. The expansion of NATO remained a touchy issue. Russian nationalists hated the thought of NATO troops at their doorstep. After years of talks, Russia signed a historic agreement in 1997 that gave it a voice in NATO. In return, Russia would allow Eastern European nations to join. In 1999, NATO admitted three new members—Poland, Hungary, and the Czech Republic.

After the Cold War, the most explosive region of the world was the Balkan Peninsula in Eastern Europe. It would provide NATO with its first post–Cold War task. The former Communist country of Yugoslavia had consisted of a complex variety of competing ethnic groups. It broke up into five countries.

A bitter civil war erupted in 1992 in Bosnia, one of the former Yugoslav republics. Three ethnic groups—Muslims, Serbs, and Croats—fought each other in a savage three-way war. The UN sent 23,000 peacekeepers, but they were powerless to stop the bloodshed. George H. W. Bush, who was president at the time, refused to commit American troops. During the 1992 election campaign, Clinton challenged him for not taking action to stop the "ethnic cleansing" (the systematic murder of ethnic minorities). But Clinton changed his position after he became president. For the next three years, he wavered between silence and threatening to bomb.

Meanwhile, American advisors secretly trained Croatian troops. Those troops launched a surprise attack in 1995. They drove out Serbs living in eastern Croatia and threatened Serbs living in Bosnia. Clinton sent U.S. jets to bomb the Serbs. As a result, the Serbs agreed to negotiations. In November 1995, Clinton invited the warring factions to meet in Dayton, Ohio. To encourage negotiations, he promised to send 20,000 American peacekeepers to Bosnia.

The warring leaders signed the **Dayton Accords**, and an uneasy peace settled over the Balkan Peninsula. The peace was uneasy because the new government in Bosnia would have two separate armies, two legislatures, and two courts. To avoid criticism, Clinton promised that U.S. troops would stay only "about one year." However, as of 2009, they were still there.

Air War in Kosovo

Though Clinton promised the involvement would be limited, U.S. involvement grew when rebels took up arms in Yugoslavia's southern province of Kosovo. Clinton demanded that Yugoslavia make peace with them or be bombed. When the Yugoslav government refused to back down, NATO forces bombed the country. It was the first time NATO had ever attacked a sovereign nation. After more than fifty days of bombing, the Yugoslav leader gave in. But by

An American crew readies a B-1 bomber for a bombing run over Yugoslavia.

U.S. Marines land in Greece on their way to the peacekeeping mission in Kosovo.

ting the FBI question them. One month later, a three-thousand-pound bomb in a truck killed nineteen American servicemen at their housing complex, Khobar Towers, near Dharan. The Saudis also failed to cooperate in the investigation of the Khobar bombing. Some observers thought that the Saudi government might be trying to hide its failure to protect the Americans from Syrian military officials it had allowed into the country. President Clinton suspected Iran in the Khobar blast.

Still further attacks occurred in Africa. On August 7, 1998, terrorists bombed U.S. embassies in Nairobi, Kenya, and Dar es Salaam, Tanzania, killing 258 and wounding more than 5,000. Those bombings seemed to be linked to wealthy Islamic radical Osama bin Laden. He reportedly sponsored an international network of terrorists that targeted the United States. The United States responded to the attacks with quick, decisive military action. On August 20, cruise missiles were launched both at a terrorism training center in Afghanistan and a pharmaceutical manufacturing facility in Khartoum, Sudan. The pharmaceutical facility was believed to be a manufacturing site for nerve gas. The United States chose a military response because of the lack of cooperation on terrorism it had been receiving and because of the need to deter further aggressive actions against American diplomatic facilities.

Compromise to Extend NATO

As part of its agreement with Russia, NATO promised that it had no "intention" of moving troops or nuclear weapons into Eastern Europe.

Updates on Countries

Ask the students to report on conditions in one of the countries mentioned in this chapter. In particular, ask for reports on countries in which the U.S. military has intervened, such as Somalia or Haiti.

Calendar Capers

Have the students design and make an illustrated calendar of events pertaining to our country's history or to events that center on a single theme. Divide the class into twelve groups. Post a list of events and the dates they occurred. Have each group illustrate one month with pictures of their own design or with prepared pictures. (Examples: individual presidents, authors, artists, composers, inventors, wars, etc.) Sources include historical almanacs and encyclopedias.

The American Ideal

Ask your students, "If you could make an ideal America, what would it be like?" Then have them write a paper describing their ideas. Consider the political, economic, religious, and social features of America. Lead them in their thinking by asking the following questions. What would be your ideals for each of the areas mentioned? How do your ideals differ from what exists today? How could you rally the public behind your goals? What would you do about those who do not share your ideals? What hindrances would keep America from reaching your ideal?

Trade with Vietnam

To "open markets" for American business, Clinton lifted a ban on trade with Vietnam. Veterans were outraged because the Communists had not made a serious effort to locate 1,609 American soldiers who were listed as missing in action since the end of the Vietnam War.

Confused Policy toward Cuba

The president sent conflicting signals to Fidel Castro, the Communist leader of Cuba. Clinton wanted to open trade despite Republican opposition. In the summer of 1994, Castro opened the door for boat people to flee to the United States. He also released many criminals from jail and told them to leave with the other refugees. Clinton's solution was to reverse America's thirty-six-year-old open-door policy and to confine the refugees to tents at the American base at Guantanamo Bay. As talks wore on, the squalor of the twenty-three thousand refugees became an embarrassment to the administration. Clinton agreed to increase the number of legal immigrants if Castro promised to stop future illegal immigration. Clinton also agreed to accept the Guantanamo refugees, and he promised to use the U.S. Coast Guard to turn back illegal refugees. Cuban-Americans and conservatives were furious at that policy. "What if such a policy had been adopted at the Berlin Wall?" they asked.

As the number of Cuban boat people declined, a group of Cuban-American pilots known as "Brothers to the Rescue" switched their activity from rescuing rafters from the ocean to dropping leaflets calling for revolt. On February 24, 1996, Cuban fighter jets shot down two of their unarmed planes, killing all four men on-

Many Americans opposed the passage of the North American Free Trade Agreement because they feared the loss of jobs to cheaper foreign labor.

Trade with China boomed under Clinton and brought greater prosperity for urban Chinese.

then, Serb attacks had forced approximately one million Kosovars from their homes.

Increasing World Trade

Clinton claimed two major successes in foreign trade. One was the passage of an agreement with Mexico and Canada called the North American Free Trade Agreement (**NAFTA**). Though Clinton had opposed free trade during the 1992 election, after taking office, he reversed course and supported NAFTA if it included labor and environmental guarantees. With strong Republican support, Congress passed NAFTA late in 1993.

Clinton's other success in world trade was the passage of the eighth round of the General Agreement on Tariffs and Trade (GATT). After World War II, the nations held seven "rounds" of negotiations to make trade easier. By 1990, tariffs had fallen from 40 percent to 5 percent. The volume of world trade had exploded. An eighth round of talks in Uruguay sought to reduce tariffs by another 30 percent. It also addressed unfair trade practices.

But the nations could not agree. Clinton brokered a deal that critics said changed the basic purpose of the agreement as he had done with NAFTA. Clinton's version included new environmental standards and a large bureaucracy. In 1994, the member nations finally approved a permanent **World Trade Organization** (WTO) to enforce GATT. Critics said Clinton had changed free trade into "managed free trade" under international bureaucrats.

Section Quiz

1. Who was the first woman to serve as secretary of state?
2. Under Bill Clinton, how did the United States deal with the threat of nuclear weapons in North Korea?
3. What effect did American casualties in Somalia have on American foreign policy?
4. What three ethnic groups fought each other in Bosnia? What peace agreement was an attempt to calm the conflict?
5. What two successes did Clinton achieve in foreign trade?
★ In Clinton's view, what role should the UN and NATO play in promoting peace in the post–Cold War era? Do you agree with him?

Activity 5: Impeachment

Use this activity to help the students understand the history and process of impeachment and to encourage them to learn how their own representatives and senators voted on both the impeachment charges.

Section Quiz Answers

1. Madeleine Albright
2. The United States agreed to build two nuclear power plants for North Korea if that country promised not to build nuclear weapons.
3. Clinton became hesitant to commit U.S. troops to combat.
4. Muslims, Serbs, and Croats; Dayton Accords
5. NAFTA and GATT
★ Policeman of the world; answers will vary, but God Himself opposed a one-world government when He told the descendants of Noah to spread throughout the world.

Chapter Review

Review Questions

Identify each of the following people.

1. This independent counsel presented evidence for impeaching Bill Clinton.

2. This was the first woman to serve as secretary of state.

3. This man became speaker of the House after Republicans took control in the 1994 elections.

4. This independent presidential candidate promised serious measures to fix the economy.

5. This conservative broadcaster gained a large following through his radio show.

Match these terms to their definitions.

6. consulting many nations about decisions

7. power to cut individual budget items

8. lawyer who investigates government corruption

9. existence of different cultures side by side without one leading the others

a. independent counsel
b. line-item veto
c. multiculteralism
d. multilateralism

Answer these questions.

10. What was the 1994 Republican campaign promise to take prompt action on popular legislation?

11. How did the failed raid in Somalia affect President Clinton's foreign policy?

12. What was President Clinton's solution to America's education problems?

13. What was the grassroots political movement of the Religious Right?

14. What organization was created to enforce fair trade practices?

People, Places, and Things to Remember:

Bill Clinton
Democratic Leadership Council
Ross Perot
centrist
Janet Reno
Freedom of Access to Clinic Entrances
Hillary Rodham Clinton
David Koresh
AmeriCorps
Newt Gingrich
Contract with America
balanced budget amendment
line-item veto
Welfare Reform Act
worldview
multiculturalism
Religious Right
Christian Coalition
Goals 2000
educational vouchers
partial birth abortions
Defense of Marriage Act
Bob Dole
Whitewater scandal
Kenneth Starr
independent counsel
Madeleine Albright
Non-Proliferation of Nuclear Weapons Treaty (NPT)
multilateralism
al-Qaeda
Osama bin Laden
Jean-Bertrand Aristide
Dayton Accords
NAFTA
World Trade Organization

board. In response, President Clinton gave up his efforts to normalize relations with Cuba. He agreed to sign a Republican bill to tighten economic sanctions.

Activity 6: Chapter Review

Use this activity to help the students review the chapter content and prepare for the test.

Chapter Review Answers

Review Questions

1. Kenneth Starr
2. Madeleine Albright
3. Newt Gingrich
4. Ross Perot
5. Rush Limbaugh
6. d
7. b
8. a
9. c
10. Contract with America
11. He avoided sending American forces on combat missions and limited them to "peacekeeping" missions.
12. Goals 2000
13. Christian Coalition
14. World Trade Organization

Chapter Goals

Students should be able to

1. Define and use the basic terms of the chapter.
2. Understand and explain the controversial disputed election of 2000.
3. Recount the events of September 11, 2001.
4. Analyze the effects of the September 11 terrorist attacks and the subsequent war on terror in Afghanistan, Iraq, and around the world.
5. Analyze the economic and political effects of Hurricane Katrina
6. Identify recurring problems with other countries, notably Iran, North Korea, and Venezuela.

Chapter Motivation

In this chapter, your students should see that sometimes events in history force a president to alter or adjust the national priorities to deal with more pressing matters. This chapter shows how George W. Bush's goals were preempted by the terrorist attacks and the subsequent war on terror. Ask the students to look for problems that he faced in building and maintaining an effective coalition of nations to help fight that war. Help them to identify new challenges to individual rights that the war brought and the effects of that war on politics and economics.

CHAPTER 29

The terrorist attacks on the United States on September 11, 2001, defined the Bush administration and set the national agenda for the foreseeable future.

A New Millennium

I. The Bush Administration

II. America in the New Millennium

III. America and the World

Chapter 29 Lesson Plan Chart			
Section Title	**Main Activity**	**Pages**	**Days**
I. The Bush Administration	Activity 1: "Let's Roll!" The Story of the Passengers of United Flight 93	559–66	1–2 days
II. America in the New Millennium	Activity 2: The Faith of George W. Bush	567–76	1–2 days
III. America and the World	Activity 3: Katrina: A True Story of Grace	577–82	1–2 days
TOTAL SUGGESTED DAYS (INCLUDING 1 DAY FOR REVIEW AND TESTING)			4–7 DAYS

MATERIALS LIST

SECTION I
- CD: Party Platform Summaries, 2000; Electoral College Results, 2000; George W. Bush, 43rd President; Scenes from the War on Terror; Electoral College Results, 2004; .
- Activity 1 from the *Student Activities* manual

SECTION II
- Activity 2 from the *Student Activities* manual

SECTION III
- Activities 3 and 4 from the *Student Activities* manual
- CD: Barack Obama, 44th President

The twenty-first century opened with great promise and great challenges. The first year, an election year, ended with a controversial presidential election. Near the end of the second year, terrorists launched the largest terrorist attack in U.S. history. The third year into the new century, the nation found itself involved in a new style of warfare in two foreign countries and at home. As the end of the first decade of the century approached, the nation still faced unprecedented challenges and dangers. Yet it also embraced great advancements in science and technology.

I. The Bush Administration

As the millennium opened, the nation was on the verge of choosing a successor to Bill Clinton. The Democrats had controlled the White House for eight years. The Republicans were eager to recapture that prize just as they had captured the Congress in 1994.

The Election of 2000

The race between Vice President Al Gore and Texas governor George W. Bush showed how divided Americans were. Gore pushed for a more active federal government—spending more on social programs, protecting the environment, and increasing taxes on businesses and the wealthy. He also defended America's global military actions under Clinton.

Bush promised a tax cut, a voucher program for private schools, a greater role for the states, and policies generally favorable to

Politics as a "Family" Business

George H. W. Bush and George W. Bush were the second father and son who both served as president. The other father-son presidential combination was the Adamses—John and John Quincy. John became president in 1796. Like the first Bush president, he failed to win reelection. In 1824, John Quincy was elected in a controversial election, just like the second Bush. John Quincy Adams failed to win a majority of the Electoral College vote and the election went to the House of Representatives, where he won.

Another political family was the Harrisons. In 1840, America elected William Henry Harrison president. In 1888, voters chose his grandson, Benjamin Harrison, as president.

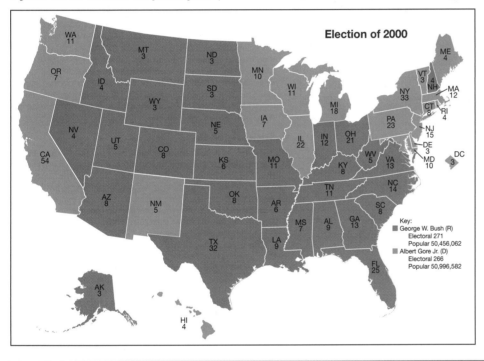

Election of 2000

Key:
George W. Bush (R)
Electoral 271
Popular 50,456,062
Albert Gore Jr. (D)
Electoral 266
Popular 50,996,582

 CD: Party Platform Summaries, 2000

Refer to the CD for a summary of each major party's platform for the presidential election of 2000.

 An Earlier Disputed Election (1876)

Compare and contrast with the students the disputed elections of 1876 and 2000. An excellent resource about the 1876 election is *Centennial Crisis: The Disputed Election of 1876* by the late Chief Justice of the Supreme Court William Rehnquist.

CD: Electoral College Results, 2000

Refer to the CD for a map showing the Electoral College results for the presidential election of 2000.

Section I
Objectives

Students should be able to

1. Define and illustrate George Bush's "compassionate conservatism."

2. Describe the issues involved in the disputed election of 2000.

3. Recount the events and effects of the September 11, 2001, terrorist attacks on the United States.

4. Outline the chronology of the war on terror.

5. Define and use the basic terms of the chapter.

Compassion Wars

For years, American liberals have tried to brand conservatives as being hardnosed and callous toward the unfortunate and others who were often the victims of conservative budget cuts. Liberals portray themselves as the only people who have real compassion for the needs and problems of others. George W. Bush campaigned for president as a "compassionate conservative," trying to prove that the label was not an oxymoron. He promoted improvements in education and advocated a partnership between government and religious organizations to solve social problems, especially those in urban areas. In a sense, this removed the stigma that had long plagued conservatives.

Focus on Florida

The focal point of the disputed election of 2000 was Florida, particularly Miami-Dade County. On November 8 at 2:15 a.m., the national news networks projected that Bush was the winner in Florida, and fifteen minutes later Gore called him to concede.

An hour later, Gore called Bush to retract his concession. At that point, the vote stood at 2,909,135 for Bush and 2,907,351 for Gore.

That set in motion a series of legal challenges stretching from local courts to the Florida Supreme Court all the way to the U.S. Supreme Court between November 9 and December 13. At issue were recounts in four Florida counties, but those recounts produced further arguments over which ballots should be counted. The "butterfly ballots" used in those counties were marked by punching a hole through the ballot with a stylus. On some of the ballots, the holes had not removed the paper completely, resulting in "hanging chads." On other ballots, the chads were not even hanging but only indented, or "dimpled." Should those dimples also be counted as legitimate votes?

On November 26, the Florida Secretary of State, Katherine Harris, certified the new vote totals, which showed Bush with a 537-vote lead. The next day, Gore filed an appeal. Two days later, he filed for a recount of 14,000 disputed ballots. On December 1, the U.S. Supreme Court heard oral arguments in the case. On December 9, the U.S. Supreme Court halted the recount and on December 12 reversed an earlier Florida Supreme Court decision. The next day, Gore finally conceded the election to Bush in a nationally televised speech.

Comparing and Contrasting Bush and Reagan

The Reagan presidency brought a major change in American government—some people even called it the Reagan Revolution. In contrast to the prevailing liberalism of the two previous generations,

CD: George W. Bush, 43rd President

Refer to the CD for more information on George W. Bush.

Gore and Bush faced each other in a close and hotly contested campaign.

Florida voters became the brunt of jokes featuring hanging chads and questioning Floridians' ability to vote.

business. He wanted to allow companies to drill for oil on federal lands. As a candidate, Bush questioned the wisdom of Clinton's use of the U.S. military around the world.

Cultural issues played a big role in the campaign. Gore defended abortion as a right. Bush strongly opposed it. Bush also generally opposed gun control. Gore favored it. Bush talked often about "**compassionate conservatism**" as a means of improving education and working with religious organizations to fight urban problems.

Each candidate had challenges to overcome. Gore was burdened by the legacy of the Clinton scandals, so he tried to distance himself from Clinton during the campaign. Bush appeared to many as a Washington outsider who lacked the expertise necessary to govern well.

The election was extremely close, and the outcome was disputed for weeks. In the national popular vote, Gore got over 540,000 votes more than Bush. But Bush won the election with 271 electoral votes to Gore's 266. Bush's victory in the Electoral College hinged on the outcome in Florida. Election night and the following morning, television networks first declared Florida had gone to Gore; then they switched the call to "too close to call." Then they gave it to Bush but later switched back to saying it was "too close to call." Earlier, Gore had conceded. But he took it back when the result in Florida remained in doubt.

In close races, Florida law required a manual recount. For weeks, the nation endured court challenges and decisions by Florida election boards as the recount continued. Finally, on December 12, the U.S. Supreme Court brought an end to the election. In a 5–4 decision, it ordered the recount to stop. Yet another recount, it ruled, would violate Florida law. Bush officially won Florida by a mere 537 votes. Despite the uncertainty, the outcome of the election showed that American democracy was strong. The people, including the defeated Gore, accepted the verdict. But many Democrats continued to refer to the "stolen" election.

Bush's Agenda

When Bush took office in 2001, the national government was sharply divided. The Republicans still had a slight majority in the House of Representatives. But the Senate was tied, with each party having fifty members. The vice president would have to break any tie votes if the Republicans were to have control. Later that year, Republican James Jeffords of Vermont became an Independent, giving the Democrats control of the Senate, 50–49. (Jeffords was a liberal who typically voted with the Democrats.)

Bush was unfazed by the close presidential election. To stimulate the economy, he called for a major tax cut of $1.6 trillion. He and his advisors hoped that with more money in Americans' hands, they would spend more. That would improve the economy. Democrats complained that the plan favored the wealthy and would wipe out the budget surplus. By June 2001, Bush and Congress compromised with a $1.35 trillion tax cut over eleven years. Bush had delivered on a campaign promise.

September 11, 2001

In the early fall morning of **September 11, 2001**, everything suddenly changed for Bush, America, and the world. An airliner, hijacked by terrorists, slammed into the north tower of the World Trade Center. Soon, a second plane crashed into the south tower. A third plane hit the Pentagon in Washington, D.C. A fourth plane, possibly headed for the White House, crashed in rural Pennsylvania. Heroic passengers, who had learned of the plot over cell phones, fought with the terrorists for control of the plane. America had entered a time of escalating danger from ruthless and violent enemies—Muslim terrorists.

That attack was the worst terrorist attack in the nation's history. More than three thousand people were killed or injured. Extensive property damage occurred. The terrorists had killed innocent men, women, and children; military personnel, policemen, and firefighters; and Americans and foreigners from about eighty countries who worked in the World Trade Center. They had struck at symbols of the heart of America—its wealth in New York City and its government in the nation's capital.

Americans responded with both anger and patriotism. They gave generously of their time and money to help the victims, especially those in Manhattan. They flew American flags from front porches and car windows. Americans of both political parties joined in public ceremonies all across the country to show unity. Bush rallied the nation when he stood at "Ground Zero," the site of the destruction of the World Trade Center, and promised victory over terrorism. People across the globe publicly displayed their sympathy for Americans during that tragedy.

Officials quickly identified the nineteen terrorists. They were connected to an international terrorist network called **al-Qaeda**. It was led by **Osama bin Laden**. He was linked to several earlier terrorist attacks against America and its allies. He and other Muslim extremists resented American troops in Saudi Arabia during the Gulf War in 1991.

To bin Laden, the United States was an obstacle to the expansion of Islam. He despised the Saudi government's cooperation with America and sought the destruction of Israel, which, he believed, occupied land that belonged to Palestinian Muslims. He operated from his base in Afghanistan, where the terrorist-friendly Taliban government protected him and aided his global terrorist activities. His personal wealth came from his Saudi

The terrorist attacks of September 11, 2001, totally rearranged the agenda of the Bush administration.

FDNY firefighters rescue one of their own from the World Trade Center.

Firefighters sift through the rubble of the World Trade Center for bodies of victims.

which had come to look to government for help, Reagan believed that government was part of the problem. He wanted to reduce the size of government. He cut taxes dramatically, to the lowest point since Coolidge in the 1920s. He also cut domestic spending while increasing defense spending. One result, however, was a huge budget deficit.

George W. Bush continued the Reagan Revolution in some ways. Like Reagan, he achieved a significant tax cut at the beginning of his administration. Also like Reagan and Coolidge, he believed that cutting taxes put more money in the hands of people and businesses. As a result, they would spend that money to purchase more or expand businesses, and the economy would improve. Bush also increased military spending, out of necessity, with the War on Terror and the Iraq War. A large federal deficit returned because government spent more than it received in tax revenues.

Why Did It Happen?

Confronted with the horrible events of September 11, 2001, many Americans asked why it had happened. The historical books of the Bible reveal that God often has multiple reasons for directing the affairs of history in the way He does. Often it is impossible to discern these reasons without special revelation from Him. Nevertheless, Luke 13:1-5 provides an answer that could be applied to the World Trade Center disaster. In that passage Jesus instructed his listeners about how to respond to two disasters that occurred in their day: the slaughter of some Galileans and the death of eighteen people when a tower fell on them. Jesus said they should not conclude that the people who suffered in these disasters were worse sinners

---

Online Research Project

Have the students conduct an online search on a concordance website for verses that could offer comfort to victims of disasters and also encourage Christians as they face the prospects of a more dangerous world.

Activity 1: "Let's Roll!" The Story of the Passengers of United Flight 93

Use this activity to help the students understand how the passengers aboard United Flight 93 helped foil one of the terrorist attacks on Washington, D.C.

than themselves. Instead they should realize that death is the consequence that all sinners face. Disasters should cause men to realize that they must repent of their sins and turn to Christ for eternal life with Him. God probably had many purposes for the September 11th tragedy, but surely one of them was to cause people to reflect on their need for salvation.

Osama bin Laden

The most-wanted man in FBI history, Osama bin Laden, was born in 1957 in Saudi Arabia to a Syrian mother and a Yemeni father. Because his father had numerous wives, Osama was one of about fifty children and of relatively low status in the family. His father owned a construction company with close ties to the Saudi royal family, and he became a billionaire through its contracts with the Saudis. Osama was heavily influenced by radical Wahabi Muslim teachings, which insisted on returning to strict observance of Islam.

When the Soviet Union invaded Afghanistan, Osama supported the mujahideen. He set up numerous Islamic schools in Afghanistan and Pakistan from which came many recruits for radical Islam and, later, his terrorist network known as Al Qaeda. He also opposed the Saudis' permitting the U.S. military bases on Saudi soil from which they conducted the war that pushed the Iraqi military from Kuwait. The Saudis expelled him in 1991 and revoked his citizenship in 1994 because he allegedly was plotting the overthrow of the Saudi royal family.

Osama bin Laden was purported to have been behind the 1993 World Trade Center bombing, the 1998 bombings of U.S. embassies in Kenya and Tanzania, and the 2000 bombing of the U.S.S. *Cole*, as well as

Bush's presence at Ground Zero bolstered emergency workers' morale.

U.S. troops fought Taliban troops in the rugged mountains of northeastern Afghanistan.

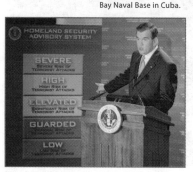

Enemy combatants (Taliban and al-Qaeda) were housed temporarily in Camp X-Ray at Guantanamo Bay Naval Base in Cuba.

Former Pennsylvania governor Tom Ridge, the first Secretary of the Department of Homeland Security, explains the terror threat-level system.

family's business fortune, and he supported the Taliban financially and militarily in its fight against a rival Afghan faction. The biggest threat from bin Laden was his worldwide band of Muslim extremists, numbering in the thousands, who trained at al-Qaeda's camps. In addition to religious instruction in radical Islam, recruits learned terrorist techniques for killing and destruction through bombings and suicide missions. Al-Qaeda attracted educated and wealthy Muslims who shared a hatred for the West.

The War on Terror

After the Cold War, the United States was the world's only superpower. Conflicts over race, religion, and culture replaced old issues, such as capitalism versus communism. Some groups in the developing world thought the Western culture they saw in news stories and films was corrupt. These people resisted the encroachment of Western culture on their way of life. For a growing minority of Muslims, hatred of the West, especially America, fueled a network of terrorist groups in some sixty countries. Most of those countries were in the Middle East, Africa, and Asia. They operated in secret. No tactic, not even the slaughter of civilians, was deemed too violent for achieving their goals. Sometimes rogue nations protected those terrorist groups. But the terrorists were not part of those governments, so fighting the terrorist groups proved difficult.

Despite the challenges, after 9/11 America began a war against terrorists both at home and abroad. Bush called it the "first war of the twenty-first century." He promised an all-out pursuit of the terrorists and the governments that helped them. He warned that it would be a long struggle and, unlike other wars, sometimes it would have no front line.

First, Bush assembled a multinational coalition to fight the Taliban government in Afghanistan. The Taliban had supported bin Laden and provided training camps and safe haven for his terrorists. On October 7, coalition forces invaded Afghanistan. They used "smart" weapons to minimize military and civilian casualties. The anti-Taliban Northern Alliance in Afghanistan and neighboring Pakistan aided them.

The Taliban collapsed in two months. In December, the other political factions in Afghanistan met in Germany and signed a peace agreement. Afghan leaders set up a temporary government and worked toward a permanent one. Then they began to rebuild their country. It had been ravaged first by the invading Soviet Union in the 1980s and then by the Taliban in the 1990s. The Afghan people celebrated their freedom from the strict Islamic rule of the Taliban.

To handle the threat in the United States, Bush created the **Office of Homeland Security**. It was the first major reorganization of the federal government in about fifty years. It streamlined existing agencies to fight terrorism at home. (It later became a cabinet-level department.) Bureaucrats covered security issues related to U.S. borders, transportation (especially at airports), chemical and biological attacks, and preparations for emergencies. Americans accepted longer delays and lines for check-in at airports as officials screened for potential terrorists.

CD: Scenes from the War on Terror

Refer to the CD for a variety of photos from the various aspects of the war on terror.

The Face of Terrorism

Who are the terrorists who would commit such atrocities as the 9/11 attacks on America, the car bombings in Iraq, and the suicide bombings in Israel? None of the nineteen terrorists who hijacked the airliners on 9/11 particularly looked like a terrorist. So what is it that makes terrorists commit such senseless and horrendous acts of violence? Are they insane? Do they have deep psychological problems that manifest themselves in senseless violence? What are their motives? What do they hope to achieve by their violence?

In the past, terrorists typically wanted maximum publicity for their cause. They were not attempting to produce maximum casualties. In fact, they knew that becoming too violent or killing too many people would actually bring public reaction against them. More recent terrorists—especially Islamic terrorists—however, have sought both violence and publicity. They know that the more "infidels" they can kill or injure and the more destruction they can cause, the greater the publicity they will get. They do not fear public disapproval. They can justify the most horrific acts of violence in the name of Allah. They can even kill innocent people—including women and children—of their own religion and countries.

One common theory is that the terrorist is poor, unemployed, and hopelessly trapped. Therefore, he has nothing to lose in committing

11 SEPTEMBER 2001 HIJACKERS

These Muslim men hijacked four commercial airliners and used them as weapons in their war of terror against the United States.

violence, even committing suicide in the process. But studies of the backgrounds of many recent terrorists often show them to be quite normal. It is that normality that allows them to blend in with the general population and work their violent deeds—and often escape—undetected. They tend to be young (20–25), male, (although increasingly more females are becoming terrorists) and well educated. Many of the terrorists have been chemists, biologists, engineers, computer specialists, or other highly trained experts. A foiled plot in Great Britain in 2007 even involved several medical doctors.

Earlier terrorists were linked to specific groups and specific coun-

tries. For example, one immediately associates the Irish Republican Army with Irish Catholics and the Basque terrorists with northern Spain. The modern terrorists, however, often operate independently from any hierarchy or central organization. This fact makes it even harder to foil planned acts of terrorism, catch the terrorists, and destroy their leadership. They also generally have no direct link to a specific country. Rather, they come from multiple countries and even include citizens of non-Islamic Western countries. Their common links seem to be their radical Islamist beliefs and their intense hatred of Western culture and society, especially America—"the Great Satan."

At the president's urging, Congress overwhelmingly passed the **Patriot Act**. That law made it easier for law enforcement officials and the courts to catch and imprison terror suspects. One feature of the act allowed government to listen to phone conversations of people suspected of having terrorist connections. Bush explained that if al-Qaeda called anyone in America, security personnel needed to know it. Most Americans agreed with his practical, commonsense approach.

Another feature of the act reduced the rights of the accused in court. Some captured terrorists could be treated as enemy aliens with very little legal protection. Critics complained that the government, in its zeal to protect citizens from terrorism, had gone too far in

other attacks on U.S. troops and facilities in the Middle East. In 1998, he called for all Americans and Jews, including women and children, to be killed. Then in 2001, he plotted the infamous attacks on the World Trade Center and various sites in Washington, D.C.

The United States sought to capture or kill Osama in its war against the Taliban in Afghanistan. So far, their efforts apparently have proven unsuccessful because Osama continues to issue periodic audio and video recordings condemning the United States and rallying Islamic terrorists to continue the war against the West. The FBI now has a reward on his head—$25 million—dead or alive.

Why Do Muslims Dislike the West?

One reason given by some Muslims is a lingering resentment about the Crusades in the late Middle Ages when Europeans fought to reclaim the Holy Land from the Muslims. Today, however, that memory is not a primary motivation for anti-Western feelings.

Muslims resent the collapse of their last great empire, the Ottoman Empire, built by the Turks over centuries. In 1683, Austria defeated the Turks and prevented further penetration of the Muslims into southeastern Europe. In the 19th century, the Turkish Empire became the "sick man of Europe" because of its increasing weakness. Greece gained independence from it, and Russia, Austria-Hungary, and Great Britain exerted increasing influence over it. In World War I, the Turks, along with Germany and Austria-Hungary, lost both the war and their empire.

Russia and Spain had expelled Muslim groups that threatened them. When Europeans built colonial empires in Asia

Topics for Discussion

Discuss with the students the issue of whether enemy combatants have the rights of U.S. citizens or those granted under the Geneva Convention since they (1) are not U.S. citizens and (2) are not fighting for any single country. Another topic for discussion is how far the government should be allowed to go in spying on its own citizens—phone calls, library usage, etc. How far may anti-terrorist activities impinge on individual rights?

and Africa, they defeated Muslims in the process. Muslims, who had experienced great power in certain parts of the world when Europe was weak, now witnessed a reversal of fortunes. Muslims resent their gradual loss of power and influence to the West.

Today, many Muslims point to America's support for Israel, which was created as a state in 1948, as the reason for their anger. Palestinian Arabs, especially, want their land back. Muslims also resent the decadence often found in Western culture, especially American popular culture (e.g., music and movies). They are offended that such influences have corrupted Muslim culture.

Knowing that they cannot compete with the West on the traditional battlefield, Muslims have resorted to terrorism and infiltration of Western societies by increasing immigration.

Capture and Trial of Saddam Hussein

After months of searching, U.S. troops finally found Saddam Hussein hiding in an underground room. U.S. troops captured him and turned him over to Iraqi judges for trial. He was found guilty of war crimes and sentenced to hang. That sentence was carried out.

U.S. Secretary of State Colin Powell tries to convince the U.N. Security Council that Saddam Hussein had weapons of mass destruction.

U.S. Marines conduct a search for enemy soldiers who had been firing at them from an abandoned school.

curtailing the rights of Americans. Some of its provisions were declared unconstitutional by a sharply divided Supreme Court.

The War with Iraq

In the war on terror, American leaders used a different strategy than they had used in the Cold War. Presidents tried to contain communism, with limited military actions if necessary. But overall the threat of nuclear force usually restrained the enemy. However, Muslim extremists were not restrained by such thinking. They followed no rules of war. They resorted to suicide bombings. They targeted innocent civilians. They even threatened to use weapons of mass destruction (such as biological or chemical weapons). Americans and Europeans feared that terrorists might even get nuclear weapons.

Bush decided that America should be aggressive in the war on terror. He proposed a policy called the **preemptive strike**. Rather than wait for another terrorist attack, the military would act before one could be carried out. Since the 1991 Gulf War, Saddam Hussein, the Iraqi dictator, had continued to threaten the Middle East and surrounding regions with the possible development of chemical and biological weapons of mass destruction (WMDs). He had even used chemical weapons against the Kurdish people in Iraq. Despite his objections, U.N. officials inspected Iraq for such weapons. In 1998, he kicked out the inspectors.

After September 11, 2001, Bush and other world leaders feared that Saddam had not only dangerous weapons but also links to global terrorism. In 2002, Bush asked the U.N. to support his actions against Iraq. The Security Council complied by issuing a resolution. It threatened Saddam with "serious consequences" if he did not destroy his weapons. Congress endorsed Bush's Iraq policy in a resolution calling for the use of force if necessary.

Saddam gave in, allowing U.N. inspectors to return. But he refused to cooperate fully. Frustrated, American, British, and Spanish officials pursued a U.N. resolution authorizing force against Iraq if Saddam did not destroy his weapons. Bush warned that the United States would act alone if necessary. Germany, France, Russia, China, and other countries opposed military action. They wanted more time for inspectors to do their work. American Secretary of State Colin Powell tried in vain to get U.N. approval for military force against Iraq.

On March 17, 2003, Bush issued an ultimatum to Saddam. He rejected it. Two days later, the United States and other nations (mostly Great Britain), in a "**coalition of the willing**," invaded Iraq. The assault began with a bombing attack meant to "shock and awe" the enemy. It was followed by a ground invasion. The coalition defeated Saddam's forces in only two weeks. Baghdad fell rather easily. The toppling of a statue of Saddam there symbolized his defeat.

But stabilizing the country after the war proved harder. Terrorists continued their fight in a guerrilla war. They launched terrorist attacks and encouraged suicide bombings. They set up ambushes and set off improvised explosive devices (IEDs) along roads. Many of the terrorists were from other Muslim countries.

Often, religious and ethnic groups within the country fought against each other. Sunnis attacked Shiites and bombed their mosques. The Shiites conducted revenge attacks. Sunnis and Shiites attacked Kurds. Iraq moved closer to a civil war.

On the other hand, the Iraqis made steps toward establishing their own democratic government. They held elections and approved a constitution. Chaos and violence, however, continued. A U.S. air strike in June 2006 killed Abu Musab al-Zarqawi, a top leader of al-Qaeda in Iraq. His death boosted the morale of coalition forces and the Iraqi people.

Like the Vietnam War, the Iraq War was controversial. Americans were divided over the need for the invasion. Some people argued that it was unnecessary, especially when the military found no evidence of WMDs in Iraq. Critics pointed out that the Muslim world was even angrier with the United States after the war. Muslims thought that Iraq was a victim of the West's desire for oil. They saw the war as one more episode of Western imperialism.

Supporters of the war countered that the attack on Iraq was part of the war on terror. Al-Qaeda might not have been in Iraq before the conflict, but terrorists were there afterward. They had to be defeated. Fighting them there made more sense than fighting them in the United States. In addition, Saddam had acted as though he was concealing WMDs throughout the buildup to the invasion of his country.

Some people who had opposed the war earlier argued that America had to stay and finish the job. They had to ensure stability in the Middle East. Also, the war had divided the world, especially Europe. Germany and France, for example, opposed the war. They worked against U.S. interests in other parts of the world. These countries claimed that America was abusing its position as the world's only superpower.

U.S. soldiers, Iraqi policemen, and innocent Iraqi civilians were the victims of numerous suicide car bombings following the fall of Saddam's regime.

The Election of 2004

Republicans faced the 2004 presidential election with confidence. They had been encouraged by successes in the 2002 congressional races. They picked up two Senate seats and regained control of the Senate. They added four seats to their majority in the House of Representatives. Usually, the party that occupies the White House *loses* seats during off-year (nonpresidential) elections.

National security shaped the 2004 election. Opposition to the war in Iraq energized the Democrats' left wing. Howard Dean, the former governor of Vermont, attacked the war. He emerged as the early favorite for the nomination. Dean organized support through the Internet. But most Democrats thought he was too liberal to be a national candidate. Dean quickly faded after doing poorly in early primaries.

A more traditional liberal, Senator **John Kerry** of Massachusetts, won the nomination. Kerry tried to campaign as a centrist, following the mold of Bill Clinton. Clinton had been successful in building a moderate image, but Kerry could not. He could not escape his liberal voting record in the Senate. He supported the old liberal groups—homosexuals, feminists, and labor unions.

Although he was a decorated Vietnam veteran, Kerry had returned home to oppose that war. He went on to a career in politics. His opposition to the Vietnam War hurt him among veterans. Kerry also seemed indecisive. After voting for the Iraq War, he later opposed measures necessary for fighting it. His effort to defend his actions—"I actually voted *for* the war before I voted *against* it"—only cemented his image as a "flip-flopper."

Senator John Kerry was often criticized for his confusing positions on the war in Iraq.

John Kerry, Vietnam, Swift Boats, and the Election of 2004

John Kerry campaigned in 2004 touting his experience as a medal-winning hero as a swift boat commander in the Vietnam War. Some of his comrades in arms, however, contested his telling of the story and his record, especially his actions after he returned from Vietnam. Kerry served as a lieutenant (junior grade) for only four months and twelve days in 1968–69. He seems to have been the only known swift boat crewman to return to the States earlier than the standard one-year tour of duty. The standard practice was to permit Navy personnel to request transfer out of Vietnam when they had earned three Purple Hearts.

When Kerry returned to the United States, he joined antiwar protestors. He testified before Congress that the United States troops and sailors had performed atrocities and war crimes in Vietnam. He also allegedly threw his service medals over the White House fence in protest. During the election of 2004, however, Kerry wanted people to view him as strong on defense and touted his military career.

His comrades, however, told a different story of his service, saying that no atrocities were ever committed and that even his account of how he got the wounds that supposedly qualified him for the Purple Hearts was suspect. Some political commentators blame (or credit) those veterans with costing Kerry the election. They also coined a new term, calling similar negative attacks against political opponents "swiftboating."

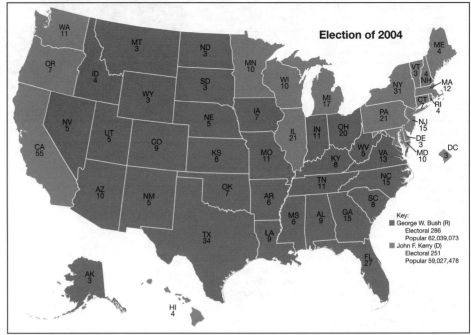

Election of 2004

WA 11
MT 3
ND 3
MN 10
ME 4
OR 7
ID 4
SD 3
WI 10
VT 3
NH 4
NY 31
MA 12
WY 3
MI 17
CT
RI 4
NV 5
NE 5
IA 7
PA 21
NJ 15
UT 5
CO 9
IL 21
IN 11
OH 20
DE 3
MD 10
DC 3
CA 55
KS 6
MO 11
WV 5
VA 13
KY 8
AZ 10
NM 5
OK 7
AR 6
TN 11
NC 15
SC 8
MS 6
AL 9
GA 15
TX 34
LA 9
FL 27
AK 3
HI 4

Key:
- George W. Bush (R)
  Electoral 286
  Popular 62,039,073
- John F. Kerry (D)
  Electoral 251
  Popular 59,027,478

Problems plagued Bush's reelection bid. Daily accounts of violence and mounting casualties in Iraq drove his approval ratings down. A scandal involving mistreatment of prisoners of war at the Abu Ghraib prison in Iraq also tarnished his image. Economic news was mixed. And the public believed that Kerry had won the three presidential debates.

In the end, voters believed that Bush was better able to deal with the war on terror. That was the most important issue in the campaign. Bush won by 3.3 million votes, avoiding a repeat of the disputed 2000 election. Republicans also increased their majorities in both houses of Congress.

The South and the central states—areas with more traditional values—gave solid support to Bush and other Republicans. Evangelical voters again were highly organized. They helped Republicans win key states. For example, evangelical voters played a major role in winning Ohio, where the vote was extremely close. For them, moral values often were more important than the economy or national security. Bush also gained more votes from women and Hispanics than he had in 2000.

Section Quiz

1. Who were the candidates in the election of 2000? in the election of 2004?

2. How was the election of 2000 finally determined?

CD: Electoral Results, 2004

Refer to the CD for a map showing the Electoral College results of the presidential election of 2004.

Section Quiz Answers

1. 2000—Al Gore and George W. Bush; 2004—John Kerry and George W. Bush

2. The U.S. Supreme Court stopped any further recounts of Florida votes, and at the last count Bush had 537 more votes than Gore.

3. What event became the defining moment of the Bush presidency?

4. The action of what one person tipped the balance of power in the Senate from the Republicans (with 50 votes plus that of the vice president) to the Democrats?

★ Is it right for sovereign nations to make preemptive strikes against other sovereign nations? Why or why not?

II. America in the New Millennium

The United States has always been a nation of immigrants. However, the late twentieth and early twenty-first centuries witnessed the largest increase in newcomers since before World War I. Most of the new immigrants came from Latin America and Asia rather than Europe.

A More Diverse America

Several changes in immigration law have resulted in a more diverse America. Important changes removed limits on the number of relatives who could join immigrants in America. Asians and Latinos benefited the most from the change. Family ties are strong in these cultures. Family members already here encouraged relatives to join them. Western Europeans, who enjoyed better economies, were less likely to come to America. Eastern Europeans still under communism before it collapsed were not allowed to come. These factors ensured that most new immigrants were Hispanic and Asian.

Other changes in the law also encouraged immigration. In 1986, Congress granted amnesty (legal status) to 1.4 million illegal aliens. In 1990, Congress increased immigration quotas. By 2000, Hispanics were about 11 percent of the population, almost equal to the percentage of blacks. Asians were about 4 percent of the population.

Hispanics came from various places, but most of them were from Mexico. Others were from Central America and the Caribbean, including Puerto Rico and Cuba. But language, more than race or nationality, was what identified Hispanics.

In 2005, Bush named the first Hispanic Attorney General in American history. **Alberto Gonzales** became the nation's top law enforcement and legal authority with an urgency to protect Americans from terrorists while protecting citizens' liberties from government interference. Earlier, he had been be a law professor, the Texas secretary of state, and a justice on the Texas Supreme Court. A controversy involving the firing of several attorneys in the Justice Department forced him to resign in 2007.

Asians also came from many regions: China, India, Japan, Korea, and Southeast Asia. New immigrants settled in predictable places—Asians on the west coast and Hispanics along the southern border. But many also moved to large American cities, as earlier immigrants had done.

Estimated Illegal U.S. Residents by Country of Origin (2005)

Country	Residents
Mexico	5,970,000
El Salvador	470,000
Guatemala	370,000
India	280,000
China	230,000
Philippines	210,000
N/S Korea	210,000
Honduras	180,000
Brazil	160,000
All other countries	2,250,000

Alberto Gonzales was the first Hispanic Attorney General.

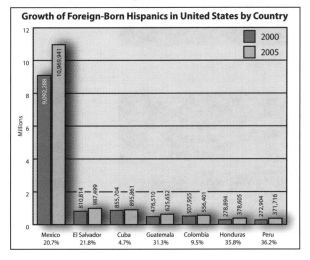

Growth of Foreign-Born Hispanics in United States by Country

Legend: 2000, 2005 (Millions)

Country	2000	2005
Mexico 20.7%	9,092,288	10,969,941
El Salvador 21.8%	810,814	987,499
Cuba 4.7%	855,704	895,861
Guatemala 31.3%	476,510	625,652
Colombia 9.5%	507,955	556,401
Honduras 35.8%	278,894	378,605
Peru 36.2%	272,904	371,716

Section II
Objectives

Students should be able to

1. Illustrate how America became a more diverse nation after the turn of the century.

2. Define and give examples of faith-based initiatives.

3. Describe the involvement of evangelical Christians in the Bush administration.

4. Define religious trends in the new century.

5. Identify economic developments, including technological advancements, at the turn of the century.

6. Describe the trend toward a more conservative Supreme Court.

Immigration Debate

America has become racially diverse, and racial identity can be confusing. For example, the Census Bureau has no official record of the Hispanic population because that classification is so ambiguous. It could include several racial groups living in the United States: descendants of European whites (Spanish or Portuguese), Africans, Latin American Indians, or Asians (Filipinos, for example) or those with mixed-race ancestry. Officially, the bureau does not consider Hispanic a "race" but a "category" with members from different races. With those factors in mind, Hispanics probably are the largest minority in America today. The Census Bureau also allows Americans to select from either fourteen different races and "subcategories" or "some other race." One option includes "two or more races" for those of mixed racial ancestry.

3. the September 11, 2001, terrorist attacks

4. Jim Jeffords, who switched parties from Republican to Independent

★ Answers will vary.

🔵 Immigration: Balancing Law and Obligation

Discuss with the students the need for a balance between enforcing immigration laws and the obligation of Christians to show compassion and to share the gospel with immigrants. Our national security demands strict adherence to and enforcement of the laws to prevent undesirables from entering the country. Society's need for order demands a clear process for legal immigration. But Christians also have obligations concerning the proper treatment of "strangers."

Have the students do an online search for Bible verses that contain the word *strangers* that apply to foreigners who lived among the Israelites. They might be surprised at the instructions from Moses, especially in Leviticus and Deuteronomy. Discuss with them any possible application to America's problems with immigrants today. Also mention the commands of Christ in the New Testament to love others as ourselves. Consider, also, the command to evangelize.

According to the History News Network (February 12, 2008), by 2050 whites will be a minority in the United States.

Faith and Politics: Coolidge, Reagan, and Bush

Calvin Coolidge, Ronald Reagan, and George W. Bush were all religious presidents who allowed their faith to influence their political actions, which were decidedly conservative in most areas. As governor of Massachusetts, Coolidge opposed the Boston police strike, just as Reagan opposed the air traffic controllers strike. In both cases, strikers were not allowed to keep their jobs. Coolidge and Reagan both were pro-business. Coolidge favored high tariffs that protected businesses from cheaper imports. Reagan cut taxes for businesses and reduced government regulations for businesses. Bush held similar views in that he supported free trade, which allows American businesses to move overseas to obtain cheaper labor. Coolidge, Reagan, and Bush invoked religion often in speeches and in their political and personal lives.

The Faith of Our Fathers

For more information on the role of faith in government service, see David L. Holmes, *The Faiths of the Founding Fathers*, Oxford University Press, 2006.

Activity 2: The Faith of George W. Bush

Use this activity to help the students understand how George Bush's faith shaped his administration, from his choice of advisors and nominees to the priorities and emphases of his administration.

President and Mrs. Bush pay their respects to Rosa Parks, the "First Lady of the civil rights movement." When she passed away in 2005, she lay in state in the rotunda of the Capitol in Washington, D.C.

President Bush was more open with his religious faith than many of his predecessors.

Bush promoted the active involvement of faith-based organizations in solving the nation's social problems.

The new wave of immigration raised an old debate. With low birthrates, the country relied on immigrants for population increases. Immigrants were also important to supply workers for a growing economy. Many Americans celebrated the nation's multicultural heritage as essential to its success. Others worried that immigrants caused problems: their illegal status, increase in crime, higher costs for social programs, loss of jobs for other Americans, and a threat to the common use of English.

African Americans at the Turn of the Century

After the civil rights movement in the 1960s, blacks made significant gains. New laws helped them gain greater equality. Household incomes improved. Record numbers of blacks pursued a college education. Toward the end of the century, many African-Americans, looking for better opportunities, returned to the South. That reversed a trend that started after World War II. More blacks served in Carter's administration than in any before it. He also had close ties to the family of Martin Luther King Jr.

Churches were still one of the most vibrant parts of African American life. Black preachers led the ongoing struggle for even greater opportunities. Bishop T. D. Jakes, a Dallas pastor, founded The Potter's House in 1996. In seven years, it had 28,000 members. It was one of the fastest growing churches in the country. The Church of God in Christ, a Pentecostal group with almost 5.5 million members, became the largest black denomination in America. (Historically, the two most popular African American denominations were Baptist and African Methodist Episcopal.)

During the 1980s, many Americans began to question some civil rights policies, particularly affirmative action. Affirmative action favored minorities in hiring and college admissions. Increasingly, courts ruled that race could not be a dominant factor in such decisions. In 1996, California voters approved Proposition 209, which banned affirmative action there. Even some minorities wanted affirmative action ended. Special treatment, they argued, demeaned them. Rather than preferential treatment, they wanted reward based on merit or ability. Others saw the need for affirmative action to continue.

An Evangelical Surge

The role of evangelical religion in politics increased significantly with the 2000 campaign and the presidency of George W. Bush. The "red" states in the heartland that Bush won contrasted with the "blue" states in the Northeast and on the West Coast that Gore carried. The "red" states were more culturally and religiously traditional. The "blue" states were more secular and liberal. Some observers noted that Bush's states reflected the Judeo-Christian heritage in Western civilization in contrast to the secular culture of the other states. Bush won easily in the South and the West (excluding California and Washington), in rural areas, and among male voters. Gore's base of support was in the more liberal Northeast and urban areas.

Bush personally made religion a more prominent issue. In a debate during the 2000 campaign, when the candidates were asked to name the person who had had the greatest influence in their lives, Bush cited Jesus Christ. Later, he shared his personal testimony of

George W. Bush's Faith in Historical Context

George W. Bush is certainly not the first president to rely on and refer to his religious faith. Other recent presidents with clear religious testimonies are Gerald Ford and Jimmy Carter. Carter announced during his 1976 campaign that he was a "born-again" Christian. Ronald Reagan talked about his religious faith but did not practice it as publicly as Carter and others did. Reagan, however, enjoyed strong support from evangelical Christians.

In historical context, Bush and these other presidents of faith were not exceptions by any means. But what about the Founding Fathers? They generally embraced deism, a philosophy/religion that respected Christianity, used Christian and biblical language, and admired Christ's ethics. They believed that Christianity helped society, but they did not believe in a supernatural Christianity. To them, Christ was not divine. Some deists even doubted the existence of God.

George Washington is something of a mystery as to his religious views, but evidence suggests that he was probably a deist. John Adams was a Unitarian, but an early version, unlike the nineteenth-century deists. He could be called a Christian Unitarian because he accepted biblical miracles, a personal God, and Jesus as Redeemer. All of those views are in contrast to other deists' beliefs. James Madison, although friendly to religion, remains a mystery as to his specific views. To James Monroe, religion was not important. Two of the Founding Fathers with the strongest orthodox Christian views are Samuel Adams and John Jay.

conversion, which occurred after he had struggled with a drinking problem.

Bush embraced a greater role for evangelical Christians, enlisting pastors, both whites and minorities, to help administer government social programs that put into practice his "compassionate conservatism." Such **faith-based initiatives** became an important part of his domestic program to combat problems in the inner cities. But he did not just enlist the support of prominent pastors; he sought the support of "the people in the pews." Critics from the left opposed these faith-based initiatives as violations of the "separation of church and state." Some conservative Christians also questioned the wisdom of these initiatives. They worried about government involvement in their programs.

Bush also tapped several evangelical Christians to serve in his administration. **John Ashcroft** was Bush's first-term attorney general. A Pentecostal, he had served as Missouri's attorney general, governor, and U.S. senator. **Condoleeza Rice** served first as Bush's National Security Advisor and later as his Secretary of State. She was an expert on Russia and Eastern Europe. Don Evans, a successful Christian businessman, served as Secretary of Commerce. Michael Gerson was one of Bush's leading speechwriters. He wove in phrases from hymns and Scripture that resonated with believers. Other Christians in the Bush administration were Chief of Staff Andrew Card and Karen Hughes, the Undersecretary of State for Public Diplomacy.

Bush was influenced not only by Christians inside his administration but also by some outside. They included James Dobson of Focus on the Family and Marvin Olasky of *World* magazine. Bush used their vast networks of radio, magazines, publishing companies, and cable television networks to communicate with their followers.

Evangelical groups represent a sizable voting force, with the largest groups being Southern Baptists and the Pentecostals/Charismatics. In 2000, Evangelicals had not voted in the numbers that the Bush campaign expected. But in 2004, they flocked to the polls in

Attorney General John Ashcroft and National Security Advisor (later Secretary of State) Condoleeza Rice were prominent Christians on the Bush administration's leadership team.

More on the Christians in the Bush Administration

Some excellent books by or about the professing Christians in the Bush administration are *Lessons from a Father to His Son* by John Ashcroft, *Condi: The Condoleeza Rice Story* by Antonia Felix, *Ten Minutes from Normal* by Karen Hughes, and Bush's autobiography, *A Charge to Keep: My Journey to the White House*.

Intelligent Design, Creationism, and Evolution

In the early twenty-first century, the controversy regarding the teaching of evolution in public schools continued. Recently, however, a change has occurred in the arguments against evolution. Initially, creationism developed as the early response to evolution. Scientifically trained believers, such as the members of the Creation Research Society, used both scientific and biblical arguments against evolution. Recently, Intelligent Design (ID) has emerged as an alternative to evolution that could be acceptable within public schools. Its proponents argue that, contrary to Darwin's view that life developed as the result of a chaotic process, life is the result of a creation that can be studied scientifically and objectively, and the study of creation leads to the conclusion of a designer. Other developments have made the debate even more lively. Evolutionists who are critical of Darwin have emerged after being convinced that Darwin was wrong. Advocates of both ID and creationism have stronger scientific and academic credentials than they did a generation or two ago. Some of the new critics include Michael Behe of Lehigh University, Scott Minnich of the University of Idaho, and William Dembski of Baylor University.

Creationists appreciate the scientific contributions by those in the ID movement. Nevertheless, Creationists differ from ID about the role Scripture should play in doing scientific work. Creationists accept the testimony of God's Word concerning creation. They recognize that there is no such thing as scientific objectivity. All facts must be interpreted within a theory. The Bible provides the only true worldview from which to practice science.

 Understanding the Conservative Cultural Mindset

To better understand the mindset of the cultural conservatives, you might consider reading Dan Quayle's two books, *Standing Firm: A Vice Presidential Memoir* (1999) and *The American Family: Discovering Values that Make Us Strong* (1996).

record numbers. Seventy-eight percent of white, conservative Christians—23 percent of all voters—voted for Bush's reelection.

Other Religious Trends

Religion helped shape opposing views in American society, and those cultural divisions made political compromise harder. Earlier conflicts had focused on abortion and prayer and Bible reading in schools. Increasingly, however, the focus was the meaning of the word "family."

Marriage and the Family

Like the church and the government, the family is a God-created institution. Therefore conservatives, especially Christian conservatives, have insisted that marriage is for only a man and woman, as God intended. But gay rights supporters have pushed for homosexual "marriages." Some people, including President Bush, pressed for a constitutional amendment that would ban homosexual marriage. Others wanted the issue to be addressed by individual states.

Some liberal churches actively supported the homosexual agenda. In 2003 the Episcopal Church elected Gene Robinson, an open homosexual, as bishop of New Hampshire. The result was a fierce debate within the denomination, and many conservative congregations split from the Episcopal Church in the United States of America. Some even placed themselves under the oversight of evangelical bishops in Africa.

Religious Controversies in Popular Culture

Other religious controversies occurred in the realm of popular culture. In 2004, the film *The Passion of the Christ* presented the extreme violence of the Crucifixion. Some critics said that it blamed the Jews. But the film was a huge financial success.

In 2006, a film and a novel both titled *The DaVinci Code* became very popular. They claimed that the Catholic Church had covered up unsavory details about Christ and the beginnings of Christianity. Catholics and Evangelicals feared that people would regard those works of fiction as fact.

Around the same time the *DaVinci Code* was released, National Geographic ran a program about the recently translated *Gospel of Judas*. According to the National Geographic program, the *Gospel of Judas* revealed that Judas' "betrayal" was arranged by Jesus as a way for him to escape his body.

In 2007 a film called *The Lost Tomb of Jesus* claimed that archaeologists had discovered the tomb of Joseph, Mary, and Jesus. It further claimed that Jesus had been married, probably to Mary of Magdalene, and that he had a son.

These public challenges to Christianity gave Christians the opportunity to respond publicly to a large audience. News organizations interviewed Christian scholars for their perspective on the controversies, and several Christian scholars authored popular books in response to the charges made against Christianity.

Religion and Social Welfare

The urgency of the AIDS crisis became increasingly apparent through the mid-1980s and early 1990s. At first, religious conservatives (particularly Roman Catholics and evangelical Protestants) resisted some measures to fight acquired immune deficiency syndrome (AIDS). They wanted the government to promote abstinence because the vast majority of AIDS patients were homosexuals and drug addicts. They believed that resources devoted to medical treatment should instead be directed at problems like cancer.

Despite conservative opposition, the Clinton administration stressed treatment. Eventually, the number of more effective drugs led to reduced deaths from the disease. Even so, by 2000, about 800,000 Americans had AIDS. At first, President Bush, influenced by Evangelicals, did not make the fight against AIDS a priority. However, Franklin Graham and others convinced Bush to support treatment. His administration became the first to commit funds to fight the disease throughout the world.

The growing diversity in American religion became more apparent at the opening of the twenty-first century. The largest Hindu temple in America was completed in the Atlanta suburb of Lilburn in 2007.

Where Religion Grew

The twenty-first century opened with a changed religious landscape. Membership of liberal Protestant denominations continued to decline. The public influence of these denominations remained strong, however, because their members still served in powerful places in society. While the mainline denominations declined, other religious groups grew. About one-half of Americans were either Roman Catholics, Pentecostals, or Charismatics. The number of Mormons also grew dramatically.

The Southern Baptist Convention was still the leading Protestant denomination. In the suburbs, large "**megachurches**"—such as Willow Creek Community Church in South Barrington, Illinois— attracted thousands of "seekers" for contemporary worship services. Immigrants from Asia, the Middle East, and Africa brought with them Hinduism and Islam. American cities soon had temples and mosques where those people worshiped.

Willow Creek Church became a symbol of evangelical megachurches.

Economic Developments

In the 1990s, the American economy was like a roller coaster. In the first half of the decade, it was weak, but during the second half it boomed. Clinton's free-trade agreements in world markets—NAFTA and GATT—contributed to the growth. American workers produced more. Computer technology and the Internet boosted business. The value of stocks on Wall Street rose dramatically. With the Cold War over, less had to be spent on defense. The federal government had a budget surplus. The American economy at the end of the twentieth century thrived. The German and Japanese economies, and those of other major countries, struggled.

But by early 2001, as the Clinton era ended and the Bush era began, the economy slowed dramatically. Stock values, especially those in new high-tech companies—the "dot coms" of the Internet boom—declined. Companies went out of business. Unemployment rose. Many investors had expected the Internet to generate greater riches.

Bush inherited a sluggish economy from Clinton. But his first tax cut in 2001 had good results. He and Congress cut taxes again in 2002 and 2003. Most Americans, even those in lower tax brackets, benefited. The tax laws also abolished the "marriage penalty." That

The Islamic Center of Greater Toledo beside I-75 in Ohio made the presence of Islam readily visible.

clause had required married couples to pay more than single tax-payers.

Although Bush pushed for more tax cuts, federal spending increased between 2001 and mid-2005. The main reason for the increase was greater expenditures for the military and security after 9/11 and the wars in Afghanistan and Iraq. With a sometimes weak

The Marvel of Wal-Mart

Sam Walton began his career in the discount retail business right after World War II when he operated a Ben Franklin store in Newport, Arkansas. He realized quickly that he could make more money by reducing prices—as long as he increased volume. He continued that philosophy when he opened his first Wal-Mart store in 1962 in Rogers, Arkansas. Walton focused relentlessly on keeping prices low. He made that possible by stressing efficiency in operating the business, demanding lower prices from suppliers (by purchasing in large quantities), and keeping wages low. Sam Walton fiercely fought unions for his employees.

Walton also had a passion for expanding his business. By 1970, Walton had 32 stores. A decade later, he had 276 stores. Expansion continued after his death in 1992. By 2006, Wal-Mart was one of the two biggest companies in the world (ExxonMobil being the other), with two million employees and annual sales in 2006 of more than $300 billion. Wal-Mart is the largest retailer in North America. In about two-thirds of the states of the United States, Wal-Mart is the largest employer. It is also now international, with stores in China, Germany, and the United Kingdom.

Given its size, Wal-Mart has important effects on society. Lower prices help people with low incomes and work against inflation. When a Wal-Mart opens, it helps reduce unemployment. The retail giant also has a global impact. If it were a country, it would be China's eighth-largest trading partner.

But Wal-Mart also has its critics. Although they hire a lot of people, the stores also put a lot of local "mom-and-pop" stores out of business because small stores cannot compete with Wal-Mart's low prices. For that reason, some towns have resisted the coming of Wal-Mart to their areas. Other people complain that Wal-Mart wages, although far above minimum wage, are not adequate for the average American family. Occasionally, Wal-Mart has to defend itself from charges that it takes advantage of even cheaper labor overseas or uses illegal immigrants in the United States.

Good or bad, Wal-Mart remains an incredible American success story.

Wal-Mart, the largest retail establishment in the nation, has large numbers of both supporters and critics.

China, which has become one of the world's largest commercial powers, is the major supplier of Wal-Mart products.

economy, reduced revenues from the tax cuts, and more spending, the federal budget deficit reached record levels. The budget deficit for 2004 reached $639 billion. That was the highest since 1983 and the second highest since World War II.

Despite the deficit, the economy remained healthy under Bush. When he took office, unemployment had been 4.7 percent. It reached a high of 6.2 percent in June 2003. But it fell again to 4.8 percent in February 2006. By early 2006, the economy had grown a modest 4.8 percent. Under President Bush the country had lower inflation, lower unemployment, increased wages and benefits, and 29 percent more economic output.

The United States had 45 percent more exports. It remained the world's largest exporter. Its economy was the largest in the world. And it continued to perform better than those of Germany and Japan, the next largest competitors.

Discussion Idea

Share the following statement with the students and then guide them in a discussion: If Wal-Mart were a country, it would be China's eighth largest trading partner.

More Discussion Questions

Pose the following discussion questions to the students.

1. Should the U.S. government prevent American companies from compromising the principle of freedom in their quest for Chinese dollars?

2. How can the United States protect its national security while at the same time permitting free trade with totalitarian regimes such as Communist China?

3. What can the United States do to ensure that China "plays by the rules" and engages in truly *free* trade rather than giving its companies an unfair advantage over American companies?

The U.S. economy continued to expand throughout the world. ExxonMobil and Wal-Mart, the two largest companies in America in 2006, and other companies had an enormous impact on the world economy. With more international free trade, bigger corporations took advantage of more opportunities. In addition to older business giants such as McDonalds, Disney, and Coca-Cola, new corporations such as Starbucks spread overseas. With the Internet, Microsoft and Google became global players. Even with the end of the Cold War, the United States continued to spend billions of dollars on the military for world stability to make those economic opportunities possible.

Communist China, the world's largest emerging market, sought American business and industry. While many had hoped that China's openness to world markets would lead to a more open society, the Chinese government was interested in business, not democracy. Chinese officials pressured foreign businesses to cooperate in suppressing individual freedoms. For example, to operate in that country, Google agreed to block certain words from searches. In effect, Google served as a censor of the Internet, forbidding citizens access to certain information the government did not want them to know. Even so, globalization brought more service, white-collar jobs, and lower prices for shoppers everywhere. Increasingly, products were made in developing countries, where wages were low.

On the other hand, a global economy did not help all Americans. Trade deficits grew as Americans bought from foreign countries more goods than they sold to people overseas. Some businesspeople complained that free trade was unfair because they had to compete with foreign businesses that paid lower wages. Cheaper goods flooded the American market.

Also, many foreigners viewed globalization as Americanization. They resented the impact of not only American business but also its culture. They saw fast food, Hollywood films, popular music, television programs, and American theme parks overseas as threats to their traditional ways of life.

Business success in the early twenty-first century also brought some corrupt executives. They committed fraud. They covered up company debt, exaggerated profits, benefited from their stock sales before declaring bankruptcy, and profited from inside information

The Enron Collapse

In 2001, the Houston-based energy company Enron declared bankruptcy. It was the biggest corporate bankruptcy in American history. The company included divisions dedicated to natural gas, electricity, pulp and paper, and communications. It had employed 21,000 people and reported revenues of more than $100 billion in 2000. The company collapsed because of massive financial fraud. As a result of the scandal, Enron's accounting firm, Arthur Anderson, dissolved.

Enron became a symbol of corporate greed in the economic boom of the 1990s. Because it had contributed mostly to Republicans, that party suffered from its association with the company. As a result of Enron's scandal, Congress tightened government control over business practices. Another result was the prosecution of other businesses that had suspect financial practices.

Gasoline prices soared in the middle years of the first decade of the new millennium.

Entertainment Explosion

By 2000, more than 98 percent of U.S. homes had color televisions. In 1995, about 65 percent of American homes had cable television. Americans spend about six hours a day watching television.

Martha Stewart and Ken Lay became symbols of corporate fraud and corruption at the turn of the century.

about the companies. When the companies crashed, the executives faced criminal charges and imprisonment. But employees and other average Americans who had purchased company stock suffered financially. Many of them lost jobs and retirement accounts.

Certain executives and companies came to symbolize corporate greed and corruption. Ken Lay of Enron and Martha Stewart are two people who became synonymous with corporate misdeeds.

The dramatic increase in the price of gasoline posed a threat to American prosperity. In July 2004, the price of regular gas was under $2/gallon. By September 2005, it had shot up to a little over $3/gallon. By June 2006, it hovered a little under $3/gallon. In 2008 the price of gas exceeded $4/gallon at times. Higher prices for fuel caused the prices of other goods to go up because of increased transportation costs.

Advances in Technology

Although the personal computer and the Internet were already normal features of everyday life for millions of Americans, by the early twenty-first century new capabilities developed rapidly. The noun *Google* became a verb. With its increased speed, that search engine could perform more complex searches for Internet users. Yahoo and Microsoft improved and competed with Google. Wireless (or WiFi) technology made computers more portable.

A new generation of electronic gadgets entered the marketplace. Palm Inc.'s "Palm Pilots," handheld computers, provided note taking, calendar management, and other applications on the go. In 1999, a competitor, BlackBerry, appeared and provided those and other services, becoming the favorite of business users. Cell phones multiplied, and as their capabilities expanded to include text messaging, digital photos, and video, they began to replace Palms.

In 2000, Apple Computer introduced the iPod. It became the most popular portable media player in the world. Apple steadily improved the device, which featured music, digital photos, and videos downloaded from the Internet. The technology that once would have taken up a lot of space in a living room now could be carried in one's pocket or held in the palm of the hand. In 2007, Apple released the iPhone, which combined the functions of cell phone, palm device, and iPod.

Other technological innovations changed daily life. Videotapes, VCRs, and fax machines were followed by DVDs, high-definition television (HDTV), and TiVo.

Bill Gates and Microsoft

William H. ("Bill") Gates started programming computers at age thirteen. Gates continued his innovative computer programming work as a student at Harvard. He dropped out of college in his junior year to found, with a friend, Microsoft Corporation in 1975. Gates and his company concentrated on developing software for personal computers for the office and home. They continued to create software that was quicker, cheaper, and easier to use. From July 2004 to June 2005, Microsoft earned about $40 billion, and the company has employed 61,000 people in more than 100 countries. Gates has written two books, *The Road Ahead* and *Business @ the Speed of Thought*.

In 2008 Gates left his day-to-day work at Microsoft to concentrate on the work of the Bill and Melinda Gates Foundation, a charity for global health and education causes.

Intelligent Design, Creationism, and Evolution

Have volunteers research (in the library and online) and report to the class on the subjects of Intelligent Design, creationism, and evolution. Prepare them by sharing the information about these topics given in the side margin.

Popular Culture Activities

If you choose to discuss popular culture of this period with the students, be aware that much of the content (television, movies, books, etc.) is decadent and ungodly. One exception is the writing of J.R.R. Tolkien, such as his trilogy *The Lord of the Rings* that became popular in both written and film forms. Have the students compare and contrast John Bunyan's *Pilgrim's Progress* and Tolkien's *The Lord of the Rings* series. Have them pay particular attention to symbolism. (You might make this a cooperative project with the literature teacher.)

Another project idea involves television. By almost every measure, television dominates America's leisure time. Students, even Christian students, do not like to hear adults complain about their watching too much television, so have the students research people's TV-viewing habits in American society. They probably will be surprised at the statistics they discover, and the information will have more impact on them than if you or their parents just "lecture" them about it.

Ask the students to read Ephesians 4–5 and evaluate how popular entertainments measure up against God's standards in these chapters. Specific programs or movies could be critiqued. This will not necessitate student (or teacher) viewing. With the most popular shows there is usually enough information "in the air" to make an evaluation.

The Growing Problem of an Obese Society

Public health officials in the United States are becoming increasingly alarmed by the growing problem of obesity, which is driven by not only overeating but also eating unhealthful foods and not getting enough exercise. Have the students look at websites

Electronic changes affected daily lives in other ways. People could shop online through eBay, Amazon.com, or countless other websites. They could have their paychecks deposited in their bank accounts electronically. They could do banking online without ever seeing the money. Even politicians could use the Internet to raise funds and solicit supporters. And electronic games entertained millions of people.

The History of Google

The Internet has affected people's lives in many ways, and one way is the creation of new words. Google, for instance, is not only a proper noun but also a verb, to google.

Larry Page and Sergei Brin, graduate students at Stanford University, after working a couple of years in a dorm room, started BackRub, a search engine that could find links among websites. In 1998, after improving the technology and attracting investors, they created Google, Inc., in a garage in Menlo Park, California.

As the world's leading Internet search engine, Google has made life easier for countless people. Since its modest beginnings, Google has also garnered about 50 percent of the Internet search engine market and has become a major global company. The company's future growth seems assured as it enters markets such as China.

Those inventions did more than just make life easier. Christians could use them to evangelize. Missionaries, for so long isolated in distant places, could now communicate instantly. A person could stand in a field in rural Kenya, position a satellite phone for connecting with a satellite, import e-mails with pictures, and then connect the phone to a laptop and discover the news from home. All of this could take place where there was no electricity, running water, or indoor plumbing.

Technology and the devices it makes possible are tools. Because humans are sinful, they often use technological tools to help them sin. Because digital data is easily copied, enforcing copyright laws proved difficult, especially for music and films. The perceived anonymity of the Web also led to the rapid expansion of the pornography industry.

Technology also threatened to become a master rather than a servant. The devices that were supposed to save time ended up making the whole pace of life speed up—so people felt they had less time. E-mail sucked time out of the work day. The way people took in information changed from the static newspaper to the dynamic television to the interactive Internet. Recently some intellectuals have begun to complain that the hyperlinked Web shortens attention spans and encourages superficial thinking. Cell phone use sometimes clashes with good manners. Phones ring at inopportune times. Private conversations in public can be awkward.

Other technological advances created moral dilemmas. Cloning and stem cell research advanced quickly, and Western societies that had abandoned scriptural absolutes were at a loss to determine right and wrong in these new situations.

Right Turn at the Supreme Court

The country had experienced decades of liberal Supreme Court decisions. Those rulings ranged from taking prayer and Bible-reading from public schools to granting women the right to an

Supreme Court Justice John Paul Stevens swore in John Roberts as chief justice on September 29, 2005.

of fastfood companies and of companies that manufacture or sell foods. Have them report on the nutritional information they find. If they discover the lack of nutrition or exercise themselves, they might be more willing to make changes in their own lifestyles. Have them find Bible verses that relate to taking care of their bodies.

Gasoline Prices

A serious economic problem encountered at the turn of the century and growing every year has been the rapid increase in the price of gasoline and other petroleum-based fuels. Have volunteers investigate, either online or in the library, various aspects of this problem such as the historical data of the increase, reasons for the increase, complicating factors, or alternatives to solve the problem. Some questions they might answer include the following: What is the importance of the price of a barrel of oil? Why do events in the world (e.g., wars) affect fuel prices? Why are prices higher (or lower) at different times of the year? Do Americans pay more or less than consumers in other countries and why? What are short-term solutions to the problem? What are long-term solutions to the problem?

Christians and the Environment

Environmental concerns have increased in recent years. Conservatives typically minimize the issue, while liberals tend to be more concerned—even alarmists—about it. Have volunteers answer the following questions about the environment: What should be the attitude of the Christian toward the environment? What does the Bible say about the natural world and our attitude toward it? Focus on the following points.

1. What does the Bible say about creation and the physical world? *(The natural world is part of God's revelation; it communicates that God exists, that He is a powerful Creator, and that He is good toward the righteous and unrighteous alike. Ps. 19:1–6; Rom. 1:20; Acts 14:17)*

2. What is the role of Christians as good stewards of the physical world? *(God has commanded all people, including*

Supreme Court Nominations

Most of the presidents of the United States have had the privilege of nominating one or more justices to the Supreme Court. George Washington has the distinction of naming the most justices—eleven. FDR is close behind with nine, followed by Taft with six. Three presidents—Jackson, Lincoln, and Eisenhower—each nominated five justices. Only four presidents—William Henry Harrison, Zachary Taylor, Andrew Johnson, and Jimmy Carter—did not have the opportunity to nominate any justices.

Samuel Alito was sworn in as a justice on February 1, 2006.

abortion. But in 2005 and 2006, the Court gained two conservative justices.

Sandra Day O'Connor, the first woman to serve on the Supreme Court, announced her retirement in 2005. Bush nominated **John G. Roberts Jr.** to replace her. Later that year, before the Senate could vote on Roberts, Chief Justice William Rehnquist died. Bush chose Roberts to replace Rehnquist. Earlier in his career, Roberts had served as a clerk for Rehnquist. Roberts's qualifications and articulate responses to hostile questions impressed even his critics. The Senate easily confirmed him. On September 29, 2005, he became the seventeenth chief justice of the United States.

Roberts was well qualified. He was a graduate of Harvard Law School and had practiced law for several years. He served under earlier Republican presidents in the Department of Justice and the office of the White House Counsel. In 2003, the Senate confirmed him for a seat on the U.S. Court of Appeals. Many Americans hoped that he would be a vote against some of the liberal landmark cases that produced abortion rights and other controversial decisions.

To fill O'Connor's spot, Bush in 2005 initially chose another woman, White House Counsel Harriet Miers. But after protests from conservatives for her lack of a track record on major issues, she withdrew from consideration. Bush then tapped **Samuel Alito Jr.** Like Roberts, Alito had excellent academic credentials. He had served on the U.S. Court of Appeals, but in a different circuit. The Senate confirmed him in January 2006.

Alito had a strong conservative record. He was a member of the Federalist Society, which seeks a return to traditional legal views. His record earned him the nickname "Scalito" because his decisions agreed often with those of conservative Supreme Court Justice Antonin Scalia. Alito and Roberts are both Catholics. For the first time the Supreme Court had a Catholic majority in Alito, Roberts, Scalia, Kennedy, and Thomas.

Section Quiz

1. From which Hispanic country do most immigrants—both legal and illegal—come?
2. Who was the first Hispanic Attorney General?
3. What types of private organizations were to provided the centerpiece of Bush's "compassionate conservatism"?
4. Name two evangelical Christians in Bush's administration.
5. What company became a symbol of corporate corruption during the first decade of the twenty-first century?
6. Whom did Bush name to be the chief justice of the Supreme Court? Which other justice did Bush nominate during his administration?

Christians, to exercise good and wise dominion over the world; they should use the resources of the world for the benefit of others, but they should do so in a wise way that respects God's creation (Gen. 1:26–28).)

3. The natural world also suffers under the curse of sin. What does that mean for our attitude toward nature? (Because of sin the world groans and decays (Rom 8:19–22); man's work at exercising dominion is hindered by the fallen world (Gen. 3:17).)

4. God placed man over the natural world. What are the implications of that as we consider the environment?

(Mankind should use the world's resources, but in doing so he should act in a way that also tends and cares for the earth that is entrusted to him.)

Section Quiz Answers

1. Mexico
2. Alberto Gonzales
3. faith-based organizations
4. (any two) John Ashcroft, Condoleeza Rice, Karen Hughes, Andrew Card, Don Evans, Michael Gerson
5. Enron
6. John Roberts; Samuel Alito

☆ Why do recent technological advances like stem cell research and cloning raise moral issues that society has trouble answering?

III. America and the World

The Bush administration faced many challenges, especially on the international scene. Dealing with these challenges without making more enemies proved difficult. Bush's critics charged that he favored a unilateral approach—America acting alone rather than through the U.N. or NATO. In Bosnia and Kosovo, Clinton had acted with the approval of only the U.N. Security Council, so Bush's actions were nothing new. For the war in Afghanistan, Bush formed a large international coalition. But for the war in Iraq, far fewer countries were part of the "coalition of the willing."

British Prime Minister Tony Blair remained a staunch ally of Bush. But others in Europe—particularly the French and the Germans—strongly disapproved of the war in Iraq. They disagreed with America's preemptive strategy. Many European countries had large Muslim minorities, so they were careful not to offend them.

During the Cold War, the Soviet Union had balanced the power of the United States. After the fall of the Soviet Empire, several European leaders feared that America was too powerful.

Diplomatic Successes

Bush enjoyed some diplomatic successes. He convinced Libya to abandon terrorism and weapons of mass destruction and to seek closer ties with the West. The toppling of Saddam Hussein in Iraq might have been a lesson to Libyan dictator Qaddafi.

Bush also convinced Pakistan, one of the world's most powerful Muslim nations, to work closely with him in waging the war on terror. (Some critics wondered if Pakistani leaders did everything they could to help.)

In Asia, Bush forged closer economic and diplomatic ties with China. Japan and South Korea continued to back American interests. They, with China and the United States, negotiated with North Korea to ensure stability in East Asia.

Lingering Problems

But problems continued. North Korea, with its Communist dictator, pursued nuclear weapons. In that instance, Bush used a multilateral approach. He enlisted China, Japan, and South Korea to help confront the problem.

Iran also threatened to acquire nuclear weapons. Bush worked with Europeans—especially France, Germany, and Great Britain—to prevent it. Iran, a terrorist state with large oil reserves, could be a serious threat to nearby Israel. Its leader, Mahmoud Ahmadinejad, threatened to attack Israel if any country tried to stop his pursuit of nuclear weapons.

Bush's decision to act alone or in conjunction with other leaders depended on the circumstances. He placed America's interests first. If other nations wanted to help, that was fine. If they did not, he would act alone.

Problems between Israel and its Arab neighbors continued into the twenty-first century. The fate of Palestinians living in Israeli-

Bush and Tony Blair, British prime minister, were staunch allies in the war on terror.

Mahmoud Ahmadinejad of Iran began challenging the West after the fall of Saddam Hussein in Iraq, verbally attacking Israel and flaunting Iran's efforts to develop nuclear weapons.

Section III
Objectives

Students should be able to

1. Describe diplomatic successes of the Bush administration.
2. Identify ongoing problems for the United States in foreign affairs.
3. Describe natural disasters that struck America in 2004–2006 and their political and economic effects on the country.

Changes in British Government

One of President Bush's staunchest allies in the war on terror was British Prime Minister Tony Blair. On June 27, 2007, however, Blair resigned. He was replaced by Gordon Brown, who pledged to remain committed to the war on terror. But some reports indicate that Brown might be trying to distance himself from the United States, especially since Blair was often caricatured as Bush's lap dog.

Mahmoud Ahmadinejad

The controversial president of Iran, Mahmoud Ahmadinejad, was born in 1956. He entered college in 1975 and earned degrees in civil engineering and traffic and transportation (PhD). He joined Iran's Revolutionary Guard and was reportedly involved in covert operations during the Iran-Iraq War. In 2003, he was appointed mayor of Tehran and immediately used his contacts in the Revolutionary Guard to roll back many of the reforms that were made before him. He tried to restore Islamic law, including forcing women to wear veils.

Ahmadinejad was elected president in 2005. He gained notoriety with his confrontational, in-your-face style and derog-

☆ Western society has largely abandoned Christian reasoning in public debates. Even evangelicals don't appeal to Scripture in public policy debates. As a result, society has no moral standard to govern the use of technological advances.

atory comments concerning the West, especially the United States. He also claimed that the Holocaust was a "myth" and said that Israel should be "wiped off the map." Of especially grave concern to the United States, he insists that Iran has a "right" to develop nuclear weapons and has repeatedly defied UN inspectors. Under his leadership, the United States alleges, Iran has been instrumental in keeping insurgent activities alive in Iraq. In early 2008, Iranian naval vessels threatened U.S. naval vessels in the Persian Gulf, ensuring that relations between the two countries would remain touchy for years to come.

Hugo Chavez

Hugo Chavez, the president of Venezuela, led a failed coup d'etat in 1992. But in 1998, he was elected to the presidency by promising aid to the poor. He was reelected in 2000 and 2006, but he had to overcome a coup attempt in 2002, and his popular support has steadily declined as his promises failed to materialize and he turned many Western countries against him for his bombastic public statements. He was reelected again in 2006. He lost a referendum, however, that would have made him president for life, and he immediately began taking actions against Christians and foreigners, whom he blamed for the defeat. He has been especially at odds with the Christian missionary group New Tribes Missions. Yet he retains great power, not least of which is the military.

Ray Nagin, New Orleans, and Hurricane Katrina

Ray Nagin, the mayor of New Orleans, was born in 1956 and earned a B.S. degree in accounting from Tuskegee University and an MBA degree from Tulane University.

controlled territory gained in an earlier war remained the focus of negotiations among Americans, Israelis, and Palestinians.

In 1993, during the Clinton administration, the **Oslo Accords** made progress toward Palestinian self-rule. In 1997, Clinton convinced the leaders of Israel and the Palestinians to sign the **Wye River Memorandum**. That agreement called for Israel to withdraw from some Palestinian territory. In exchange, Palestinians would try to control terrorism against Israel. More importantly, they would accept the existence of the state of Israel and no longer seek its destruction.

Progress toward peace was further hampered by three events. First, Yassir Arafat, head of the Palestine Liberation Organization, and Israeli Prime Minister Ariel Sharon died. Then the Palestinian terrorist group Hamas won control of the Palestinian Authority parliament. Nevertheless, in 2005 Israel withdrew from the Gaza Strip and surrendered it to the Palestinians. That development raised hopes that peace could eventually come to the region.

Hurricane Charley was the first of many major natural disasters that hit the United States in the middle 2000s.

Natural Disasters

In 2004–2006, several major catastrophes, most of them weather related, struck the United States. In 2004, six major hurricanes (category 3 and higher) hit the United States, causing $42 billion in damages and killing more than 3,100 people. The worst was **Hurricane Charley**, which made landfall on August 13 in Punta Gorda and Port Charlotte, Florida, in the southwestern part of the state. Charley was a category 4 hurricane with sustained winds of 150 mph. It was the first hurricane to hit that area in nearly forty years.

In 2005, a record fifteen hurricanes developed, seven of them major. They caused more than 2,280 deaths and $128 billion in damages. The worst of those storms was **Hurricane Katrina**, a category 3 with sustained winds of 125 mph that hit the Gulf Coast of Louisiana, Mississippi, and Alabama, on August 29. But the high winds were not the major problem. Flooding from the storm broke the levees surrounding New Orleans, much of which is below sea level. Soon, 80 percent of the city was under water. The tragedy killed more than 1,800 people, the highest number of fatalities in a hurricane since 1928. Katrina caused about $75 billion in damages, making it the costliest hurricane in American history.

A Public Relations Disaster

The residents of Louisiana and Mississippi suffered greatly from Hurricane Katrina. Nonstop media coverage of the disaster focused national and world attention on the plight of the residents of New Orleans. They showed images of people trying desperately to escape the flooding. People cut holes in their roofs and tried to get the attention of rescuers. Those who managed to escape had few places to go. Patients in hospitals languished. Many of them died in the more than one hundred-degree temperatures.

During Hurricane Katrina, broken levees allowed the waters of Lake Pontchartrain to flood the city of New Orleans.

Blame for the disaster flowed freely. Most of it was directed at Bush and the **Federal Emergency Management Administration** (FEMA) for their slowness to act.

Less publicized were the faulty decisions by local officials and local residents and the crime wave that swept the area in the aftermath of the hurricane. Residents were warned to evacuate well before the hurricane hit. But thousands of them refused to do so. Dozens of school buses could have been used to evacuate people who had no other means of transport. But the buses sat unused until they were stranded in floodwaters.

Would-be rescuers were driven away from the very people they wanted to save when criminals shot at their helicopters, boats, and other rescue vehicles. Many New Orleans police officers simply walked away from their jobs.

Relief workers moved people into the Super Dome, but that sports complex quickly became overcrowded and disorderly. Gangs who were also inside terrorized the refugees. People lived in filth. The entire incident became a public relations nightmare.

As the region began to clean up and rebuild, priorities became evident. For example, in Biloxi, Mississippi, another hard-hit area, Katrina destroyed the "floating casinos." Some of them were even washed ashore. But casinos were the first businesses to be rebuilt. They were rebuilt before most homes. The legislature even passed a special law allowing them to be built on land. Within four months, gambling revenues were approaching pre-Katrina levels.

But Hurricane Katrina also brought out the best in some people. Aid workers risked their lives to help victims. Americans and even citizens of other nations gave generously to those in need. Cities throughout the nation offered to house refugees in shelters. Individuals all over America opened their homes or provided jobs for those who would have to remain away from their homes for months. They gave millions of dollars in aid. Schools, church groups, and other nonprofit organizations went to New Orleans and other surrounding cities and towns to help with rescues and rebuilding efforts. Christians took the opportunity to show love to fellow citizens and live the truth that Paul described in 1 Corinthians 13: "And now abideth faith, hope, charity, these three; but the greatest of these is charity."

The 2008 Presidential Election

The 2008 presidential election campaign began in 2006 as candidates of both parties began positioning themselves for a run at the White House. The campaign started earlier than any other race in recent history, and more money was raised and spent during that campaign than in any other presidential campaign.

Both major parties fielded several candidates. The Democrats gradually narrowed their field of viable candidates to two: former First Lady Hillary Clinton and a relative newcomer to national politics, Illinois senator **Barack Obama**. For much of the campaign, Clinton seemed to be the presumptive nominee, but she stumbled in several late primaries, and Obama surged ahead, capturing the nomination. Despite having campaigned on the theme of change, Obama chose as his vice presidential running mate a career politician, Delaware senator Joe Biden.

The Republicans also fielded a large number of candidates of various political stripes. They ranged from a former Baptist preacher

Hurricane Katrina caused terrible damages along the Gulf Coast east of New Orleans. Floating casinos in Biloxi, Mississippi, were wiped out.

Joe Biden, Barack Obama, and their wives wave to the delegates at the Democratic National Convention.

When he was elected the sixtieth mayor of New Orleans in 2002, he had never held elected office before. He had, instead, gained experience in business as the vice president and general manager of Cox Communications, a cable company.

Nagin campaigned on promises to end government corruption and run city government more like a business. After taking office, he began a crackdown on corruption amid highly publicized scenes of government officials being taken out in handcuffs. He also fired the entire city vehicle inspection department in response to corruption there.

In 2004, as Hurricane Ivan threatened the city, Nagin ordered a mandatory evacuation, and more than half a million people heeded his warning, leading to massive traffic jams lasting twelve to twenty-four hours. But the storm missed the city, and people criticized him for creating unnecessary disorder. So when Hurricane Katrina threatened, Nagin was understandably slower to order an evacuation. Finally, after Katrina rose to a Category 4 storm, he ordered a mandatory evacuation. About 90,000 people were still in the city when the storm hit. The city survived the storm itself, but about 80 percent of it was inundated with floodwaters when levees broke. The loss of life and property was horrific.

A flood of criticism followed the flood of water, and Nagin began blaming the federal disaster relief agencies, especially FEMA, for responding slowly and insufficiently as well as for subsequent problems. But criticism flowed back toward him, especially for his letting hundreds of New Orleans buses sit idle instead of using them to evacuate people. Yet, he was reelected in 2006 and has continued to work for the rebuilding of his city. Many parts

Activity 3: Katrina: A True Story of Grace

Use this activity to help the students "put a human face" on the tragedy of Hurricane Katrina and to encourage them to look to God for the grace they need in every trial.

of the city, however, remain in decay, and recovery is slow.

Federal Response to Katrina

In spite of criticisms of FEMA, the federal government has spent record amounts of money on various types of relief for victims of Hurricane Katrina. As of September 8, 2006, FEMA had taken the following actions:

- Provided $6 billion directly to victims for housing and other emergency assistance. This is the most that has been spent for any single natural disaster. Nearly 950,000 applicants were deemed eligible. FEMA spent $4.2 billion for housing, including $650 million for motels for 85,000 households as short-term help.

- Conducted 1.3 million housing inspections in Alabama, Louisiana, and Mississippi.

- Provided 101,174 travel trailers and mobile homes for victims.

- Housed more than 7,000 households, most of them New Orleans city employees and first responders and their families, on cruise ships.

- Paid out more than $4.8 billion for debris removal and restoration of infrastructure (roads, bridges, utilities, etc.), double that budgeted for 2004 across fifteen states, Puerto Rico, and the U.S. Virgin Islands. These funds paid for removal of more than 99 million cubic yards of debris.

- Paid out $126 million for crisis counseling.

- Paid out $735 million to forty-five states and the District of Columbia to reimburse them for expenses in-

The conservative Sarah Palin and the maverick John McCain failed to gain a victory for the Republicans.

and social conservative, Arkansas governor Mike Huckabee, to New York mayor Rudy Guiliani, made popular by his prompt response to the 9/11 terrorist attacks, to former Massachusetts governor and fiscal conservative Mitt Romney. However, John McCain, Arizona senator and Vietnam war hero, won the Republican nomination. In a move designed to shore up weak support among the Republican base, McCain selected Alaska governor Sarah Palin to be his running mate. Both of them had reputations as political "mavericks" who had fought wasteful government spending and unethical conduct, even within their own party.

The race for president pitted youth, inexperience, and promises of new ideas, hope, and change against age, experience, and toughness. The Republicans tried to focus voters' attention on the fact that Obama had had no administrative experience beyond being a "community organizer" and had no record of accomplishment in his short political career that included short stints in the Illinois legislature and less than a full term as U.S. senator. They pointed out that most of Obama's votes had been neither for nor against legislation but merely "present." This was designed to show that he was in attendance but did not take an official position. However, McCain proved to be an uninspiring campaign speaker who did not connect with many voters. In addition, many conservatives in the Republican Party did not trust him because of his willingness

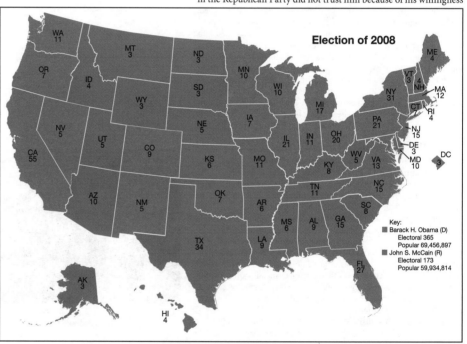

to cooperate with liberals on many issues. But his running mate was different. Palin attracted large, enthusiastic crowds wherever she appeared and rallied the base as no candidate had since Ronald Reagan. The media attacked her at every opportunity and embarrassed her with obscure questions during televised interviews. No detail of her life was considered off limits. Yet she responded with a tenacity and transparency that sustained her popularity through the campaign.

Obama was a tireless, enthusiastic campaigner who knew how to create an image of power, authority, and promise. His team orchestrated every appearance to enhance that image, from his nomination acceptance speech amid Greek columns and machine-generated smoke to his ads showing him in a mock-up of the Oval Office. Critics repeatedly argued that his speeches lacked substance, but his charisma and the support of an overwhelming majority of the media overcame those objections. The fact that he could become the nation's first African-American president energized the black electorate as never before. On November 4, 2008, Obama defeated McCain by several million popular votes. The Electoral College vote was 365 for Obama and 173 for McCain. Obama was sworn in as America's first black president on January 20, 2009.

The Democrats added to their majorities in both the House and the Senate as their candidates rode Obama's coattails to victory. In the Senate, however, although the Democrats added seats, they fell short of gaining a filibuster-proof majority.

The Bidens and Obamas wave to the crowd on Inauguration Day.

The Start of the Obama Administration

Obama's campaign had promised hope, change, and transparent ethics. However, as Obama named his cabinet there was little change. Most of his nominees were Washington insiders, and many of them had ties to the Clinton administration, including his choice of Hillary Clinton to be secretary of state. Although he had pledged that no lobbyists would be part of his administration, he named several former lobbyists to cabinet posts. Several of his nominees also came under fire for failure to pay income taxes, and some had to withdraw from consideration. In a nod toward his pledge of bipartisanship, Obama asked Republican Robert Gates to stay on as

curred in relocating and sheltering victims.

- Paid $1.6 billion to 803,470 individuals to help with immediate emergency needs (housing, food, clothing, etc.).
- Allocated $410 million for unemployment assistance to victims.

 CD: Barack Obama, 44th President

See the CD for information on President Obama.

secretary of defense and tapped Judd Gregg a Republican senator from New Hampshire to be his commerce secretary. Gregg soon resigned from his position as he became uncomfortable with the unfolding details of the Obama administration. Obama's plan to take an active role in directing the 2010 census proved to be the last straw for Gregg since it appeared that the administration would seek to use the census for political gain.

Often compared to Franklin Roosevelt, Obama remained closely watched by conservatives while retaining his charismatic influence over the press. What would he try to accomplish during his first one hundred days? Early indications of the direction his administration would take surfaced quickly. Among his first acts as president were executive orders to close the prison holding terrorists at Guantanamo Bay and to end prohibitions against federally funded abortions overseas.

Obama's top priority, however, was the passage of an economic stimulus package. Throughout the campaign, he had repeatedly said that the economy was in a crisis like no other since the days of the Great Depression. Such a crisis, he said, was beyond the power of the free market system to solve and therefore required unprecedented actions by the federal government. Building on President George W. Bush's push for government-financed bailouts of various industries at the end of his administration, Obama pressed for massive government spending to boost the economy into recovery. In response, the House passed, without a single Republican vote, a package for spending more than $840 billion. Republicans and Democrats alike complained that the bill contained billions of dollars of "pork" projects that would do nothing to jump-start the economy.

During his first administration, President Clinton declared that the era of big government was over. However, government continued to grow under Presidents Clinton and Bush, and it is expanding at an alarming pace under President Barack Obama.

Section Quiz

1. Which former terrorist-supporting nation became a U.S. ally after witnessing the fall of Iraq and Saddam Hussein?
2. Which Middle Eastern leader challenged Bush after the fall of Saddam?
3. Which major hurricane in 2004 became the first hurricane to hit Southwest Florida in nearly forty years?
4. Which major hurricane in 2005 wreaked havoc on New Orleans, Louisiana, and Biloxi, Mississippi?
★ How should Christians view natural disasters?

Section Quiz Answers

1. Libya
2. Mahmoud Ahmadinejad
3. Hurricane Charlie
4. Hurricane Katrina
★ They should recognize that God is in control of all things, and they should show His love to people by helping with recovery efforts.

Activity 4: Chapter Review

Use this activity to help the students prepare for the chapter test.

Chapter Review Answers

Review Questions

1. Alberto Gonzales
2. John Kerry
3. Condoleeza Rice
4. John Roberts
5. John Ashcroft
6. C
7. E
8. A
9. D
10. B

Chapter Review

Review Questions

Identify the following people.

1. first Hispanic Attorney General
2. Bush's opponent in the 2004 election
3. National Security Advisor and Secretary of State
4. replaced Rehnquist as chief justice of Supreme Court
5. Bush's first Attorney General

Match each term to its definition.

A. megachurches
B. faith-based initiative
C. coalition of the willing
D. "compassionate conservatism"
E. preemptive strike

6. countries that joined the United States in invading Iraq and ousting Saddam Hussein

7. strategy of hitting an enemy that presents a perceived threat before that threat can be launched

8. large suburban ministries that attract thousands of "seekers" to contemporary services

9. using religious organizations rather than government programs to help fight urban problems

10. any religious organization or program used to practice compassionate conservatism

Critical Thinking

1. Discuss the voting patterns in the 2000 presidential election and why the outcome was so rancorous.

2. Compare and contrast the Japanese attack on Pearl Harbor with the terrorists' attack on the United States on September 11, 2001.

3. In light of the circumstances facing Bush, evaluate his presidency. Rank him in relation to the other presidents of the United States. Support your assessments.

People, Places, and Things to Remember:

"compassionate conservatism"
September 11, 2001
al-Qaeda
Osama bin Laden
Office (Department) of Homeland Security
Patriot Act
preemptive strike
coalition of the willing
John Kerry
Alberto Gonzales
faith-based initiatives
John Ashcroft
Condoleeza Rice
megachurches
John G. Roberts Jr.
Samuel Alito Jr.
Oslo Accords
Wye River Memorandum
Hurricane Charley
Hurricane Katrina
Federal Emergency Management Administration
Barack Obama

Critical Thinking

1. People in large cities tended to vote for Gore, smaller cities and towns and the rural heartland tended to vote for Bush, which made the popular vote very close. The Electoral College vote hinged on the votes of about three states, of which Florida proved the most critical. The contest was rancorous because each side refused to concede to the other. Gore's supporters demanded more and more recounts, hoping to squeeze out every possible vote, and the Bush supporters used the courts to further their candidate's chances.

2. Answers will vary but might include the following ideas. Similarities: Both were surprise/sneak attacks without significant provocation. Both did great material and human damage. Both elicited massive responses from the U.S. military. Differences: The former was perpetrated by a sovereign nation; the latter was perpetrated by individuals from several countries. The former unified the entire nation in a determined effort to destroy the enemy no matter how long it took, whereas the unity produced by the latter was relatively short-lived and ended up dividing the country when people tired of it and politicians tried to use it for political gain. The former demanded sacrifices by the entire nation through either direct military service, loss of loved ones, or rationing of consumer goods whereas the latter demanded no sacrifices by the common citizen. The former elicited unified support for the president, the military, and the entire war effort regardless of political party, whereas the latter elicited partisan political wrangling and positioning for power.

3. Answers will vary.

Index

Photograph Credits

The following agencies and individuals have furnished materials to meet the photographic needs of this textbook. We wish to express our gratitude to them for their important contribution.

AAA
Alamy
AP/WireImage
Architect of the Capitol
Art Resource, NY
Associated Press
Atwater Kent Museum of Philadelphia
BACM
BigStockPhoto.com
Billy Graham Center, Wheaton, Illinois
BJU Press Files
Boston College
The Bridgeman Art Library International
Brink, Julie
Bryan College Archive
Center for American History, UT-Austin
Central Intelligence Agency
Chessie System Railroads
Civilwarphotos.net
Clineff, Kindra
Collection of the Supreme Court of the United States
The Colonial Williamsburg Foundation
Colorado Department of Transportation
Coniff, Dennis
Corcoran Gallery of Art
COREL Corporation
Delaware Art Museum
Department of Defense
Detroit News
Deutsches Bundesarchiv (German Federal Archive)
FEMA News Photo
Finley, Russ
Flyin Phil's Photos
Foskett, Stephen
Fotolia.com
Franklin D. Roosevelt Presidential Library
Frederick, Kenneth
George Bush Presidential Library and Museum
George Mason University Libraries
George W. Bush Presidential Library
Gerald Ford Presidential Library and Museum

Getty Images
Gettysburg Foundation
The Granger Collection, New York
Harper's Weekly
Harry S. Truman Presidential Library
Heisler, Gregory
The Hermitage
Historical Documents Company
The History Place
Independence National Historical Park
Indiana University Archives
iStockPhoto.com
Japanese Library of Parliament Digital Archive
Jas. Townsend and Sons
John F. Kennedy Presidential Library and Museum
Johnson Presidential Library
JupiterImages Corporation
Kansas State Historical Society
Kidder Smith Collection, Rotch Visual Collections, M.I.T.
Landis, Joyce
Library of Congress
Louisiana State Museum
Magnum Photos
The Mariners' Museum
The Metropolitan Museum of Art
Minnesota Historical Society
Mitchell, Rita
NASA
National Archives
National Aviation Hall of Fame
National Park Service
Navy.mil
Nebraska State Historical Society
Nelson, Holly
The New York Public Library
The New York World
NOAA
The Pennsylvania Turnpike Commission
Peterson, John
Photodisc, Inc.
Premiere Radio Networks
The Providence Journal

RadiolaGuy.com
Reuters
Ridgeway, Harry
Ronald Reagan Library
Saint Louis Art Museum
Savannah Area Convention & Visitors Bureau
Shutterstock Images LLC
Smithsonian Institution
Sobol, Richard
Social Security Administration
State of Illinois, NPS photo
The State Preservation Board, Austin, TX
Tennessee Tourist Development
Tennessee Valley Authority
Texas State Library & Archives Commission
TSN Archives
Tuskegee University Archives/Museum
U.S. Air Force
U.S. Coast Guard
U.S. Department of State
U.S. National Archives and Records
U.S. Naval Historical Center
U.S. Navy
U.S. News & World Report
U.S. Senate Collection
Union Pacific Museum
United Nations
University of Missouri at Columbia
Unusual Films
Vogel, Bob
W. Churchill Memorial and Library
Walmart
Westminster Theological Seminary
The White House
The White House Historical Association
Wikimedia Commons
Wikipedia.org
Woolaroc Museum, Bartlesville, Oklahoma
Worldwide Slides

Introduction

© 2009 JupiterImages Corporation xi, xiii (bottom), xiv (both), xv; © iStockphoto.com/Kriss Russell xii; Shane McMullin xiii (top)

Unit 1

Getty Images/John Elk III xvi; PhotoDisc/Getty Images xvi (gutter); The Granger Collection, New York xvii

Chapter 1

Library of Congress xviii; Debra James © Fotolia 1 (top right); © 2009 Shutterstock

Images LLC/Justin Williford 1 (top left); © iStockphoto.com/Leslie Banks 1 (bottom right); Harris Shiffman © Fotolia 1 (center left); © iStockphoto.com/James Phelps 1 (center right); © iStockphoto.com/Aiyana Paterson-Zinkand 1 (bottom left); Cahokia Mounds State Historic Park, courtesy of the State of Illinois, NPS photo 3 (top); www.iStockphoto.com/Duncan Gilbert 3 (bottom); © iStockphoto.com/Stephan Hoerold 5 (top right); Texas Council for the Humanities/Wikipedia.org. 7 (top); © iStockphoto.com/John Woodworth 7 (center); NMAH-National Numismatic Collection, Smithsonian Institution 7 (bottom); The Granger Collection, New

York 8 (top), 12 (top left and bottom); Library of Congress, Geography and Map Division 8 (bottom); Getty Images/© 2003 Stock Montage, Inc. 10 (top); © British Museum/Art Resource, NY 10 (bottom); © 2009 Shutterstock Images LLC/L. Kragt Bakker 12 (top right); U.S. Senate Collection 11

Chapter 2

Bridgeman-Giraudon/Art Resource, NY 15; Justin Kase zonez/Alamy 16; Wikipedia.org 17 (top left and right); The Granger Collection, New York 17 (bottom), 20, 23 (top), 25 (both), 28 (both), 29, 30 (center), 31 (top); Stuart Walker/Alamy 21; G.E. Kidder Smith, Courtesy of Kidder Smith Collection, Rotch Visual Collection, M.I.T. 22; Library of Congress 23 (both); Copyright New York Historical Society/Wikipedia.org 27; The Colonial Williamsburg Foundation 30 (bottom); © 2009 JupiterImages Corporation 31 (bottom); Savannah Area Convention & Visitors Bureau 32

Chapter 3

© The Metropolitan Museum of Art/Art Resource, NY 34; The Granger Collection, New York 36 (both), 39, 40 (top), 41 (bottom), 44 (top), 45 (top); Willard Clay/Oxford Scientific/Jupiterimages 38 (bottom); © 2008 JupiterImages/Photos.com 40 (bottom); The New York Public Library/Art Resource, NY 44 (bottom); Wikipedia.org 45 (bottom); Wikipedia.org/Larry Pieniazek 46

Chapter 4

The Colonial Williamsburg Foundation 50; The Granger Collection, New York 51, 53, 55 (top), 57, 58 (top and bottom), 59 (bottom), 67; Jeffery Howe, Boston College 54 (left); © James Quine/Alamy 54 (right), 55 (bottom); The Philadelphia Museum of Art/Art Resource, NY 56; Unusual Films 58 (center); Library of Congress 59 (top), 65 (top); Dover Publications, Inc. 60; The Granger Collection, New York/Erik Falkensteen 62 (top); Gene Fisher 62 (bottom); © National Portrait Gallery, Smithsonian Institution/Art Resource, NY 65 (bottom); © Maurice Savage/Alamy 68

Chapter 5

Getty/Stock Montage 70; © 2009 JupiterImages Corporation 72 (top); Wikipedia.org/photo by ScottyBoy900Q 72 (center); Library of Congress 72 (bottom), 82; The Granger Collection, New York 73 (both), 74 (both); 76, 77 (bottom); 79 (top), 83 (top), 84 (top); Jas. Townsend and Sons 77 (top); Art Resource, NY 78, 81; © The Metropolitan Museum of Art/Art Resource, NY 80; public domain 79 (bottom); Wikipedia.org 83 (bottom); Alamy 84 (bottom)

Unit 2

© 2009 JupiterImages Corporation 86 (both); National Archives 87 (left); U.S. Diplomacy Center/U.S. Government 87 (right)

Chapter 6

Architect of the Capitol 88, 98 (top), 102 (top); © iStockphoto.com/SM Photography 89 (top); Réunion des Musées Nationaux/Art Resource, NY 89 (bottom); Philip Kineyko of Flyin Philís Photos 90 (top right); © Eric Adams. Image from BigStockPhoto.com 90 (top left); The Granger Collection, New York 90 (center), 92, 95, 96 (bottom); Delaware Art Museum 90 (bottom); Library of Congress 93 (top and bottom); © iStockphoto.com/Tom Marvin 94; public domain 96 (top); © 2009 Shutterstock Images LLC/ Hatem M. Eldoronki 98 (center); Getty Images/Photo by MPI 98 (bottom); The New York Public Library/Art Resource 100; Rita Mitchell/ National Park Service 101 (top); Wikimedia Commons/Independence National Historical Park 101 (bottom); © Russ Finley/russfinley@yellowstone.net 102 (center); National Archives 102 (bottom)

Chapter 7

National Archives 105; The Granger Collection, New York 106, 111, 112 (bottom), 113 (top), 114, 121 (top); Historical Documents Company 110; Library of Congress 112 (top); Réunion des Musées Nationaux/Art Resource, NY 113 (bottom); Architect of the Capitol 115; Yale University Art Gallery/Art Resource, NY 117; Photo by Earl McDonald for the National Archives 122; © iStockphoto.com/ Olga Bogatyrenko 124; © iStock-photo.com/ Cristina Ciochina 128; © 2009 Shutterstock Images LLC/ Olga Bogatyrenko 130; Getty Images/KAREN BLEIER/AFP 136

Chapter 8

The Bridgeman Art Library International 141; Portrait of George Washington by Gilbert Stuart, Sterling and Francine Clark Art Institute, Williamstown, MA/Wikipedia.org 142; Library of Congress 143 (top), 144, 155 (top and bottom), 157 (top); The Granger Collection, New York 143 (center and bottom), 145, 146 (top), 148, 149, 150 (bottom), 151 (top), 152 (top), 156, 157 (bottom), 158; The New York Public Library, New York, NY, U.S.A./Art Resource, NY 146 (bottom); Chateau de Versailles, France/ Giraudon/ The Bridgeman Art Library 147; © iStock-photo.com/ Pierrette Guertin 150 (top); National Portrait Gallery, Smithsonian Institution, Washington, DC, U.S.A./Art Resource, NY 151 (bottom); © 1999 KINDRA CLINEFF 152 (bottom); Wikipedia.org 154

Unit 3

Library of Congress/Carol M. Highsmith Archive 160 (left); © 2009 JupiterImages Corporation 160 (right); Library of Congress/Pat Terry (OWI) 161

Chapter 9

The Granger Collection, New York 162, 165 (bottom), 172 (bottom); Wikimedia Commons/New York Historical Society 163 (top); Library of Congress, Geography and Map Division 163 (bottom); Library of Congress 164; Official U.S. Navy Photograph 165 (top); Independence National Historical Park 167 (top left and top right); © 2009 JupiterImages Corporation 167 (center), 168 (bottom), 169 (bottom); The Bridgeman Art Library International 167 (bottom); Smithsonian Institution MSC/Dept. of Anthropology 168 (top); © 2009 iStockphoto.com/ Desert Digital Images 169 (top); The Marinersí Museum, Newport News, VA 170; © iStockphoto.com/Travis Daub 171; Wikimedia.com/National Gallery of Art 172 (top); Dover/Courtesy Bureau of American Ethnology, Smithsonian Institution 172 (center); U.S. Navy Photo by John E. Gay 175 (top); William Manning/Alamy 175 (bottom); Military History, Smithsonian Institution 176 (top); National Park Service 176 (bottom); © Smithsonian American Art Museum, Washington, DC/Art Resource, NY 177

Chapter 10

The Granger Collection, New York 179, 181, 190 (top); Library of Congress 180 (top), 185 (bottom), 186, 188, 190 (bottom); Wikipedia.org 180 (bottom); National Archives 183; © 2009 JupiterImages Corporation 184 (top); Photograph by Franz Jantzen, Copyprint/Collection of the Supreme Court of the United States (178) 184 (bottom); © Corcoran Gallery of Art, Washington, DC, Museum Purchase, Gallery Fund/Photo by Mark Gulezian/QuickSilver 185 (top)

Chapter 11

Saint Louis Art Museum 193; The White House Historical Association (White House Collection) 194 (top), 206 (top), 208 (top left and top right); The Hermitage: Home of President Andrew Jackson, Nashville, TN 194 (bottom); The Granger Collection, New York 195, 199, 202, 207 (top); Wikipedia.org/Daniel Rice & James G. Clark 196; Library of Congress 197 (top), 198, 200 (top and bottom), 204, 206 (bottom); Woolaroc Museum Bartlesville, Oklahoma 197 (bottom); Getty Images/Hulton Archive/MPI/Stringer 200 (center); US Senate Collection 201; Courtesy of Atwater Kent Museum of Philadelphia, The Historical Society of Pennslvania Collection 203; Tennessee Tourist Development 205; Wikipedia.org 208 (bottom)

Chapter 12

I.N. Phelps Stokes Collection, Miriam and Ira D. Wallach Division of Art, Prints and Photographs, The New York Public Library, Astor, Lenox and Tilden Foundations 211; Washington University Gallery of Art, St. Louis, Missouri/ Wikimedia Commons 213 (top); © iStockphoto.com/J. Norman Reid 213 (bottom); The Granger Collection, New York 214, 216 (bottom), 221 (bottom), 222 (top), 223 (both), 224, 226 (top), 227 (top), 230 (bottom), 233, 234 (top and bottom); Library of Congress 215, 221 (top), 225, 229 (bottom), 231, 235, 236 (top and bottom); © 2009 JupiterImages Corporation 216 (top), 227 (center), 229 (top), 232; Chessie System Railroads 218; Wikipedia .org 220 (top); National Park Service/ Photographer: Chuck Milliken 220 (bottom); Worldwide Slides 222 (bottom); Smithsonian Institution Photo by Hugh Talman 226 (bottom); Tom Murphy VII/ Wikipedia.org 227 (bottom); Library of Congress/Harris & Ewing Collection 229 (center); BJU Press/Linda Eller 230 (top)

Chapter 13

COREL Corporation 238; Getty Images 239, 245 (bottom left), 248 (center) 251 (bottom); Library of Congress 240, 246 (top), 250 (all), 252 (top), 254 (top), 255, 256 (both); National Park Service/ Wikipedia.org 242 (top); Shanel/ Wikipedia.org 242 (bottom); Sally Pearce, Colorado Department of Transportation 243; Texas State Library & Archives Commission 244; BJU Press Files 245 (bottom right); National Archives 247 (top and bottom), 248 (top), 251 (top); Wikipedia.org 247 (center); National Geographic/Getty Images 248 (bottom); Kenneth Frederick 249 (top); © Living Legend - Fotolia.com 249 (bottom); © 2009 JupiterImages Corporation 252 (bottom); George Wilkins Kendall & Carl Nebel/Wikipedia.org 254 (center); The State Preservation Board, Austin, TX 254 (bottom)

Unit 4

Roger Viollet/Getty Images 258; © James G. Cummings 259 (right); © 2009 JupiterImages Corporation 259 (left)

Chapter 14

© Mario Savoia - Fotolia.com 260; Library of Congress 262 (bottom), 266 (bottom), 267 (top and bottom), 268 (top and center), 269, 272 (top), 273 (bottom), 274 (both), 275 (all), 276 (right); © Ekaterina Fribus. Image from Bigstockphoto.com 265 (bottom); Courtesy of the Louisiana State Museum 265 (top); Time & Life Pictures/Getty Images 266 (top); National Archives 267 (center), 271 (bottom), 273 (top), 276 (left), 279; Frederic Bancroft and William A. Dunning/ Wikipedia.org 268 (bottom); Courtesy of the Division of Special Collections, Archives, and Rare Books, University of Missouri at Columbia 271 (top); John L. Magee/ Wikipedia.org 272 (bottom);

Chapter 15

Library of Congress 283, 286 (top and center), 287 (bottom), 288, 289 (top left and bottom), 291, 293 (top and bottom), 294 (top and center), 295 (top and center), 296 (top and center), 297 (bottom), 299 (top and bottom), 300 (all), 301, 302 (top), 303 (top), 304; Provided by BACM 284, 285 (top); Joyce Landis 285 (bottom); © Harry Ridgeway 286 (bottom); National Archives 287 (top), 289 (top right and center), 293 (center), 294 (bottom), 295 (bottom), 297 (top), 302 (bottom); R.G. Skerrett/US Navy 292; Gettysburg Cyclorama, courtesy of Gettysburg Foundation 296 (bottom); civilwarphotos. net 299 (center)

Chapter 16

Library of Congress 306, 307 (center), 309, 311 (all), 313, 314 (all), 315 (all), 316 (top), 317 (top and center), 319 (all), 320; National Archives 307 (top); Unusual Films 307 (bottom); The Granger Collection, New York 312; Harperís Weekly 316 (bottom left and bottom right), 317 (bottom)

Unit 5

Photo by Picture Post/Hulton Archive/ Getty Images 324 (left), 325 (right); George Grantham Bain Collection/ Library of Congress 324 (right); Getty Images/Hulton Archive/Stringer 325 (left)

Chapter 17

Library of Congress 326, 328 (center and bottom), 329, 330 (both), 331, 335 (bottom left), 336, 338 (both), 339, 341; Nebraska State Historical Society 328 (top); National Archives 333 (bottom), 335 (bottom right); Union Pacific Museum 334 (top); Getty Images 335 (top)

Chapter 18

Library of Congress 345, 351 (center and bottom), 355 (both), 358 (both), 361 (top right and bottom right), 362 (top); © 2009 JupiterImages Corporation 346, 350, 353; National Archives 347, 351 (top), 354, 361 (top left and center); © iStockPhoto.com/ ilbusca 356 (bottom); © iStockPhoto.com/ Gary Alvis 356 (top); NOAA George E. Marsh Album 357; Wikimedia Commons 359 (top), 362 (bottom); National Park Service 359 (bottom); The Granger Collection, New York 360 (top); Getty Images, 360 (bottom), 361 (bottom left), 362 (center)

Chapter 19

The Granger Collection, New York 364, 369; Library of Congress 366, 368 (all), 371 (both), 372, 373, 375 (center, bottom left and right); Courtesy of US Navy 367; National Archives 370 (top and bottom); The New York World 370 (center); New York Times/Wikipedia.org 374; Getty Images 375 (top)

Chapter 20

Library of Congress 379, 381 (both), 382 (bottom), 383 (bottom), 385, 388 (top), 389 (bottom left and bottom right), 390 (top), 391, 392, 393, 395, 396; © Tuskegee University Archives/Museum 382 (top); Getty Images, Inc 383 (top); Archives of the Billy Graham Center, Wheaton, Illinois 386; Harperís Weekly 388 (bottom); Associated Press 389 (top); Jane Addams Memorial Collection (JAMC-1921-0049-5597). Photographer: Unknown. Special Collections, University of Illinois at Chicago Library 390 (bottom)

Unit 6

© 2009 JupiterImages Corporation 396 (right); Moes Garage/Wikipedia.org 396 (left). Photo by Fox Photos/Getty Images 397

Chapter 21

National Archives 400, 402 (both), 403 (top), 406 (top), 413; Getty Images, 401 (bottom), 404 (top); The Granger Collection, New York 401 (top), 411 (bottom); Photo Courtesy of National Aviation Hall of Fame 403 (bottom); Time & Life Pictures/Getty Images 404 (bottom); Courtesy of John Peterson 405 (top), 412 (top); Library of Congress 405 (bottom), 406 (bottom), 407, 408 (both), 409 (both), 410 (bottom), 411 (top), 412 (bottom)